T0065992

THE ART OF

Harry Potter™

MINI BOOK OF MAGICAL PLACES

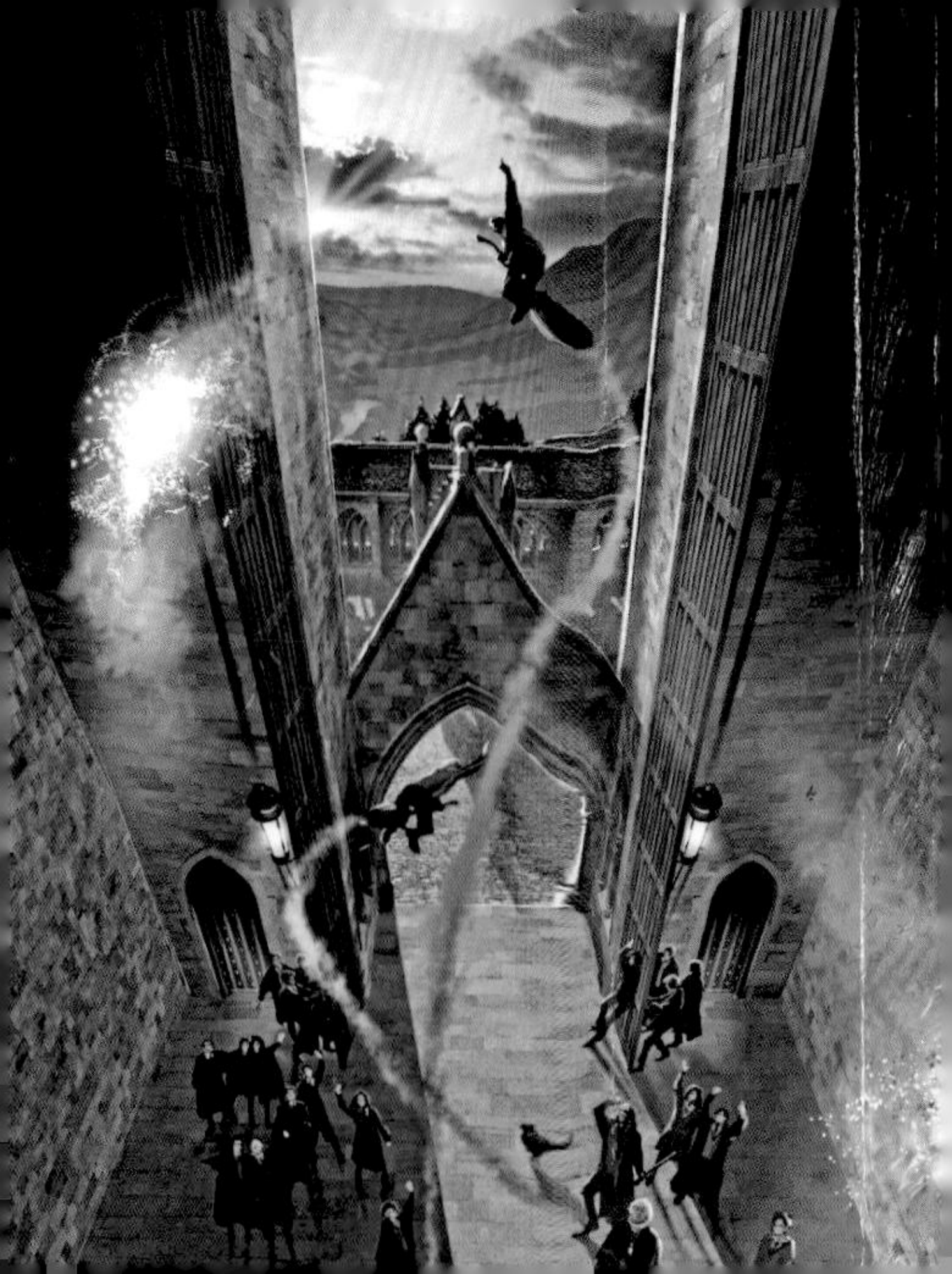

THE ART OF Harry Potter™

MINI BOOK OF MAGICAL PLACES

Marc Sumerak

INSIGHT EDITIONS
San Rafael, California

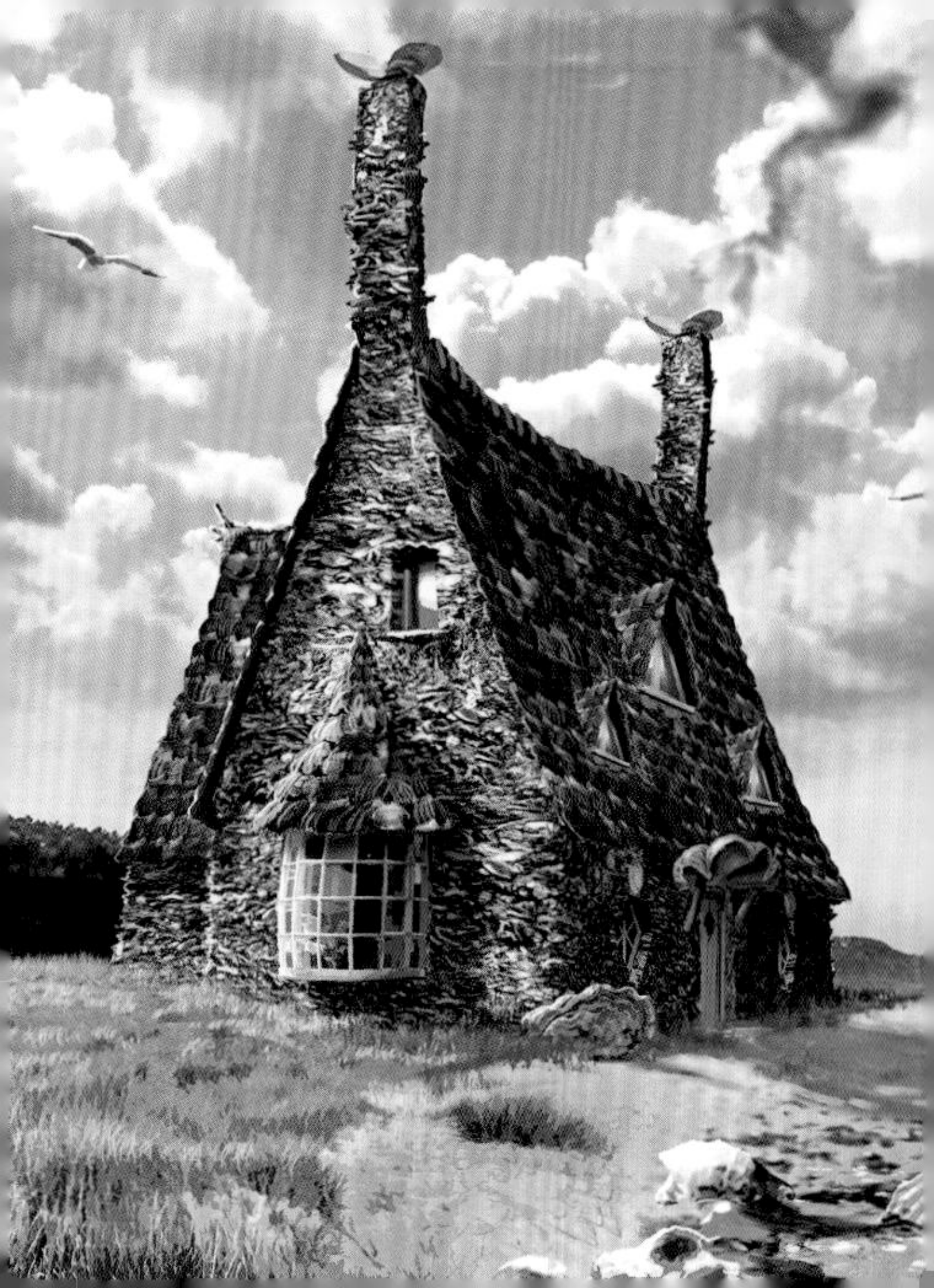

CONTENTS

Introduction 10

The Muggle World 14

- Privet Drive 16
- The Hut-on-the-Rock 24
- London 26
- King's Cross 30

Diagon Alley 32

- Gringotts Wizarding Bank 40

Hogwarts Castle 50

- The Castle Exterior 52
- The Great Hall 88
- The Front Gates 96
- Entrance Hall 100
- The Library 106
- Prefects' Bathroom 108
- Moaning Myrtle's Bathroom 110
- The Chamber of Secrets 112

The Owlery 118
The Room of Requirement 122
The Astronomy Tower 130
Hogwarts Classrooms and Offices 138
Dumbledore's Office 140
The Greenhouse 142
Defense Against the Dark Arts Classroom 146
Divination Classroom 154
Professor Umbridge's Office 160
Hogwarts Grounds 164
The Bridge 166
The Gatehouse Sundial 168
The Forbidden Forest 170
The Black Lake 178
Hagrid's Hut 194
The Whomping Willow 198
The Quidditch Pitch 202
The Triwzard Tournament 208
Dumbledore's Tomb 214
The Battle of Hogwarts 220
Hogsmeade 228
Quidditch World Cup 244
The Ministry of Magic 252
The Atrium 254

Courtrooms 256
Muggle-Born Registration Commission 260
Department of Mysteries 262
Wizarding Prisons 270
Azkaban 272
Nurmengard 274
The Cave 276
Wizarding Homes 278
The Burrow 280
Number Twelve, Grimmauld Place 284
Lovegood House 286
Malfoy Manor 288
Spinner's End 290
Budleigh Babberton 292
Shell Cottage 294
Conclusion 298

PAGE 2: Fred and George Weasley toss fireworks from their brooms in artwork by Andrew Williamson for *Harry Potter and the Order of the Phoenix*.

PAGE 4: Concept art by Andrew Williamson for Shell Cottage for *Harry Potter and the Deathly Hallows – Part 2*.

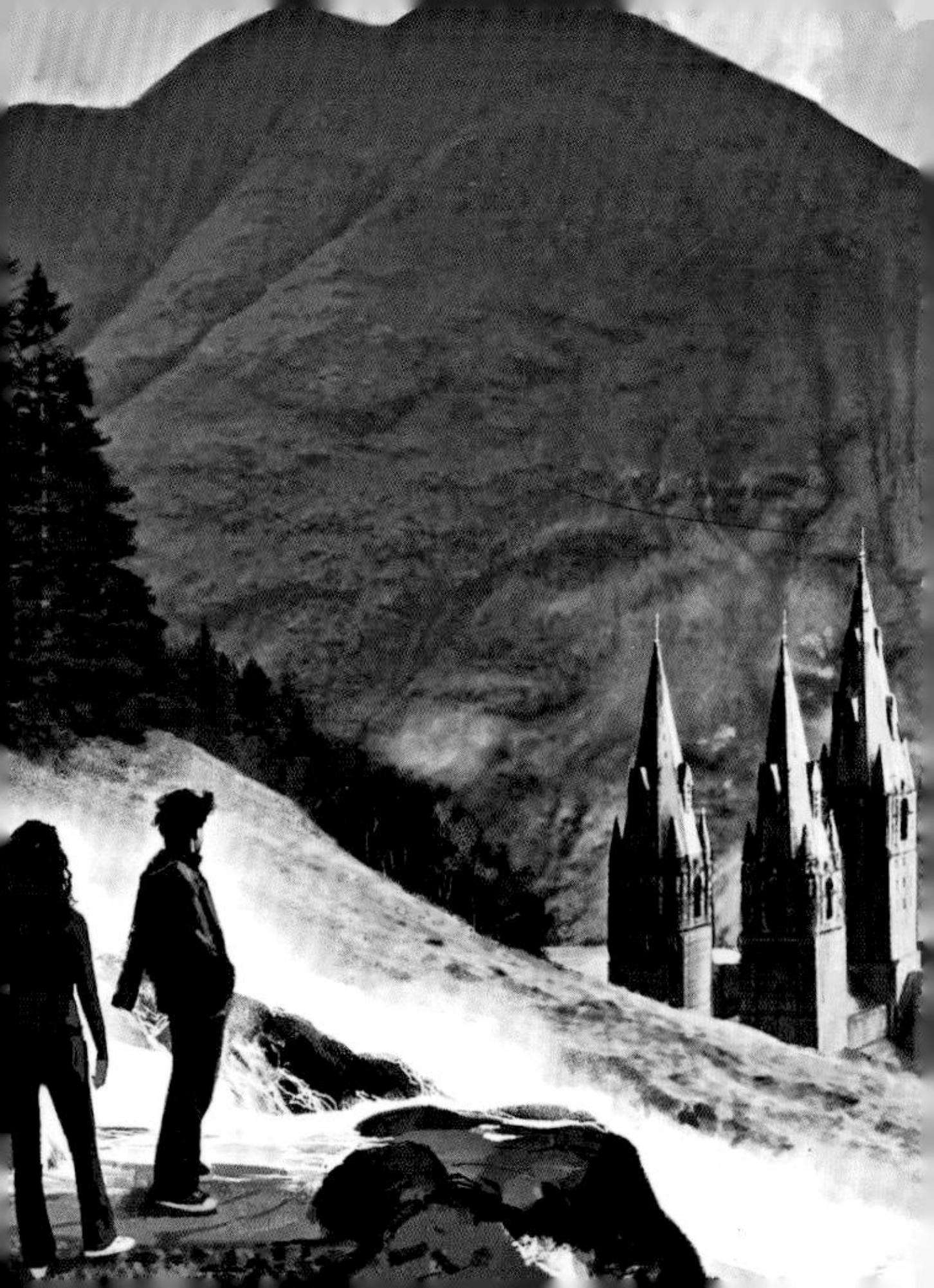

Stuart Craig was tasked with making sure that these sensational settings didn't lose their luster as they were translated from page to screen.

Similar to most other creative aspects of the films, set designs began as a series of detailed sketches and concept art. And one of the most important sketches came not from the film's design team, but from J.K. Rowling herself.

During their first meeting to discuss the visual identity of the films, Rowling sketched out a map that told Craig everything he would need to know about Hogwarts School of Witchcraft and Wizardry. While

INTRODUCTION

The most wondrous thing in the world of the Harry Potter films might be the world itself. From dark forests to ancient castles to hidden alleyways, there is magic teeming in every unique location that our young heroes visit. As head of the art department, production designer

PAGES 8–9: Harry and Hermione stare down at Hogwarts castle in artwork by Adam Brockbank for *Harry Potter and the Goblet of Fire*.

OPPOSITE: Andrew Williamson depicts the Hogwarts Express approaching the castle for *Harry Potter and the Half-Blood Prince*.

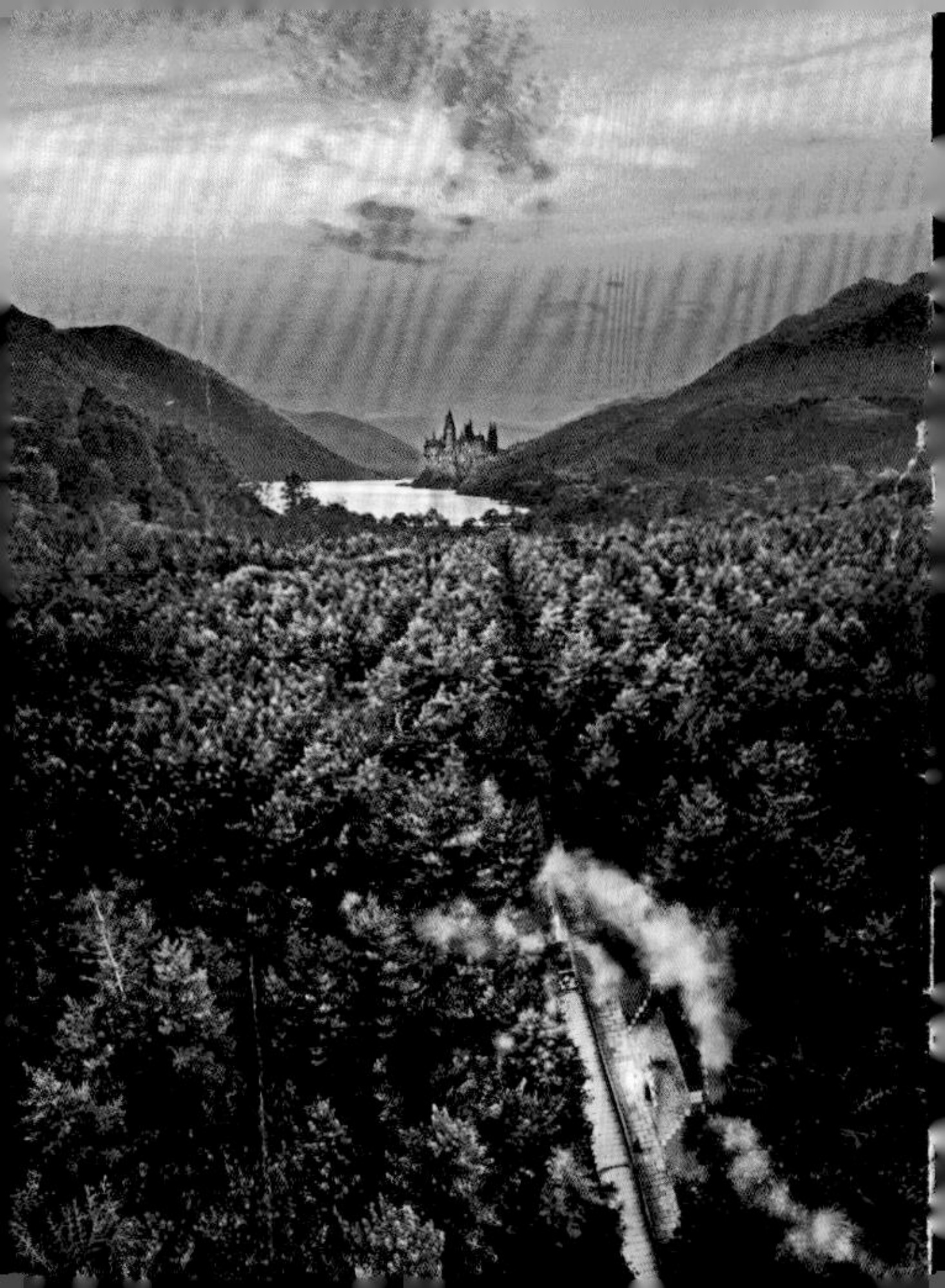

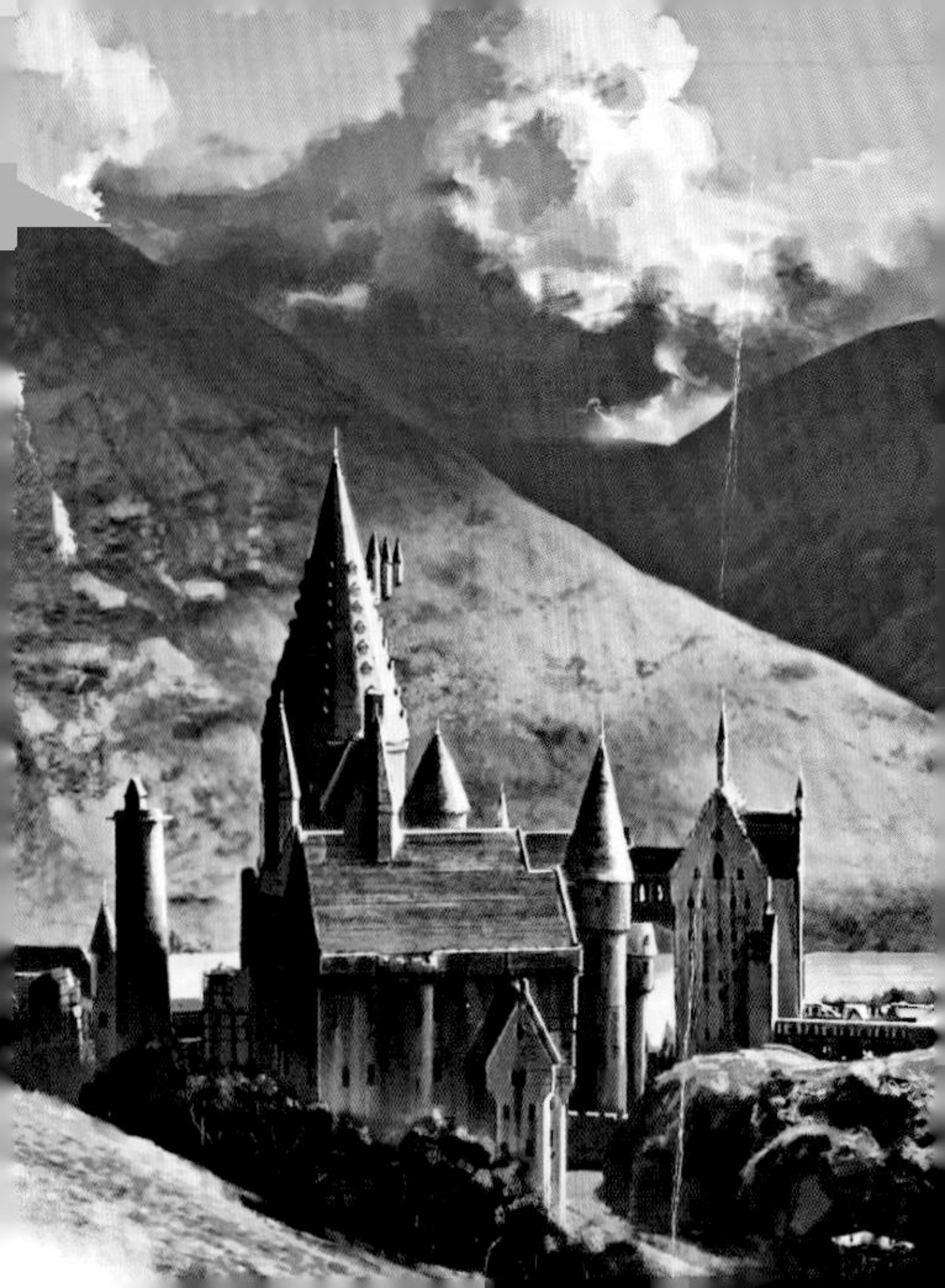

not as elaborate as the Marauder's Map, Rowling's initial sketch detailed the most important locations of the school grounds—from the Front Gates to the Forbidden Forest. Craig held on to Rowling's sketch and referenced it frequently throughout the years.

While Rowling did not provide the concept sketches for the other locations in the films, it was her written words that inspired the team of artists working under Craig to bring these iconic settings to life. In this book, we take a comprehensive tour of these unforgettable locations via the dazzling art that first gave them shape. Enjoy!

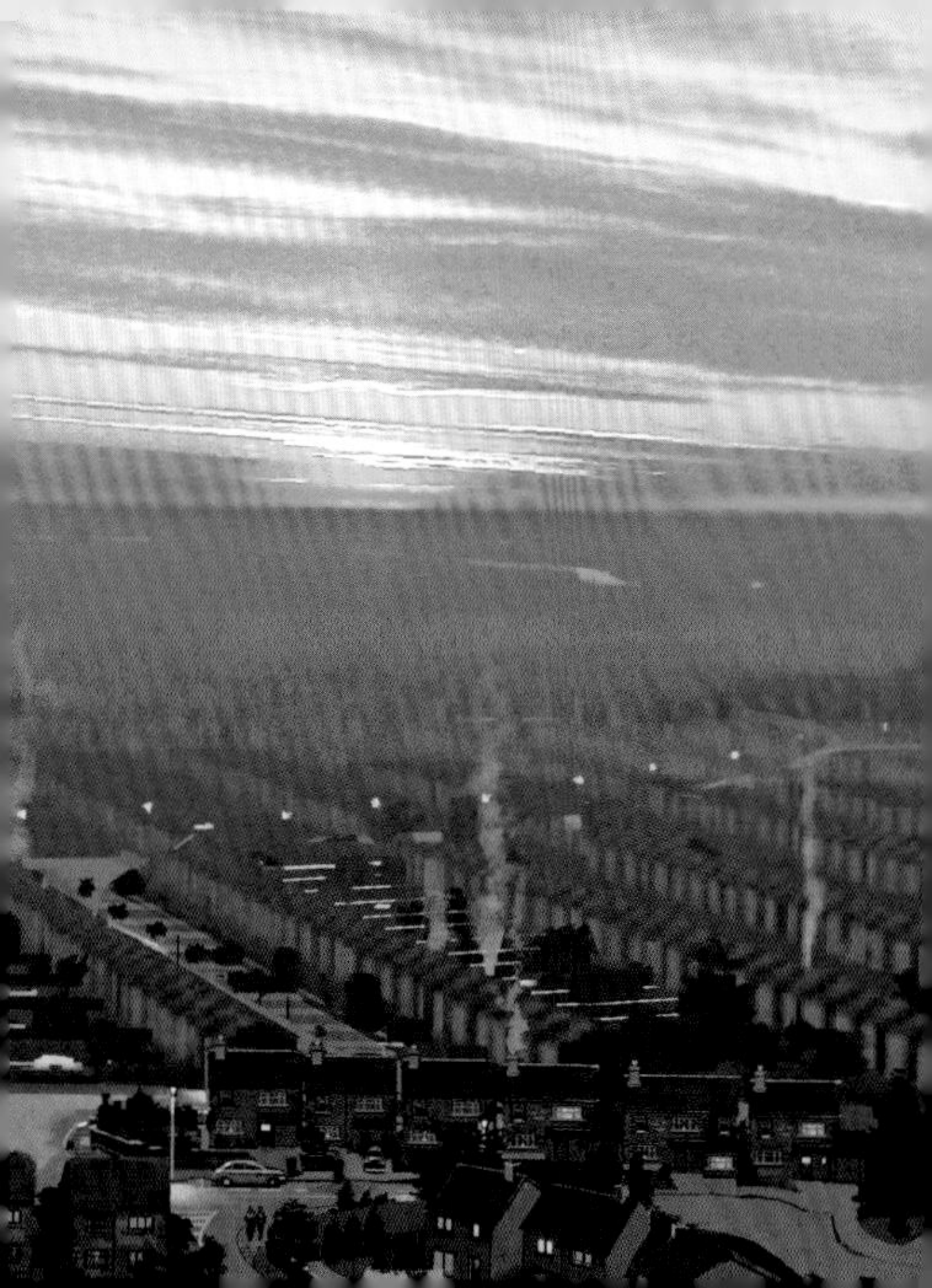

THE MUGGLE WORLD

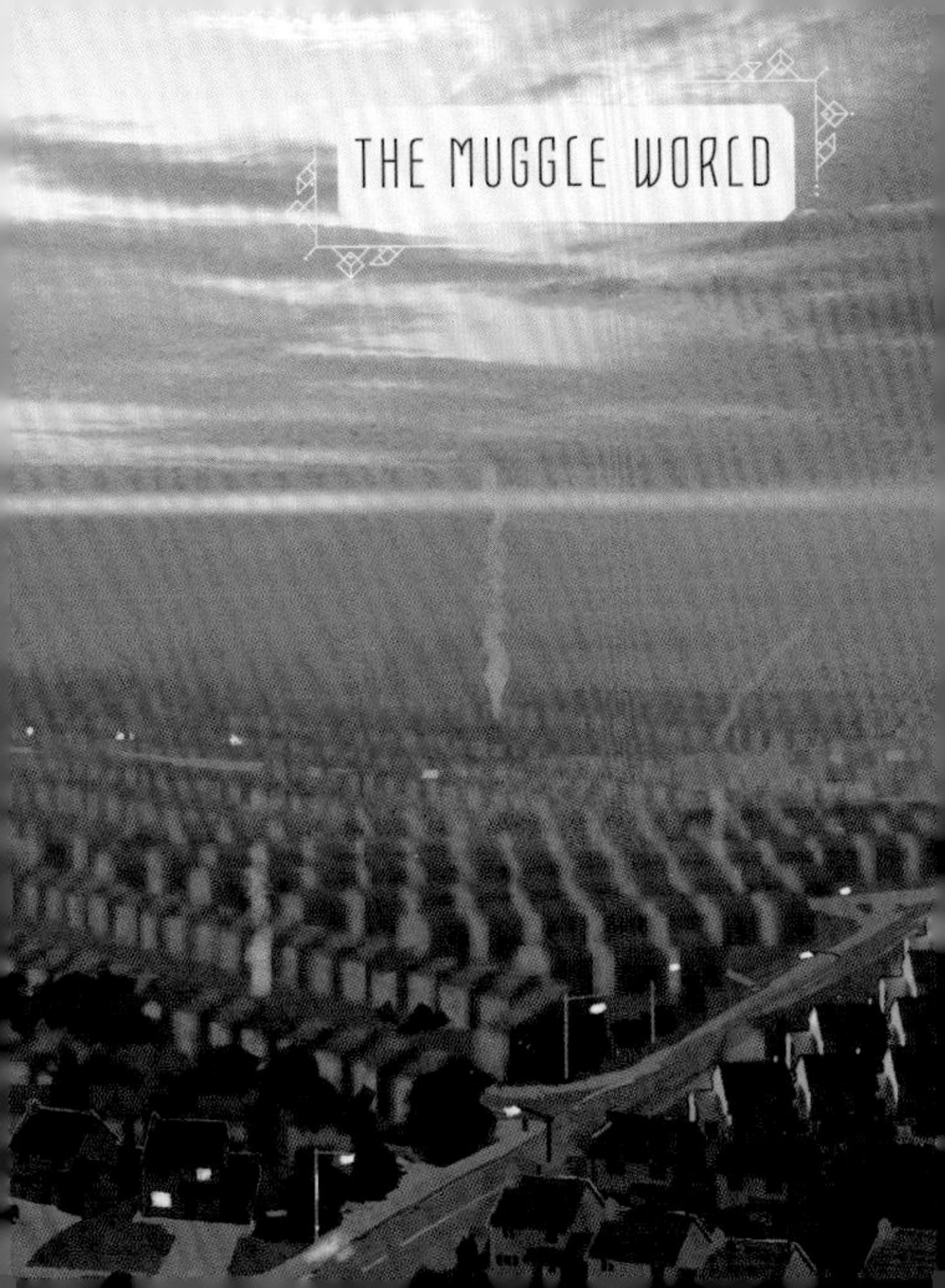

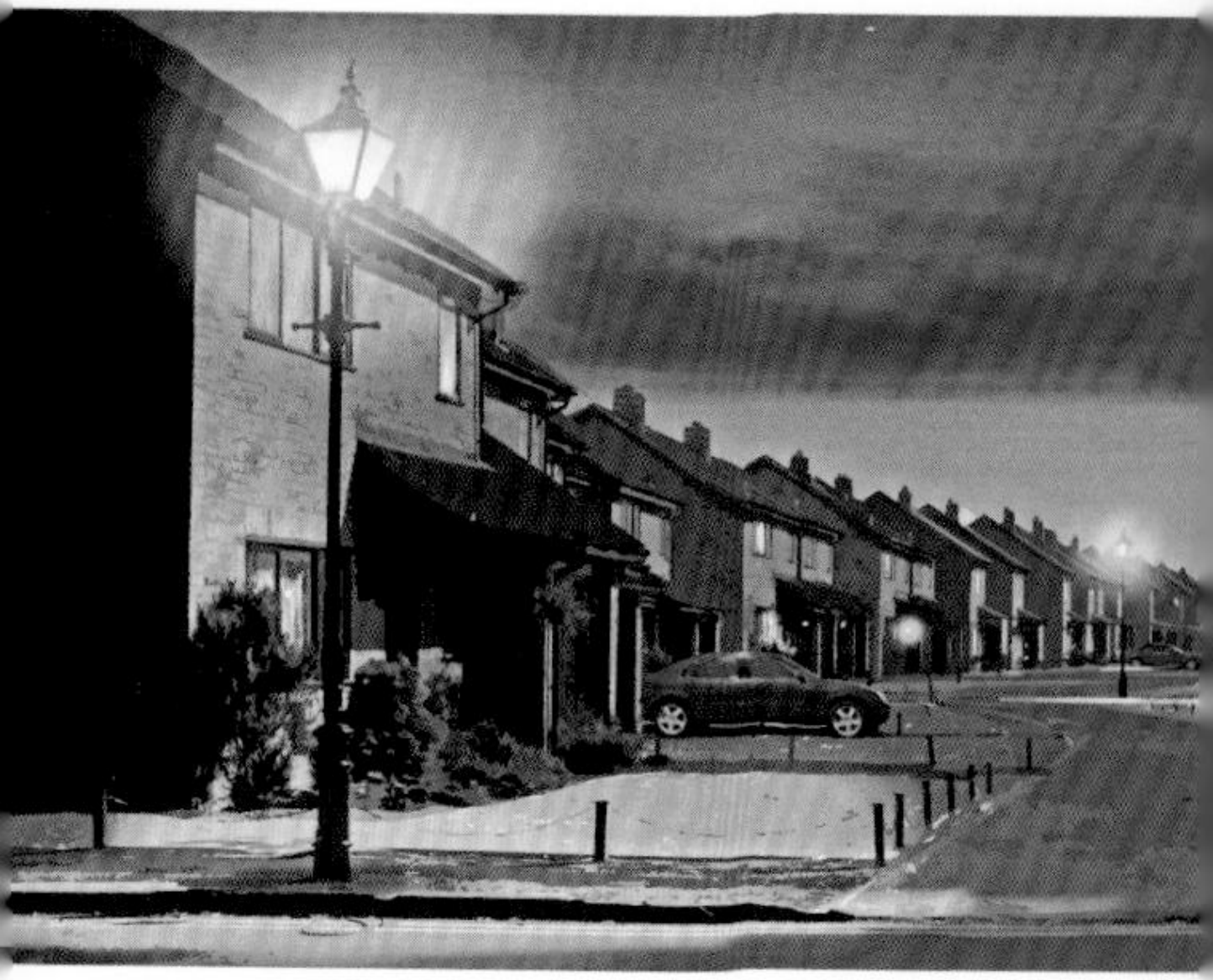

PAGES 14–15: Little Whinging at sunset by Dermot Power for the opening of *Harry Potter and the Chamber of Secrets*.

PRIVET DRIVE

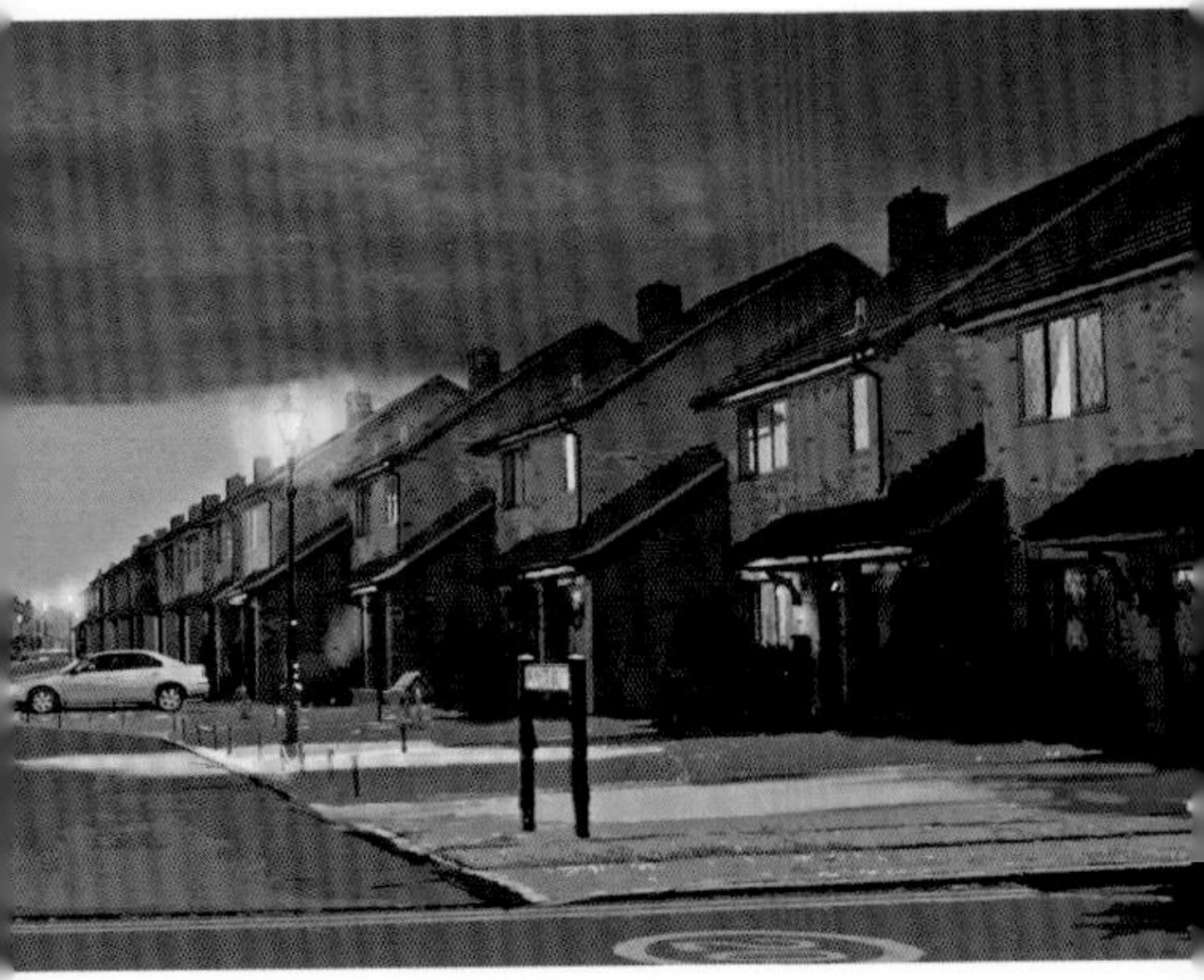

ABOVE: A look down Privet Drive by Andrew Williamson for *Harry Potter and the Order of the Phoenix*.

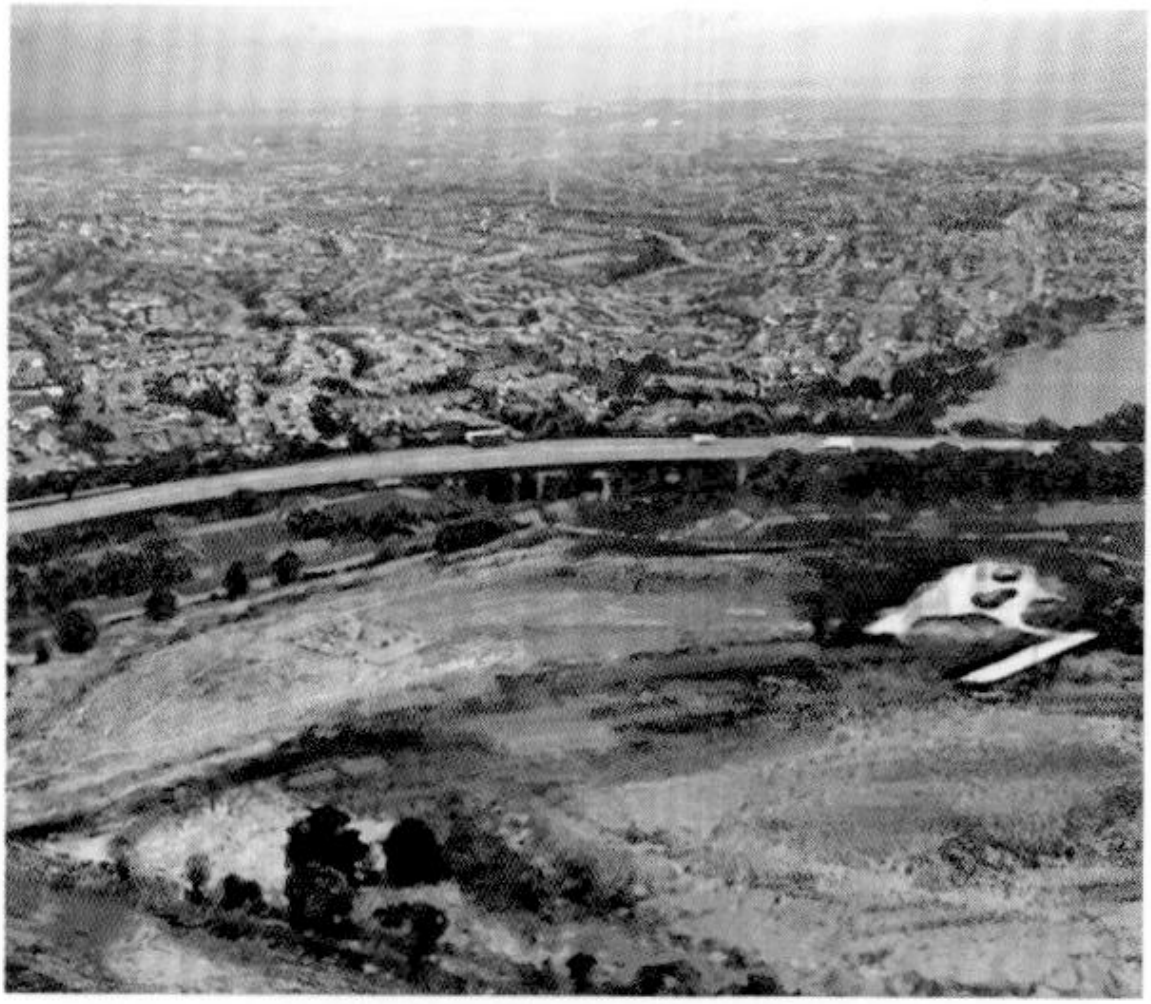

THESE PAGES: Aerial views by Andrew Williamson of the suburban neighborhood of Little Whinging for *Harry Potter and the Order of the Phoenix*.

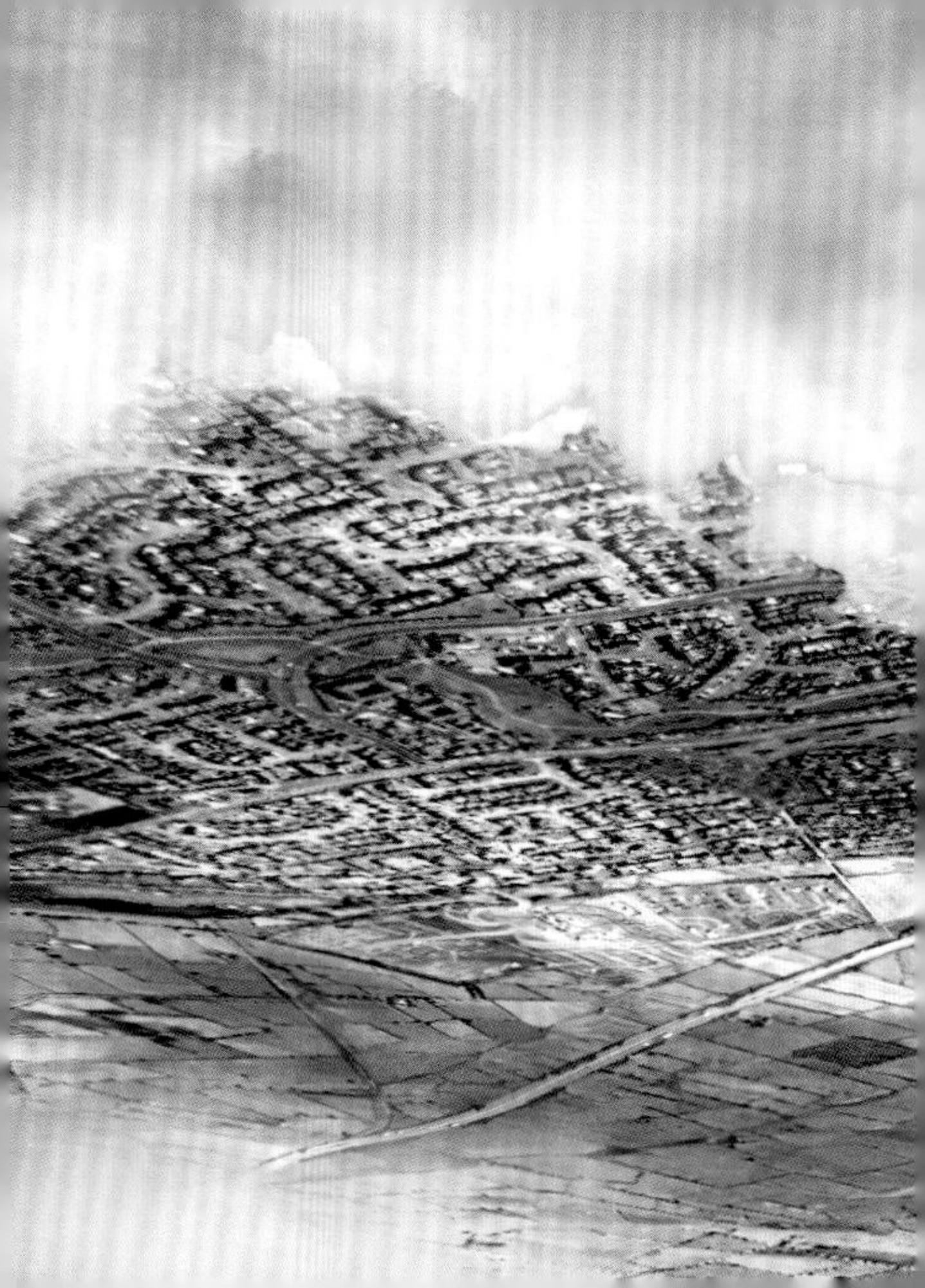

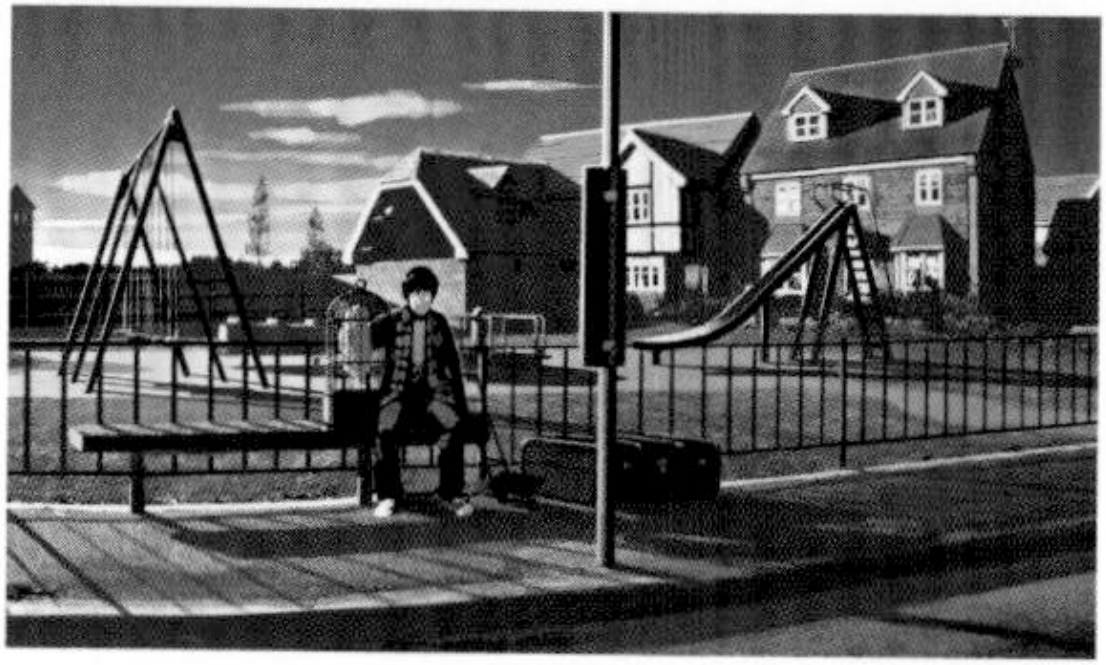

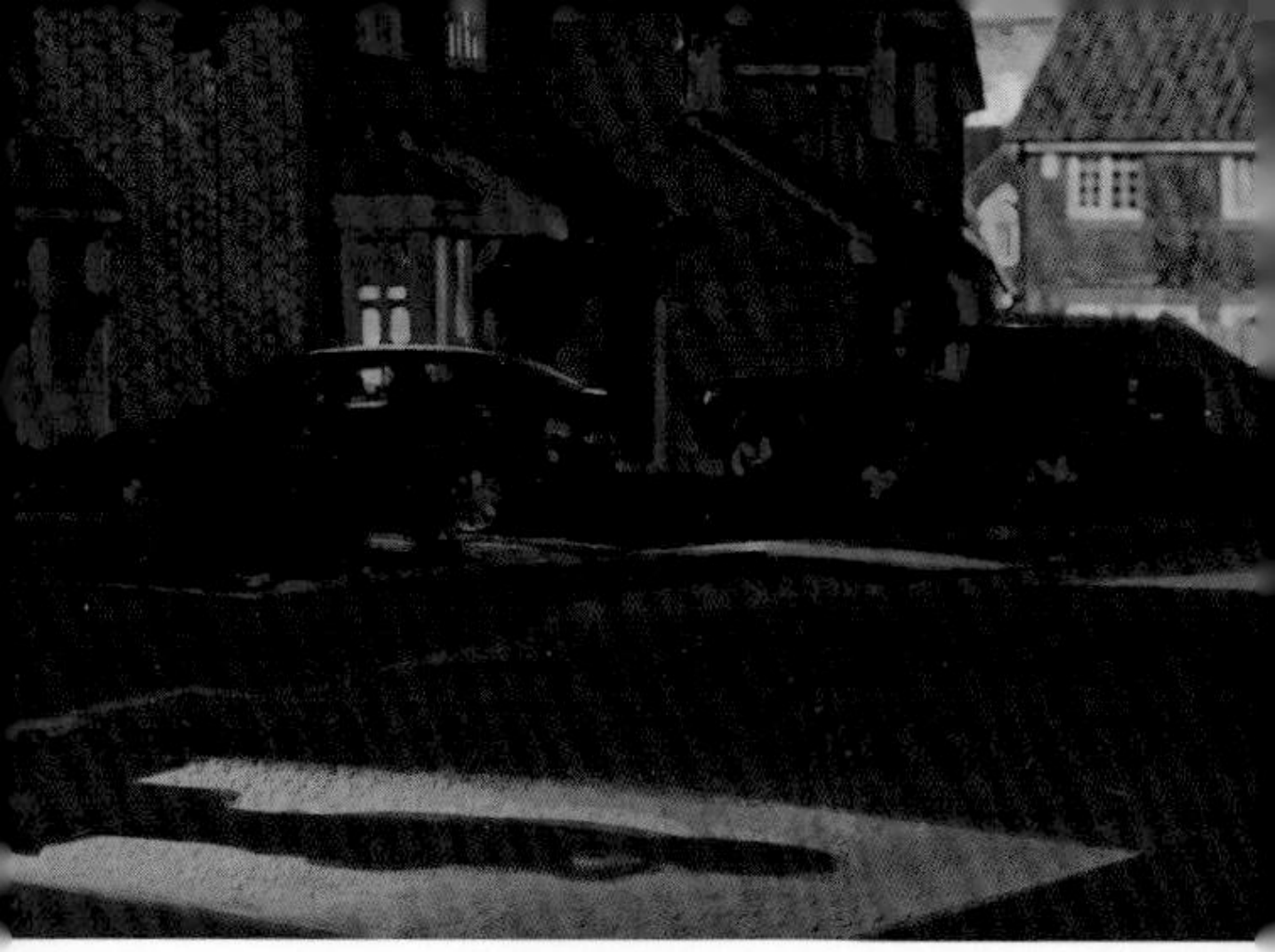

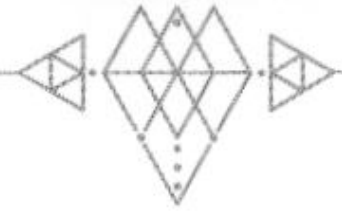

THESE PAGES: Concept art by Adam Brockbank that depicts Harry leaving the Dursley house after he blows up Aunt Marge in *Harry Potter and the Prisoner of Azkaban*.

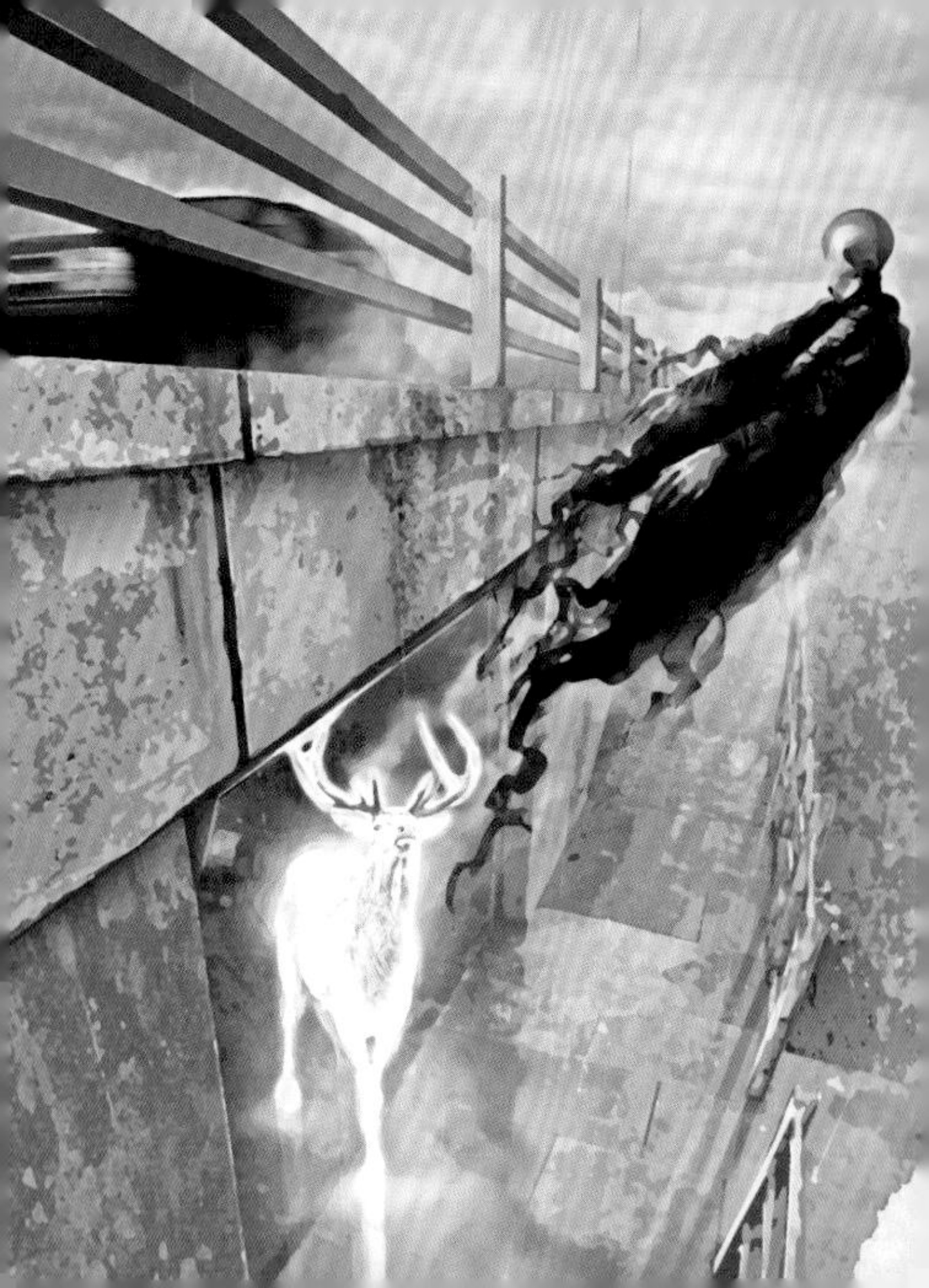

INSIGHT EDITIONS
PO Box 3088
San Rafael, CA 94912
www.insightedition s.com

Find us on Facebook: www.facebook.com/InsightEditions

Follow us on Twitter: @insighteditions

Copyright © 2019 Warner Bros. Entertainment Inc.
HARRY POTTER characters, names and related indicia are © & ™ Warner Bros. Entertainment Inc. WB SHIELD: © & ™ WBEI. WIZARDING WORLD trademark and logo © & ™ Warner Bros. Entertainment Inc. Publishing Rights © JKR. (s19)

All rights reserved. Published by Insight Editions, San Rafael, California, in 2019.

Sections of this book were originally published in *The Art of Harry Potter* by Insight Editions, San Rafael, CA, in 2017.

No part of this book may be reproduced in any form without written permission from the publisher.

978-1-68383-751-0

Manufactured in China by Insight Editions

10 9 8 7 6 5 4

That regeneration continues with a new series of films based on *Fantastic Beasts and Where to Find Them*. Written by J.K. Rowling herself, and featuring the talents of both Craig and veteran Harry Potter director David Yates, this series introduces a whole new generation of wizards, but features a few key set pieces that will be familiar to filmgoers.

It seems fans haven't yet taken their last trip to Hogwarts!

OPPOSITE: Concept art of a view of Hogwarts castle by Adam Brockbank to suggest a possible final shot for *Harry Potter and the Goblet of Fire*.

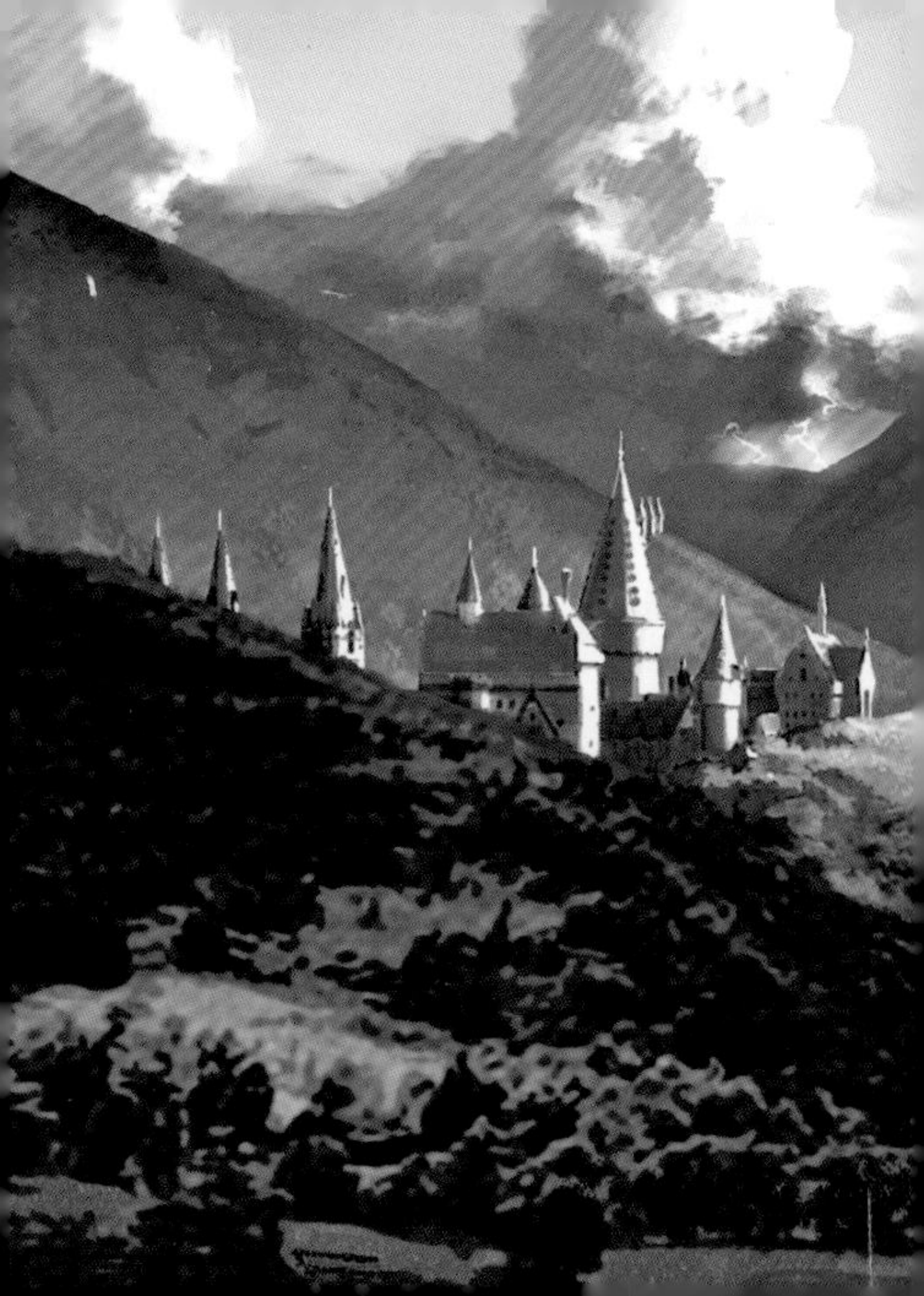

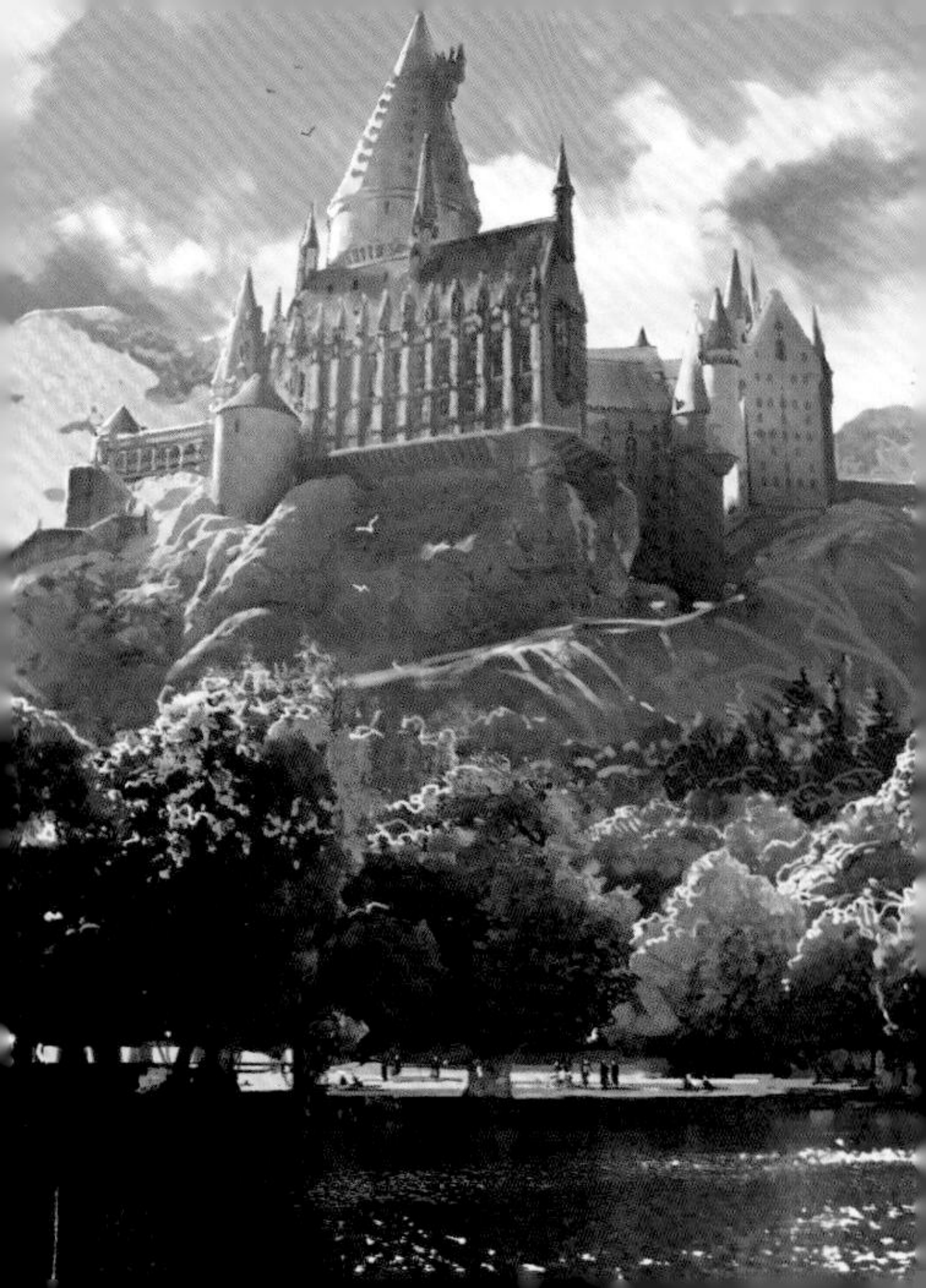

SPINNER'S END

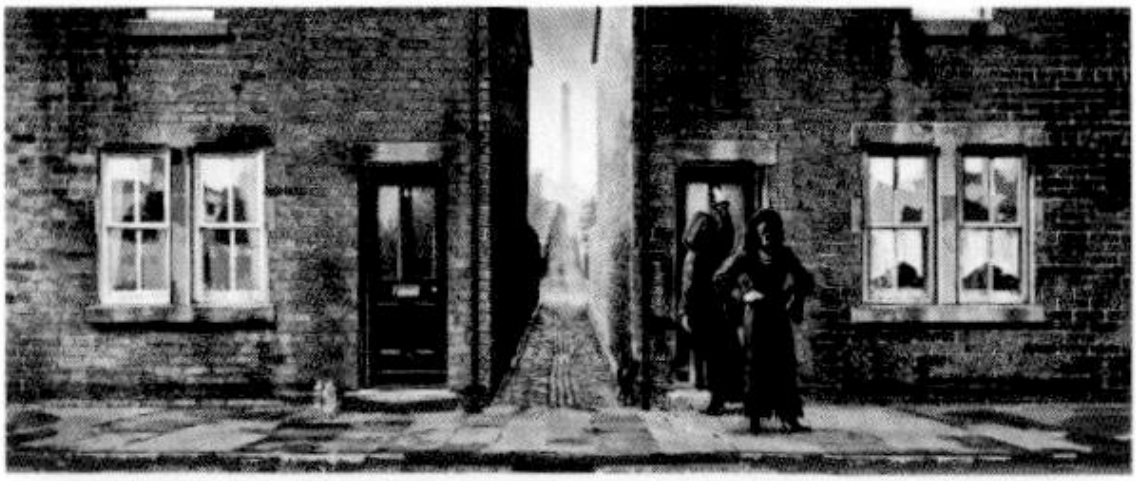

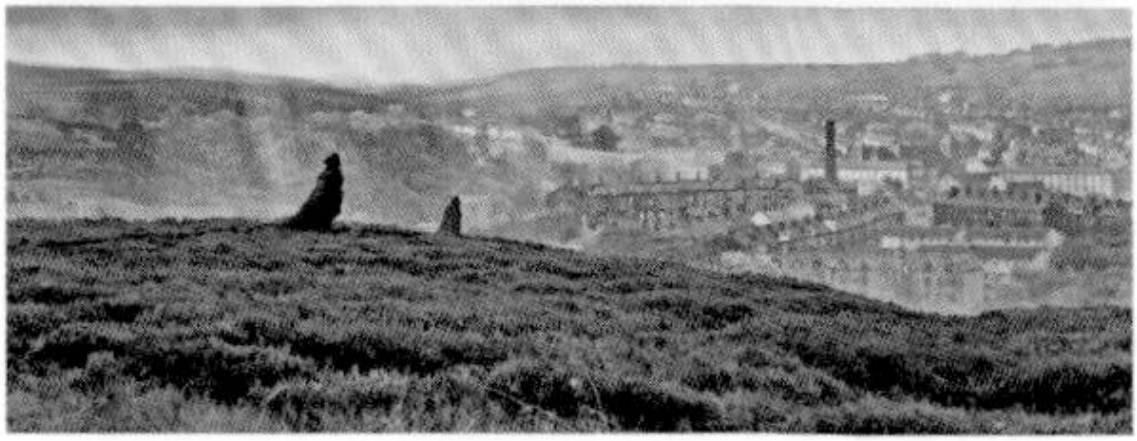

OPPOSITE: Andrew Williamson depicts the dreary village of Spinner's End, home of Severus Snape in *Harry Potter and the Half-Blood Prince*.

ABOVE: Sisters Narcissa Malfoy and Bellatrix Lestrange travel to Spinner's End to see Professor Snape in two pieces created by Andrew Williamson for *Half-Blood Prince*.

BUDLEIGH BABBERTON

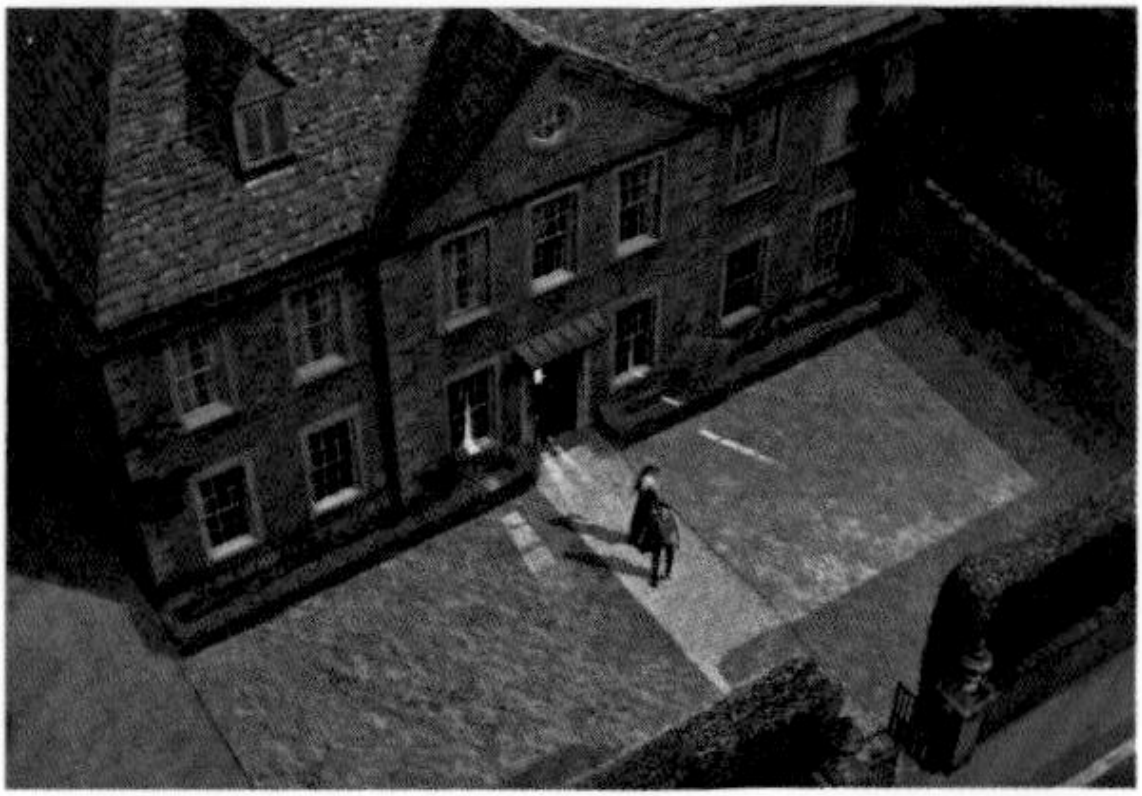

THESE PAGES: In *Harry Potter and the Half-Blood Prince*, Harry and Professor Dumbledore travel to the village of Budleigh Babberton to convince Horace Slughorn to return to his teaching position at Hogwarts. Art by Andrew Williamson.

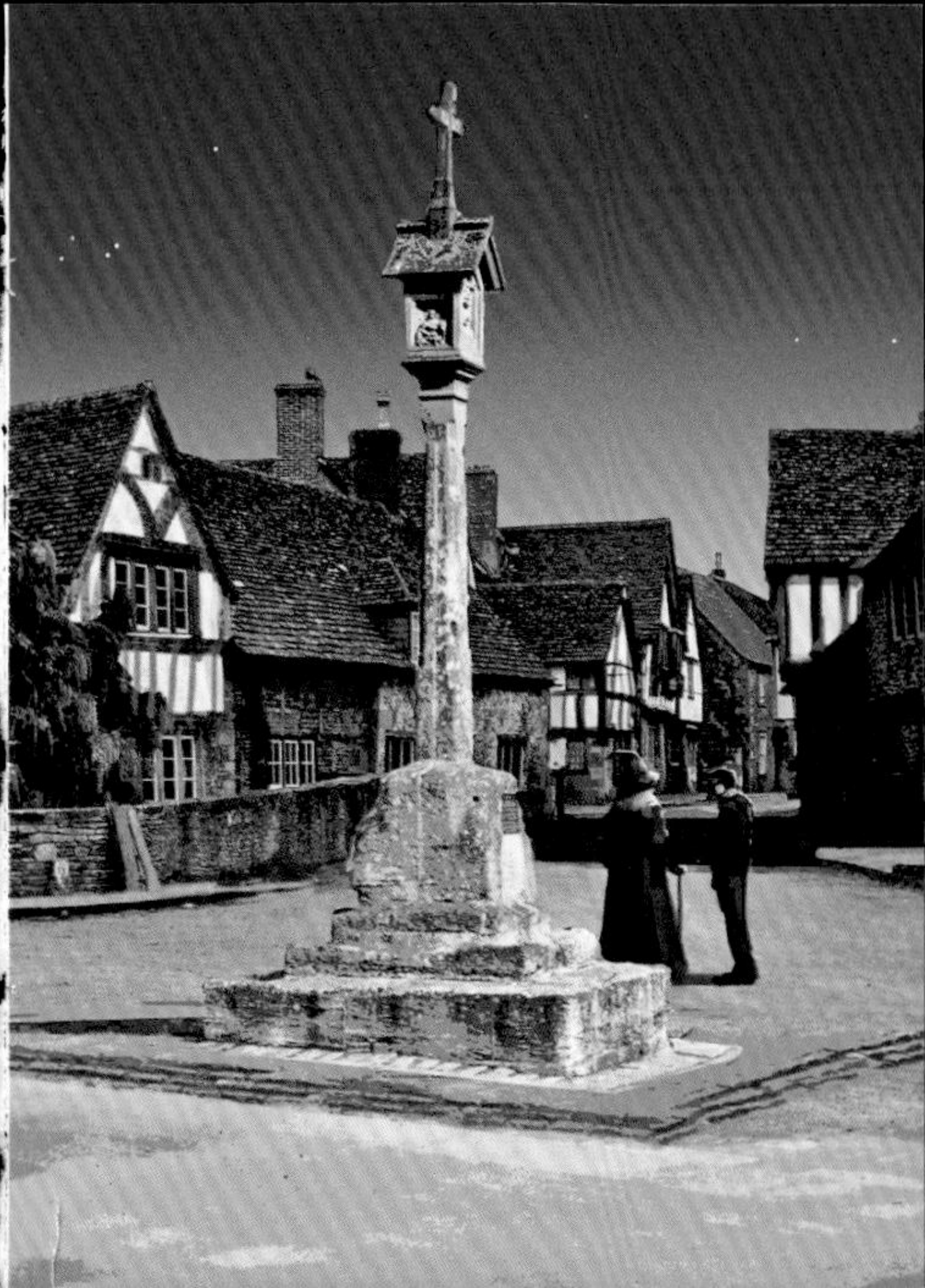

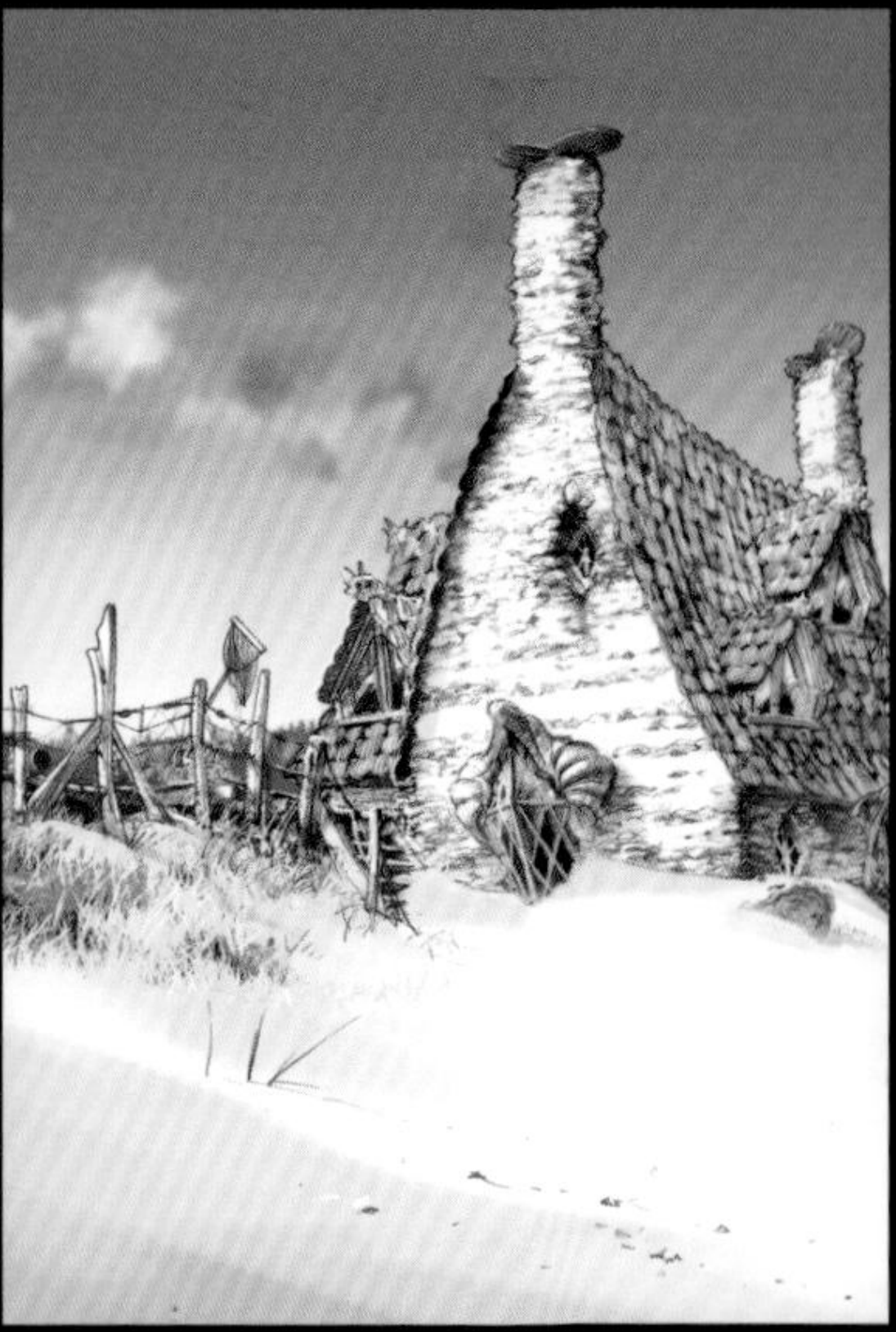

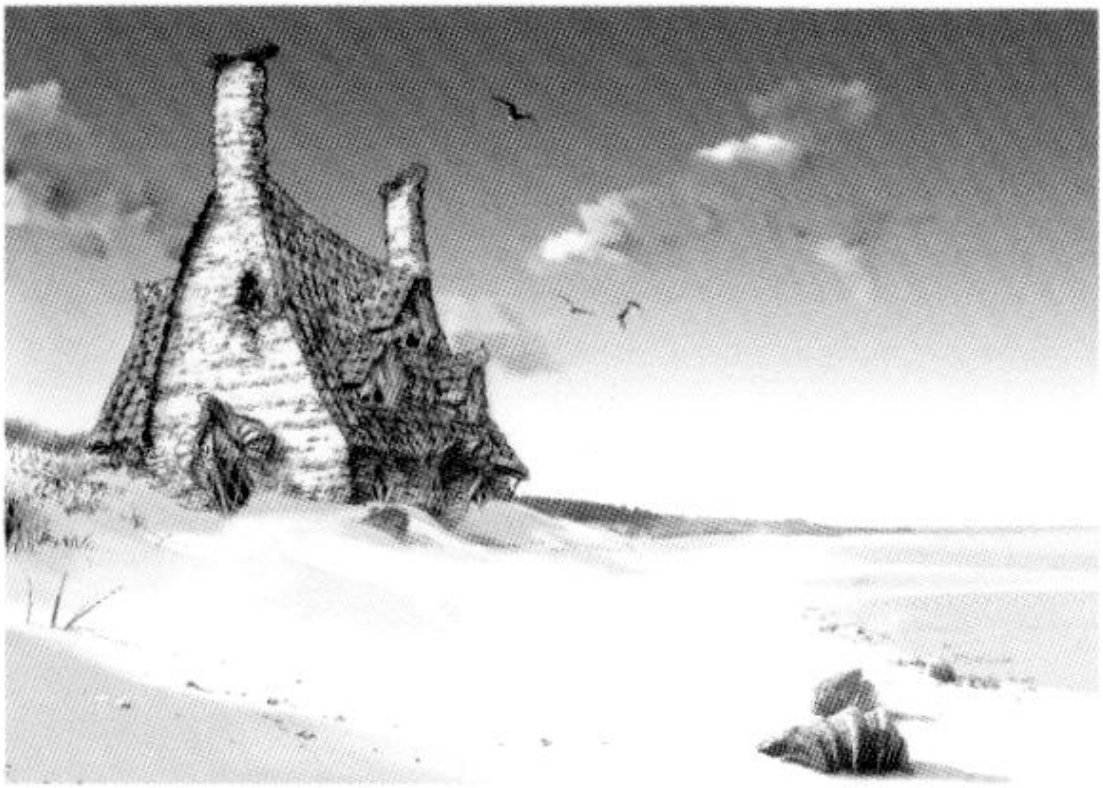

THESE PAGES: Two sketches of Shell Cottage by Andrew Williamson for *Harry Potter and the Deathly Hallows – Part 2*.

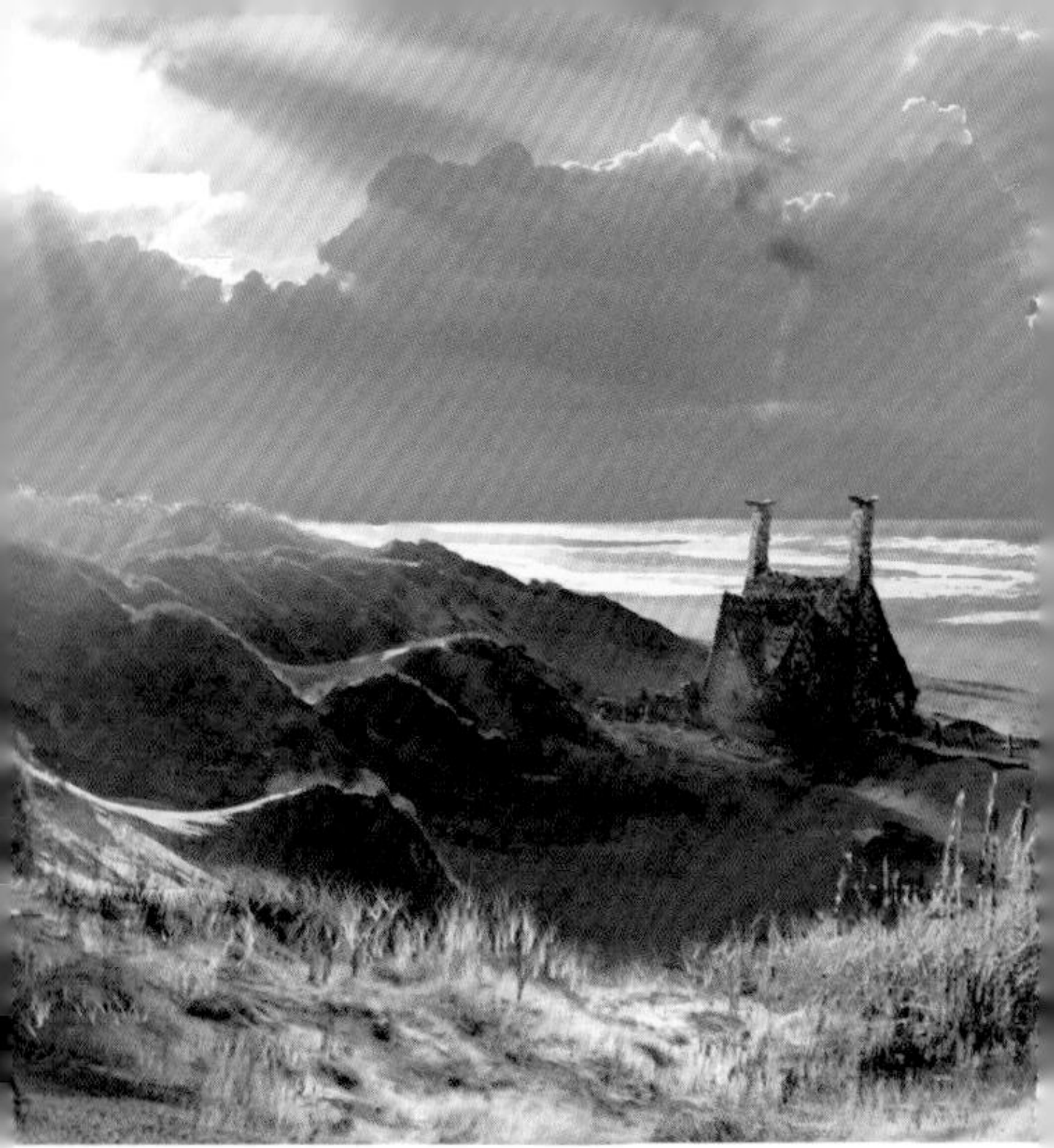

THESE PAGES: Dobby's grave sits on a hill above Shell Cottage. Art by Andrew Williamson for *Harry Potter and the Deathly Hallows – Part 2*.

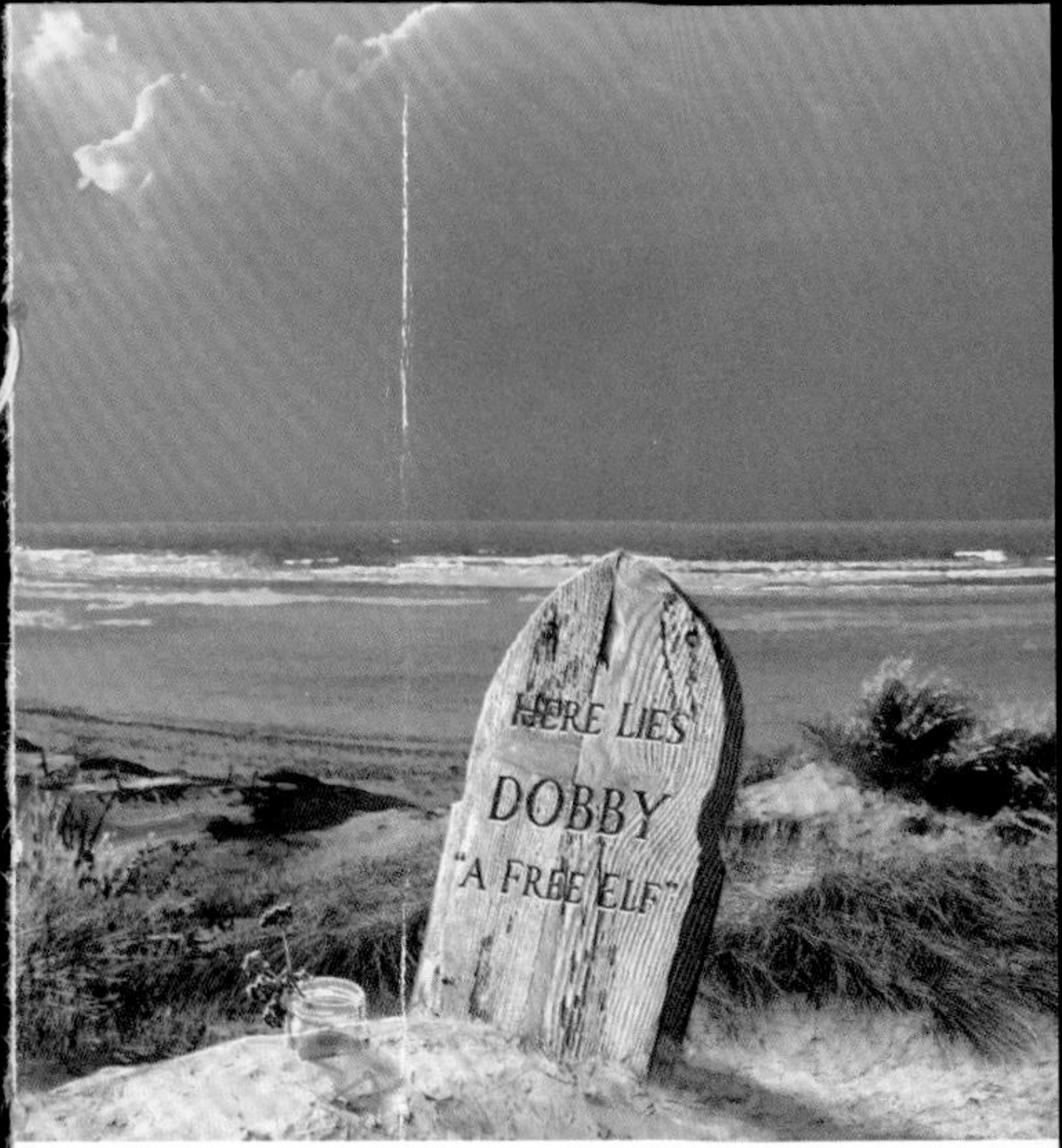
HERE LIES
DOBBY
"A FREE ELF"

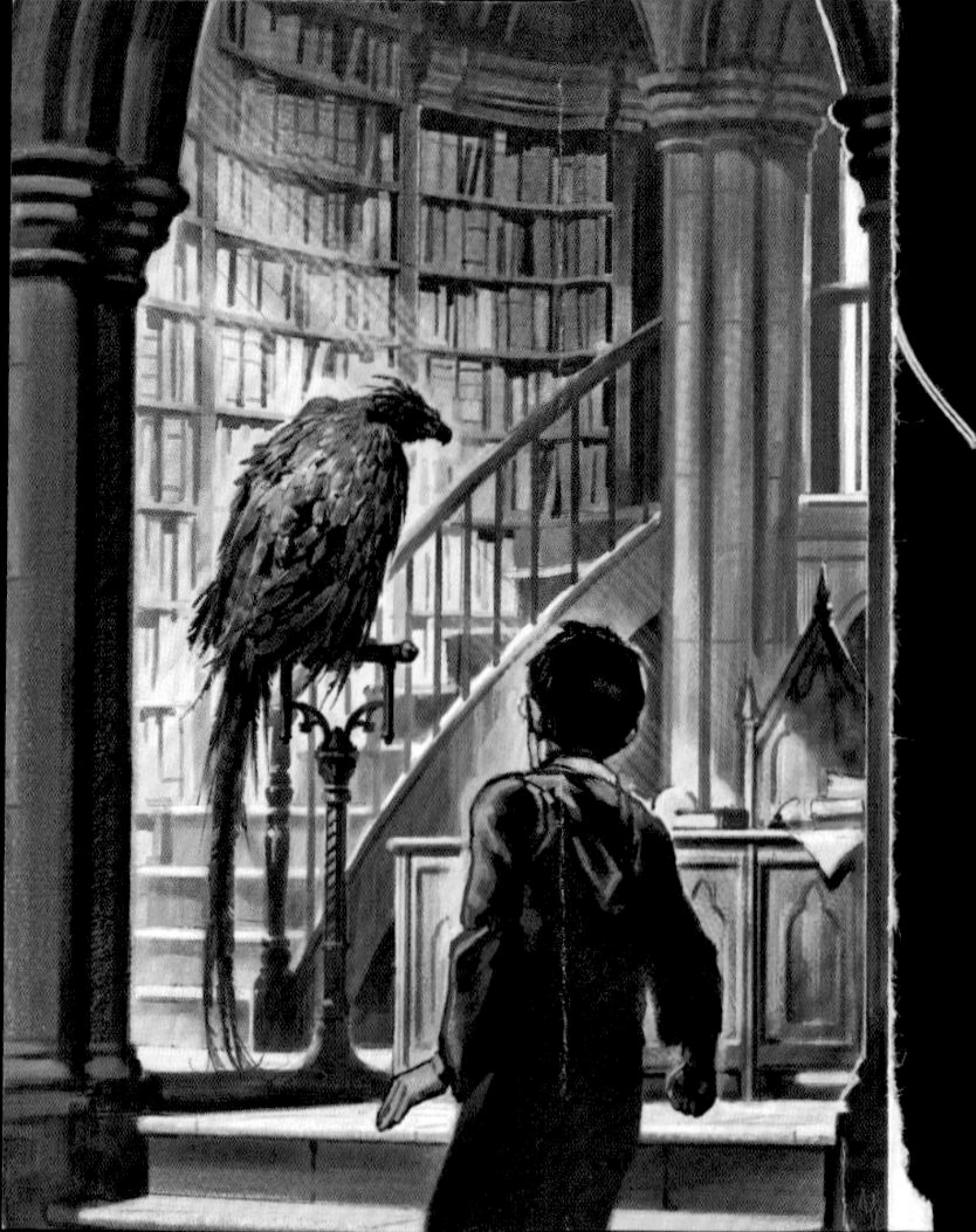

CONCLUSION

From the soaring towers of Hogwarts to the gravity-defying lean of Diagon Alley, the concept art for each mysterious location featured in the Harry Potter films explored fascinating ways to infuse the films' settings with magic. Of course, as the series progressed, the design for the sets often evolved as well. Popular

OPPOSITE: Harry Potter discovers Dumbledore's phoenix, Fawkes, on a Burning Day in concept art by Adam Brockbank for *Harry Potter and the Chamber of Secrets*.

settings, such as the Great Hall and the Dark Arts classroom, were frequently redressed for special celebrations, changes of season, and new inhabitants, which helped to keep familiar locations feeling fresh and exciting. Even the iconic exterior of Hogwarts itself gained a few new towers over the course of the series.

"They've been changed for no better reason than that it would just be nice to improve on them," says production designer Stuart Craig, noting that this is "part of the ongoing magical regeneration, from one film to another."

OPPOSITE: Artwork by Andrew Williamson for *Harry Potter and the Order of the Phoenix*.

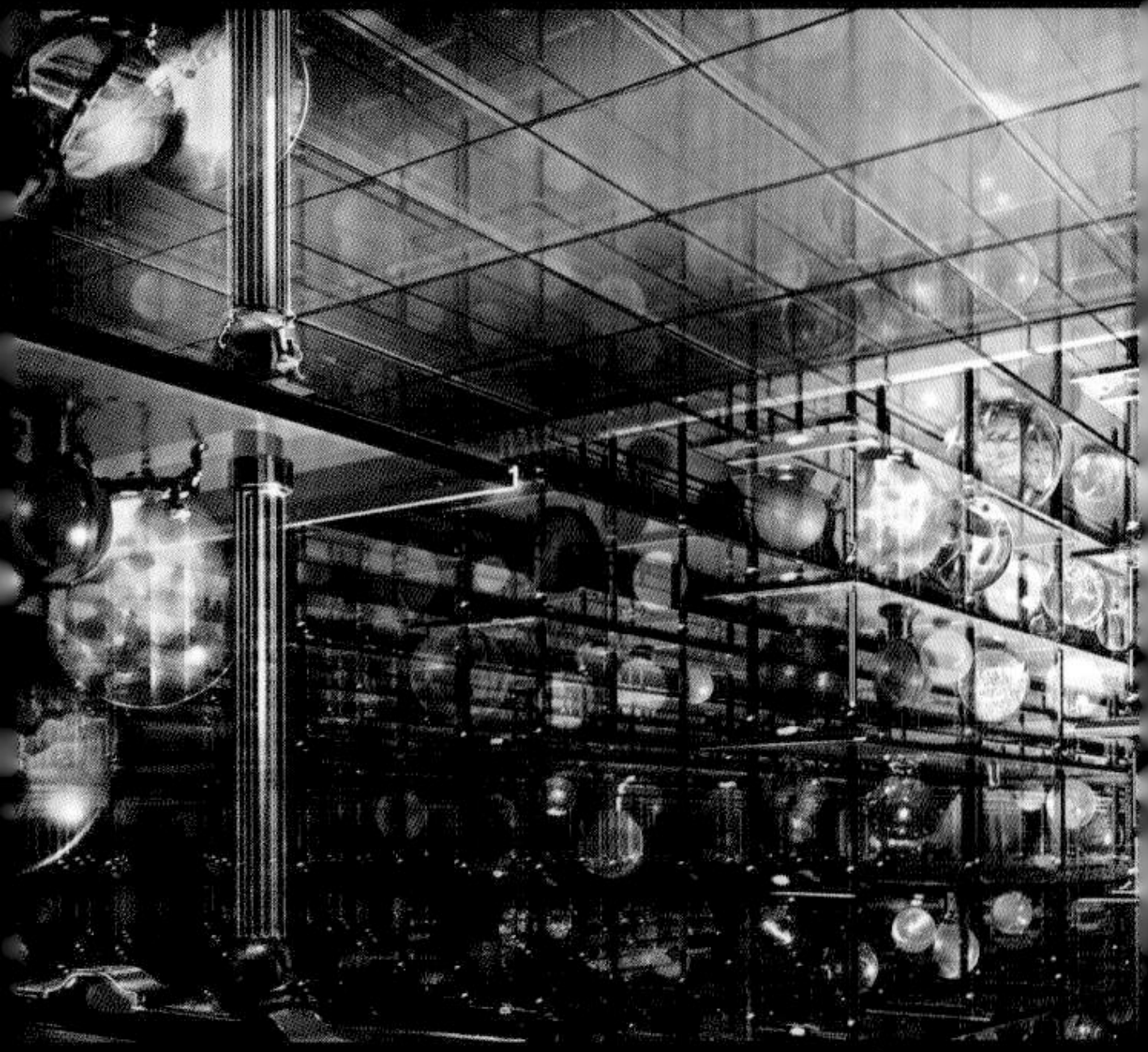

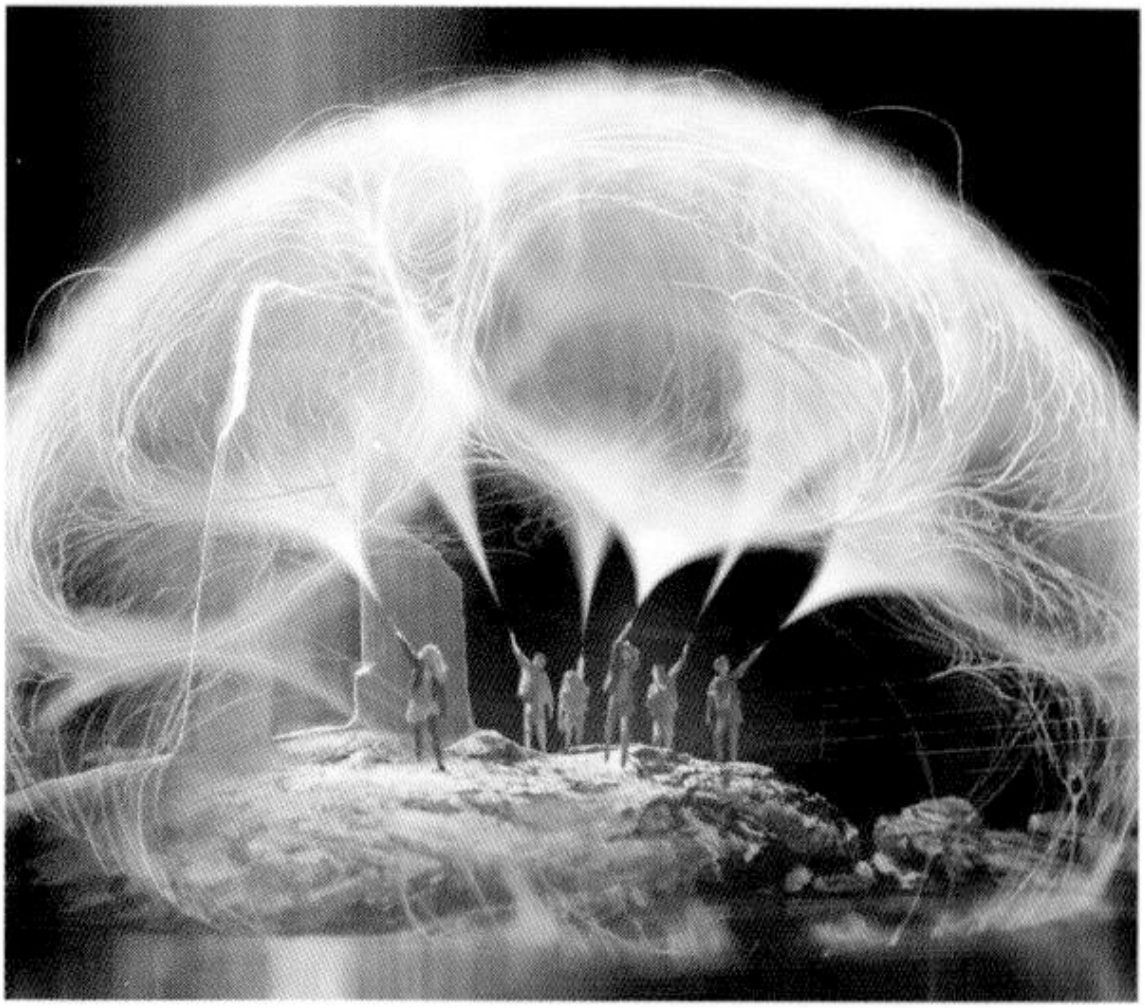

ABOVE: Adam Brockbank's concept art portraying Dumbledore's Army creating a Patronus shield in the Death Chamber for *Order of the Phoenix*. This scene did not occur in the film.

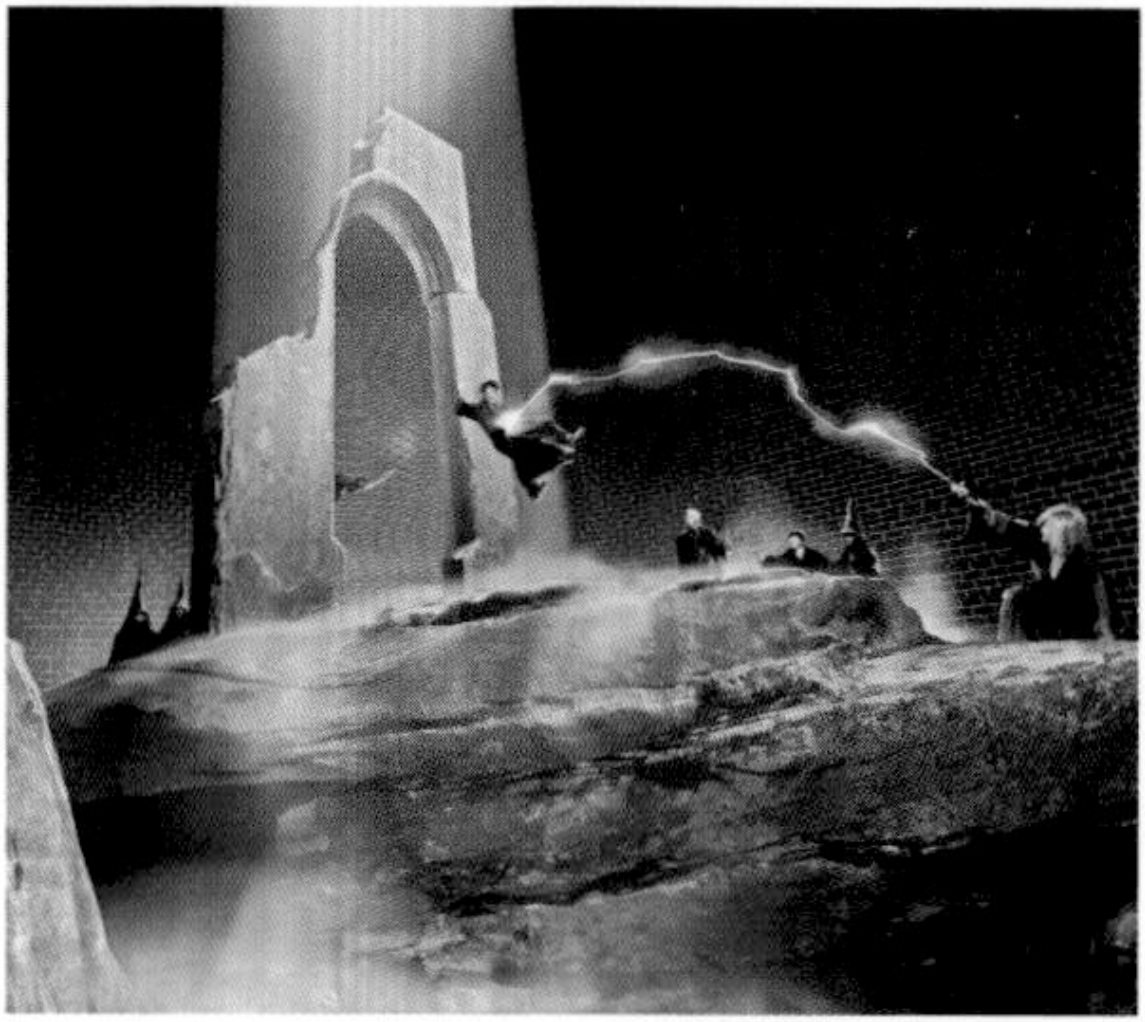

ABOVE: Andrew Williamson shows the moment when Bellatrix Lestrange casts the *Avada Kedavra* Curse at Sirius Black, sending him through the Veil, in *Order of the Phoenix*.

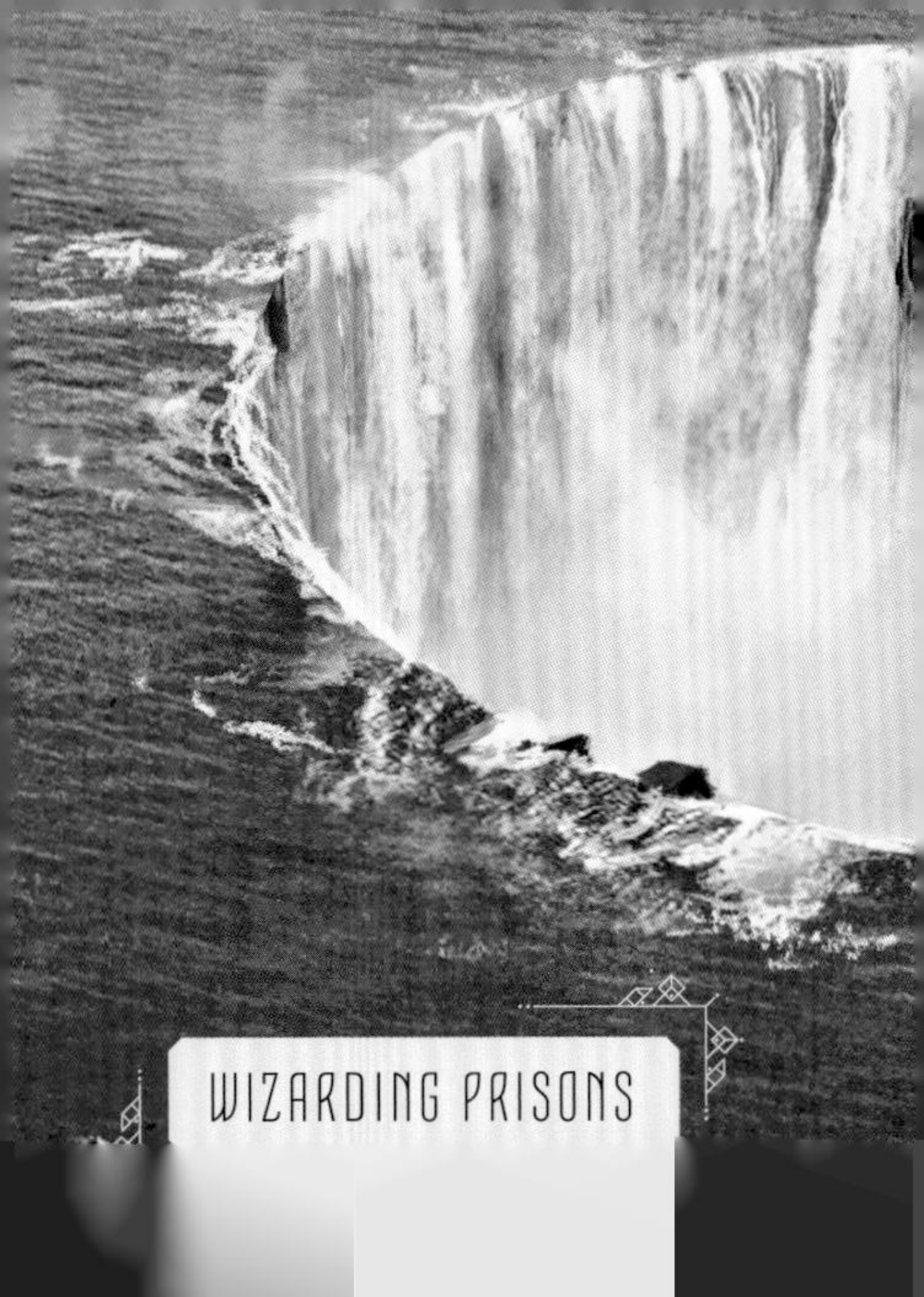

WIZARDING PRISONS

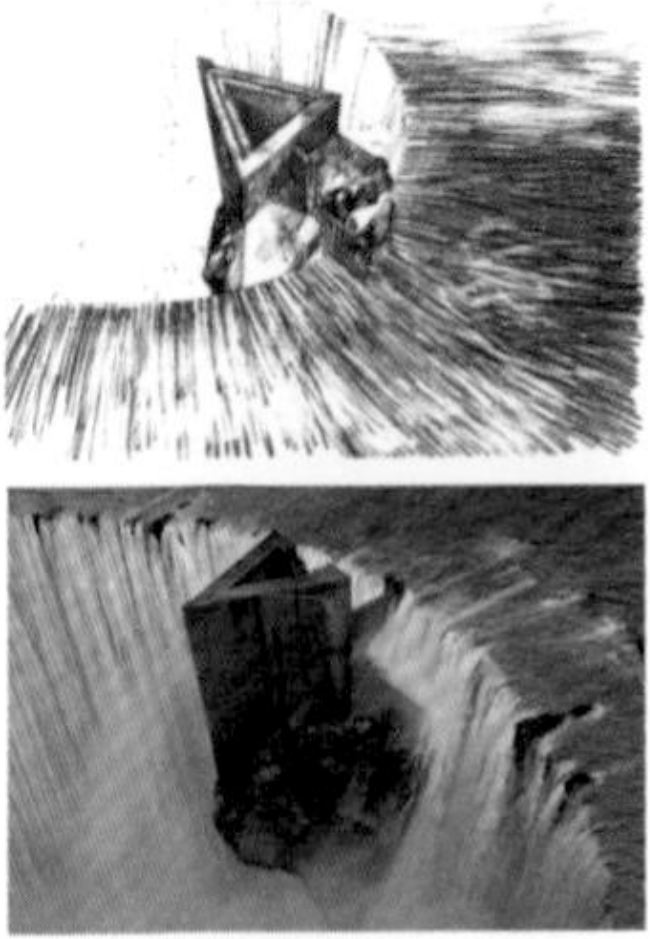

PAGES 270–273: Andrew Williamson depicts Azkaban on an island in a stormy sea.

ABOVE: The first sketch of Azkaban prison by production designer Stuart Craig for *Harry Potter and the Order of the Phoenix* (*top*) and a painting by Andrew Williamson following the design (*bottom*).

NURMENGARD

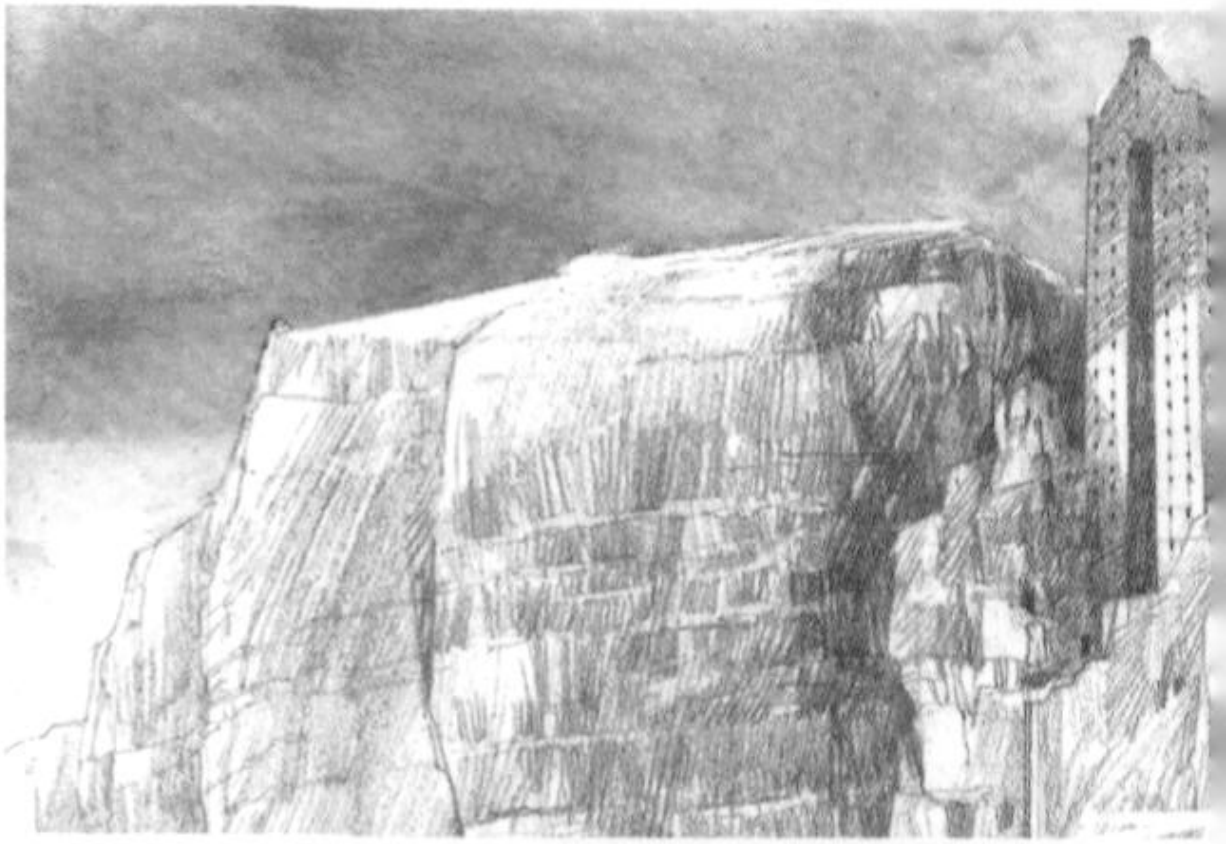

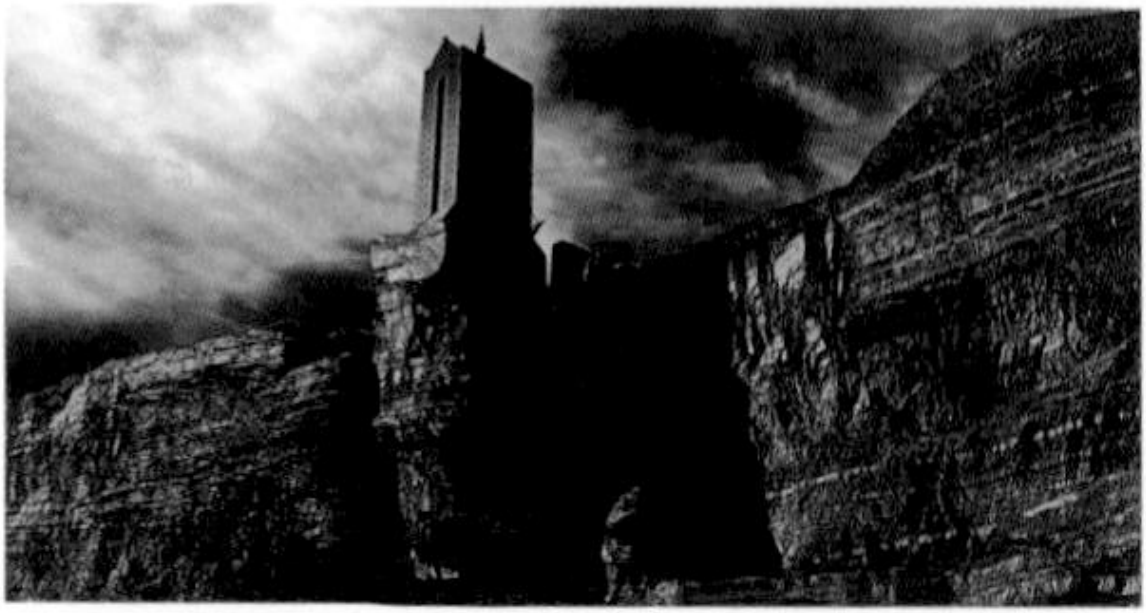

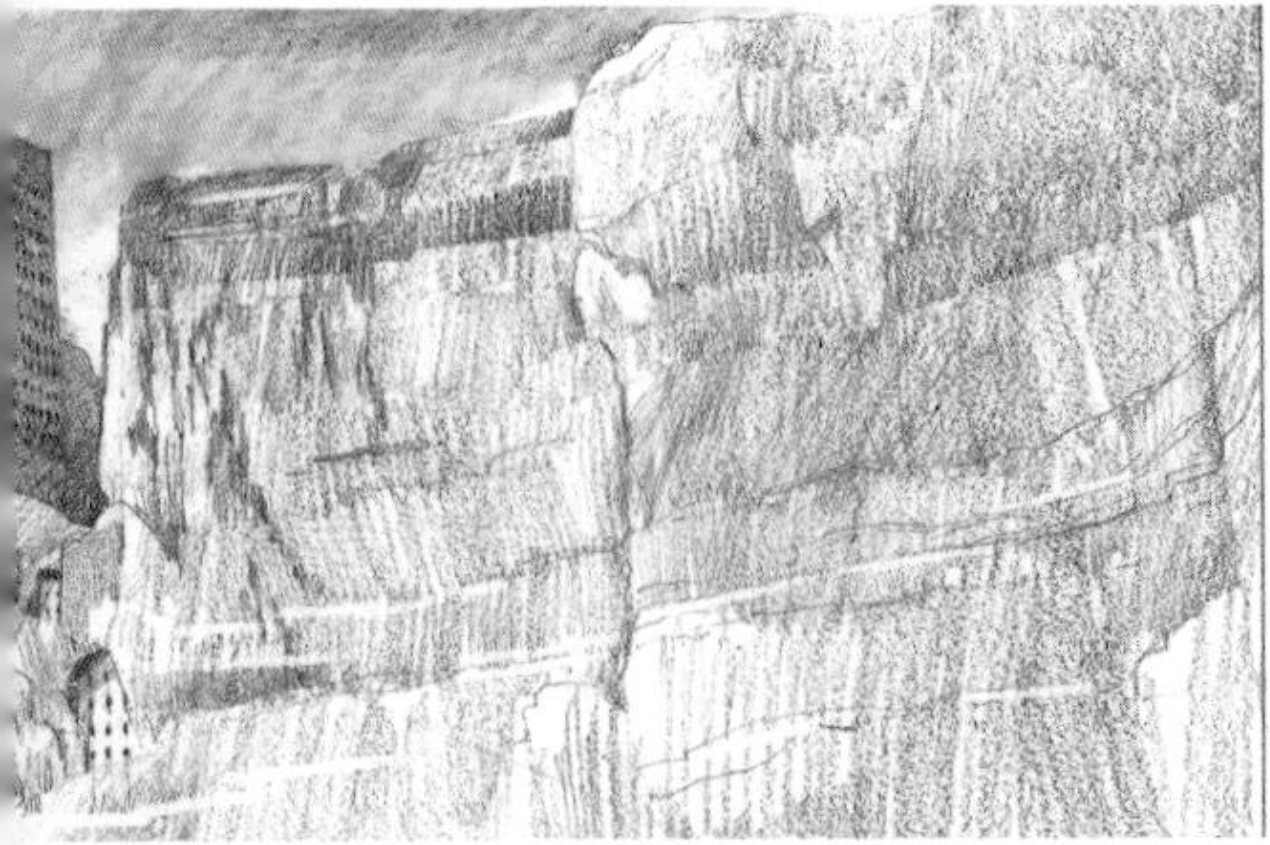

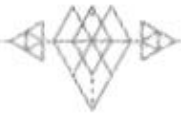

THESE PAGES: A sketch and a painting of Nurmengard prison, where Gellert Grindelwald was imprisoned and where Voldemort tortured him for information about the Elder Wand, as seen in *Harry Potter and the Deathly Hallows – Part 2*.

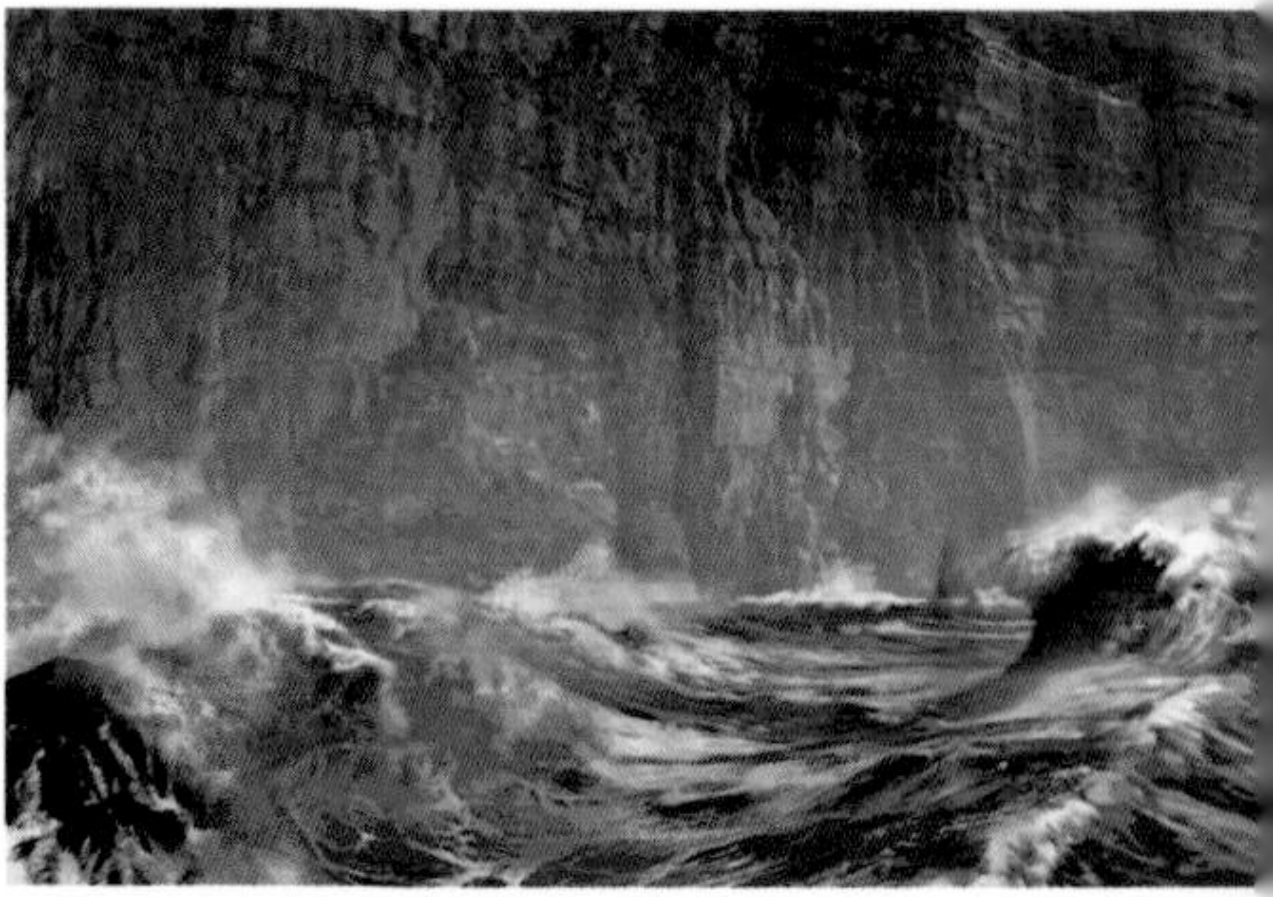

THESE PAGES: In *Harry Potter and the Half-Blood Prince*, Harry and Professor Dumbledore travel to a remote cave to retrieve one of Voldemort's Horcruxes. Visual development for this location by Andrew Williamson.

THE CAVE

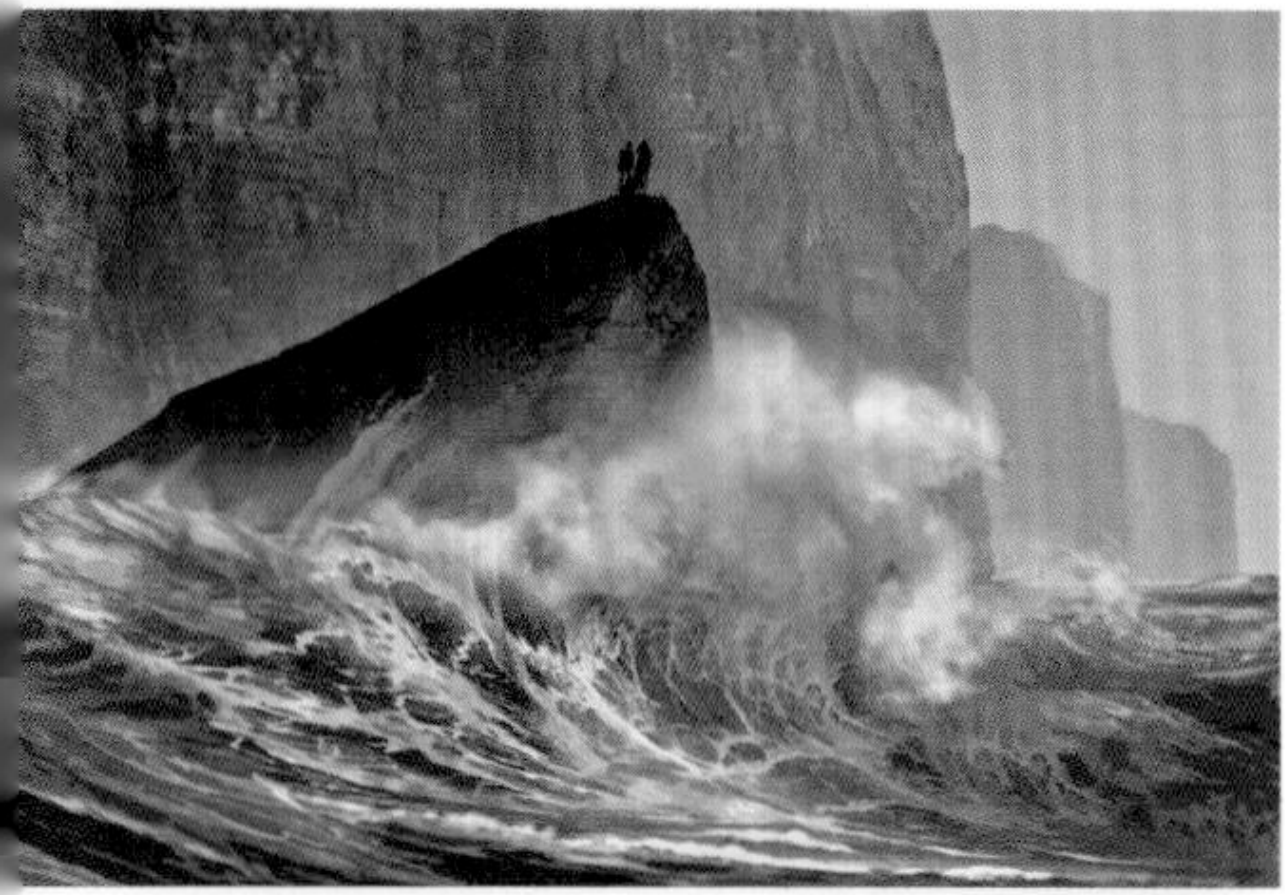

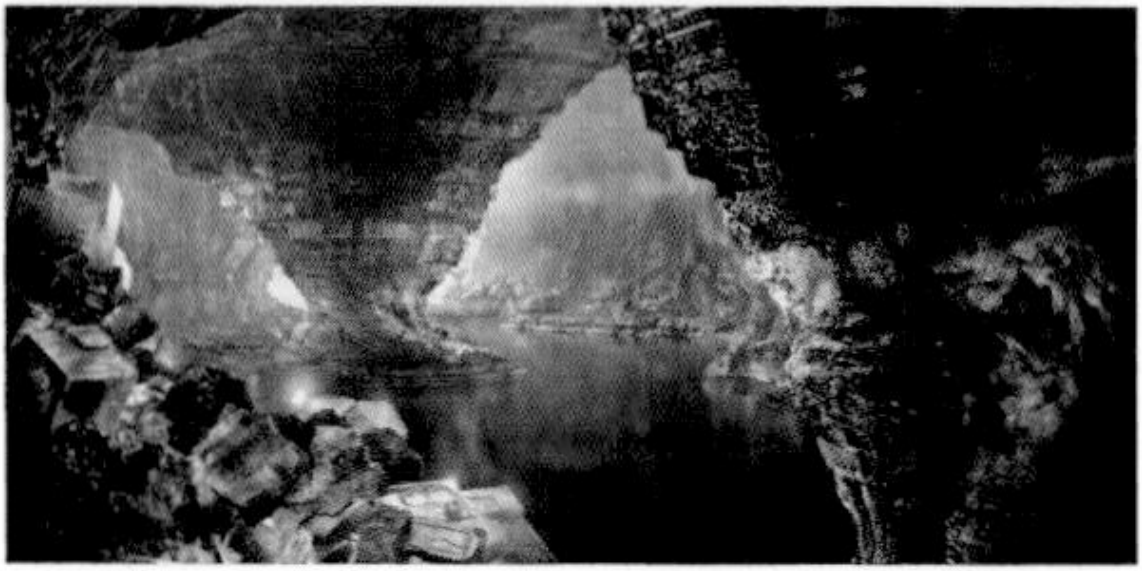

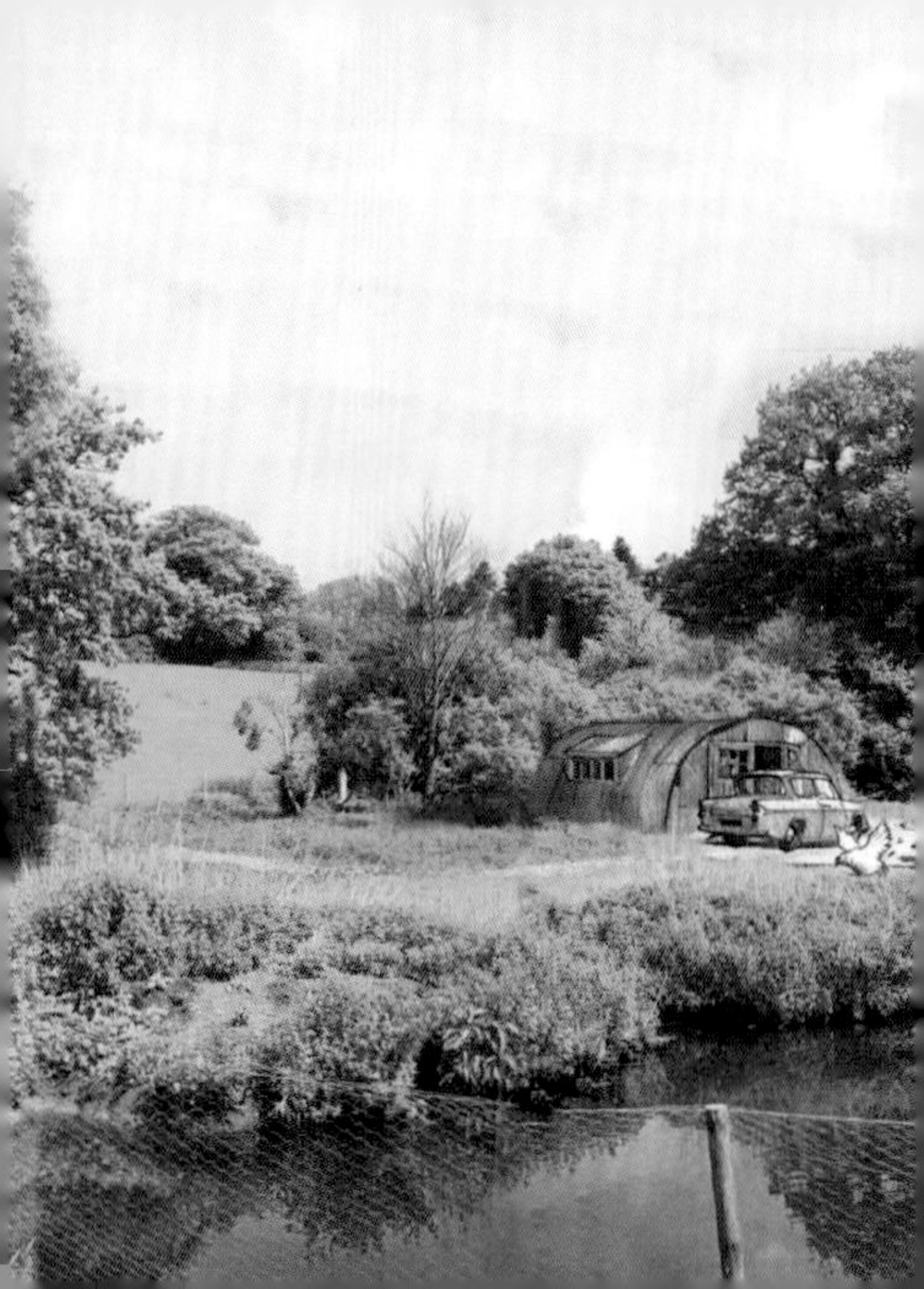

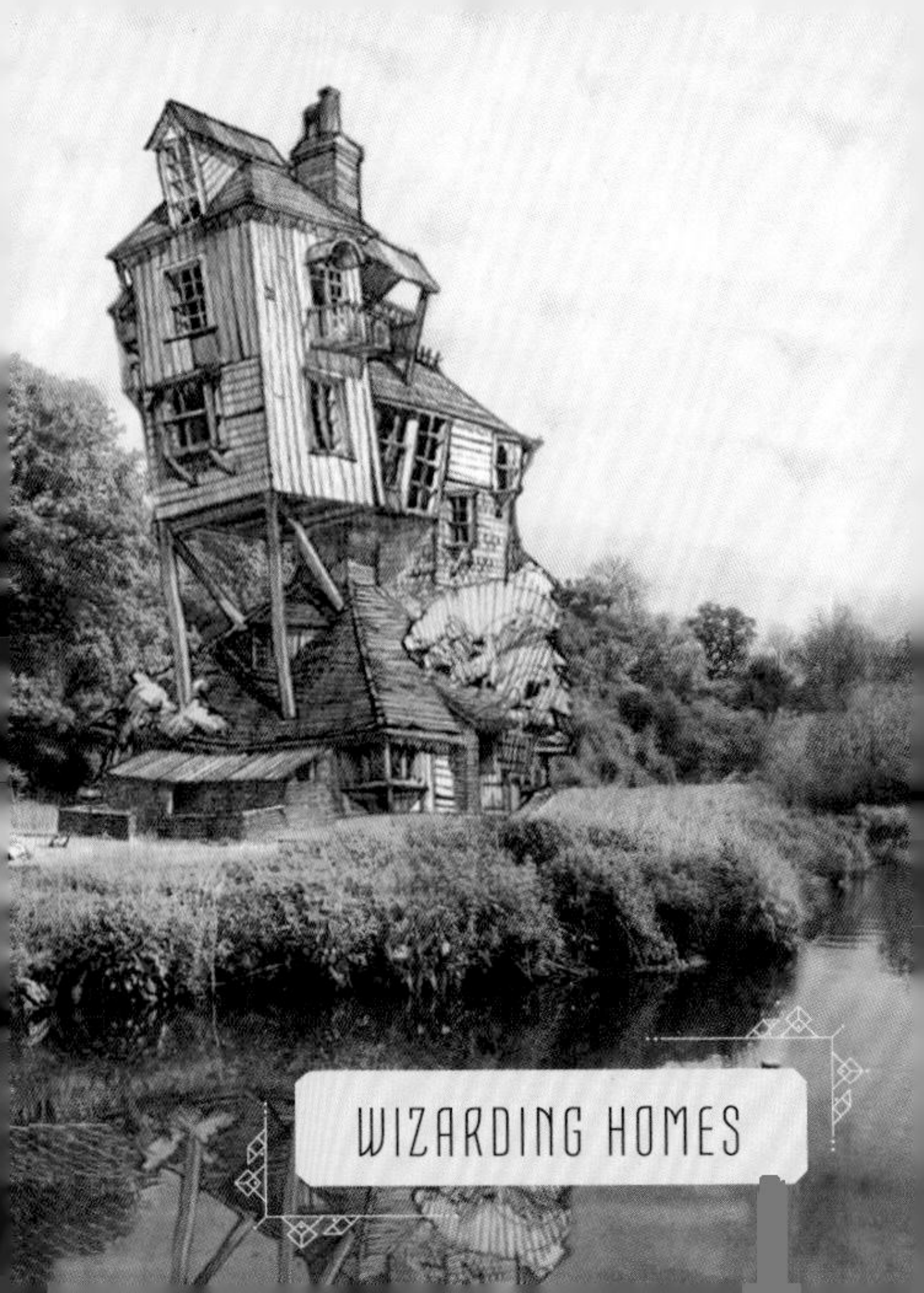

WIZARDING HOMES

THE BURROW

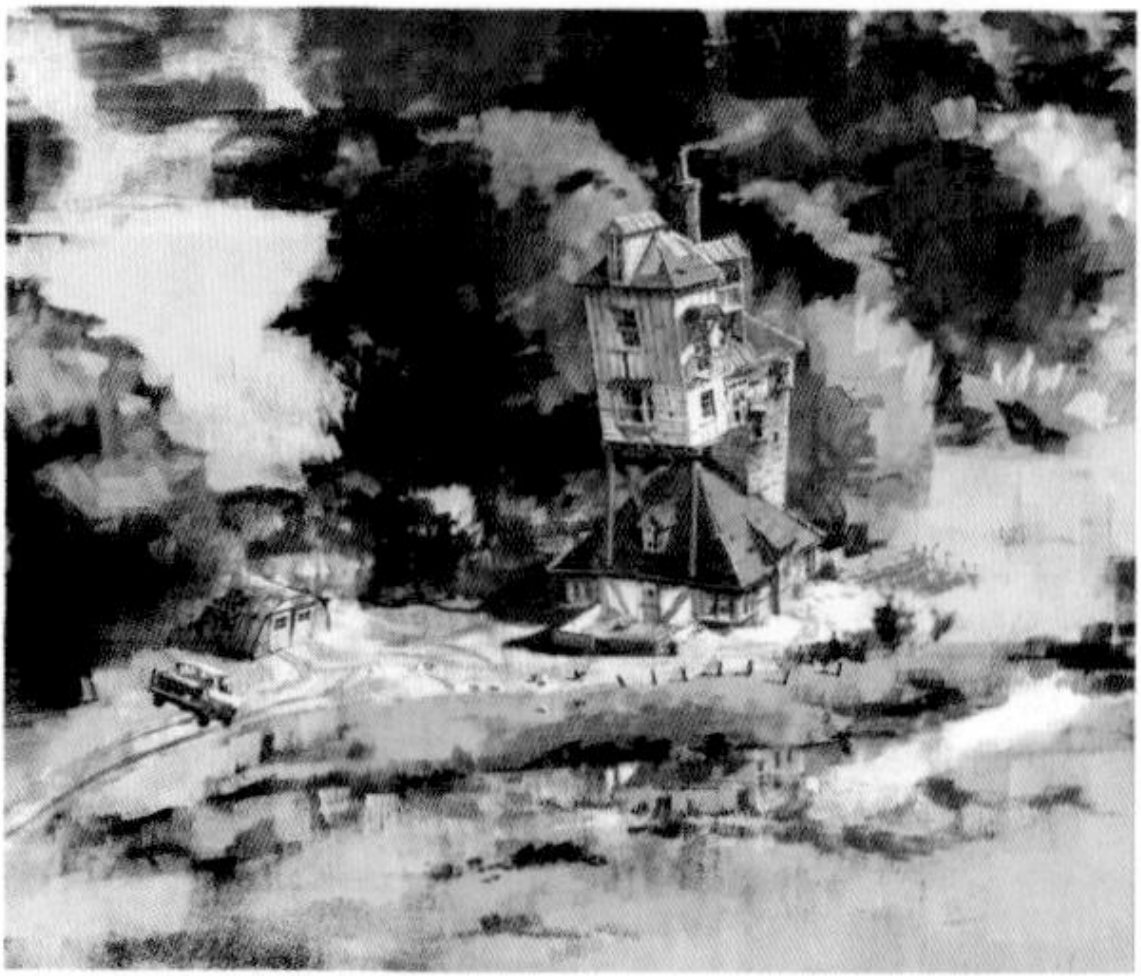

PAGES 278–280: Andrew Williamson illustrates the flying Ford Anglia at The Burrow for *Harry Potter and the Chamber of Secrets*.

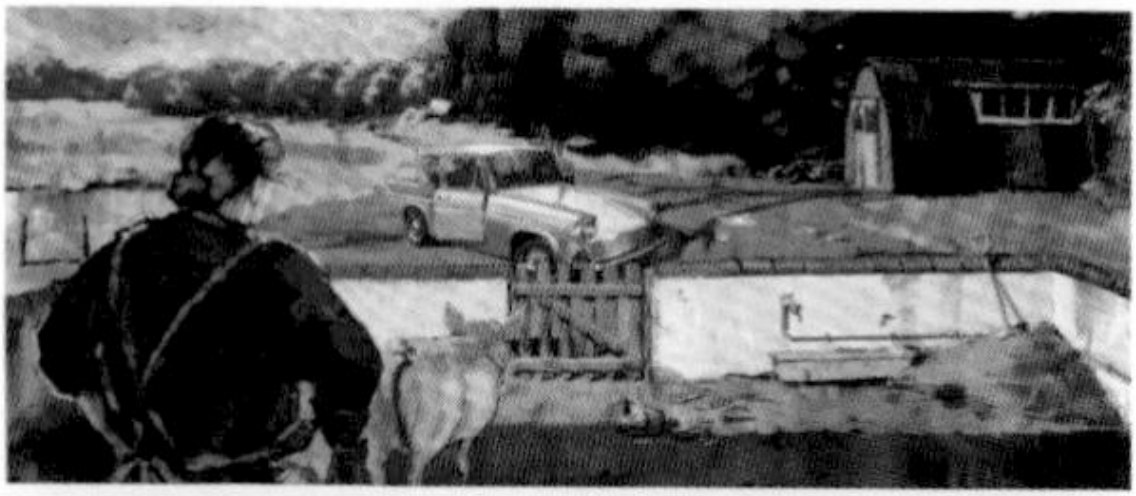

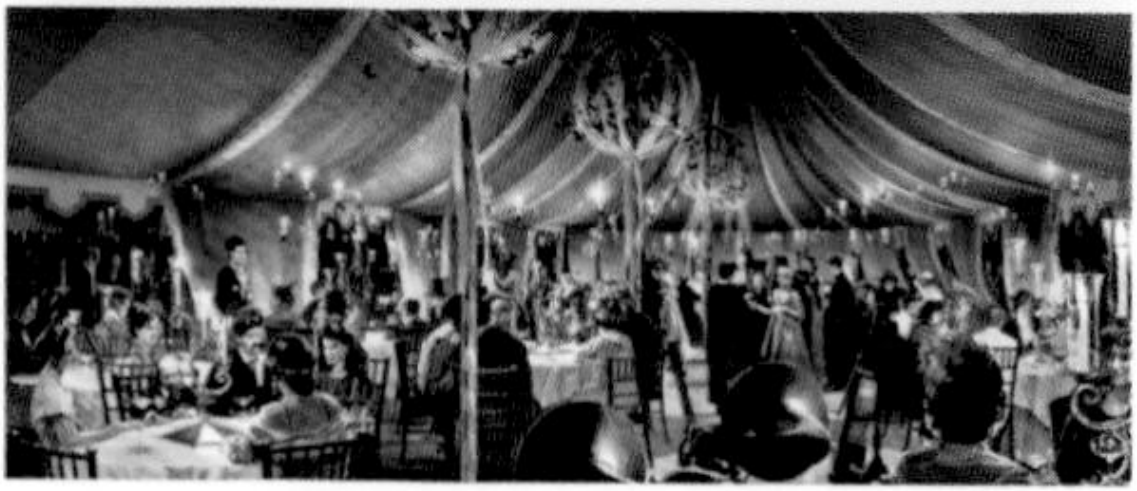

TOP: Andrew Williamson portrays Molly Weasley about to confront her sons about taking their father's car in *Chamber of Secrets*.

ABOVE: The wedding of Bill Weasley and Fleur Delacour took place in a covered tent in the garden of The Burrow. Art by Andrew Williamson for *Harry Potter and the Deathly Hallows – Part 2*.

THESE PAGES: Andrew Williamson depicts The Burrow under attack by Death Eaters in *Harry Potter and the Half-Blood Prince*.

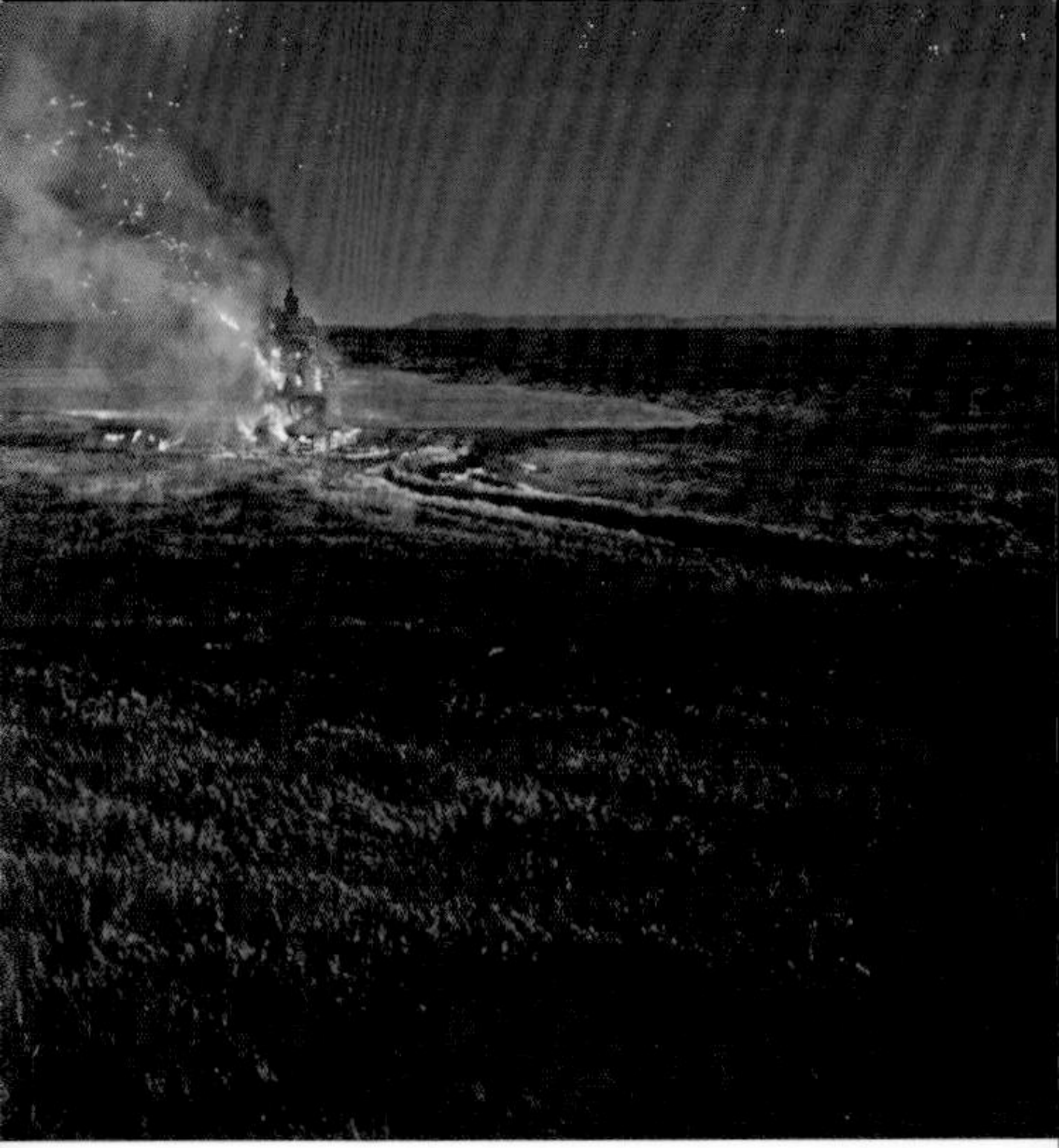

NUMBER TWELVE, GRIMMAULD PLACE

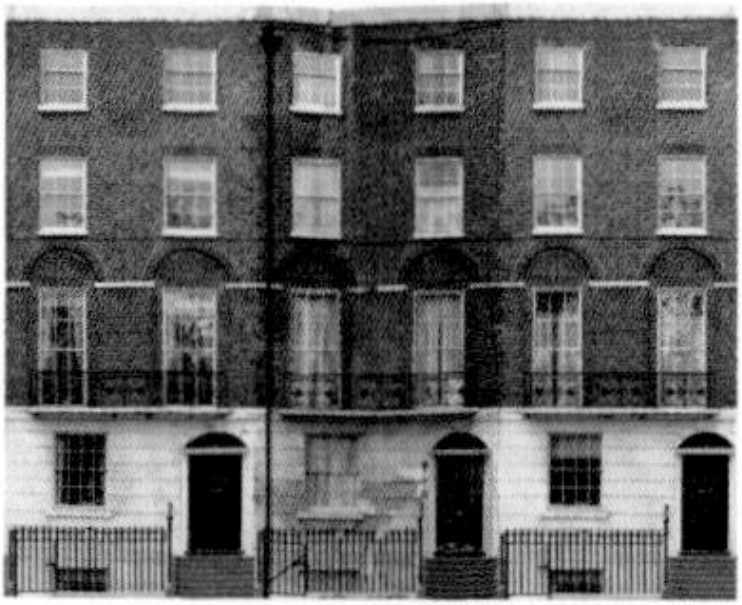

ABOVE: The façade of Grimmauld Place opens up to reveal Number Twelve, as detailed by Andrew Williamson.

OPPOSITE TOP: Number Twelve, Grimmauld Place, the ancestral home of the House of Black, as painted by Andrew Williamson for *Harry Potter and the Order of the Phoenix*.

OPPOSITE BOTTOM: The Weasley family spends Christmas at Sirius's home. Art by Adam Brockbank.

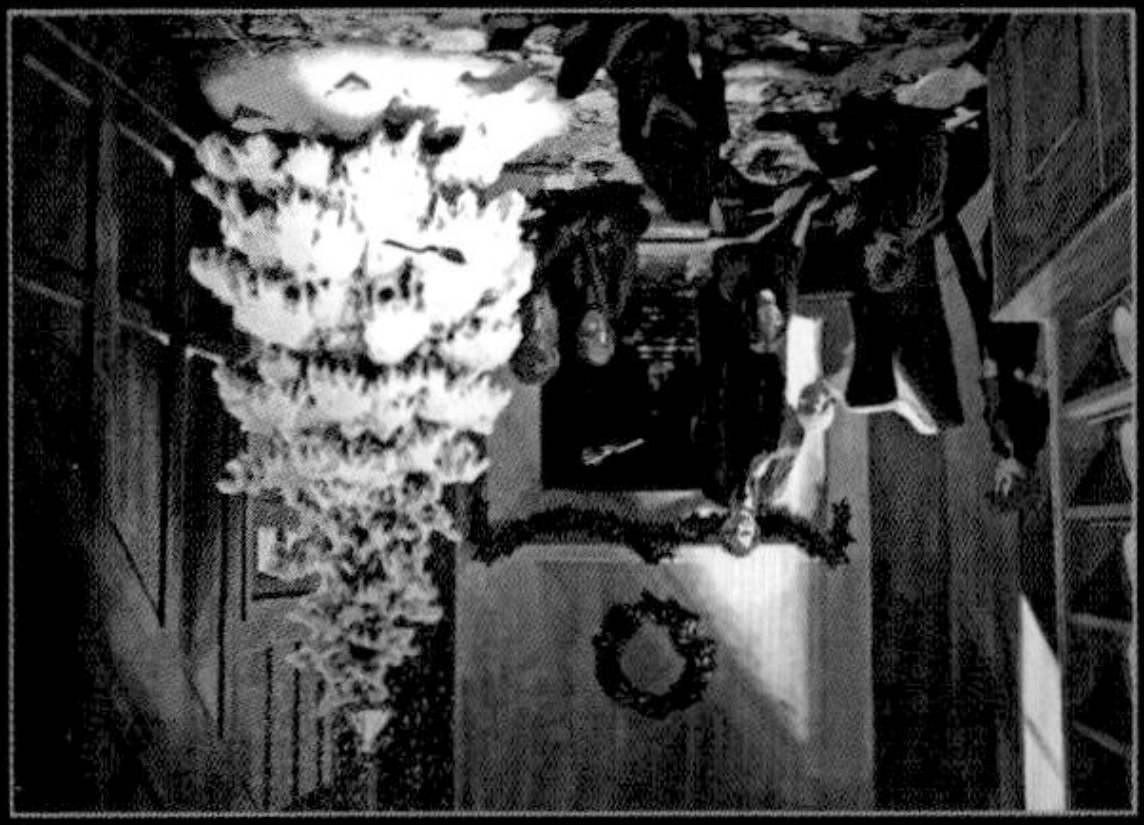

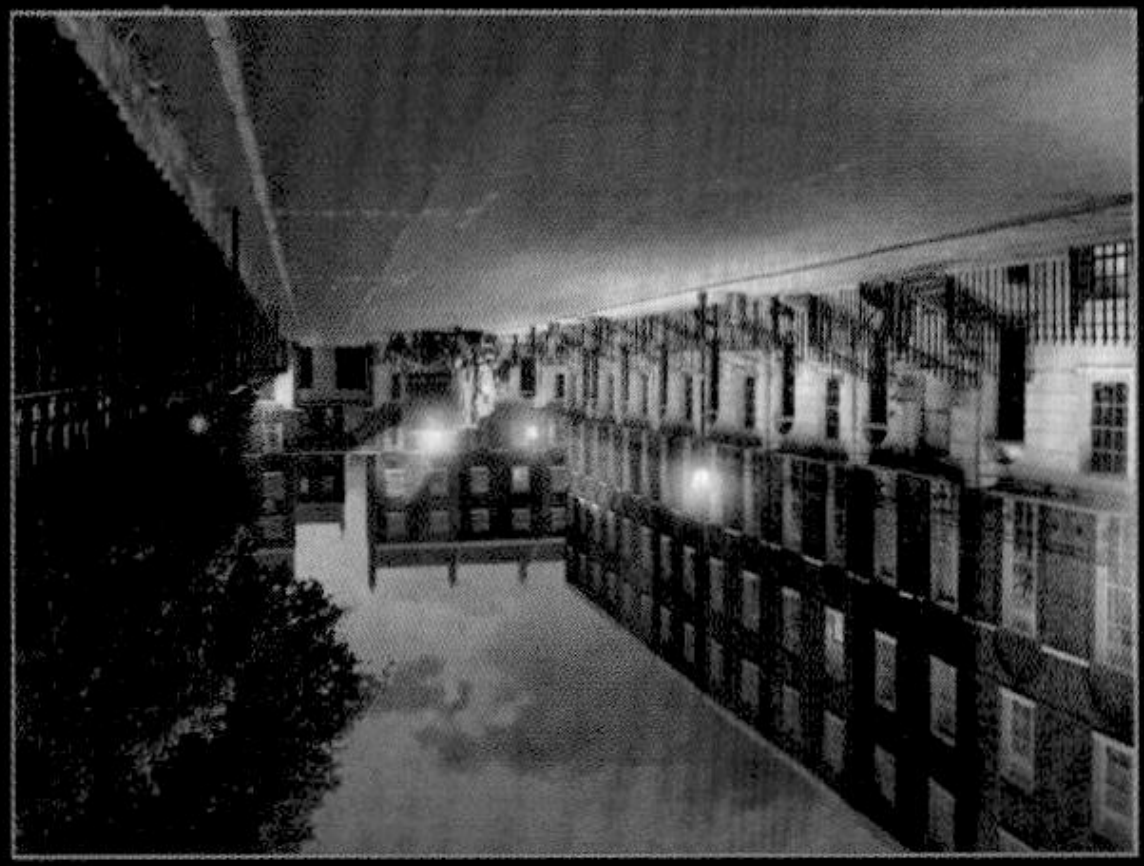

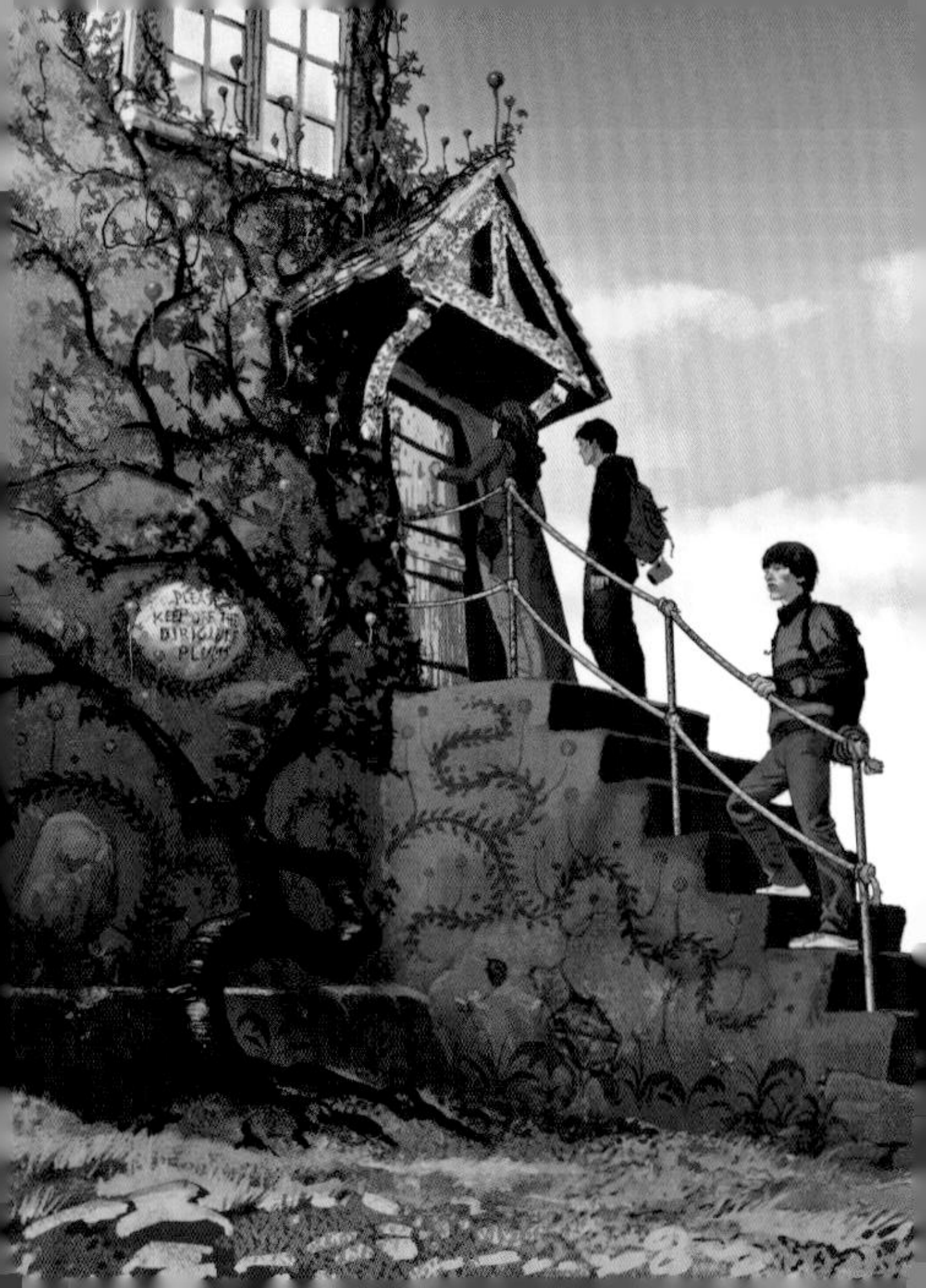
PLEASE
KEEP OFF THE
BIRKLOFF
PLUM

LOVEGOOD HOUSE

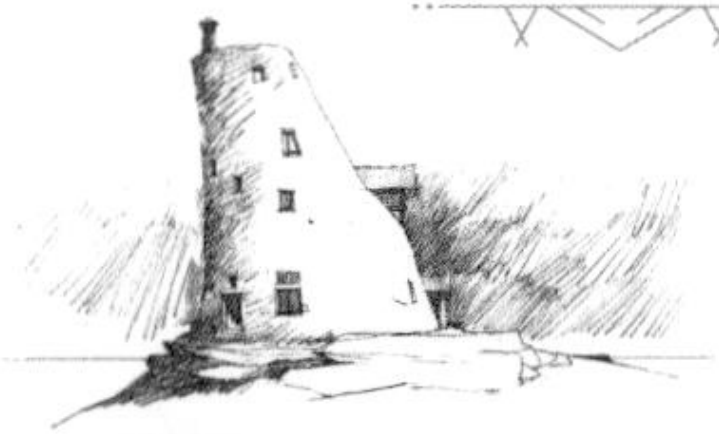

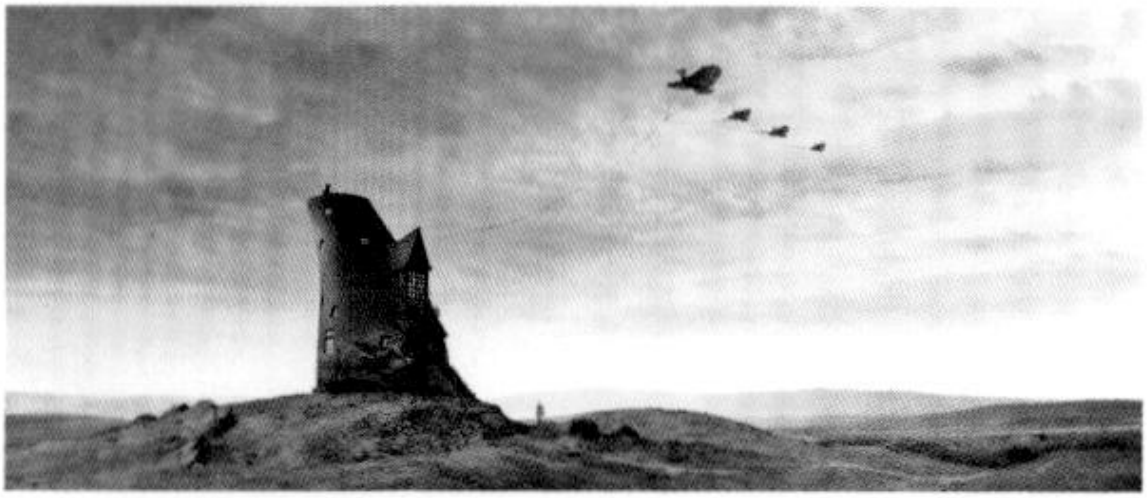

OPPOSITE: Hermione, Harry, and Ron approach the Lovegood house for help, as seen in *Harry Potter and the Deathly Hallows – Part 1*.

TOP: A sketch by Stuart Craig of the Lovegood house, noted for resembling a rook chess piece.

ABOVE: Adam Brockbank depicts the house perched on its hill with kites flying above it.

MALFOY MANOR

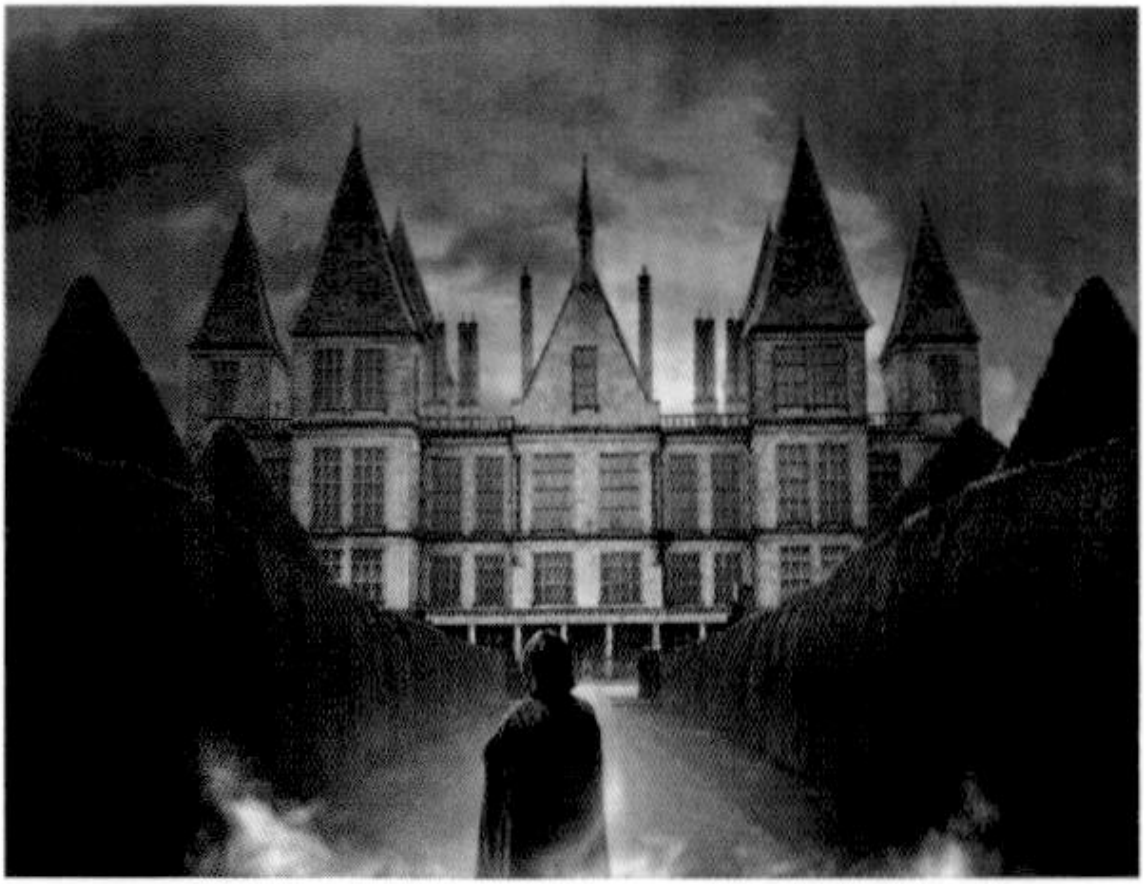

ABOVE: Severus Snape stands before Malfoy Manor in *Harry Potter and the Deathly Hallows – Part 2*. Concept art by Andrew Williamson.

OPPOSITE: Inside the dining hall of Malfoy Manor, where Charity Burbage hangs above Voldemort and his Death Eaters. Art by Andrew Williamson.

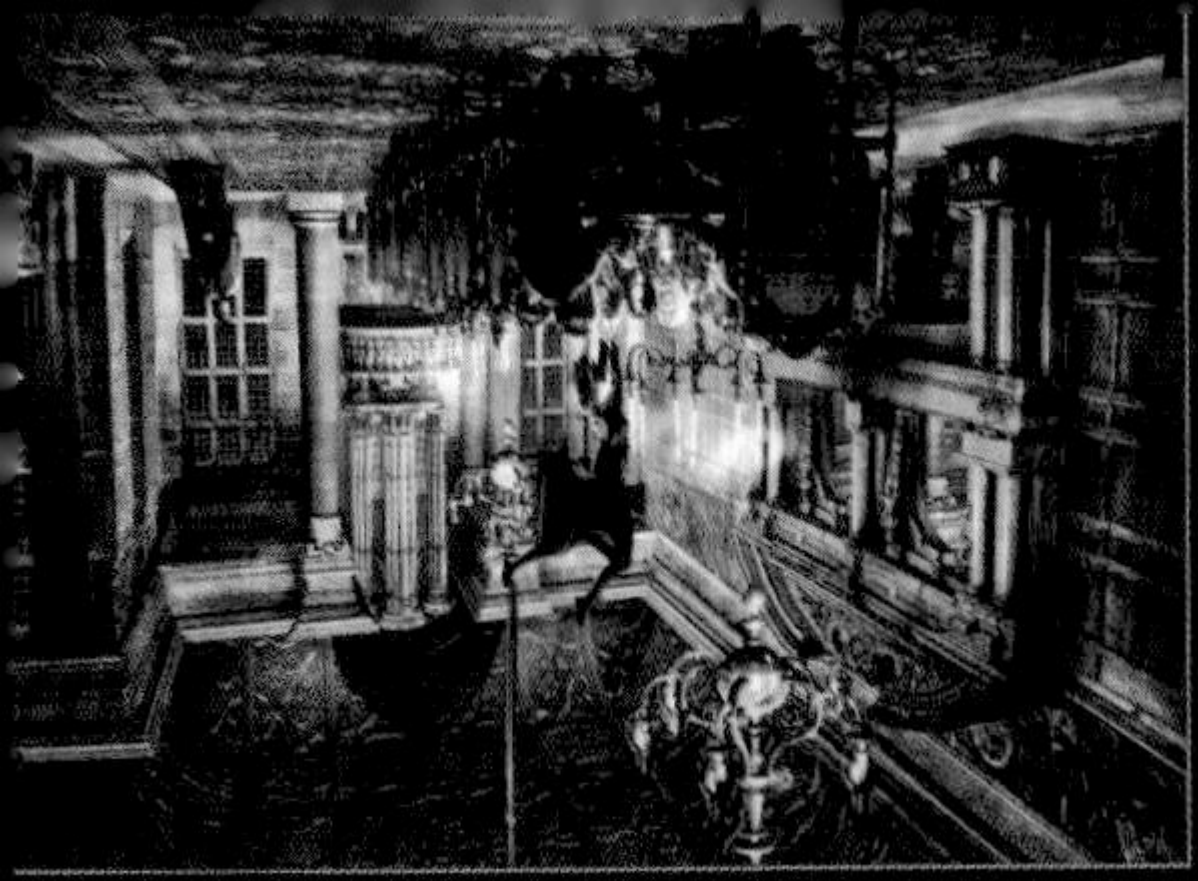

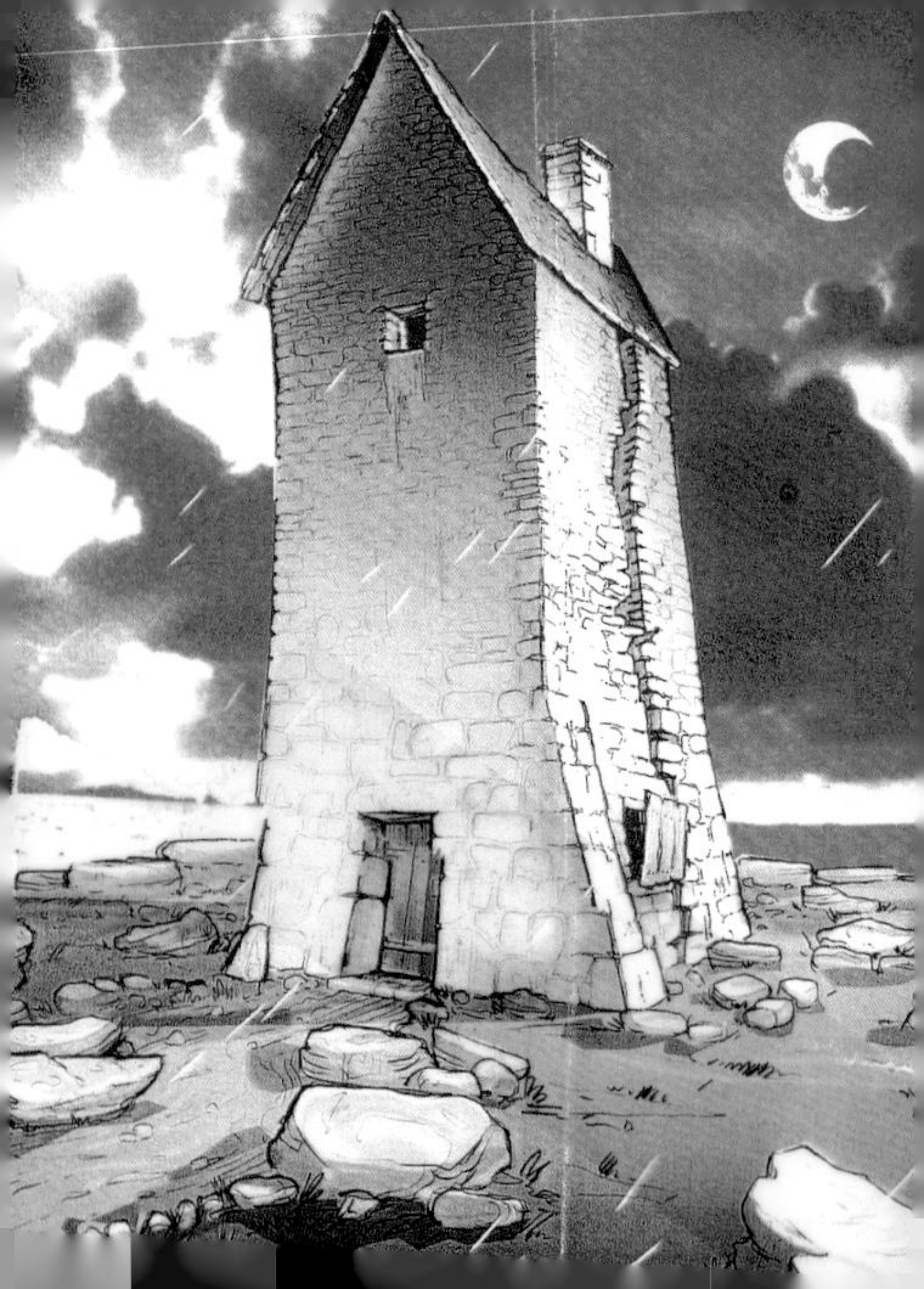

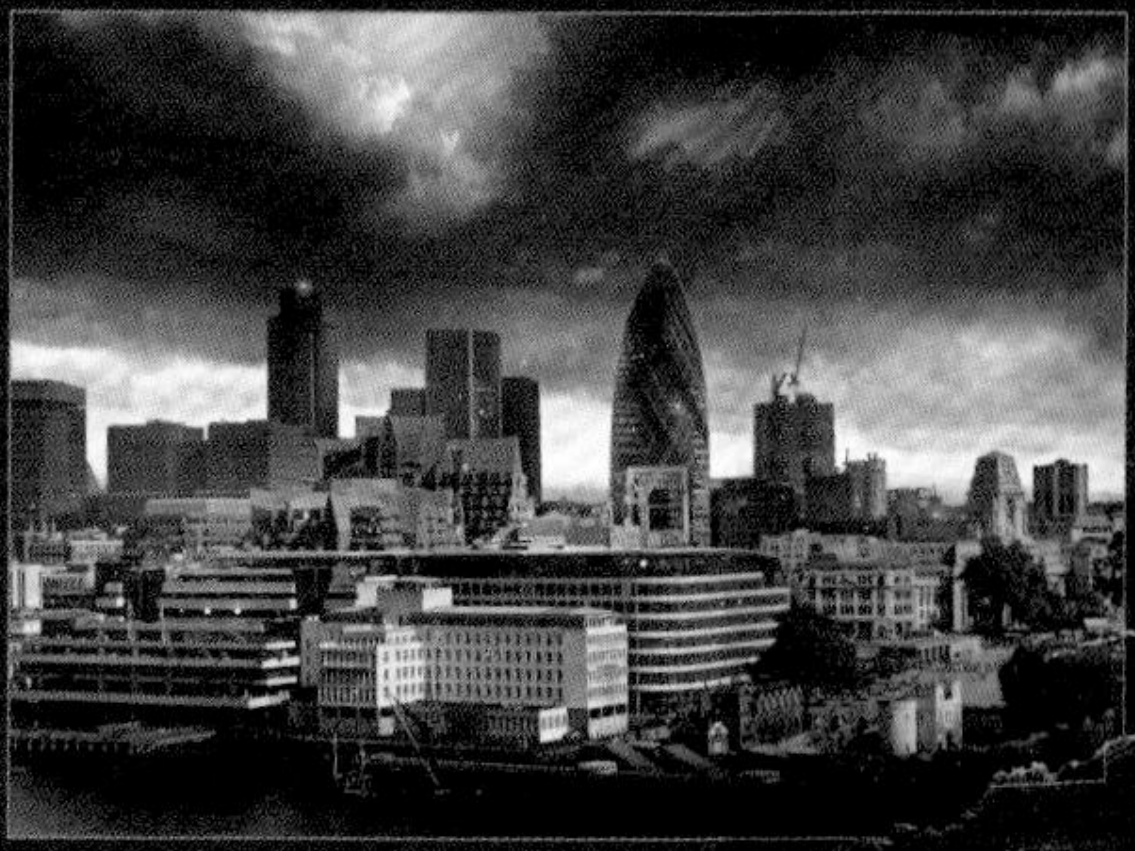

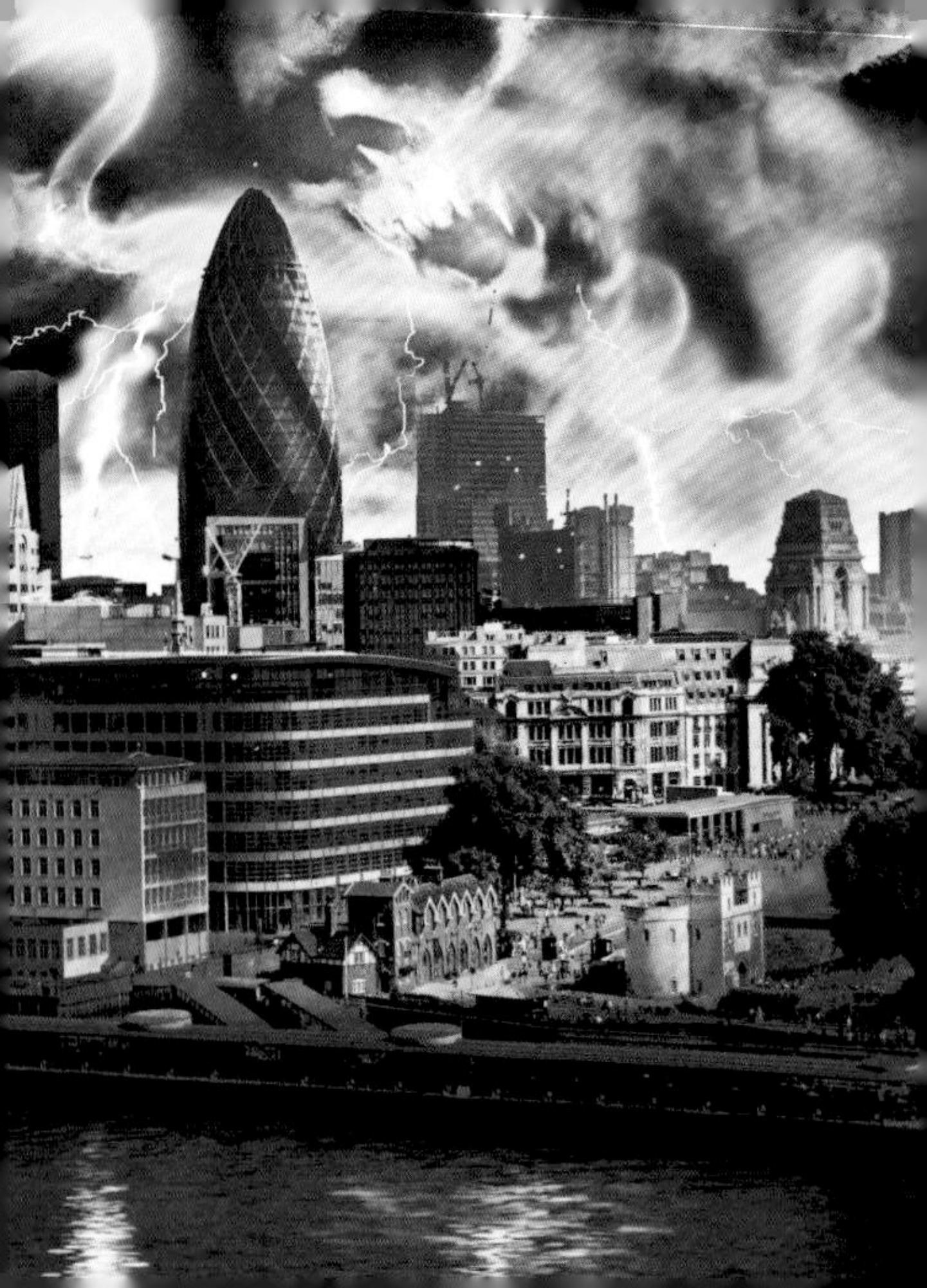

KING'S CROSS

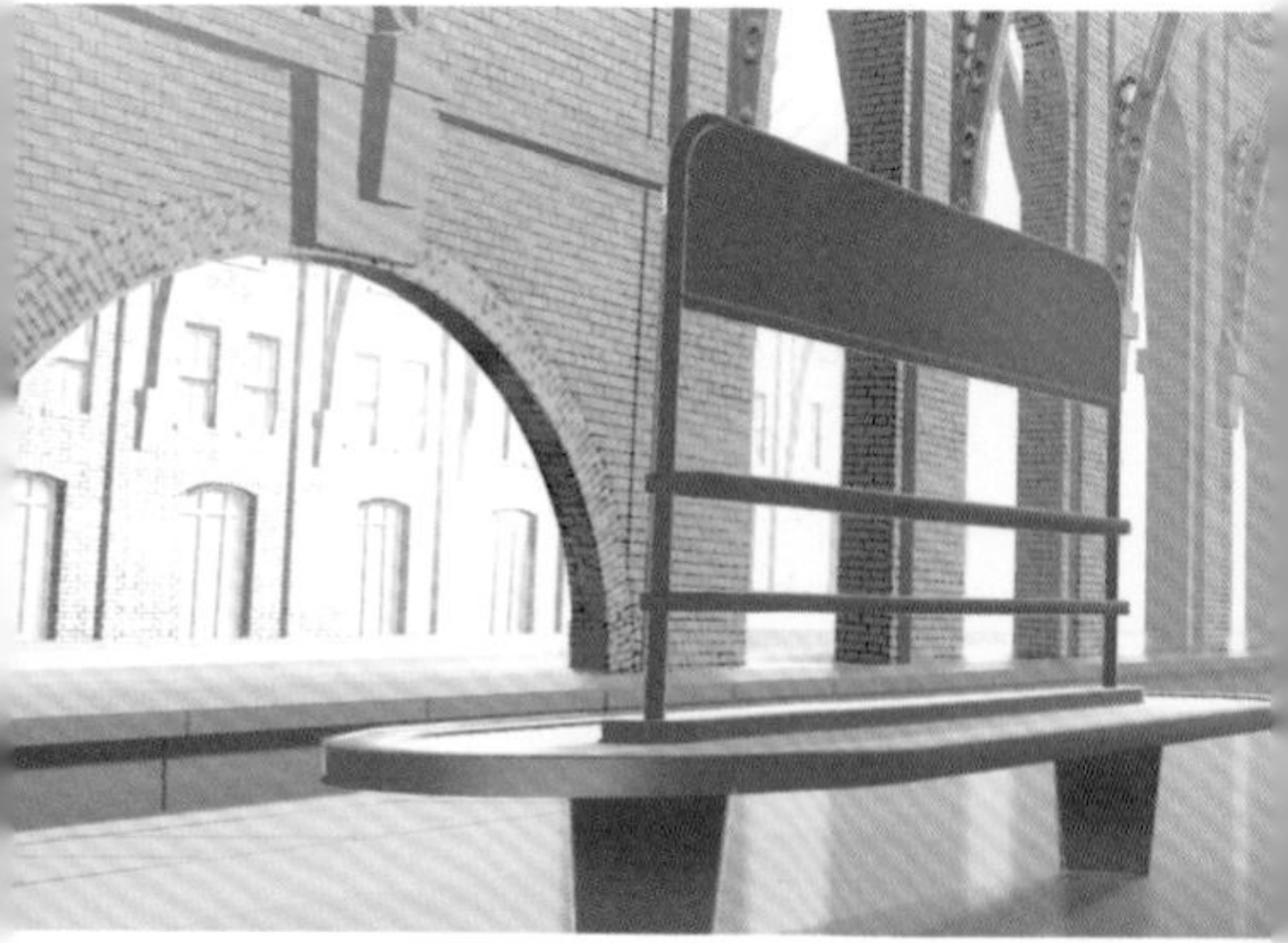

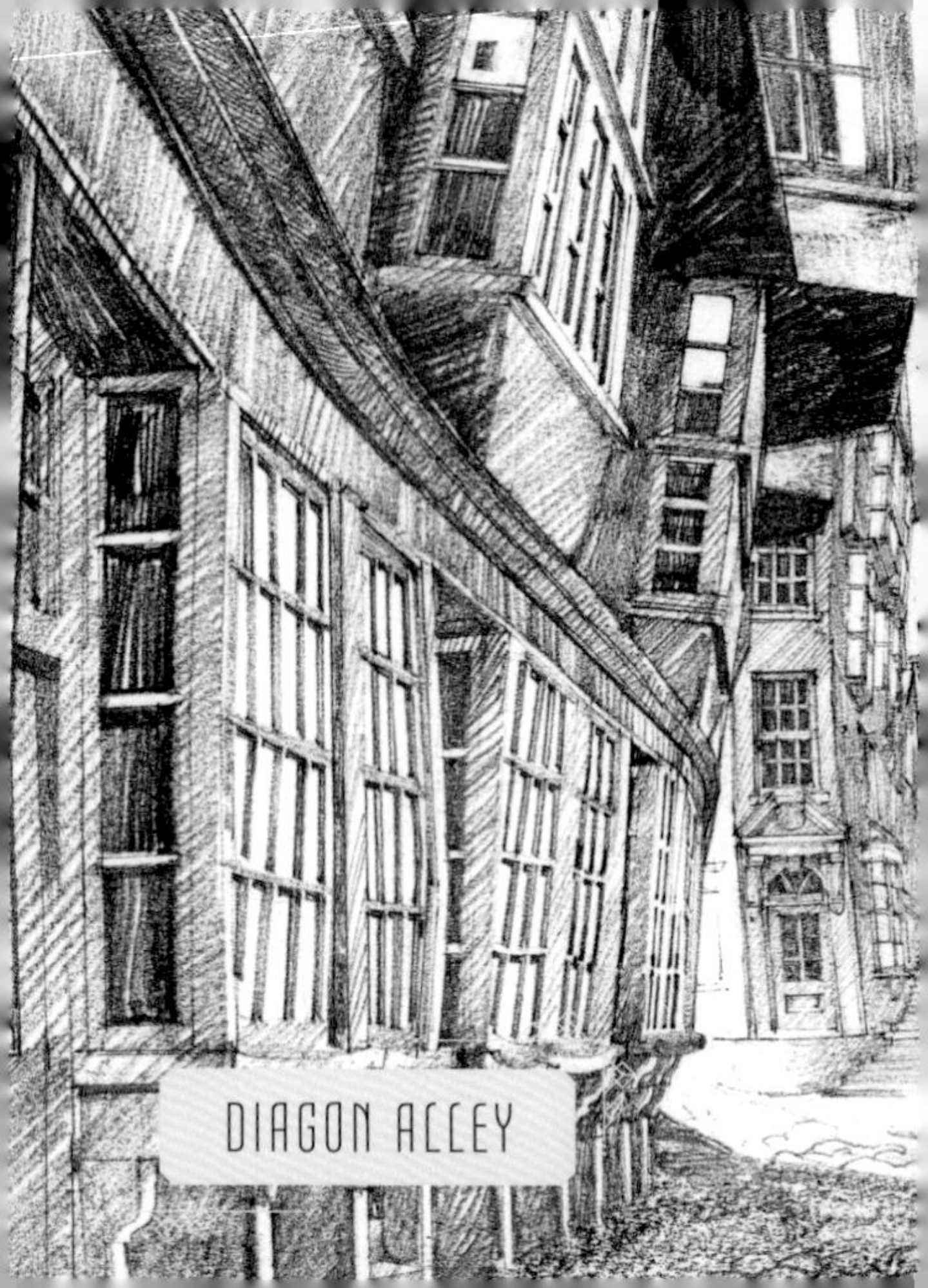
DIAGON ALLEY

THESE PAGES: Concept art by Andrew Williamson of the ethereal King's Cross Station where Harry encounters Dumbledore in *Harry Potter and the Deathly Hallows – Part 2*.

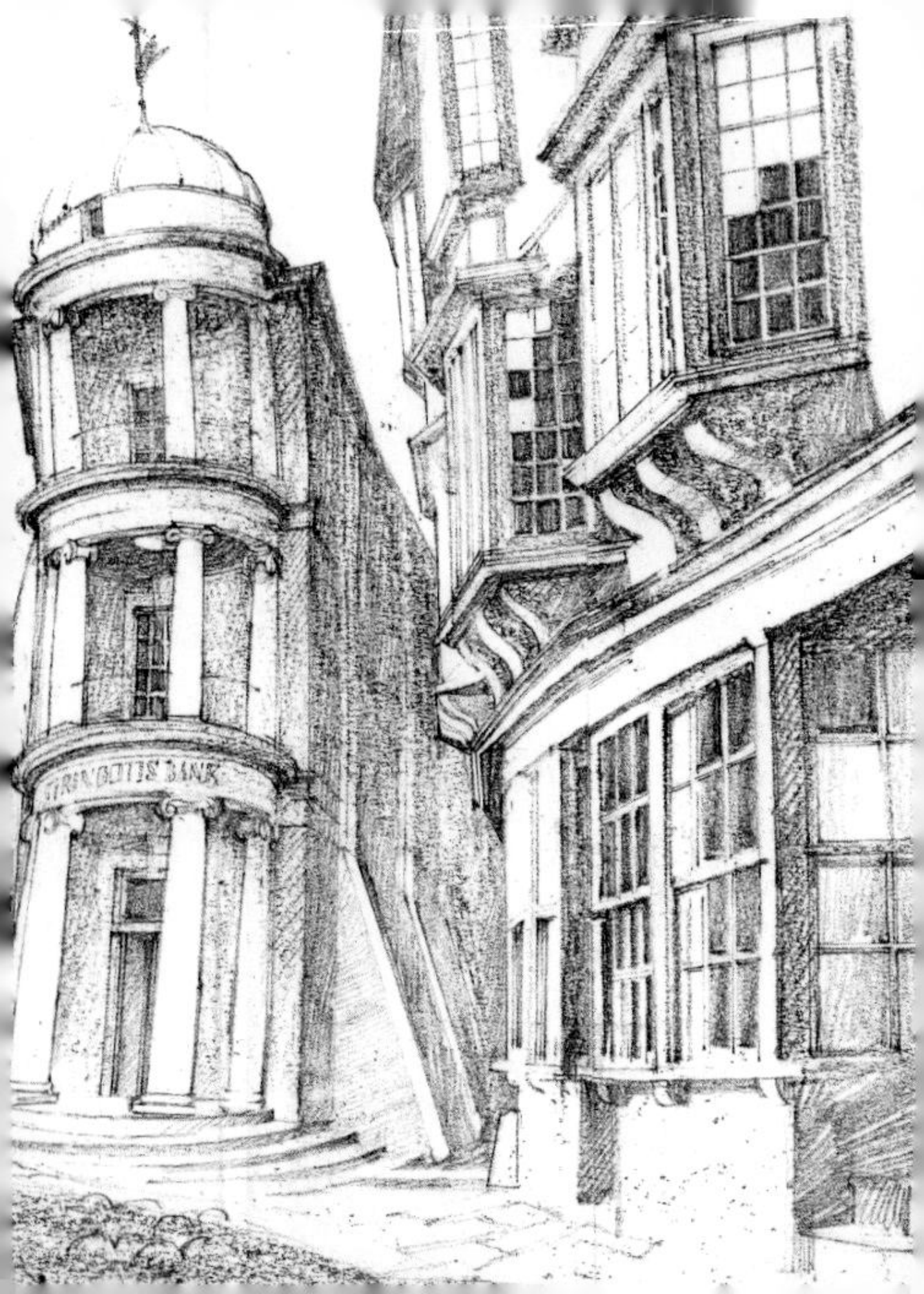
BANK

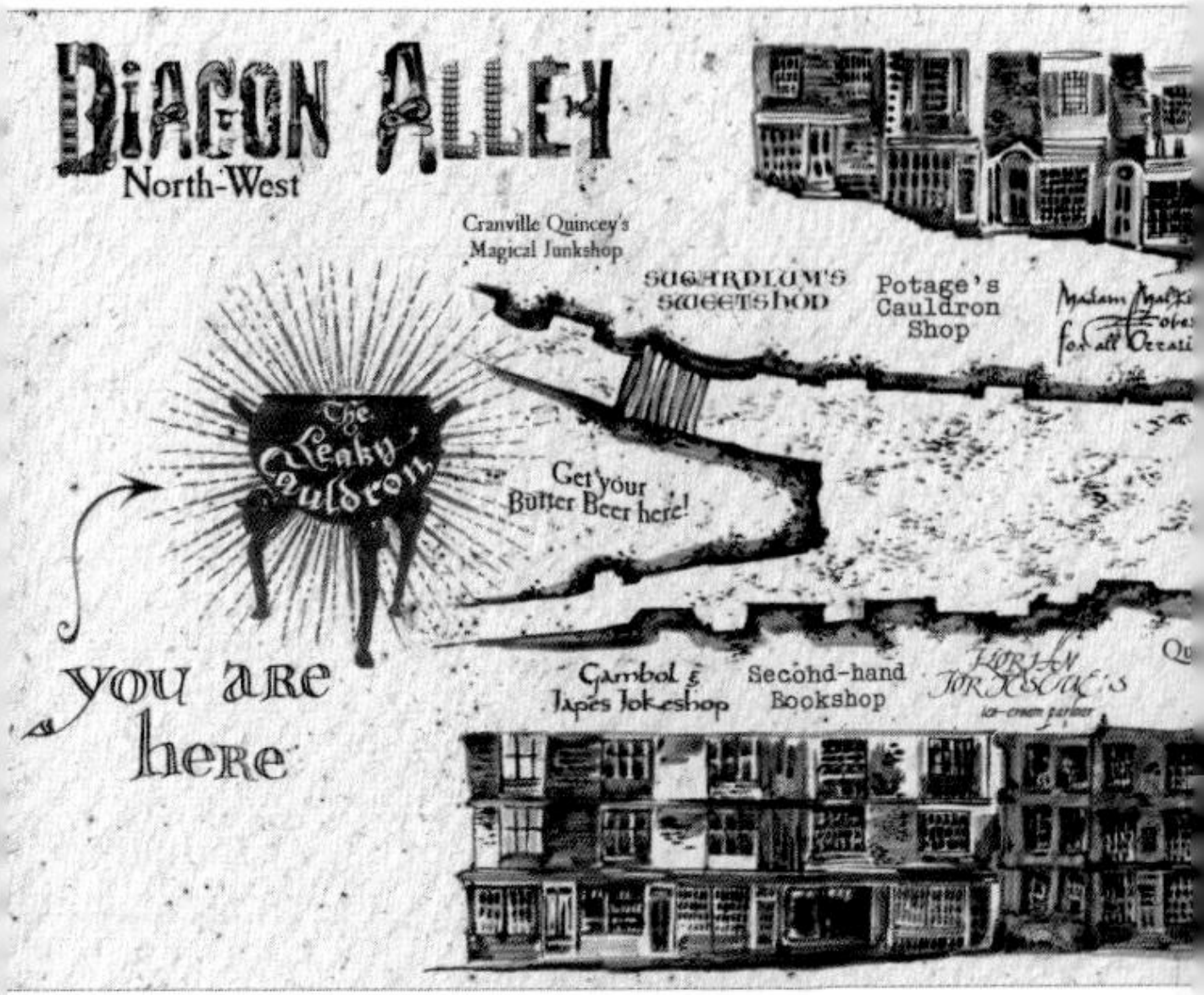

PAGES 32–33: Stuart Craig's production sketch of Diagon Alley, one of the first sets developed for *Harry Potter and the Sorcerer's Stone*.

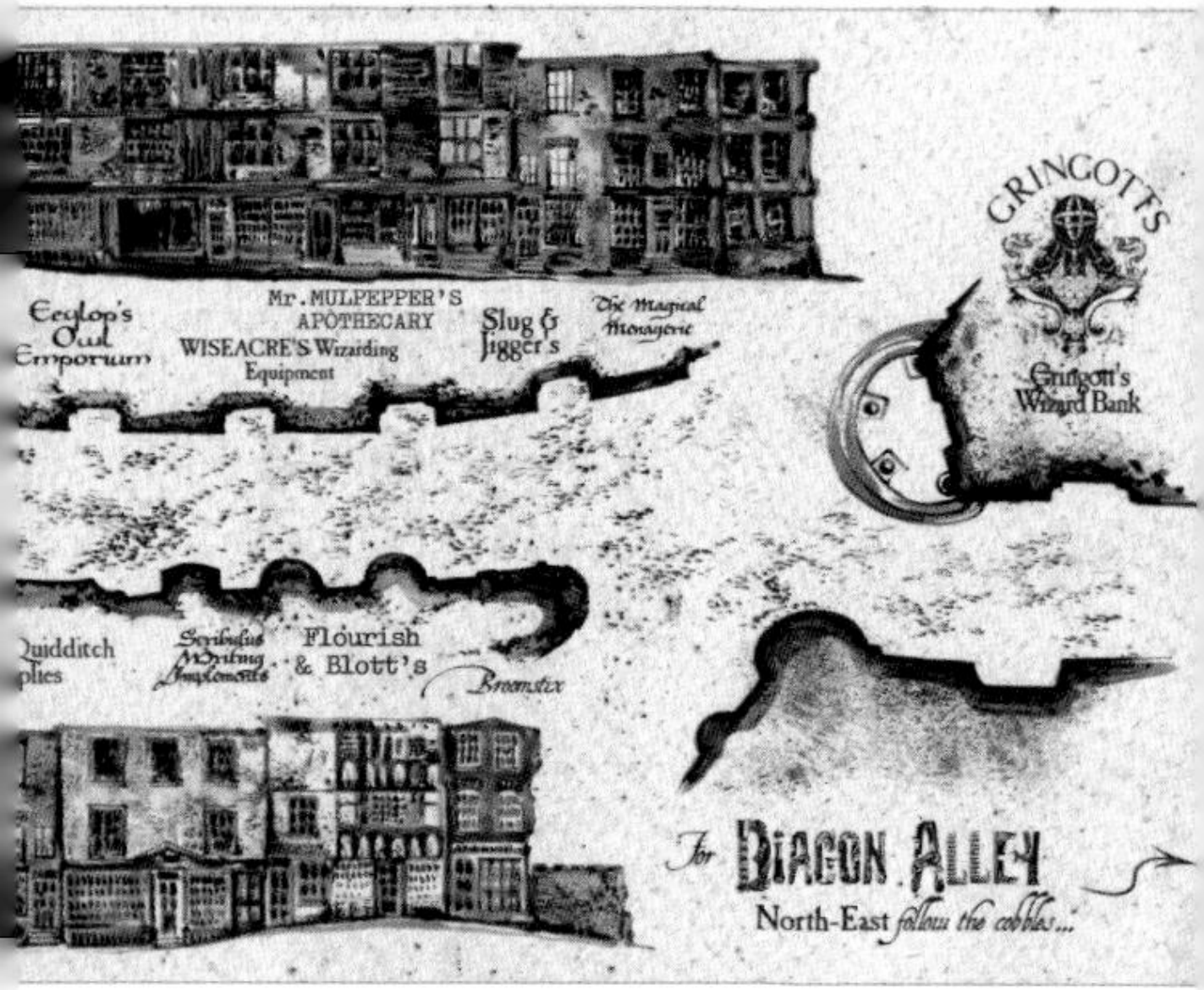

THESE PAGES: Map of Diagon Alley, that hangs on the wall of the Leaky Cauldron.

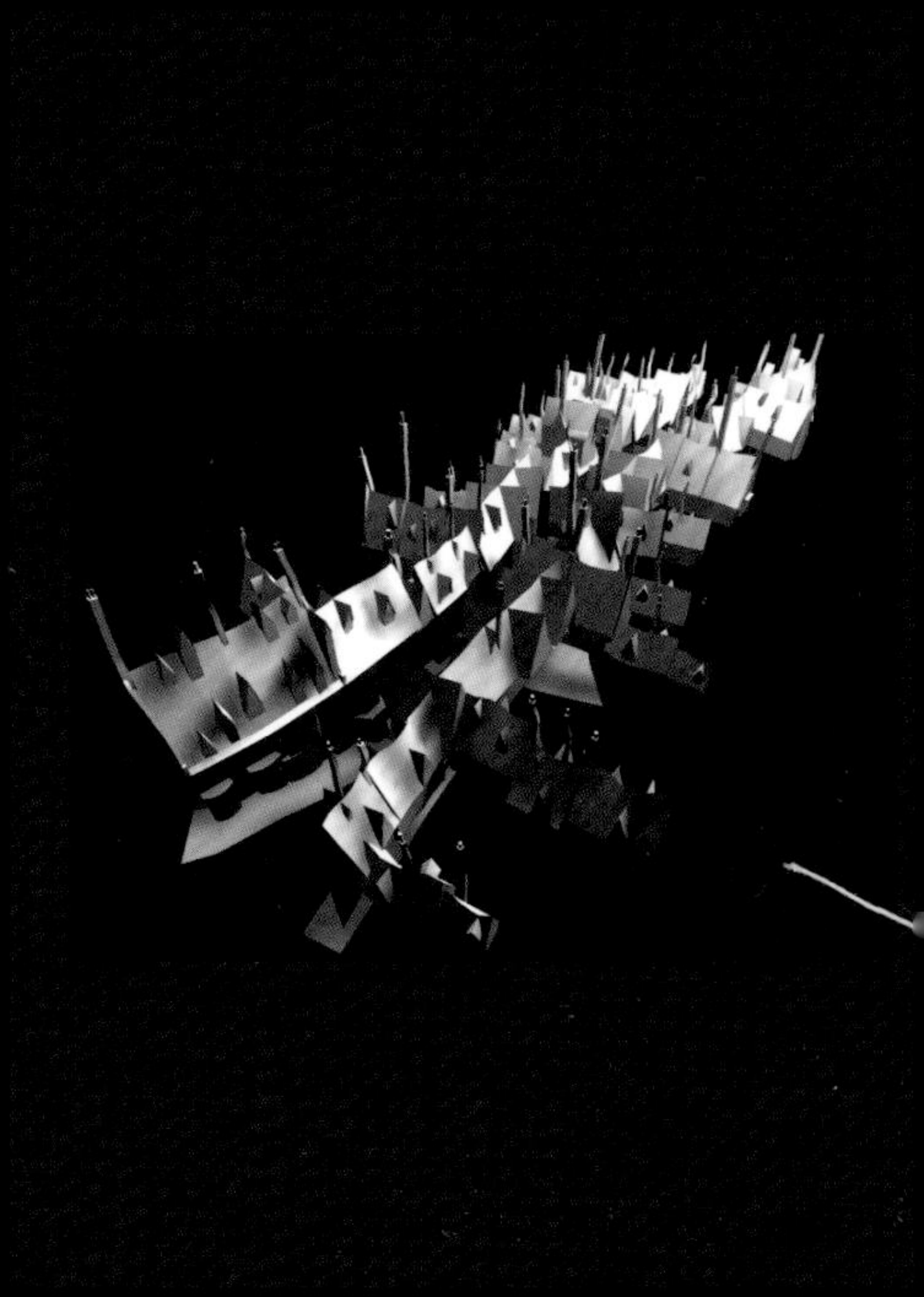

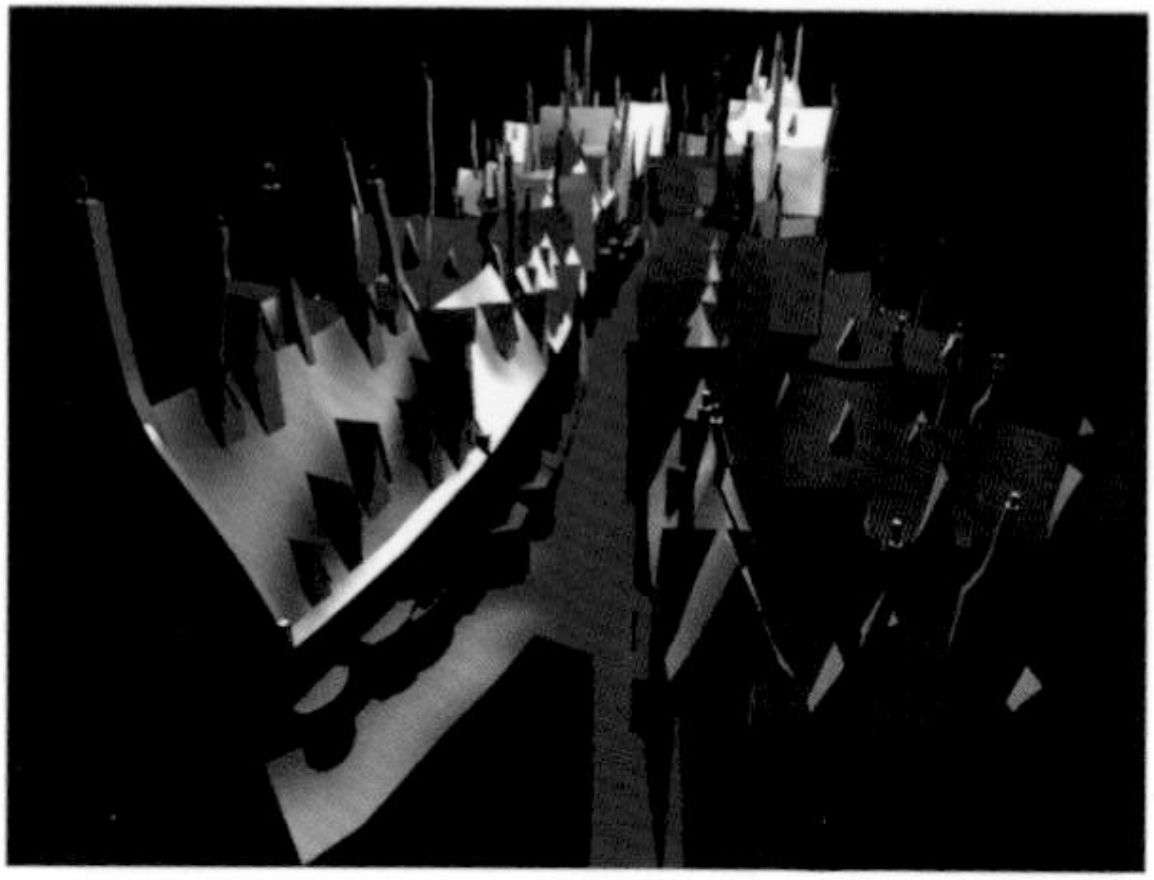

THESE PAGES: Computer-generated models map out Knockturn Alley with its towering chimneys. Harry Potter, Ron Weasley, and Hermione Granger spy from a rooftop as Draco Malfoy enters Borgin and Burkes in *Harry Potter and the Half-Blood Prince*.

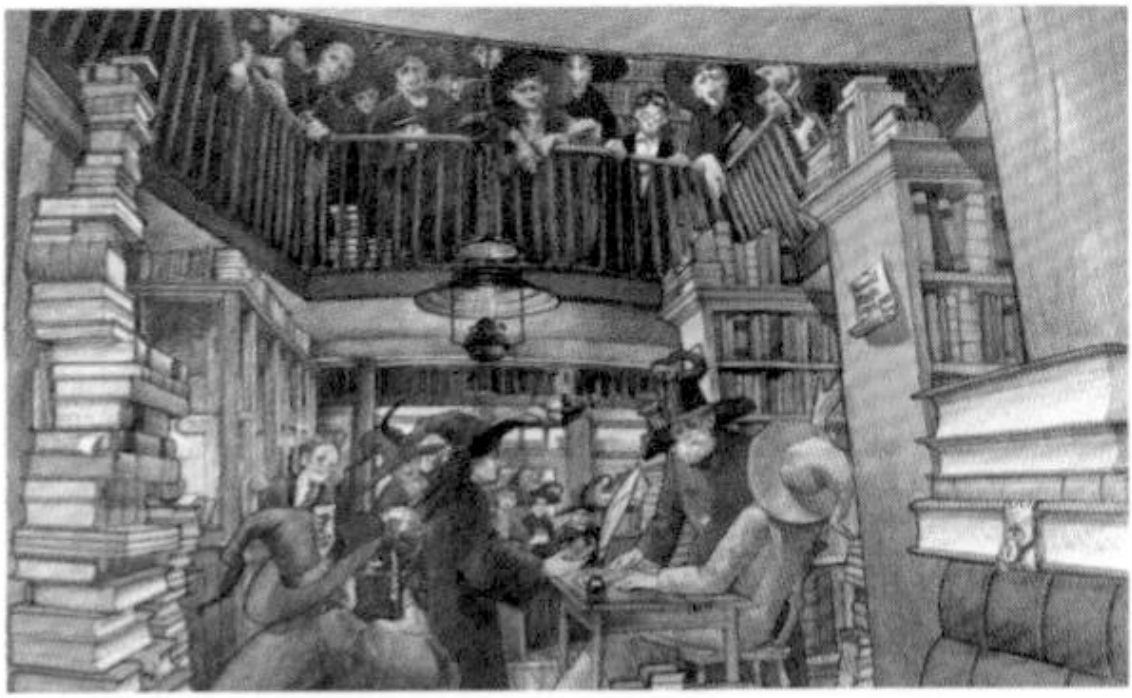

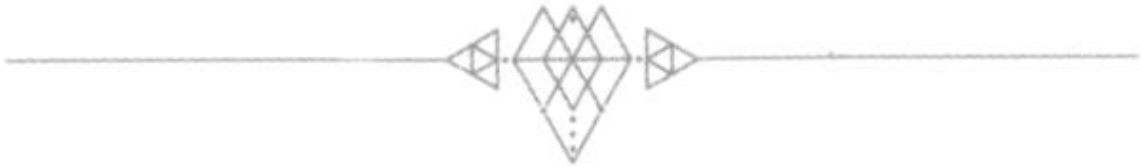

ABOVE: Artwork by Andrew Williamson of the wizarding bookshop Flourish and Blotts, where Gilderoy Lockhart sits for a signing of his autobiography, *Magical Me*, in *Harry Potter and the Chamber of Secrets*.

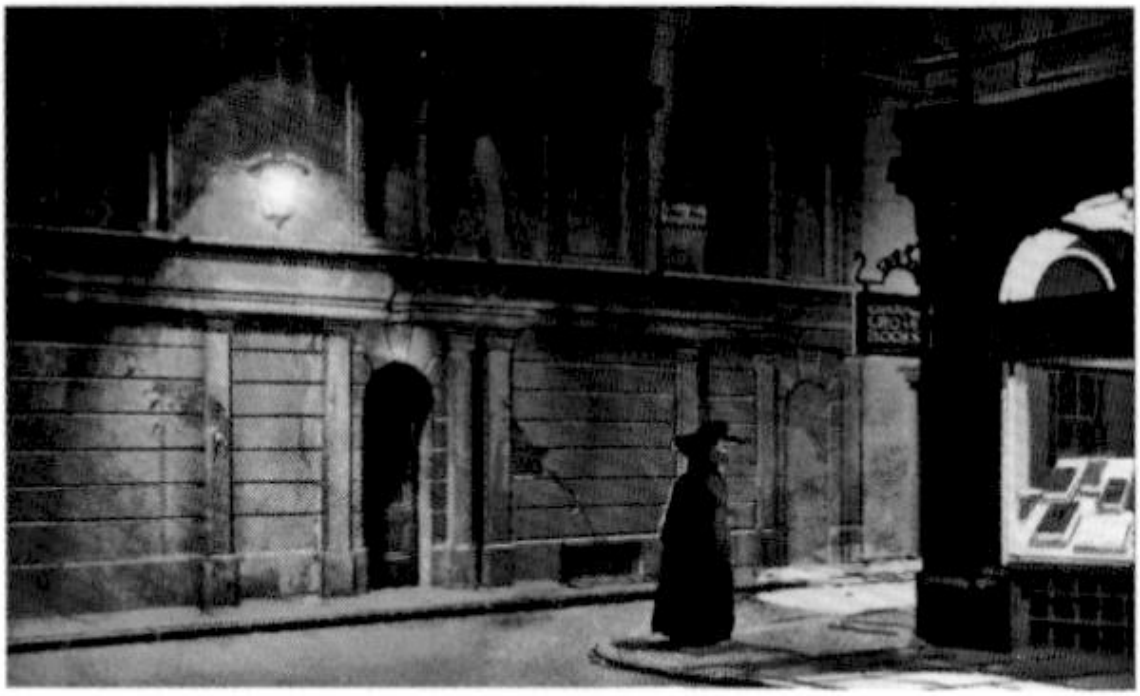

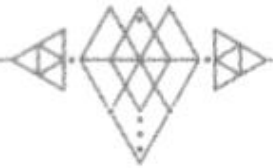

ABOVE: A witch stands outside the nondescript entrance to the Leaky Cauldron in a study by Andrew Williamson.

GRINGOTTS WIZARDING BANK

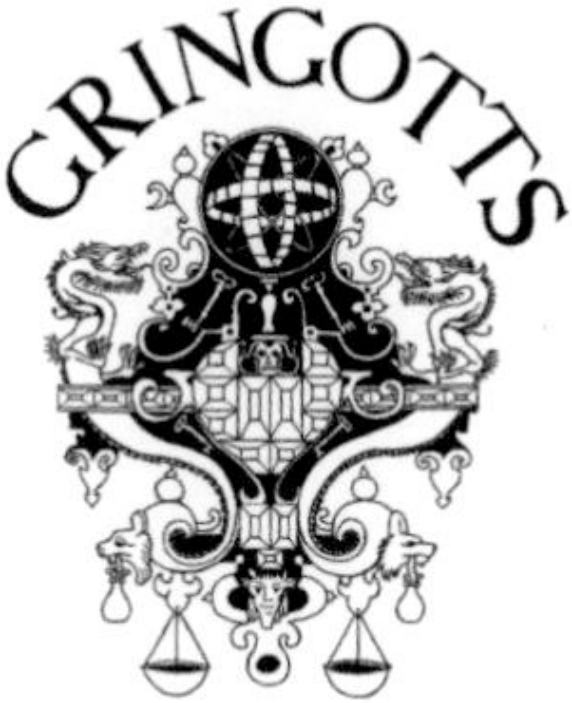

ABOVE: The Gringotts Wizarding Bank seal, as created by the graphics department.

OPPOSITE: In *Harry Potter and the Deathly Hallows – Part 2*, Harry, Ron, and Hermione escape from Gringotts Wizarding Bank on a Ukrainian Ironbelly dragon, as portrayed by Andrew Williamson.

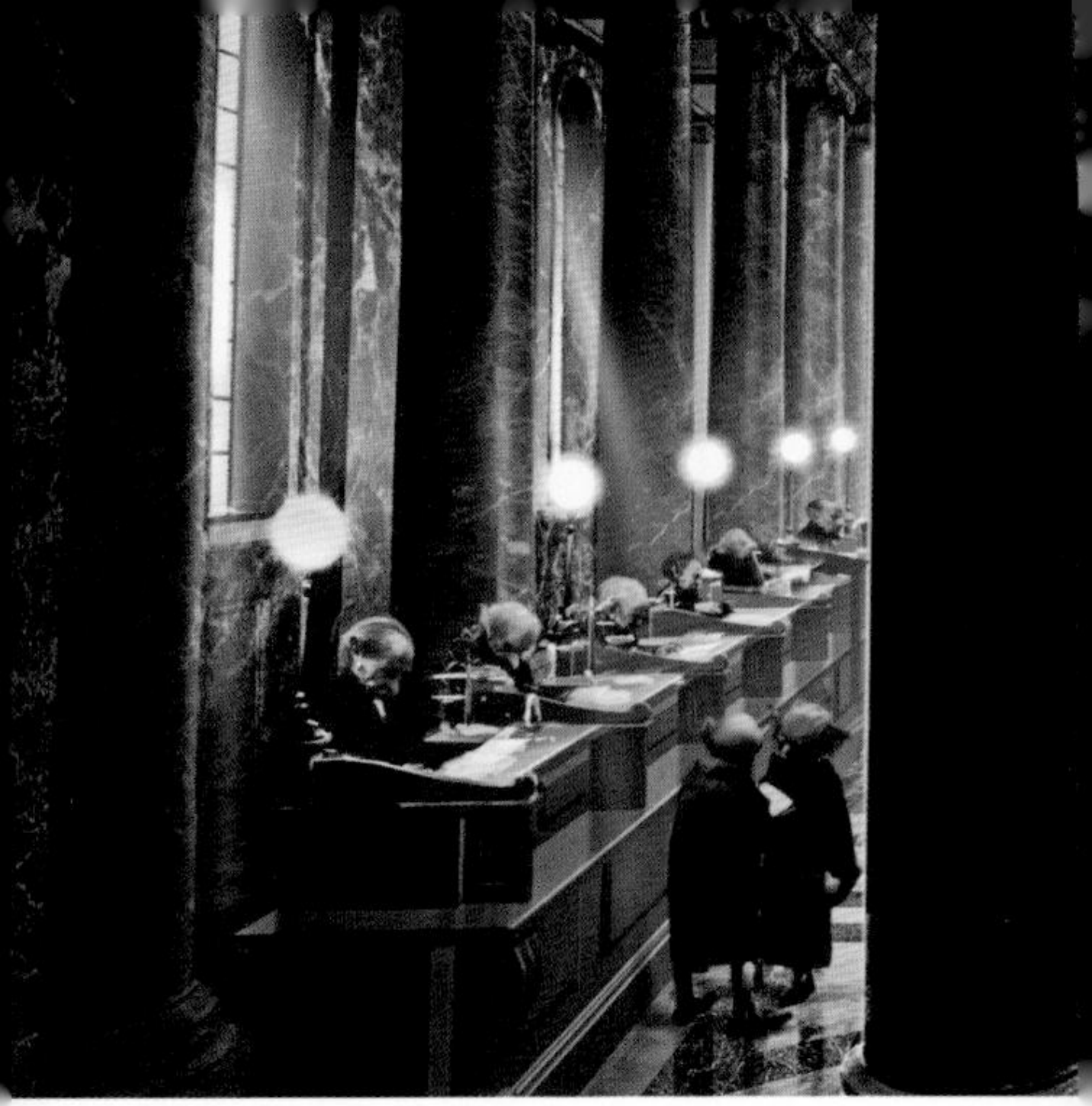

THESE PAGES: Placid views of Gringotts by Andrew Williamson before the dragon breaks through both floor and ceiling as it flees; both for *Harry Potter and the Deathly Hallows – Part 2*.

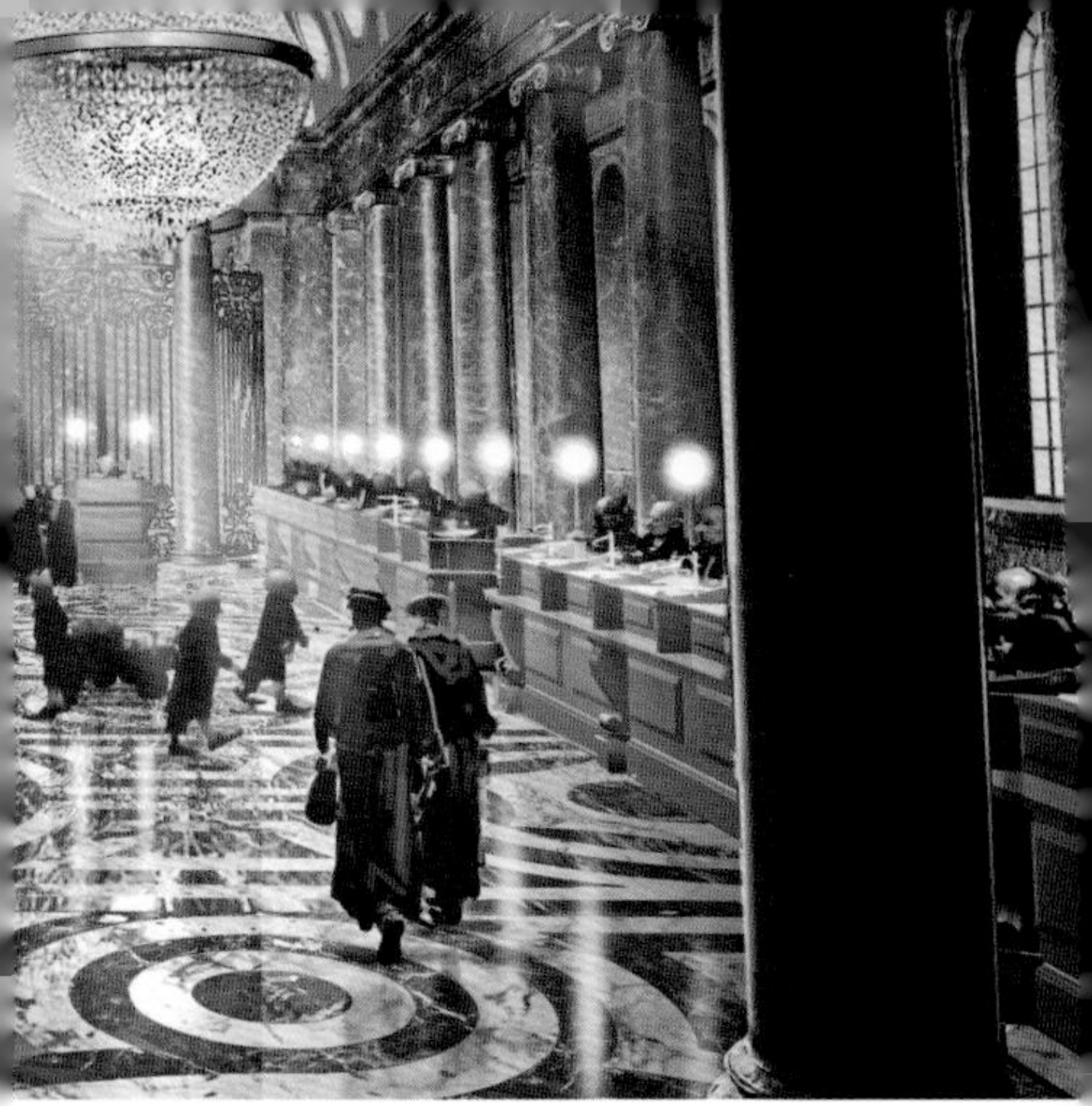

PAGES 44–47: Blueprints for Gringotts Wizarding Bank seen in *Harry Potter and the Deathly Hallows – Part 2*. A team of draftsmen and women were employed to diagram everything from buildings to brooms.

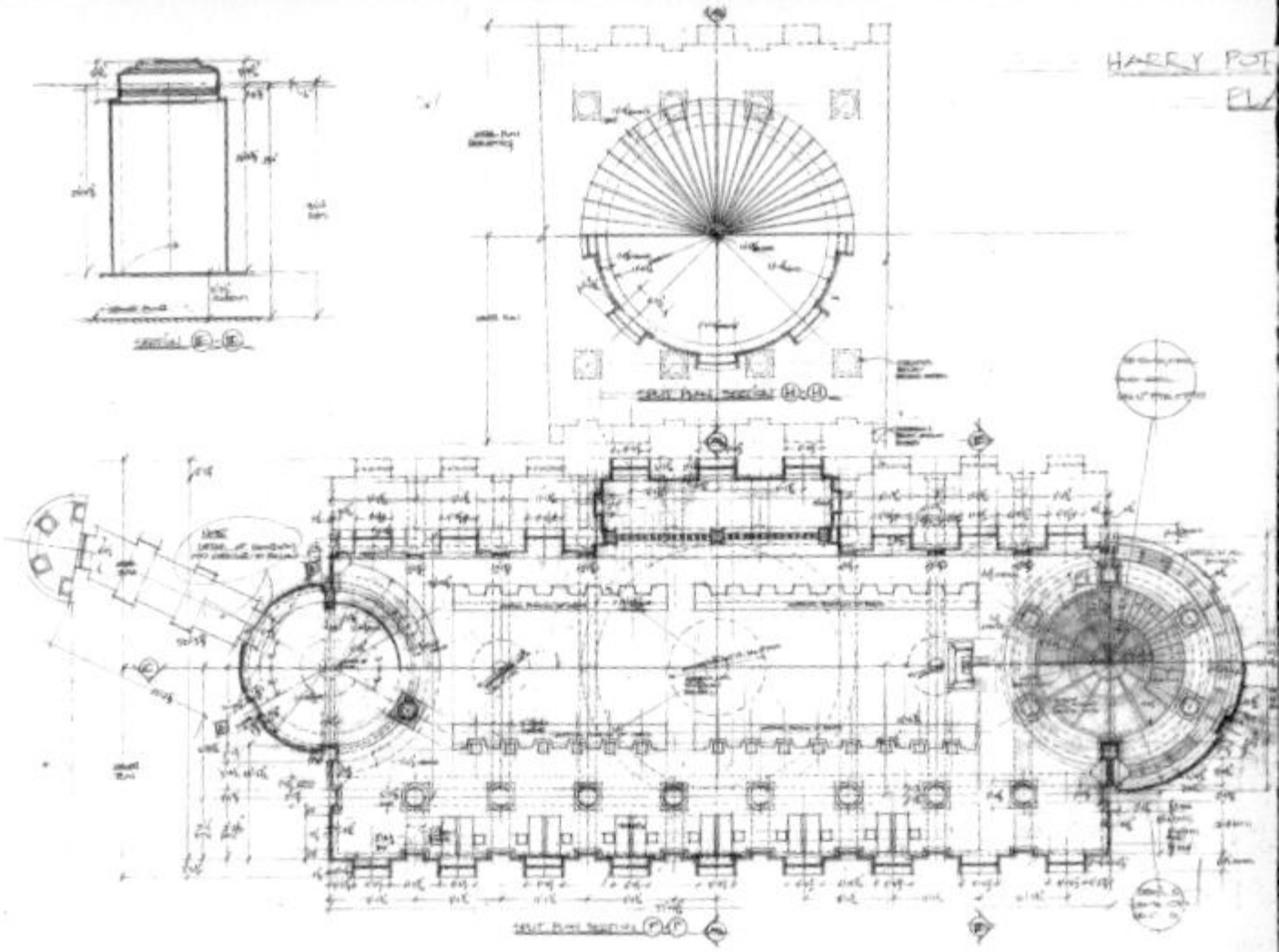
HARRY POT

AND THE DEATHLY HALLOWS INT GRINGOTTS BANK

AND SECTIONS A-A AND B-B (REVISION B)

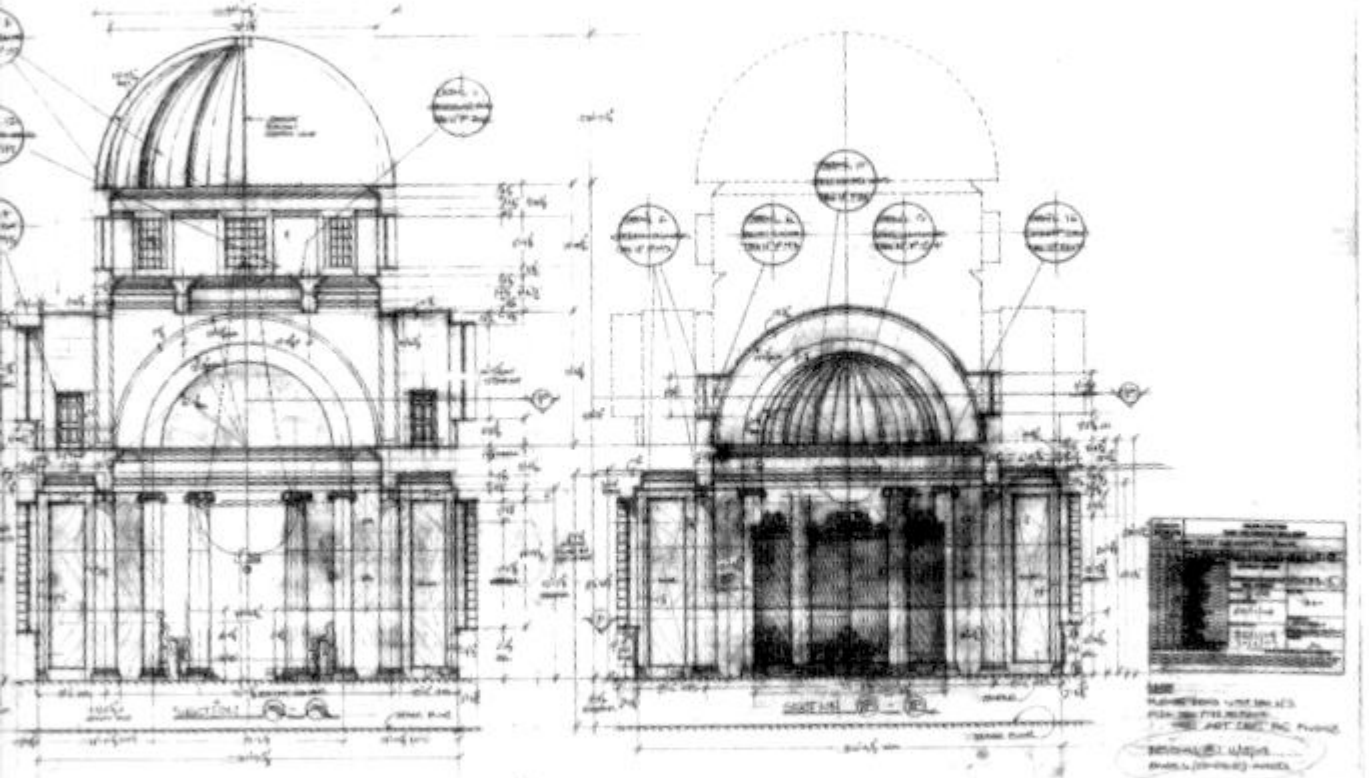

F0173 B

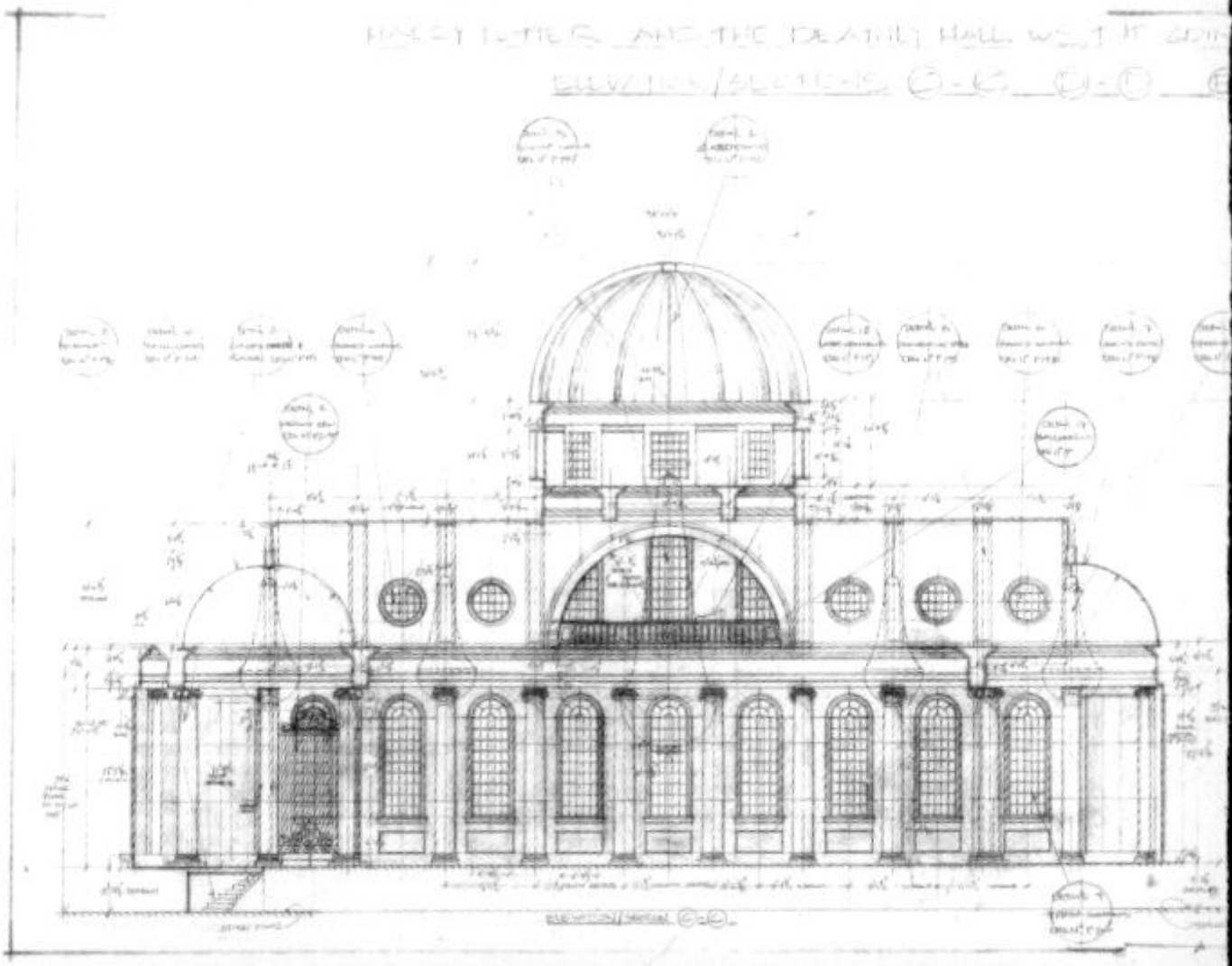
ELEVATION/SECTIONS

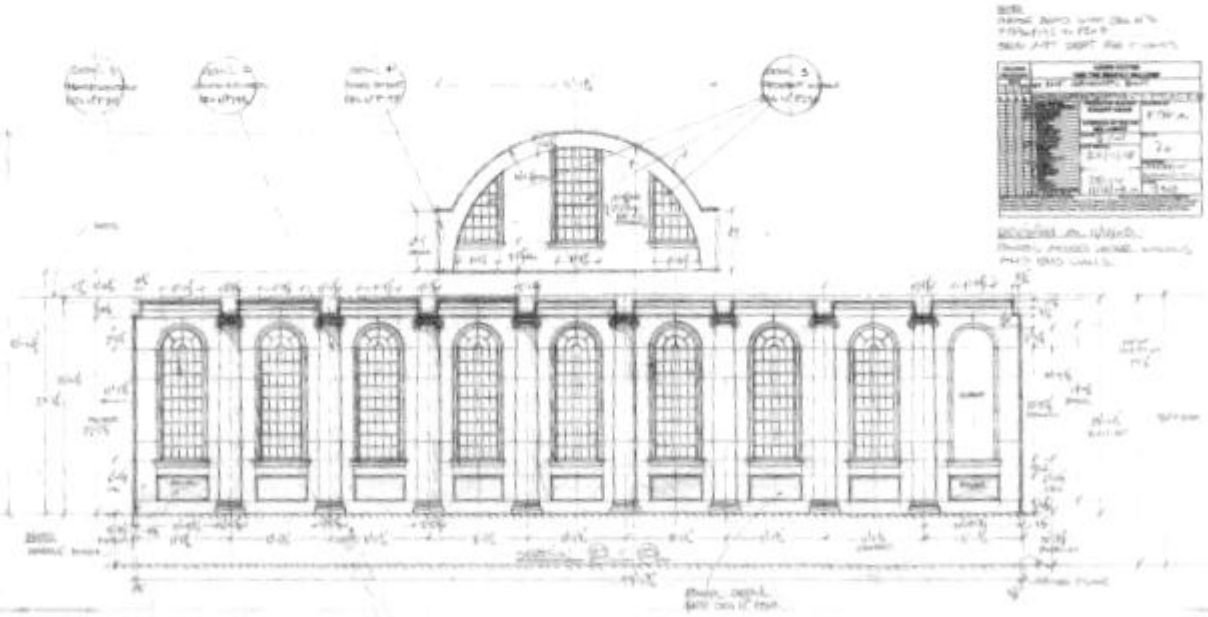

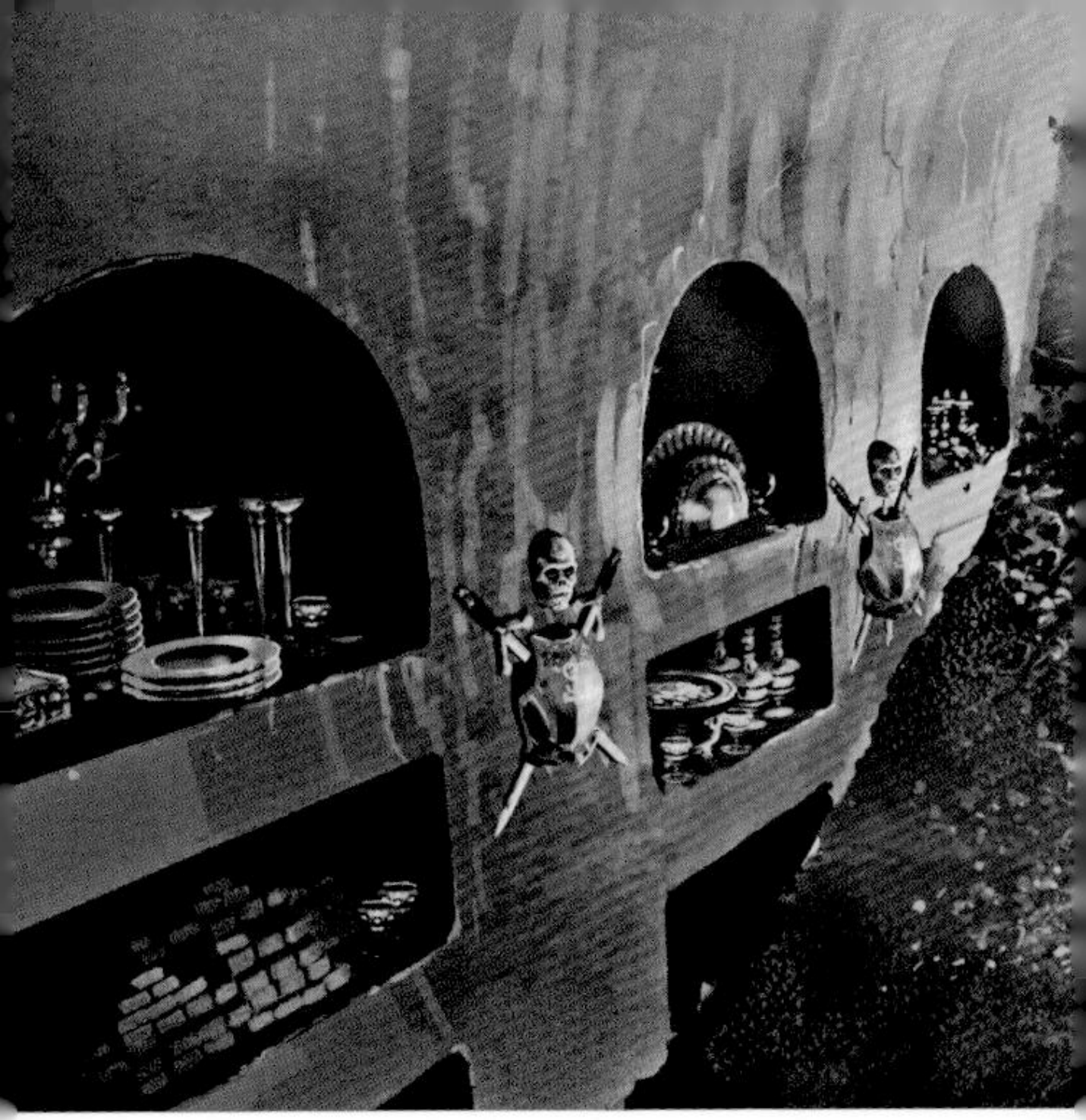

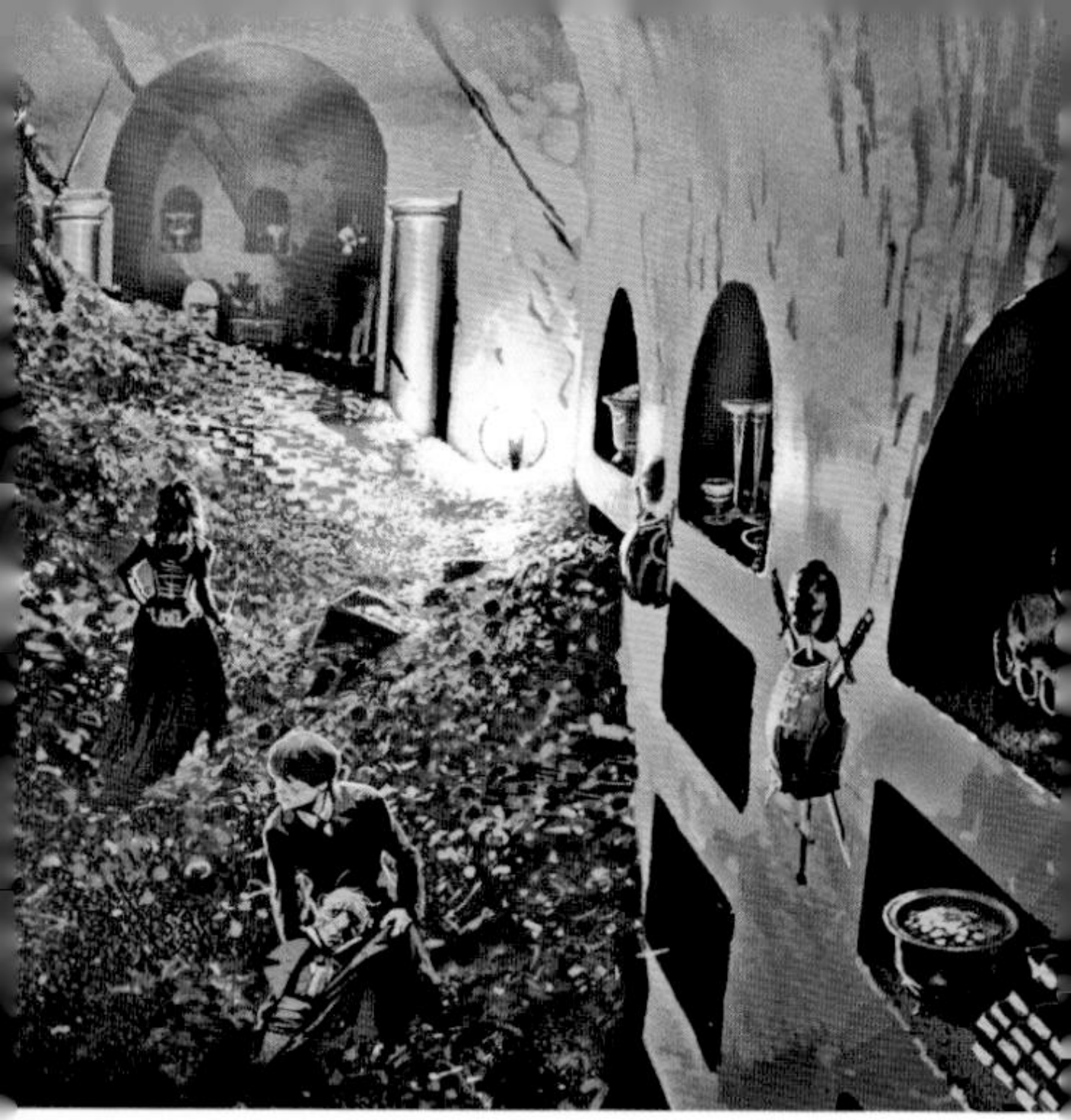

THESE PAGES: Harry, Ron, and Hermione are trapped in Bellatrix Lestrange's vault at Gringotts as gold coins and other objects multiply around them, in *Harry Potter and the Deathly Hallows – Part 2*.

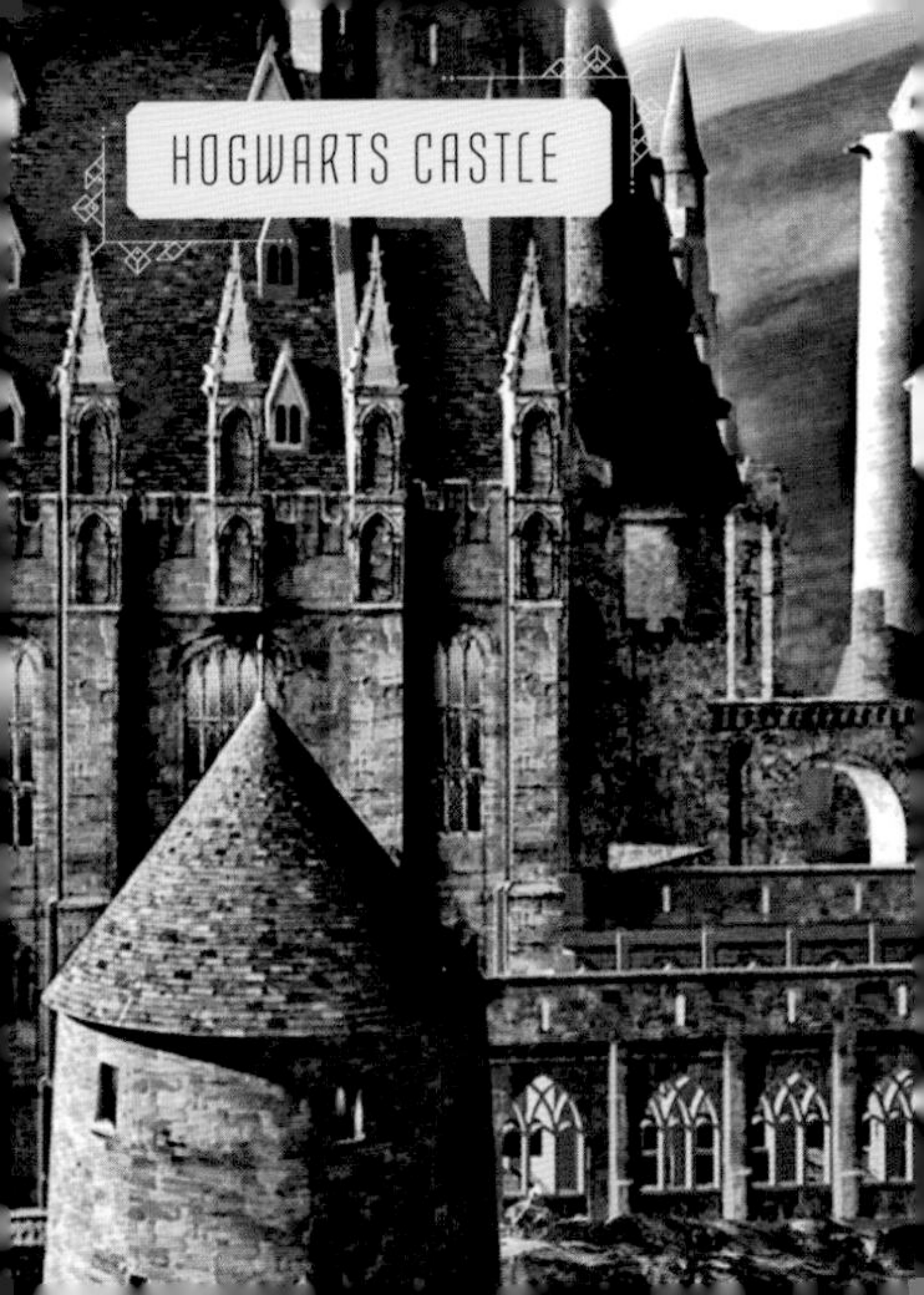
HOGWARTS CASTLE

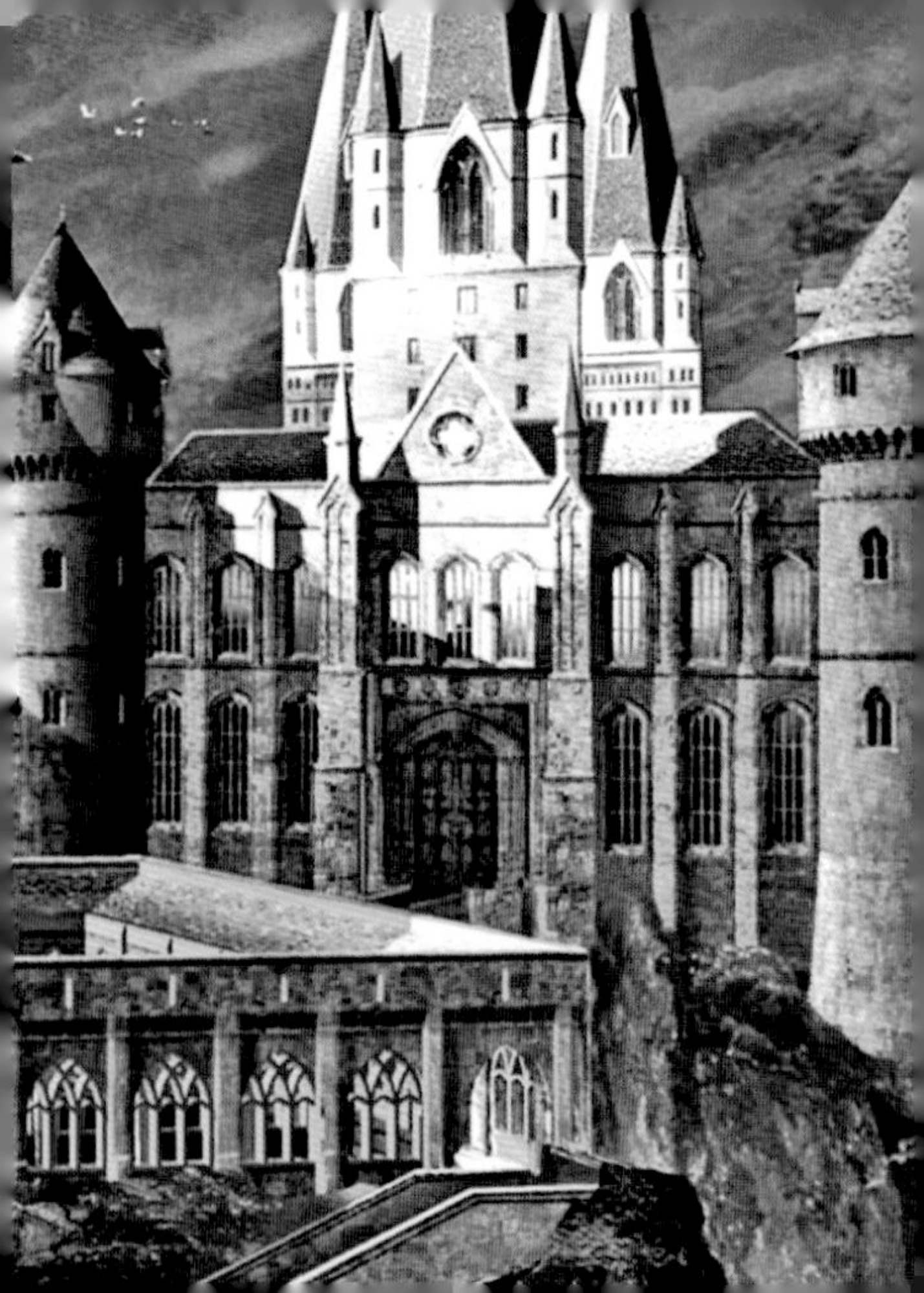

THE CASTLE EXTERIOR

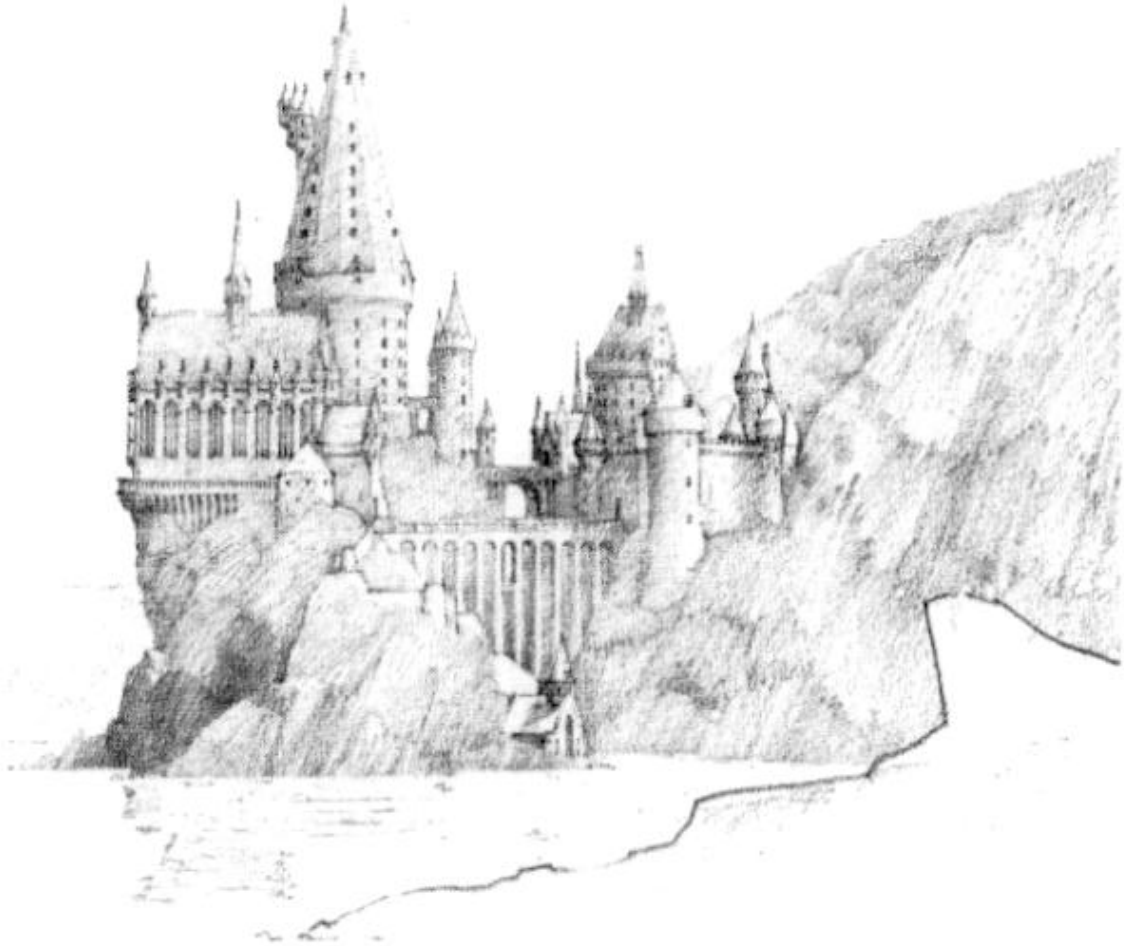

PAGES 50–51: A detailed view of the exterior of the courtyard beside the Great Hall by Andrew Williamson for *Harry Potter and the Goblet of Fire*.

ABOVE: An early sketch of Hogwarts castle by production designer Stuart Craig, visual development art of Hogwarts by Dermot Power.

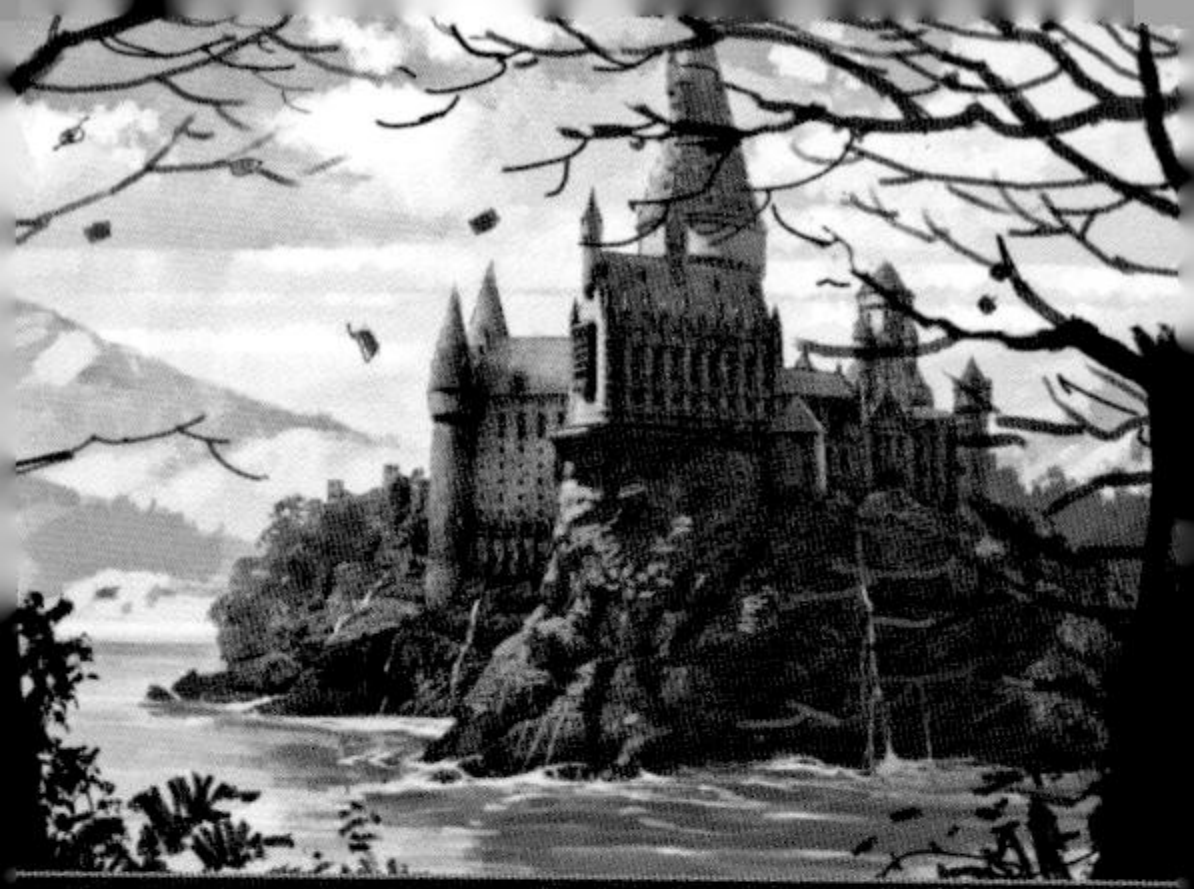

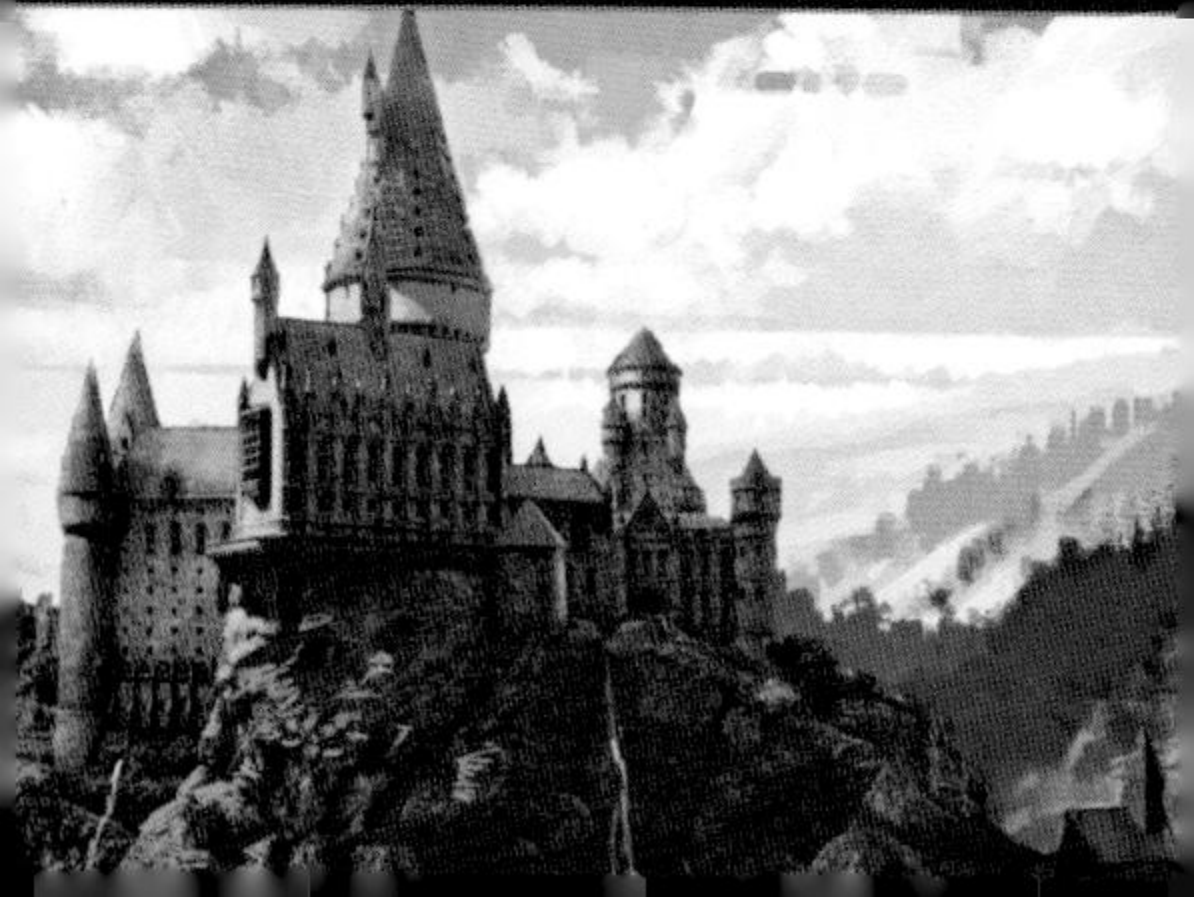

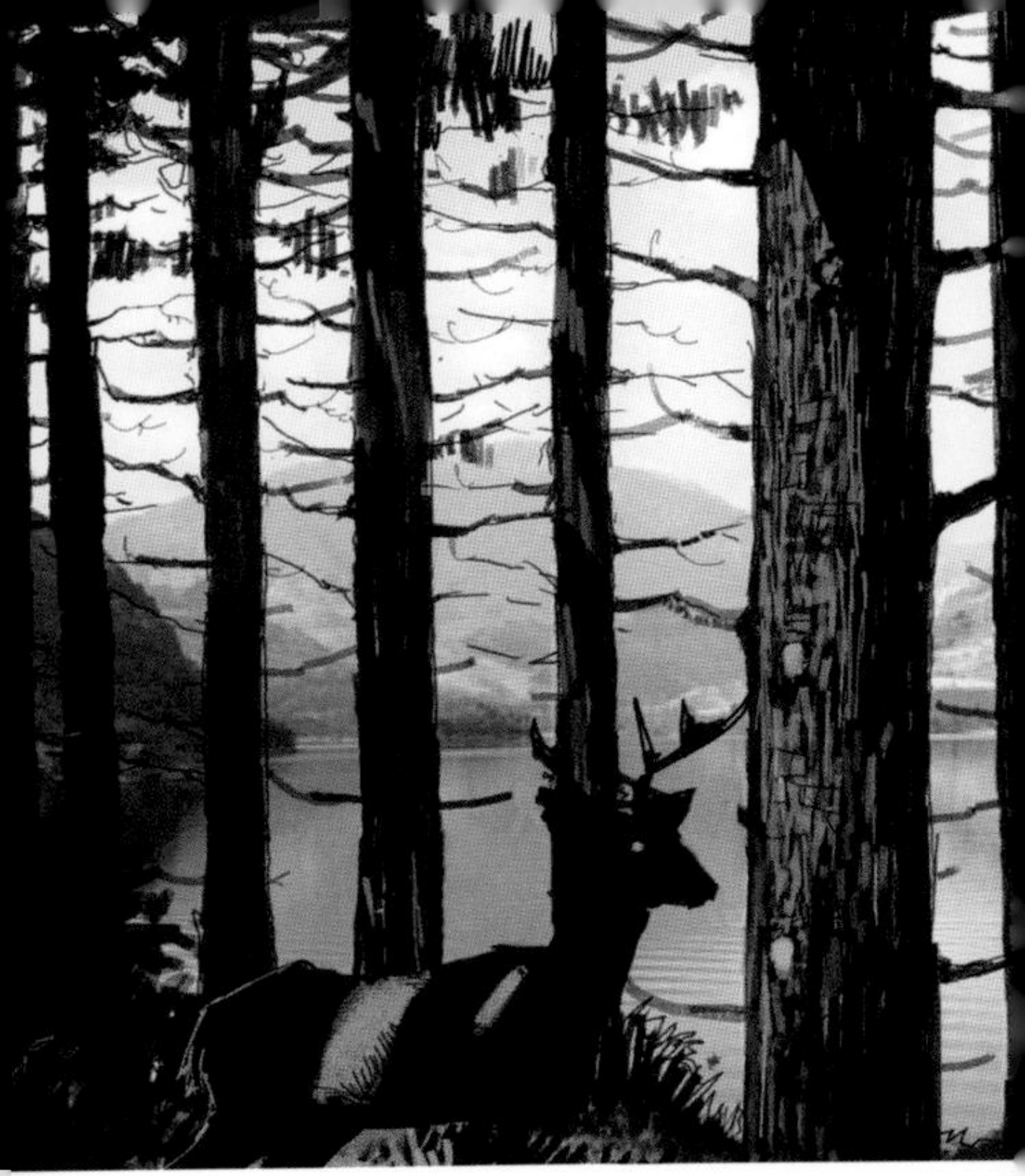

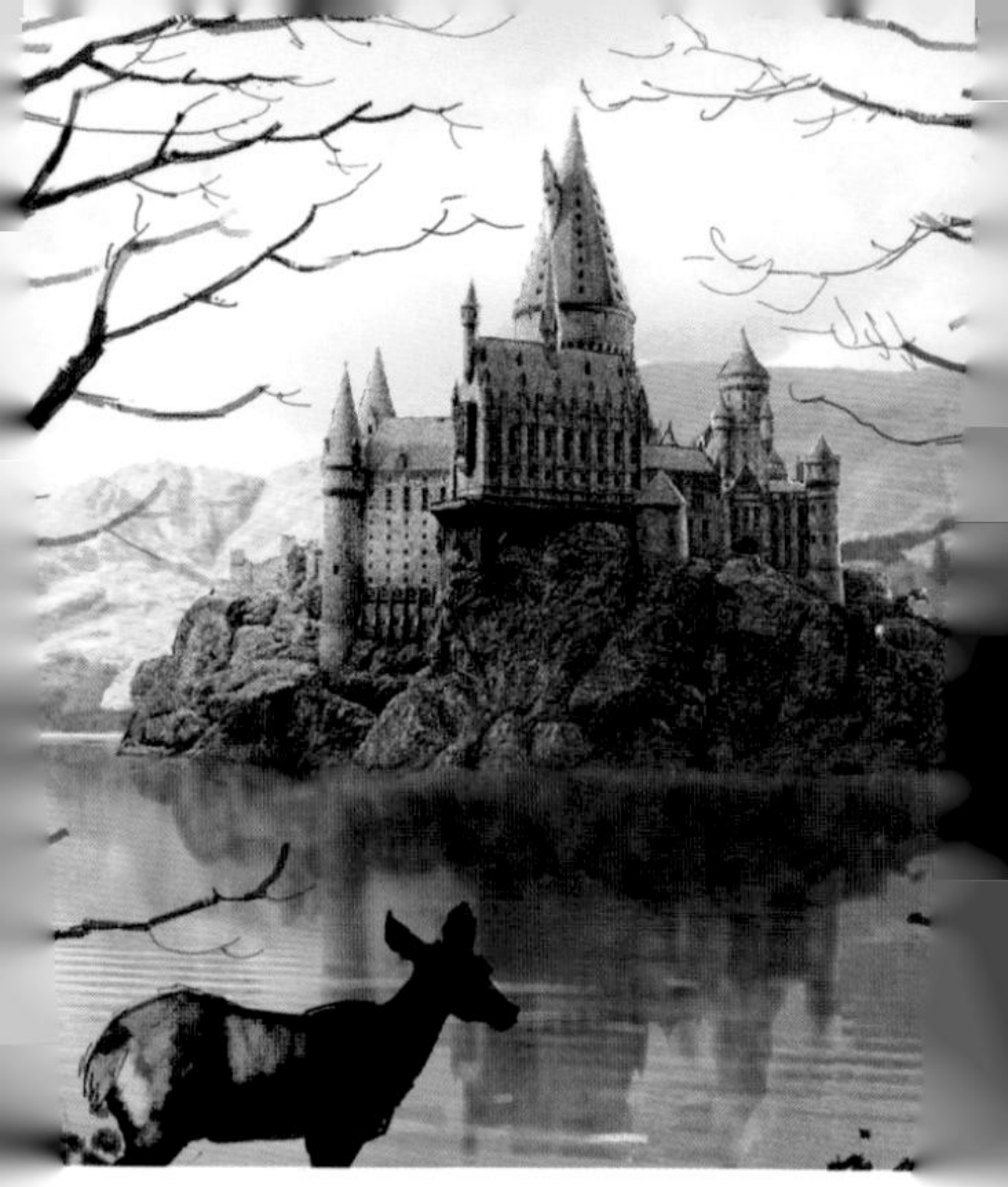

PAGES 53-55: Concept artist Dermot Power depicts Hogwarts castle from different locations for *Harry Potter and the Chamber of Secrets*.

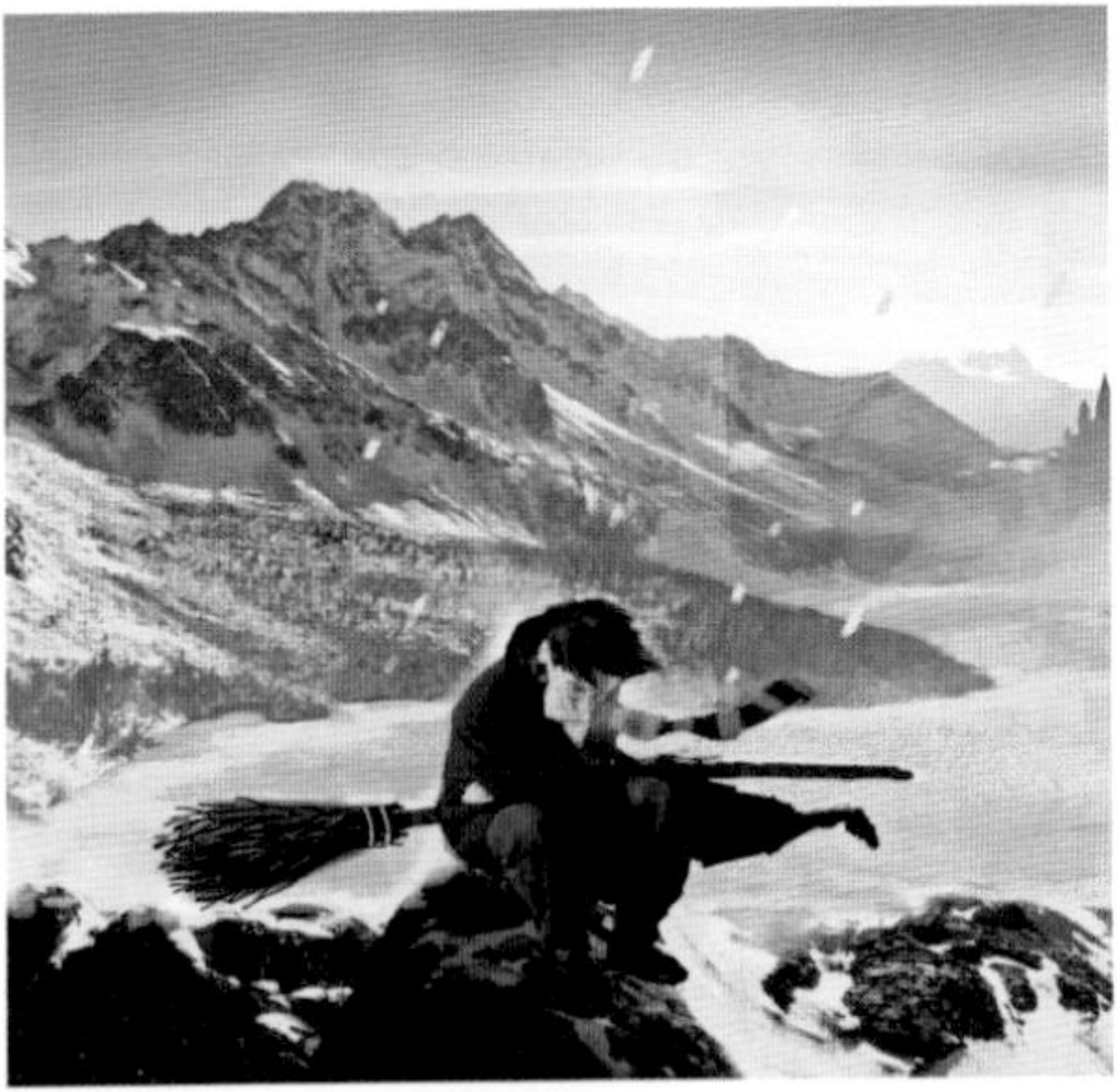

THESE PAGES: Winter scenes at Hogwarts. Art by Adam Brockbank for *Harry Potter and the Chamber of Secrets*.

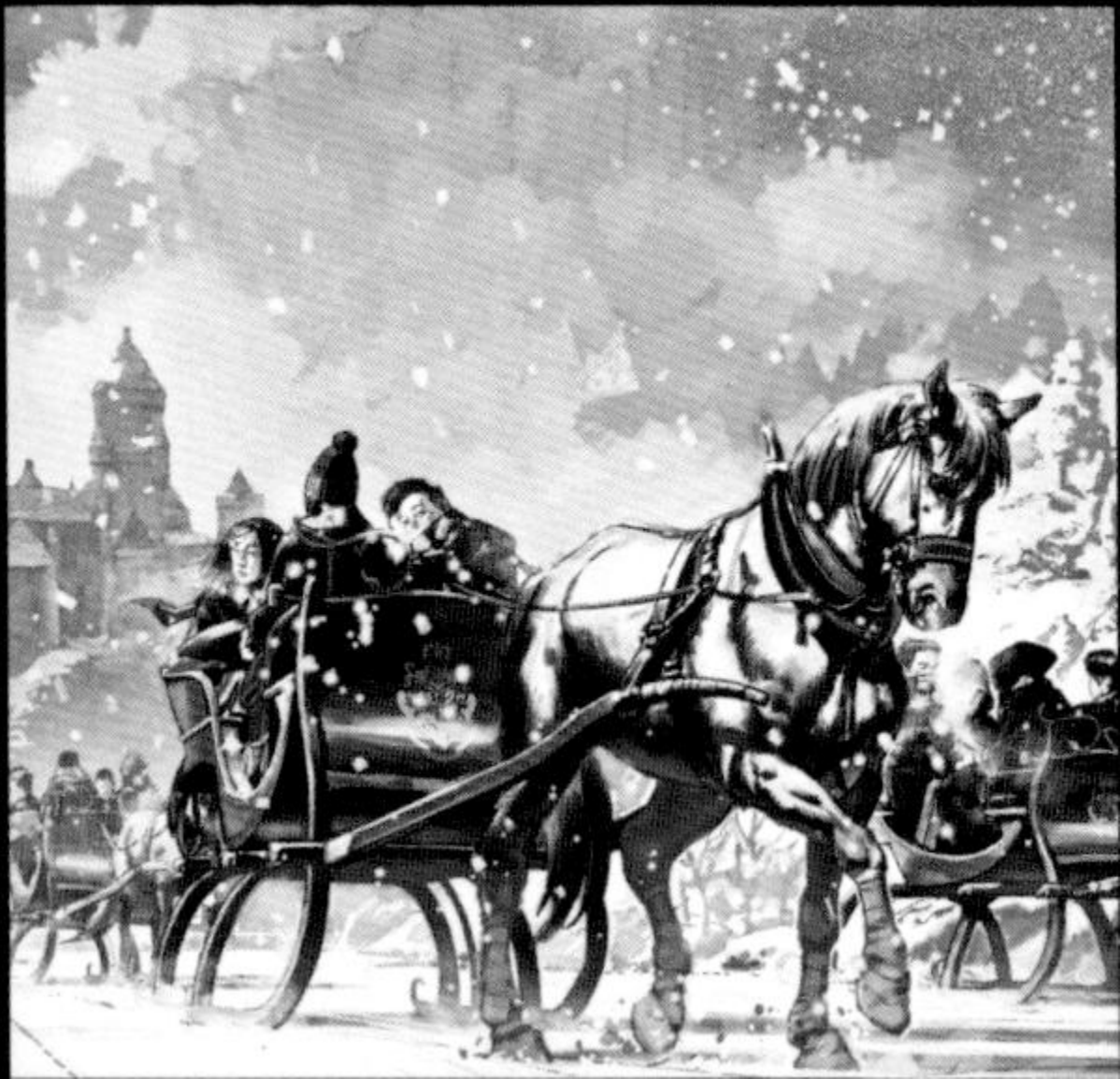

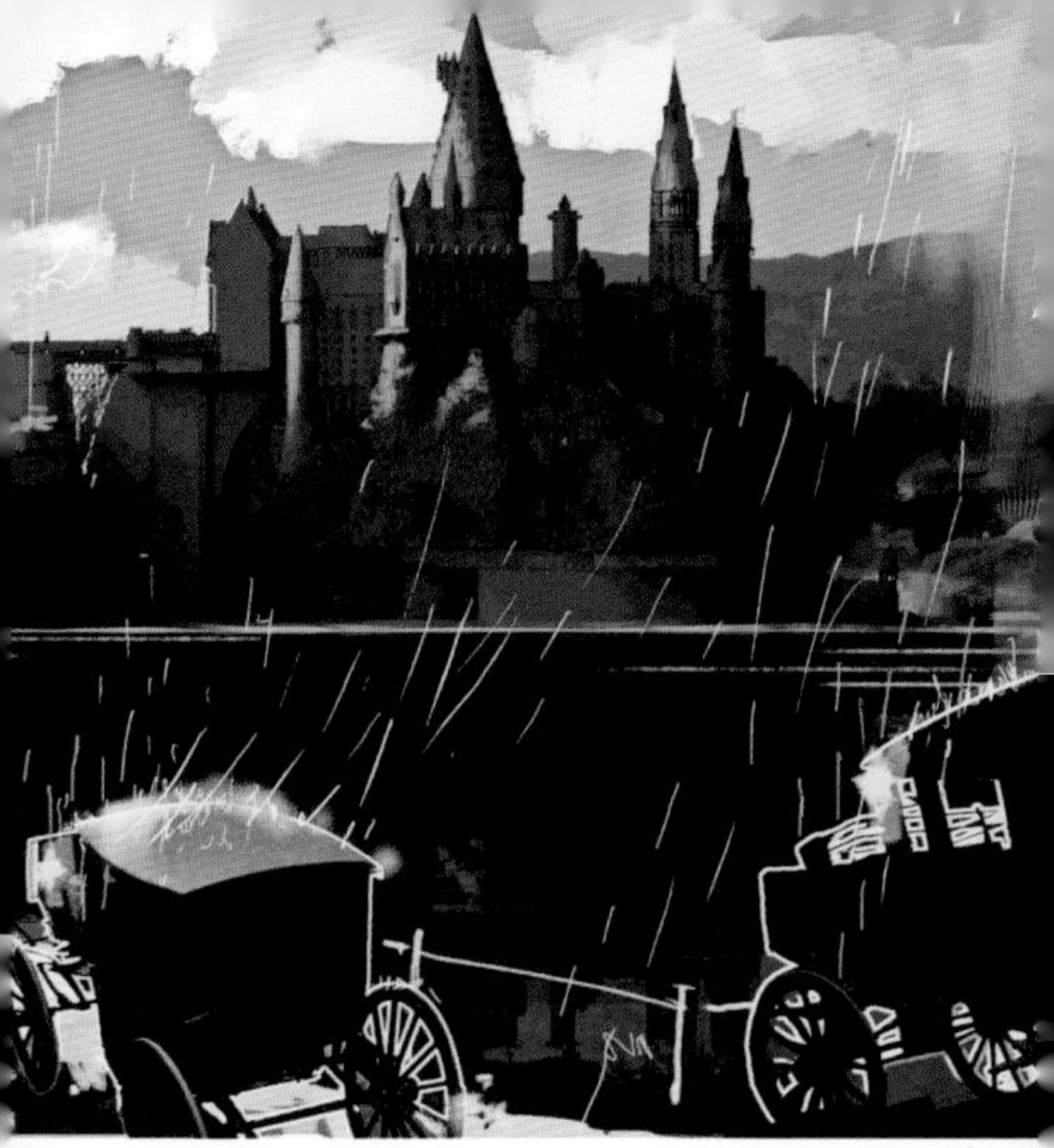

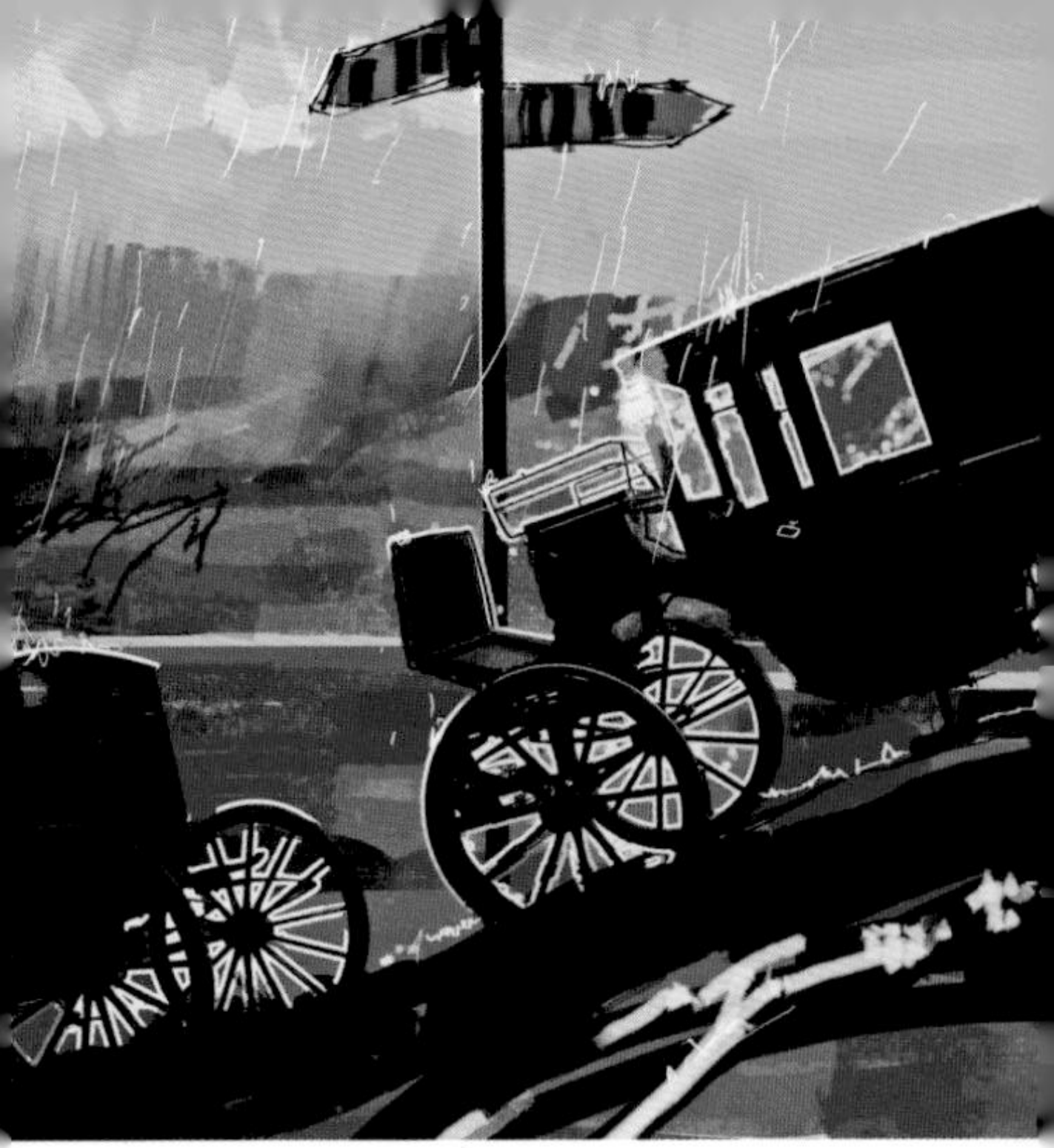

THESE PAGES: Dermot Power depicts the horseless carriages carrying students to Hogwarts on a stormy night in a scene from *Harry Potter and the Prisoner of Azkaban*.

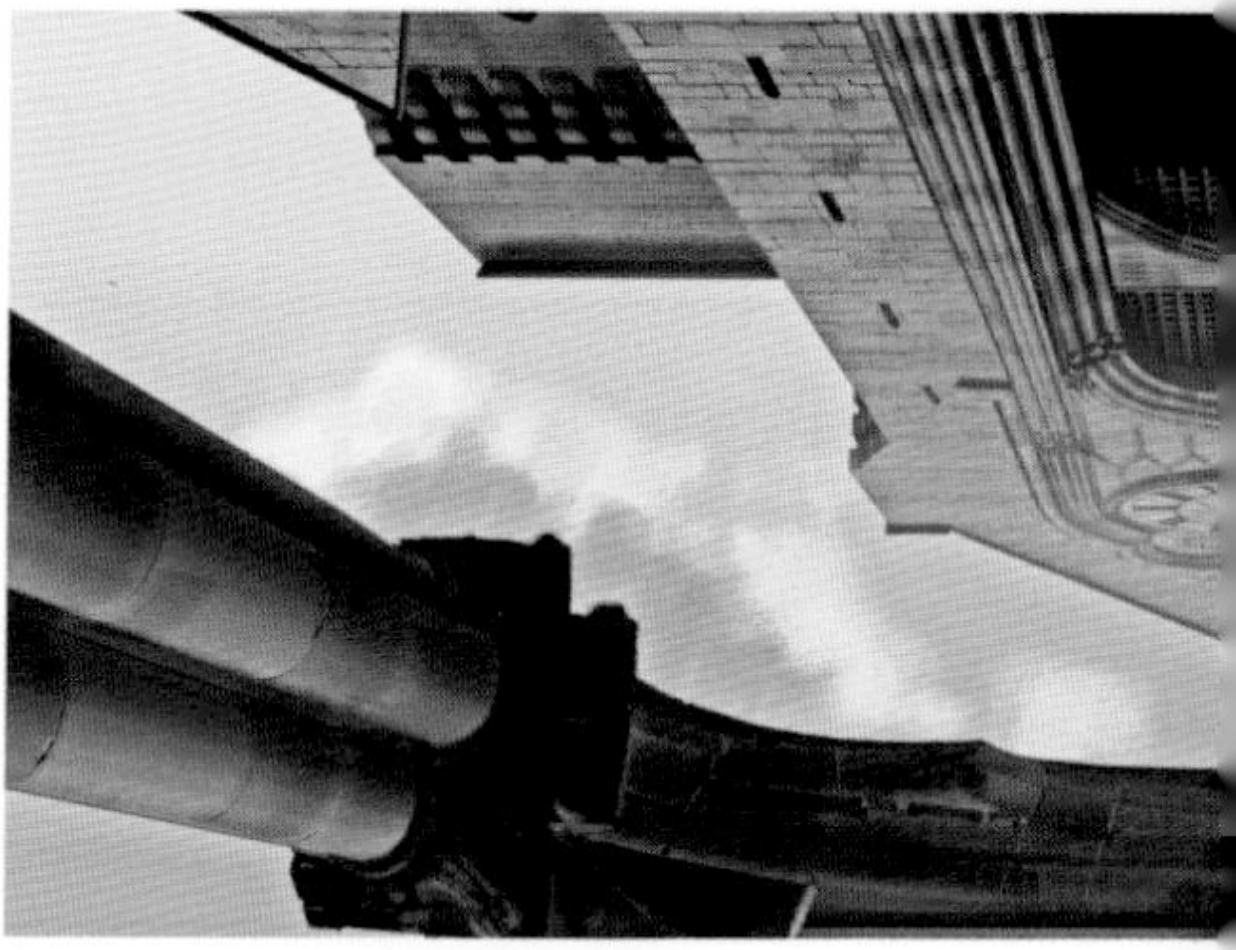

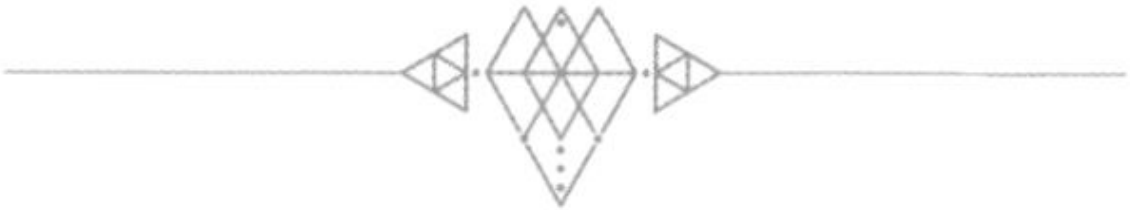

PAGES 60–69: Andrew Williamson depicts the outside of Hogwarts castle from various angles in concept art developed for *Harry Potter and the Prisoner of Azkaban*.

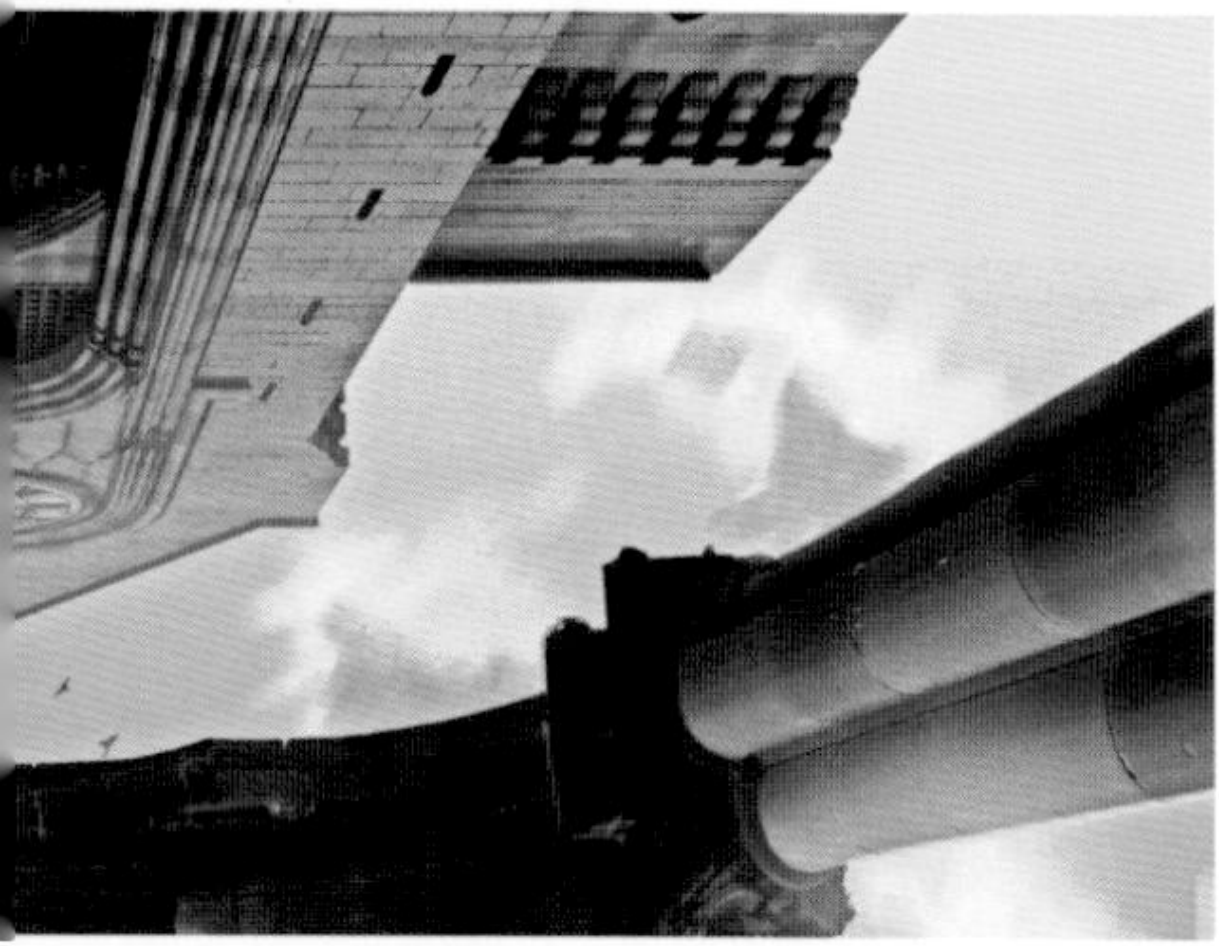

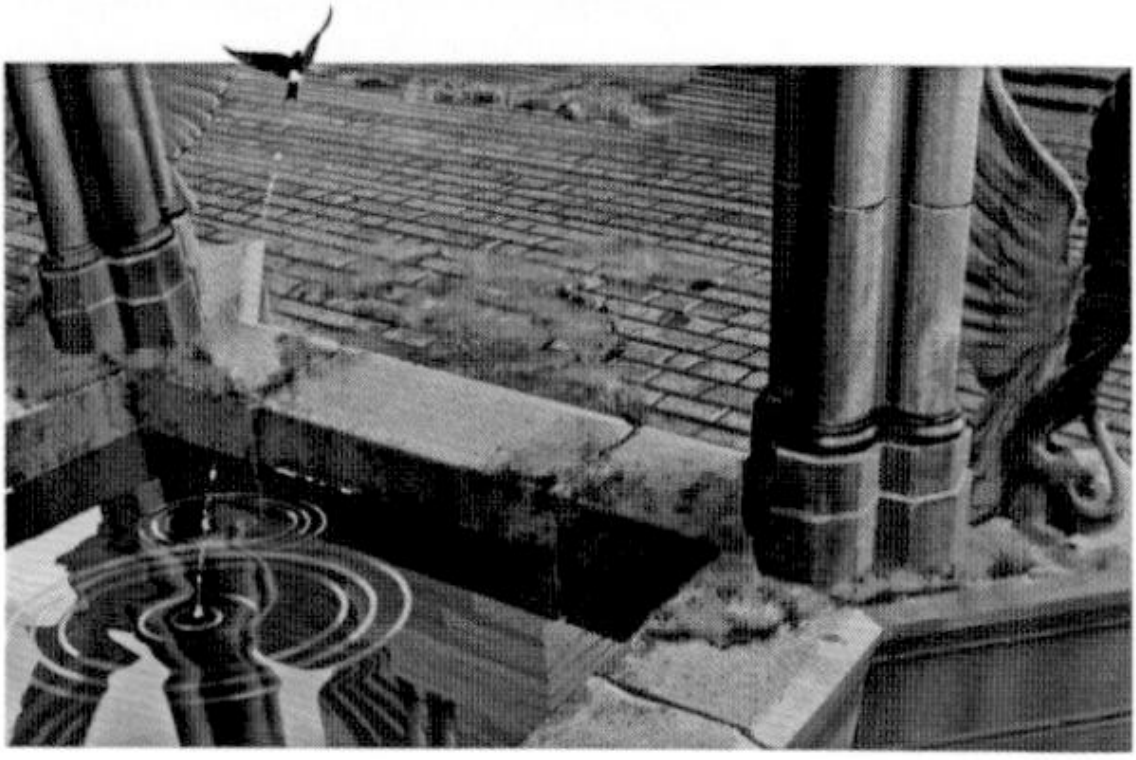

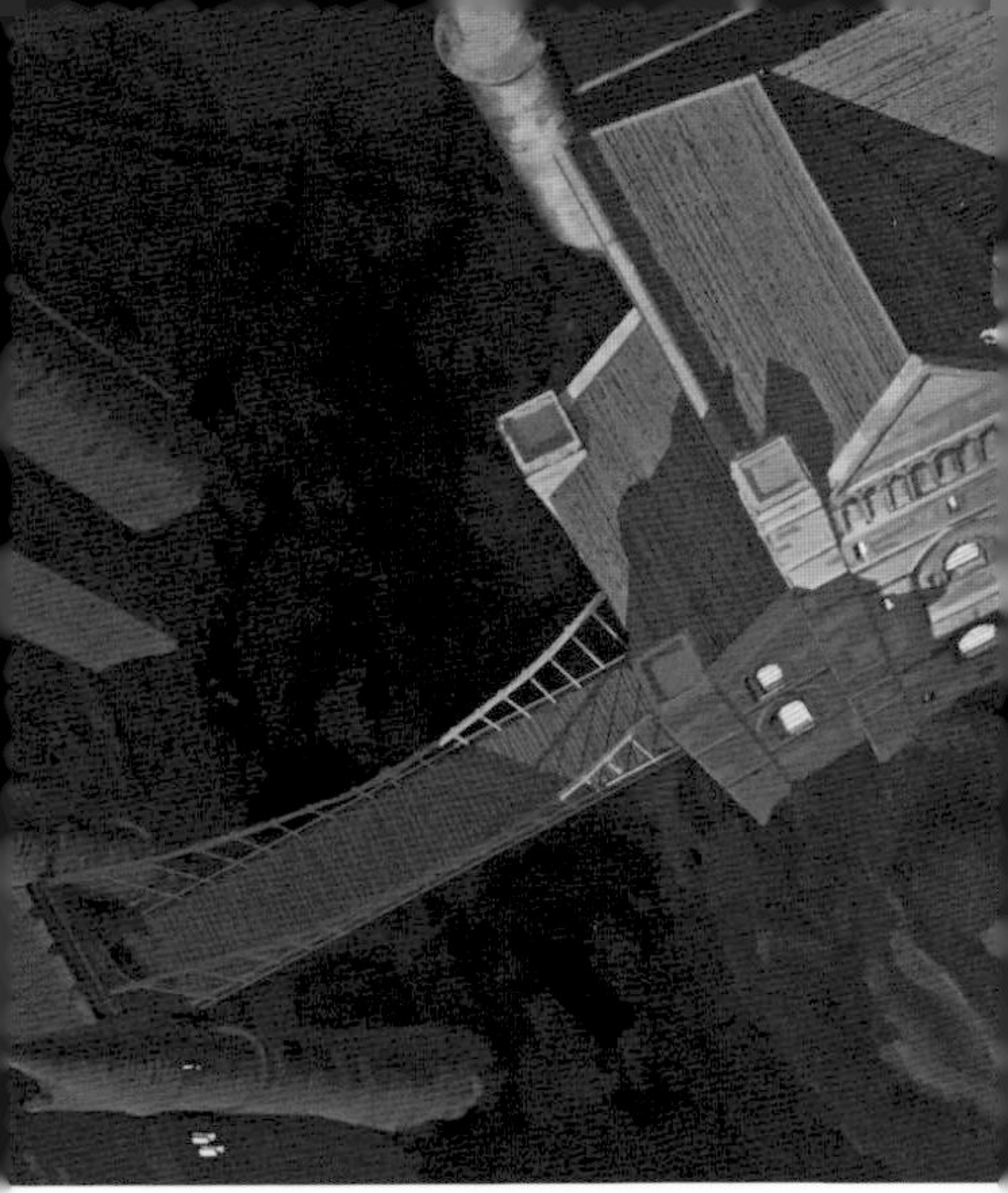

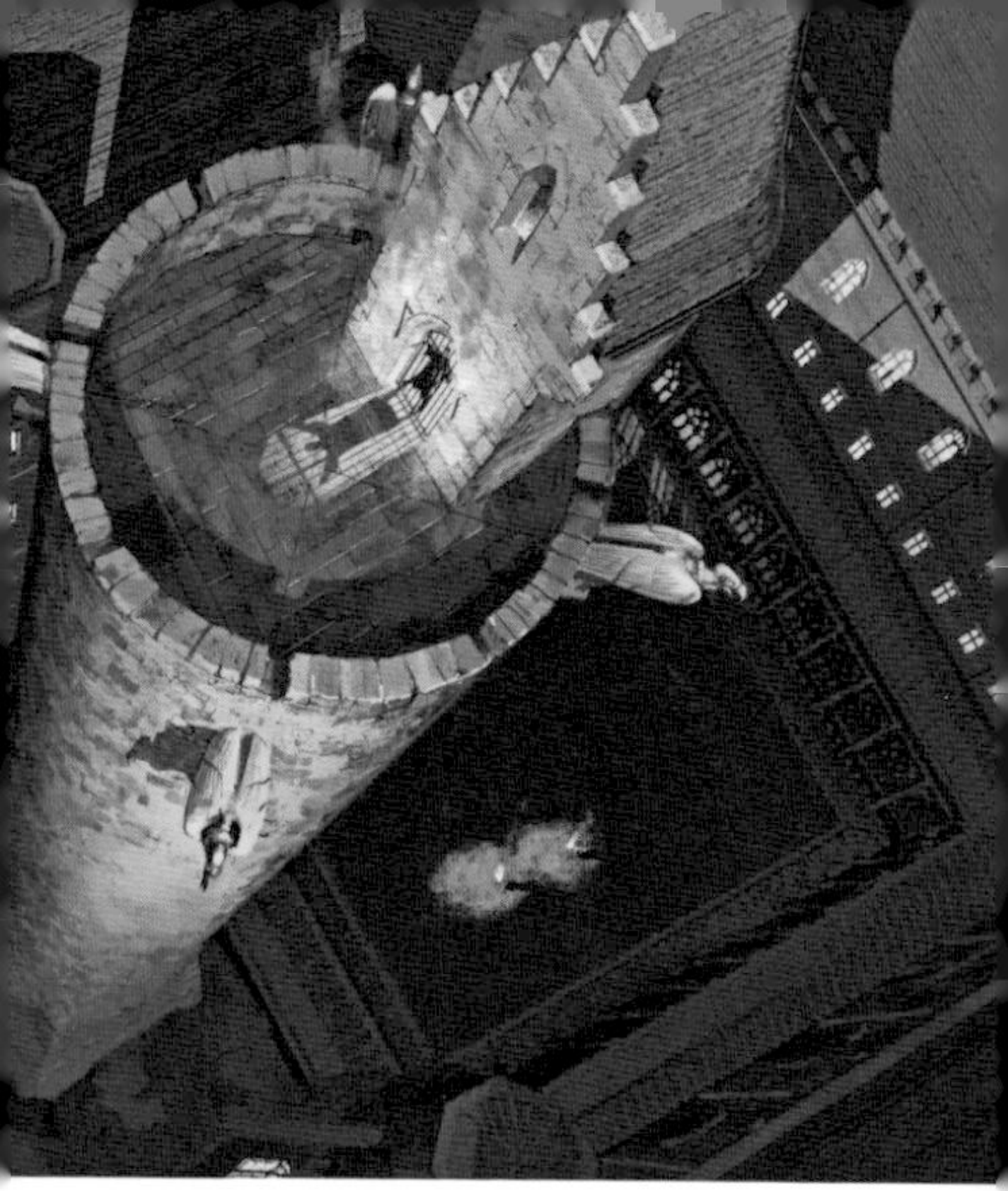

THESE PAGES: The tower in which Sirius Black is held at the end of *Prisoner of Azkaban*.

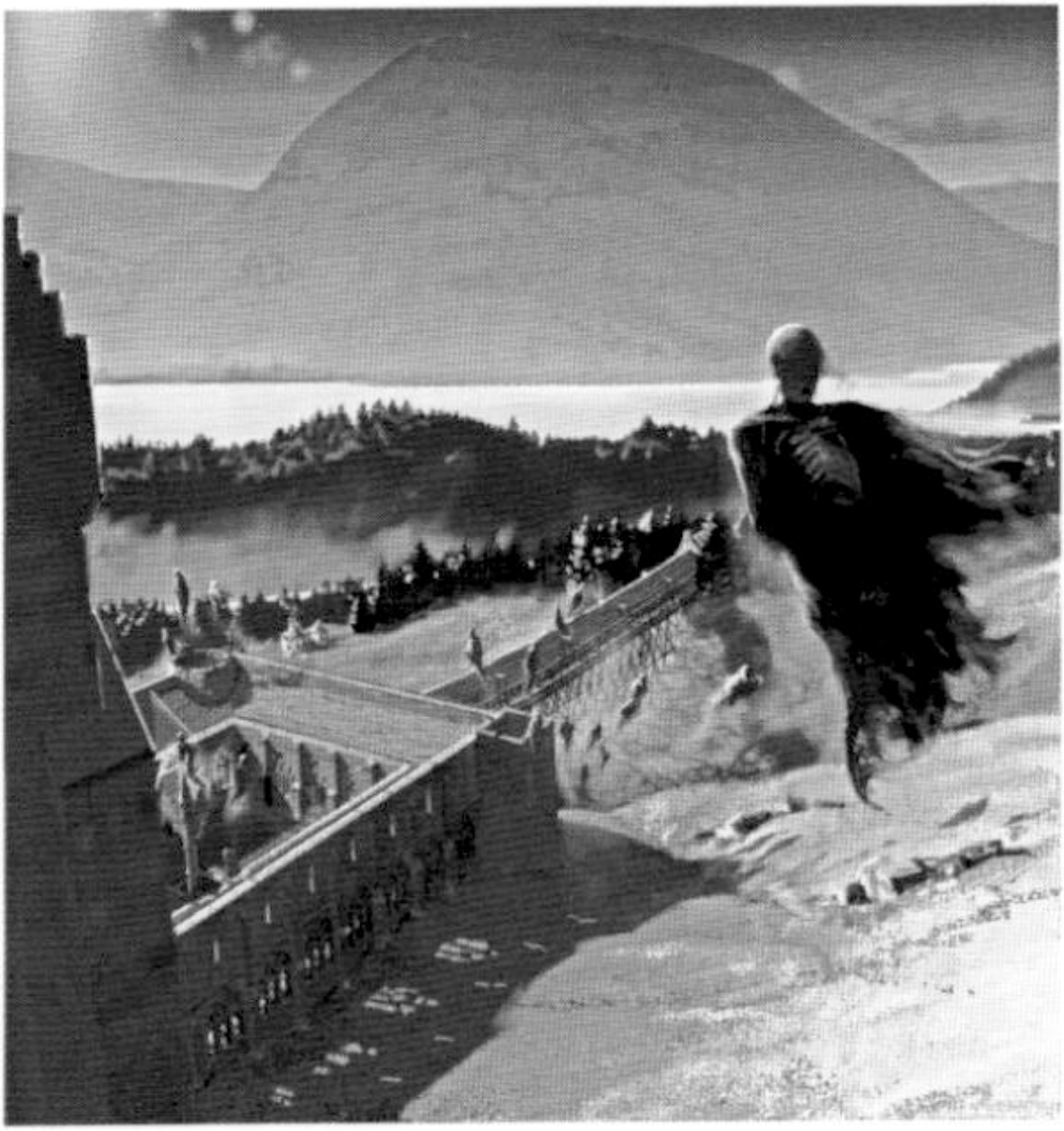

THESE PAGES: Dementors surround Hogwarts castle.

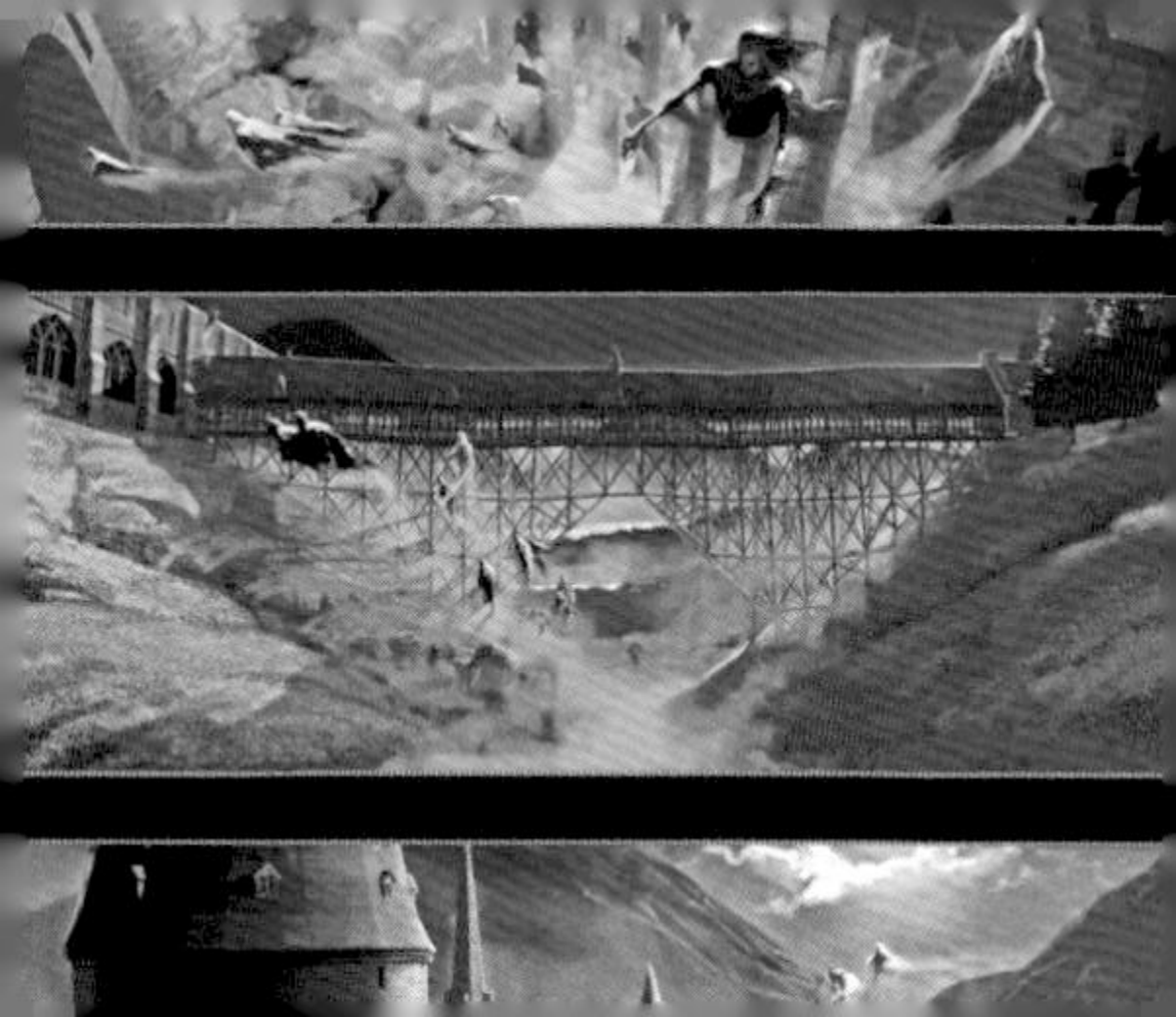

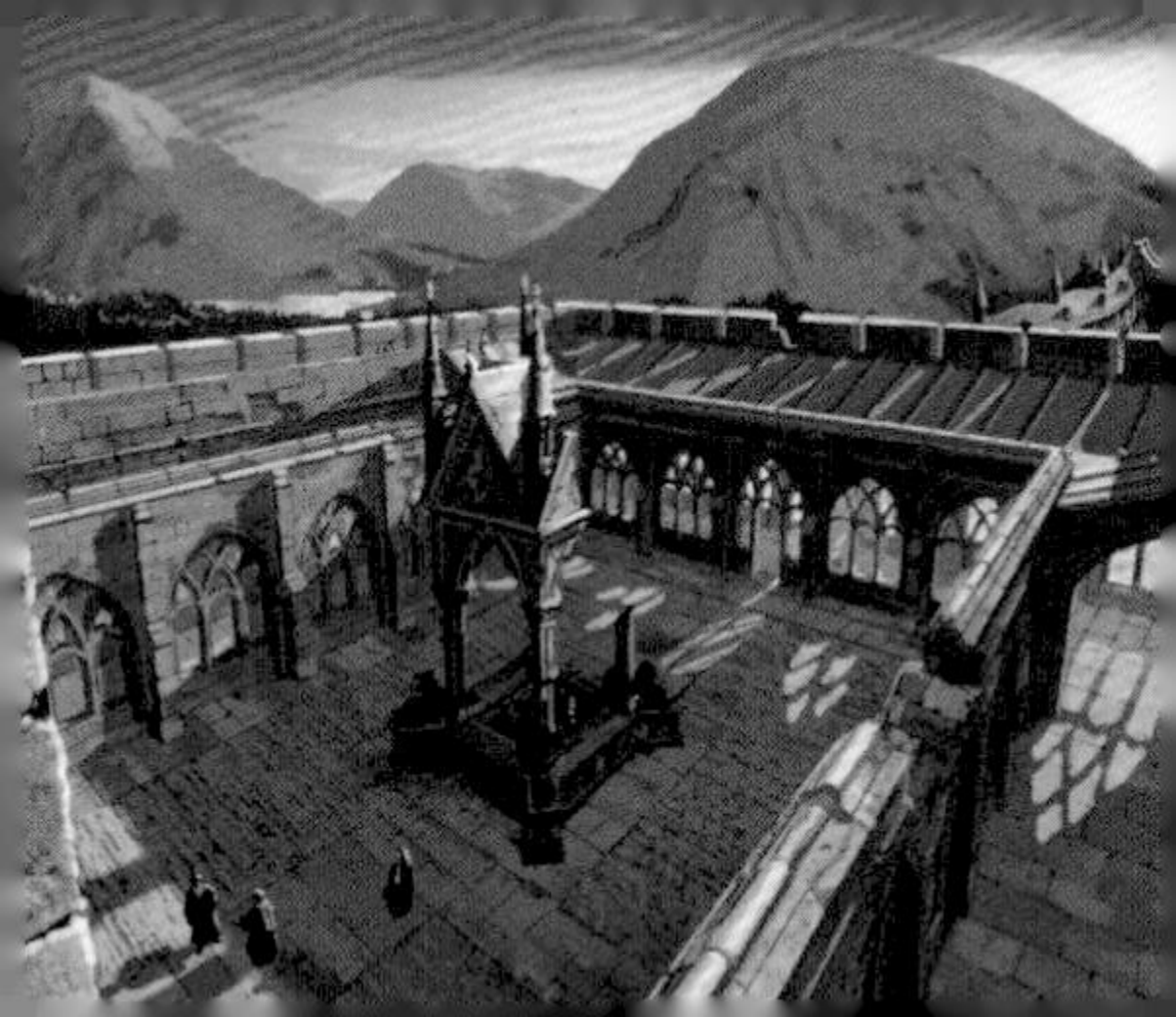

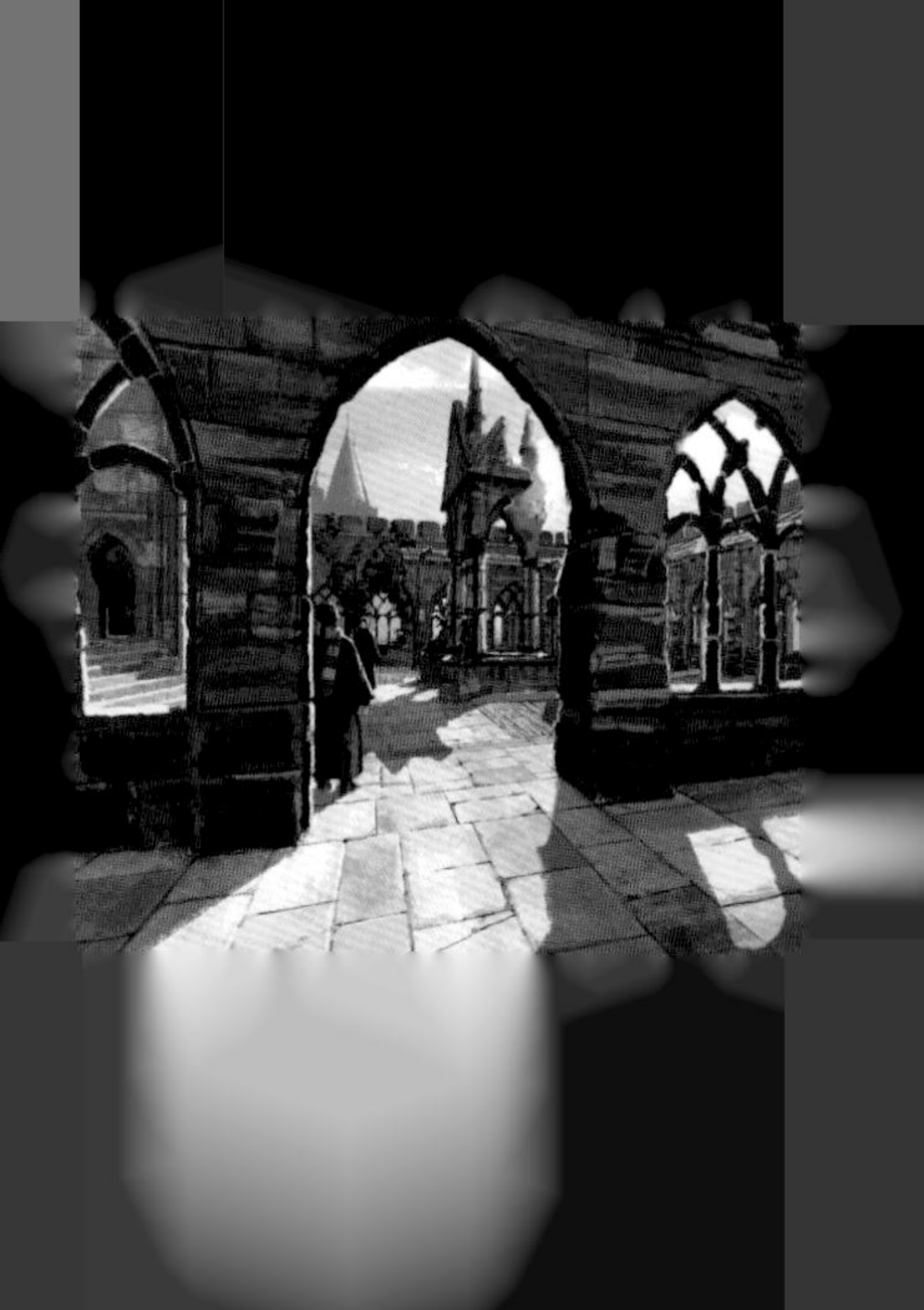

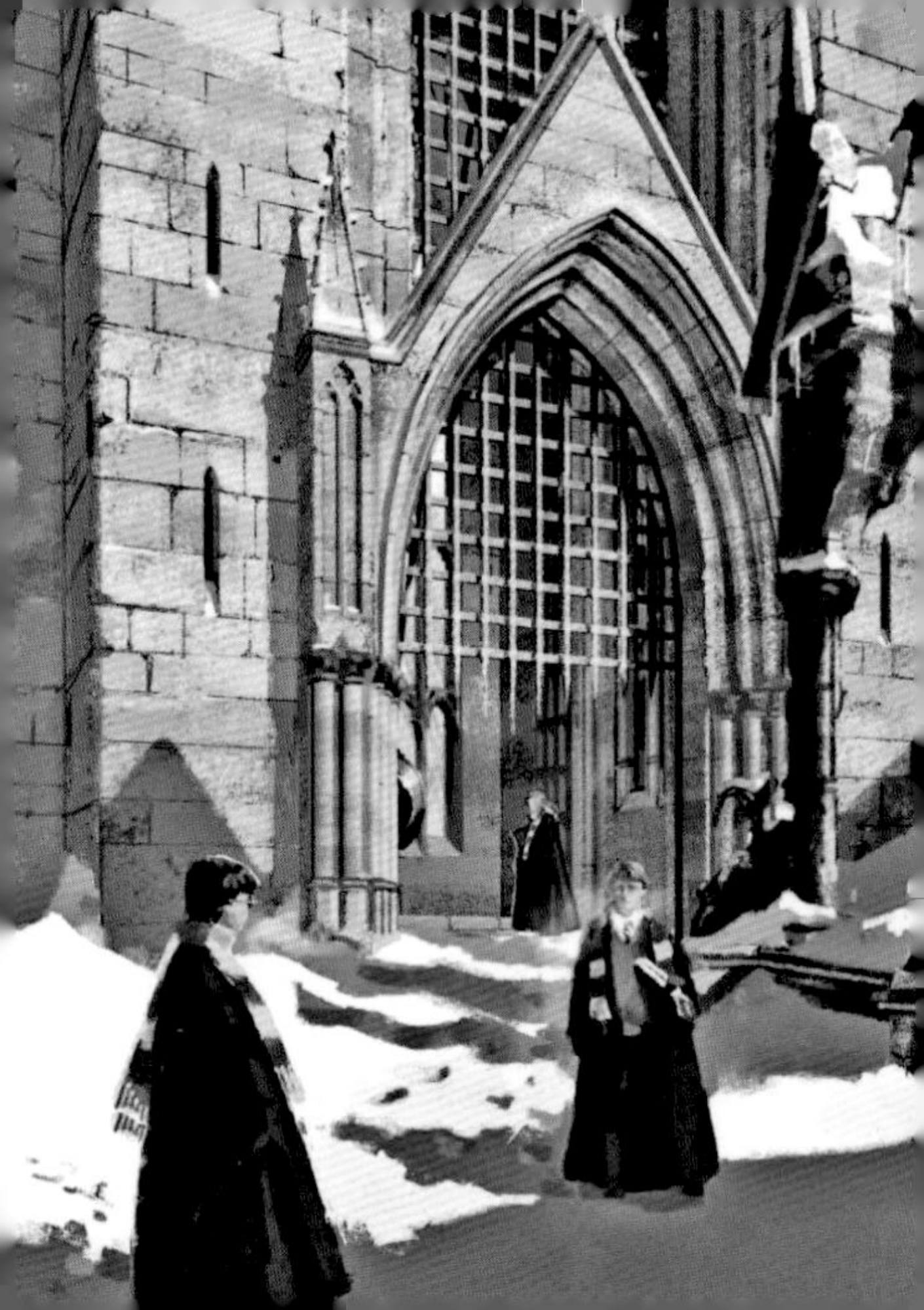

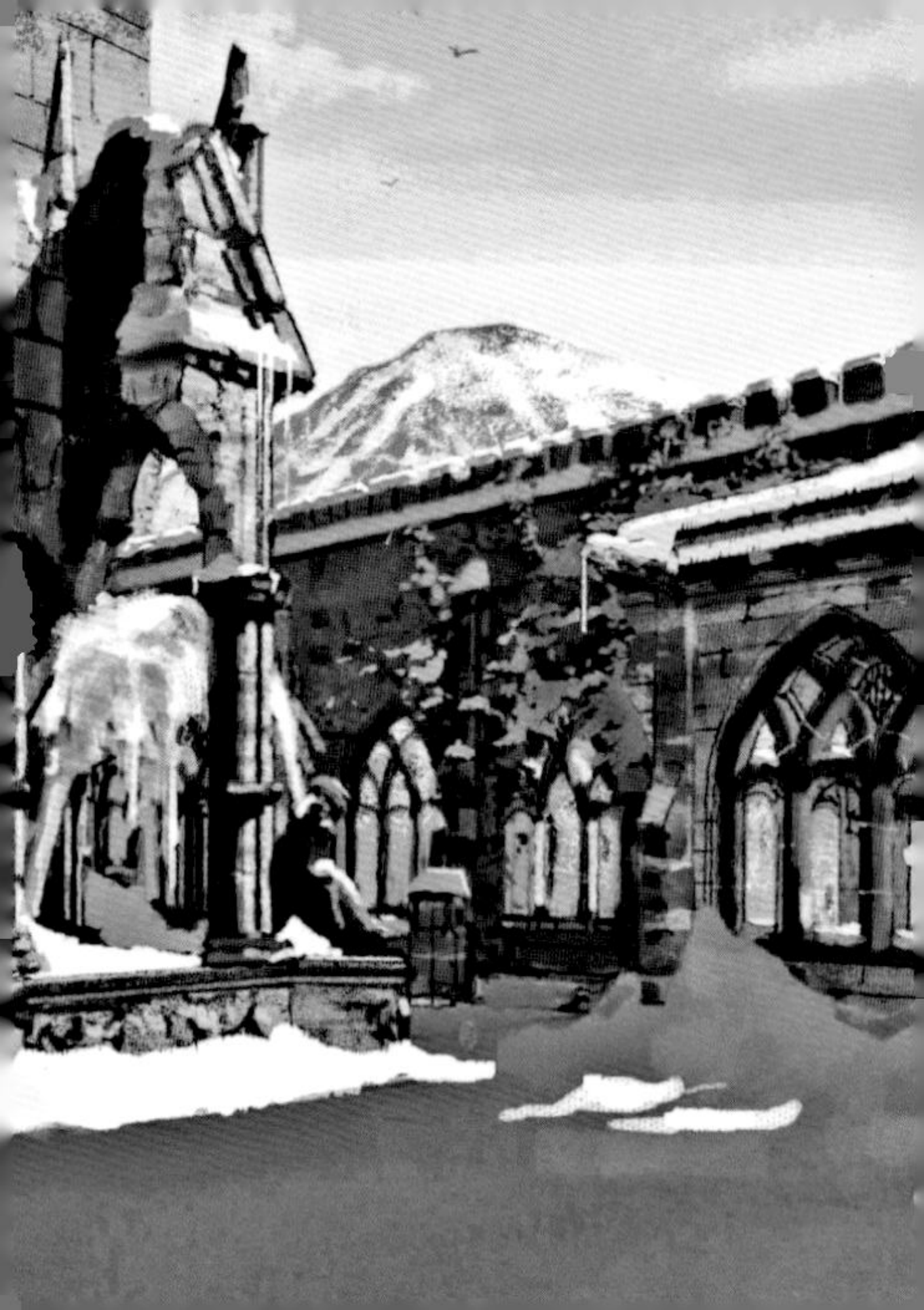

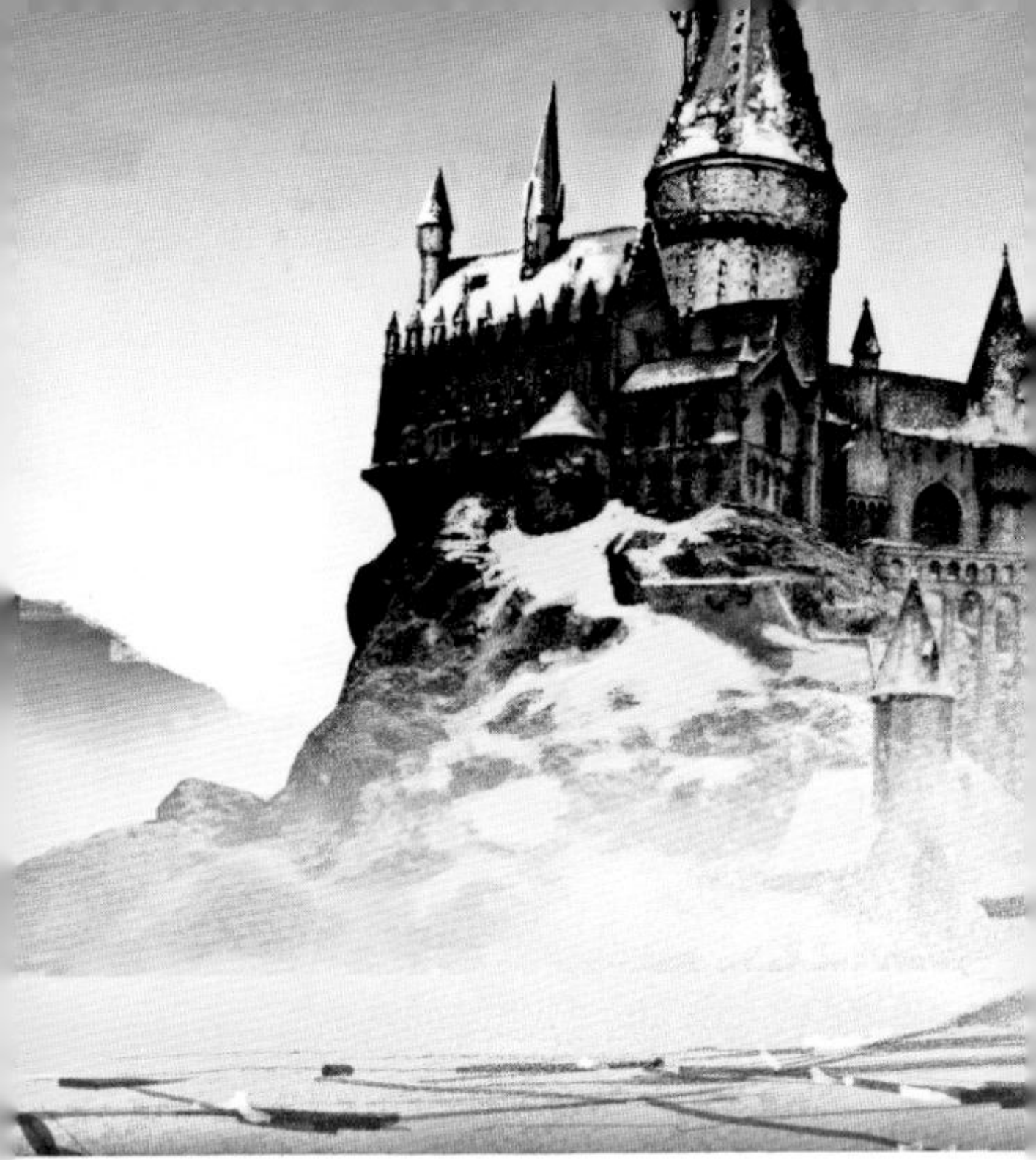

THESE PAGES: The Giant Squid bursts through the frozen Black Lake in a scene by Adam Brockbank that did not make it into the films.

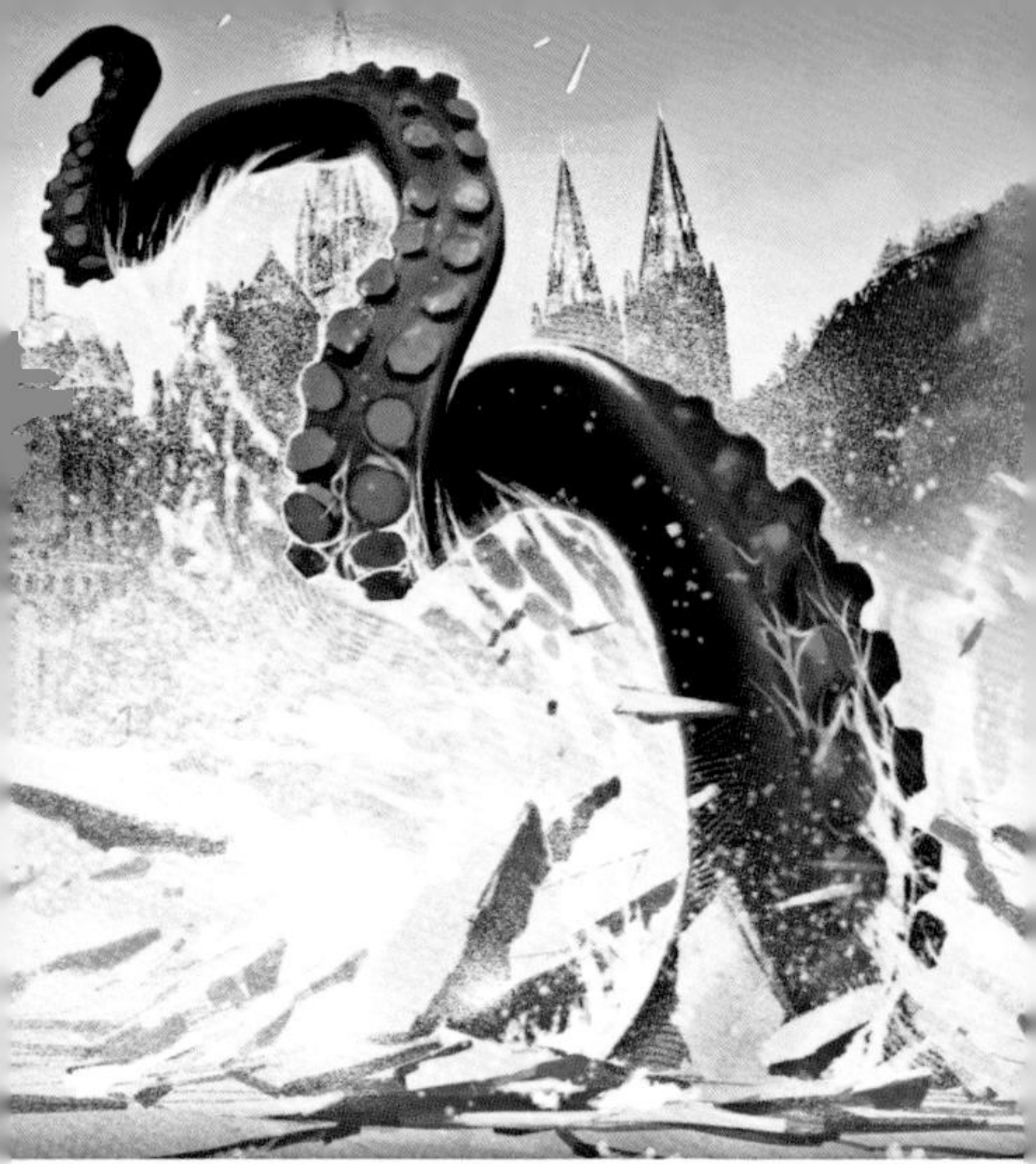

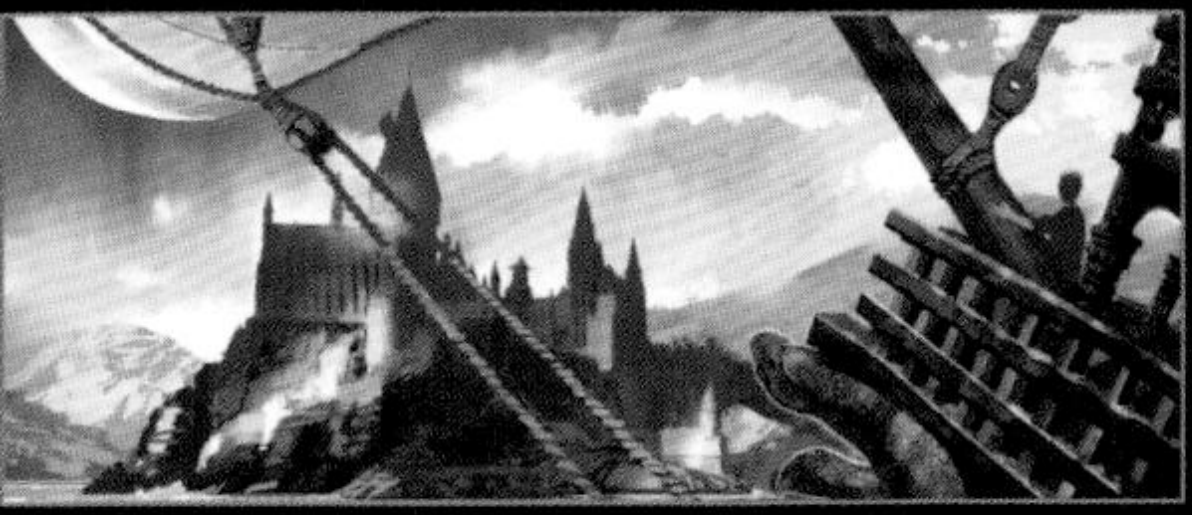

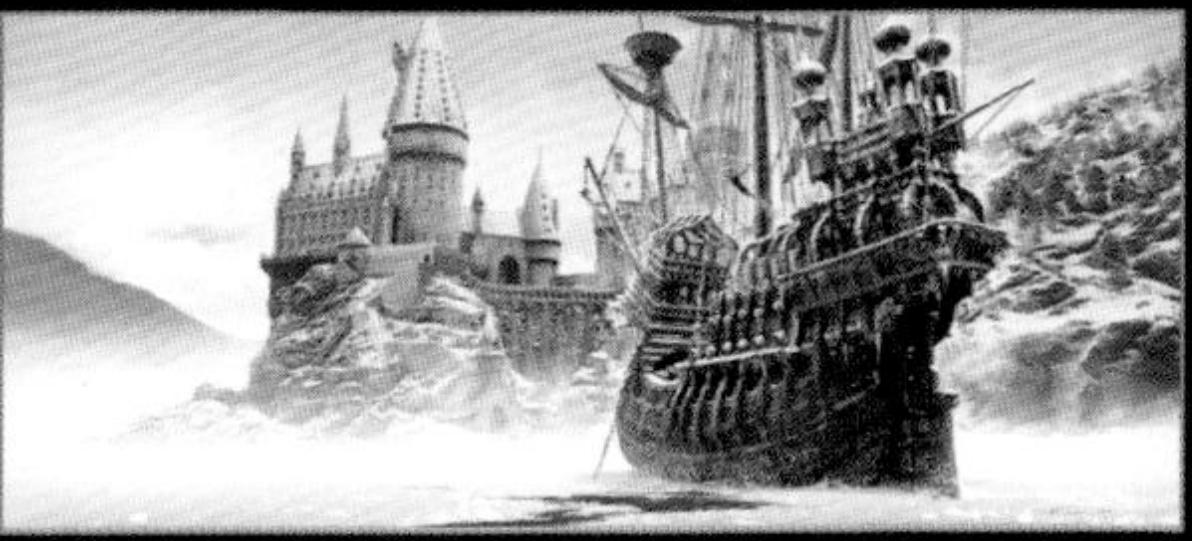

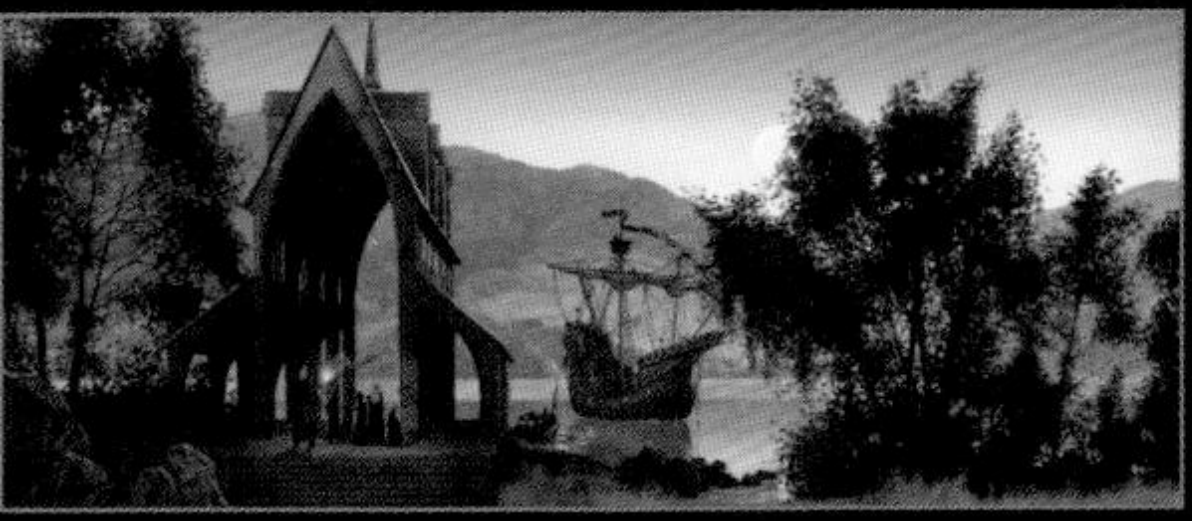

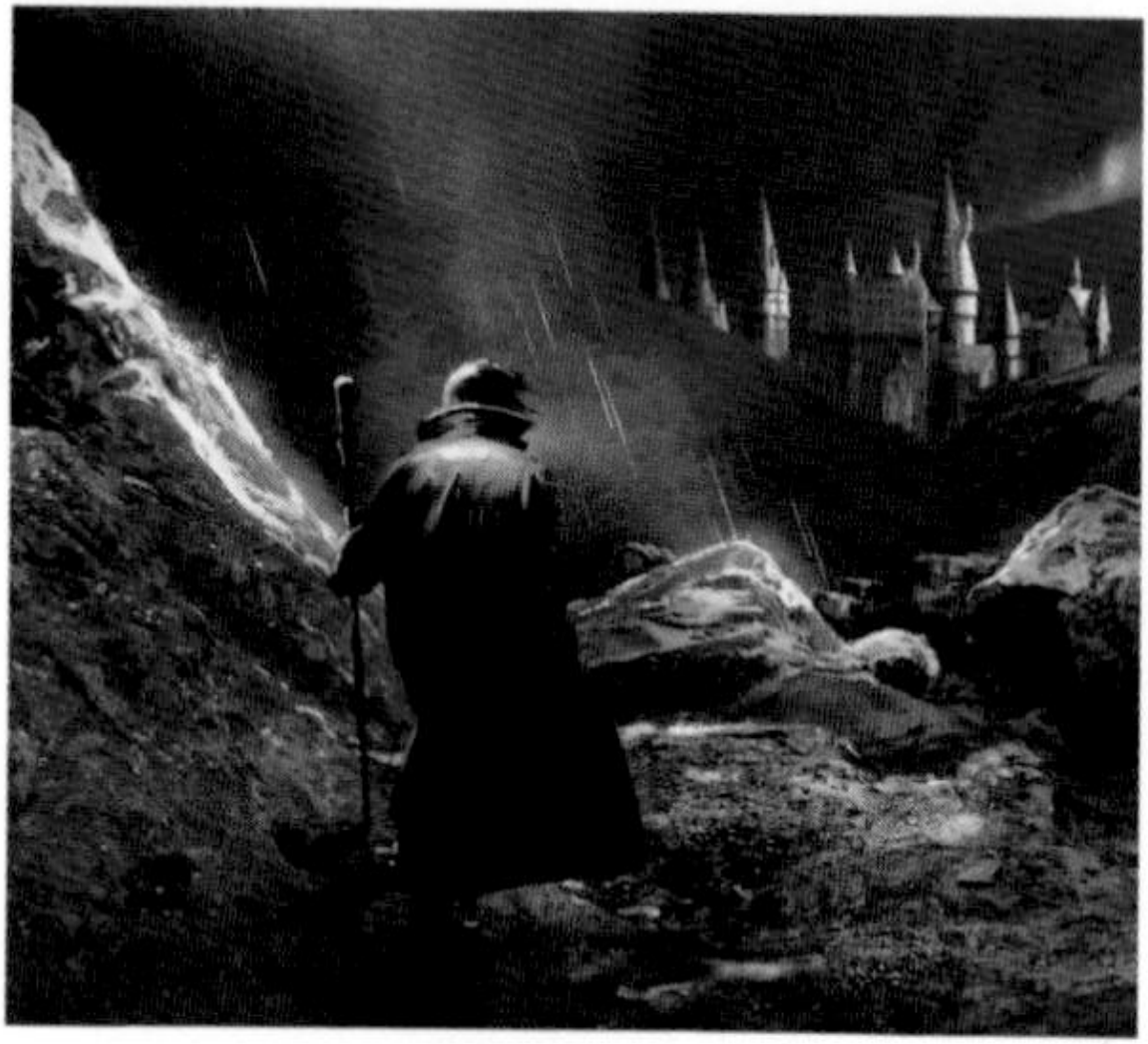

OPPOSITE: The Durmstrang ship arrives at Hogwarts. Art by Dermot Power (*top*), Adam Brockbank (*middle*), and Andrew Williamson (*bottom*).

ABOVE: "Mad-Eye" Moody arrives at Hogwarts in this piece by Andrew Williamson for *Harry Potter and the Goblet of Fire*.

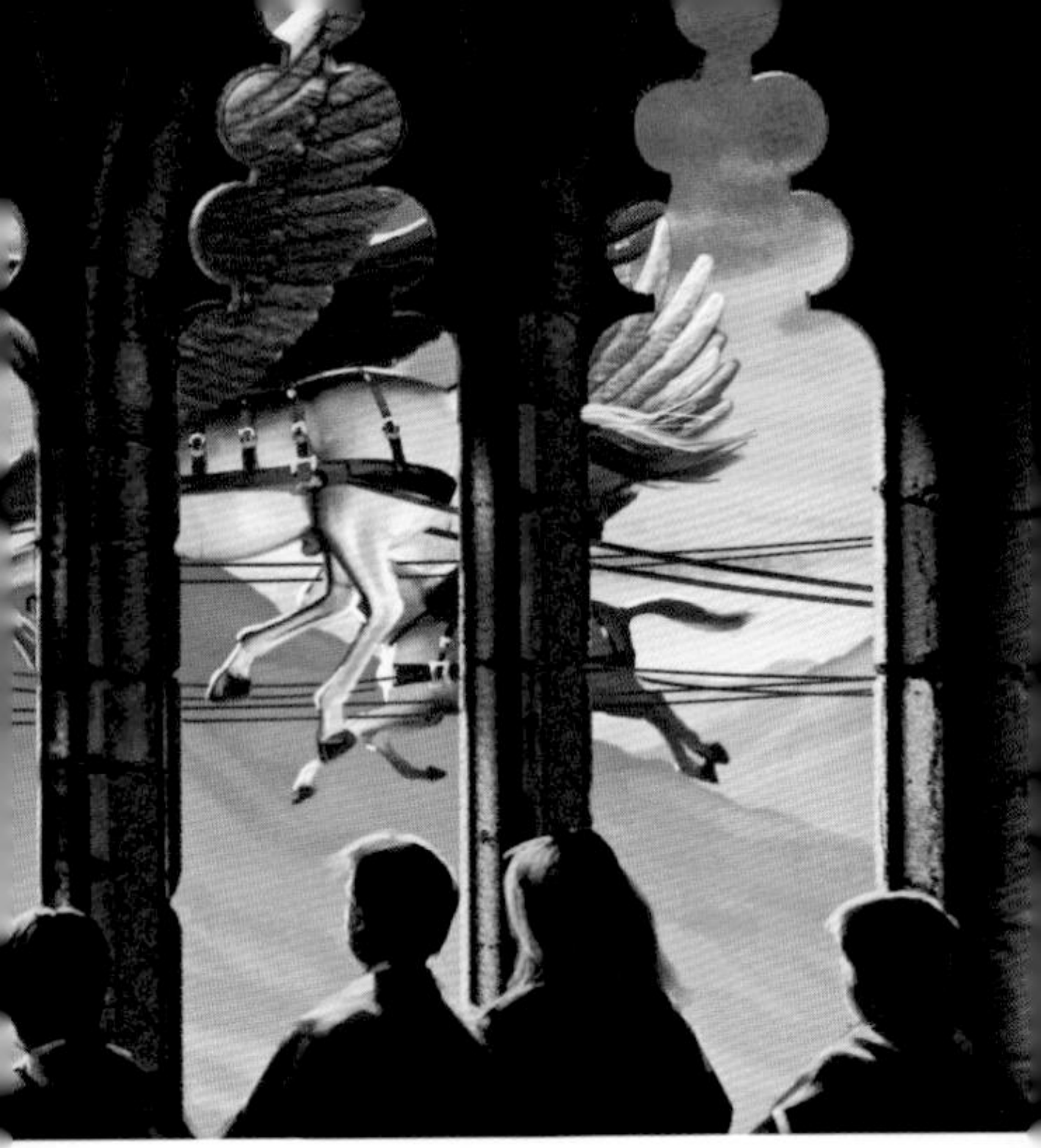

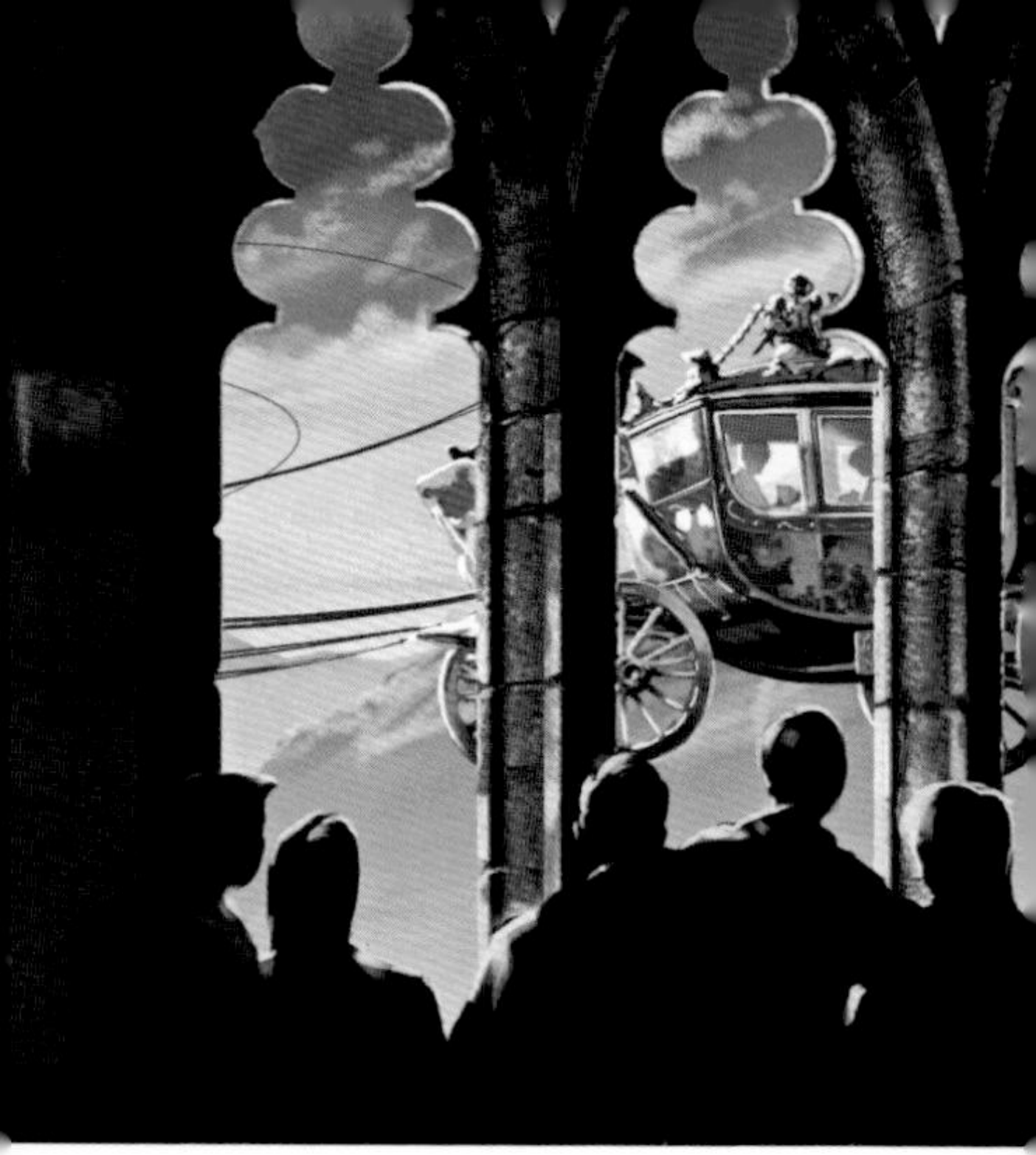

THESE PAGES: Andrew Williamson depicts the Beauxbatons carriage arriving at Hogwarts for the Triwizard Tournament.

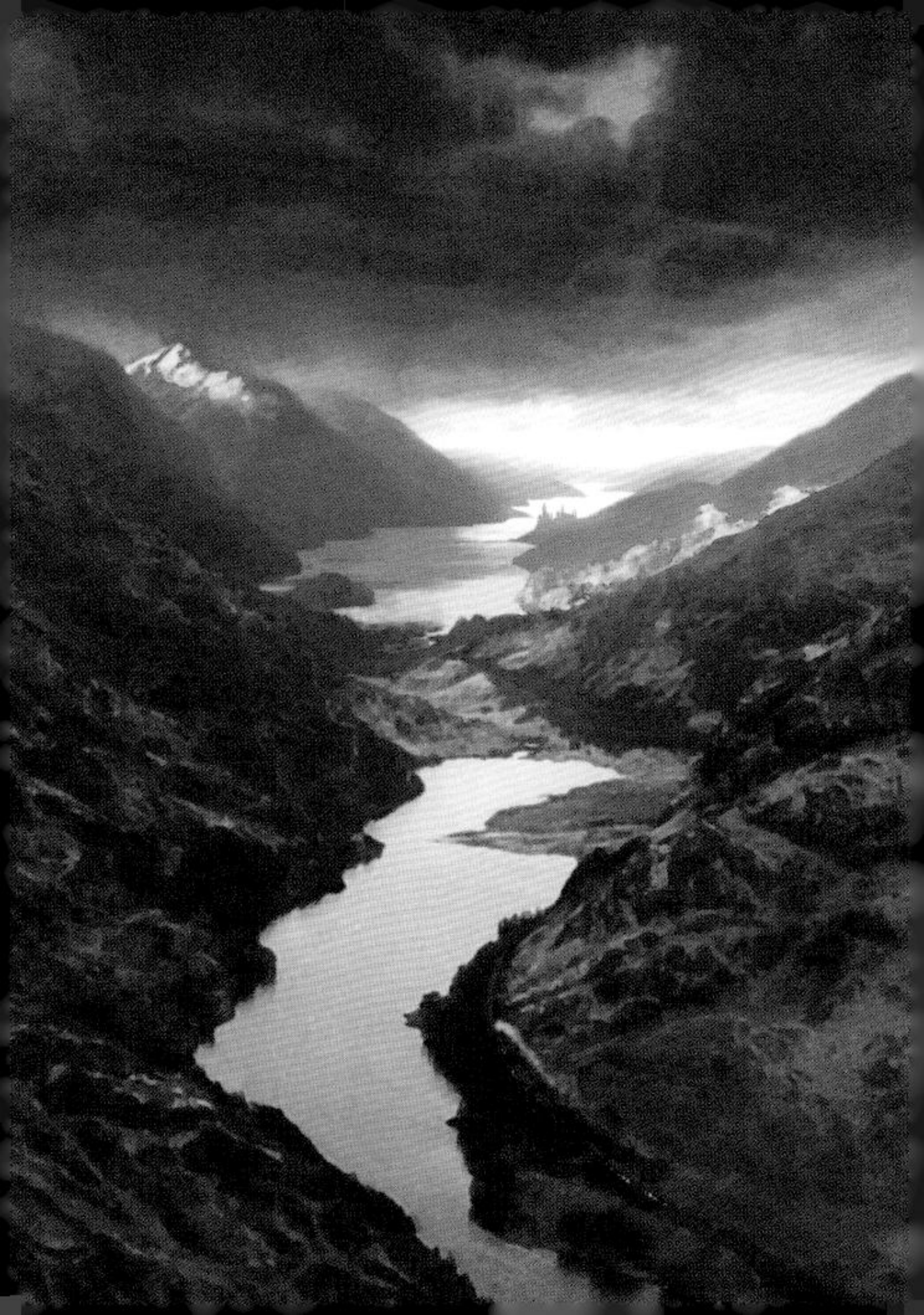

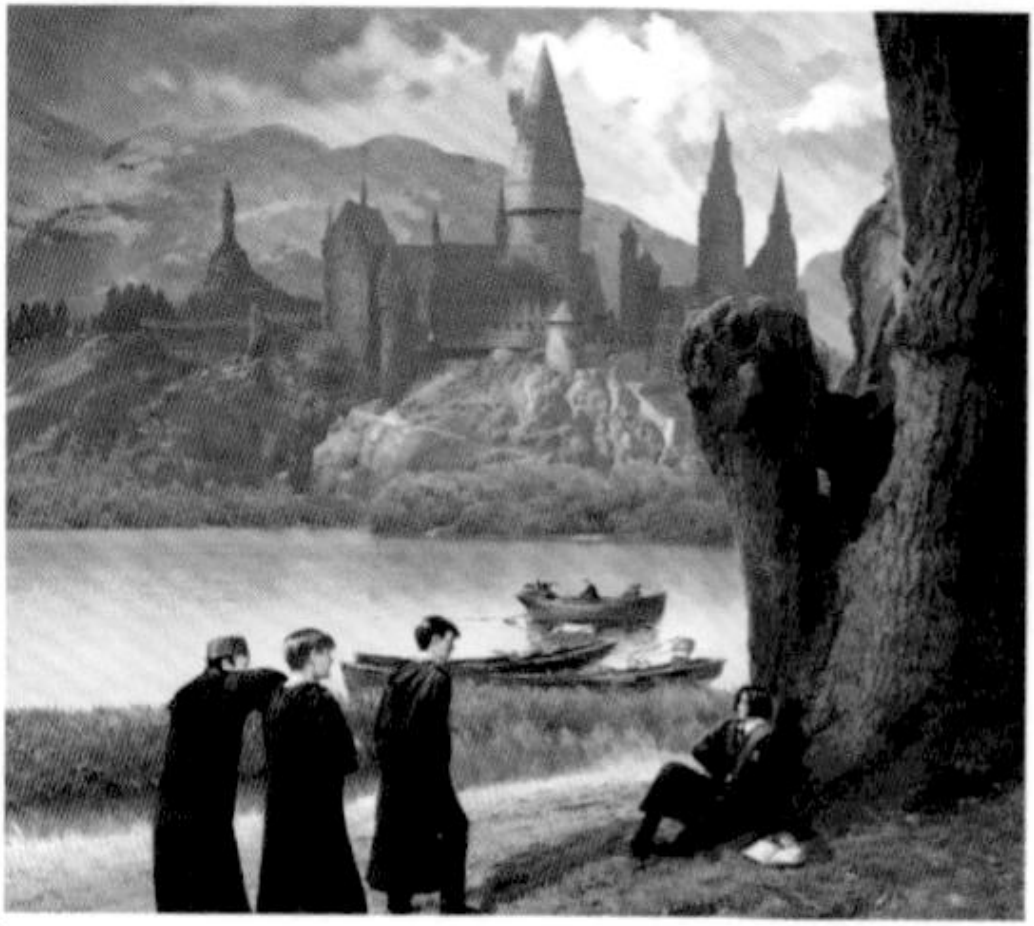

OPPOSITE: The Hogwarts Express steams through the Scottish Highlands toward Hogwarts castle in art by Adam Brockbank for *Harry Potter and the Order of the Phoenix*.

ABOVE: Andrew Williamson depicts a flashback scene that shows the Marauders confronting teenage Severus Snape in *Harry Potter and the Order of the Phoenix*.

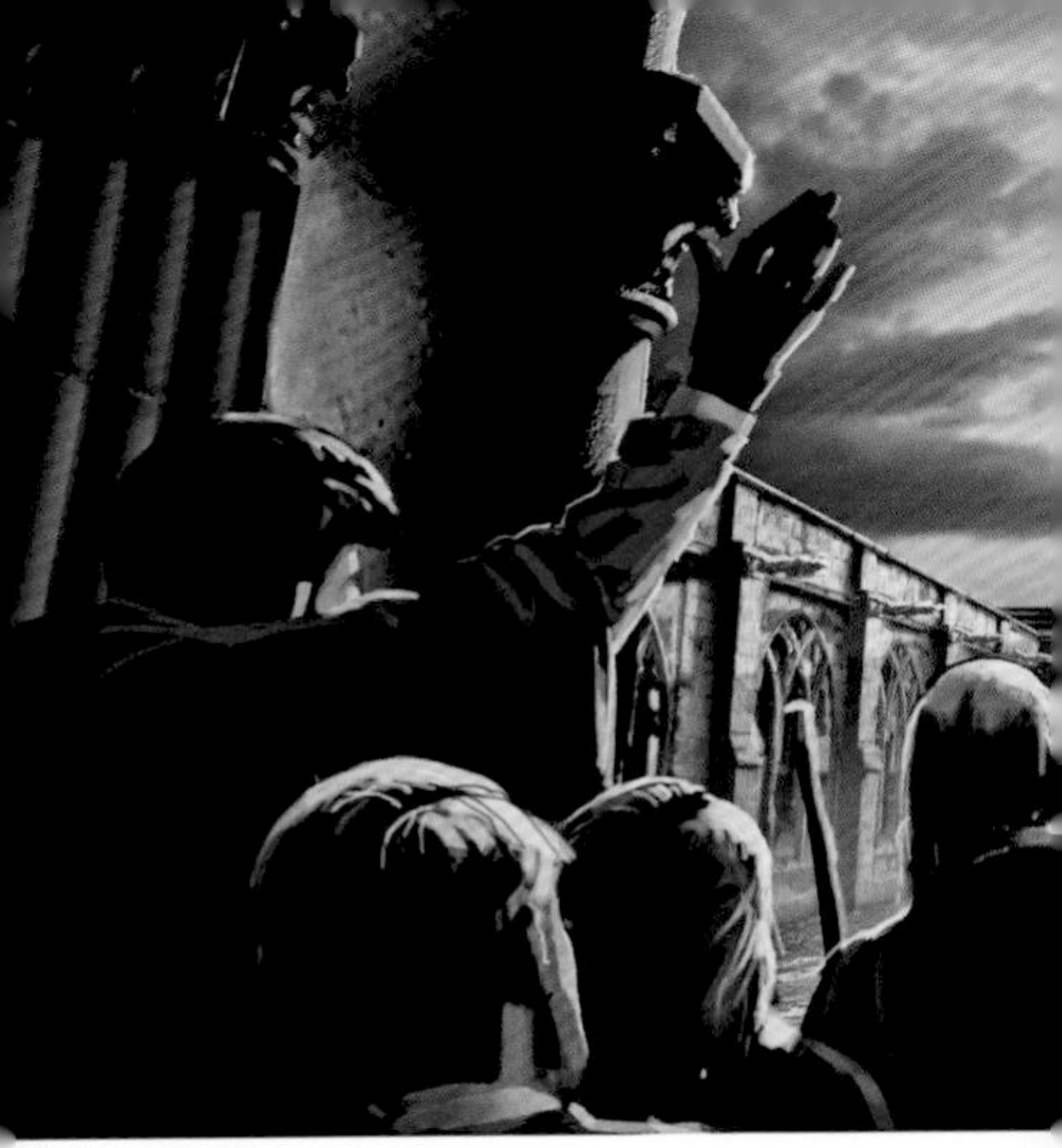

THESE PAGES: The Weasley twins escape Hogwarts on brooms as Argus Filch and other students look on. Art by Andrew Williamson for *Harry Potter and the Order of the Phoenix*.

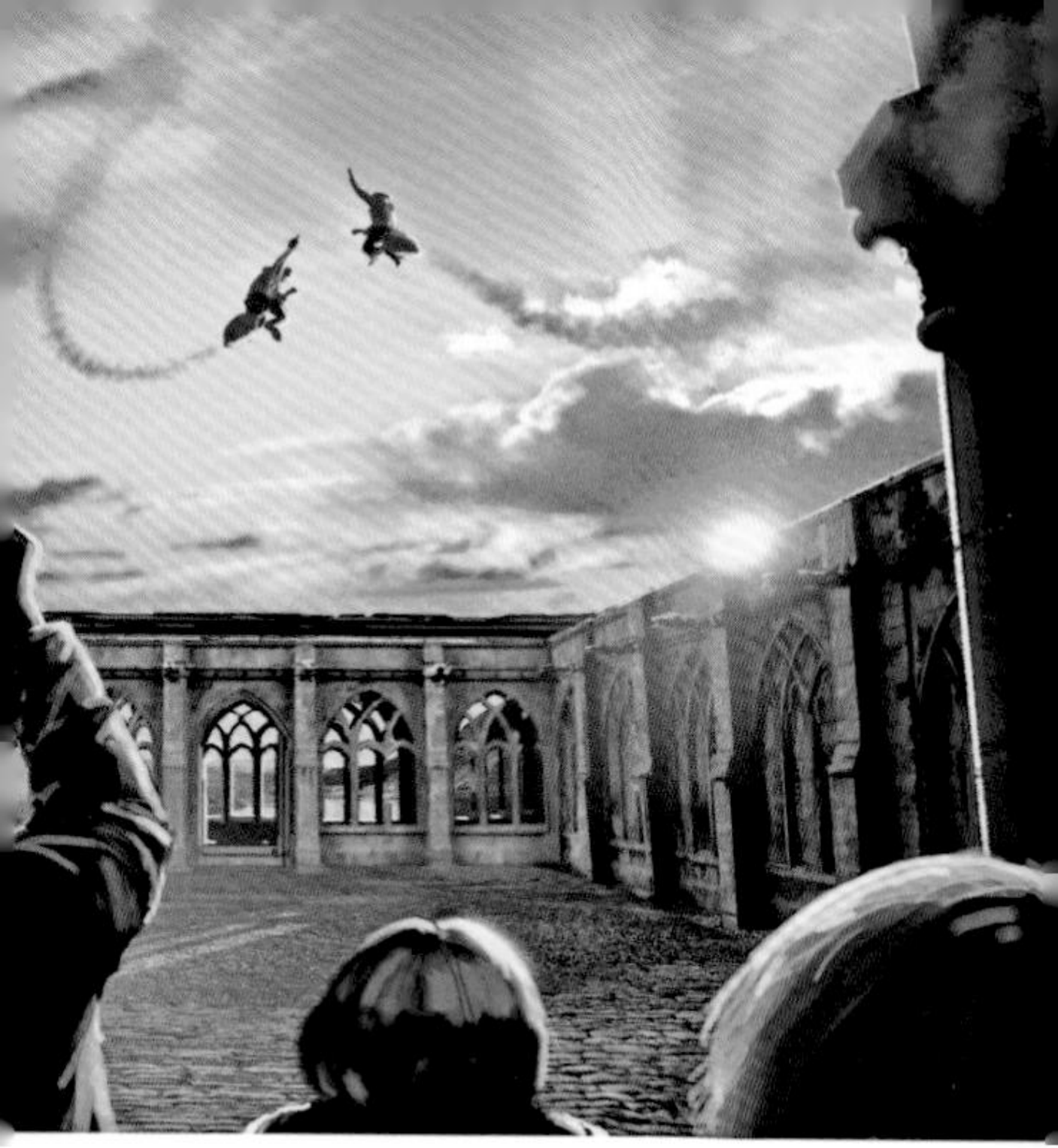

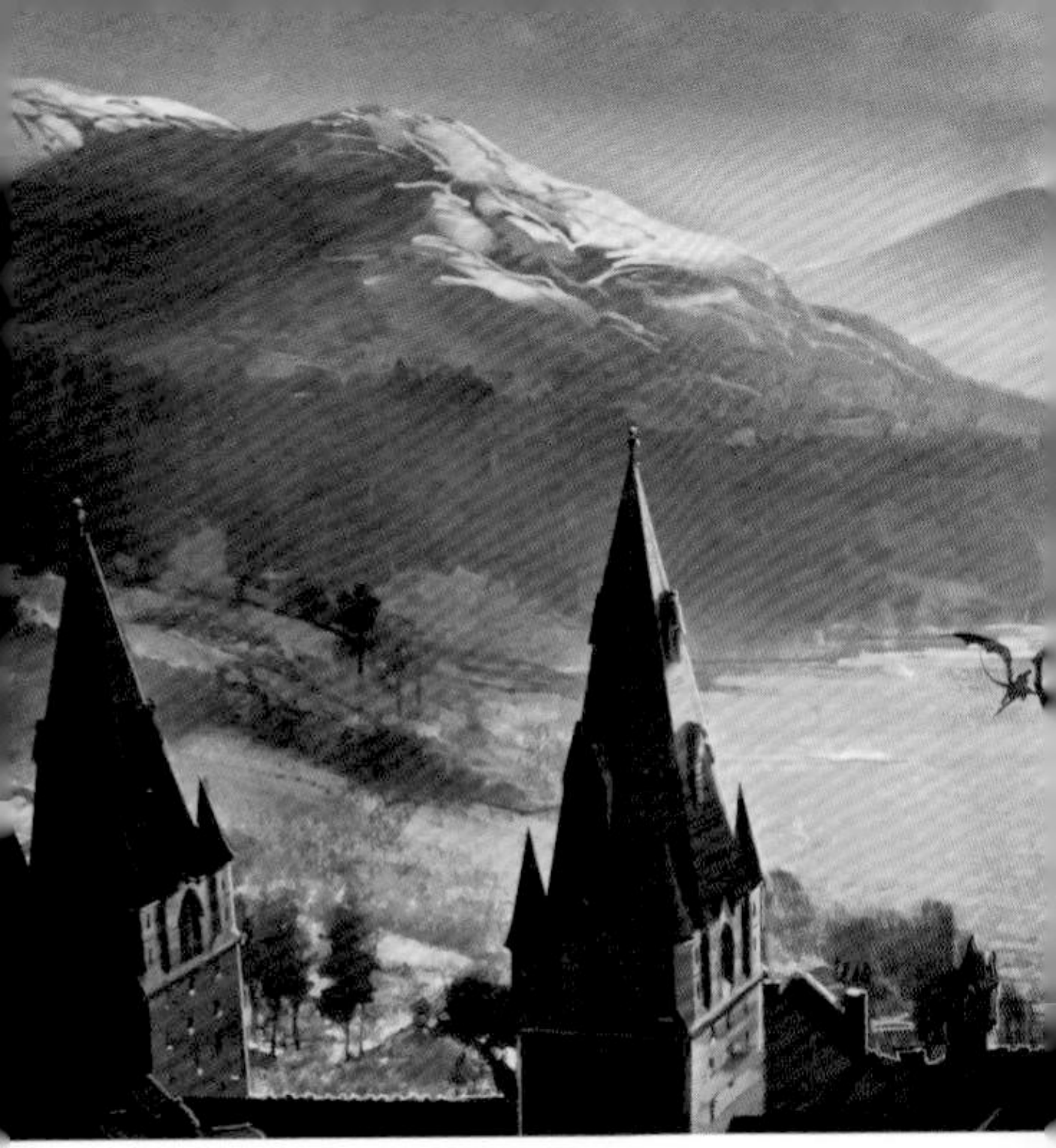

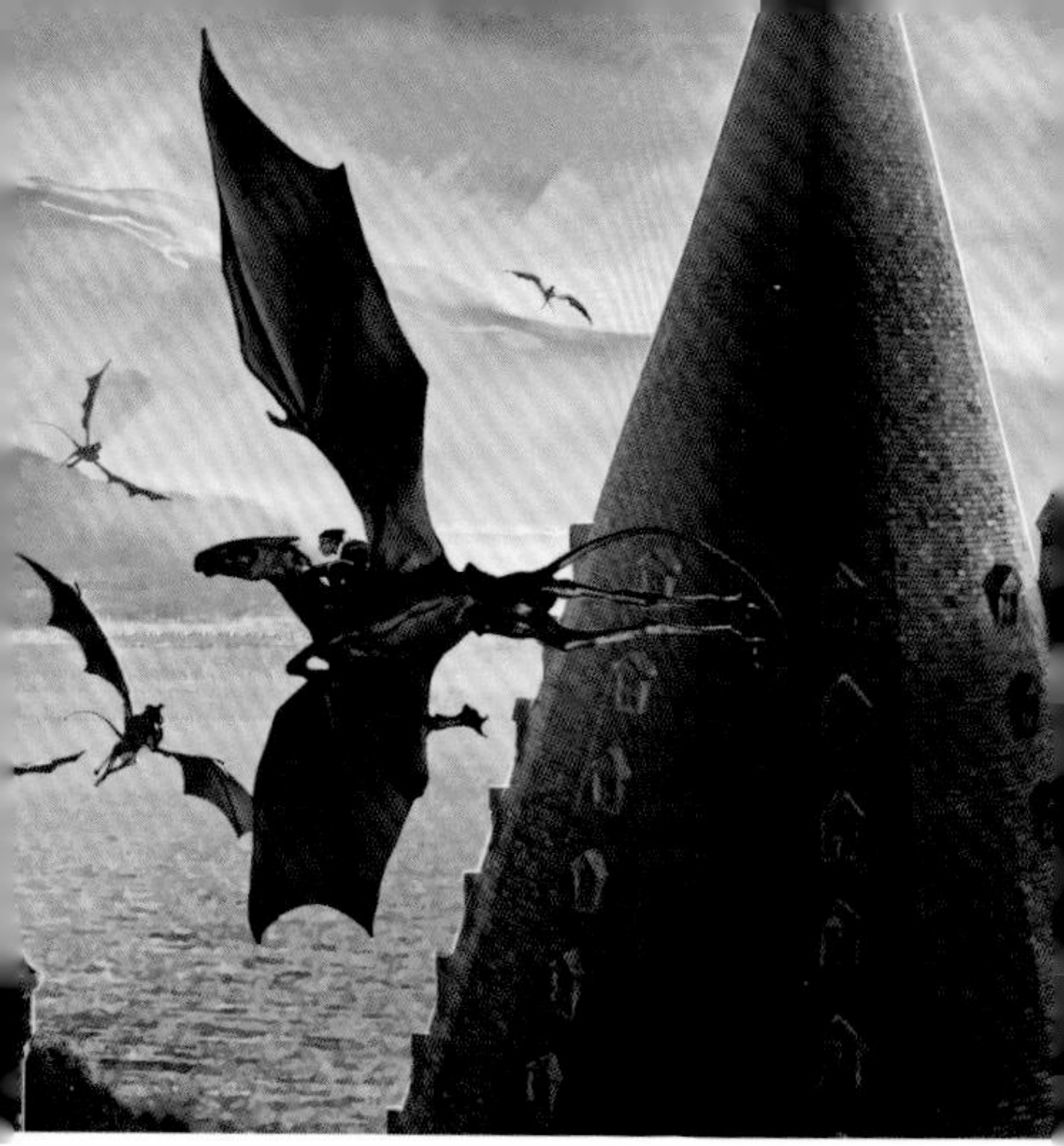

THESE PAGES: In *Harry Potter and the Order of the Phoenix*, Harry and his friends fly on Thestrals to the Ministry of Magic to rescue Sirius Black. Art by Andrew Williamson.

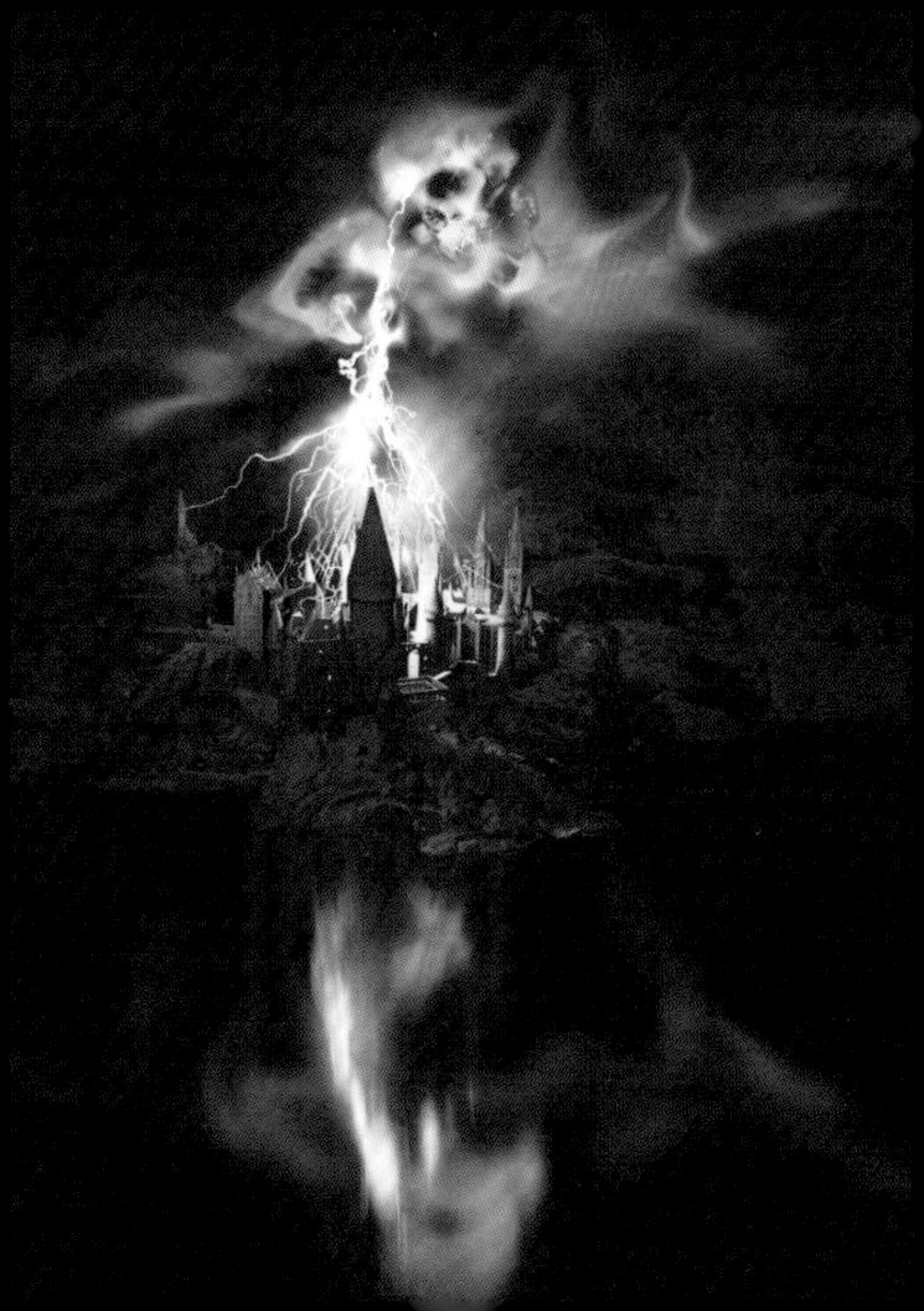

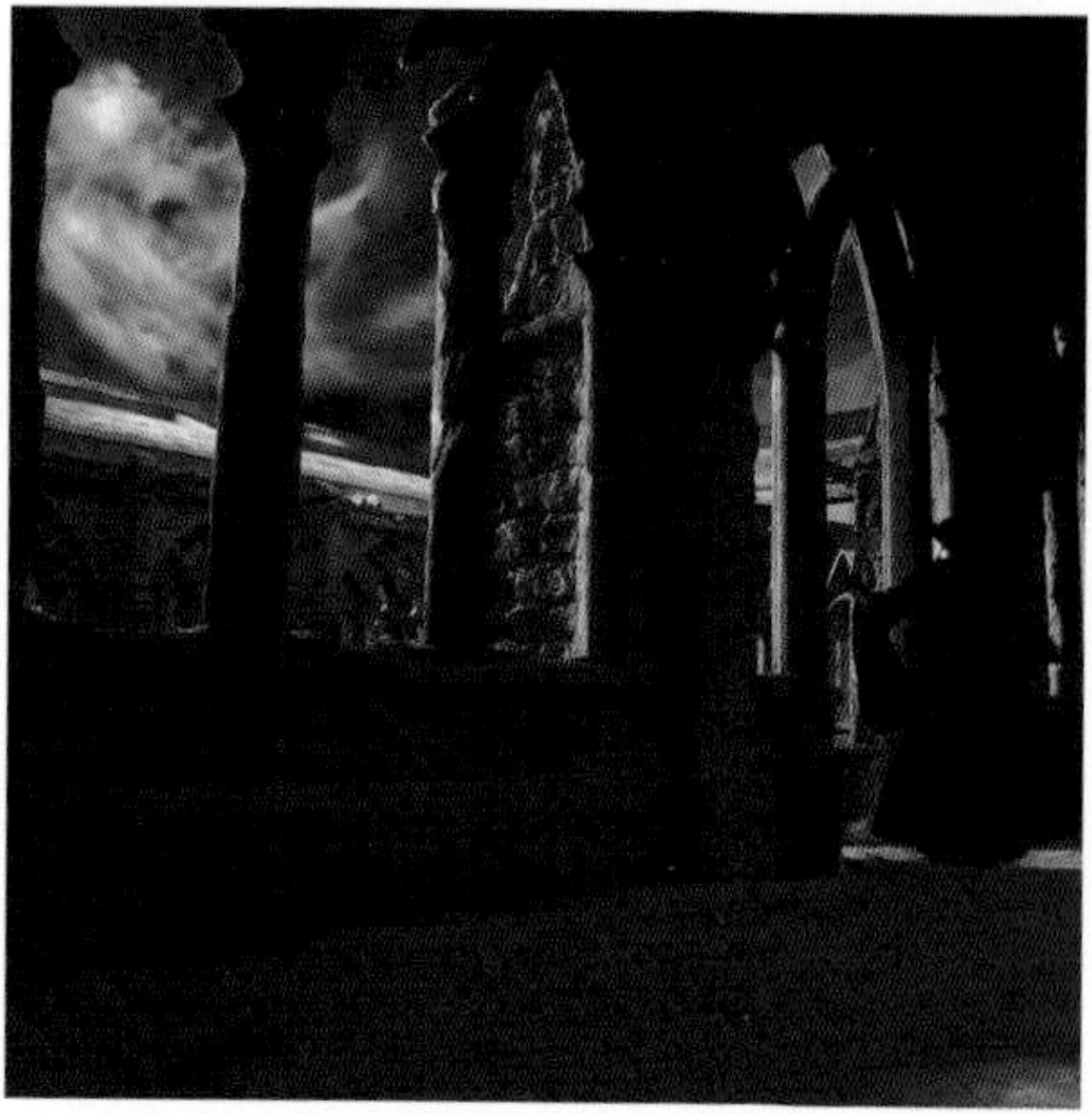

THESE PAGES: The Dark Mark hovers over Hogwarts in these pieces by Andrew Williamson for *Harry Potter and the Half-Blood Prince*.

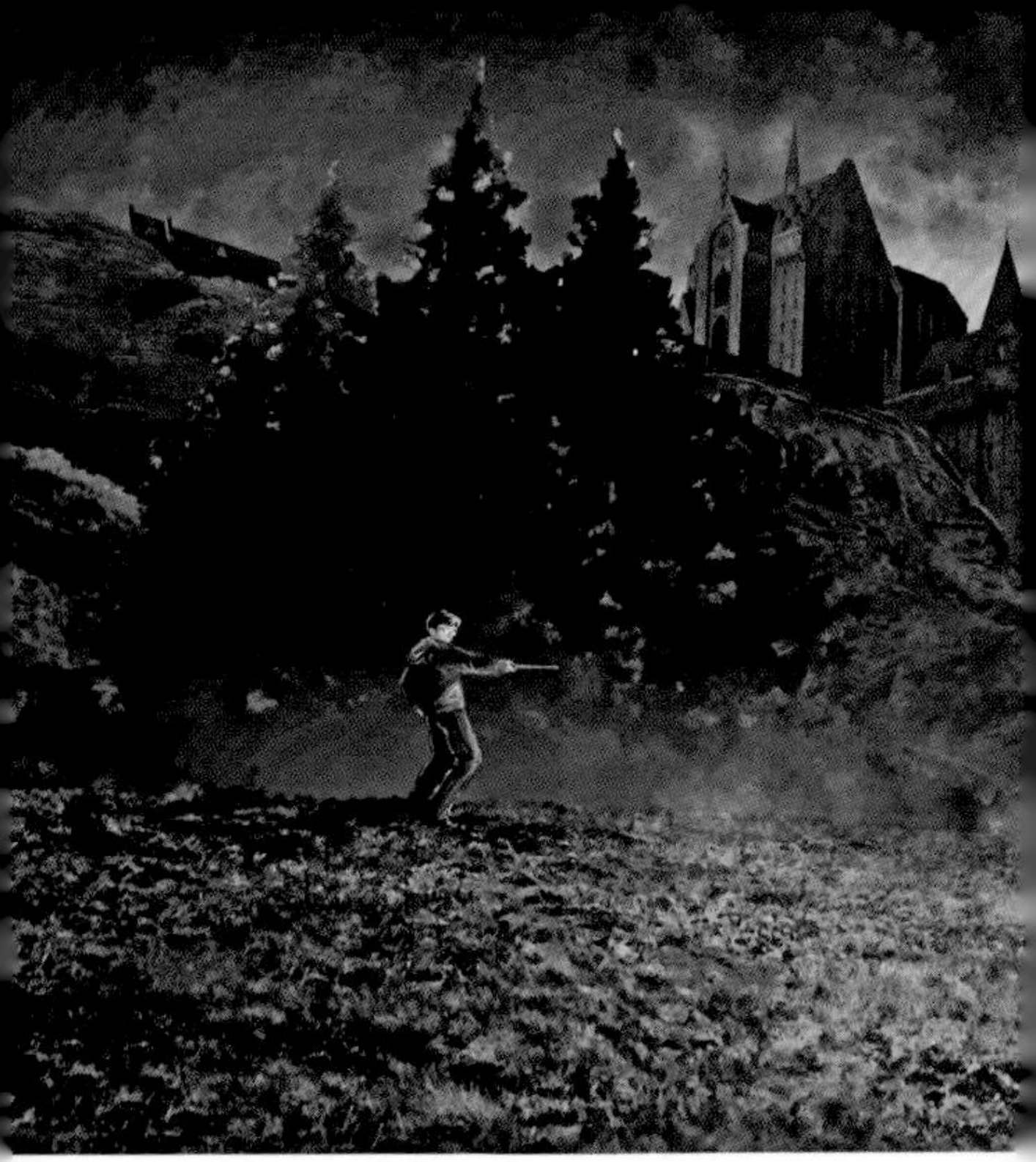

THESE PAGES: Harry faces off against Professor Snape at the end of *Harry Potter and the Half-Blood Prince*. Art by Andrew Williamson.

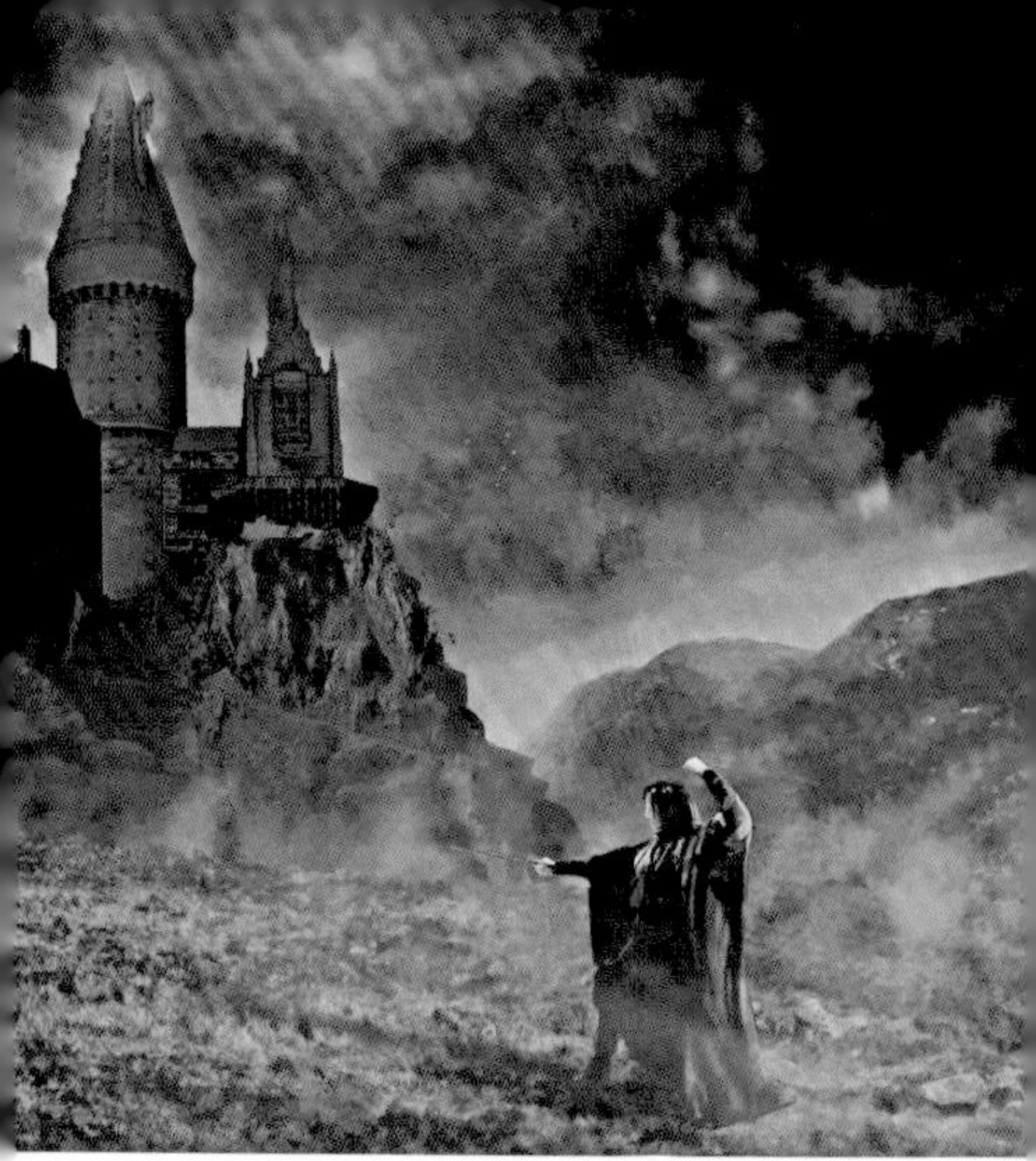

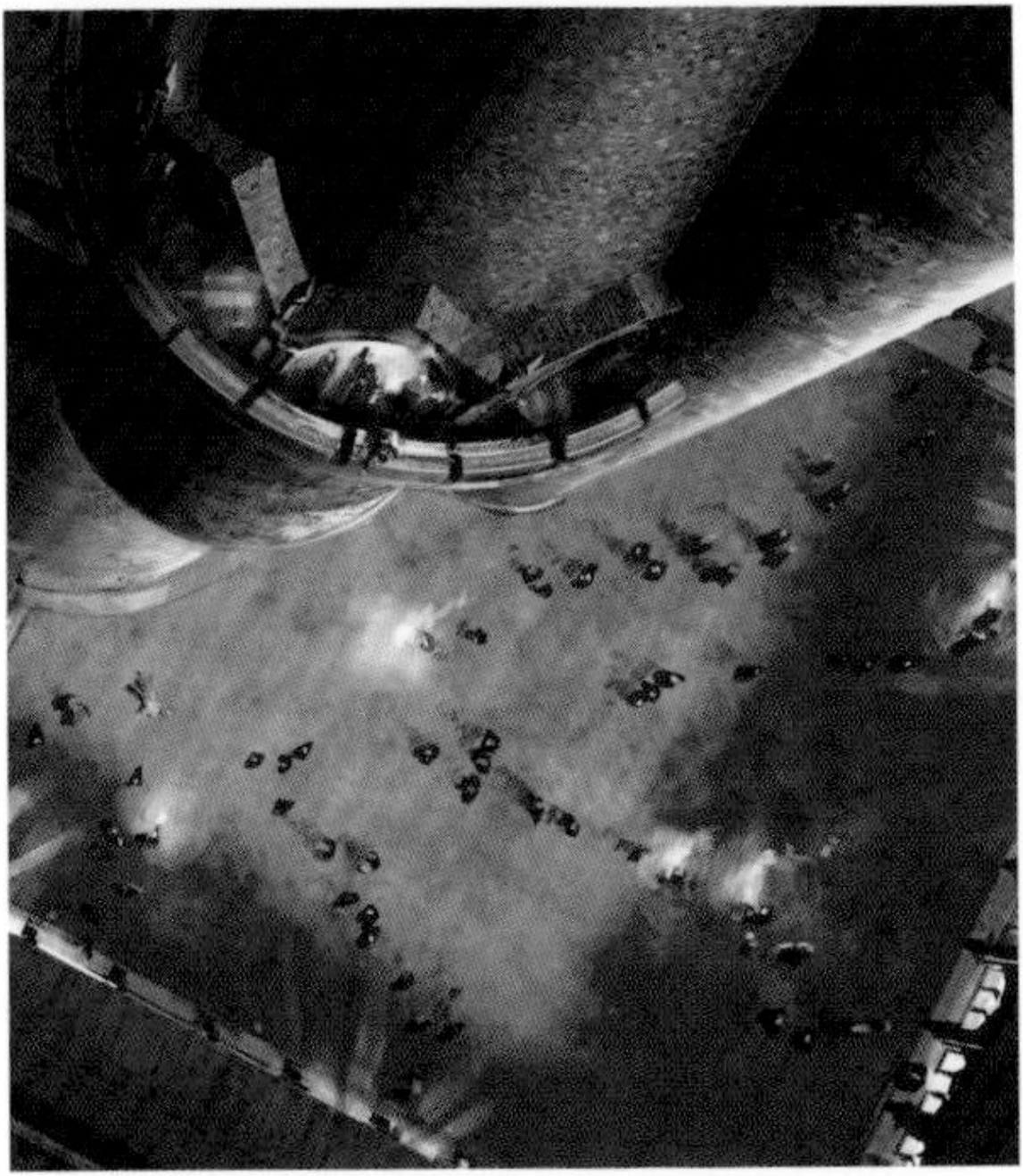

THESE PAGES: Andrew Williamson depicts Hogwarts in mourning for Professor Dumbledore in *Harry Potter and the Half-Blood Prince*.

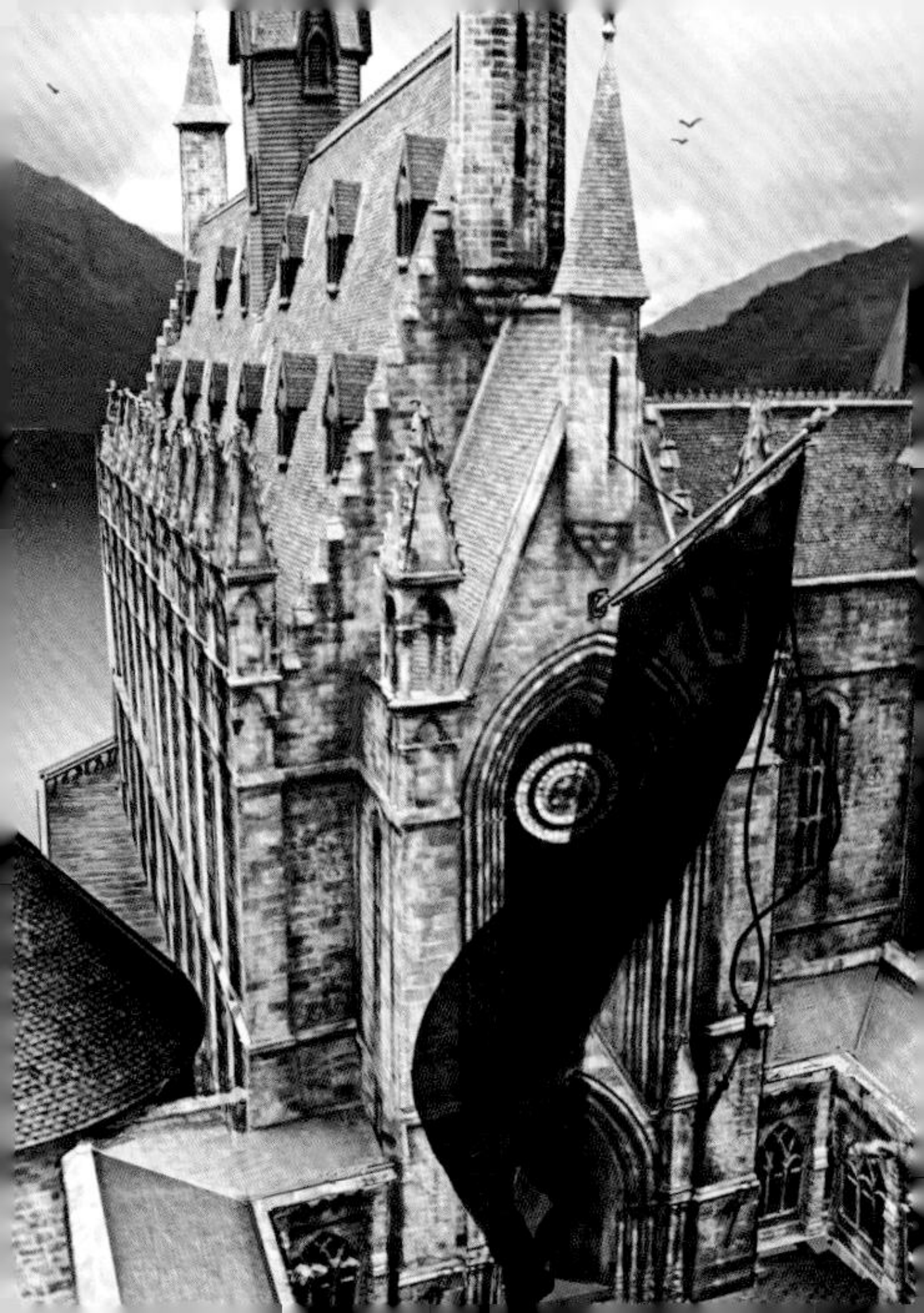

Tropicus Capricorni
Hydra

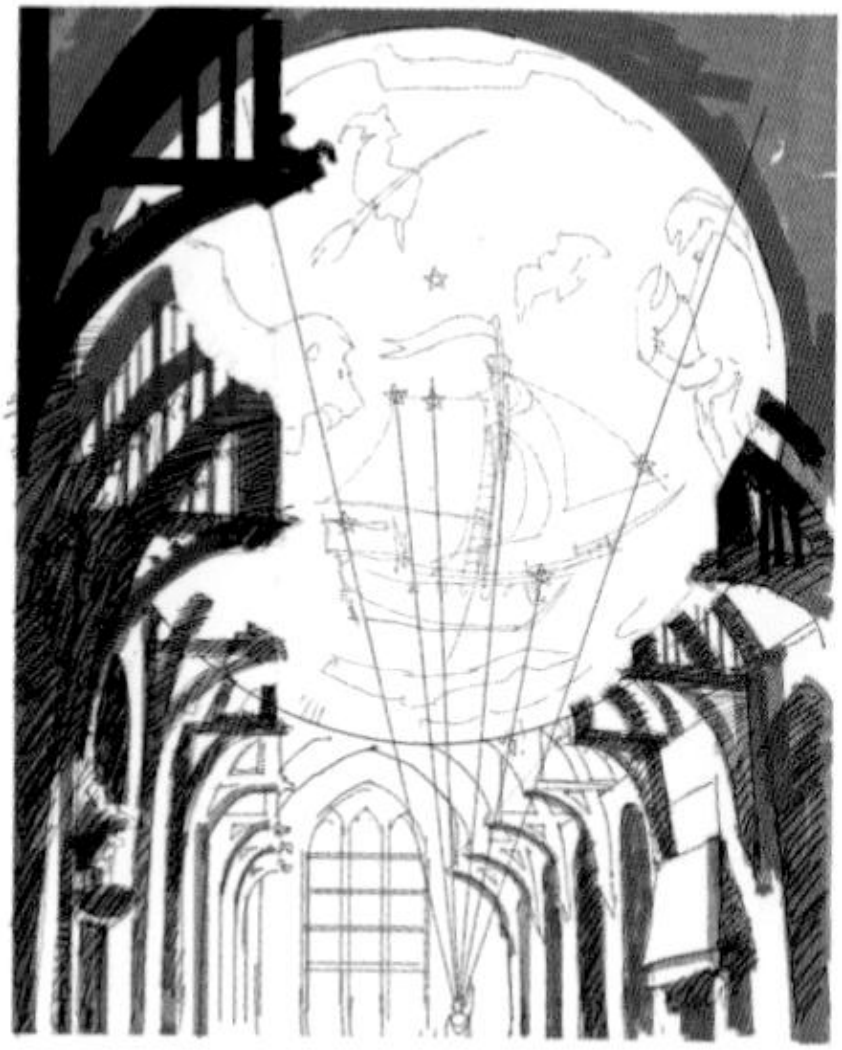

OPPOSITE: Composite of film stills and digital art of the Great Hall by Dermot Power.

ABOVE: Sketches by Dermot Power showing the position of the celestial globe in the bewitched ceiling of the Great Hall.

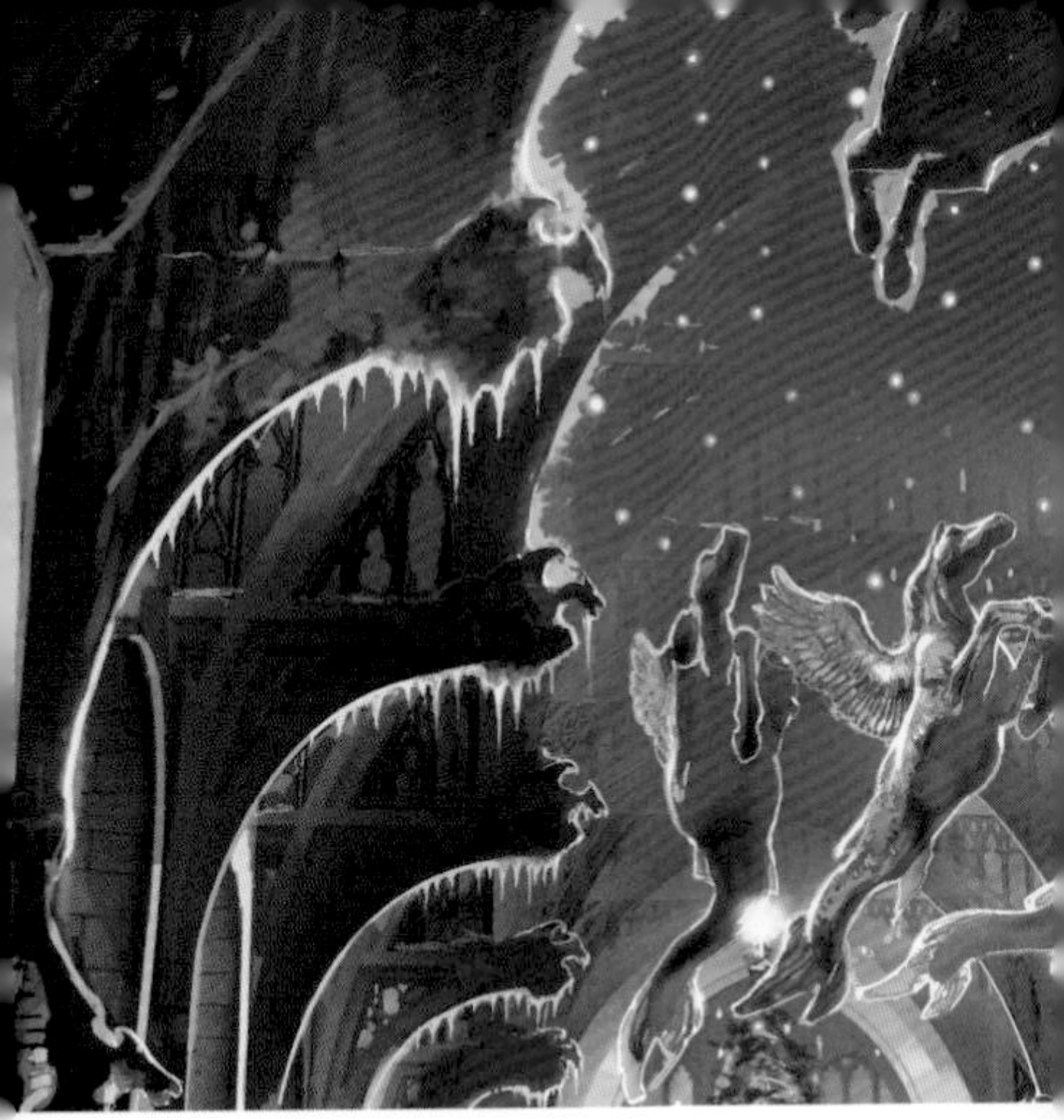

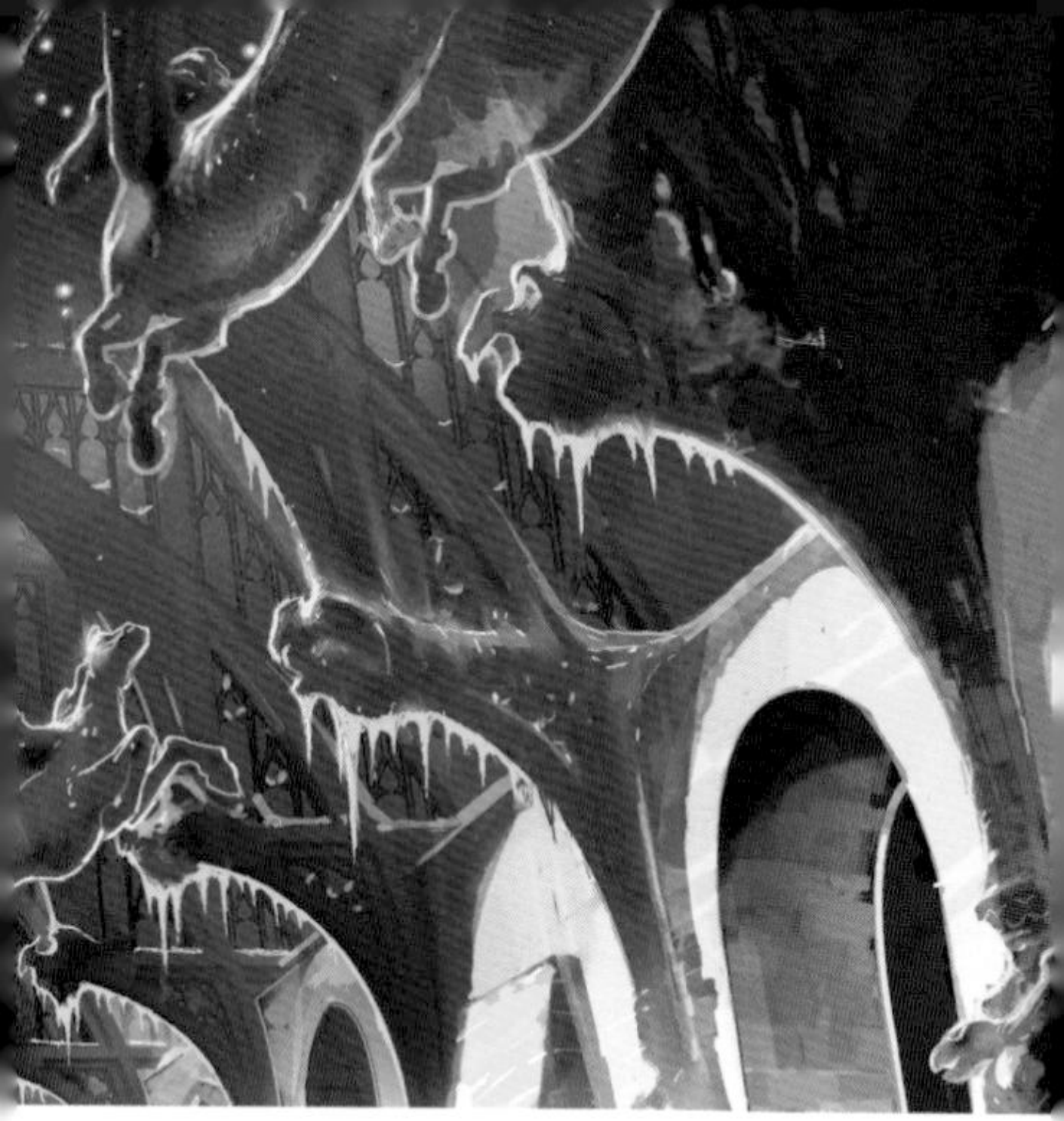

THESE PAGES: Artwork by Dermot Power for *Harry Potter and the Goblet of Fire*, showing the ceiling of the Great Hall in a shot that did not make it into the final film.

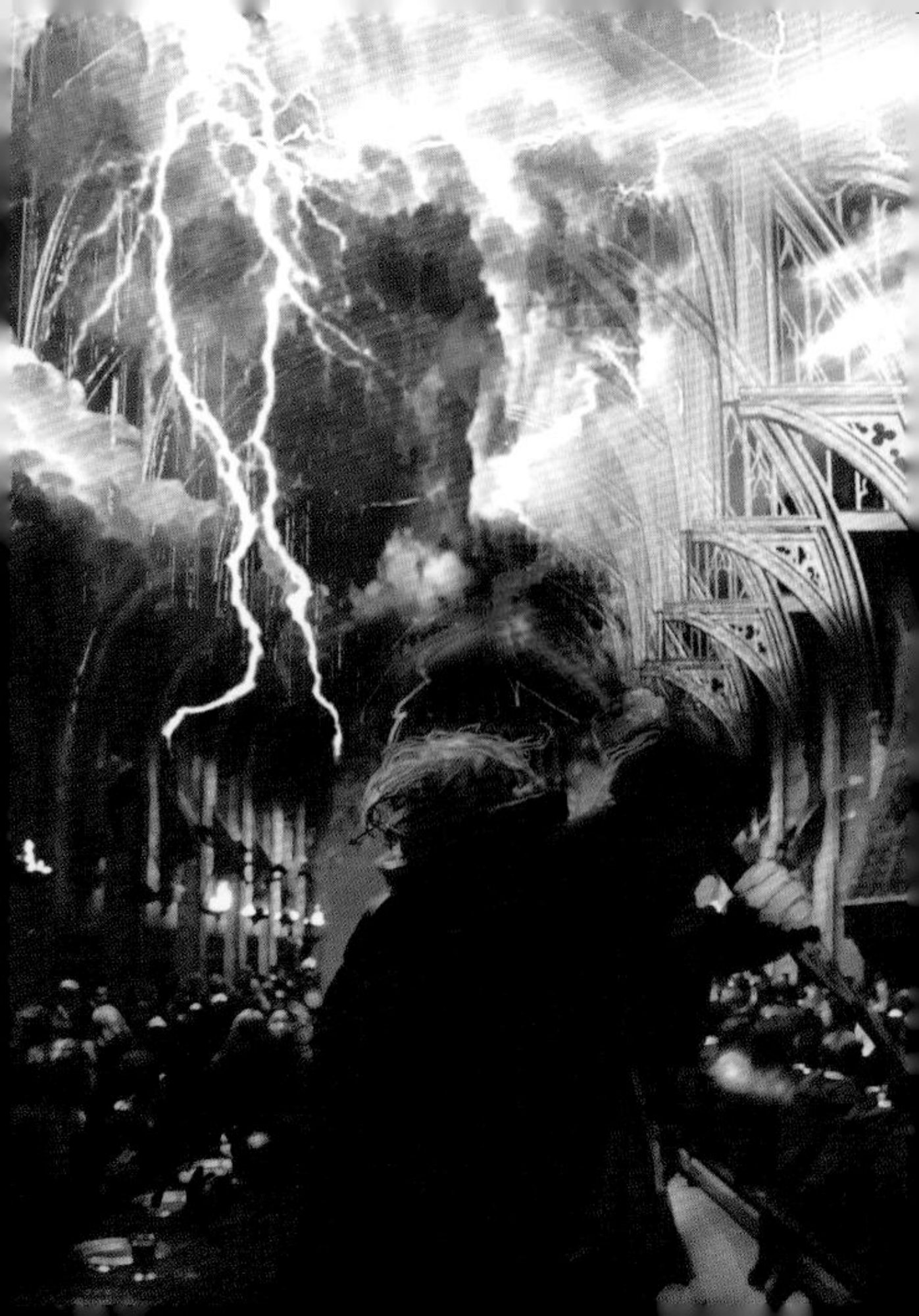

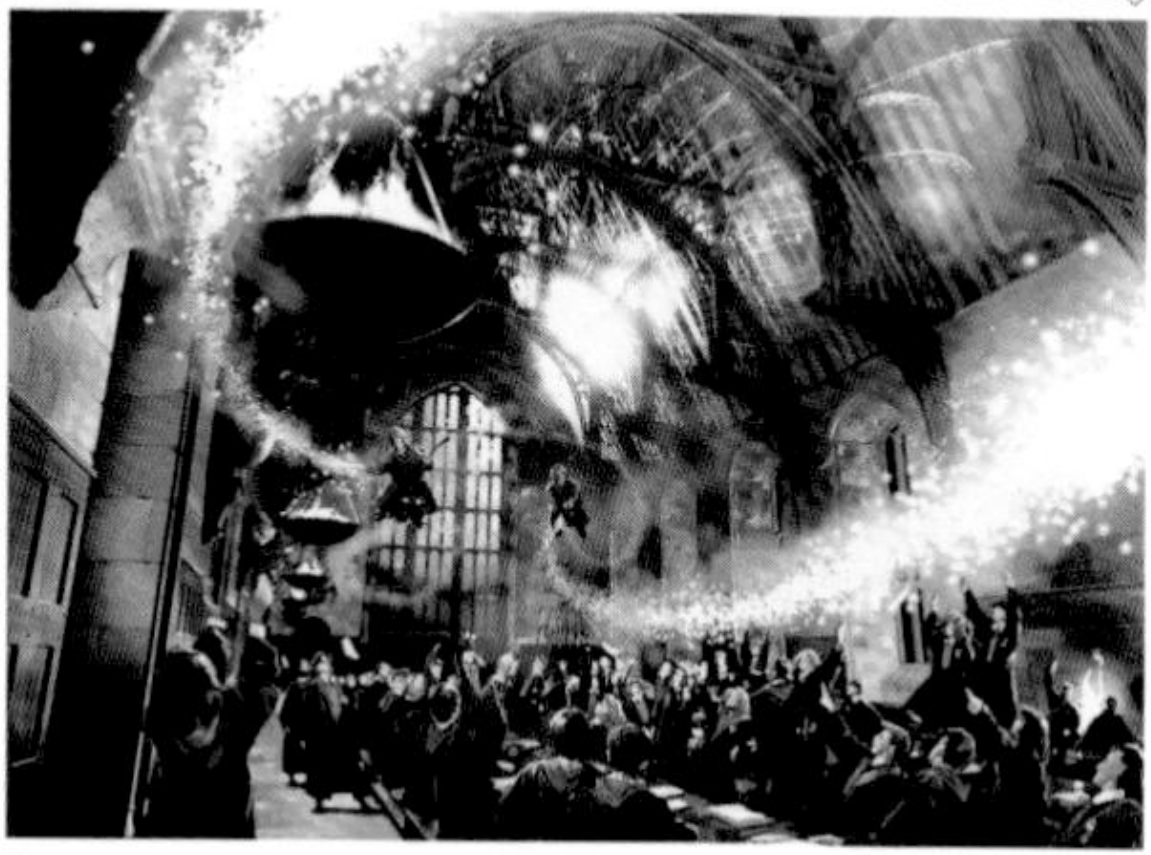

OPPOSITE: Professor Alastor Moody makes an electric entrance into the Great Hall in *Harry Potter and the Goblet of Fire* as depicted by Paul Catling.

PAGES 93–95: Fred and George Weasley interrupt Harry's O.W.L. exams with a display of fireworks. Art by Andrew Williamson for *Harry Potter and the Order of the Phoenix*.

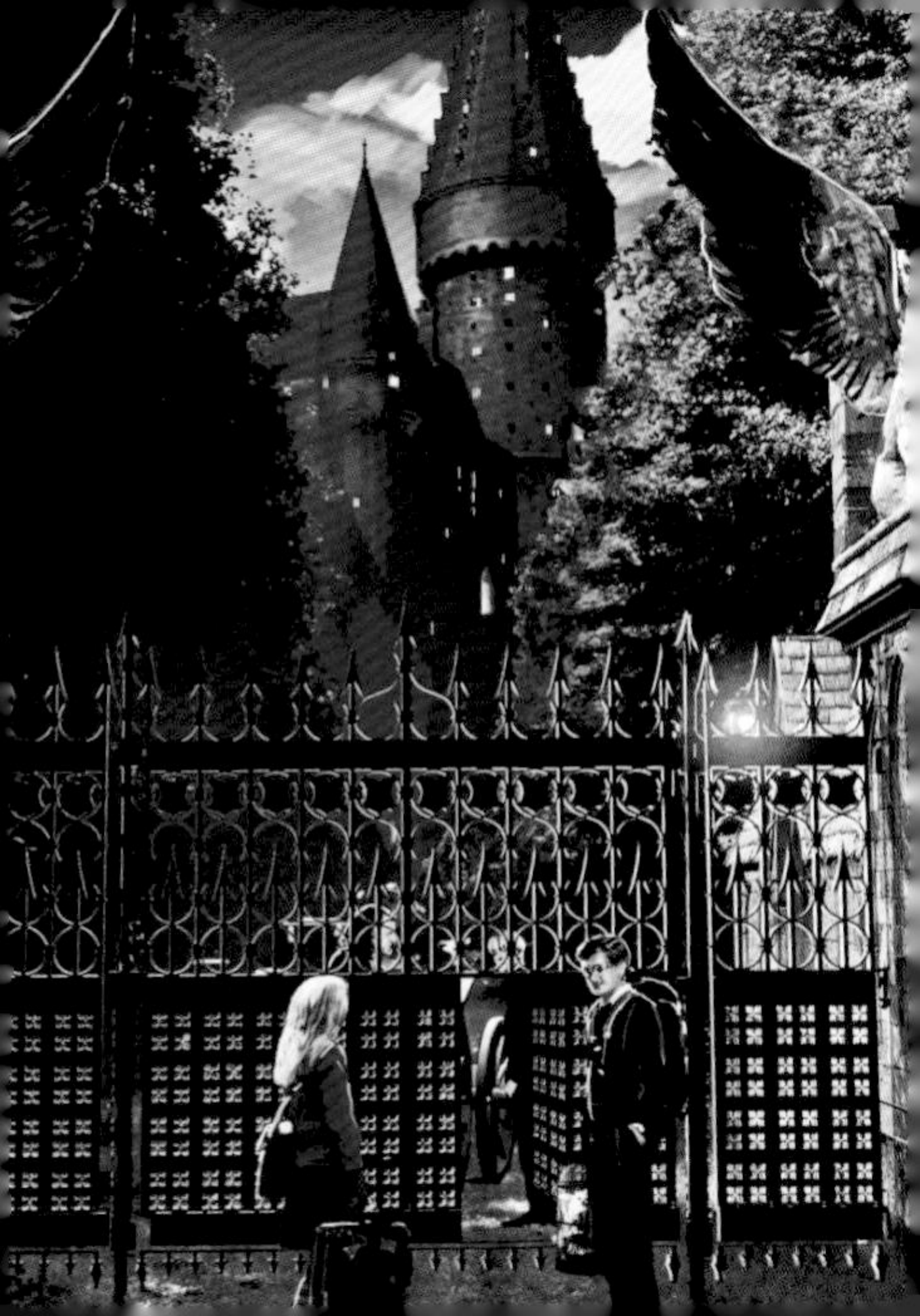

THE FRONT GATES

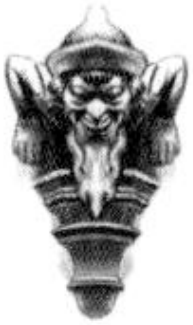

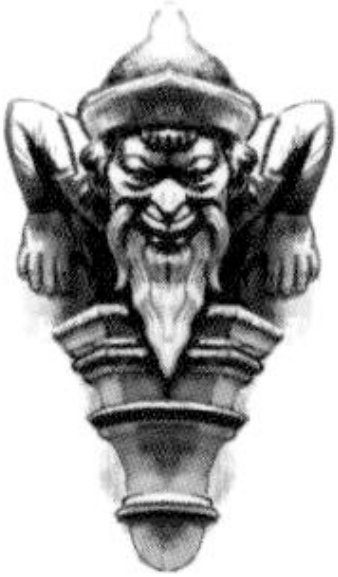

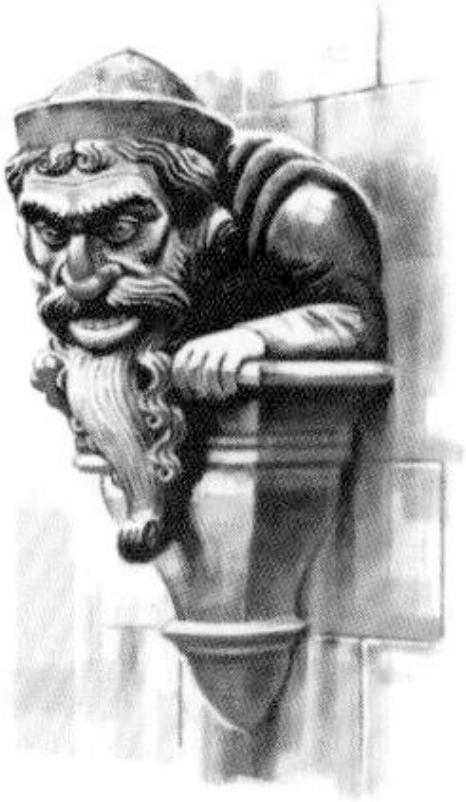

OPPOSITE: Hogwarts students are stopped at the gates of Hogwarts to be scanned for Dark items in concept art by Andrew Williamson for *Harry Potter and the Half-Blood Prince*.

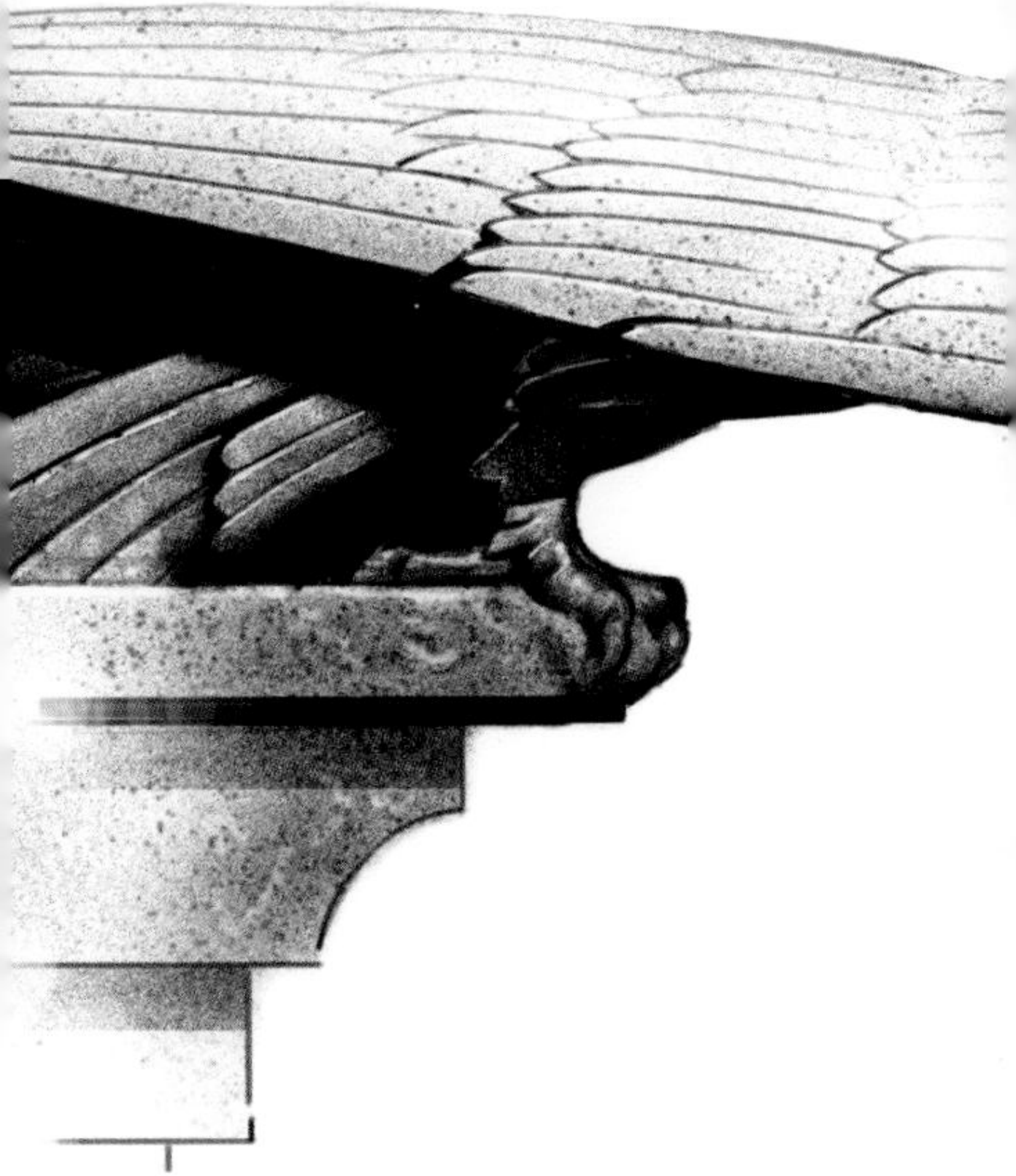

PAGES 97–99: Gargoyle studies by Adam Brockbank.

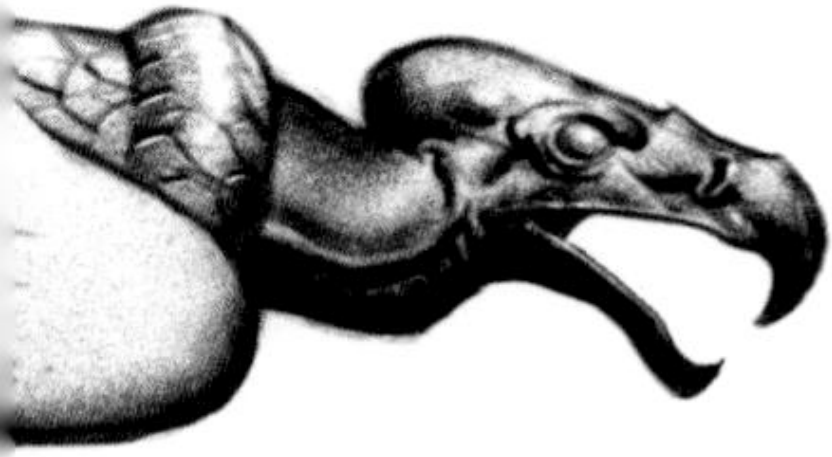

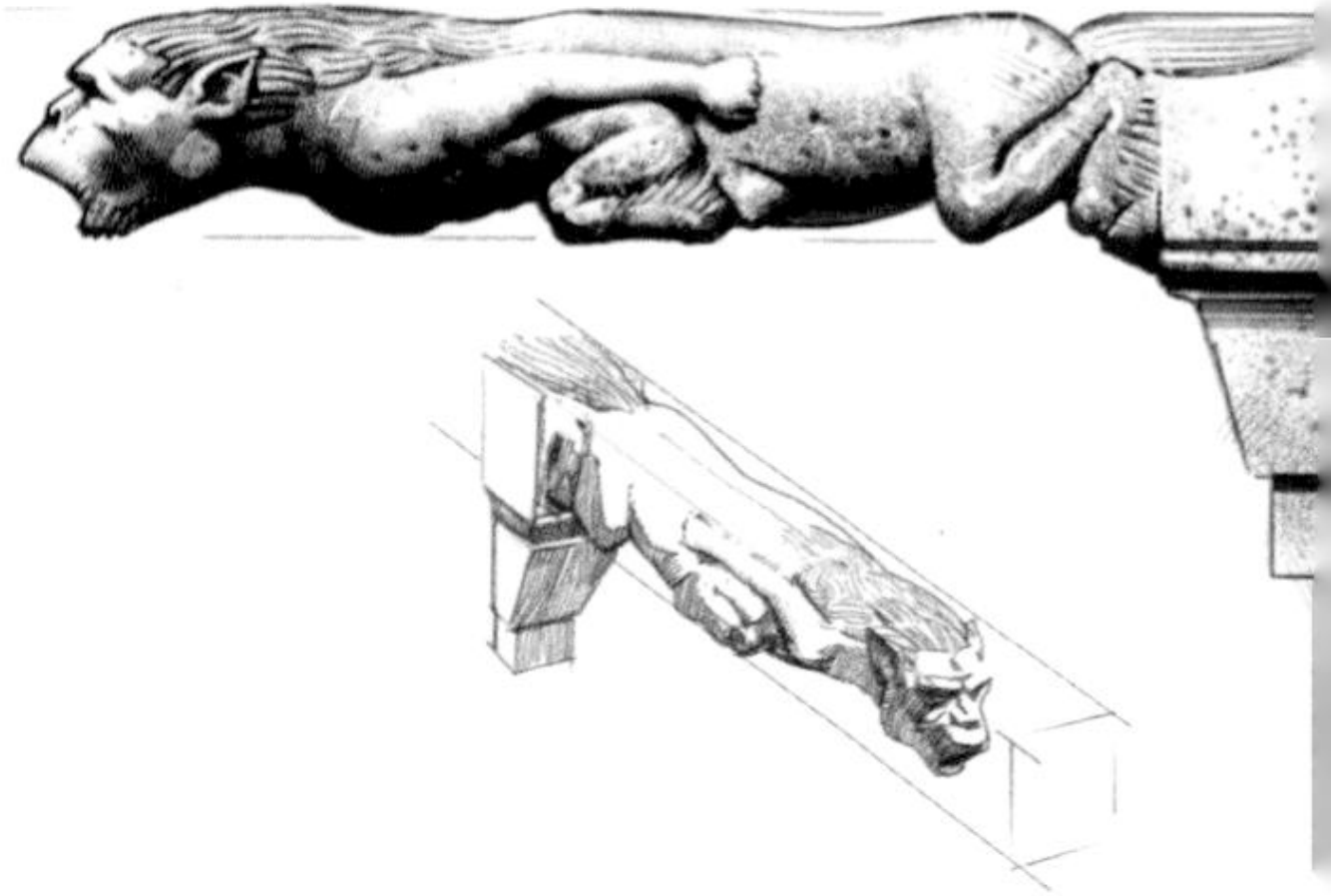

ENTRANCE HALL

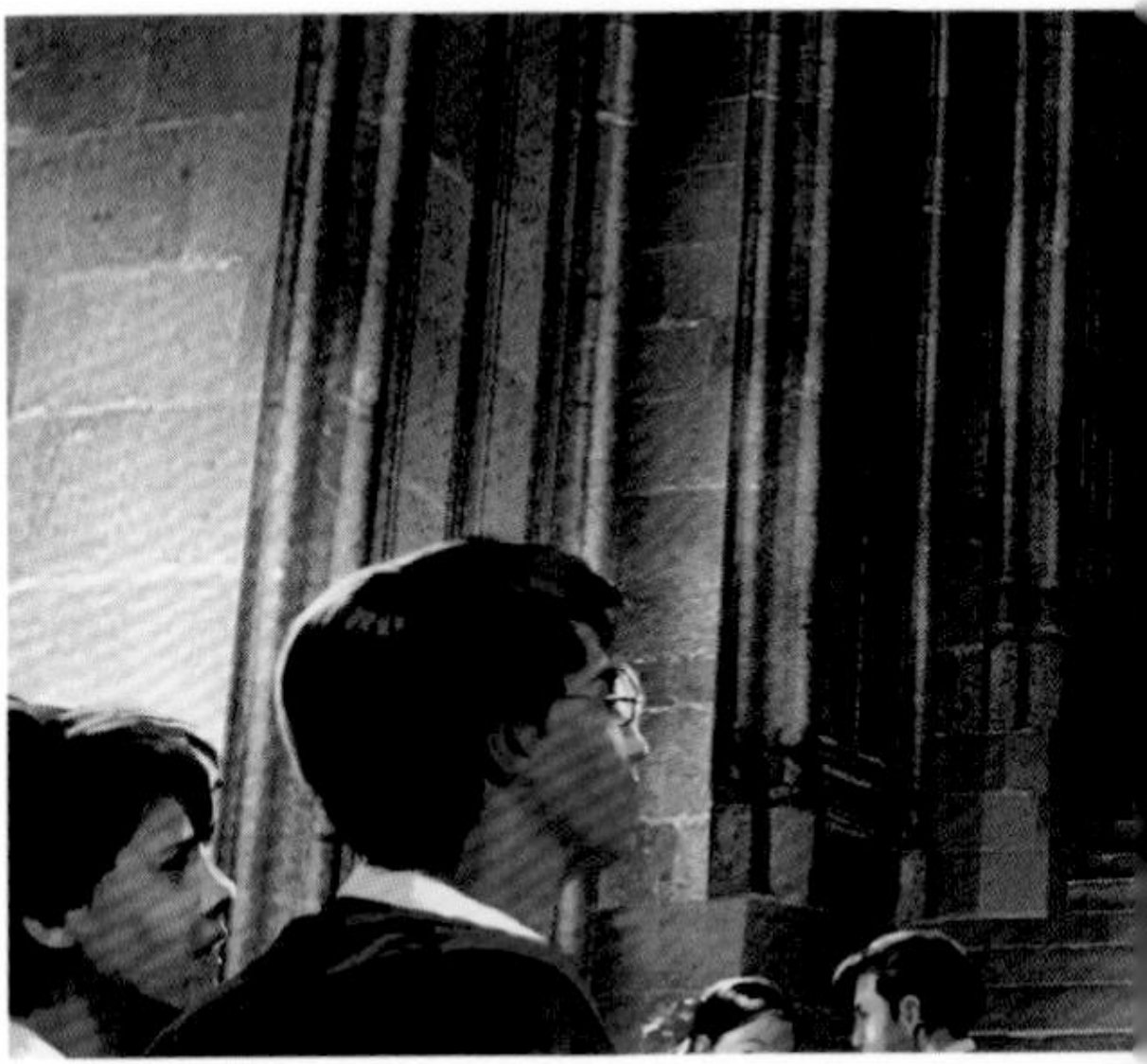

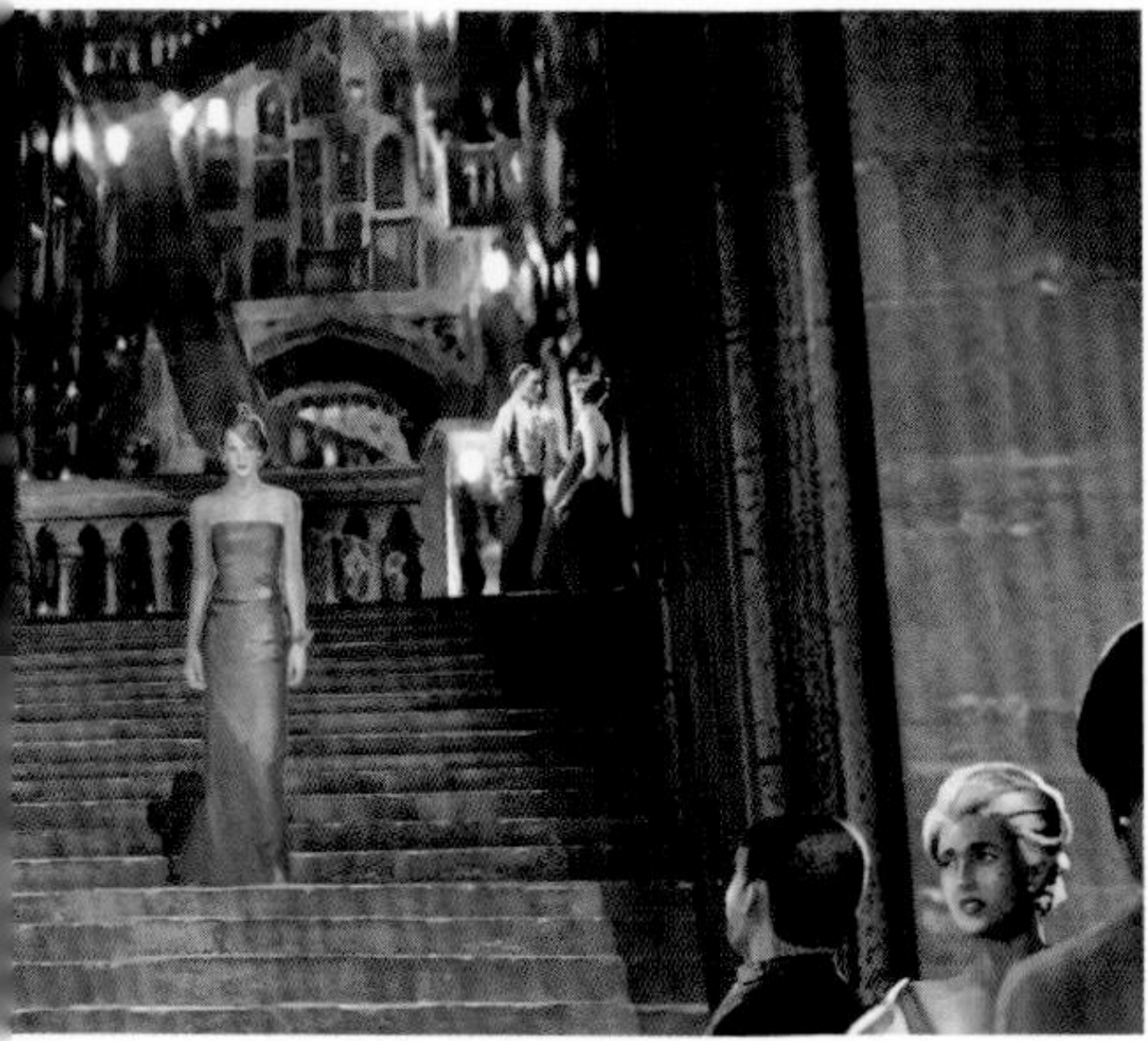

THESE PAGES: Hermione arrives at the Yule Ball in *Harry Potter and the Goblet of Fire*. Andrew Williamson painted her dress periwinkle blue, as it was described in the novel.

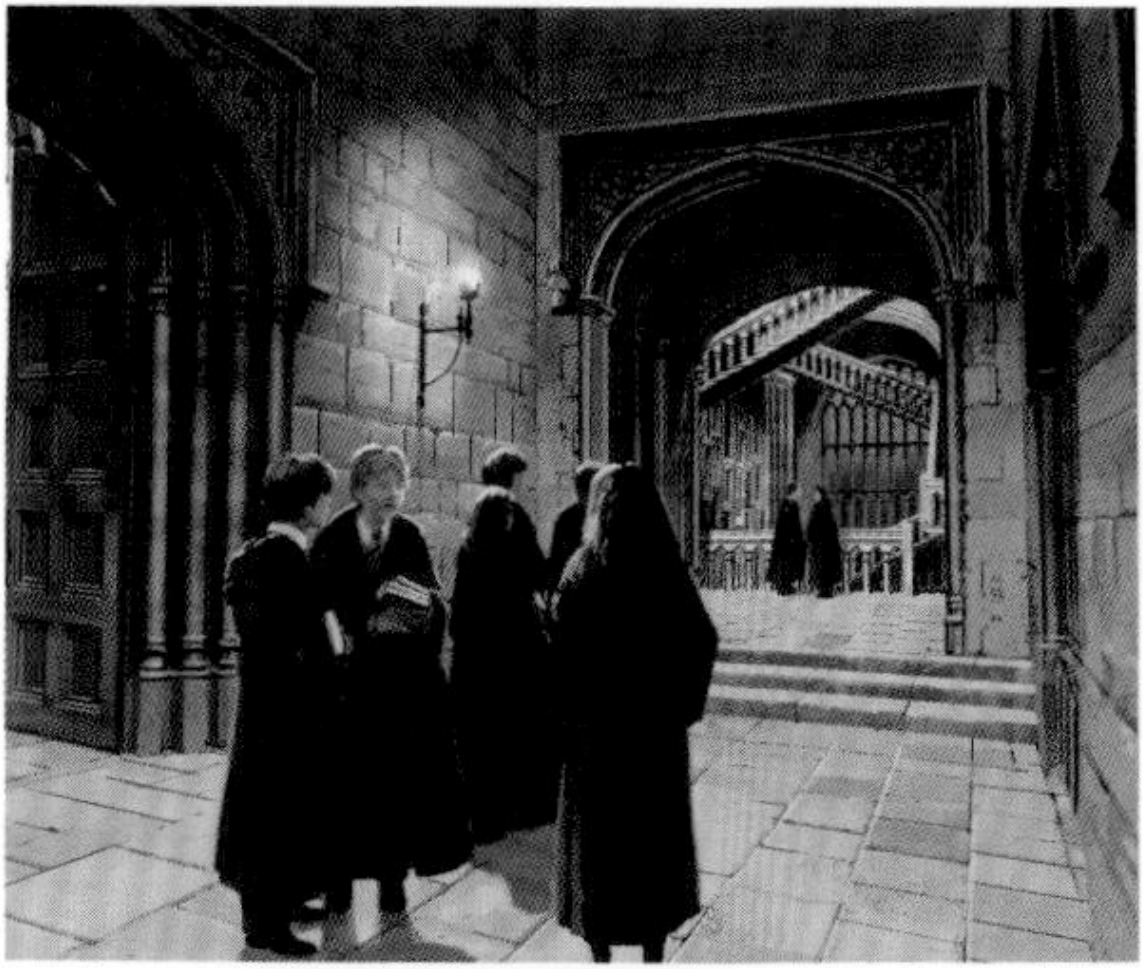

ABOVE: Study by Andrew Williamson of the Entrance Hall with marble staircases visible in the background.

OPPOSITE: Adam Brockbank illustrates Hagrid and other staff members shutting up the entrance to the Clock Tower.

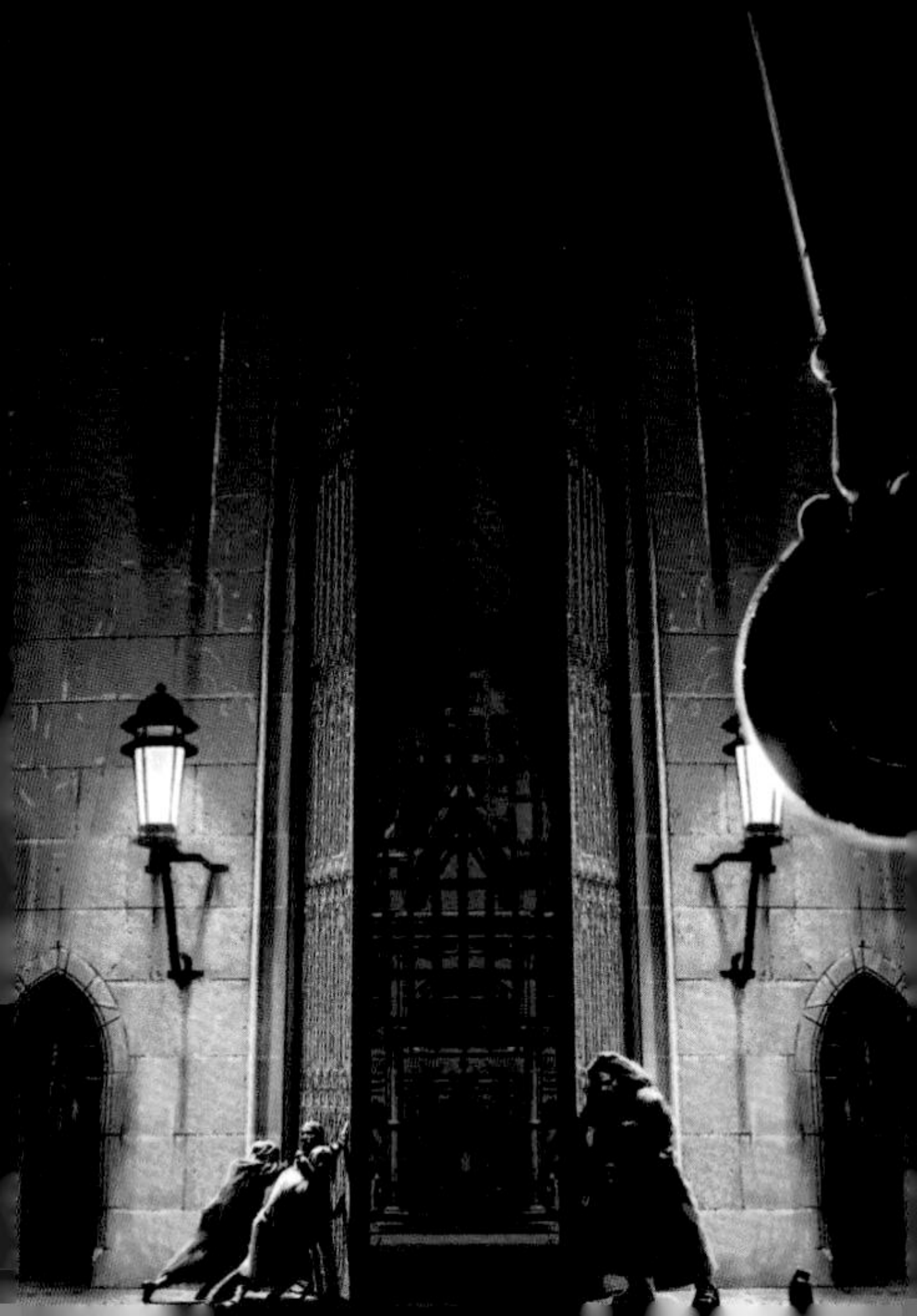

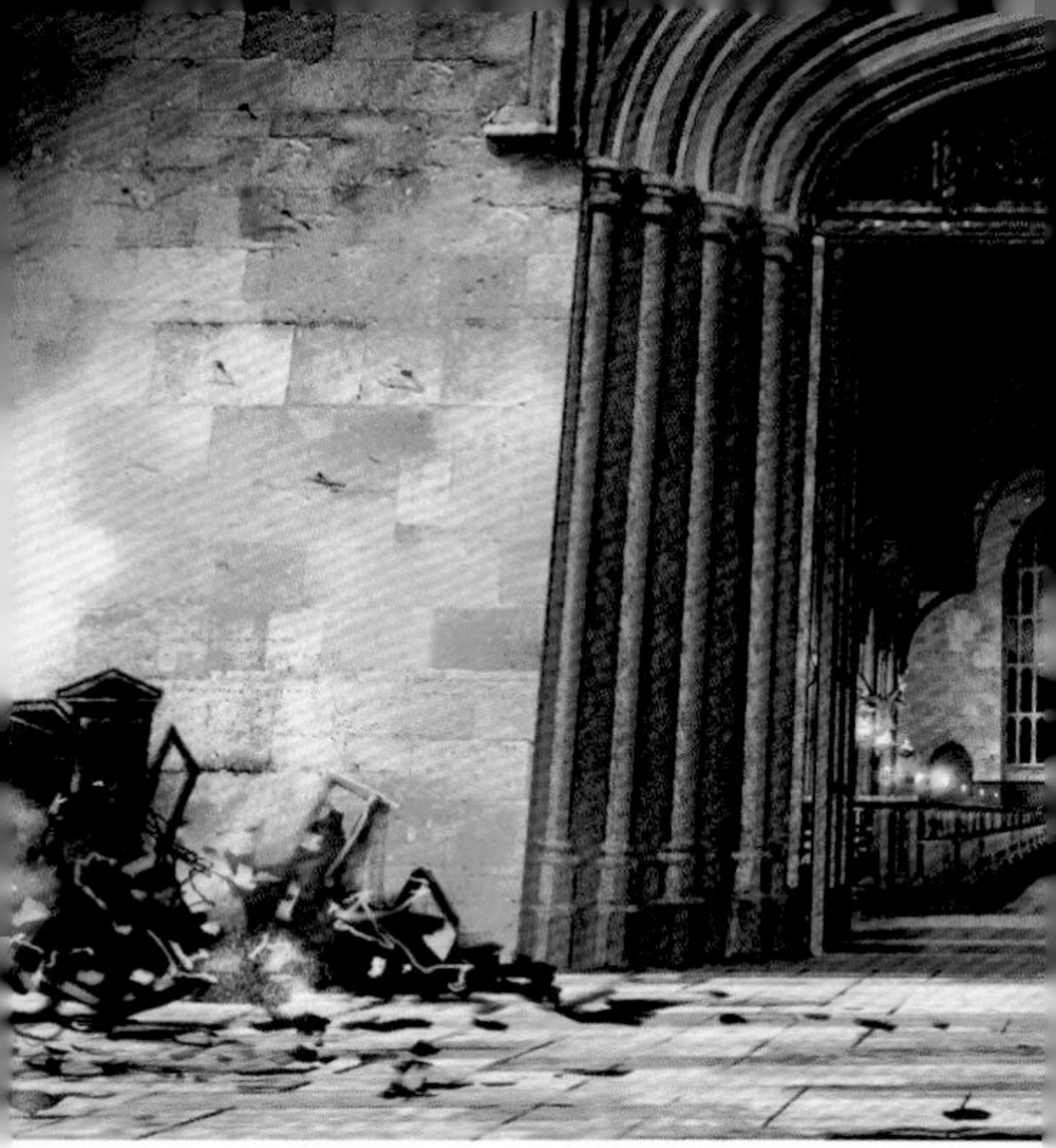

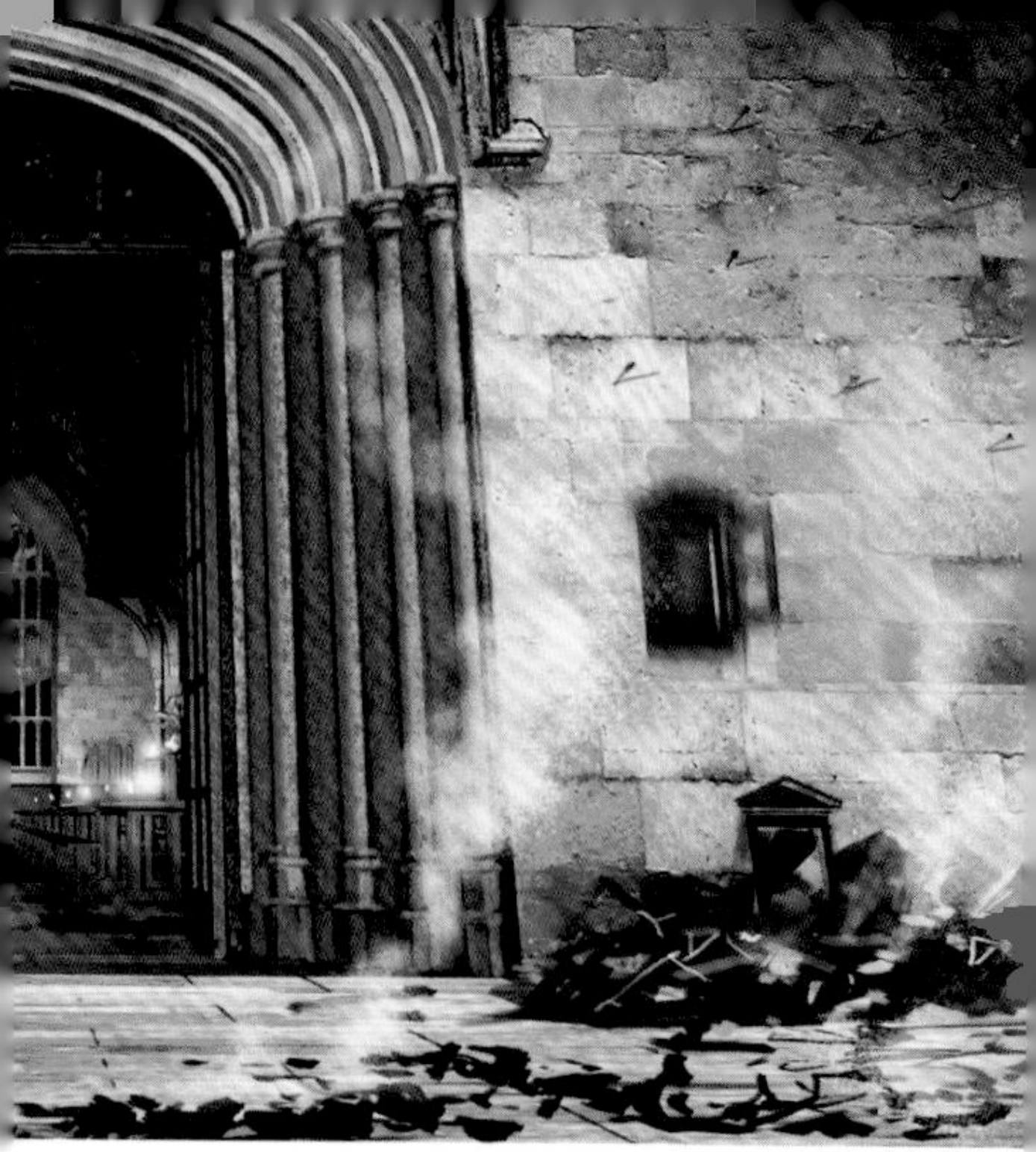

THESE PAGES: A shot of the Entrance Hall after Fred and George Weasley make their famous escape in *Harry Potter and the Order of the Phoenix*. Art by Andrew Williamson.

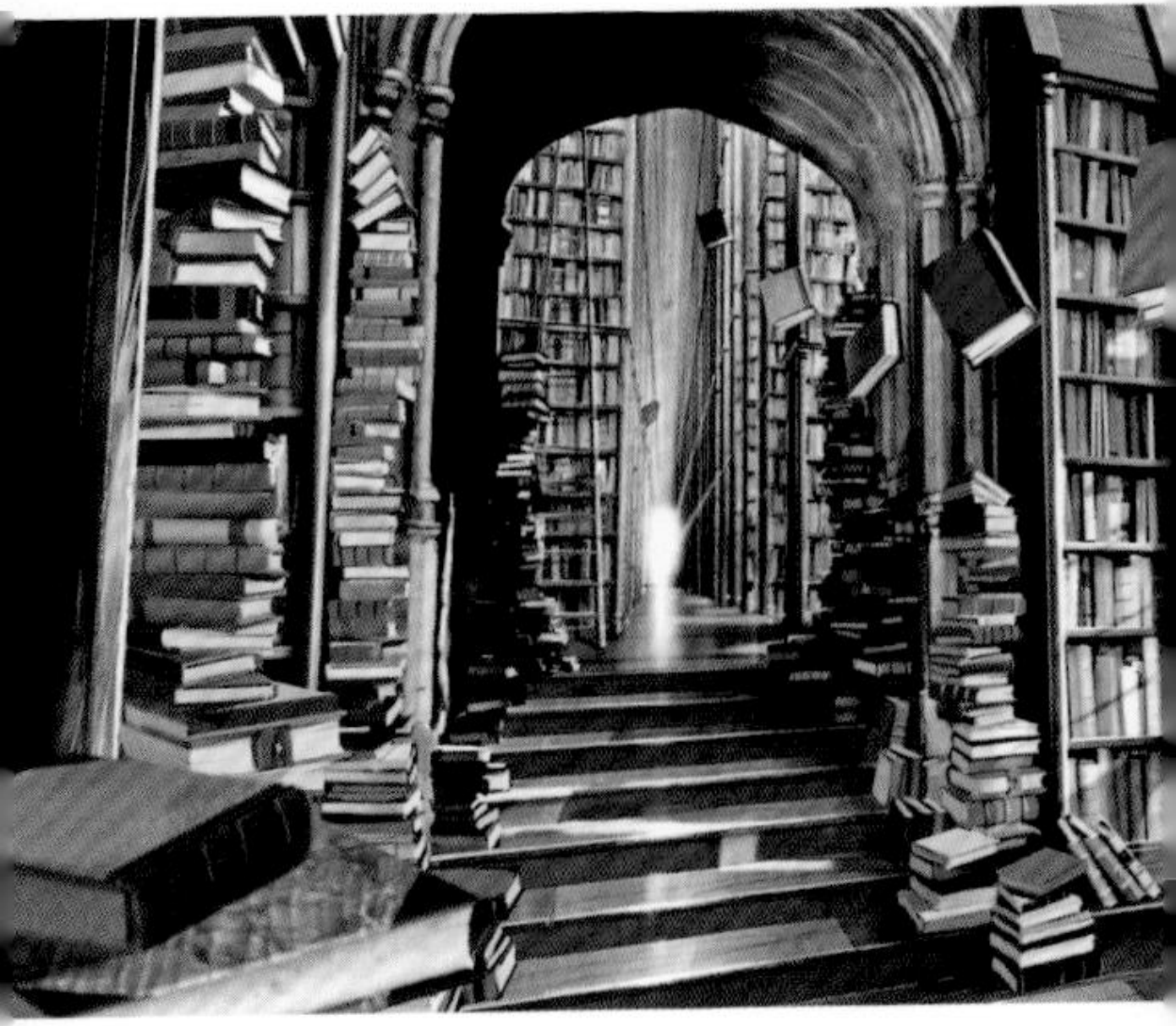

THE LIBRARY

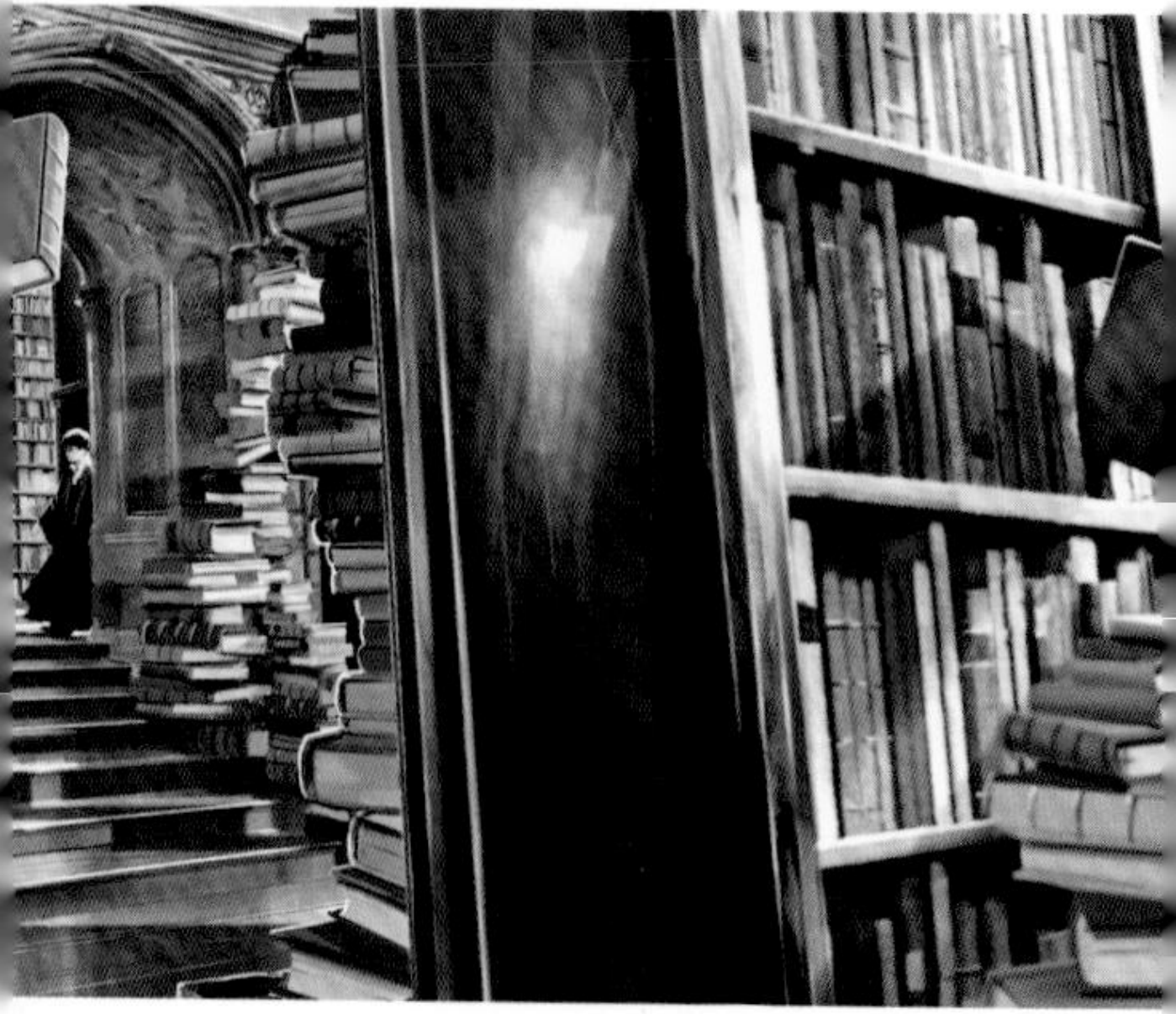

THESE PAGES: Harry and Hermione in the Hogwarts Library, complete with floating books. Artwork by Adam Brockbank for *Harry Potter and the Half-Blood Prince*.

PREFECTS' BATHROOM

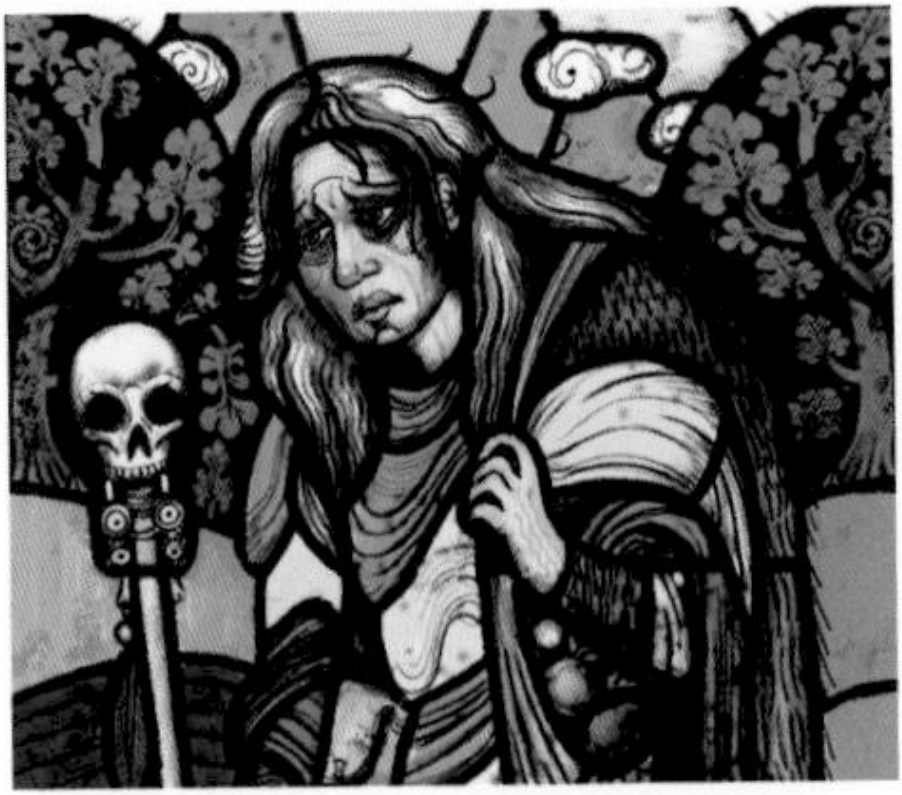

OPPOSITE: Stained glass windows by Adam Brockbank for *Harry Potter and the Goblet of Fire*. The mermaid resides in the Prefects' bathroom, where Harry deciphers the clue for the second task. Neville Longbottom stops near the window on the right after a difficult Defense Against the Dark Arts class.

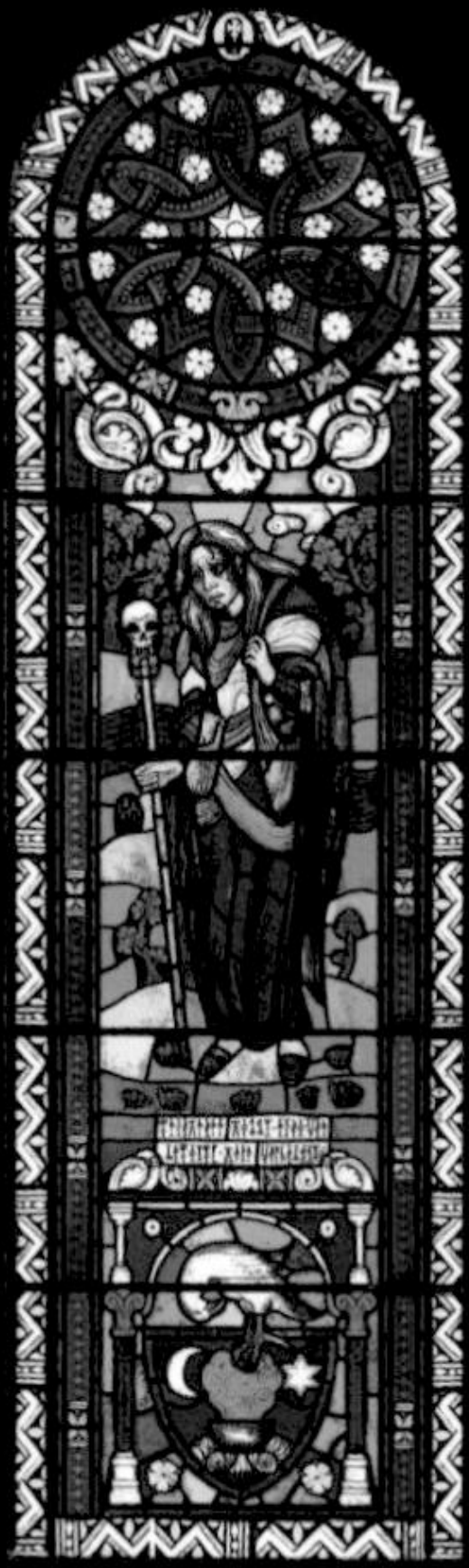

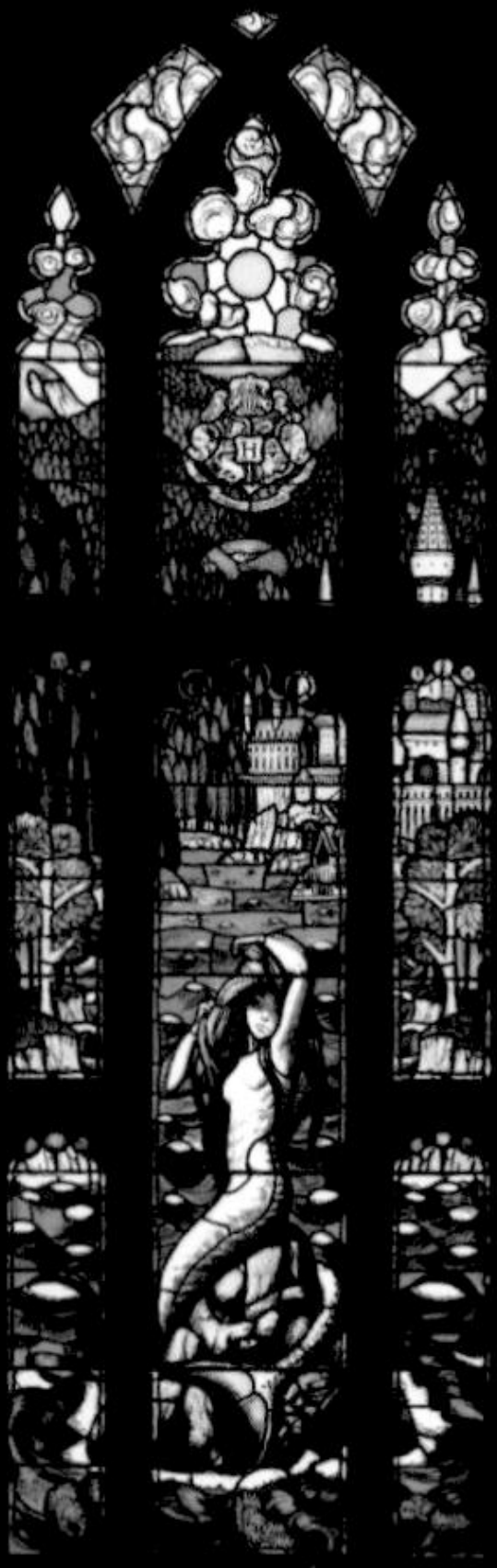

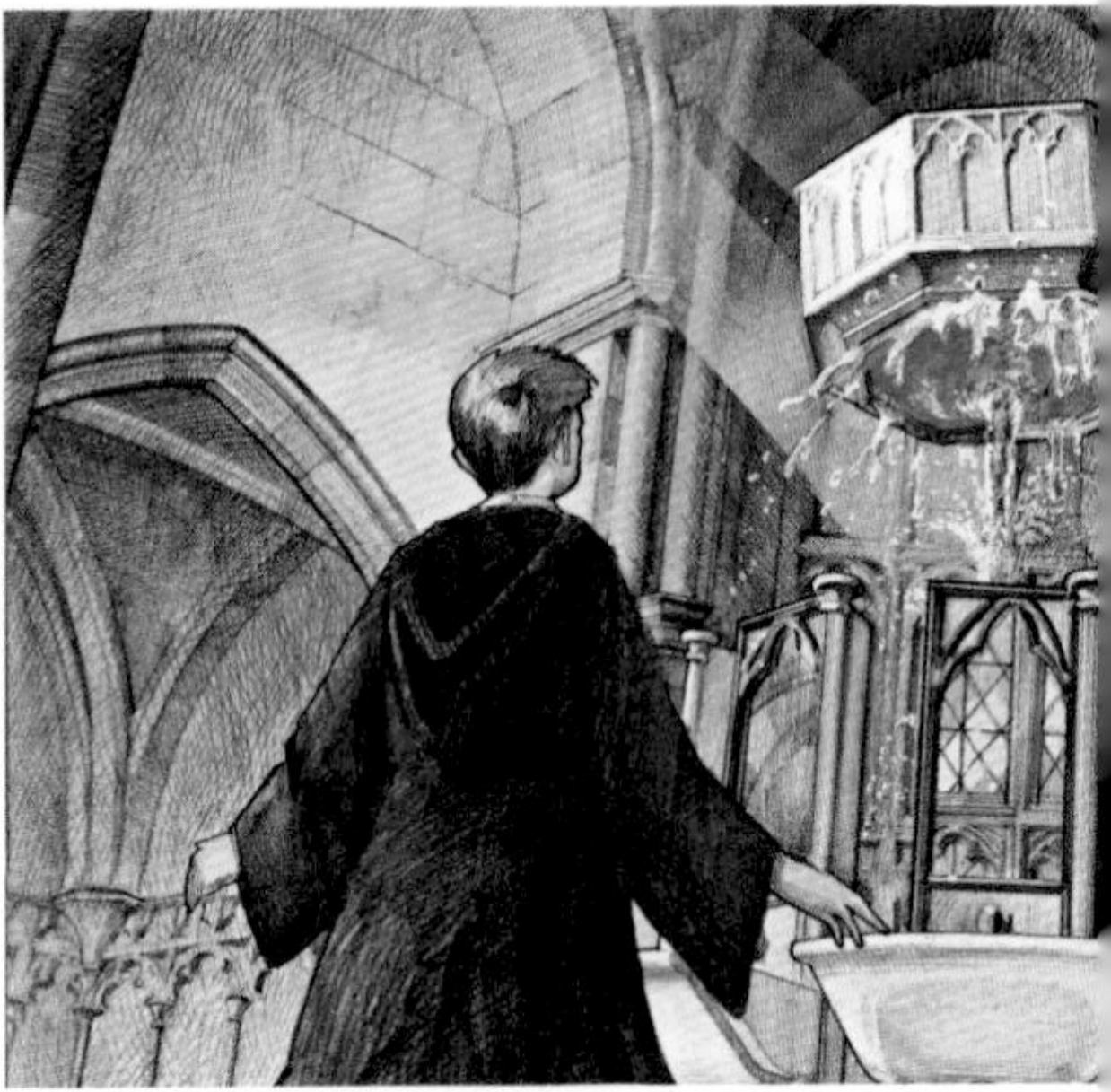

THESE PAGES: Harry and Ron unlock the entrance to the Chamber of Secrets as Professor Lockhart looks on in *Harry Potter and the*

MOANING MYRTLE'S BATHROOM

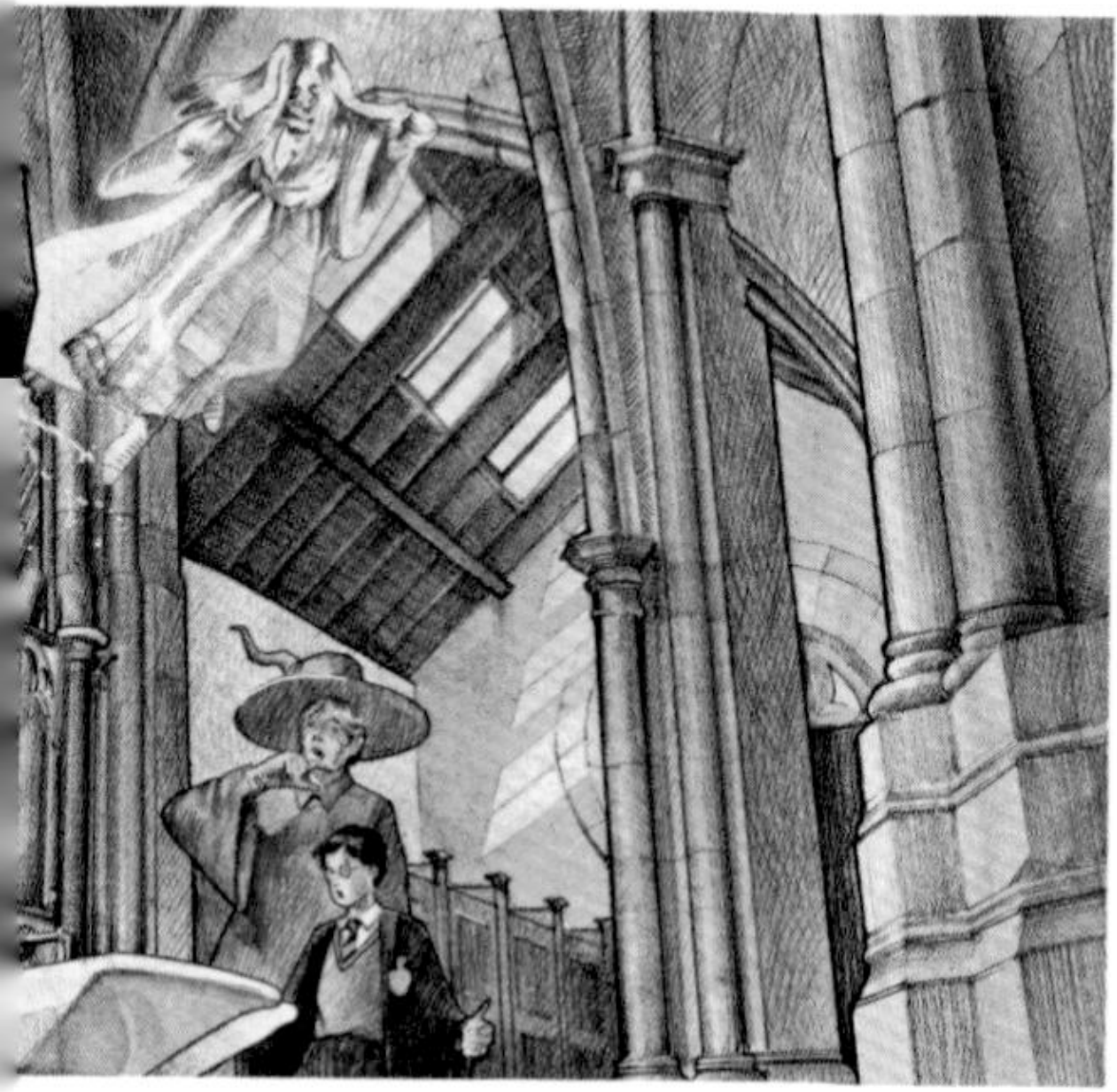

Chamber of Secrets. Andrew Williamson floated Moaning Myrtle above the sinks, though she was not in the scene in the movie.

THE CHAMBER OF SECRETS

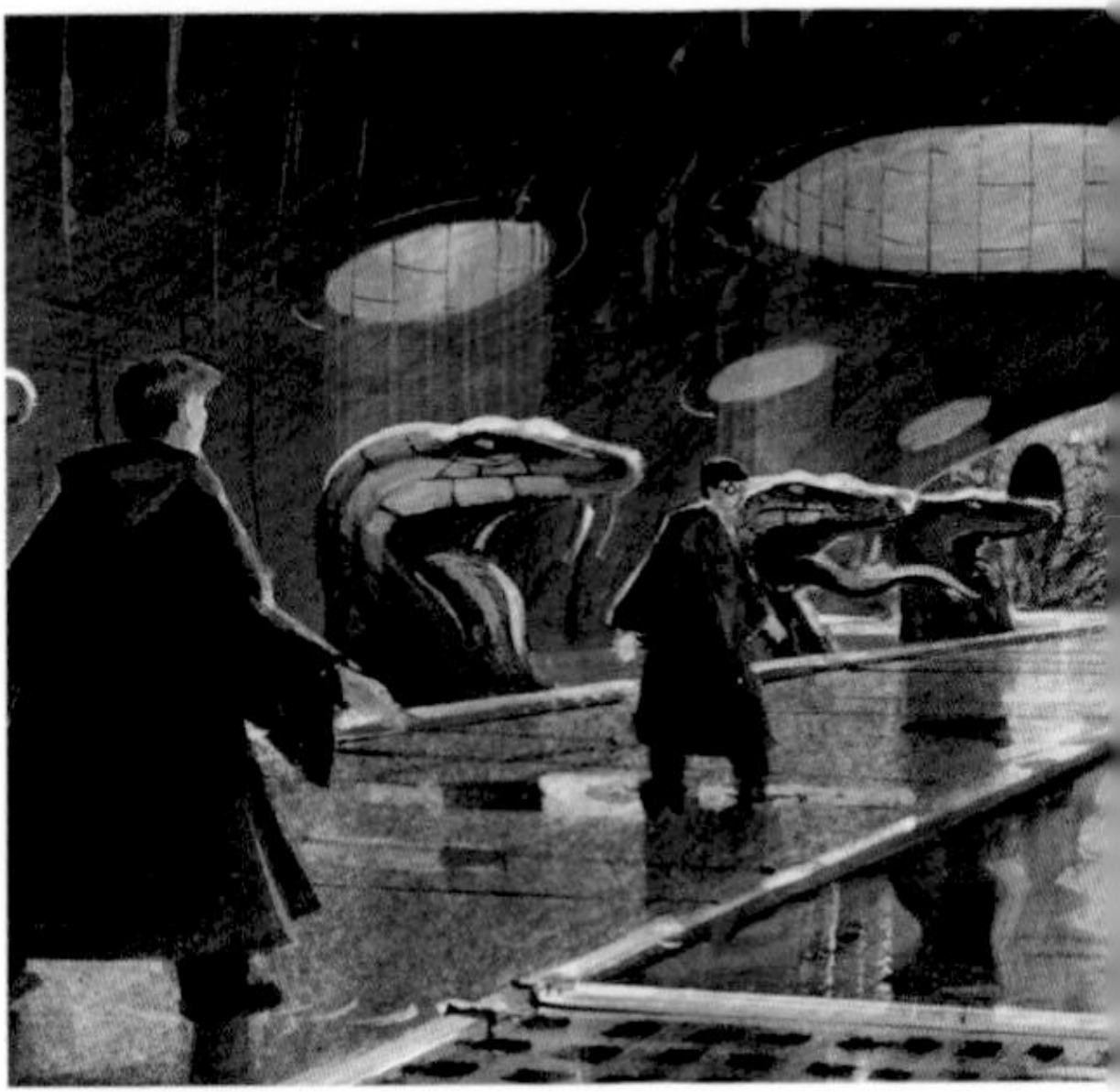

THESE PAGES: Andrew Williamson depicts the Chamber of Secrets in art for the film of the same name. This piece includes Ron Weasley, who

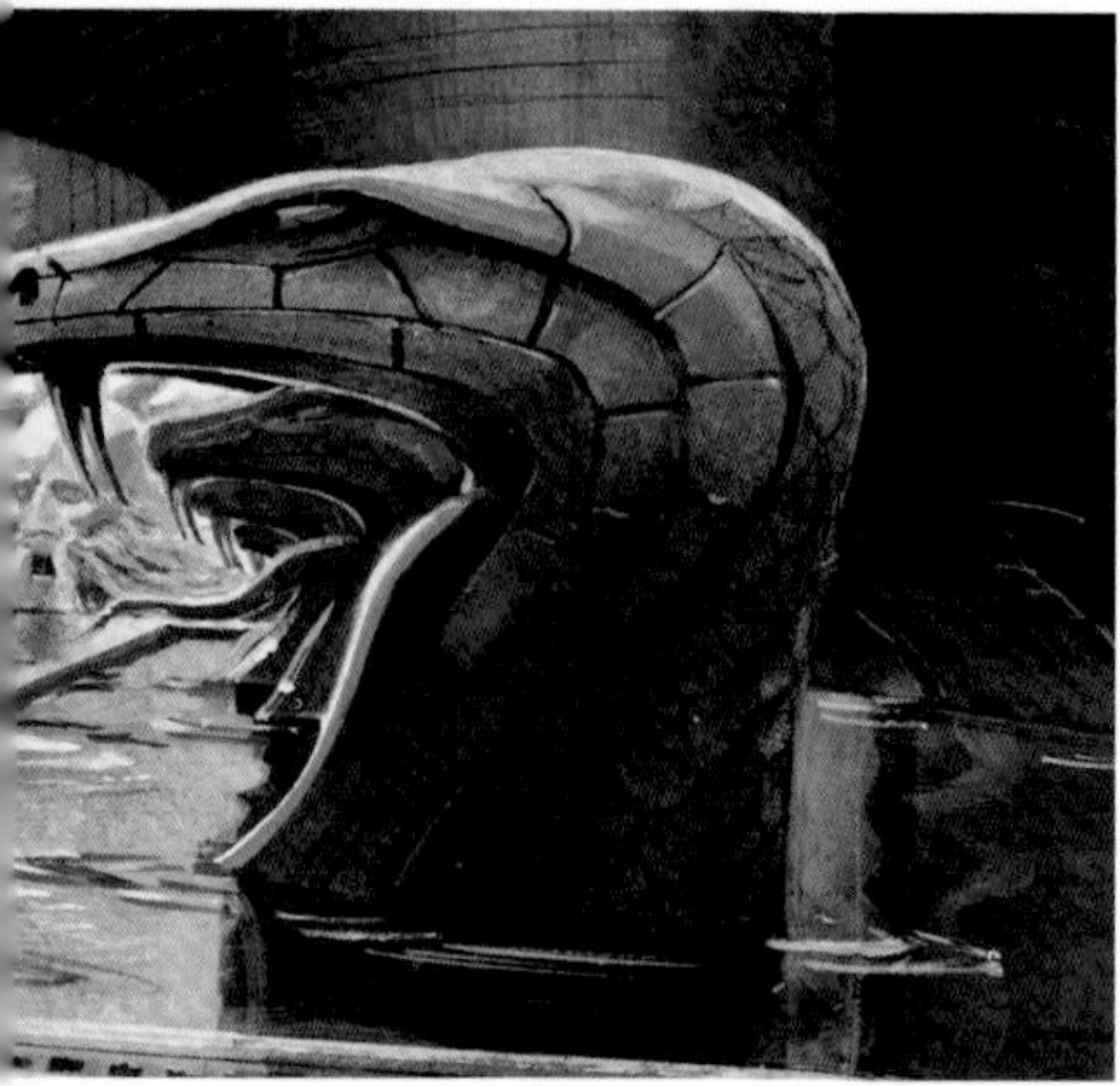

did not appear in the scene in the film. Ron was actually barricaded from entering by a rockslide that trapped him and Professor Lockhart.

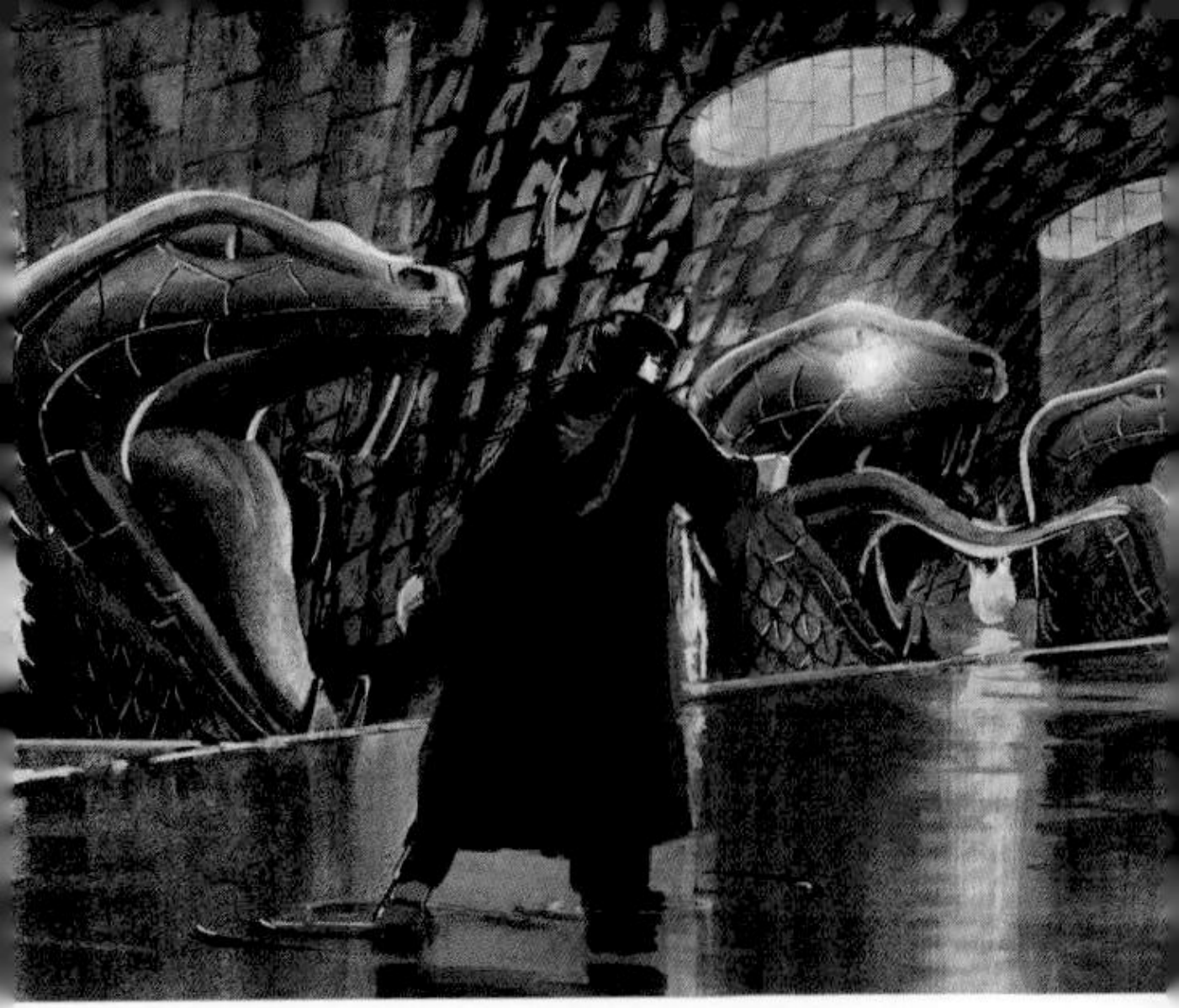

ABOVE: Another view of the Chamber by Andrew Williamson.

RIGHT: Concept art by Andrew Williamson of the Chamber's elaborate door.

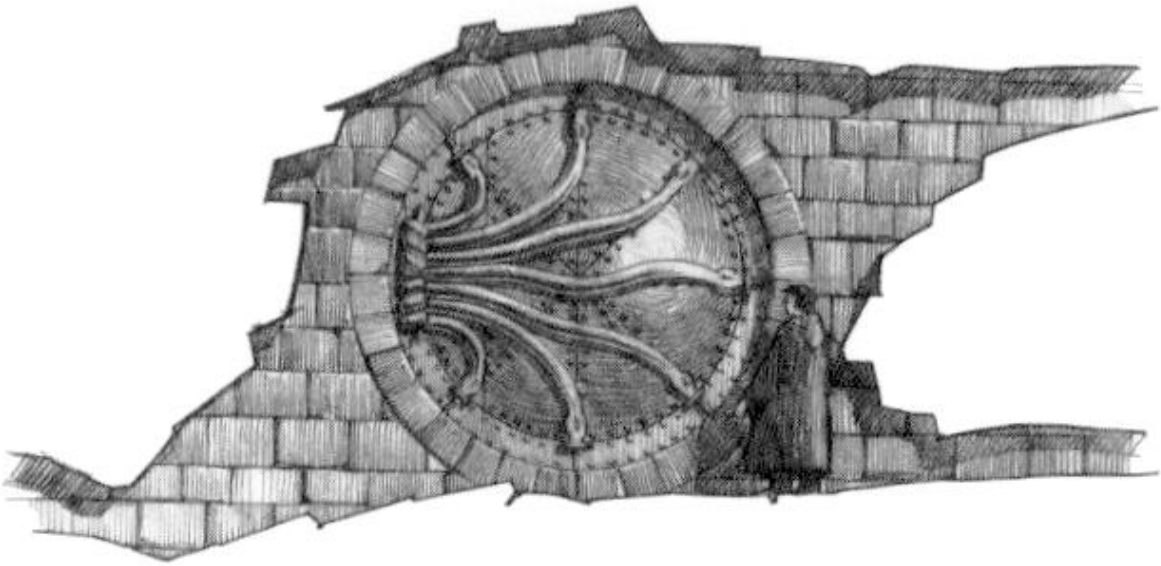

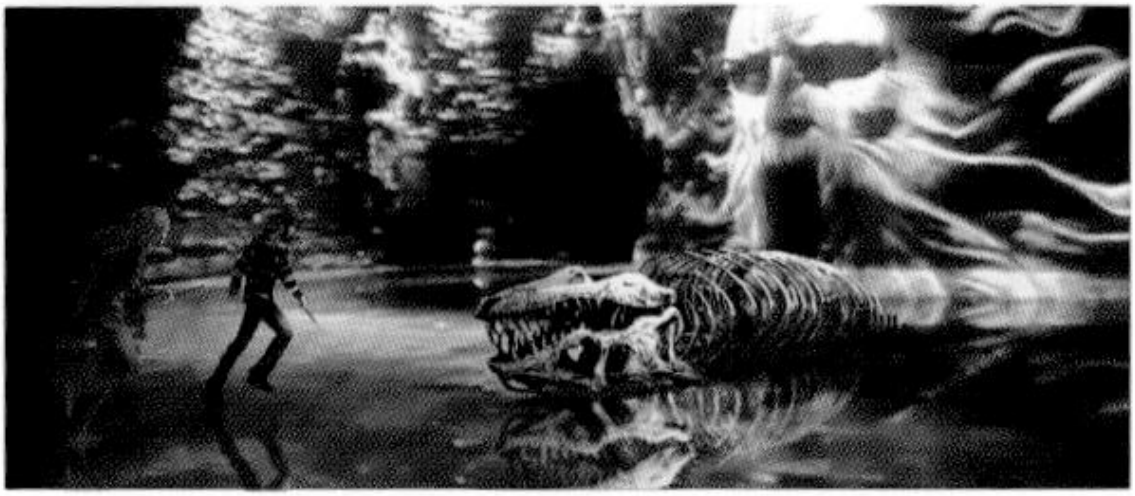

THESE PAGES: Adam Brockbank illustrates Ron and Hermione returning to the Chamber of Secrets in *Harry Potter and the Deathly Hallows* –

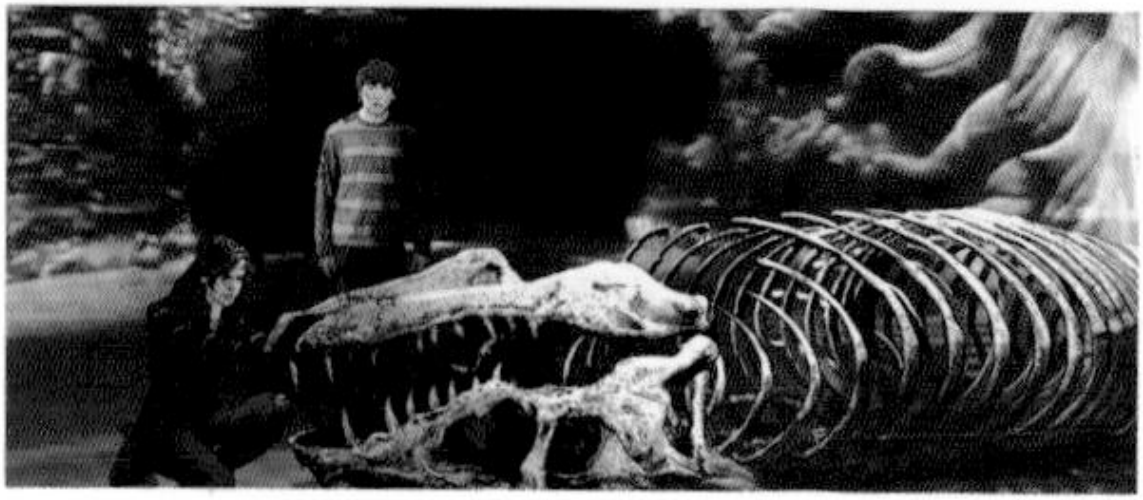

Part 2 to retrieve a Basilisk fang to destroy a Horcrux. The Chamber was re-created digitally for this scene.

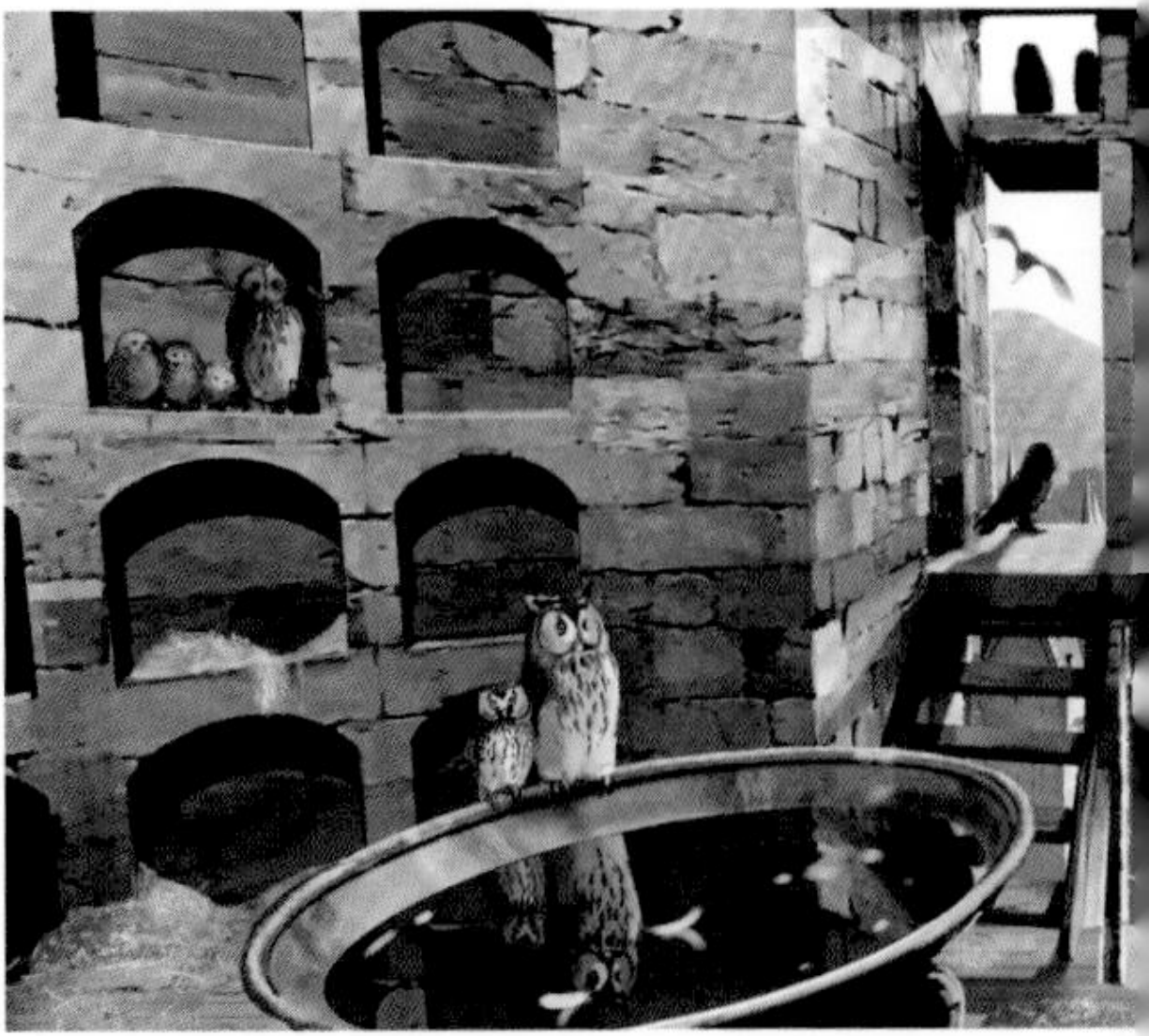

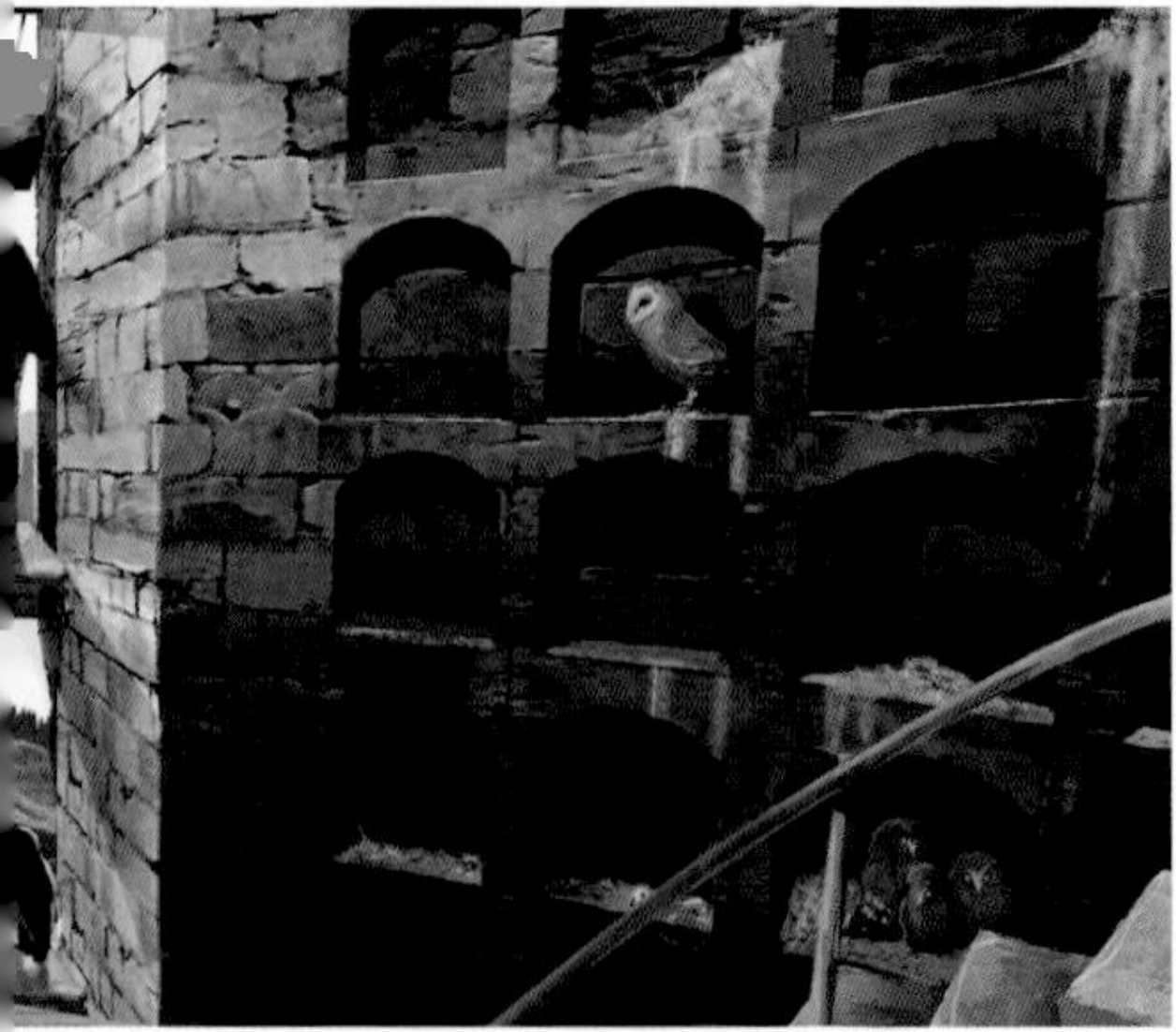

PAGES 118–121: Andrew Williamson portrays different views of the Owlery at Hogwarts. It is here that Harry encounters Cho Chang and discovers she already has a date for the Yule Ball in *Harry Potter and the Goblet of Fire*.

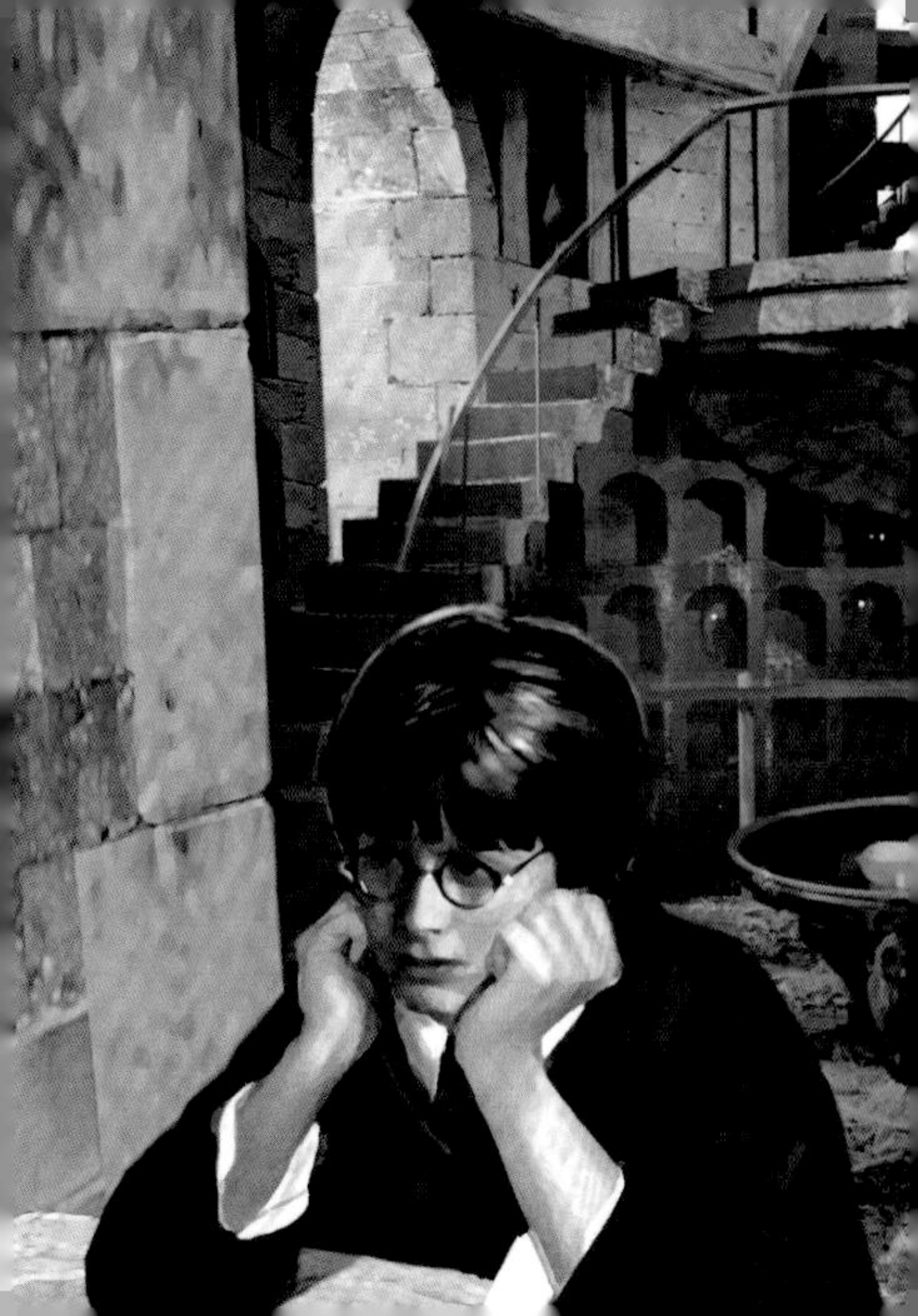

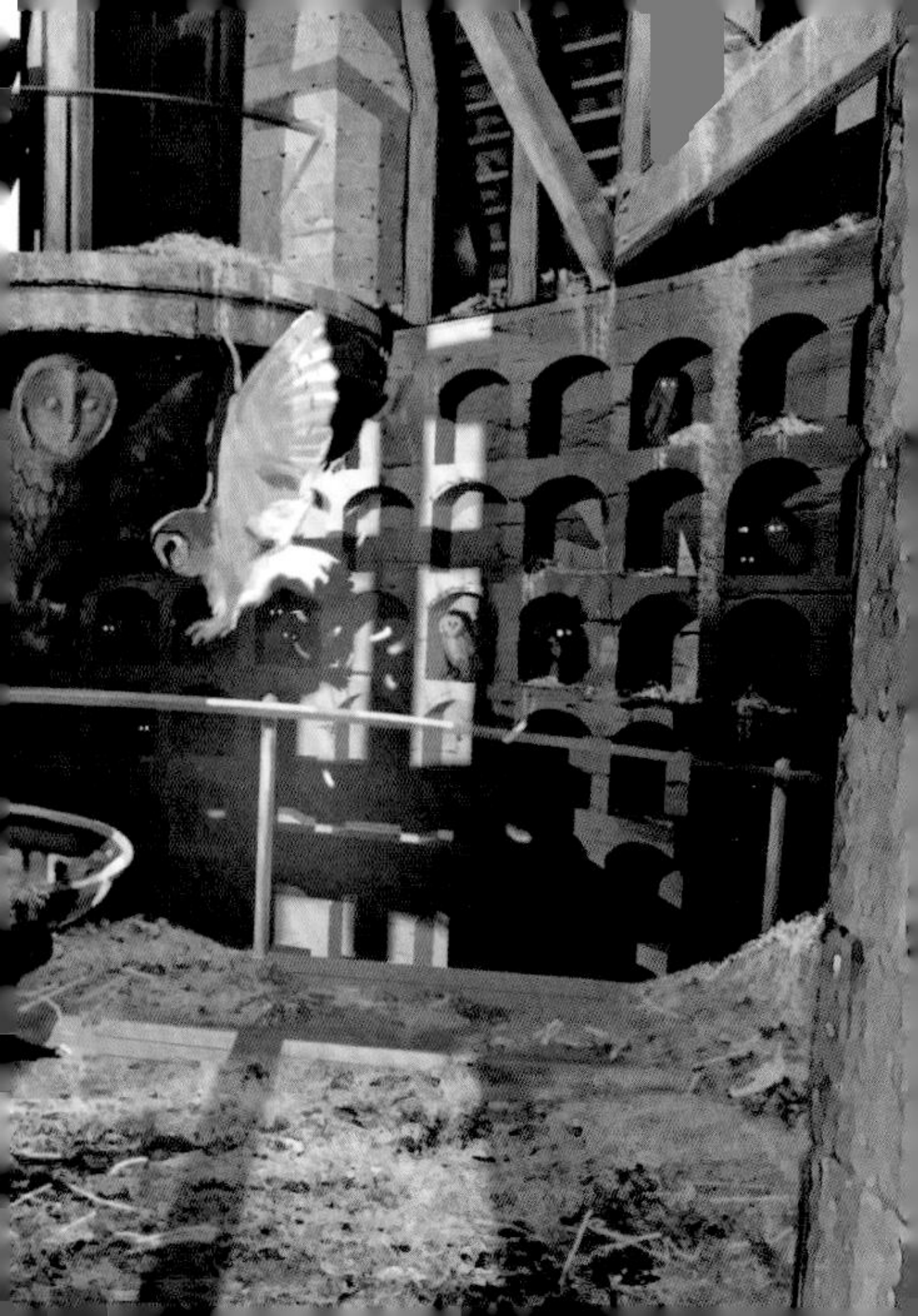

THE ROOM OF REQUIREMENT

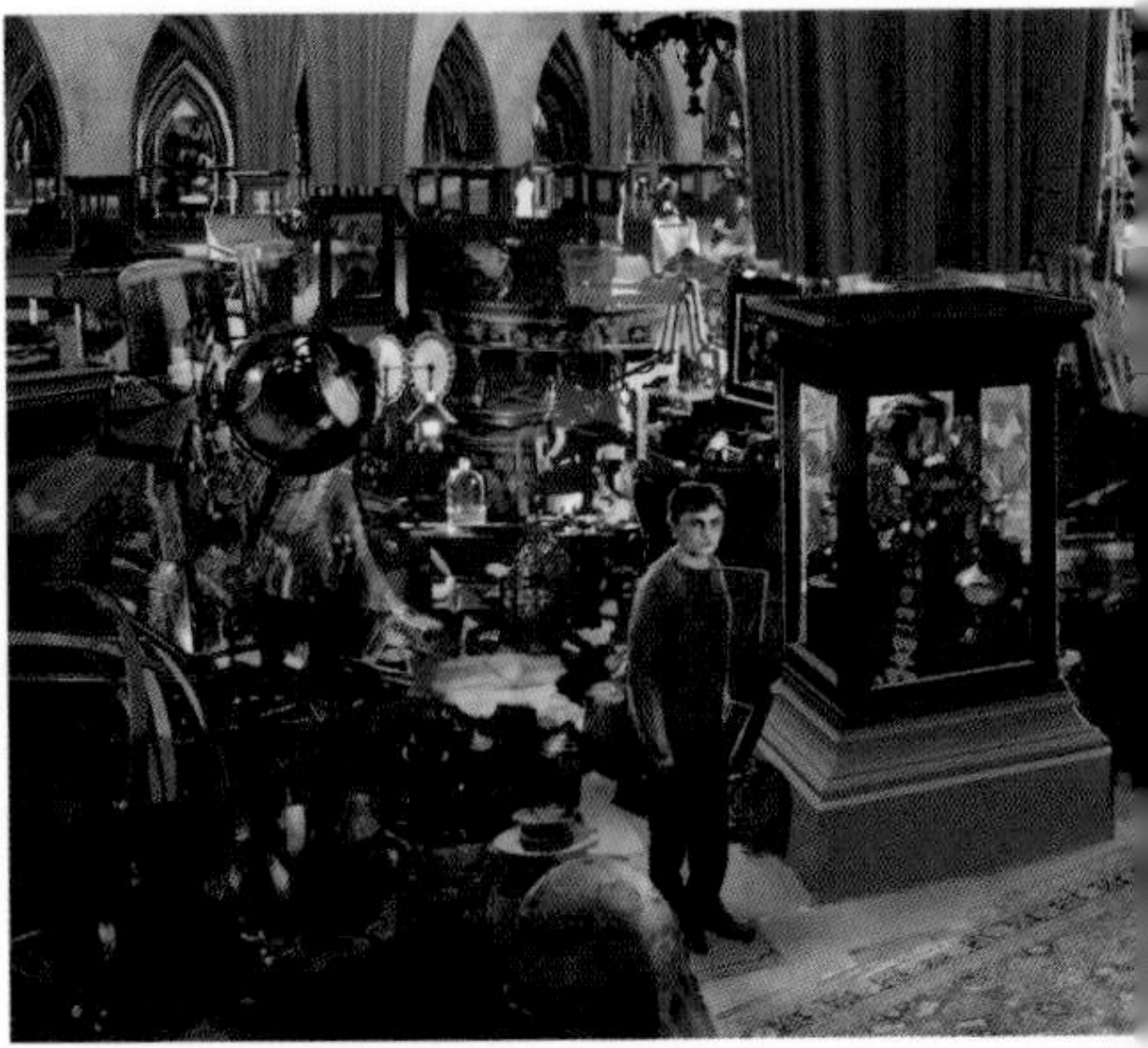

The Room of Requirement is a special room in Hogwarts that only appears when a person has great need of it, coming fully equipped to answer that person's needs.

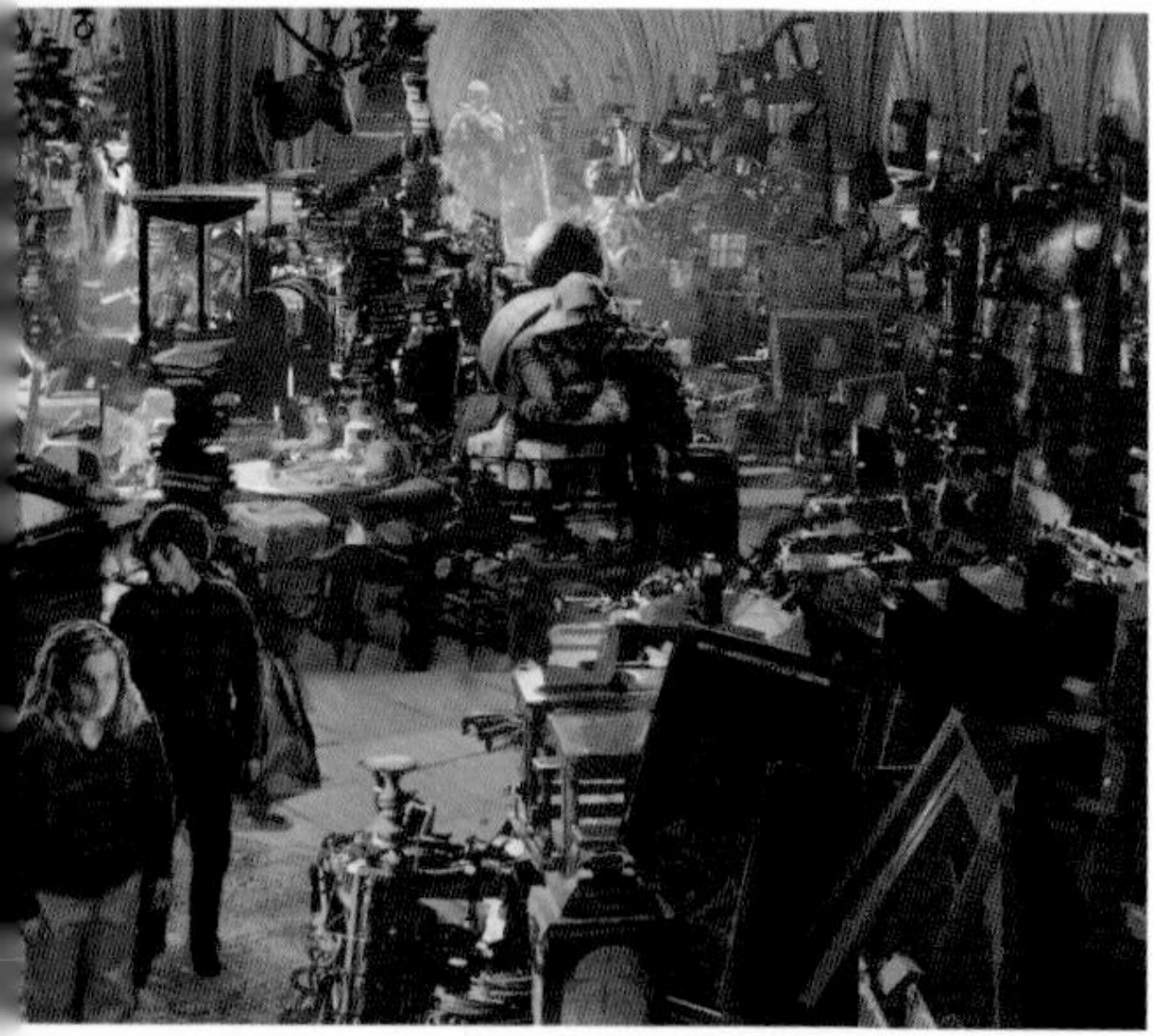

PAGES 122–129: Andrew Williamson depicts the Room of Requirement in its various incarnations.

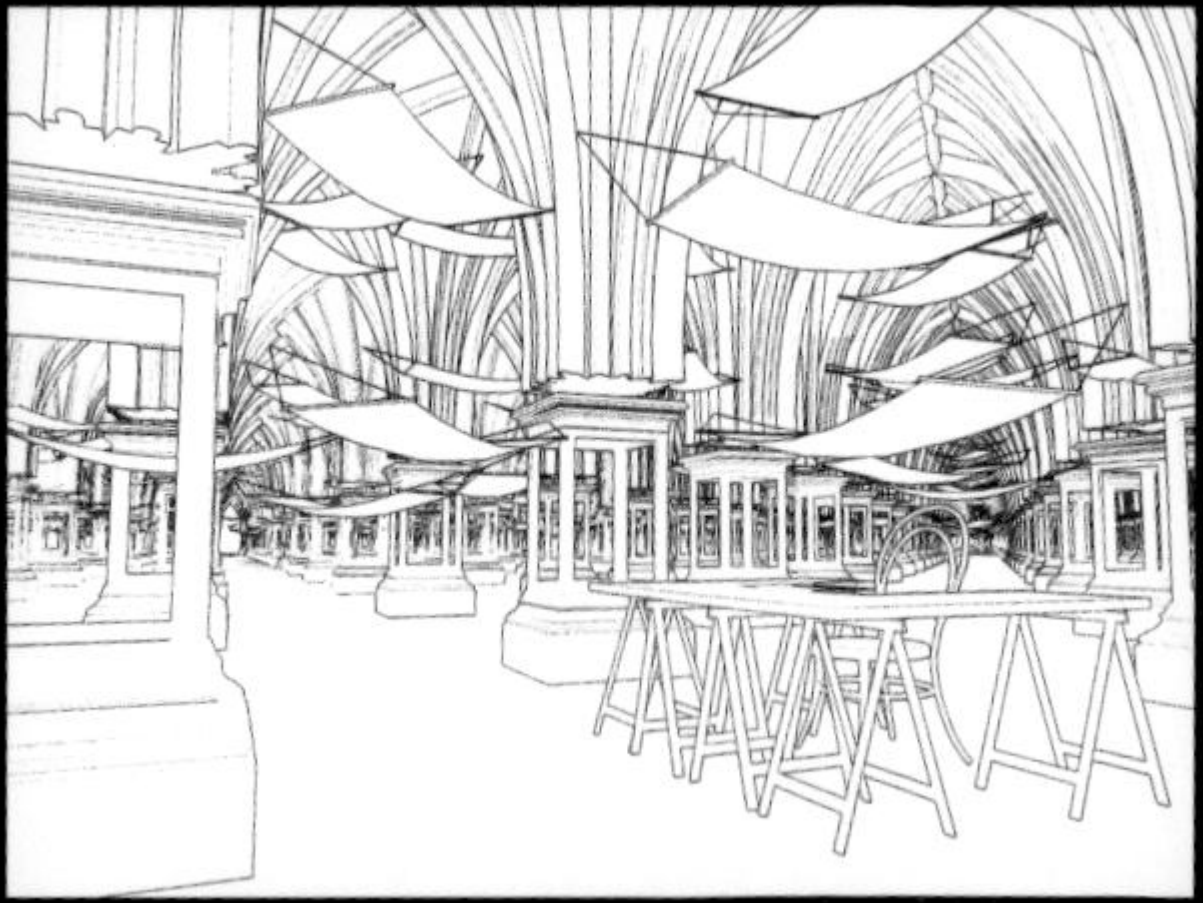

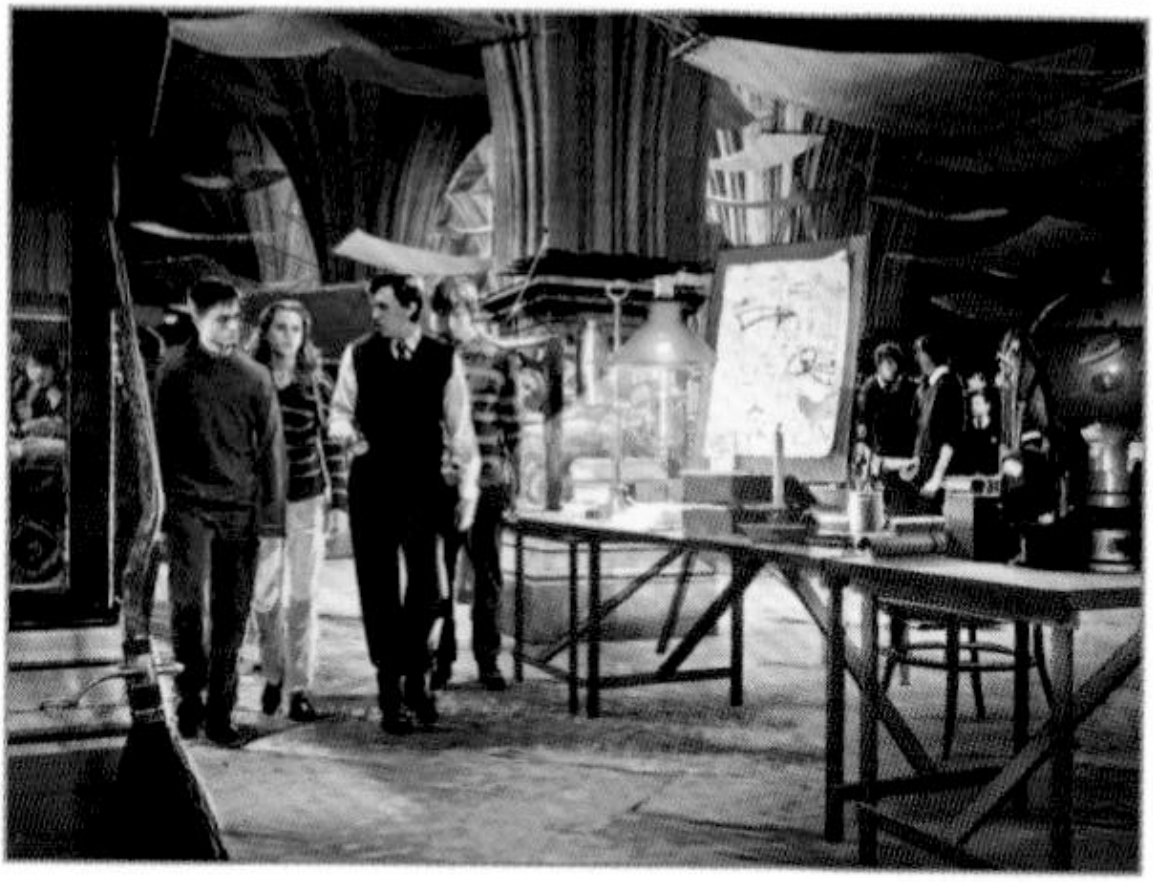

THESE PAGES: Harry, Ron, and Hermione in the Room of Requirement when Harry returned to Hogwarts for the final battle, alongside a preliminary sketch showing the placement of hammocks used by the students hiding in the room.

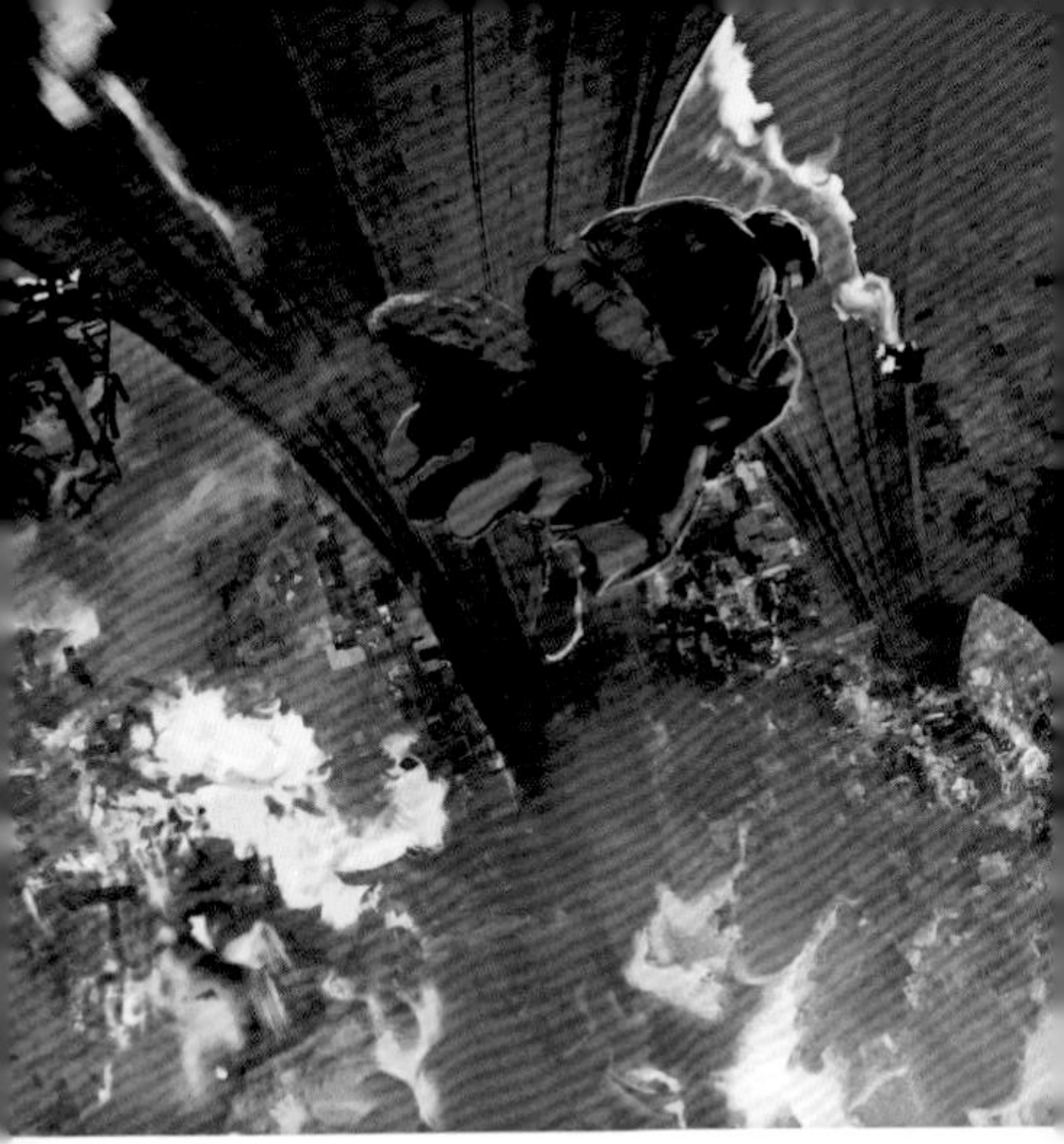

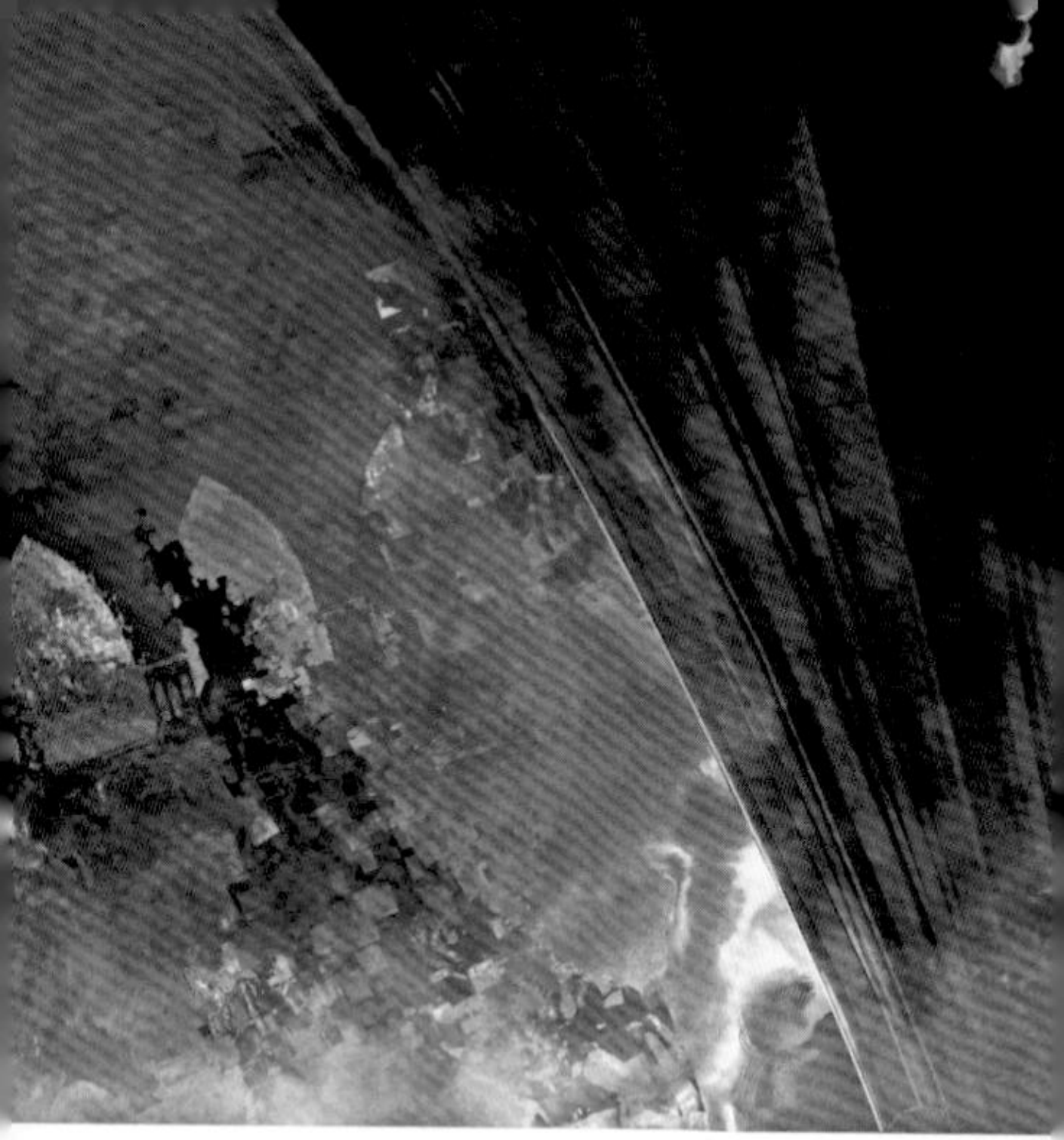

THESE PAGES: Harry, Ron, Hermione, and Draco must escape the Room of Requirement on brooms after Goyle releases Fiendfyre in *Harry Potter and the Deathly Hallows – Part 2*.

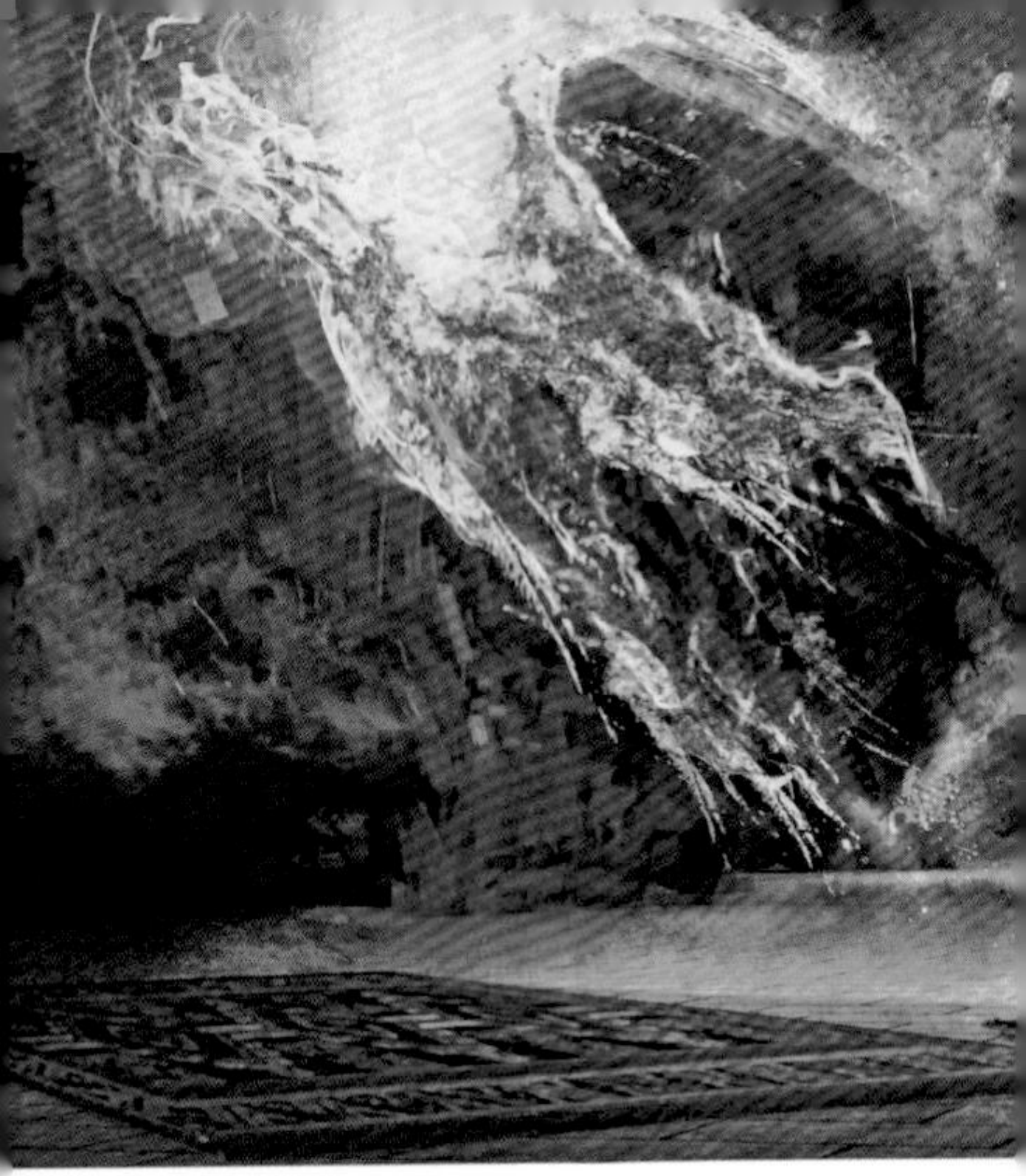

THESE PAGES: Concept art by Paul Catling of the Fiendfyre that consumes the Room of Requirement in *Deathly Hallows – Part 2*.

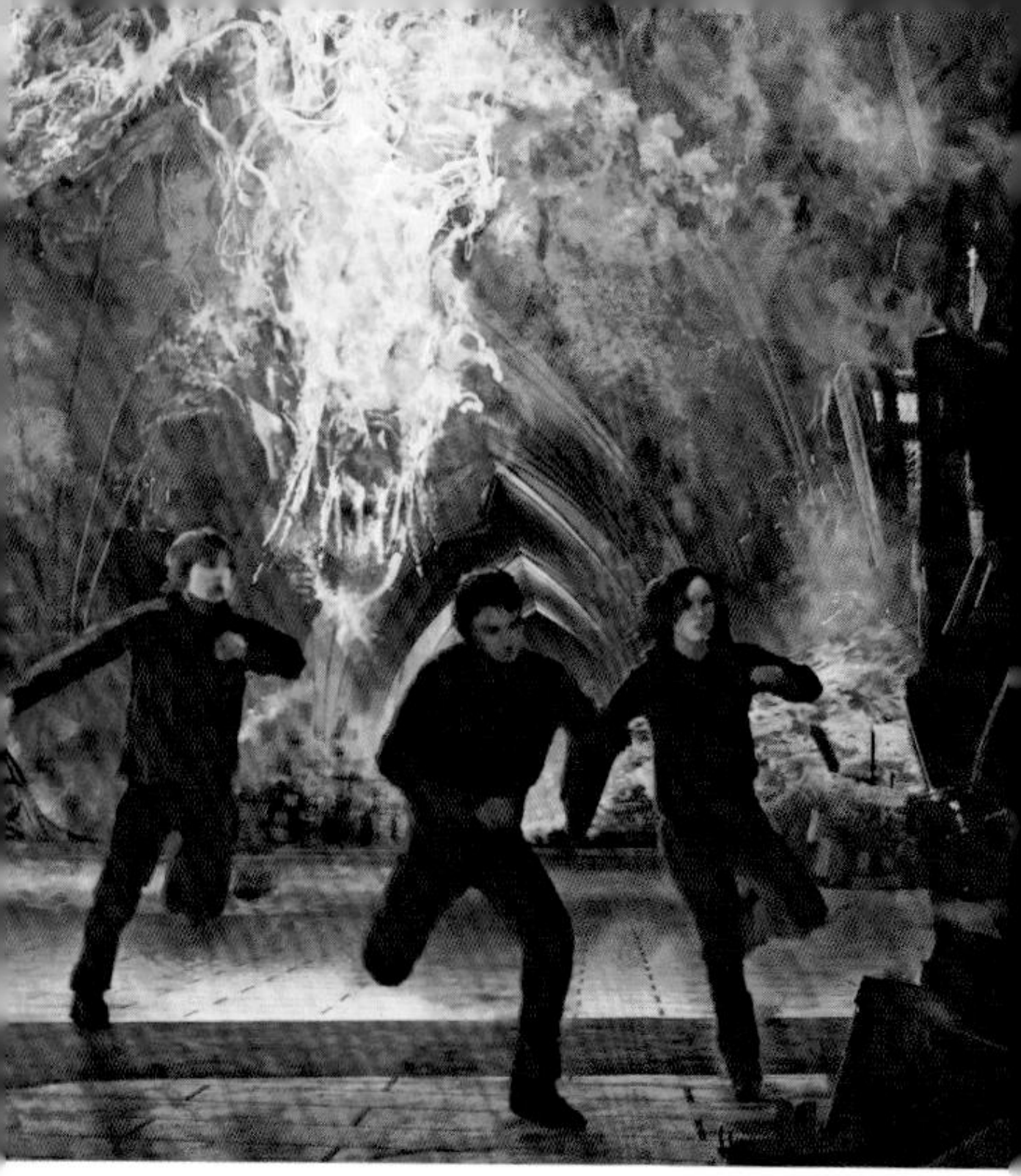

THE ASTRONOMY TOWER

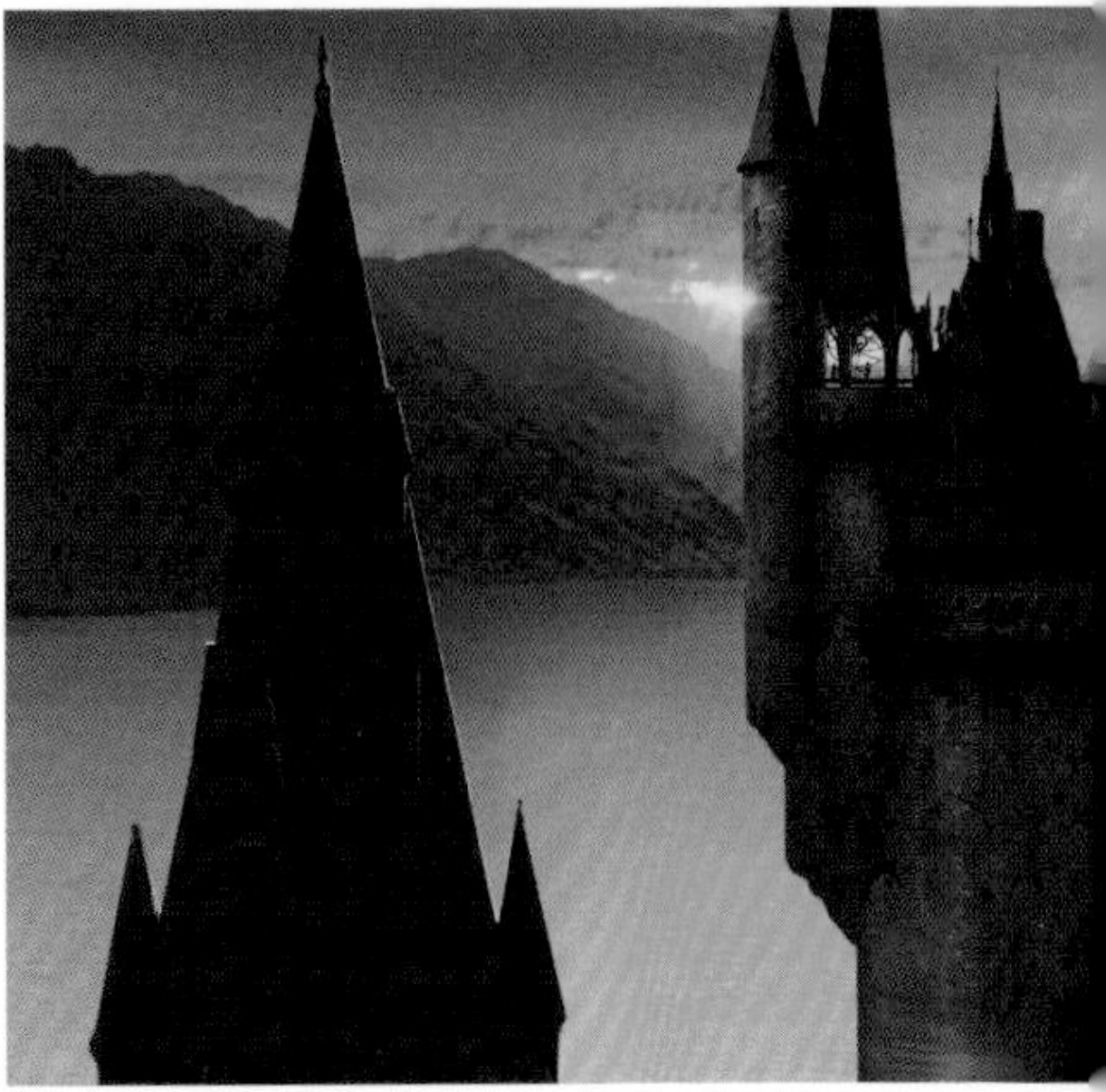

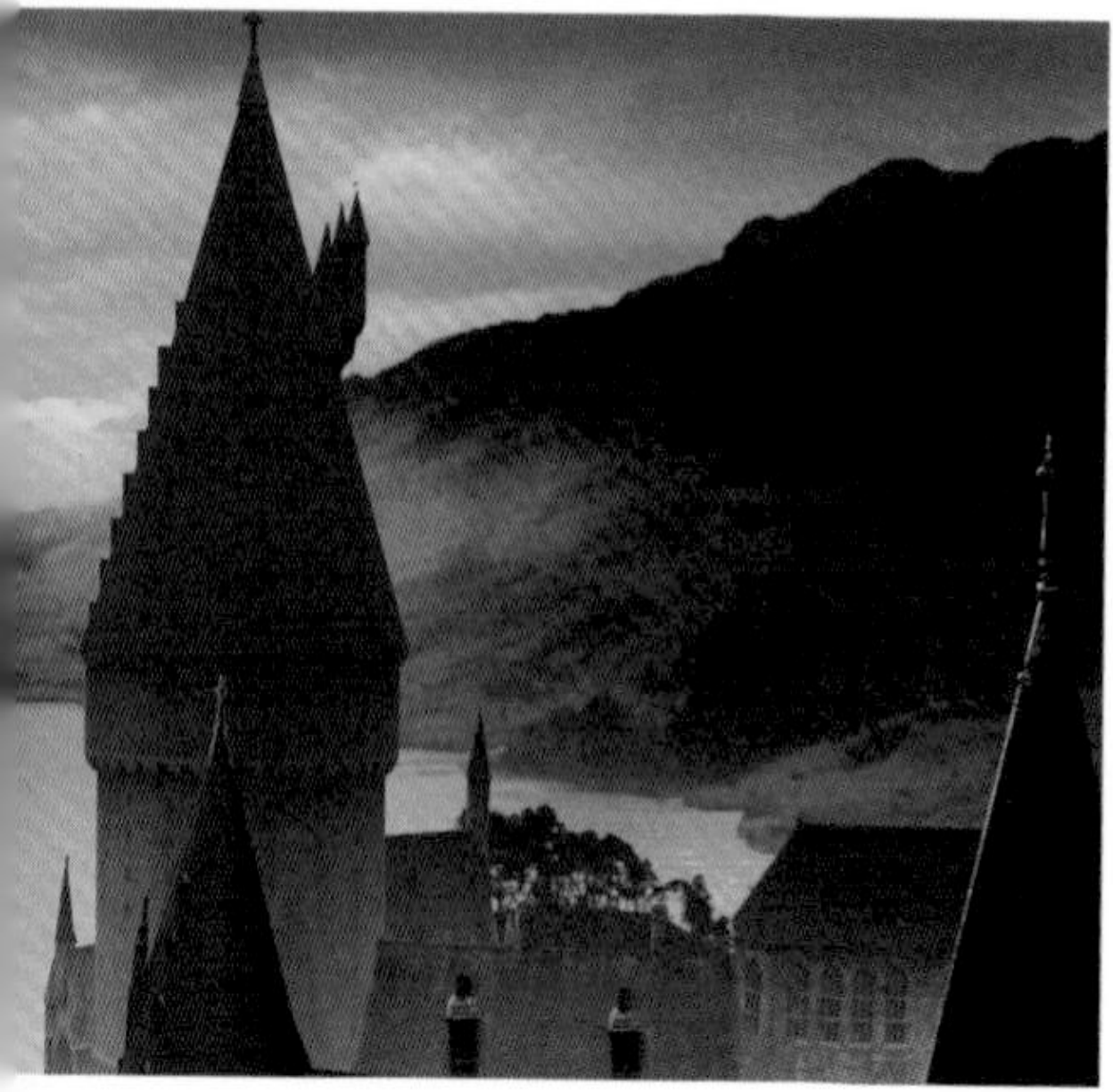

THESE PAGES: The exterior of the Astronomy Tower. Art by Andrew Williamson for *Harry Potter and the Half-Blood Prince*.

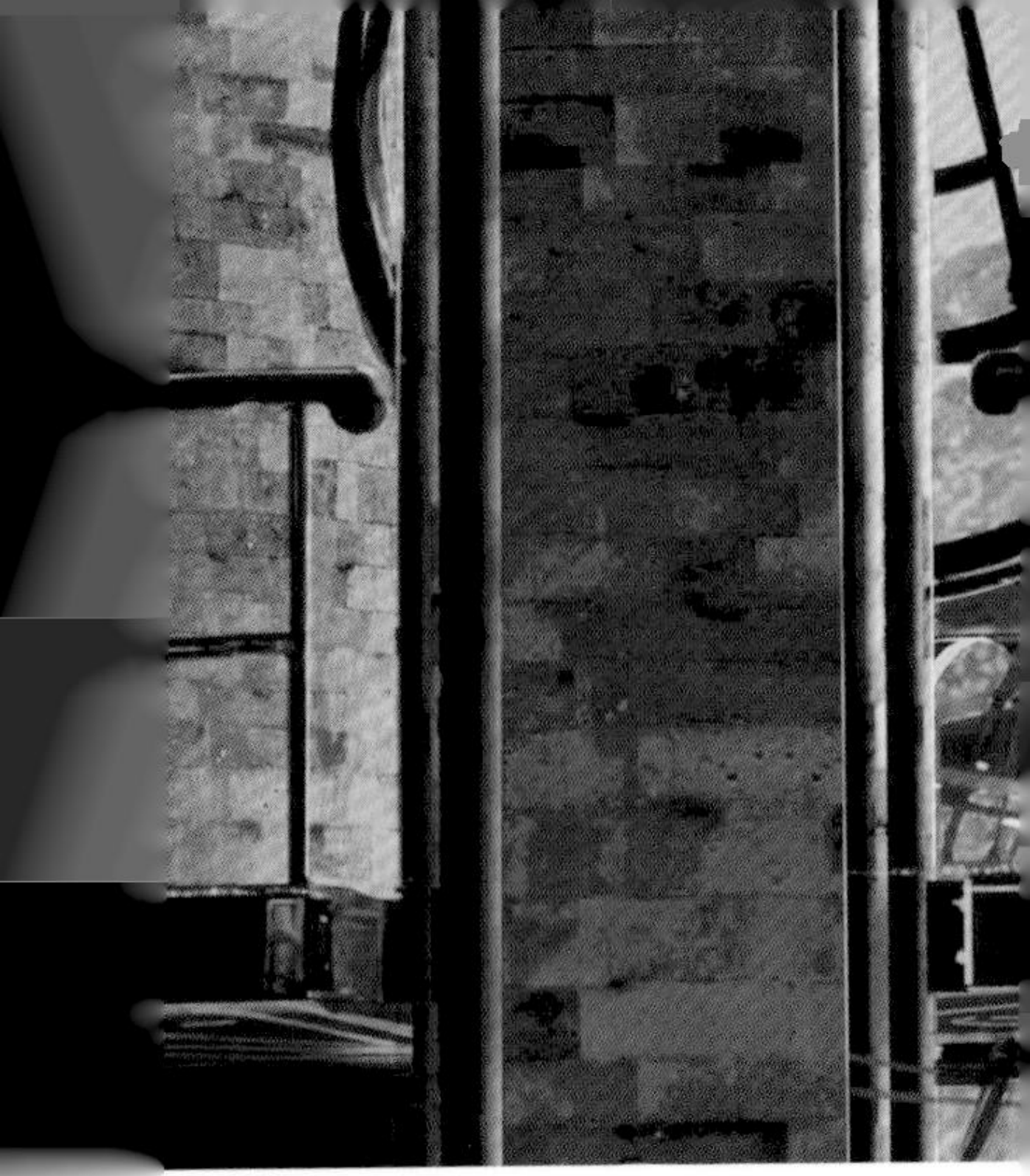

AGES 132–137: As the scene of Professor umbledore's tragic death, the Astronomy ower was a major set piece in *Harry Potter and*

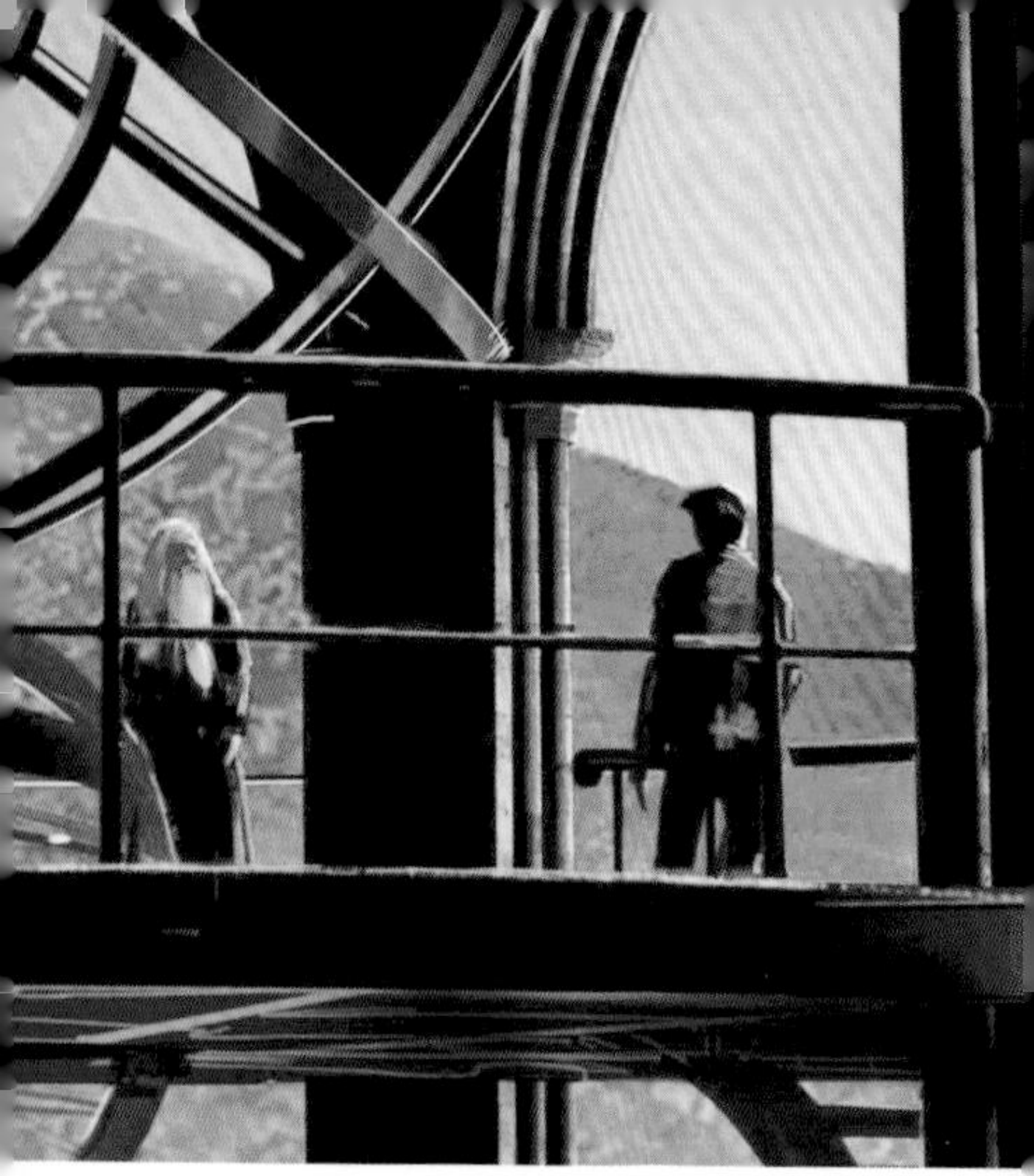

the Half-Blood Prince. In these pages, Andrew Williamson illustrates various views of the tower before, during, and after the climactic scene.

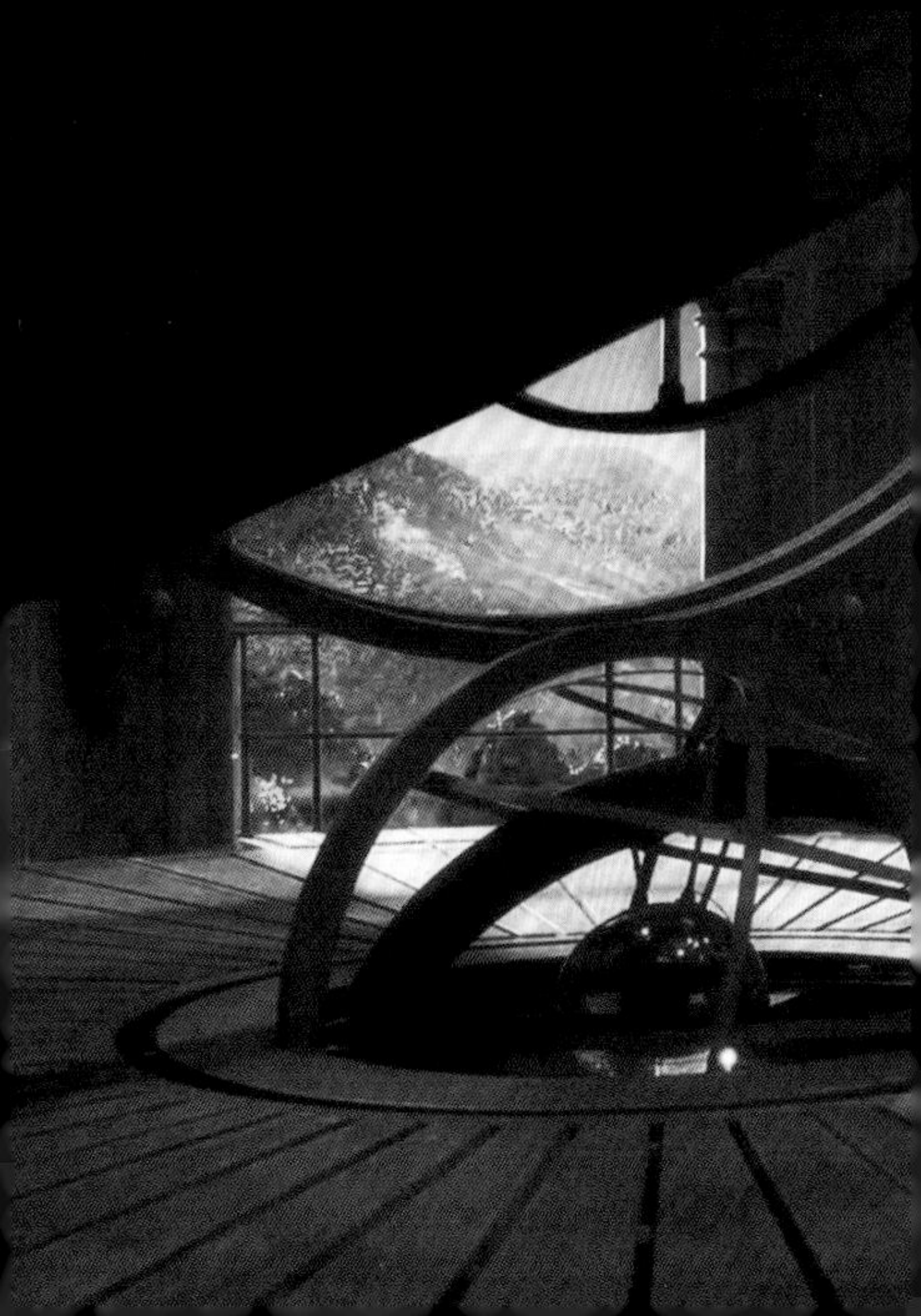

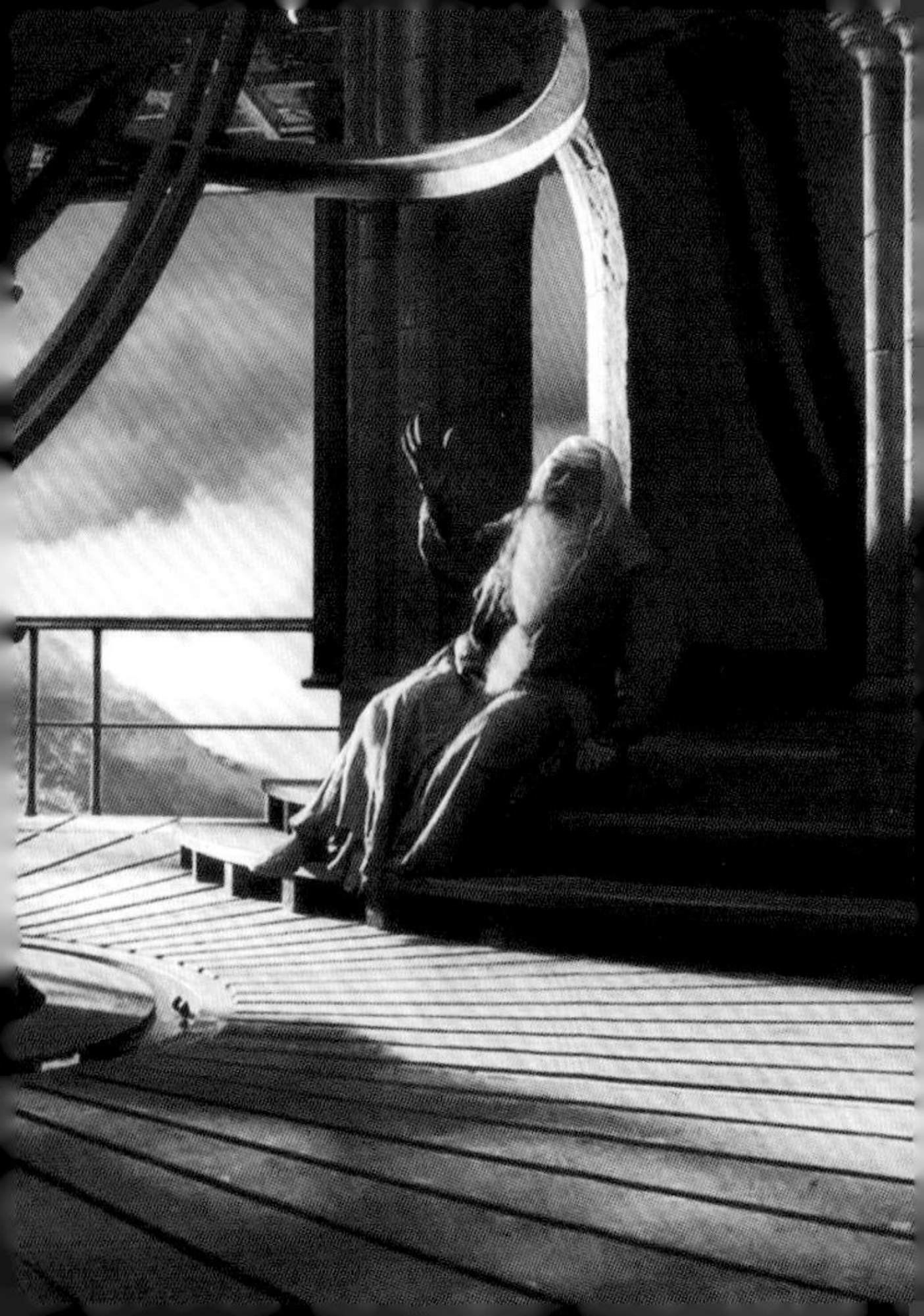

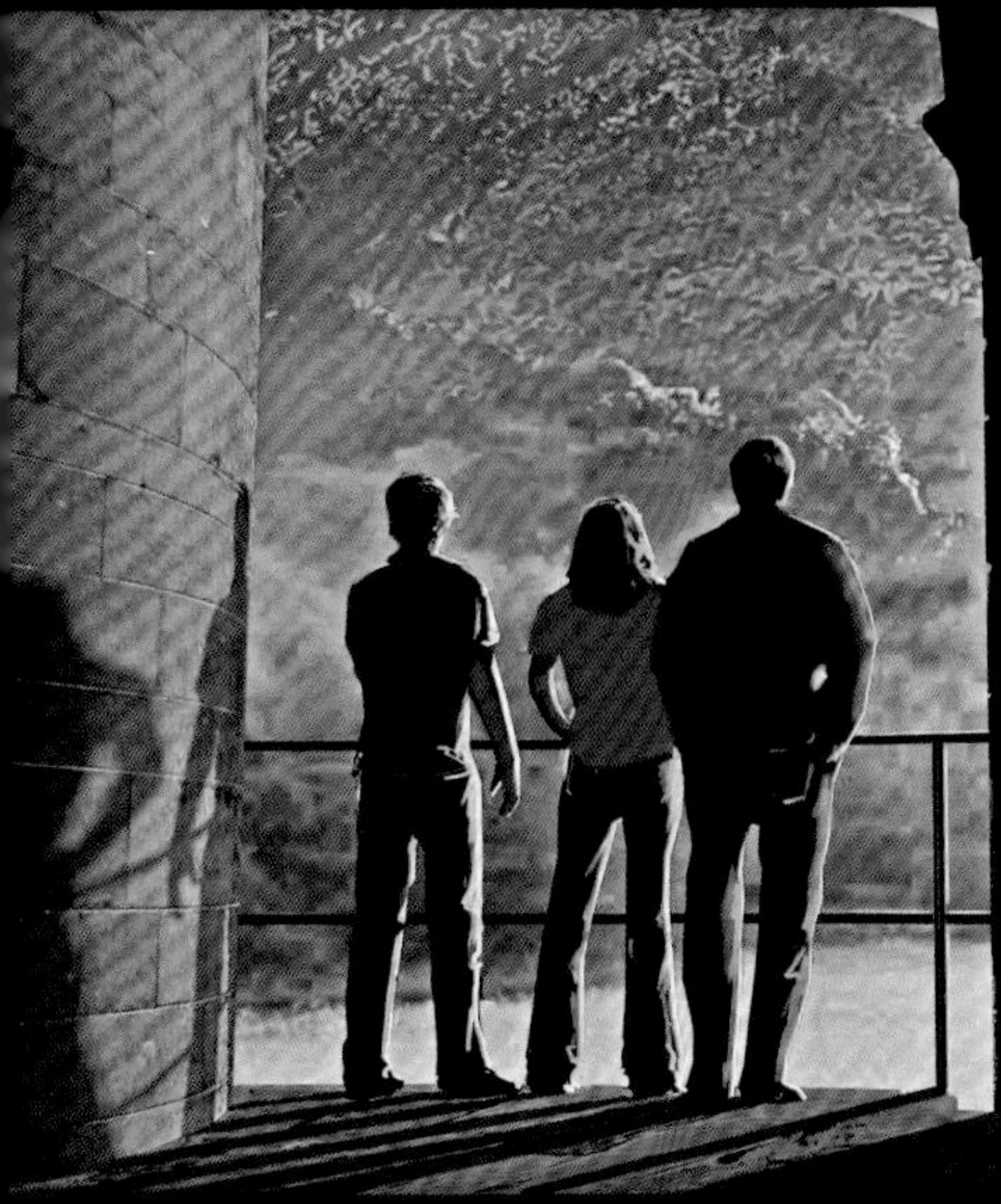

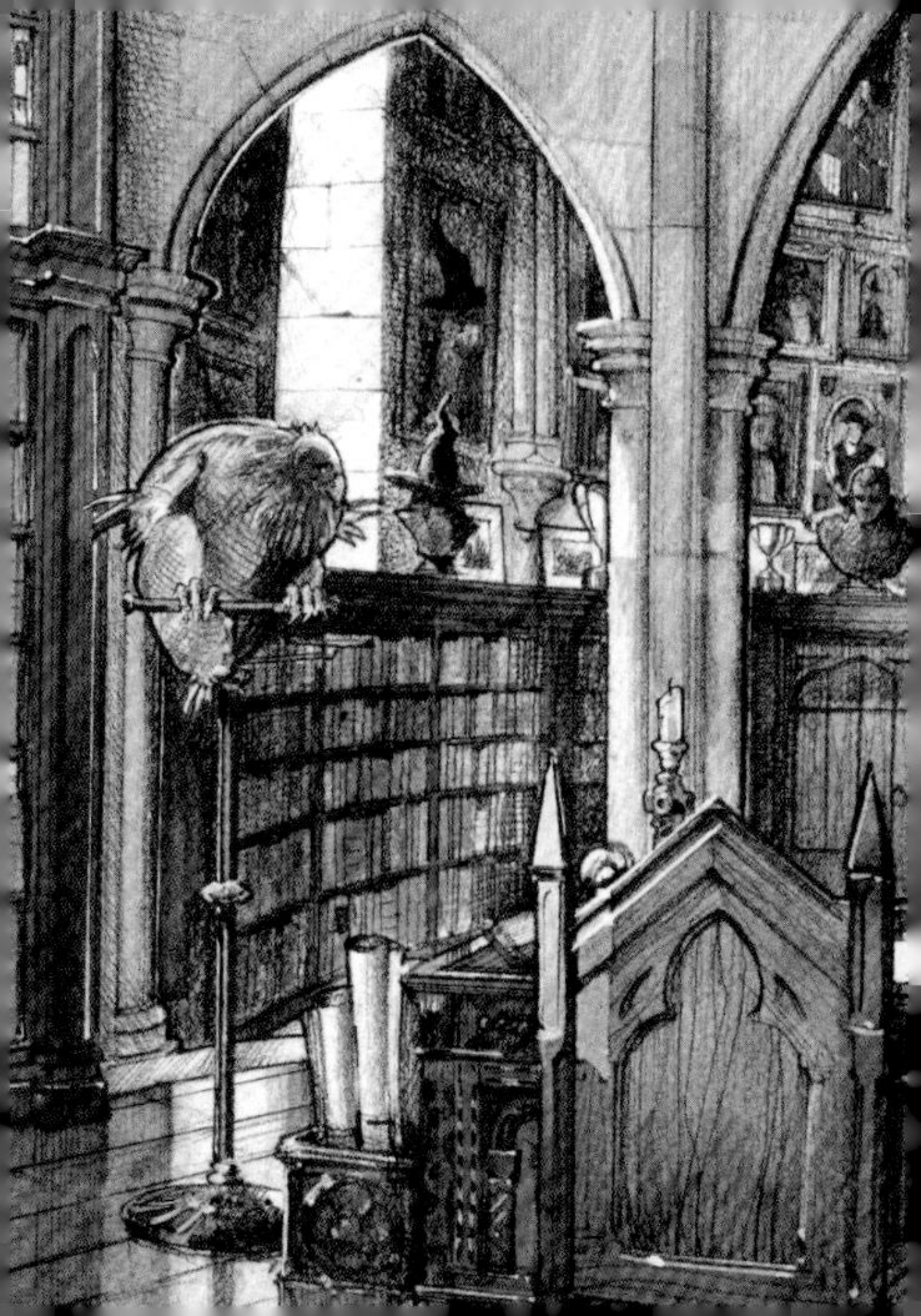

HOGWARTS CLASSROOMS AND OFFICES

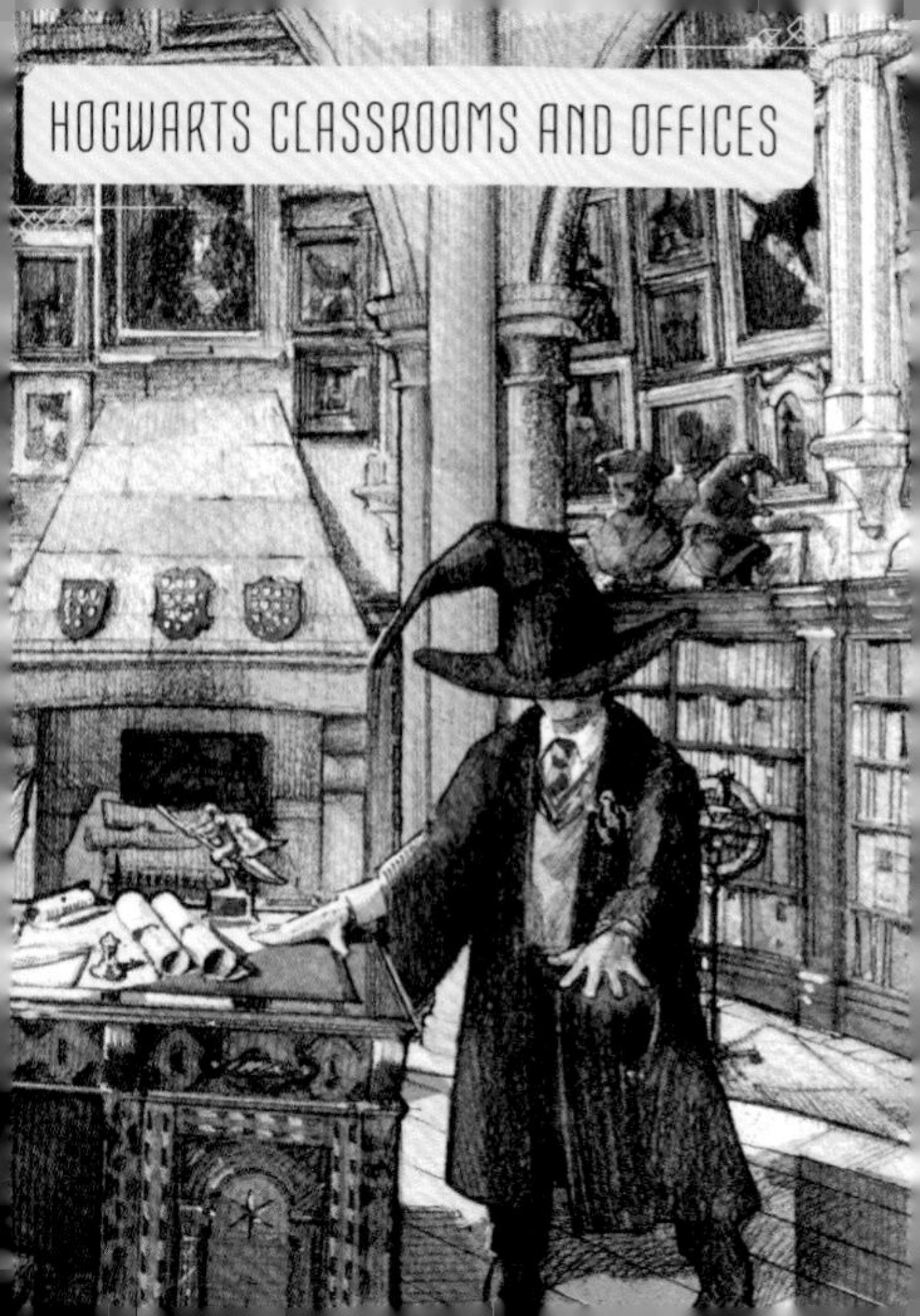

DUMBLEDORE'S OFFICE

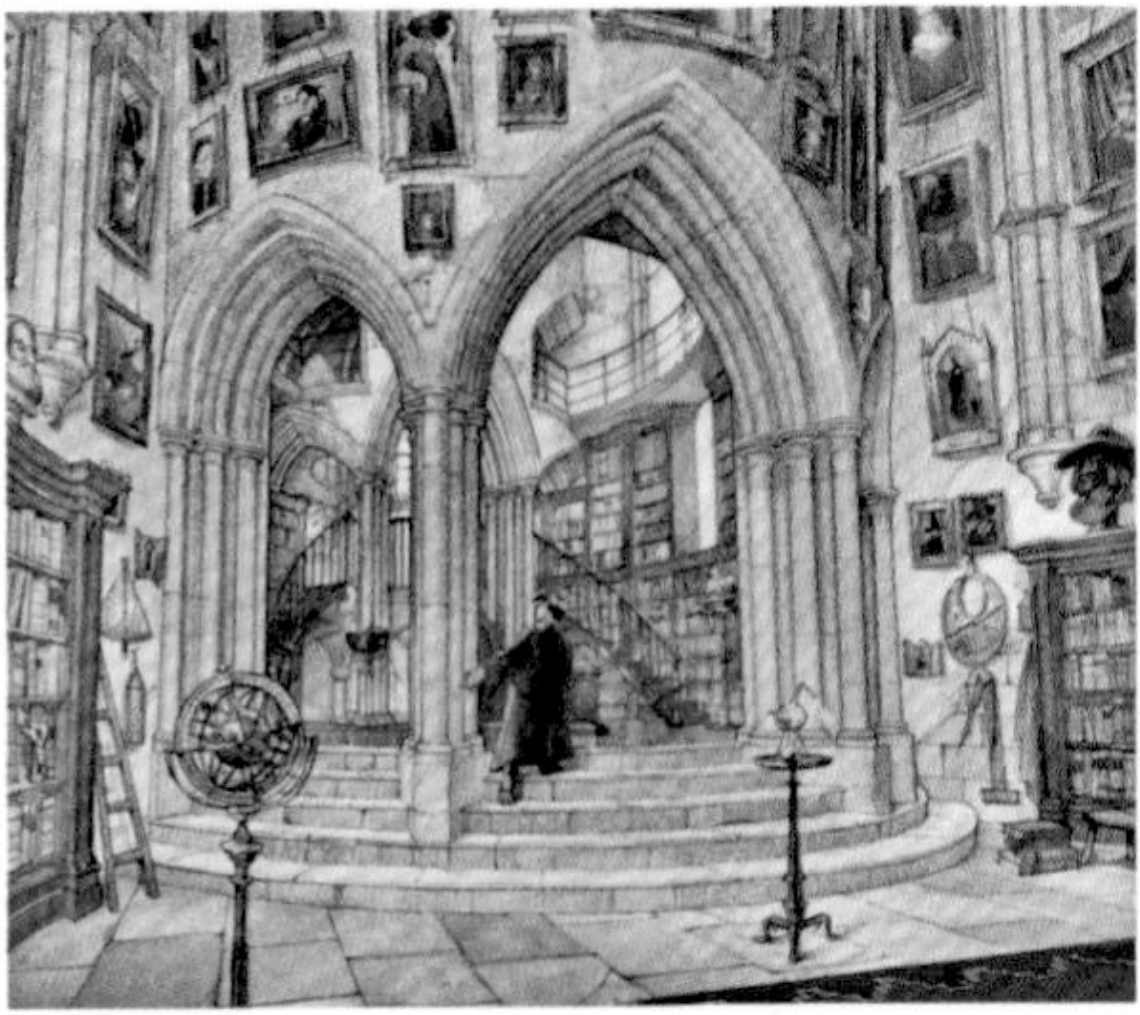

PAGES 138–140: Harry Potter awaits Professor Dumbledore in the Headmaster's office in *Harry Potter and the Chamber of Secrets*. Art by Andrew Williamson.

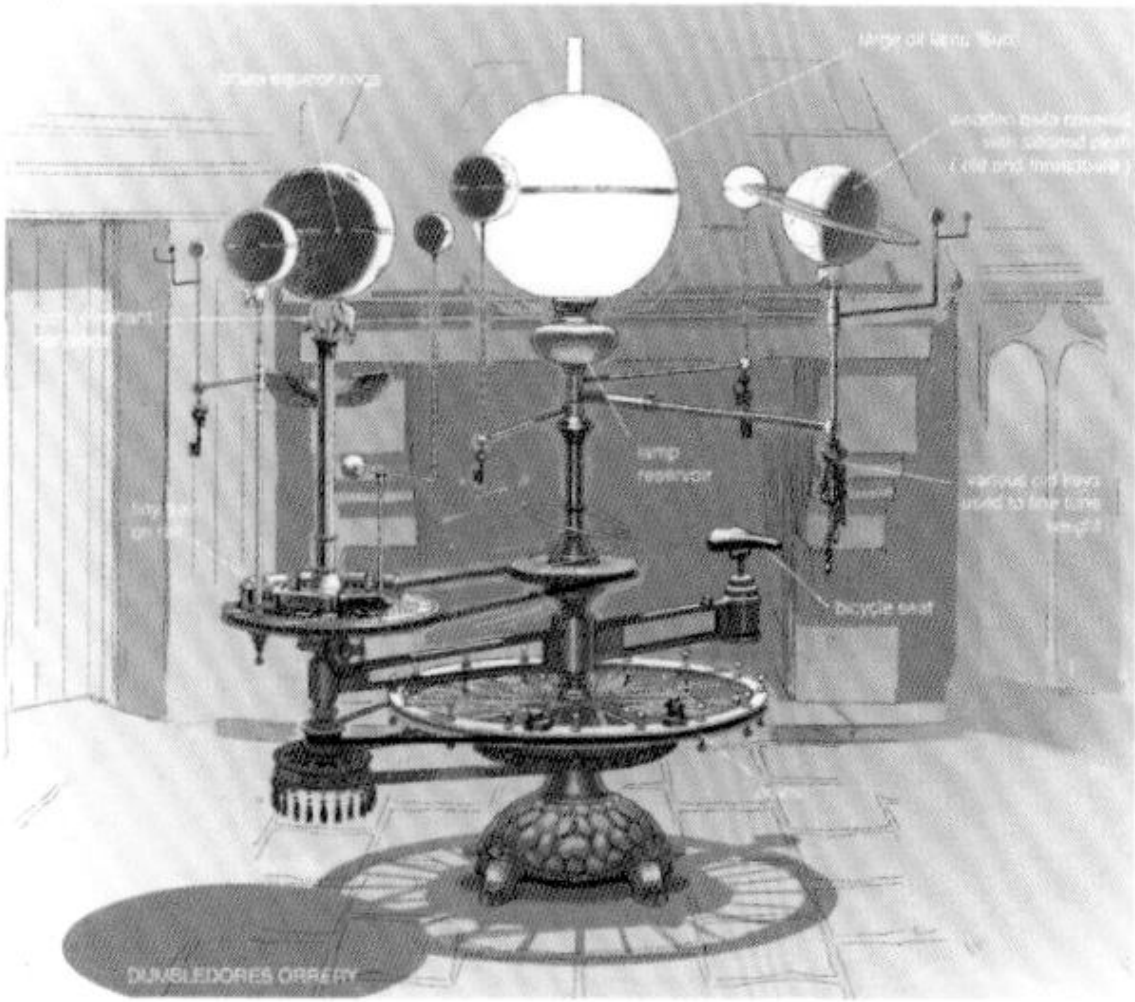

ABOVE: Adam Brockbank depicts an orrery that sat in Dumbledore's office throughout the films.

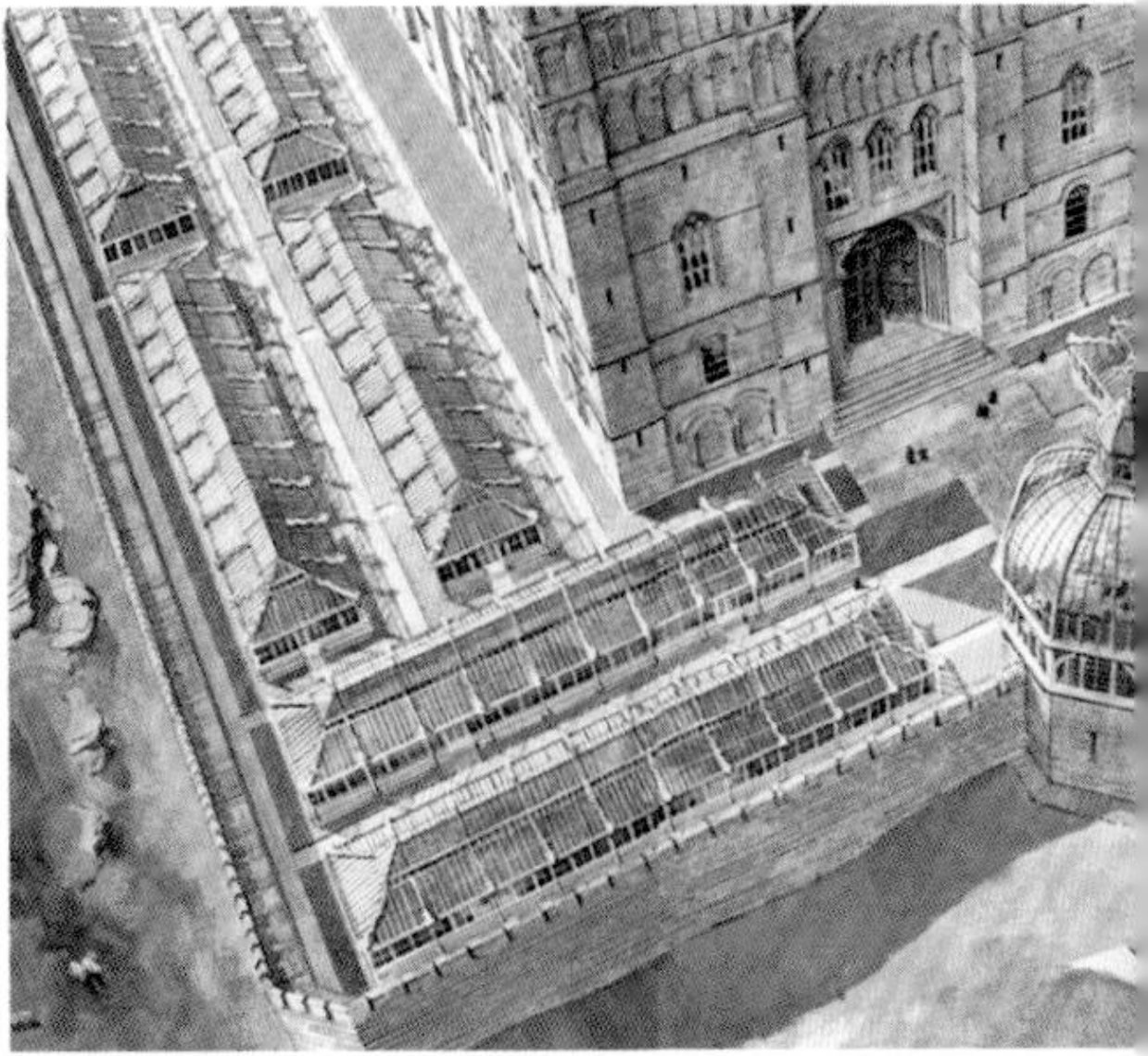

THE GREENHOUSE

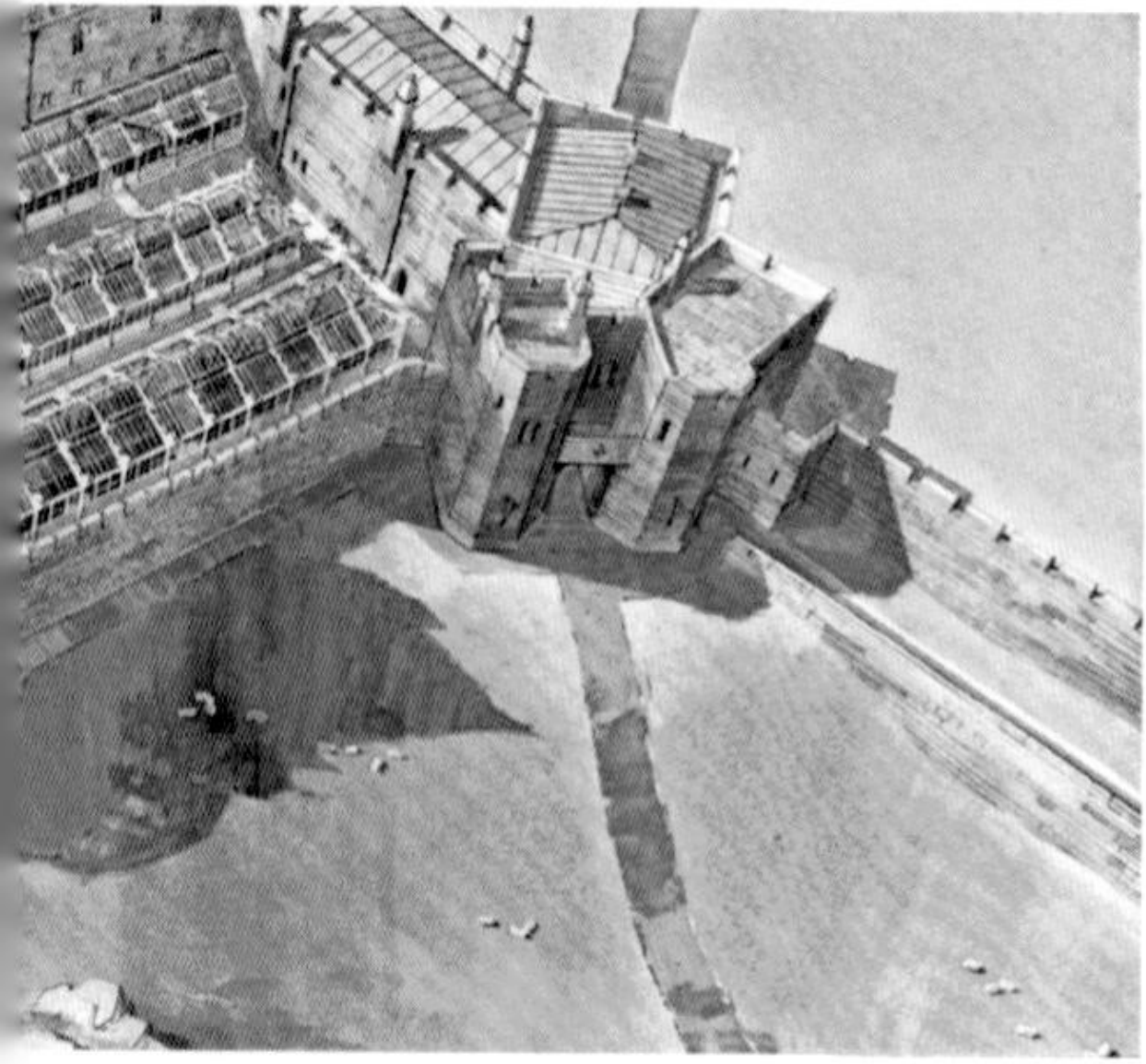

PAGES 142–144: Andrew Williamson depicts Greenhouse Three, where the second years repot Mandrakes under the tutelage of Professor Sprout in *Harry Potter and the Chamber of Secrets*.

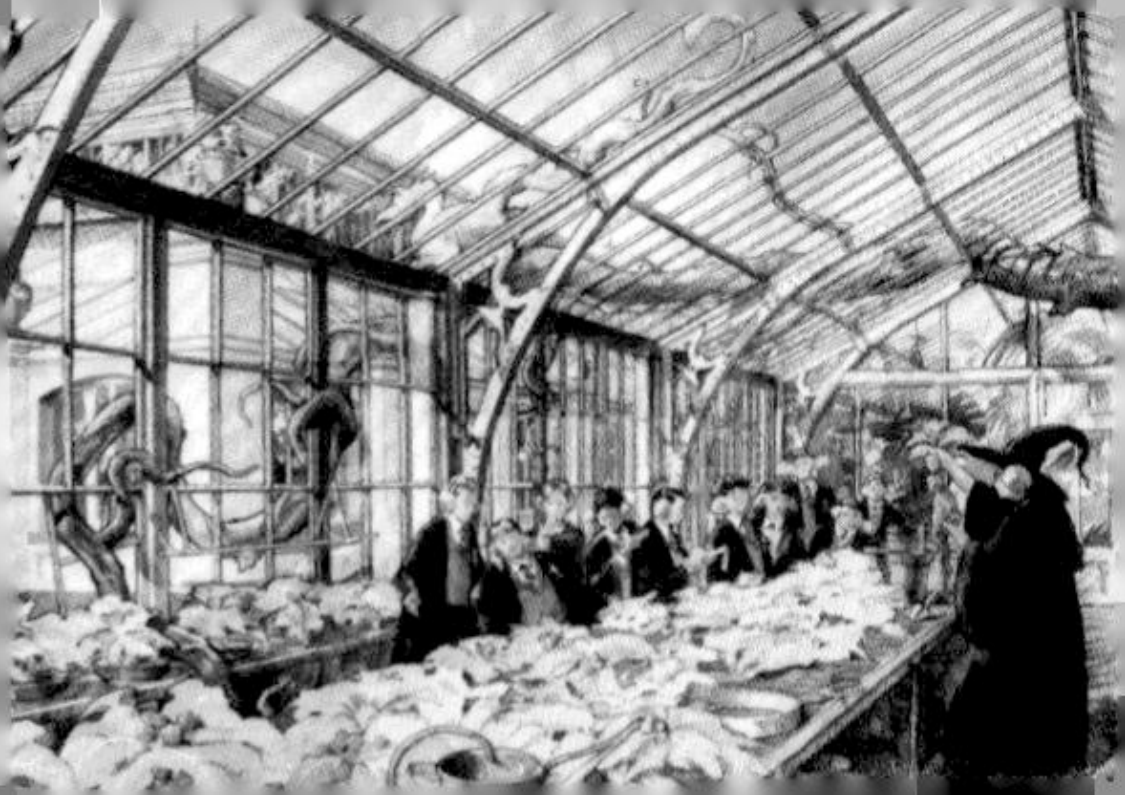

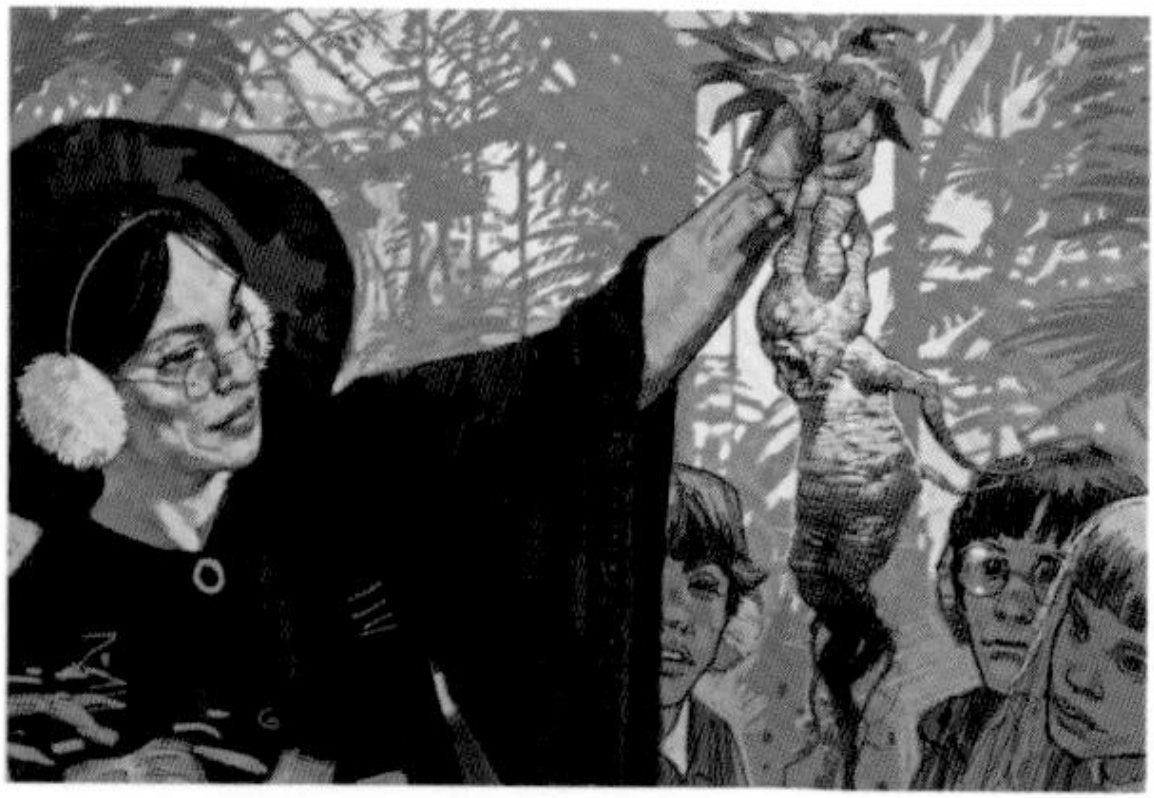

ABOVE: A close-up of Professor Sprout wearing earmuffs as auditory protection against the shrieking Mandrakes. Artwork by Dermot Power.

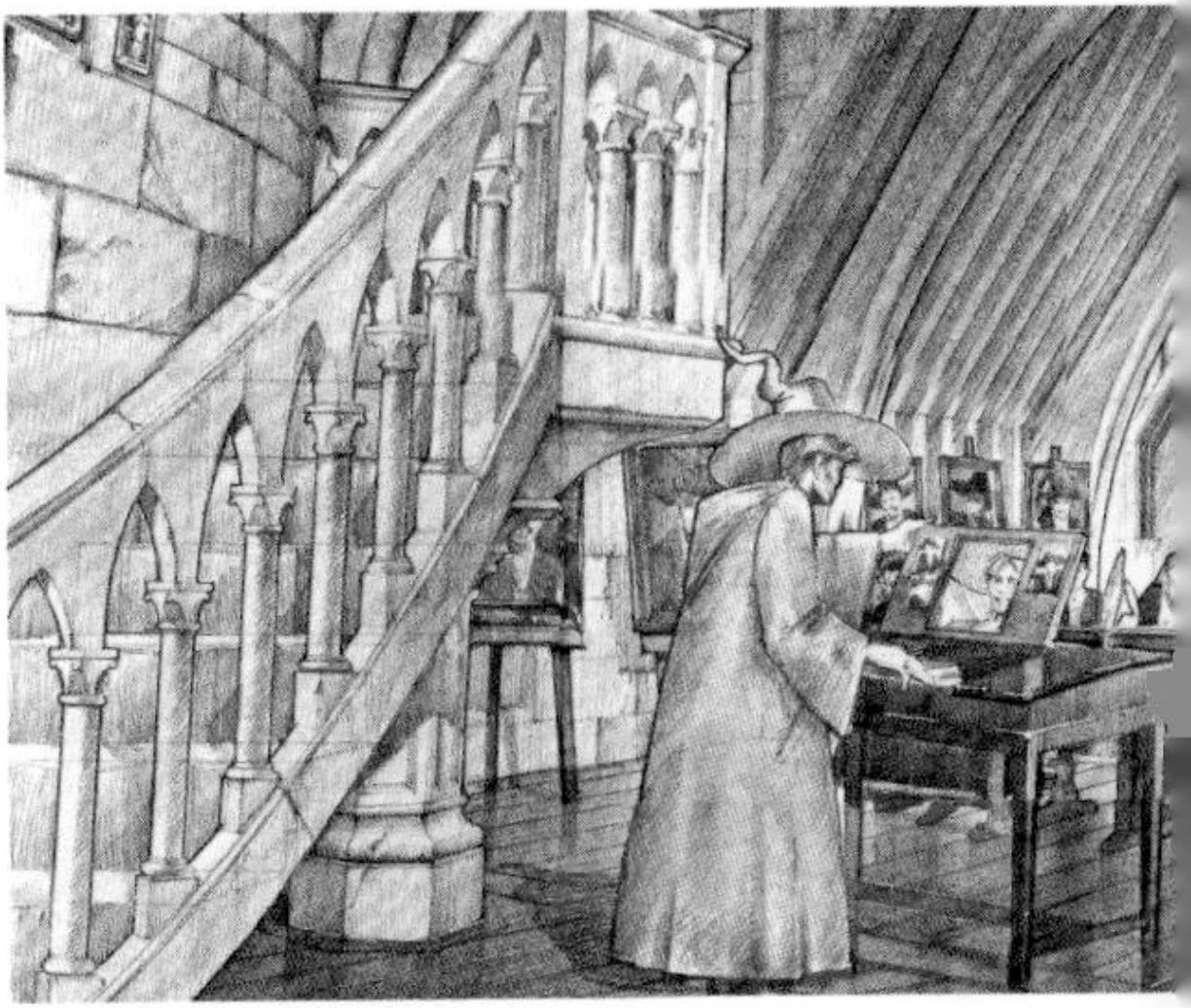

The Defense Against the Dark Arts classroom hosted seven different teachers across the eight films, and each teacher brought their own style and personality to the space.

DEFENSE AGAINST THE DARK ARTS CLASSROOM

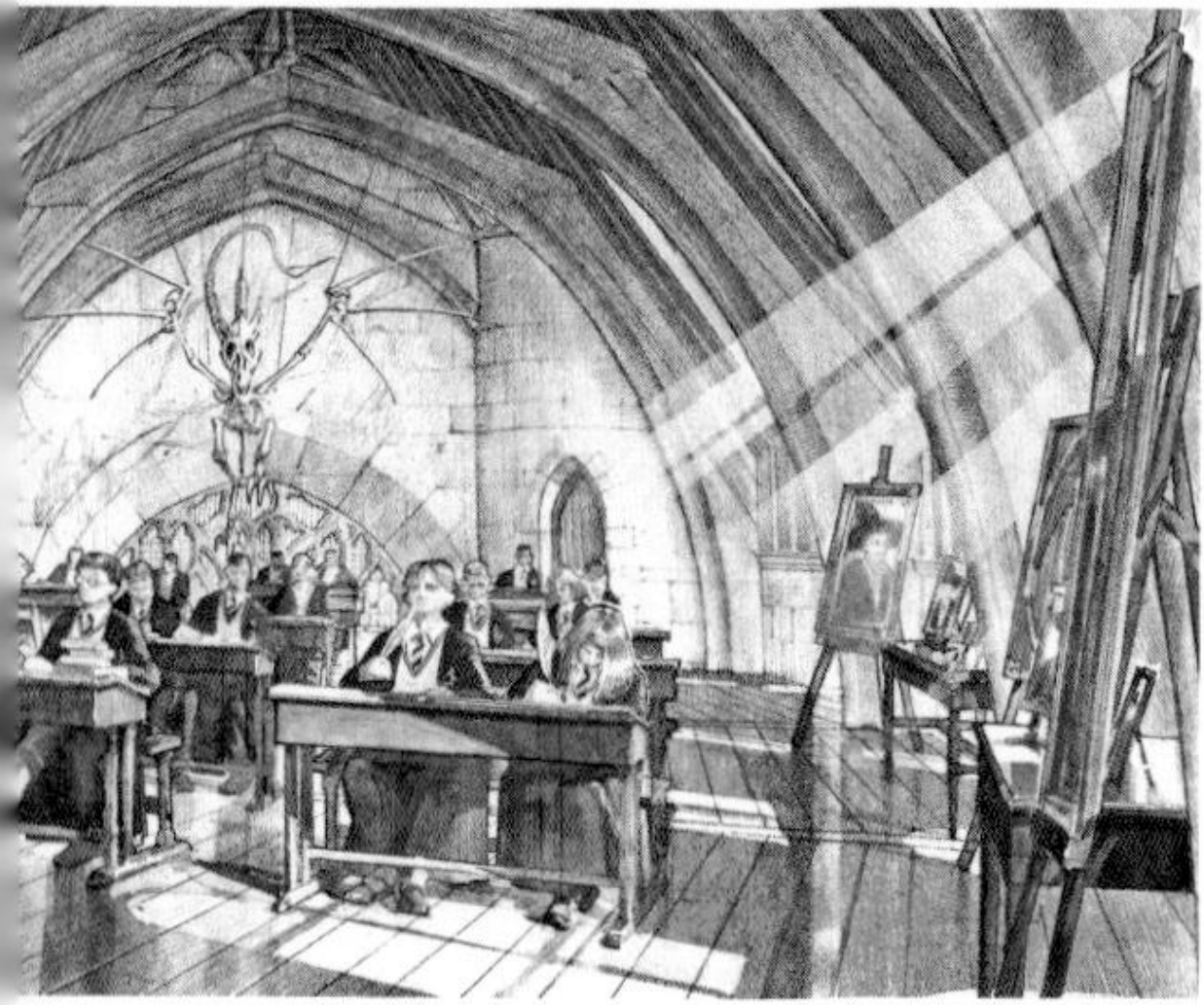

THESE PAGES: Professor Lockhart's classroom as depicted by Andrew Williamson for *Harry Potter and the Chamber of Secrets*.

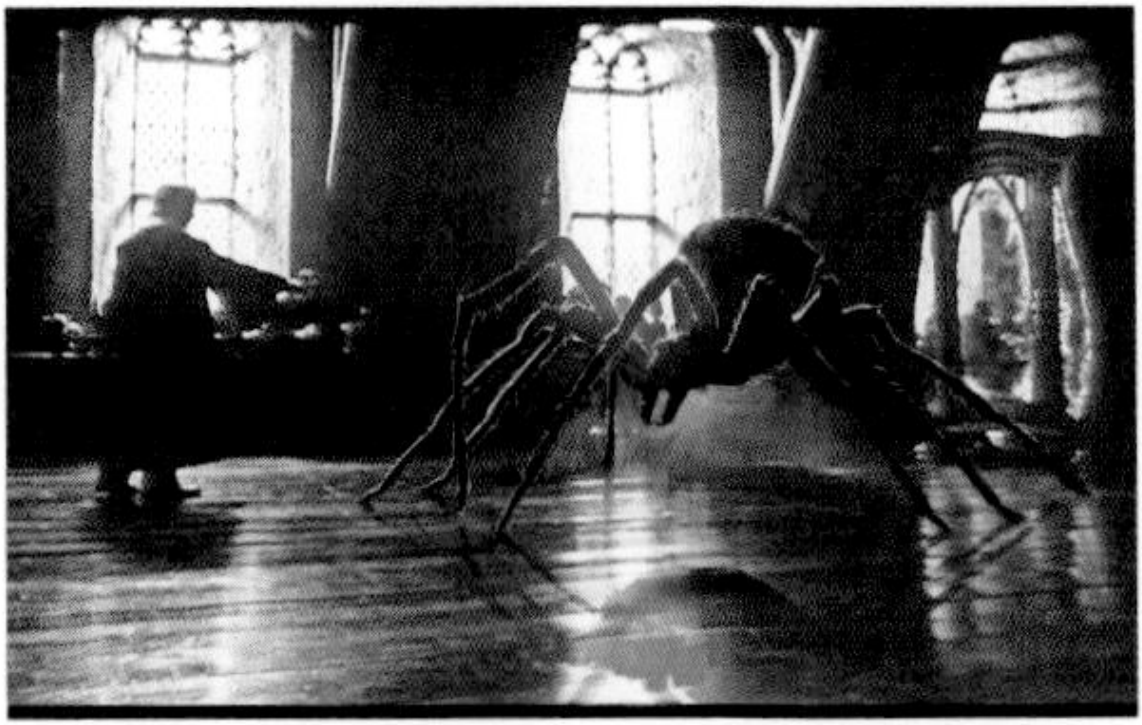

ABOVE: Dermot Power depicts the classroom during a lesson on Boggarts conducted by Professor Lupin in *Harry Potter and the Prisoner of Azkaban*.

OPPOSITE: Adam Brockbank illustrates the cabinet in which the Boggart lurks.

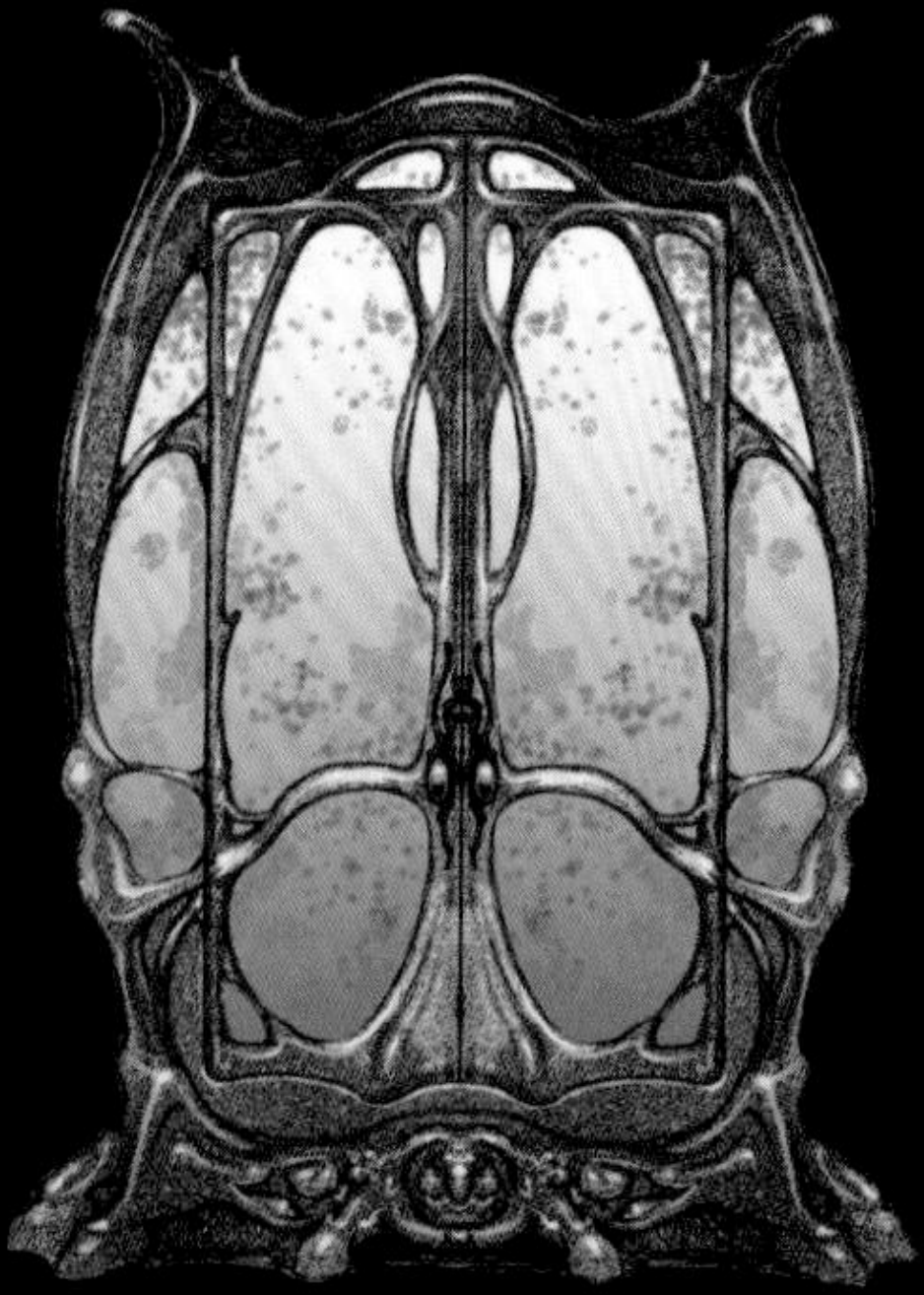

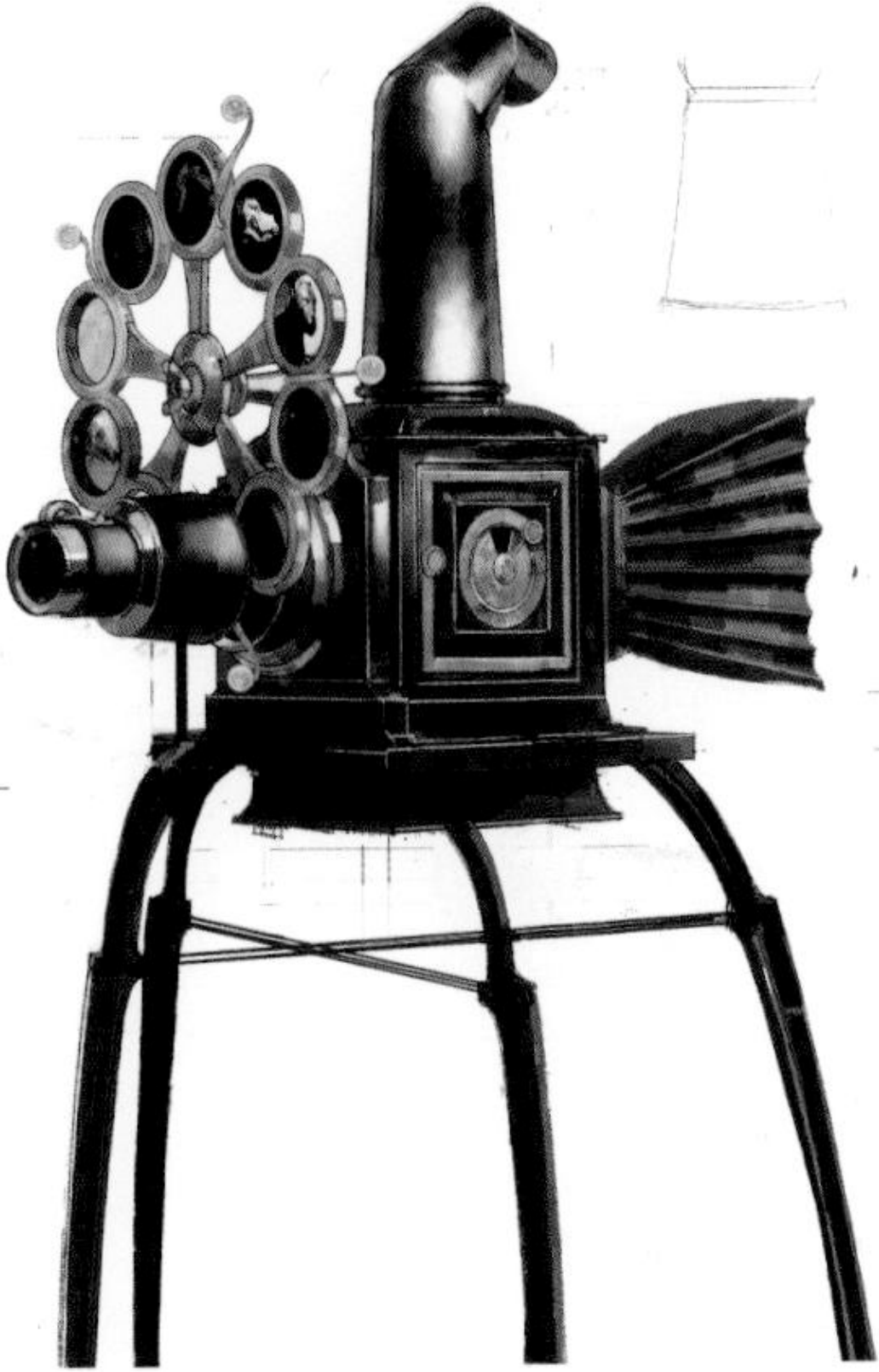

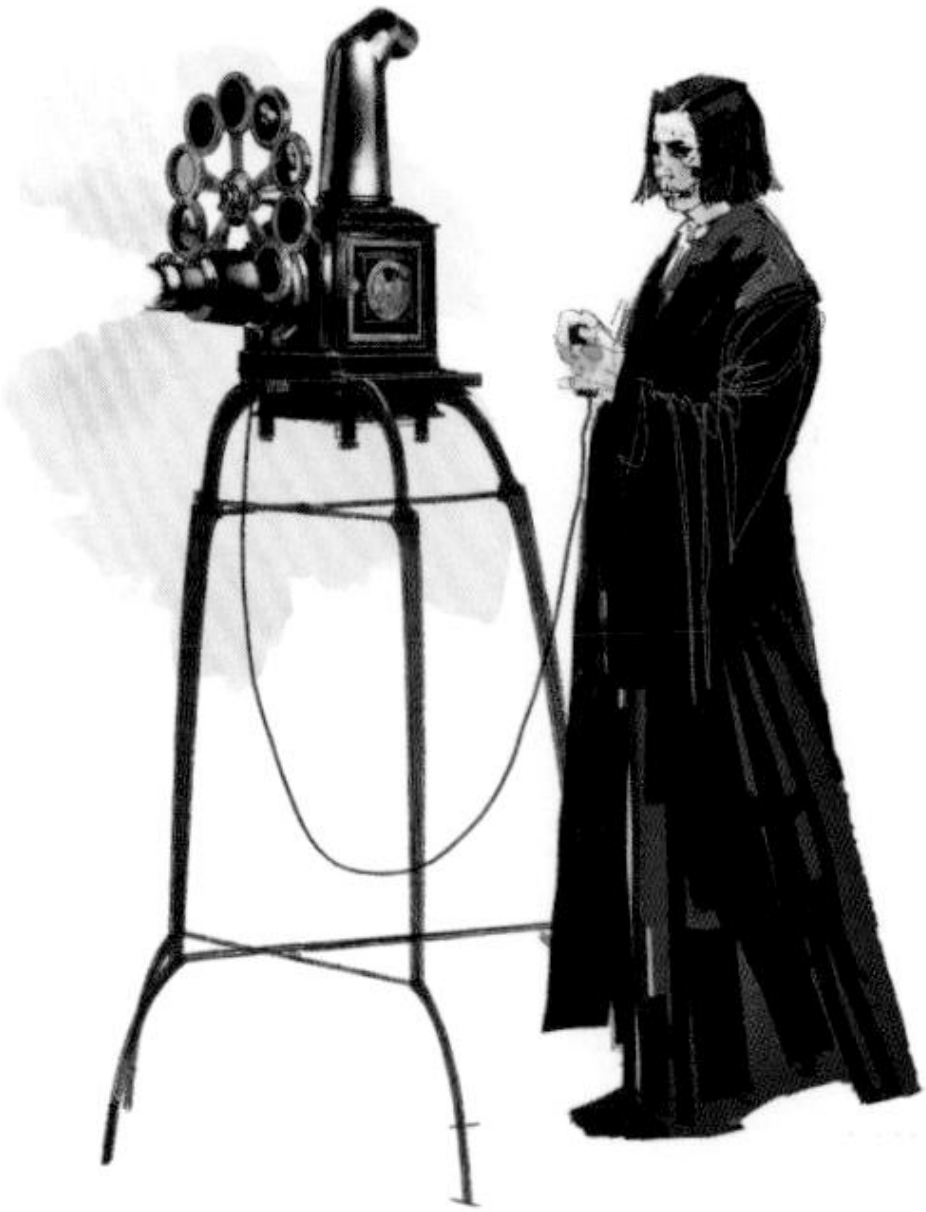

THESE PAGES: Professor Snape substitutes in the Defense Against the Dark Arts class when Professor Lupin is ill. These pages show the lantern projector he used to teach a lesson on werewolves. Art by Dermot Power.

THESE PAGES: In *Harry Potter and the Goblet of Fire*, Professor Moody keeps a large trunk in his office. Unknown to Harry, this trunk includes a chamber in

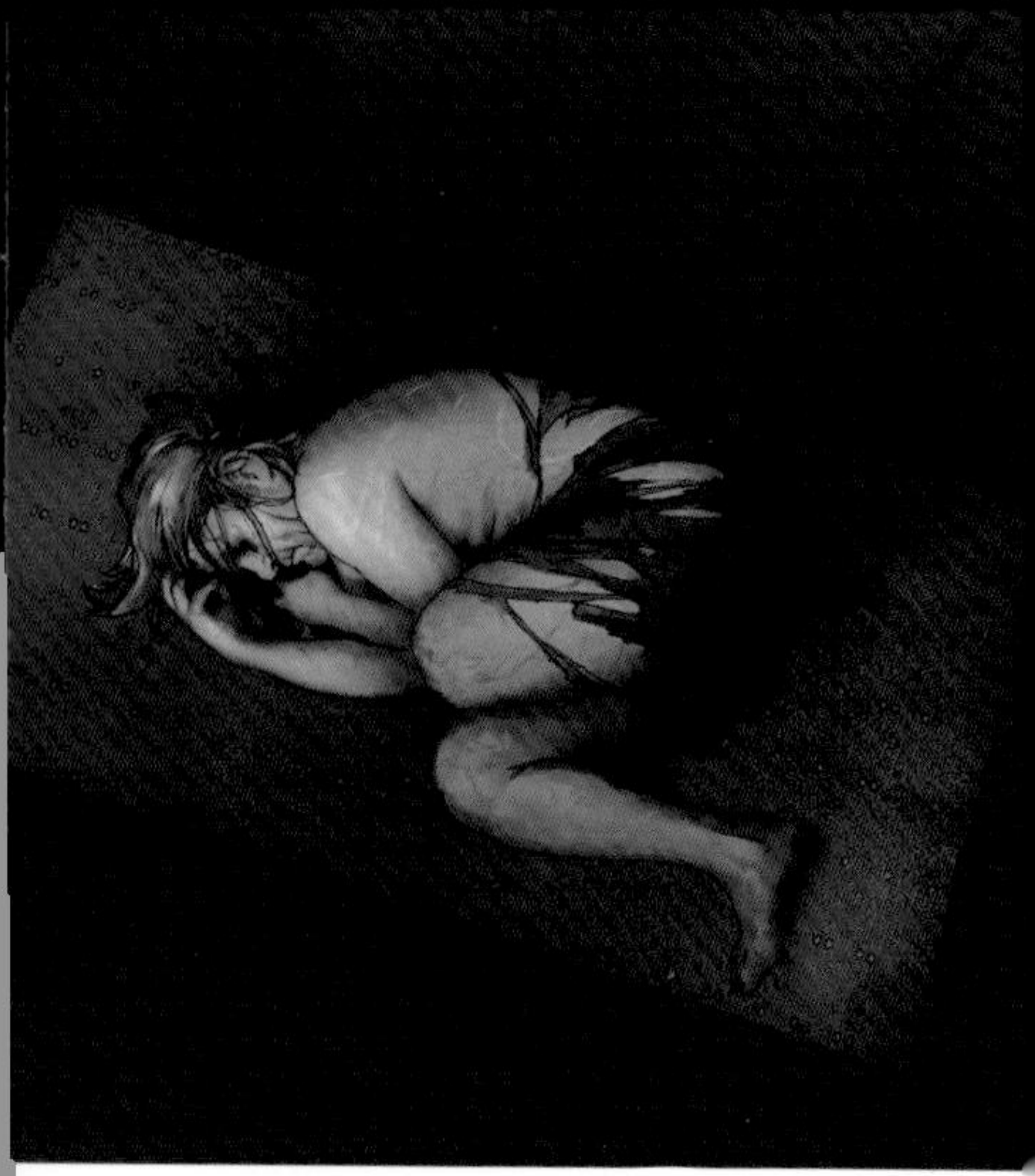

which the real "Mad-Eye" Moody is being kept while his imposter teaches at Hogwarts. Adam Brockbank illustrates this trunk with the captive Moody inside.

DIVINATION CLASSROOM

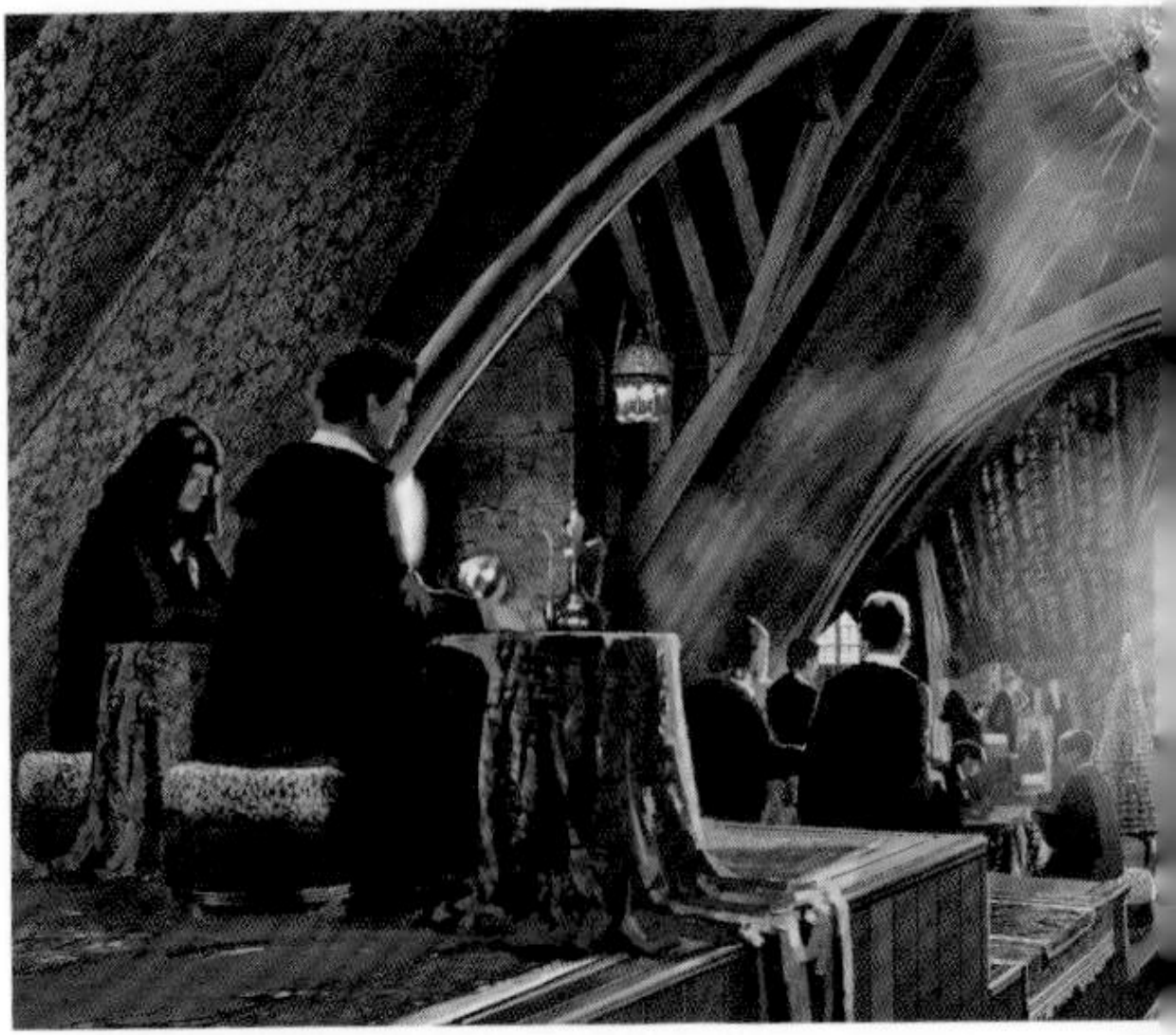

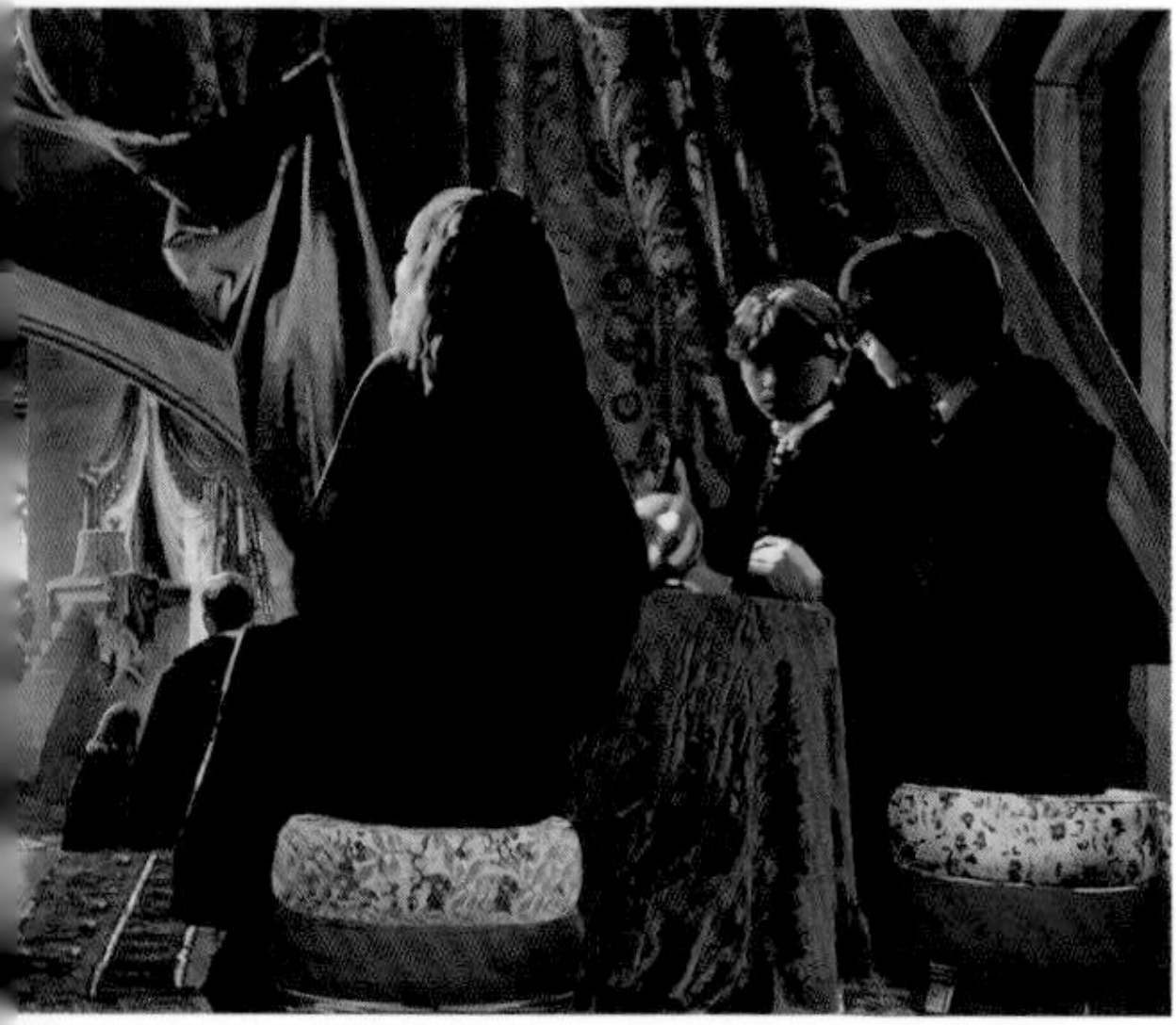

PAGES 154–159: Concept artist Andrew Williamson portrays Divination Professor Trelawany's attic classroom as lavishly draped in exotic, jewel-toned fabrics for *Harry Potter and the Prisoner of Azkaban*.

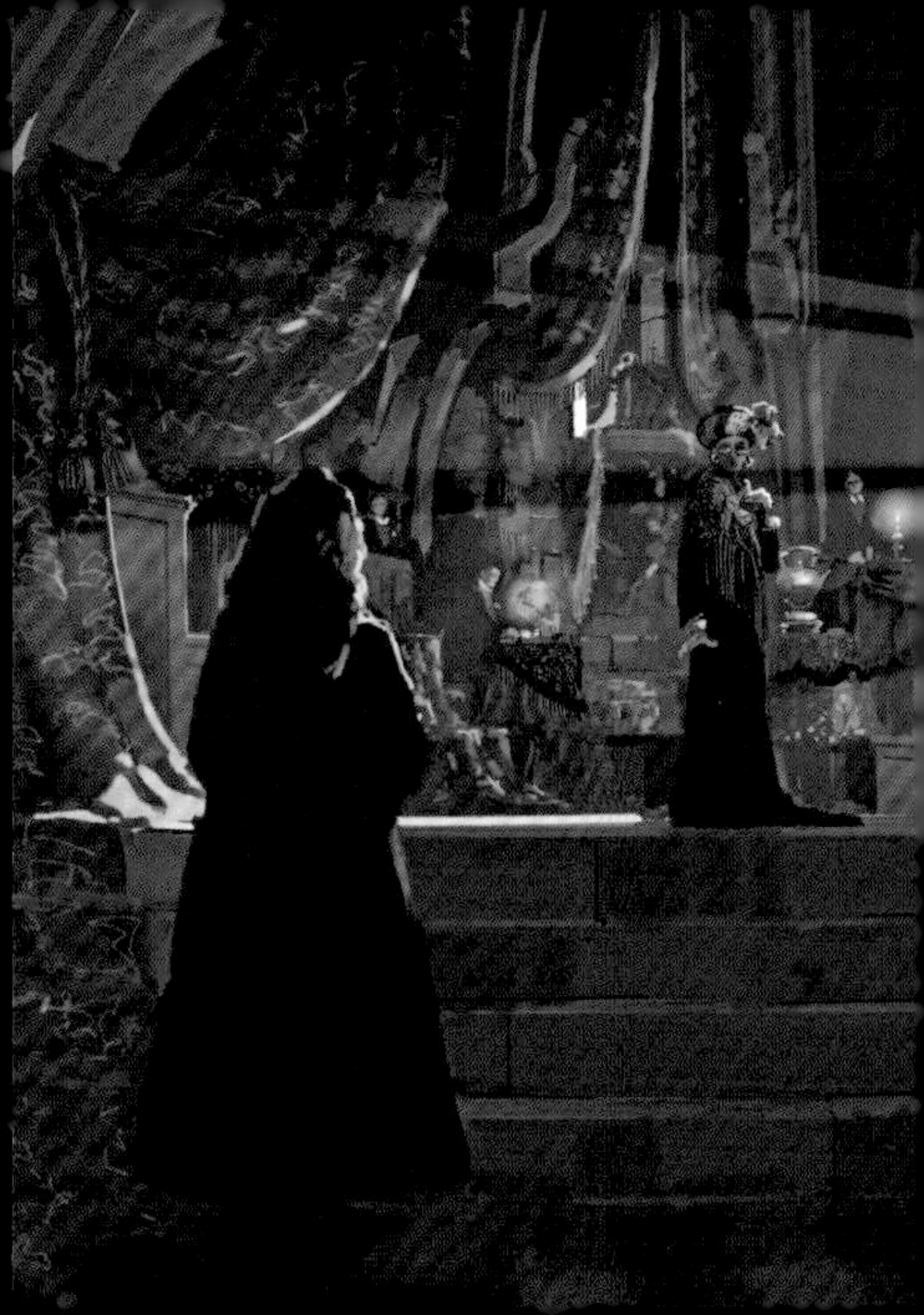

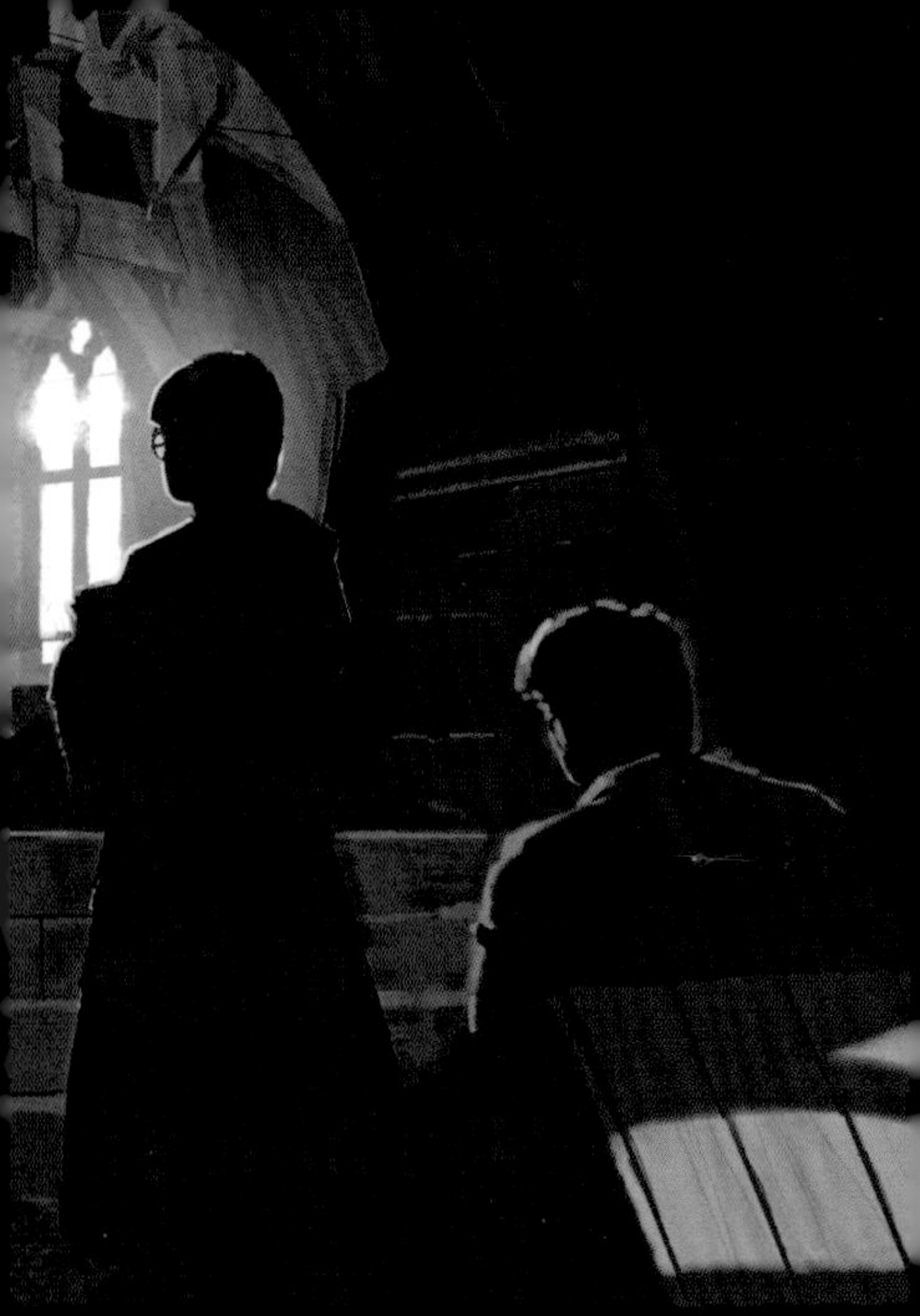

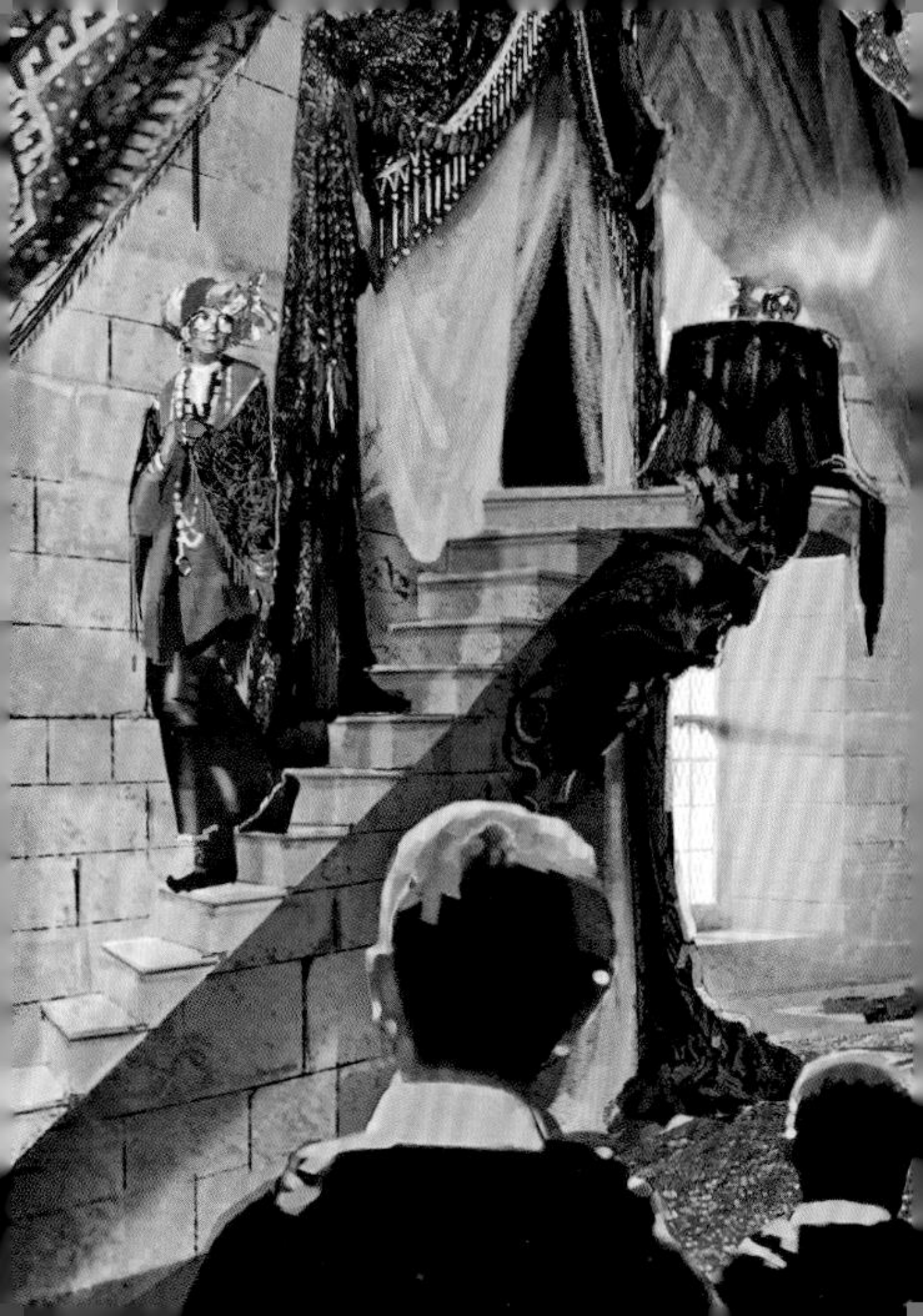

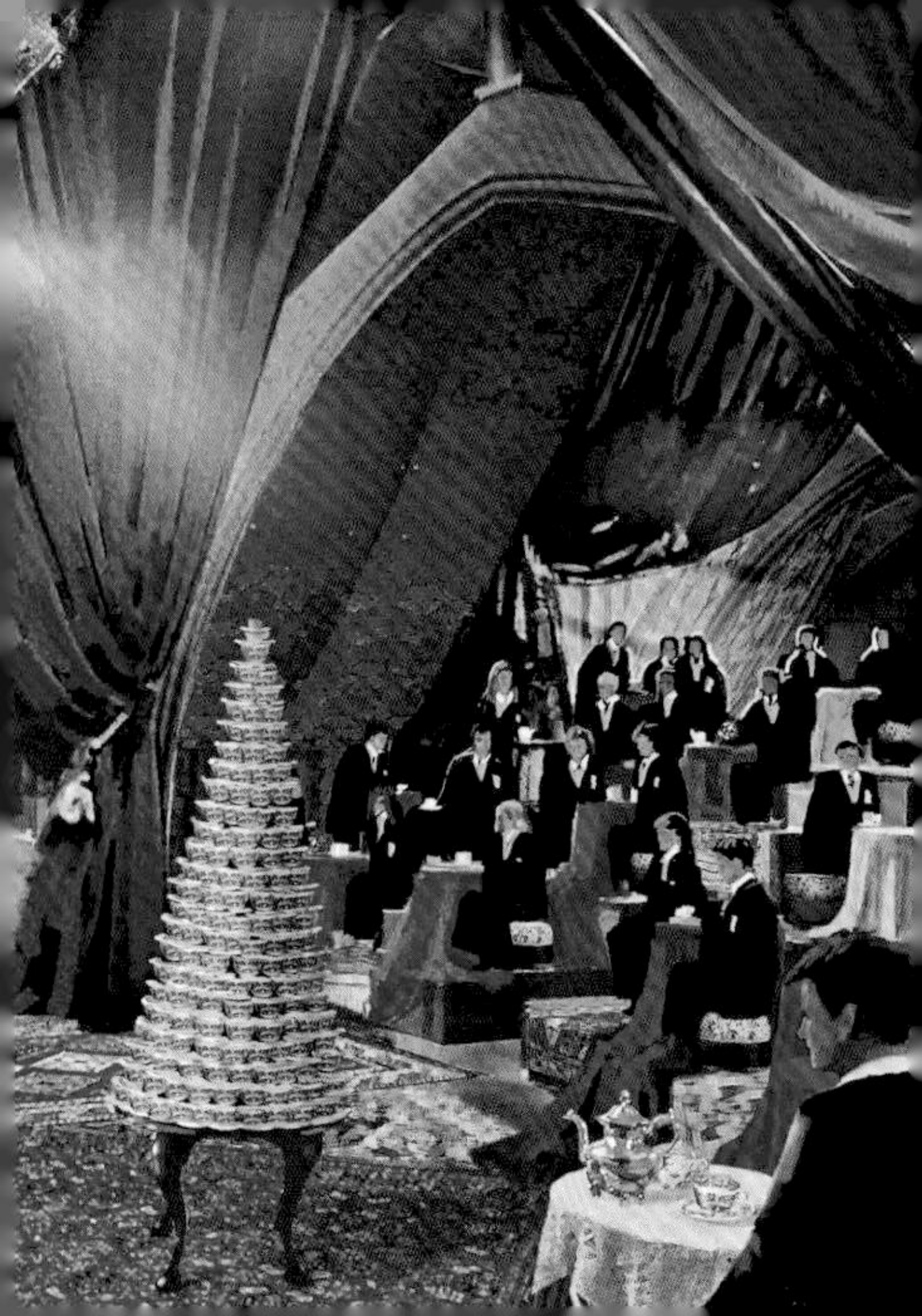

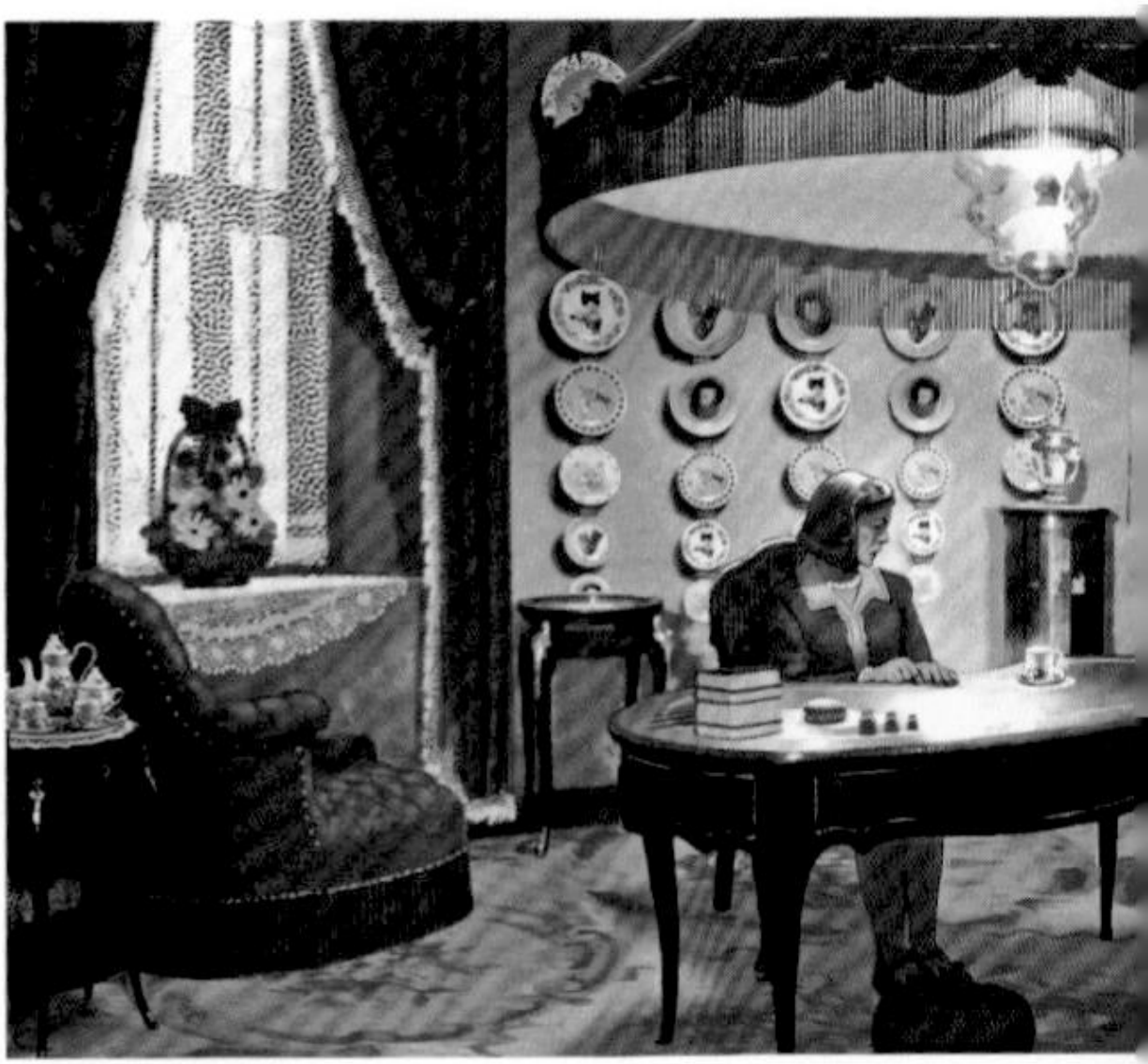

PROFESSOR UMBRIDGE'S OFFICE

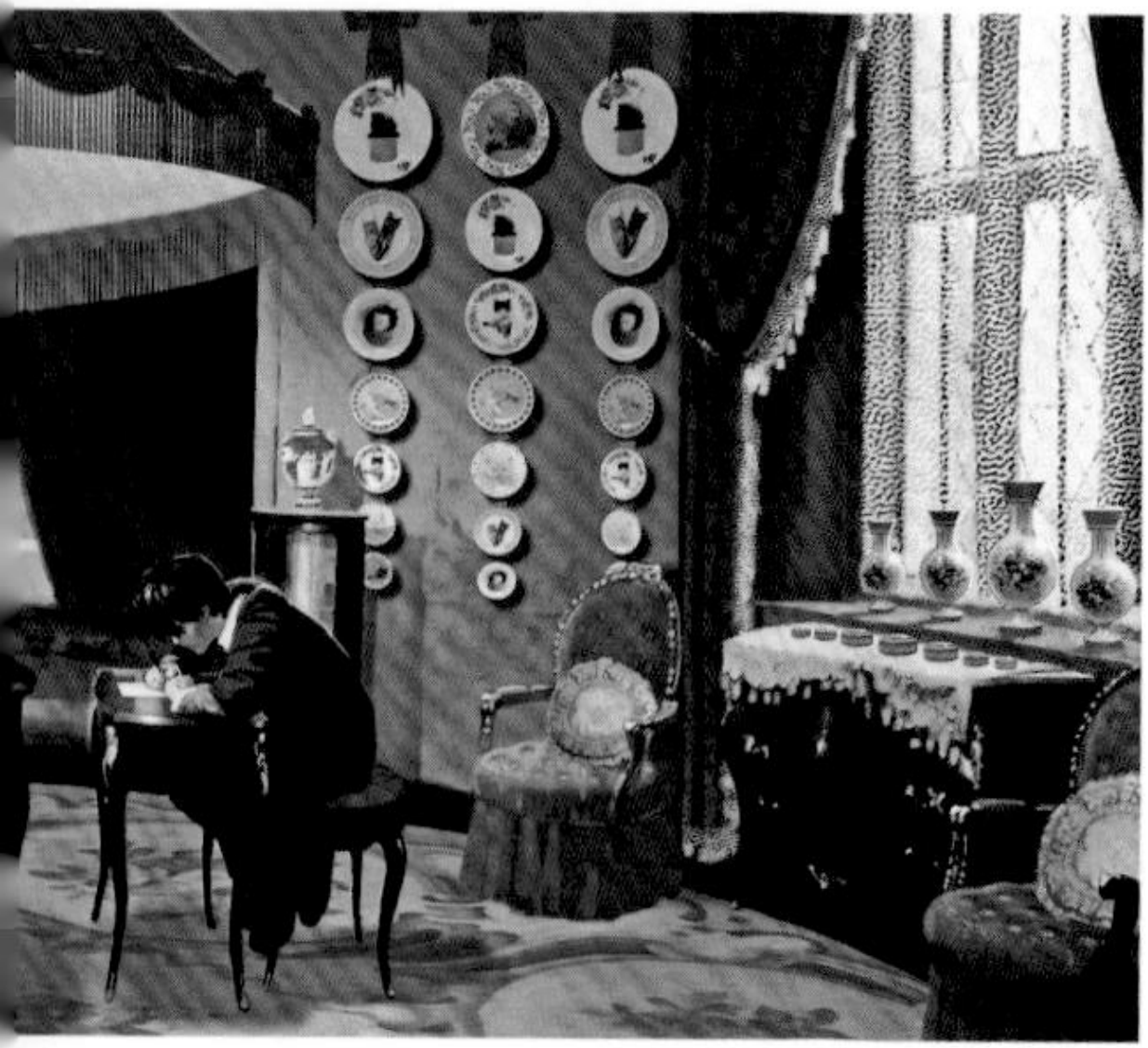

THESE PAGES: Professor Dolores Umbridge oversees Harry's detention in her office in *Harry Potter and the Order of the Phoenix*. A study in pink by Adam Brockbank.

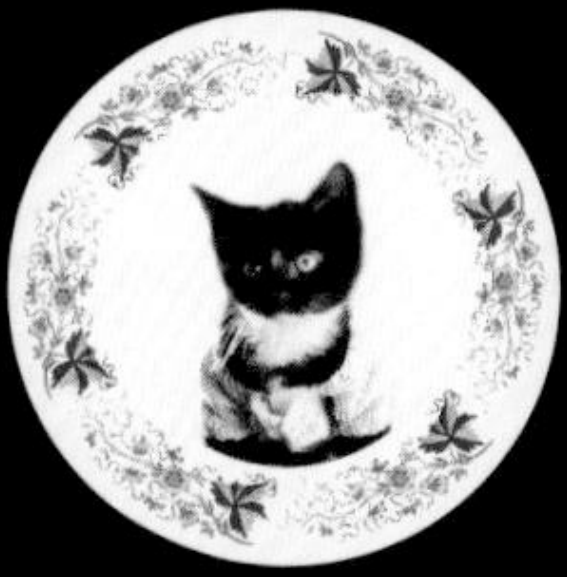

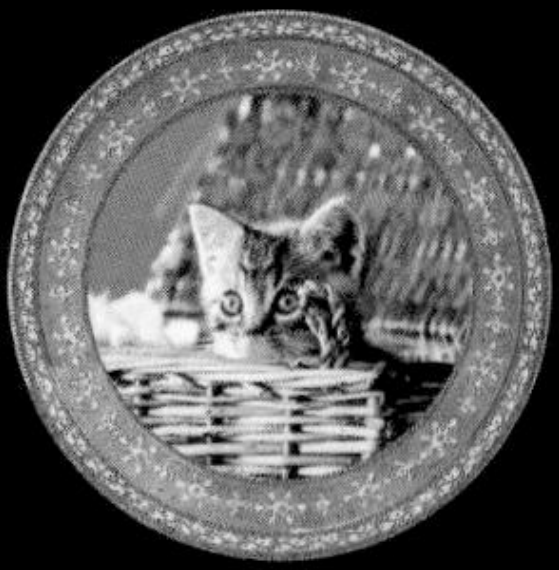

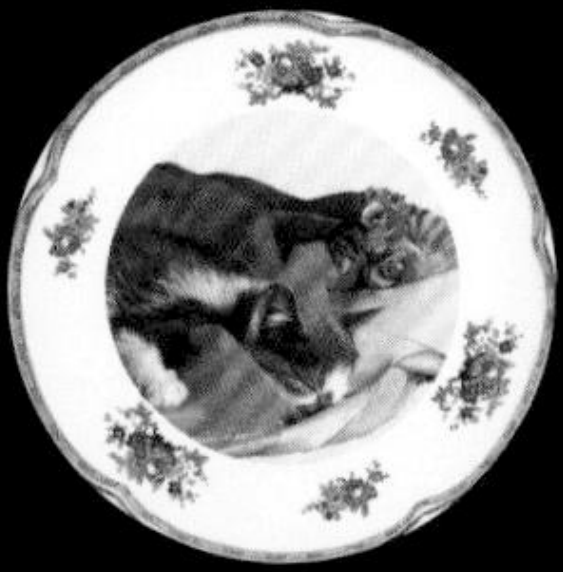

THESE PAGES: A selection of cat plates adorning Professor Umbridge's office, for which forty different cats and kittens modeled. Digitally composited by Hattie Storey.

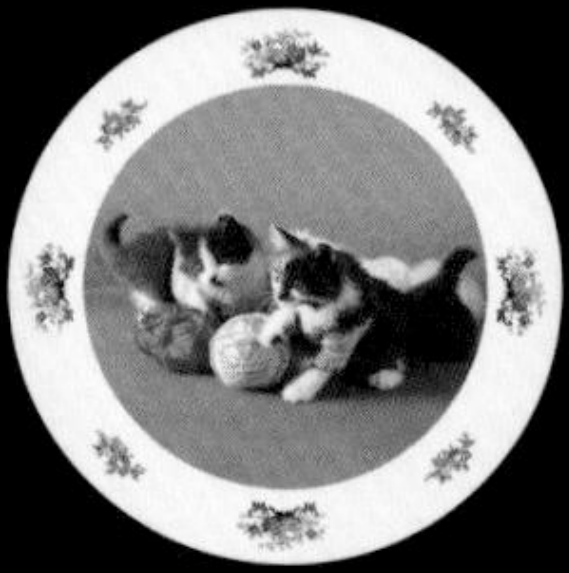

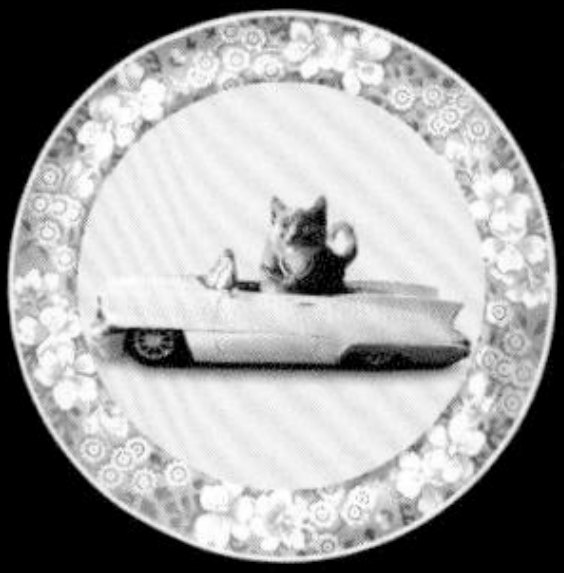

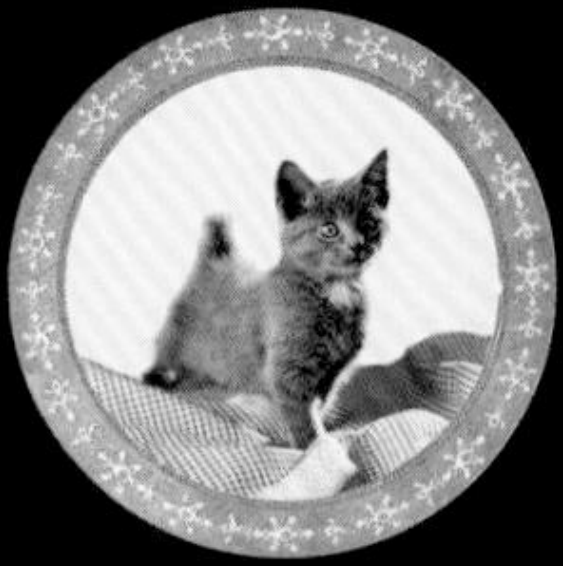

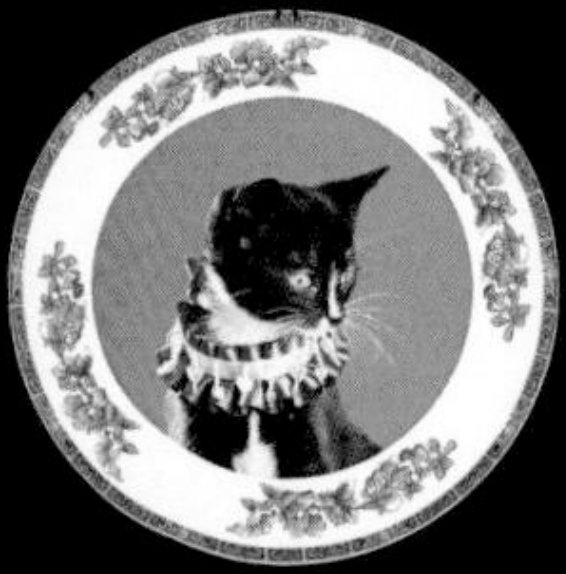

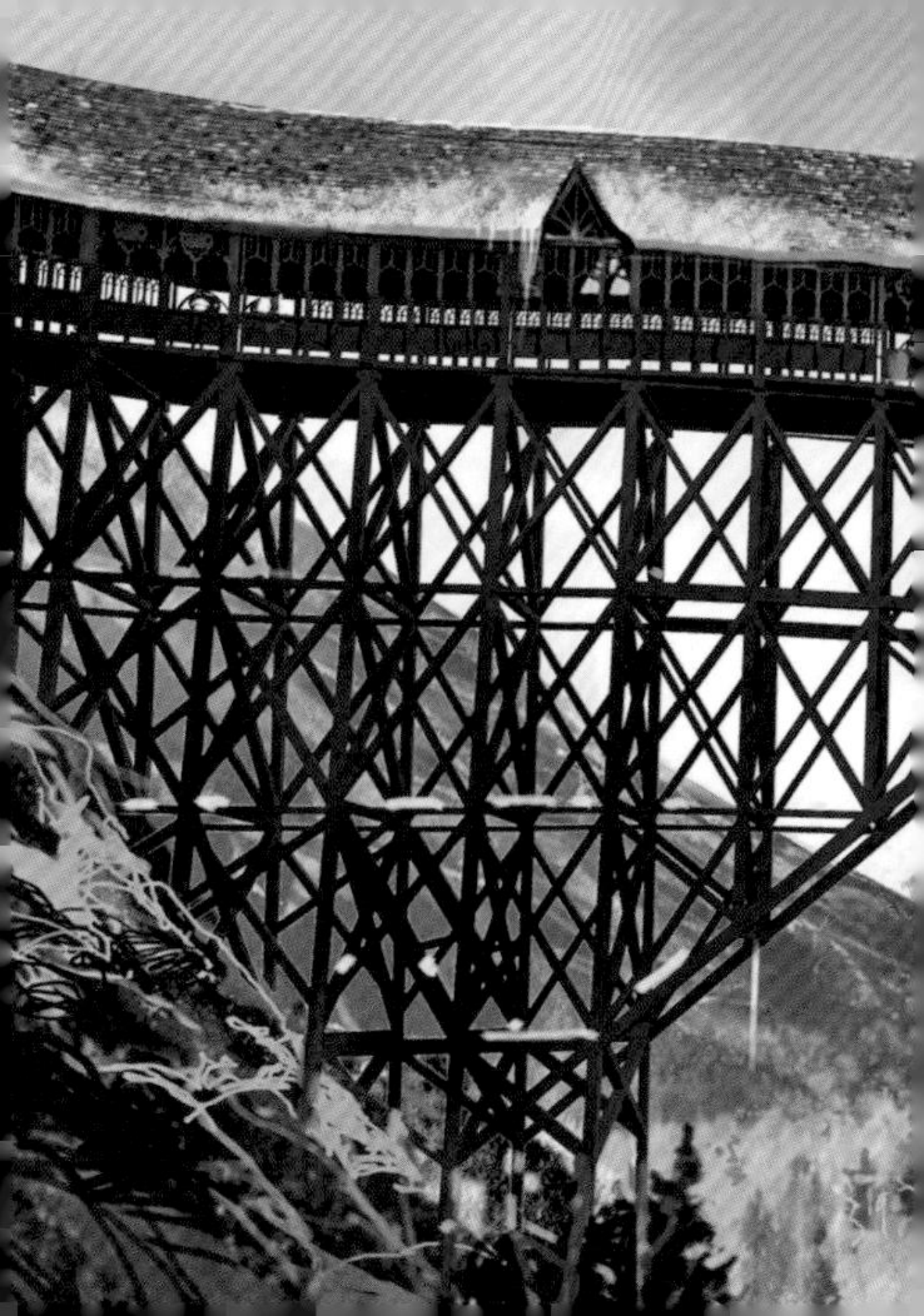

HOGWARTS GROUNDS

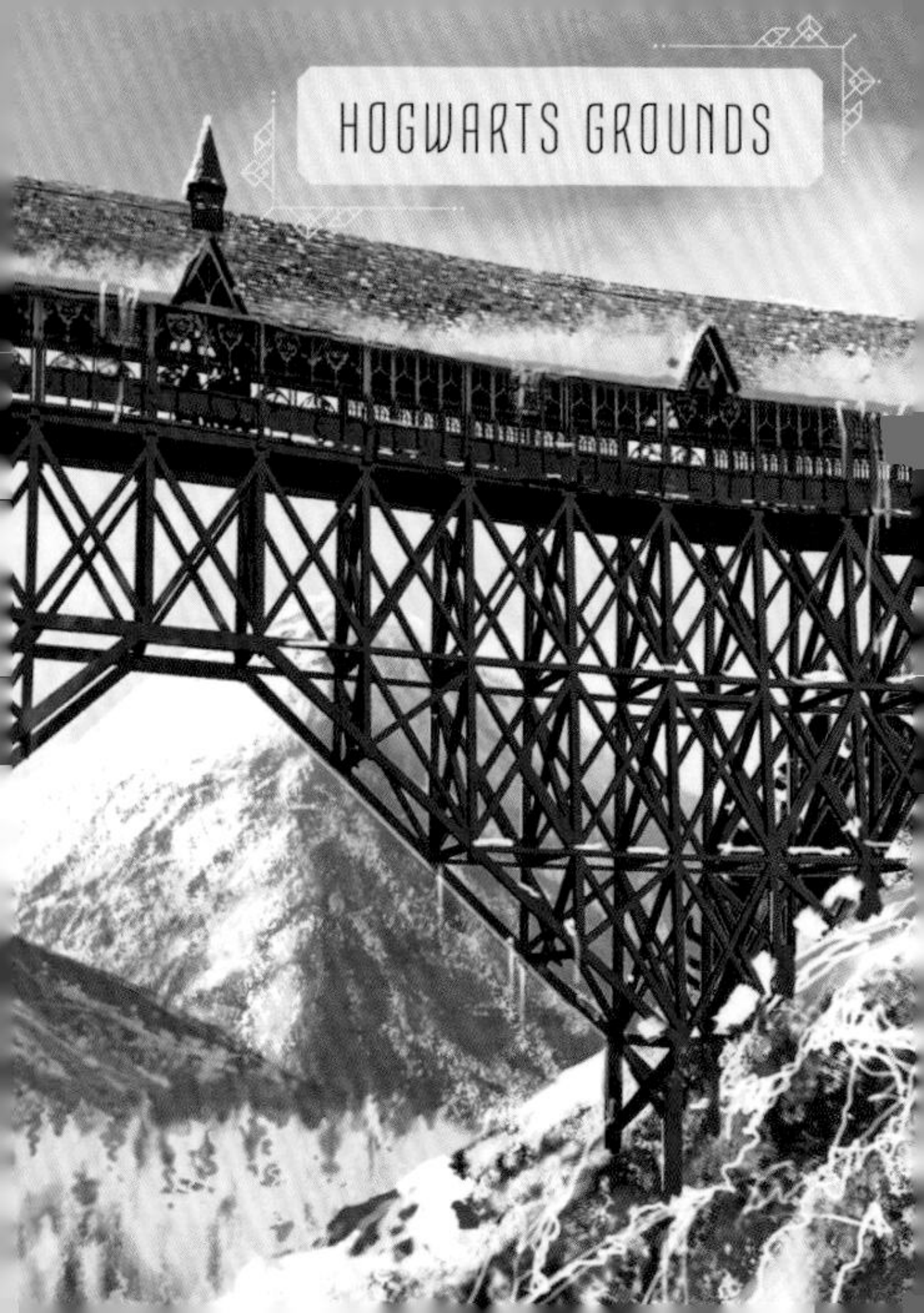

THE BRIDGE

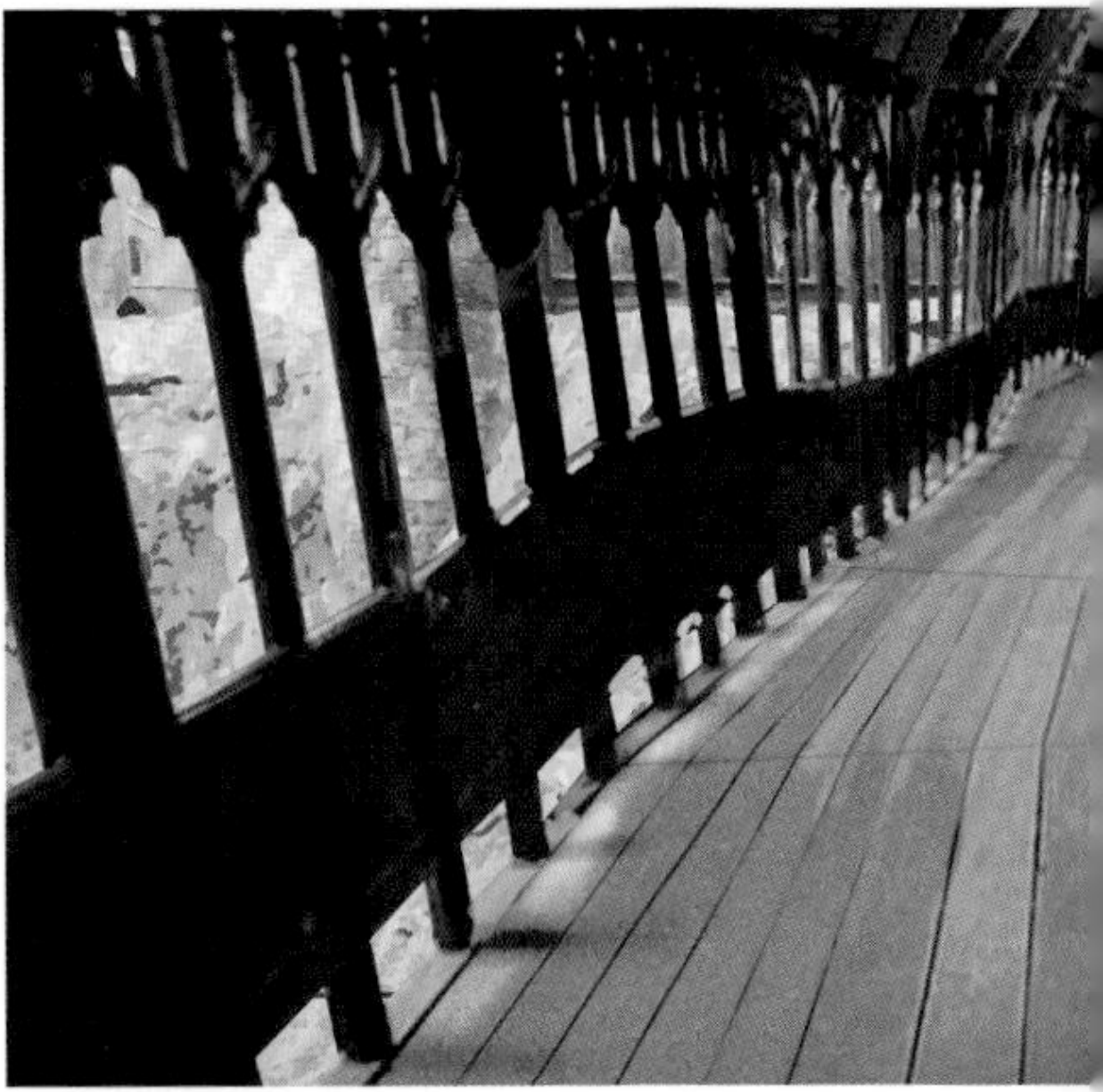

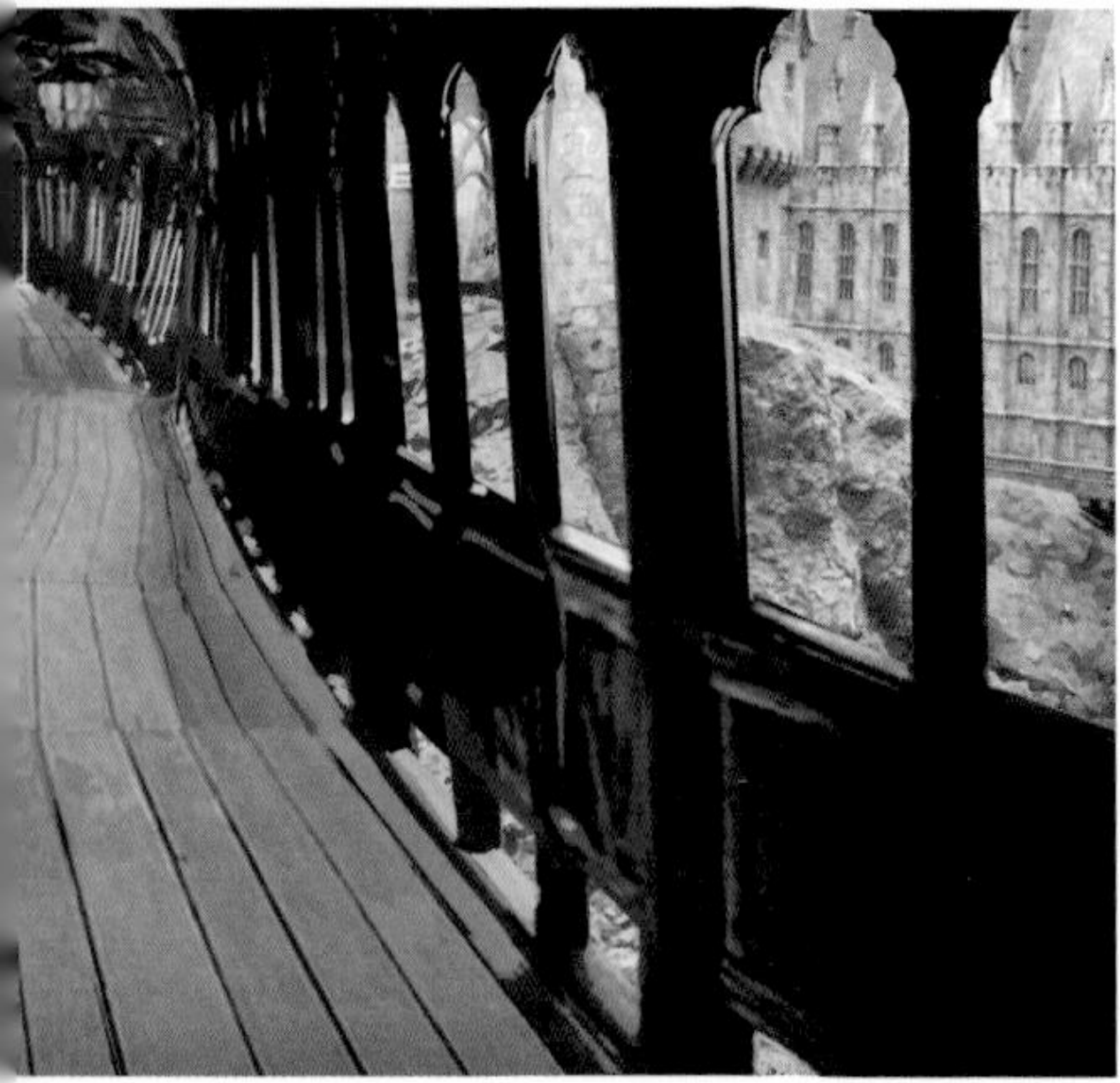

PAGES 164–167: Art by Andrew Williamson of the covered bridge and views from inside it created for *Harry Potter and the Order of the Phoenix*.

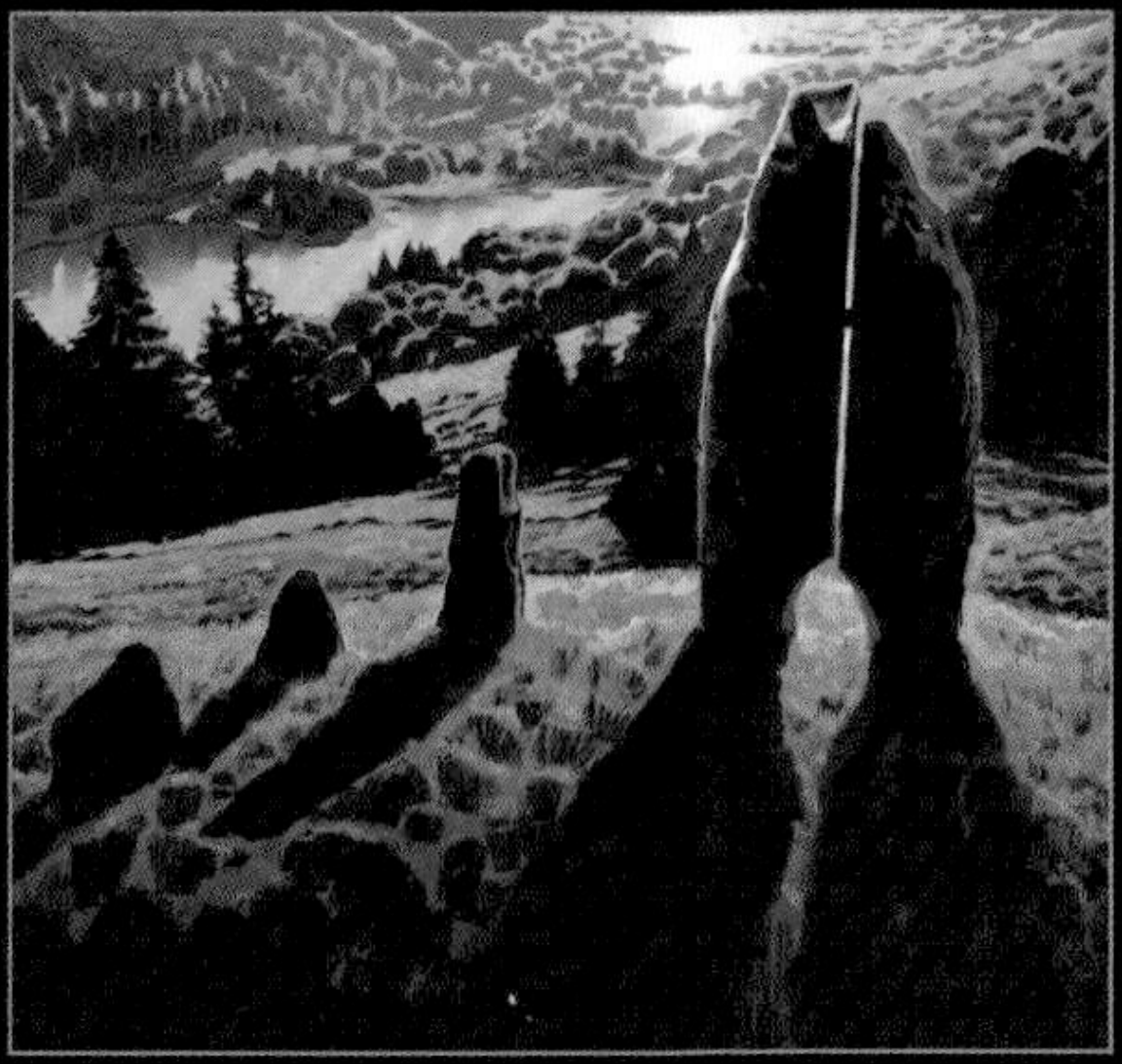

THE GATEHOUSE SUNDIAL

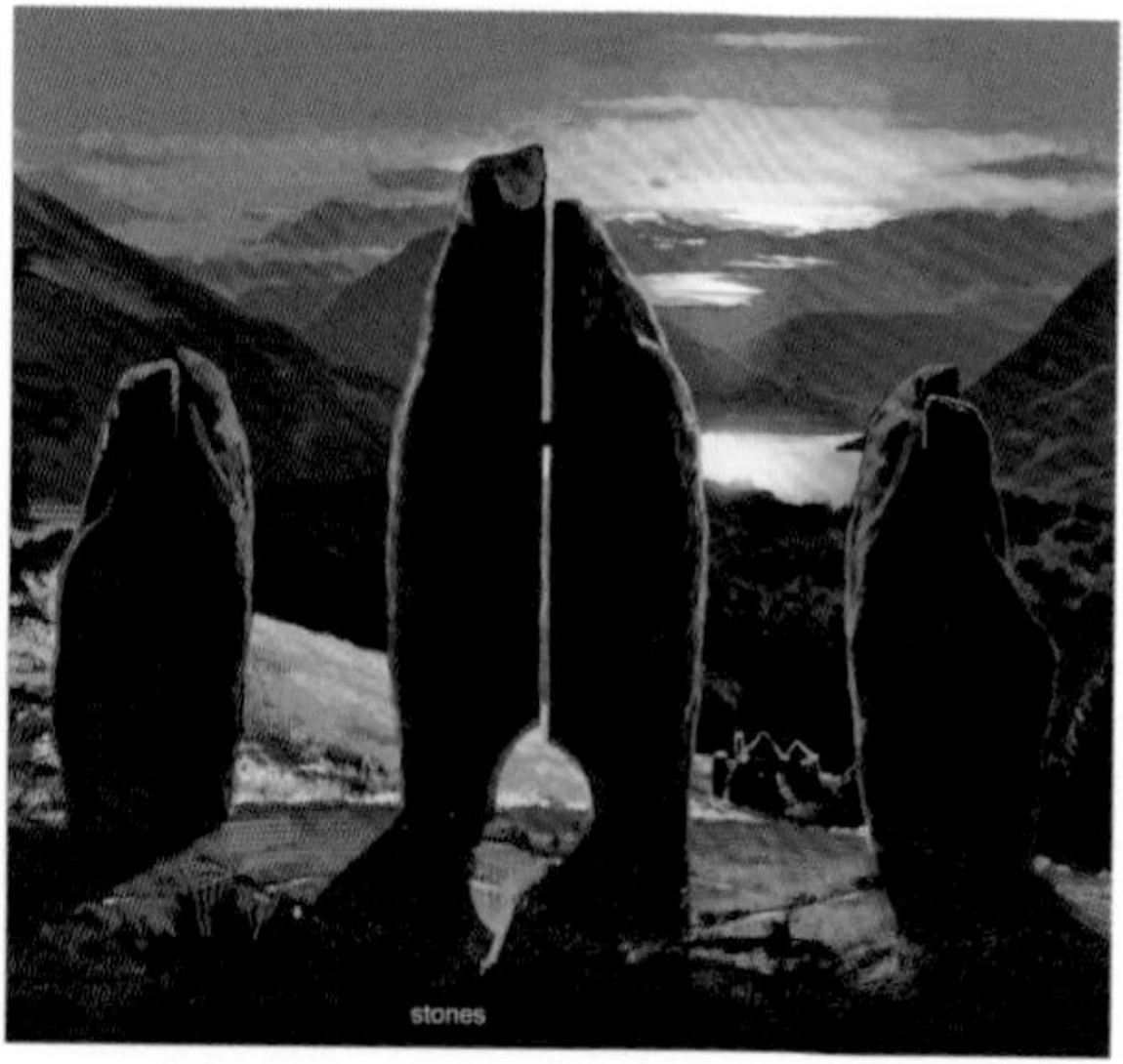

THESE PAGES: Views of the Gatehouse sundial, developed by Adam Brockbank for *Harry Potter and the Order of the Phoenix*.

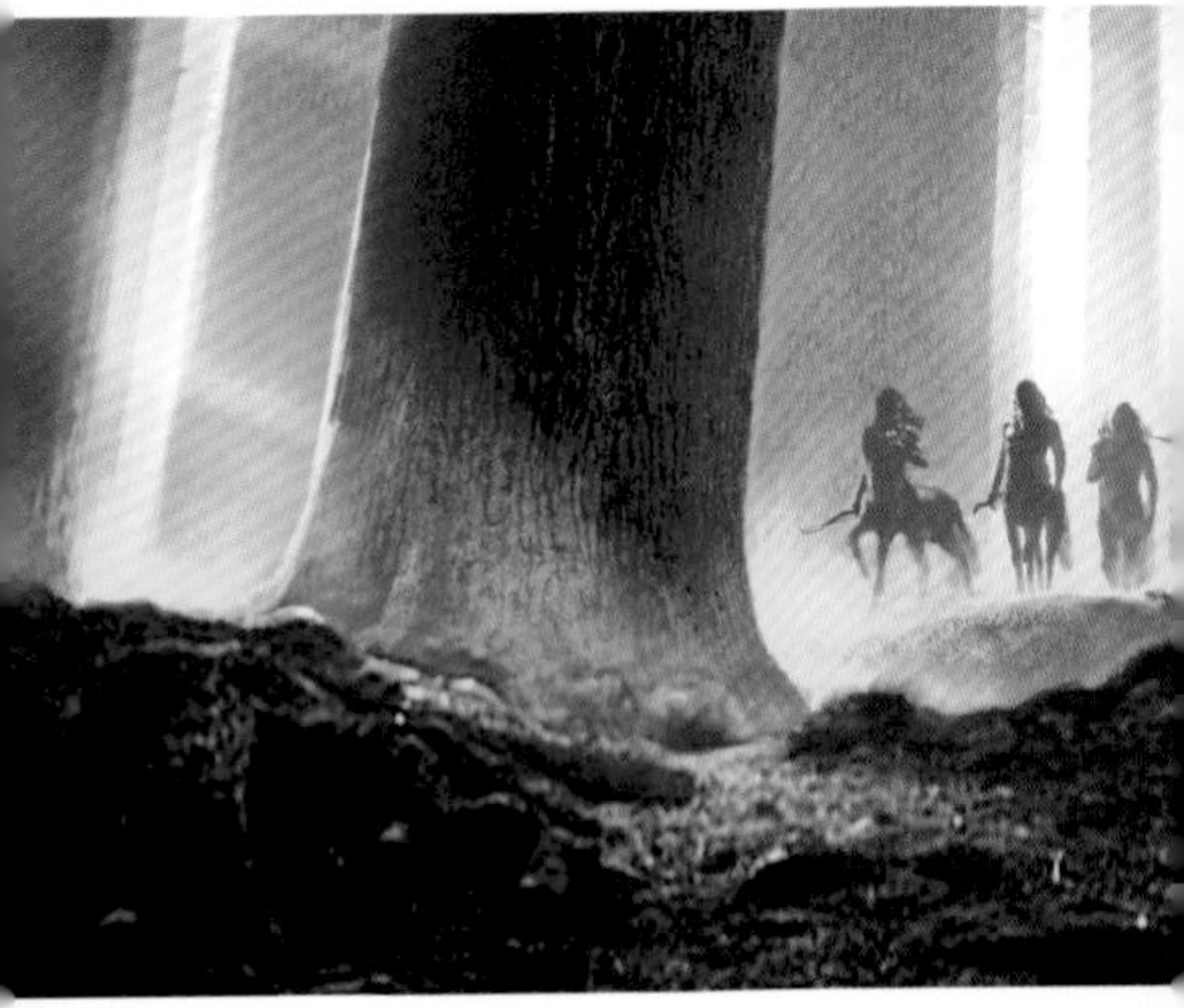

THE FORBIDDEN FOREST

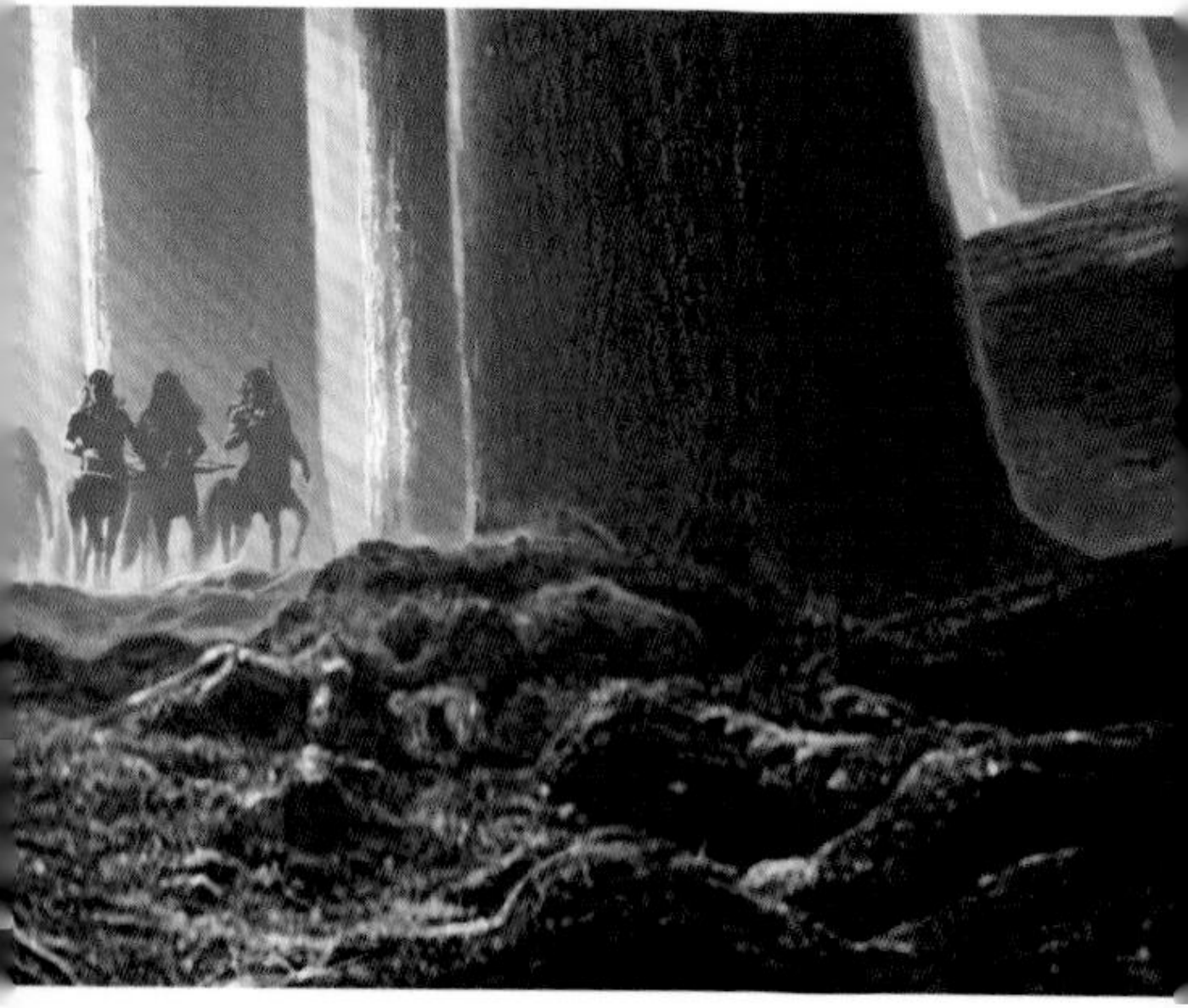

THESE PAGES: Centaurs amass in the Forbidden Forest in *Harry Potter and the Order of the Phoenix* by Adam Brockbank.

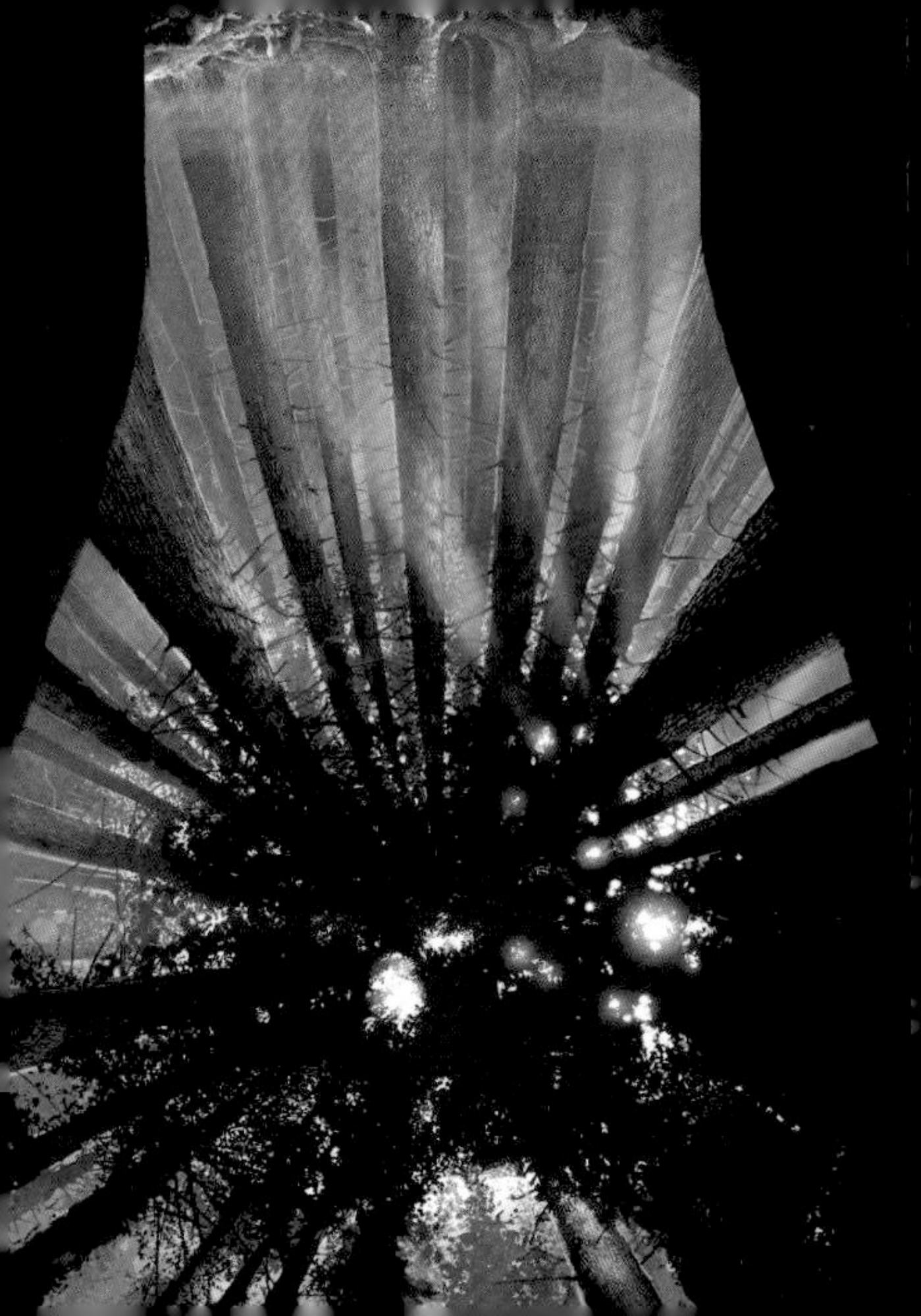

THESE PAGES: Views upward to the canopy of the Forbidden Forest by Andrew Williamson for *Harry Potter and the Order of the Phoenix* showcase shadows and beams of light.

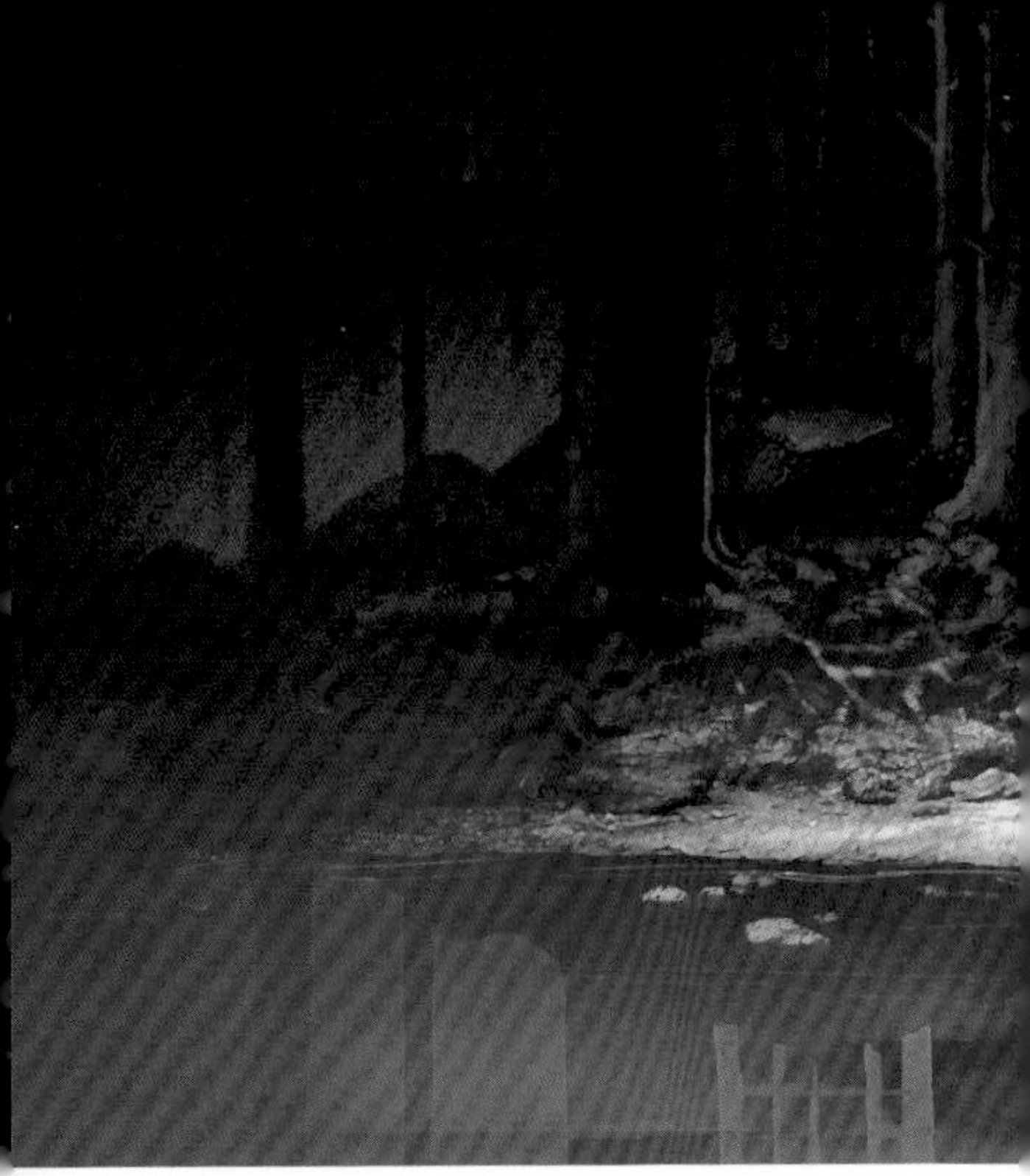

THESE PAGES: Adam Brockbank depicts the scene where Harry finds Sirius at the edge of the

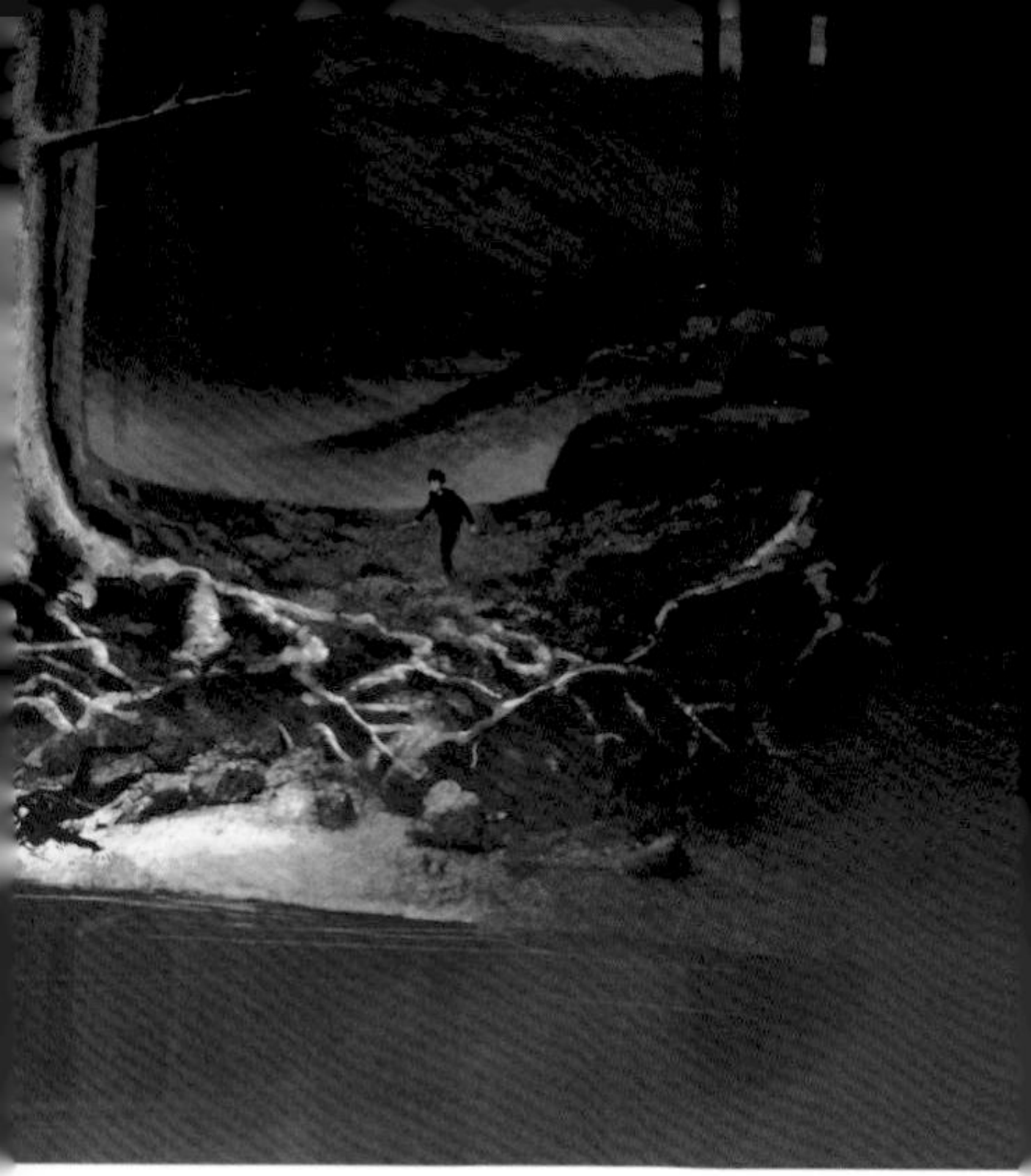

lake in the Forbidden Forest in *Harry Potter and the Prisoner of Azkaban*.

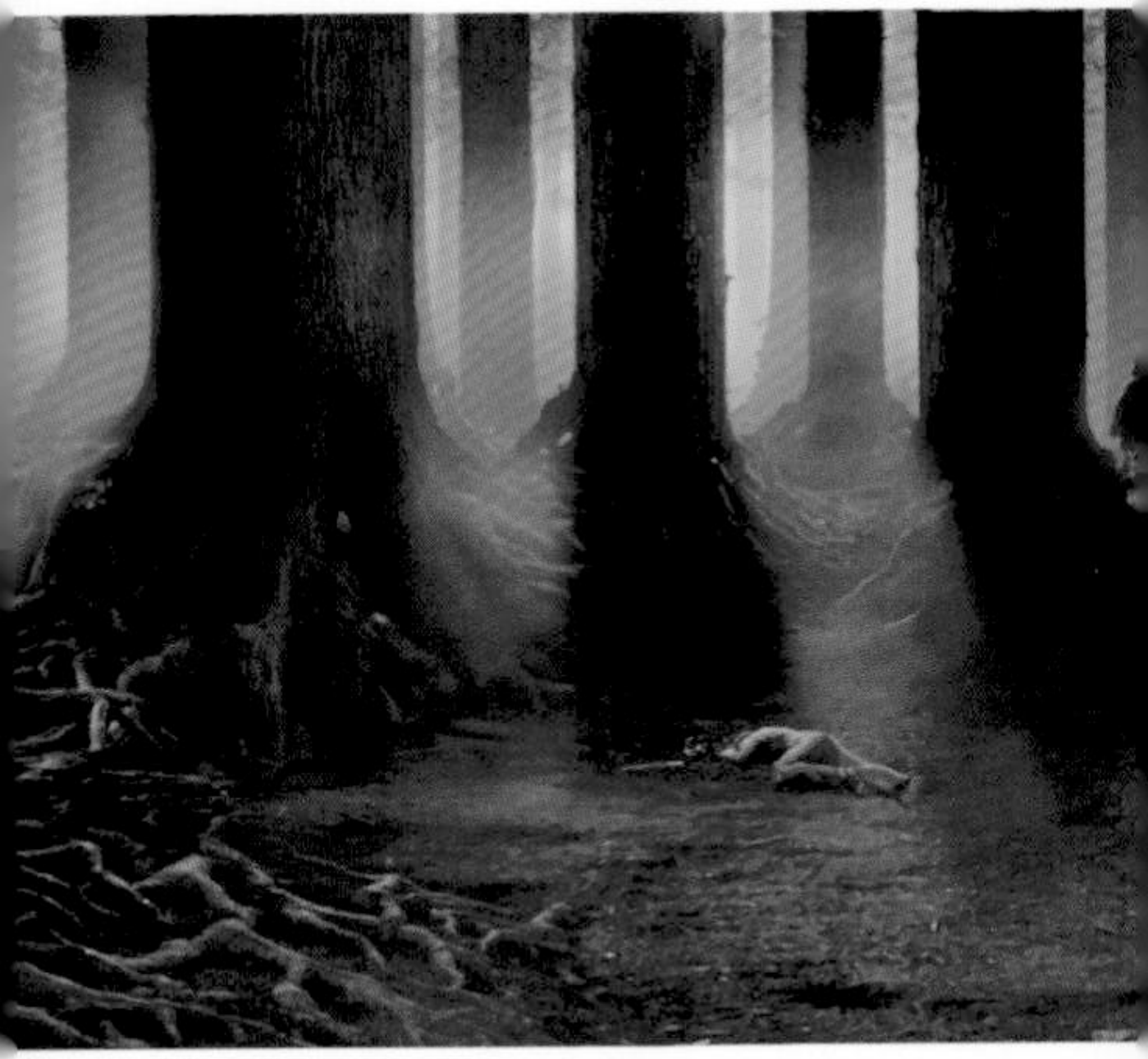

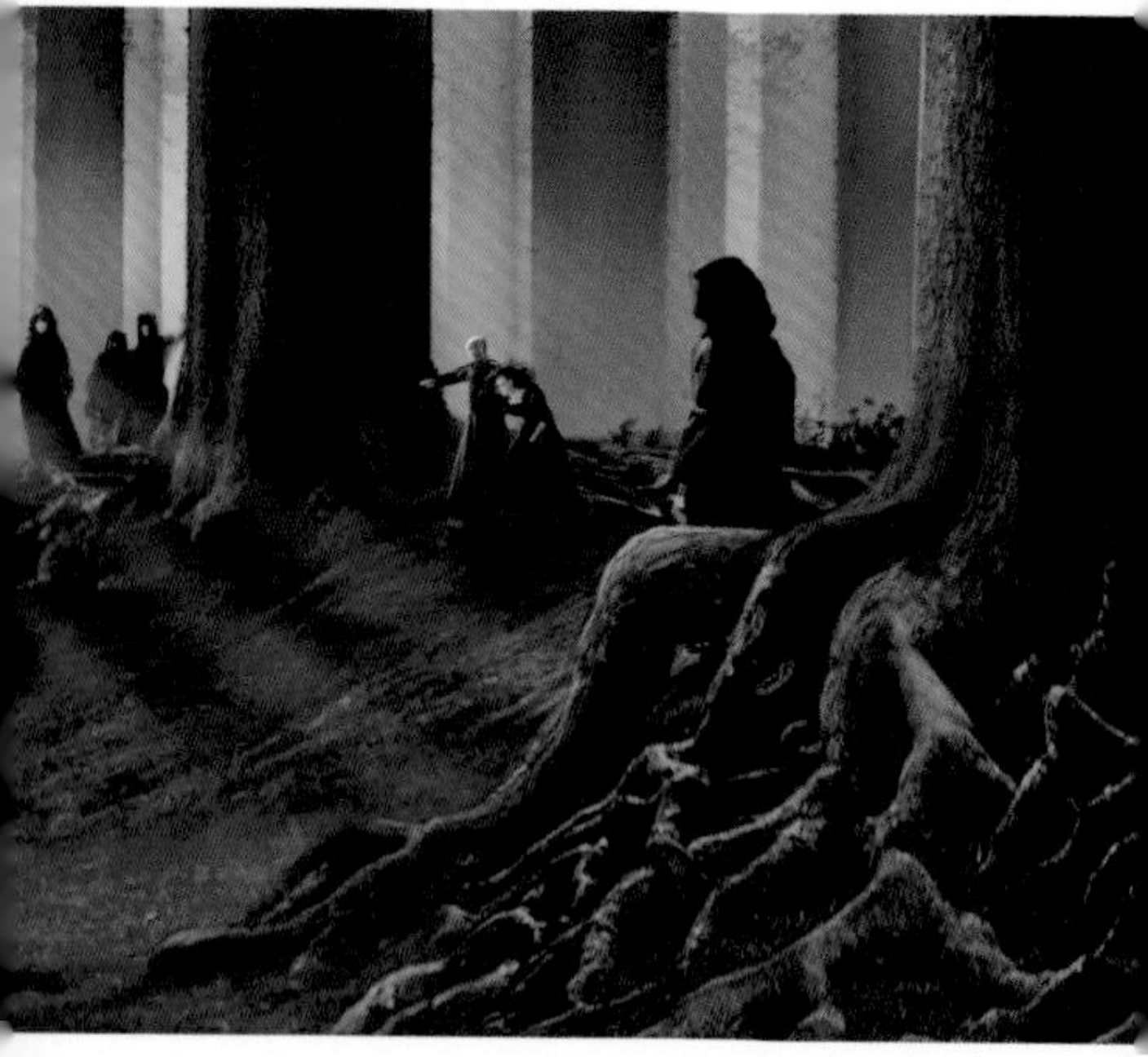

THESE PAGES: Voldemort and his Death Eaters surround Harry's fallen body in *Harry Potter and the Deathly Hallows – Part 2* after the Dark Lord casts the Killing Curse at him. Art by Andrew Williamson.

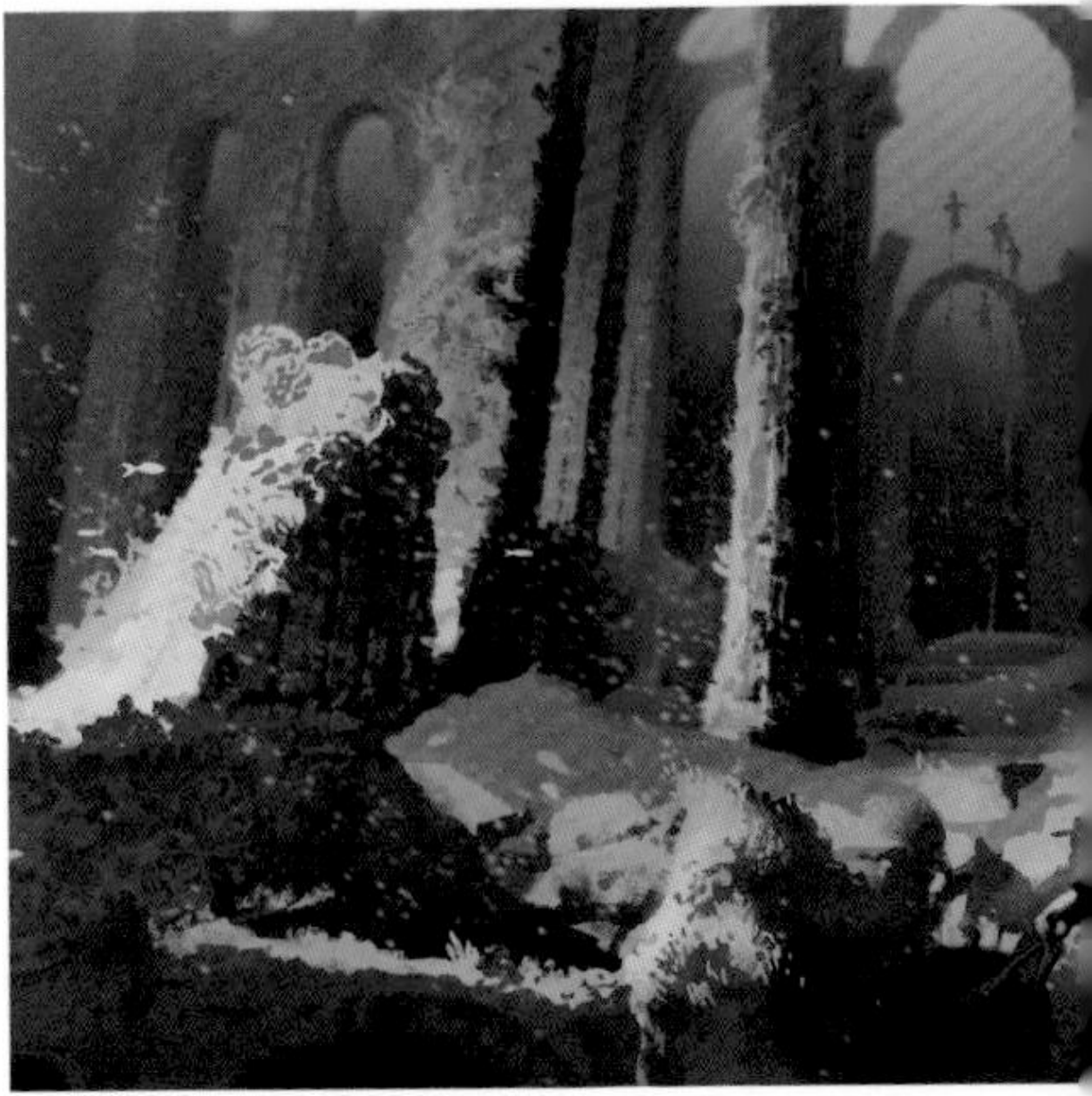

PAGES 178–183: Adam Brockbank's concept art of Harry and Fleur Delacour, the Beauxbatons champion, swimming past ruins and kelp during

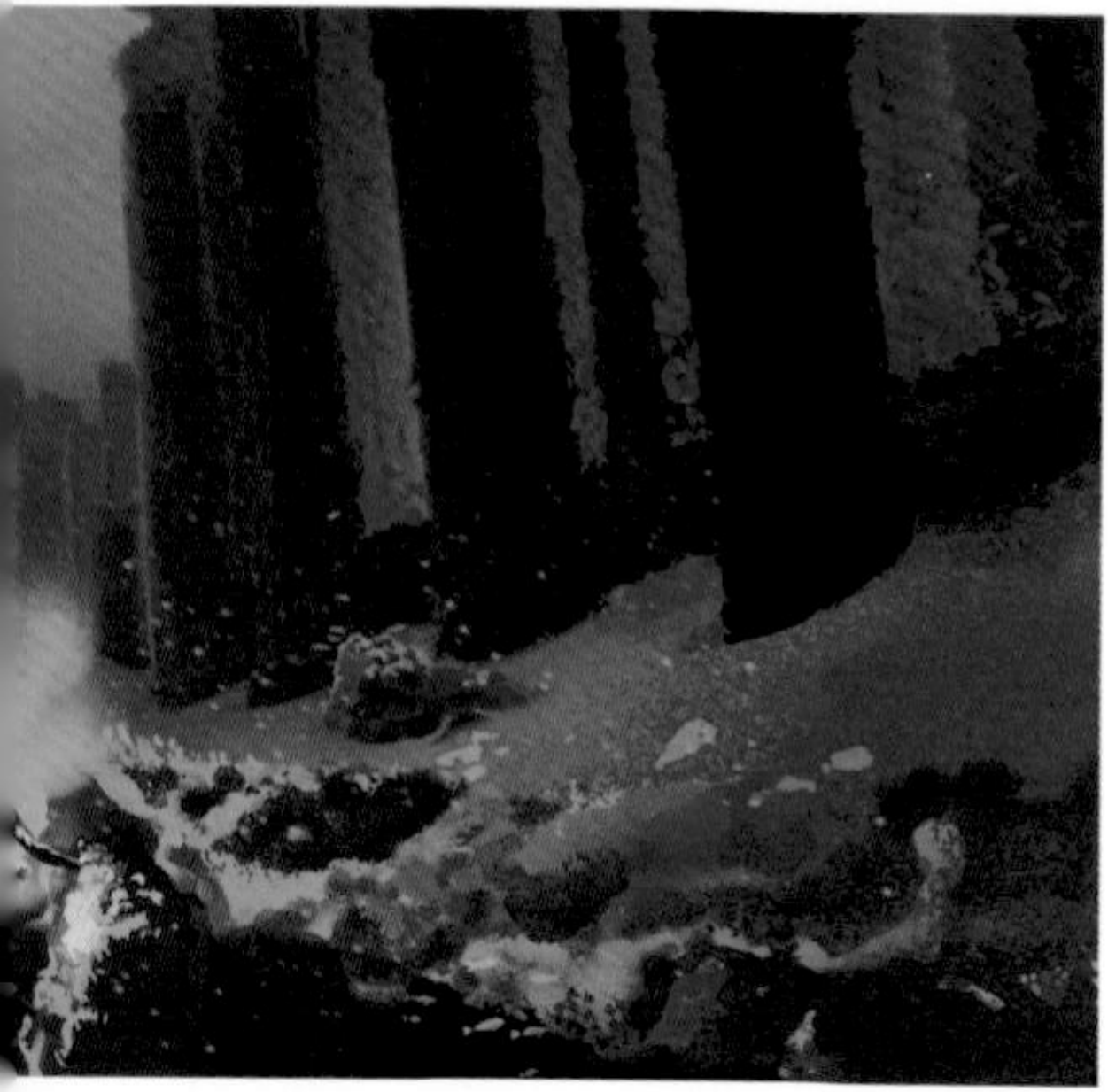

the second task of the Triwizard Tournament in *Harry Potter and the Goblet of Fire*.

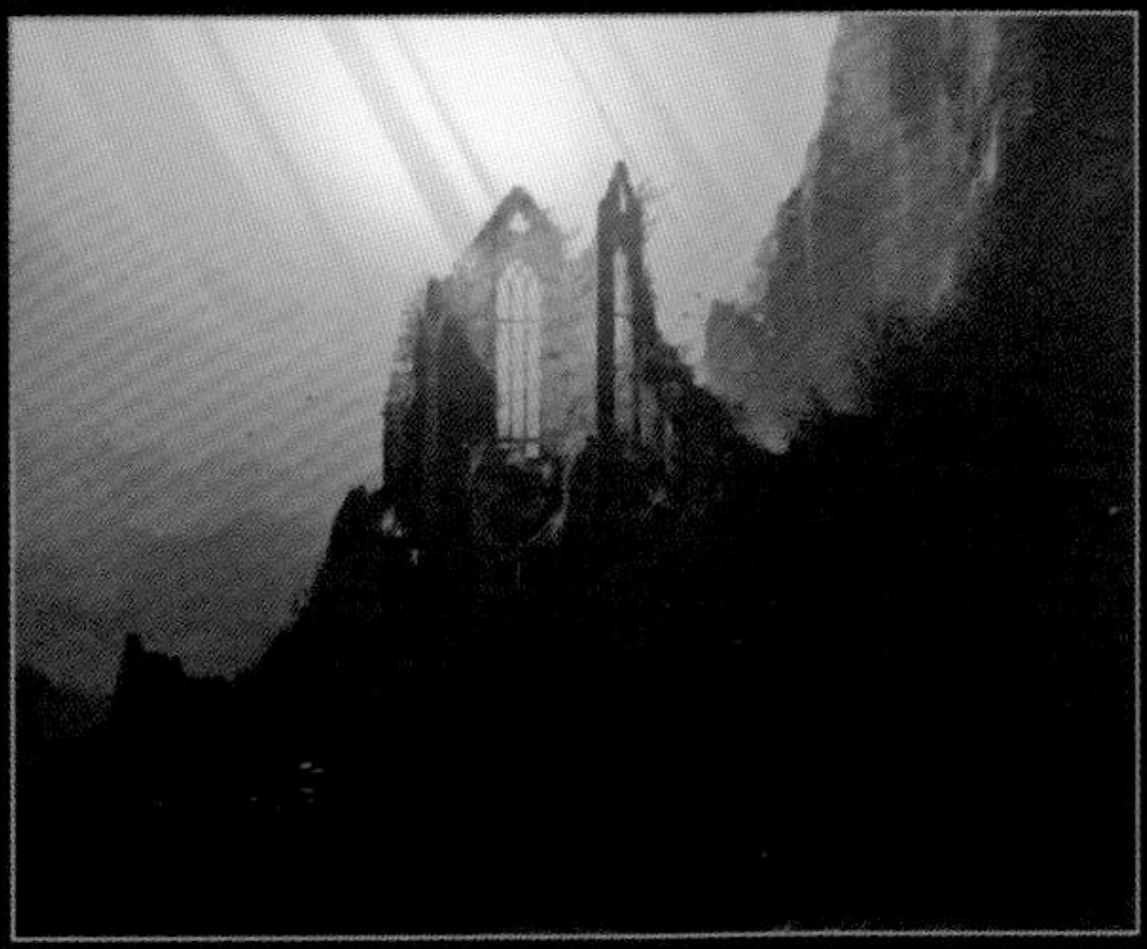

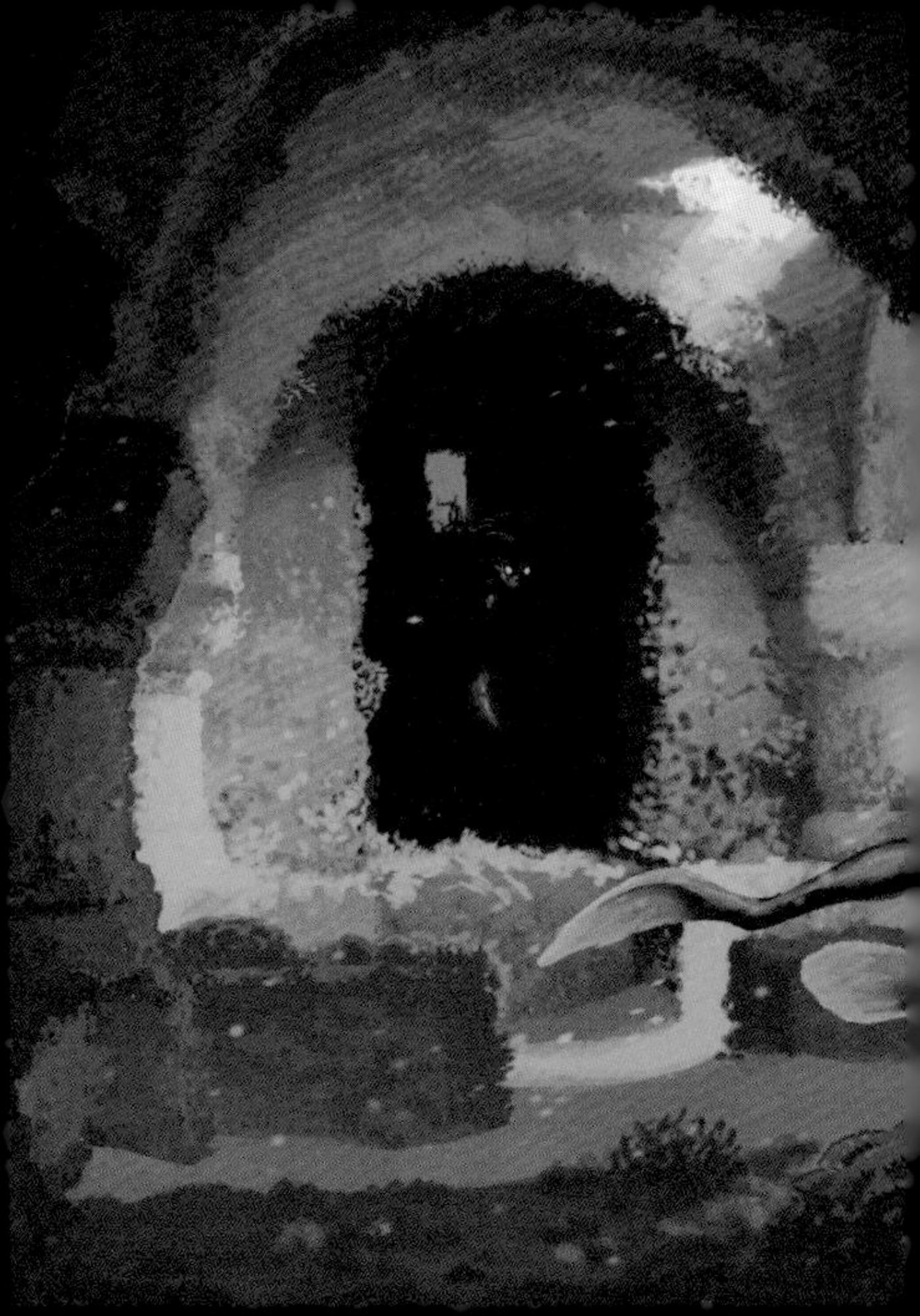

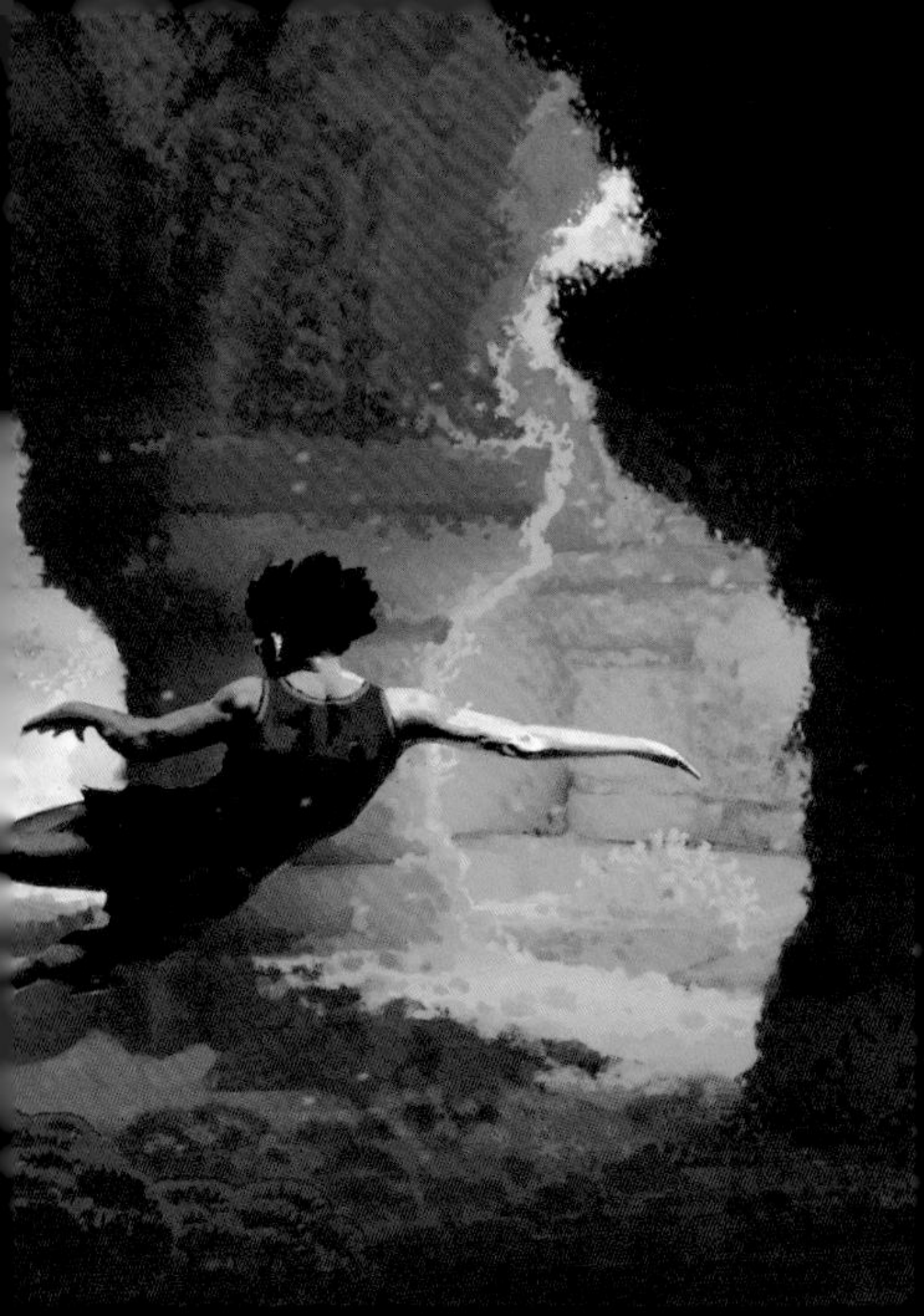

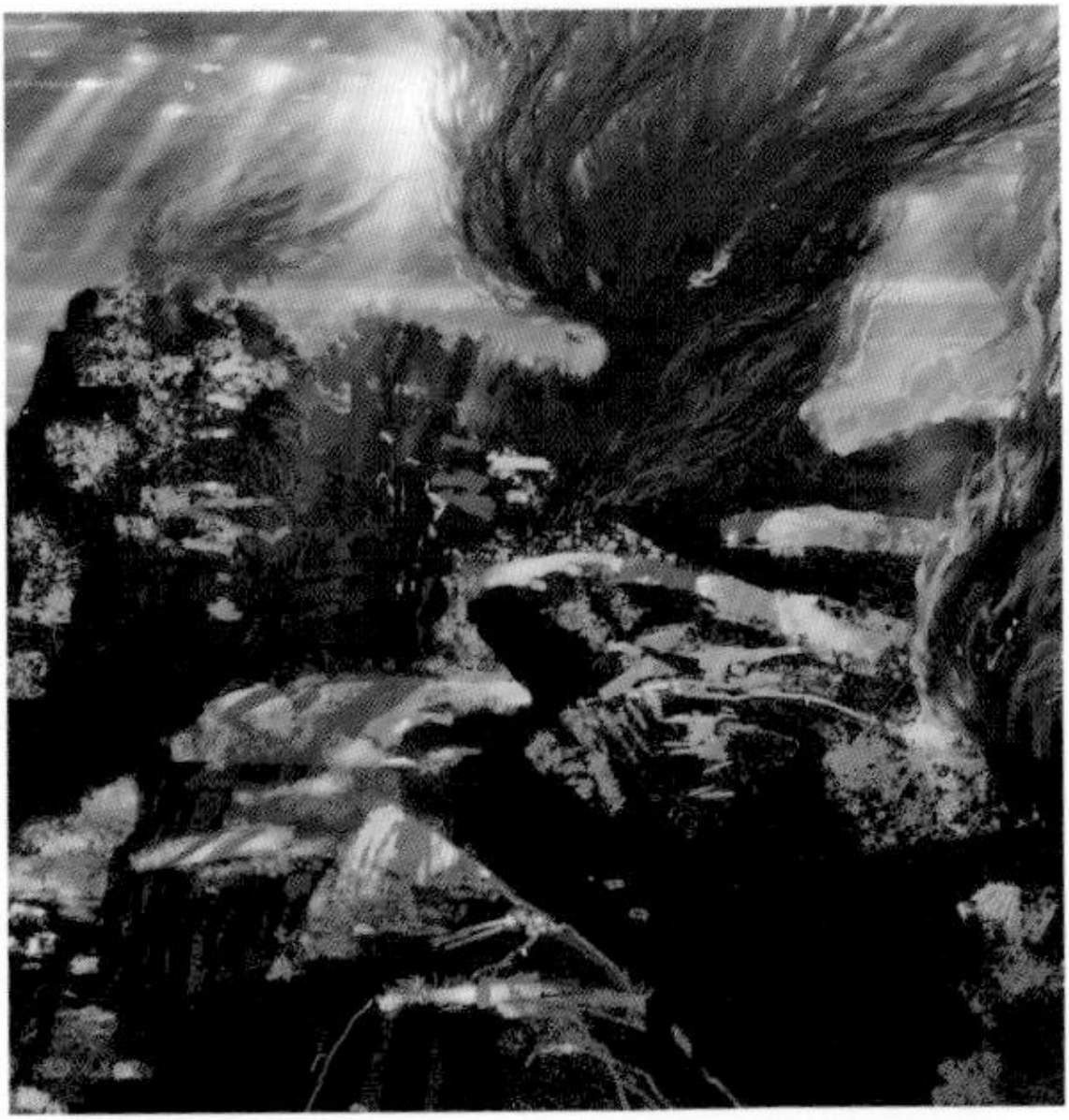

PAGES 184–189: Dermot Power offers underwater vistas of Harry trying to find what he needs to retrieve in order to win the second task.

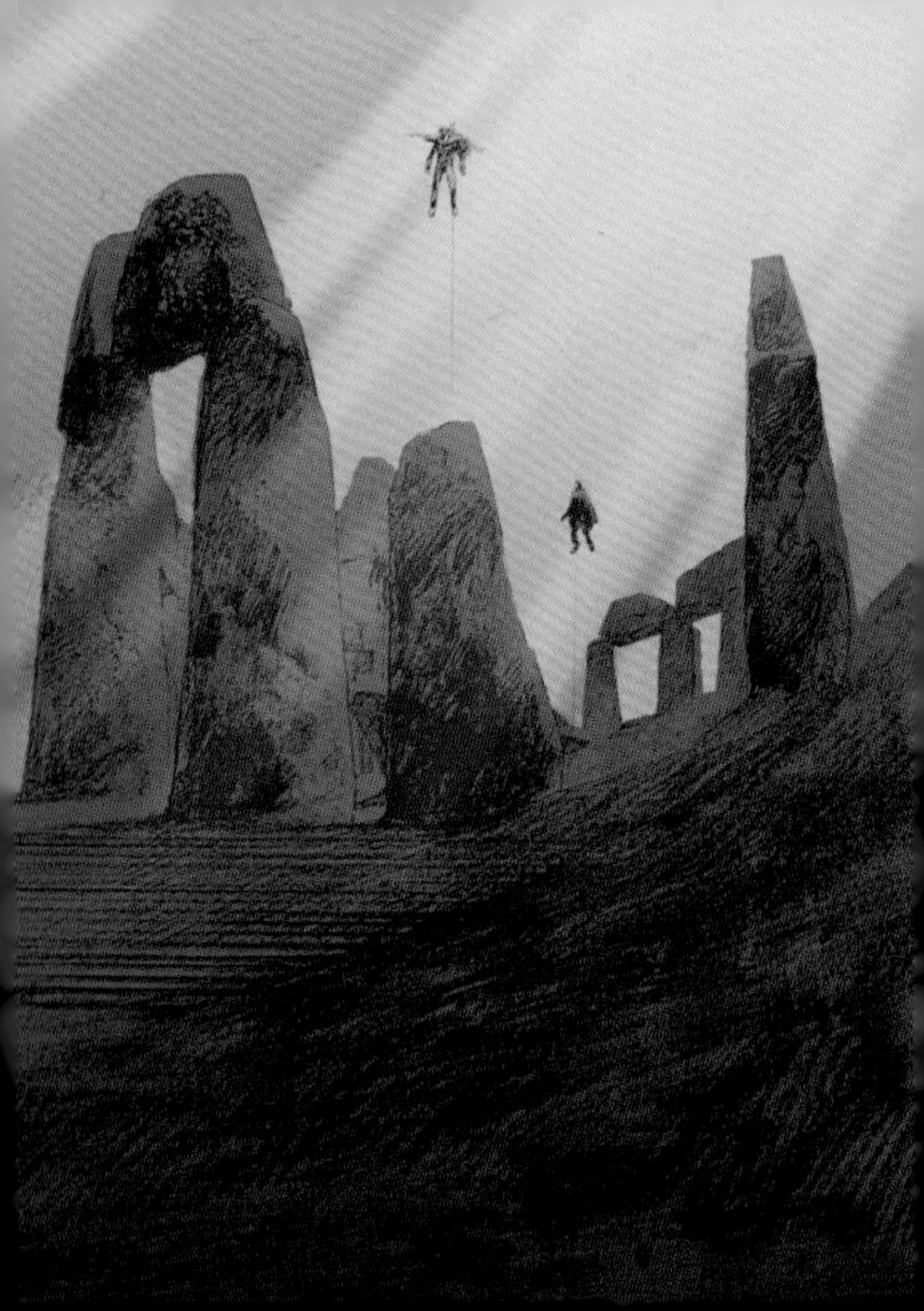

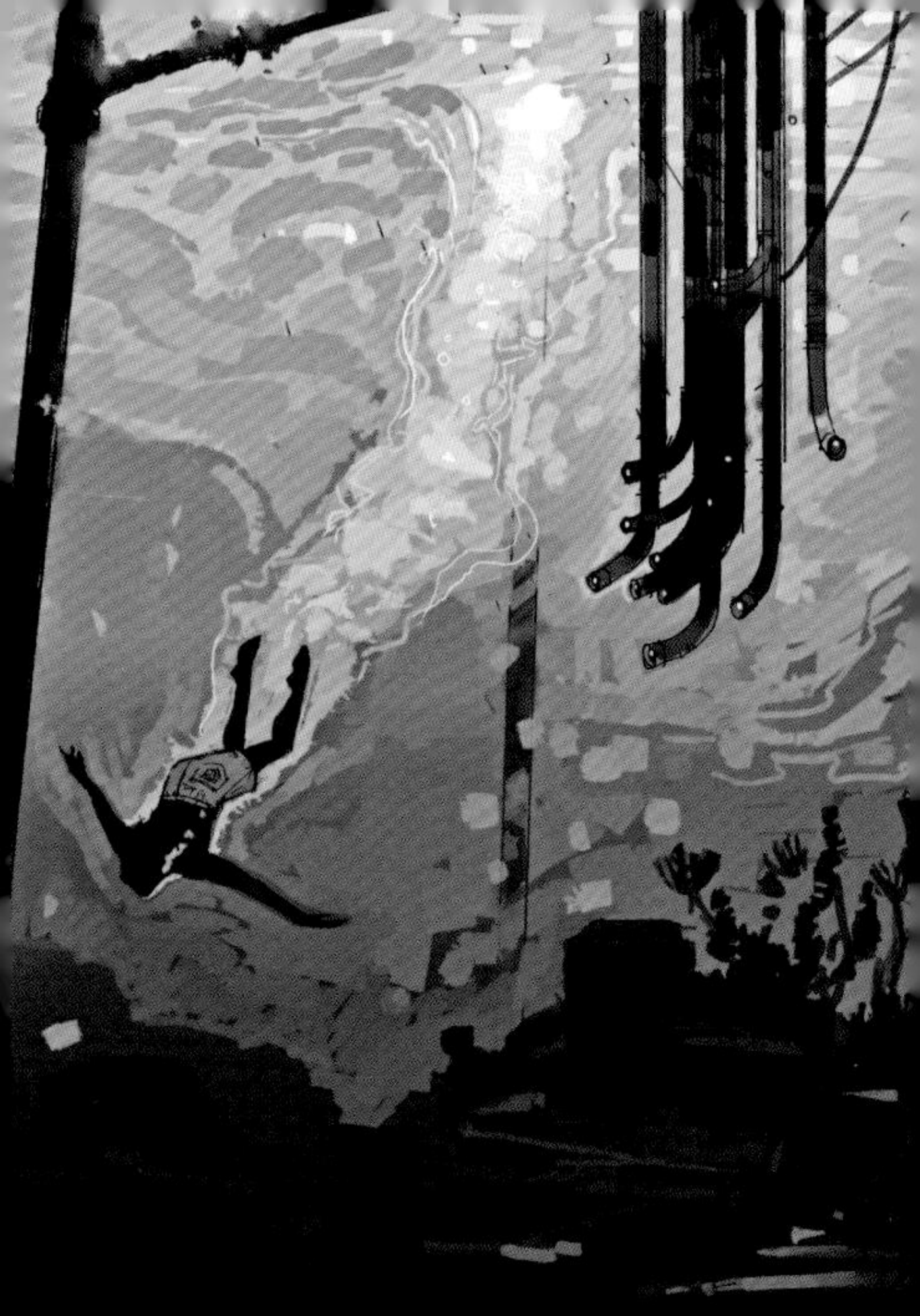

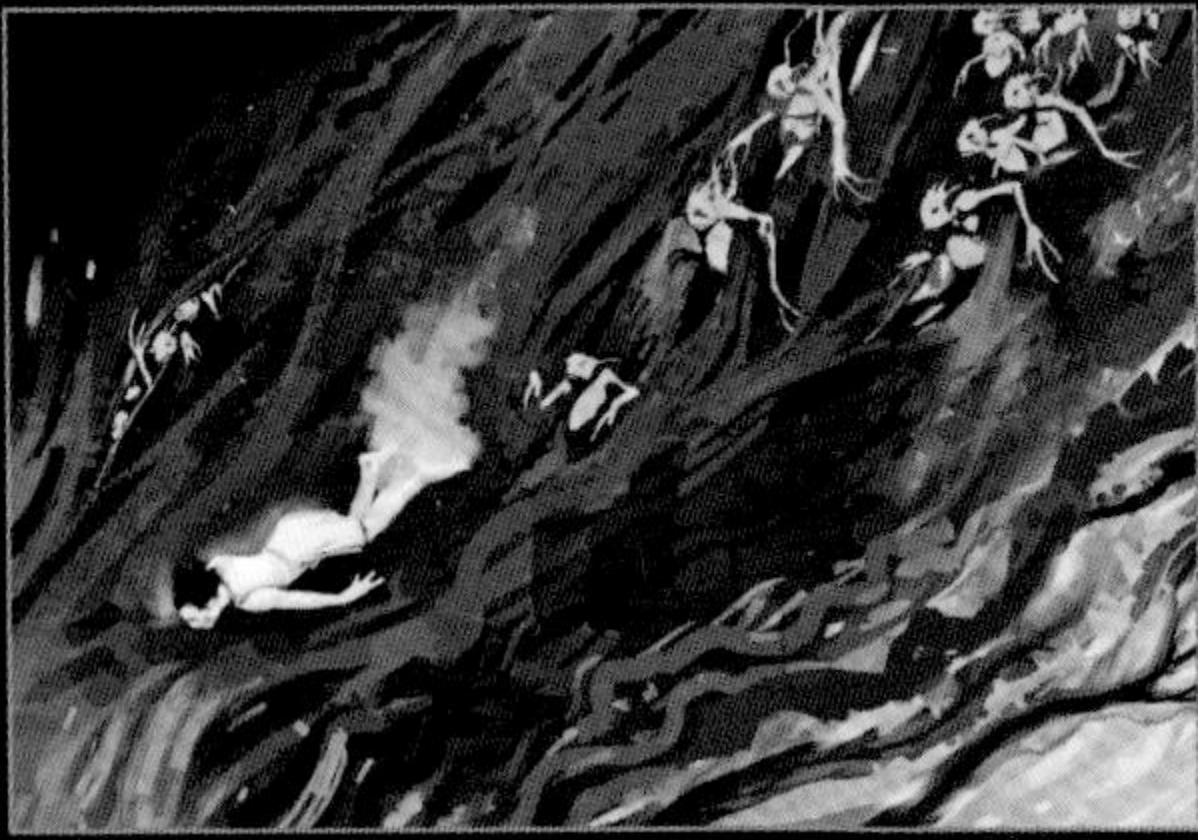

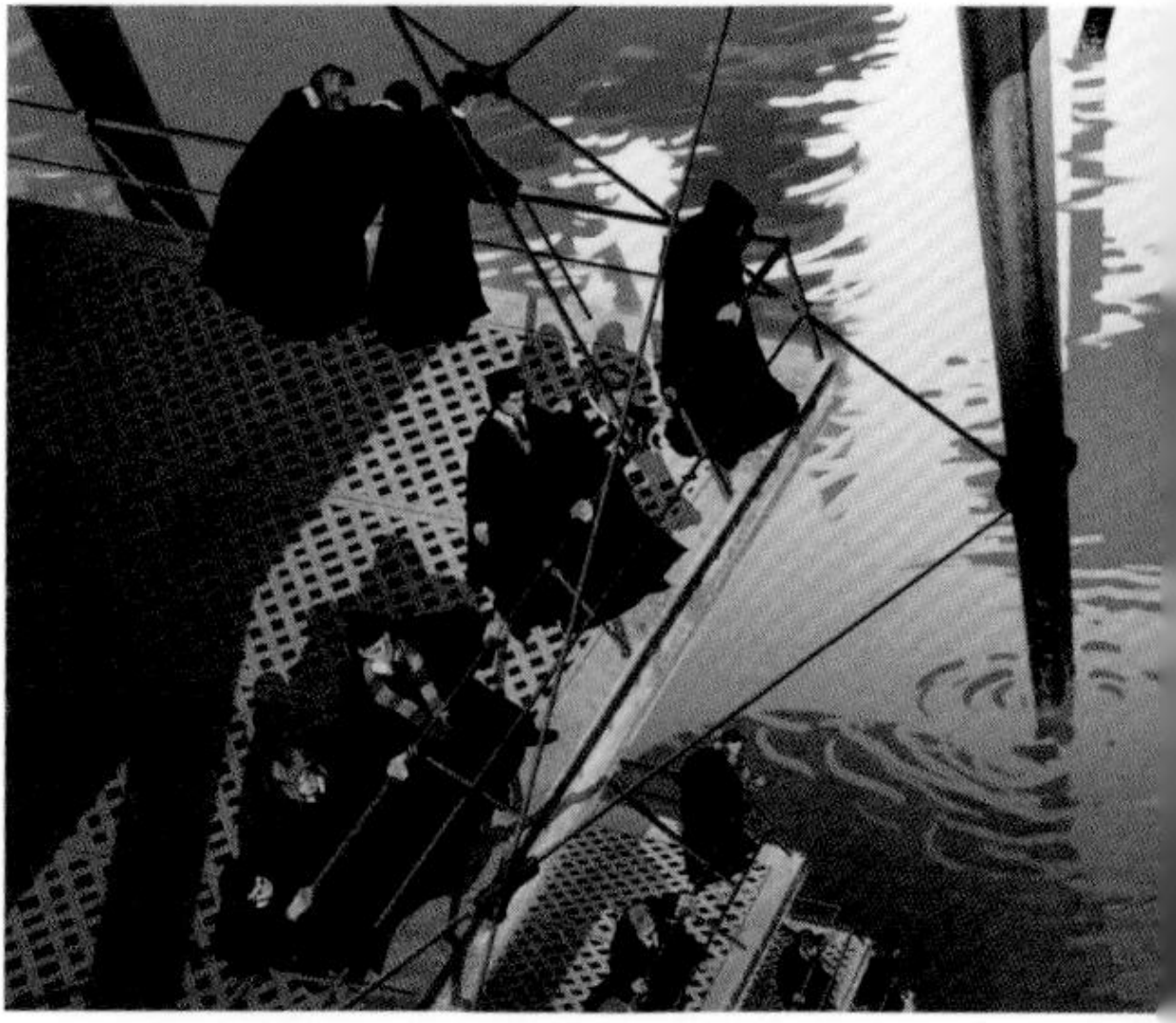

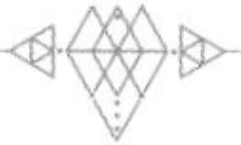

THESE PAGES: Crowded viewing towers precipitously balance above the Black Lake as viewers watch the second task of the Triwizard Tournament. Concept art by Andrew Williamson for *Harry Potter and the Goblet of Fire*.

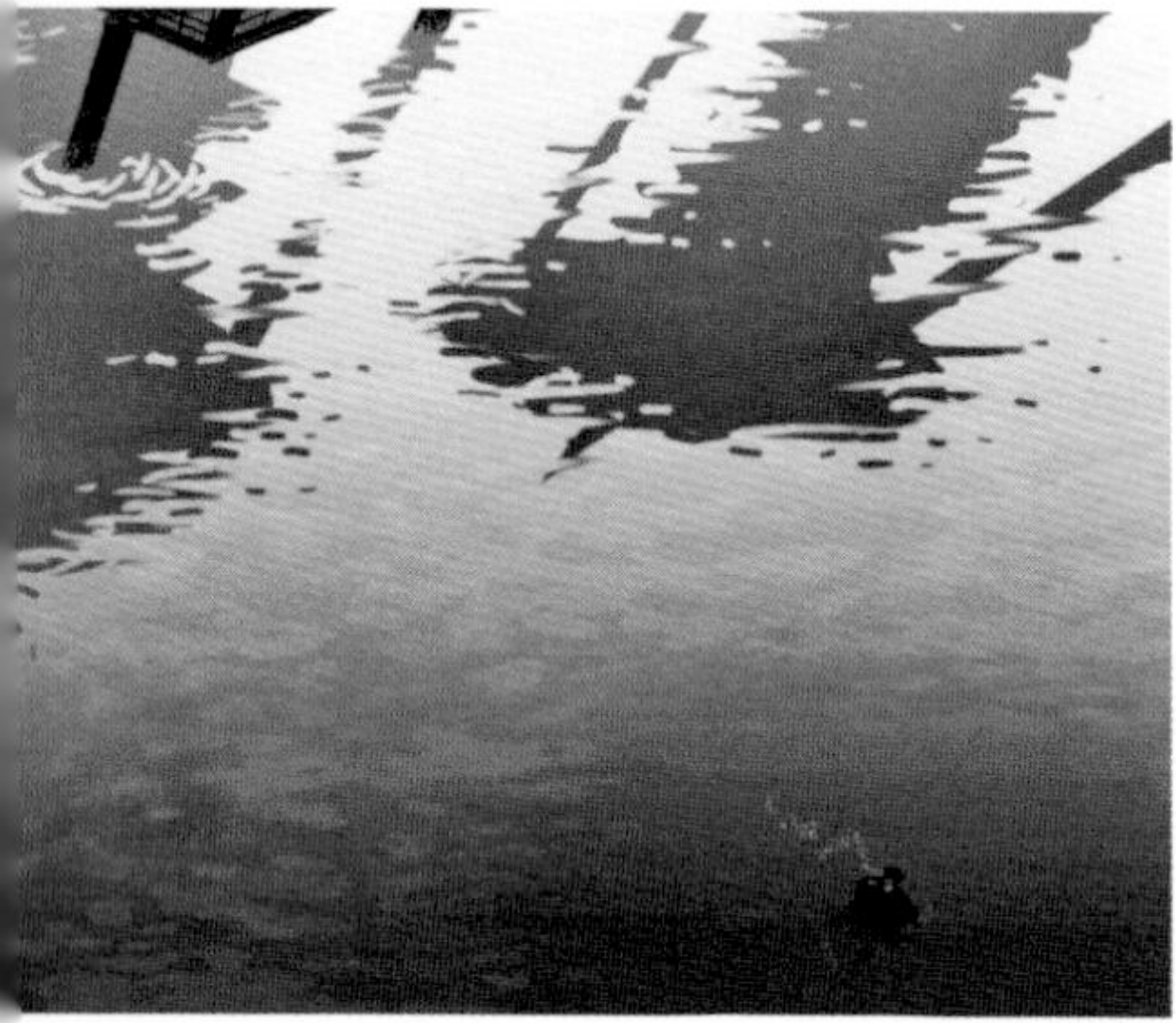

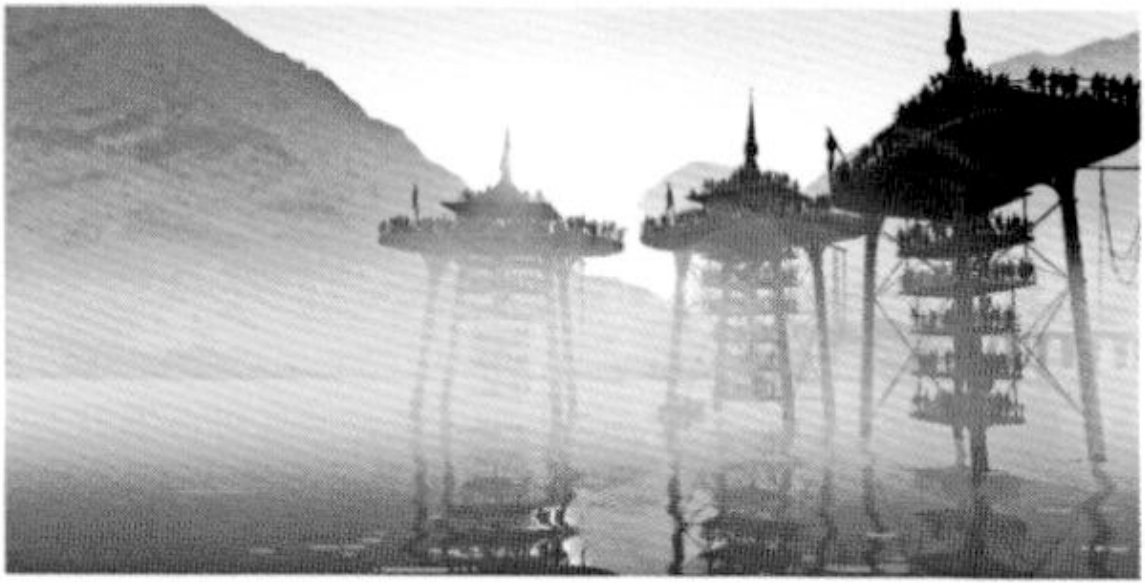

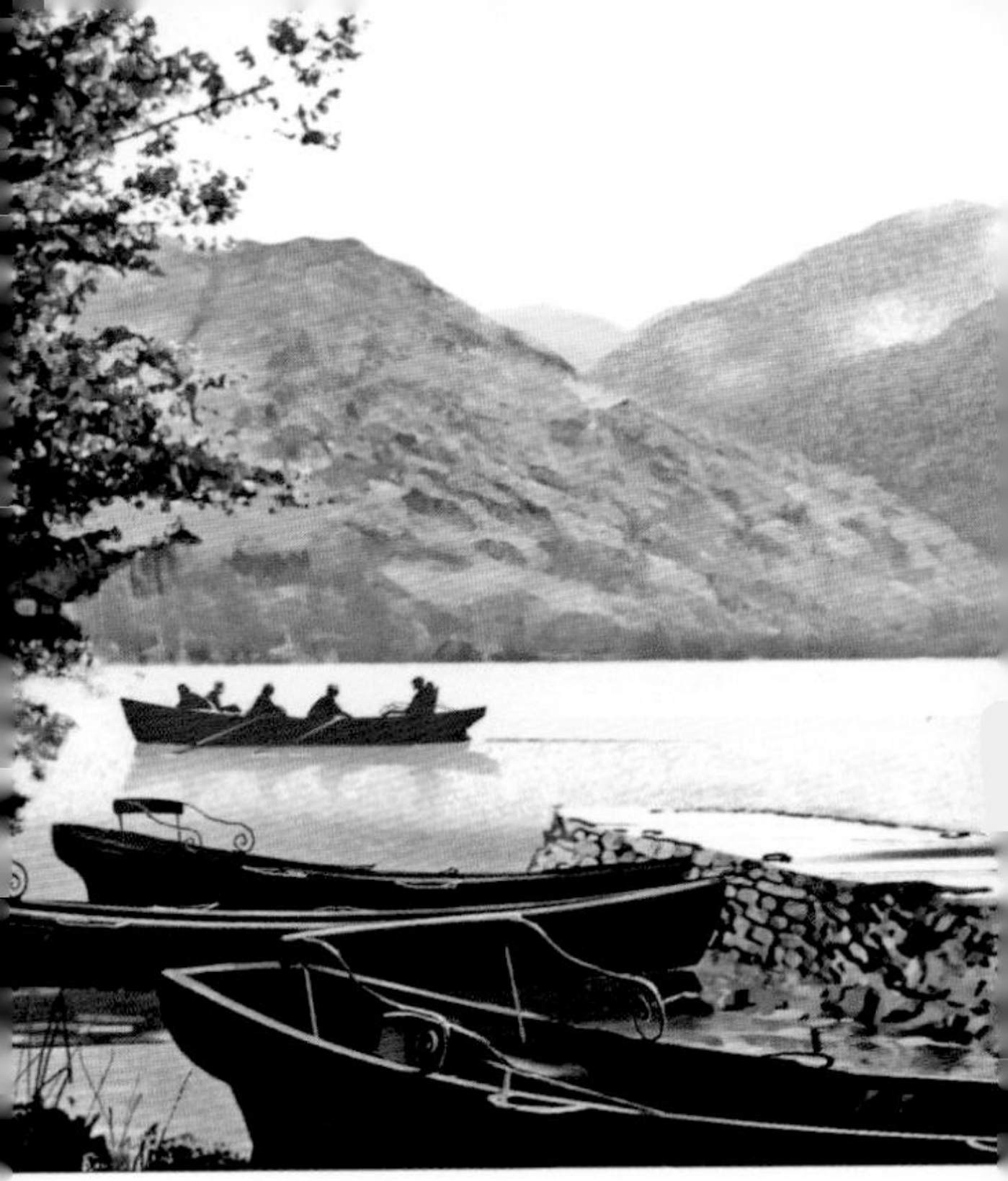

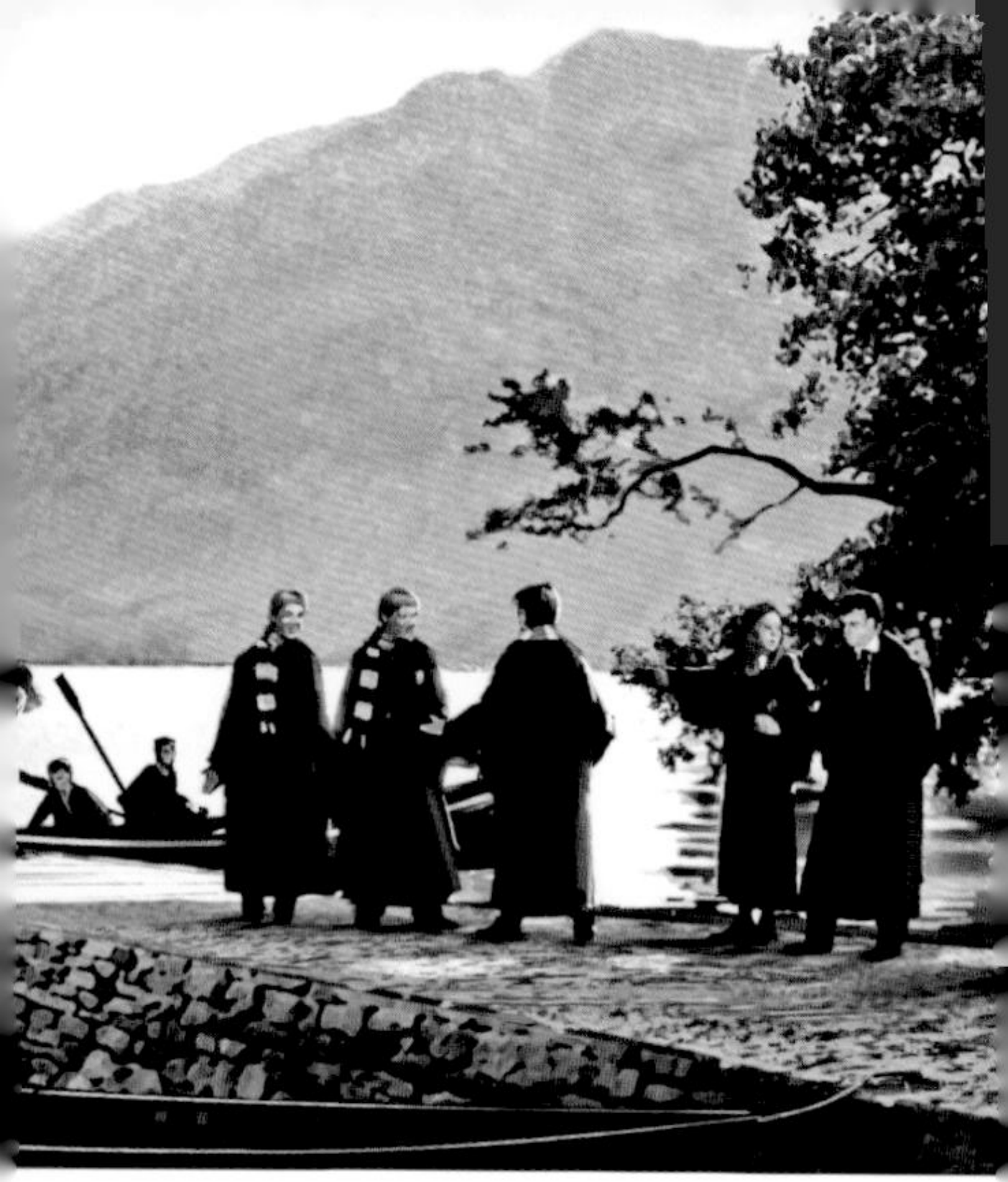

THESE PAGES: A view of the Black Lake from the boat dock, created by Andrew Williamson for *Goblet of Fire*.

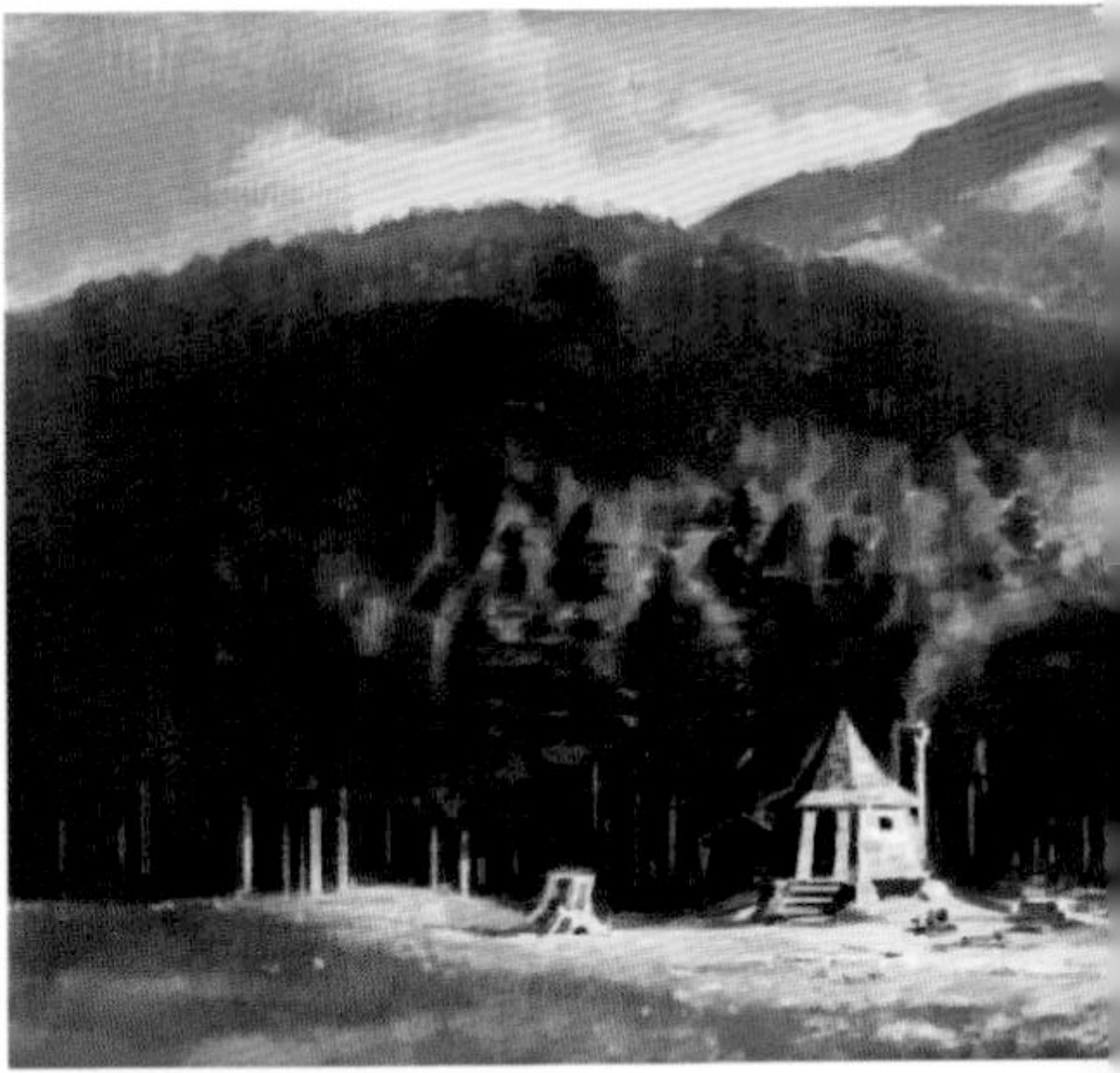

HAGRID'S HUT

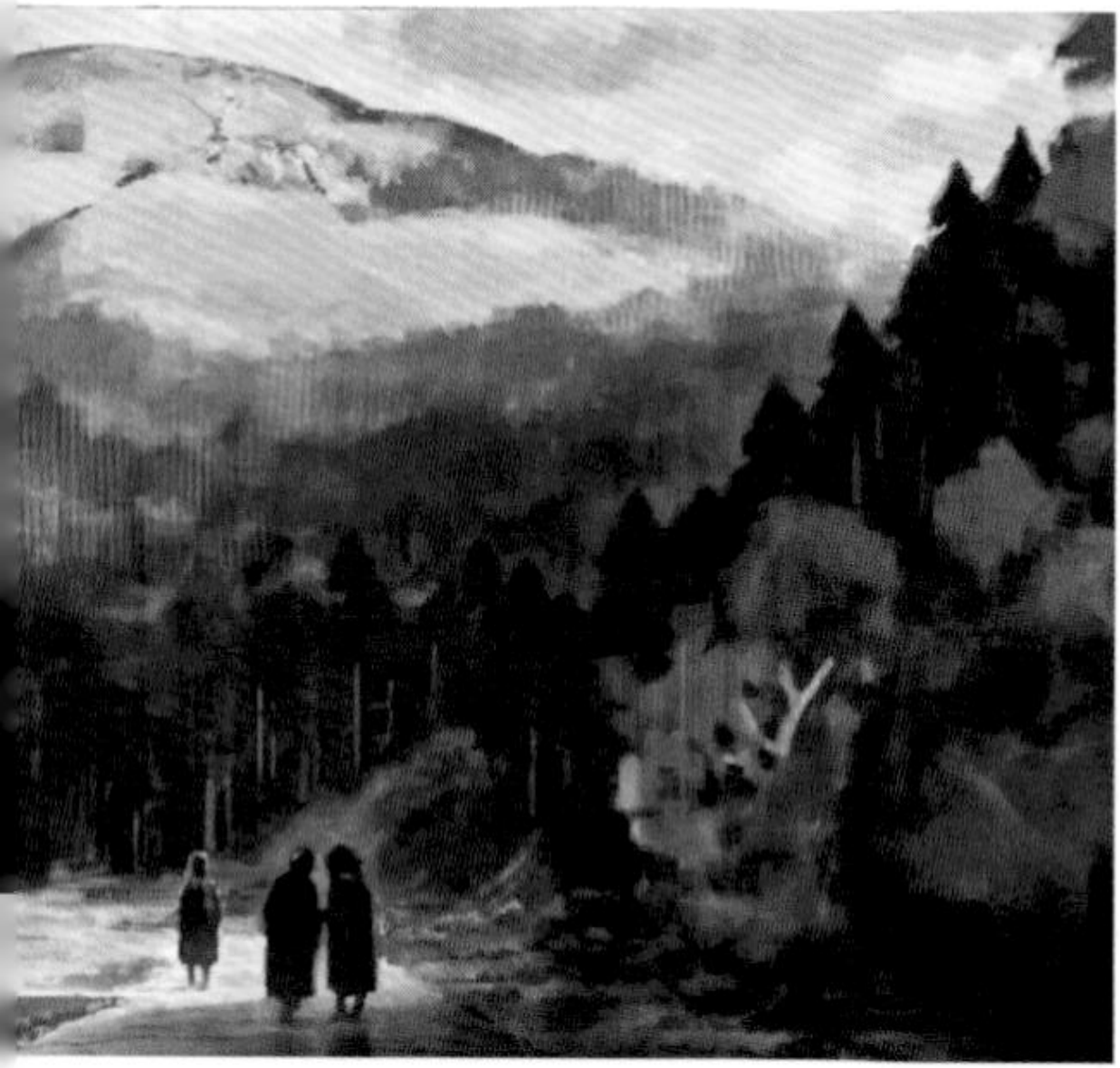

THESE PAGES: Harry, Ron, and Hermione visit Hagrid's hut many times throughout the films. Concept art by Adam Brockbank for *Harry Potter and the Chamber of Secrets*.

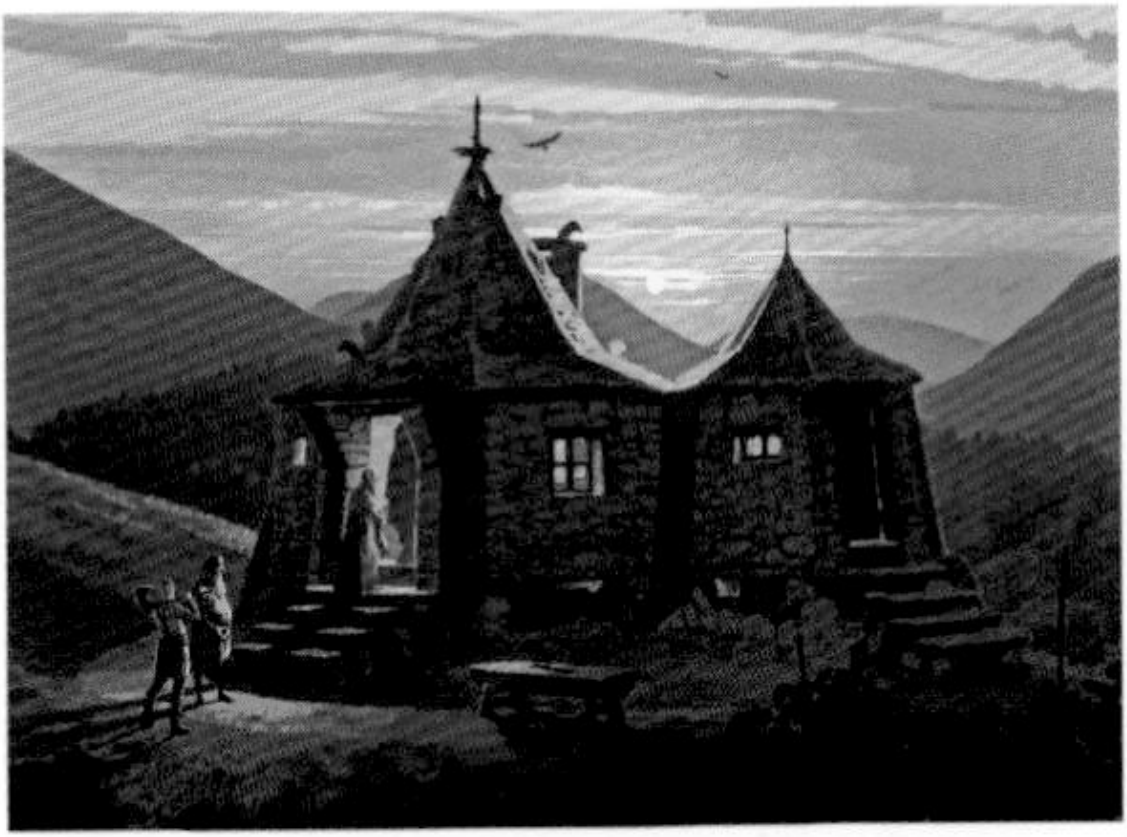

THESE PAGES: The hut acquired a second room in *Harry Potter and the Prisoner of Azkaban*, as depicted by Adam Brockbank (*above*) and Andrew Williamson (*right*), who also painted a view of Harry, Ron, and Hermione watching Buckbeak's fate being determined.

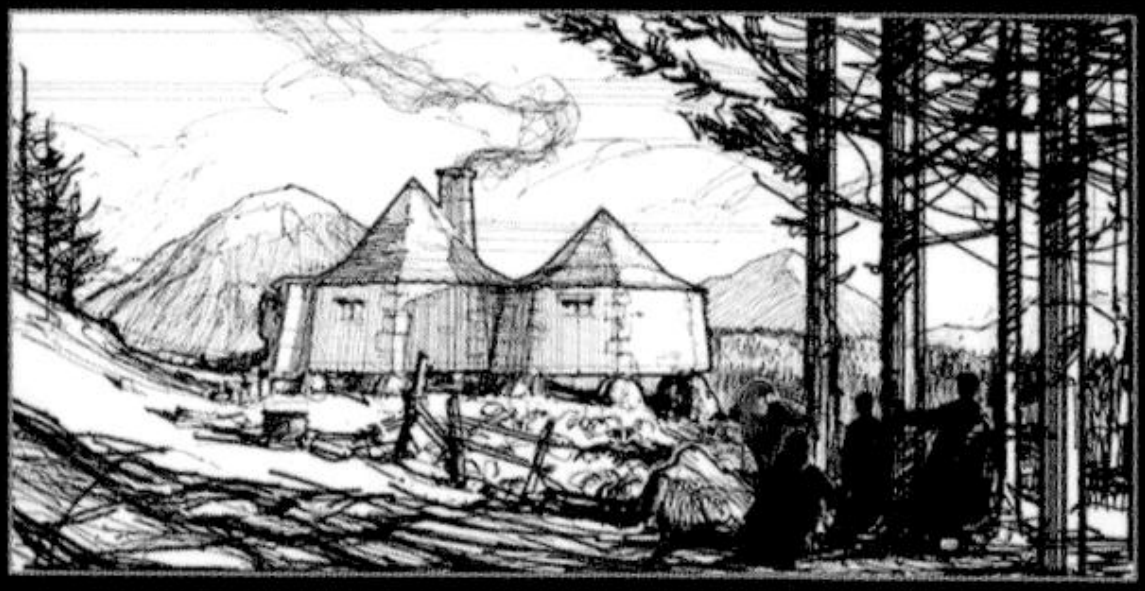

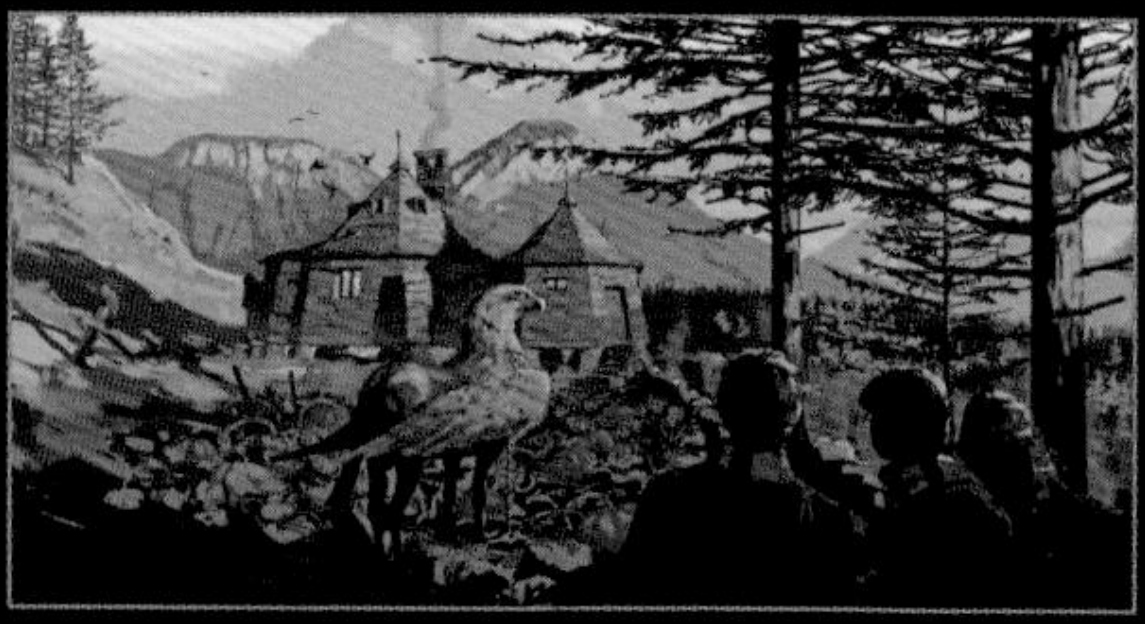

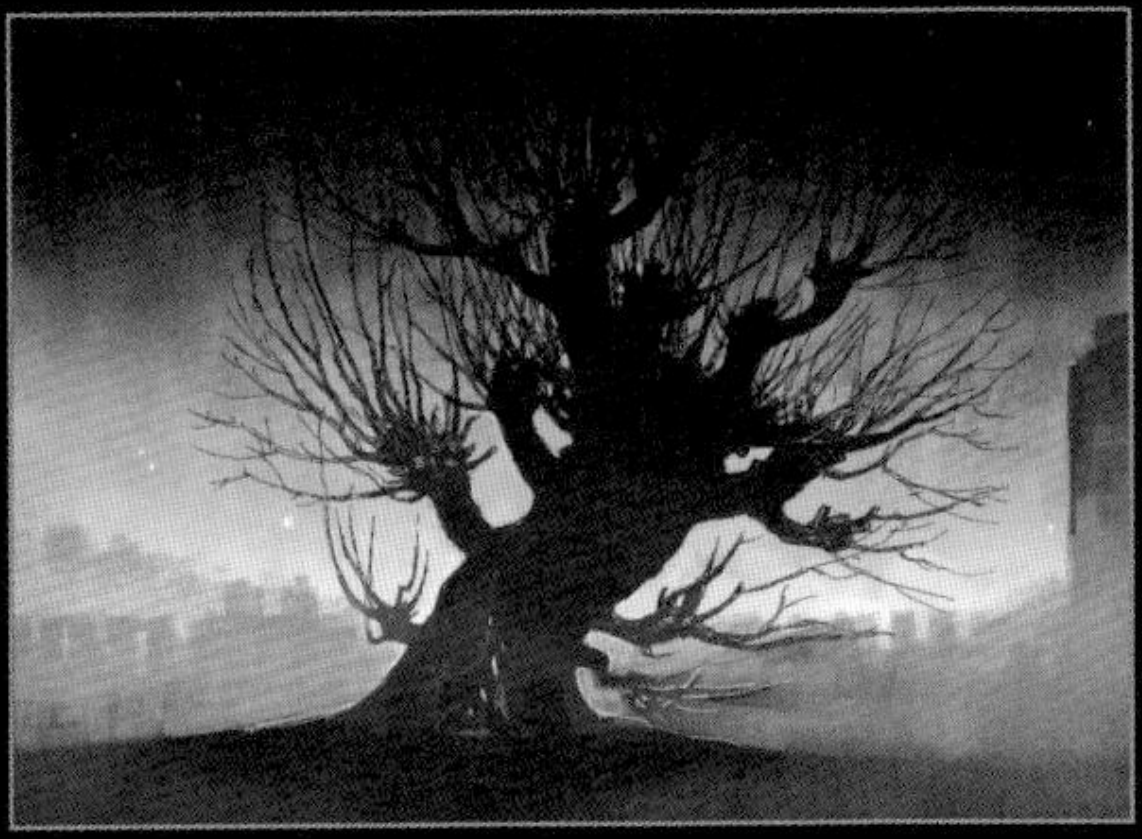

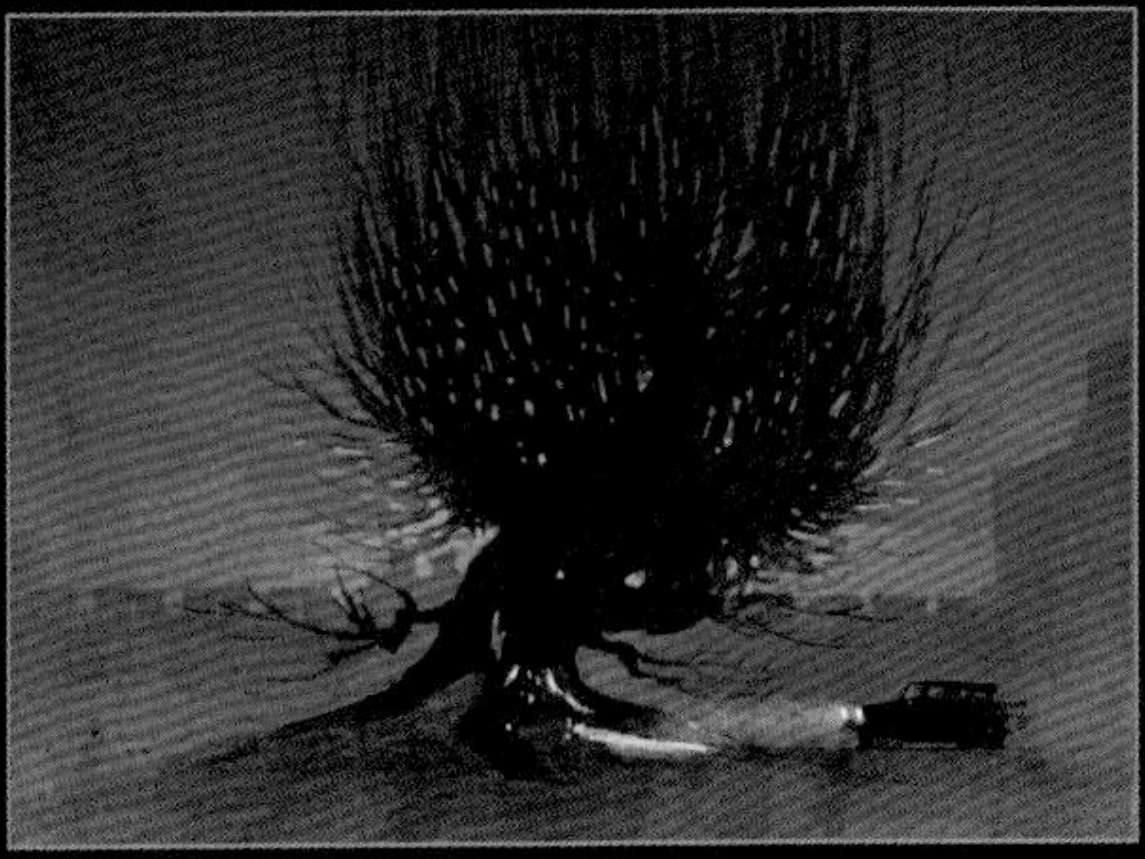

THE WHOMPING WILLOW

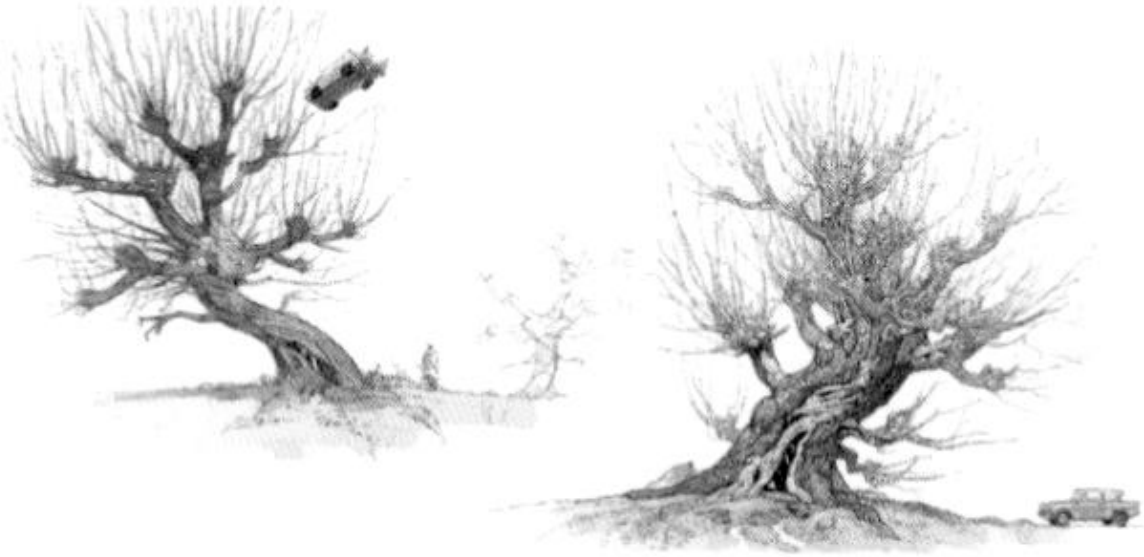

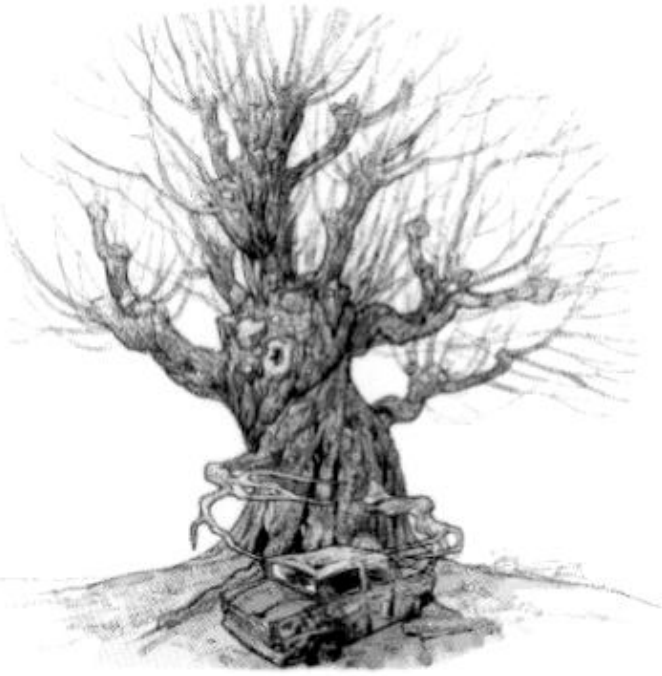

THESE PAGES: Visual development for the Whomping Willow by Dermot Power for *Harry Potter and the Chamber of Secrets*.

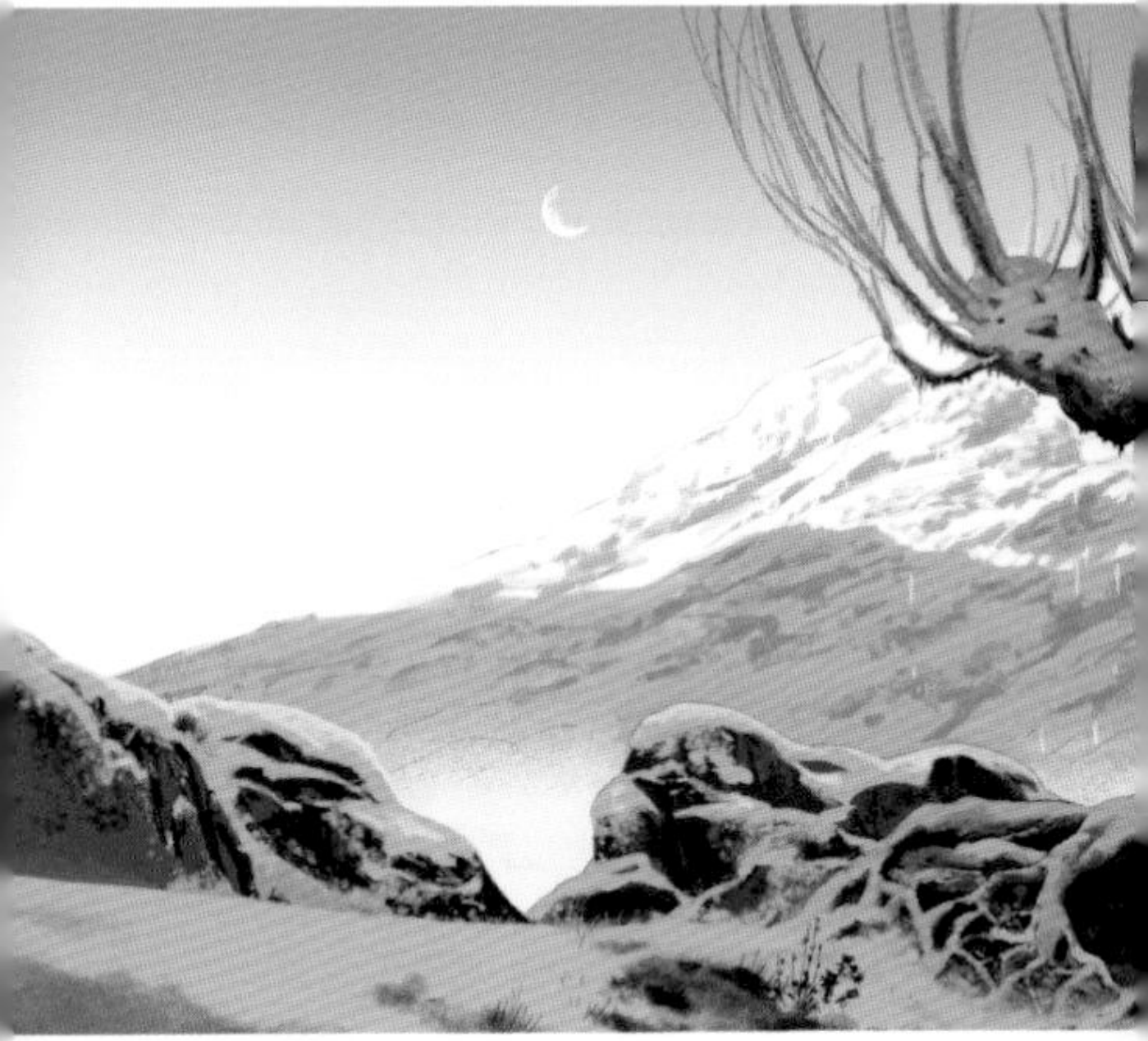

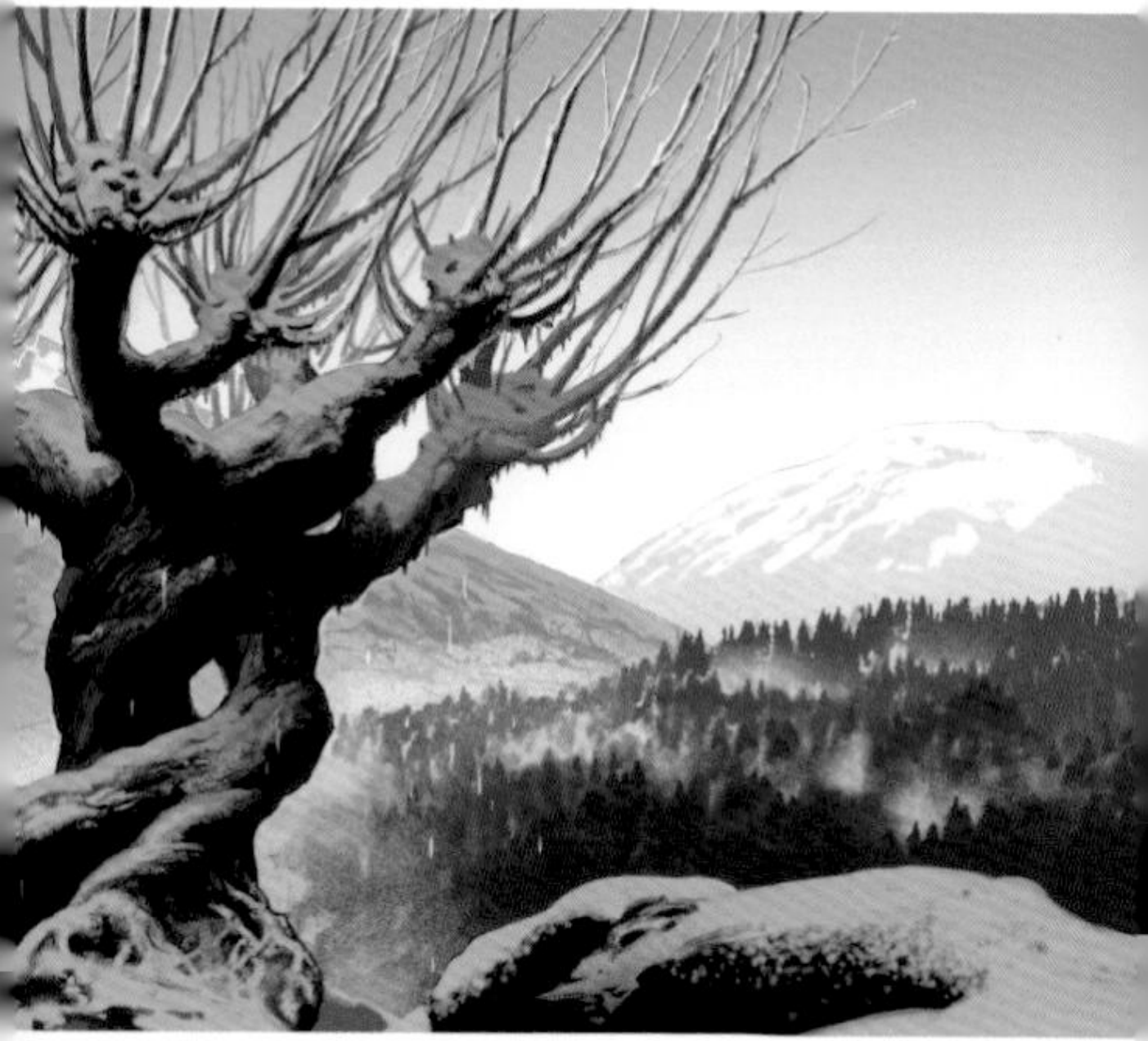

THESE PAGES: The Whomping Willow in winter by Adam Brockbank for *Harry Potter and the Prisoner of Azkaban*.

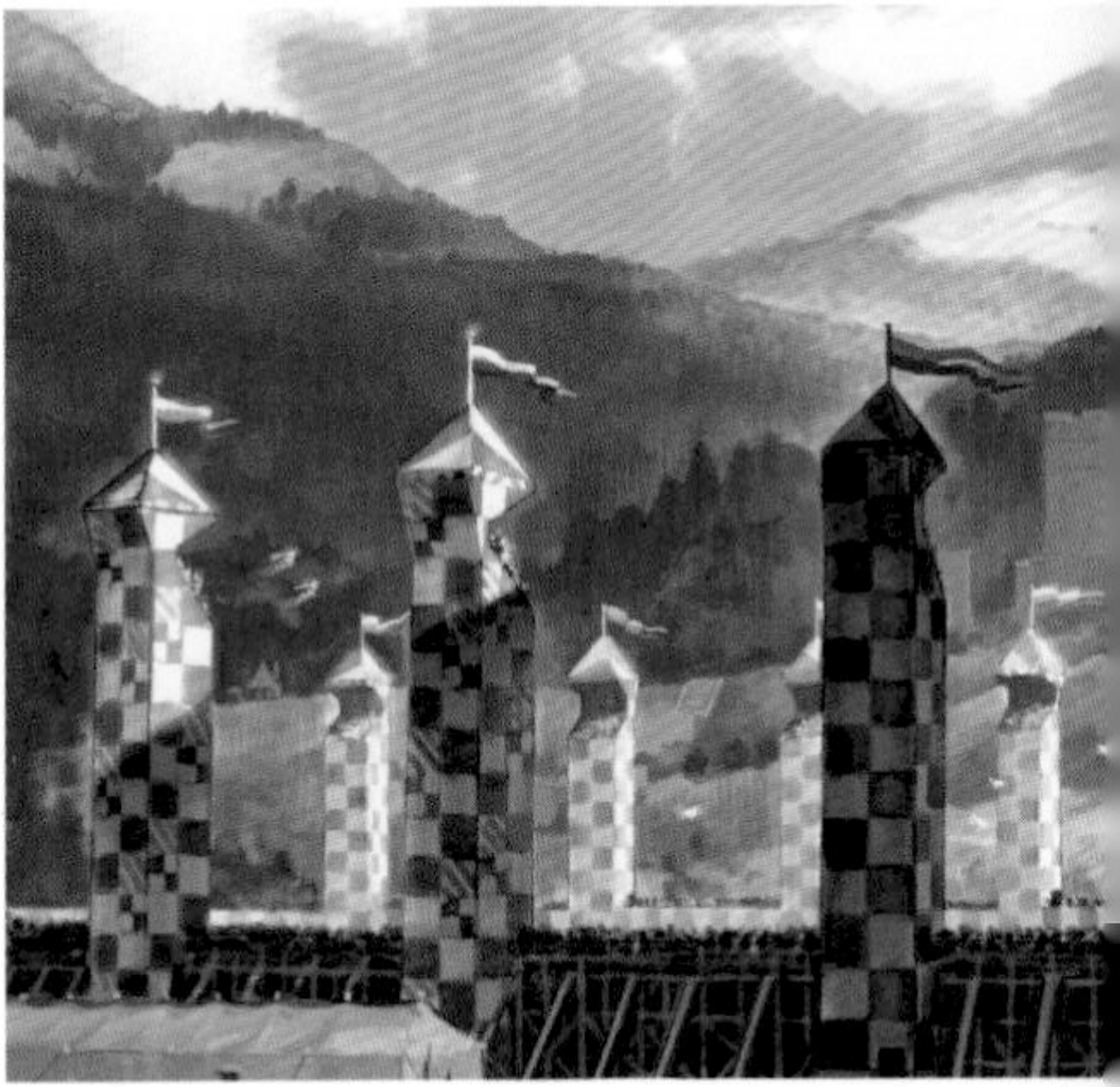

Quidditch, the favorite sport of wizards and witches, incited thrilling rivalries between the houses of Hogwarts.

THE QUIDDITCH PITCH

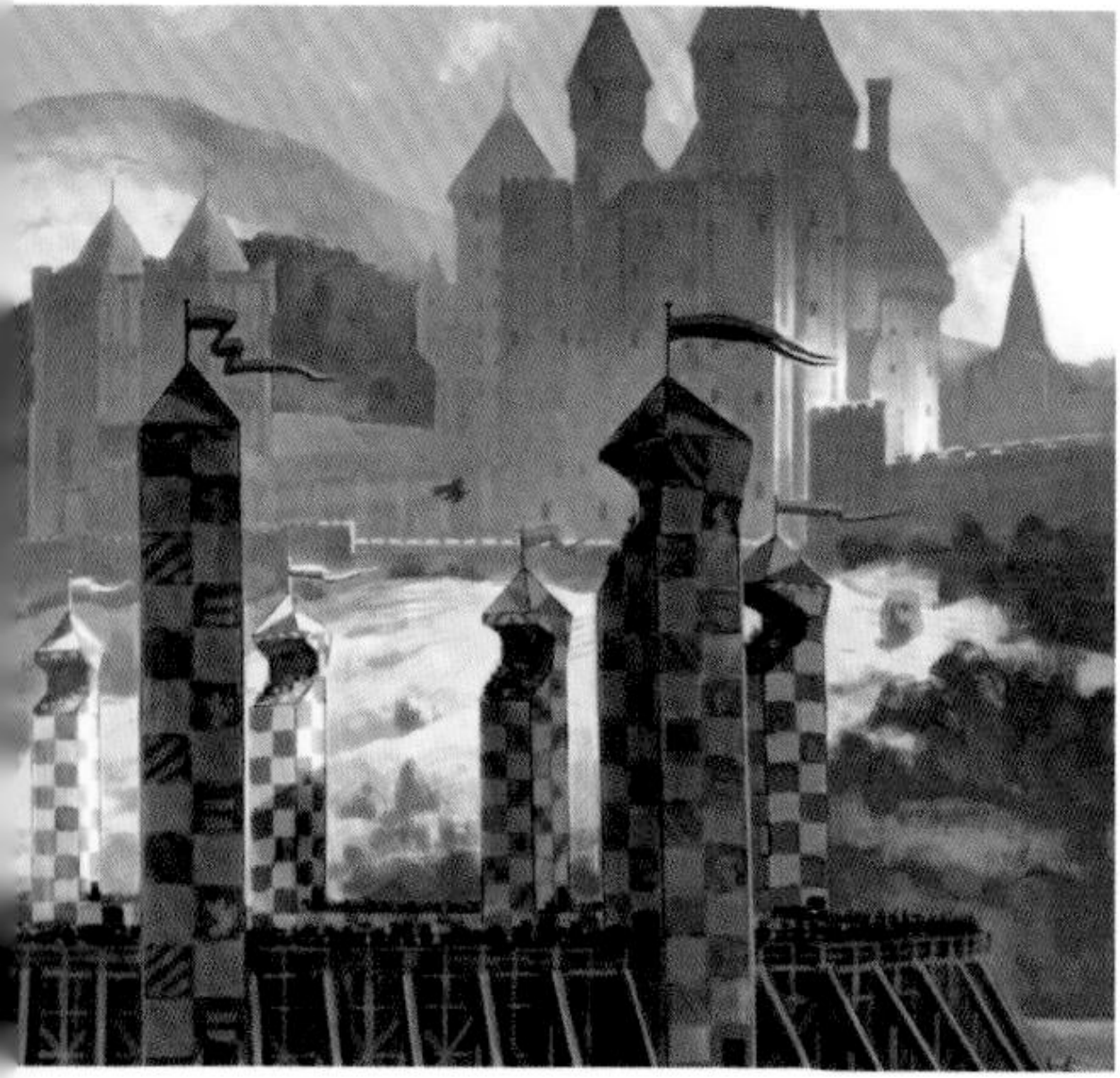

THESE PAGES: Adam Brockbank depicts the Quidditch Pitch in art for *Harry Potter and the Chamber of Secrets*.

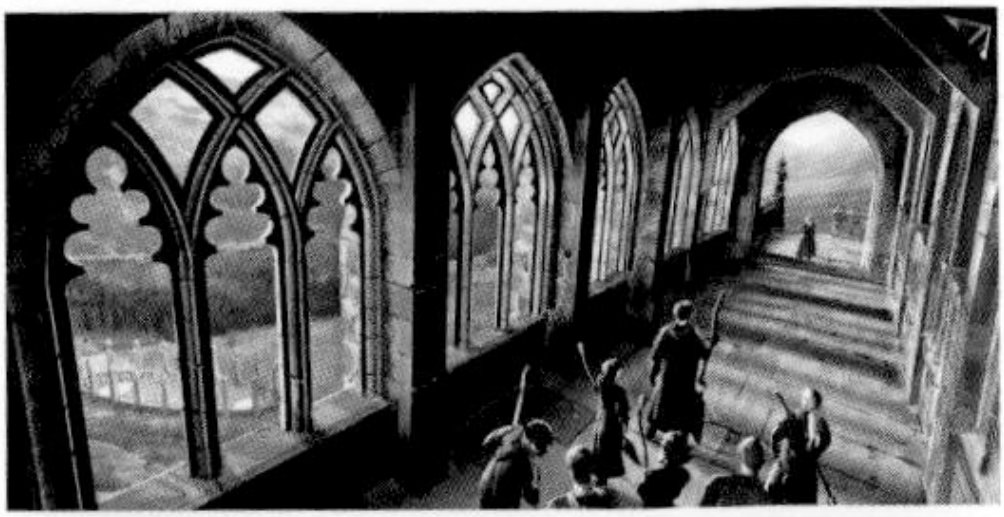

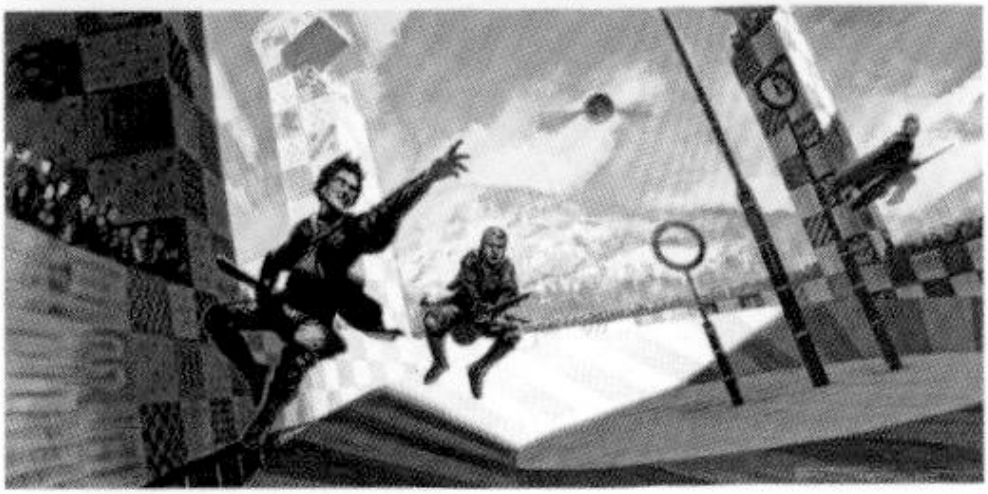

TOP: The Gryffindor Quidditch team unknowingly heads for a game that has been canceled in concept art by Andrew Williamson, for a scene for *Harry Potter and the Order of the Phoenix* that did not make it into the final film.

ABOVE: Seekers Harry Potter and Draco Malfoy race after the Golden Snitch in *Harry Potter and the Chamber of Secrets*. Art by Adam Brockbank.

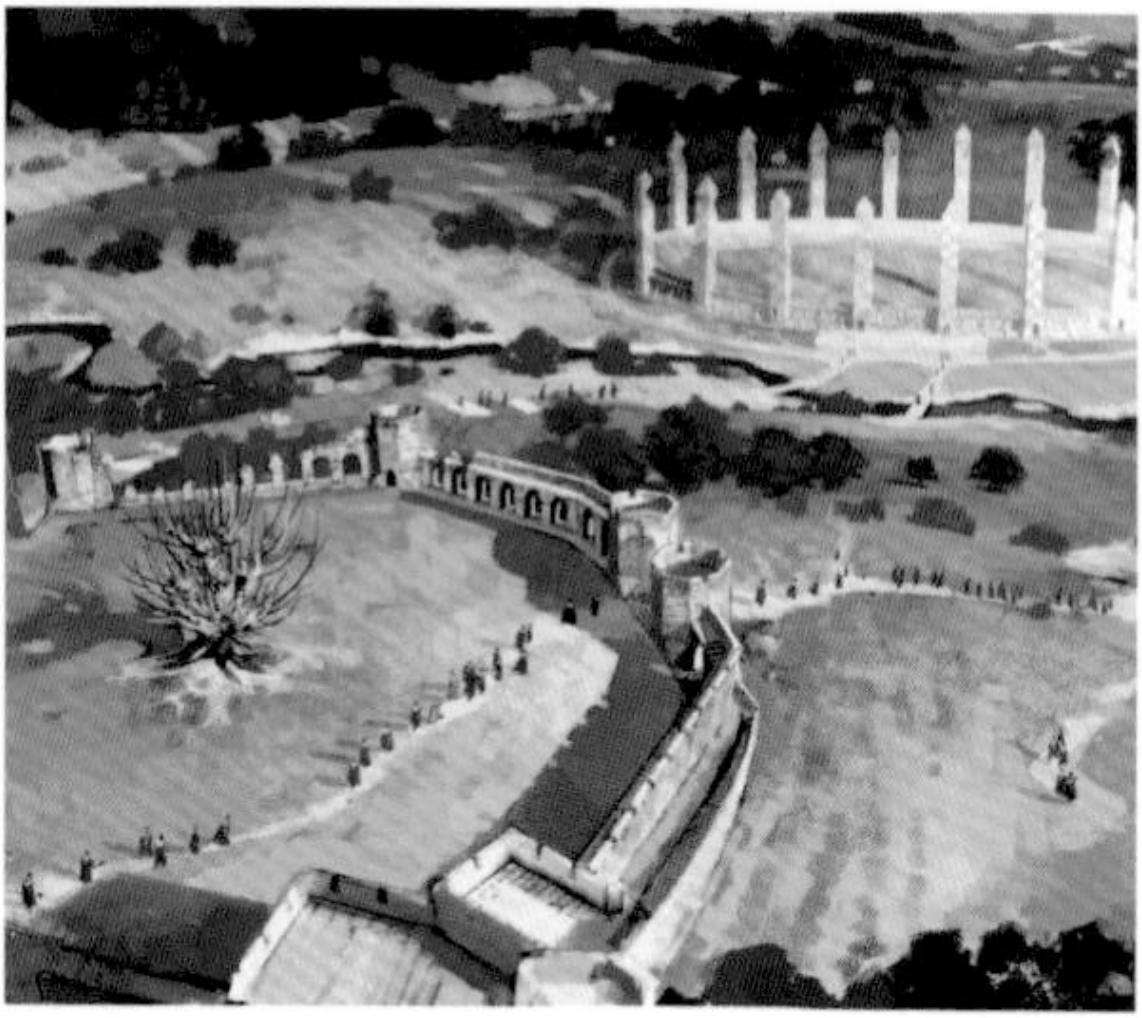

ABOVE: Dermot Power placed the Quidditch Pitch right next to a meandering river—not it's actual geography—for *Harry Potter and the Chamber of Secrets*.

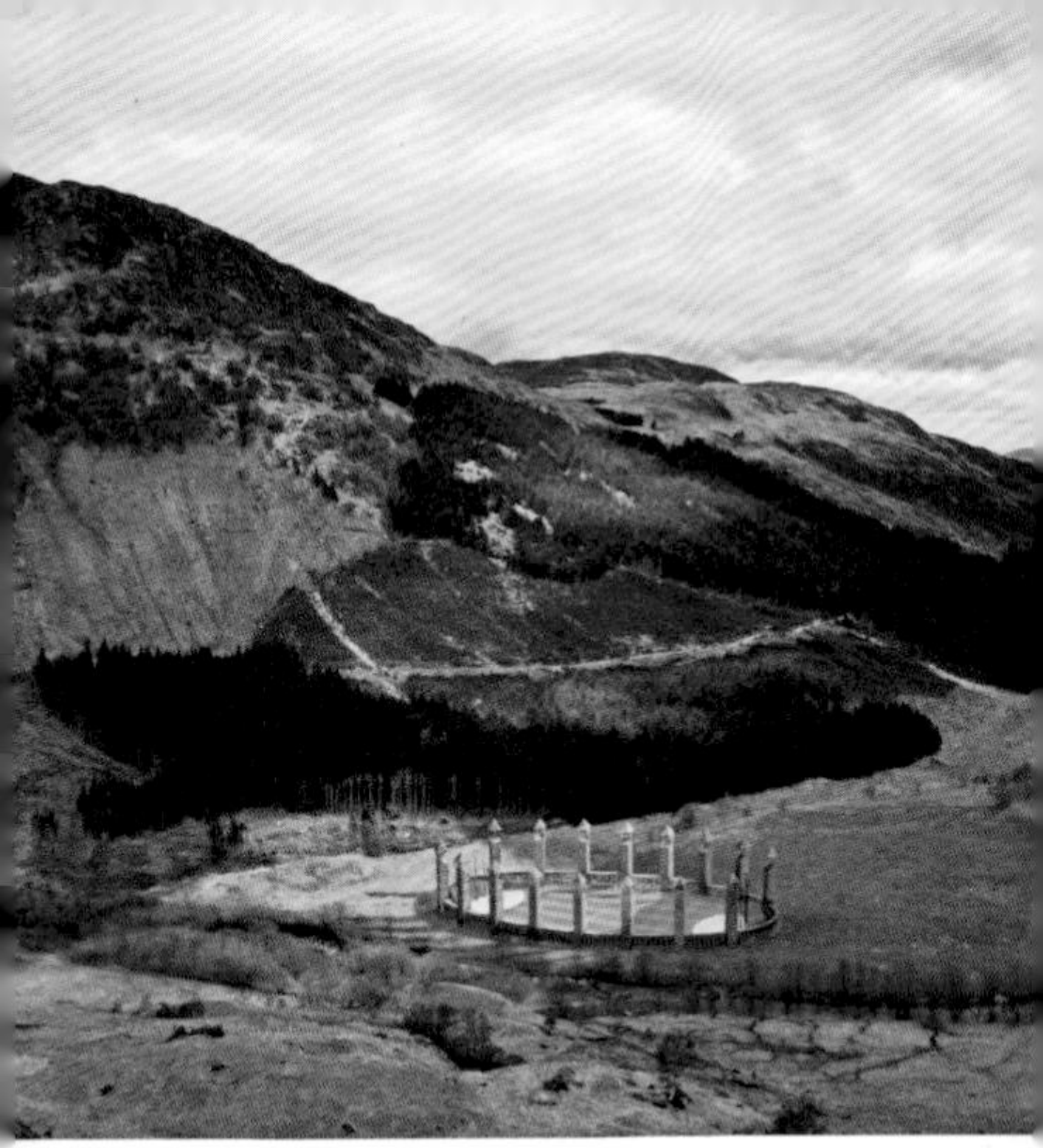

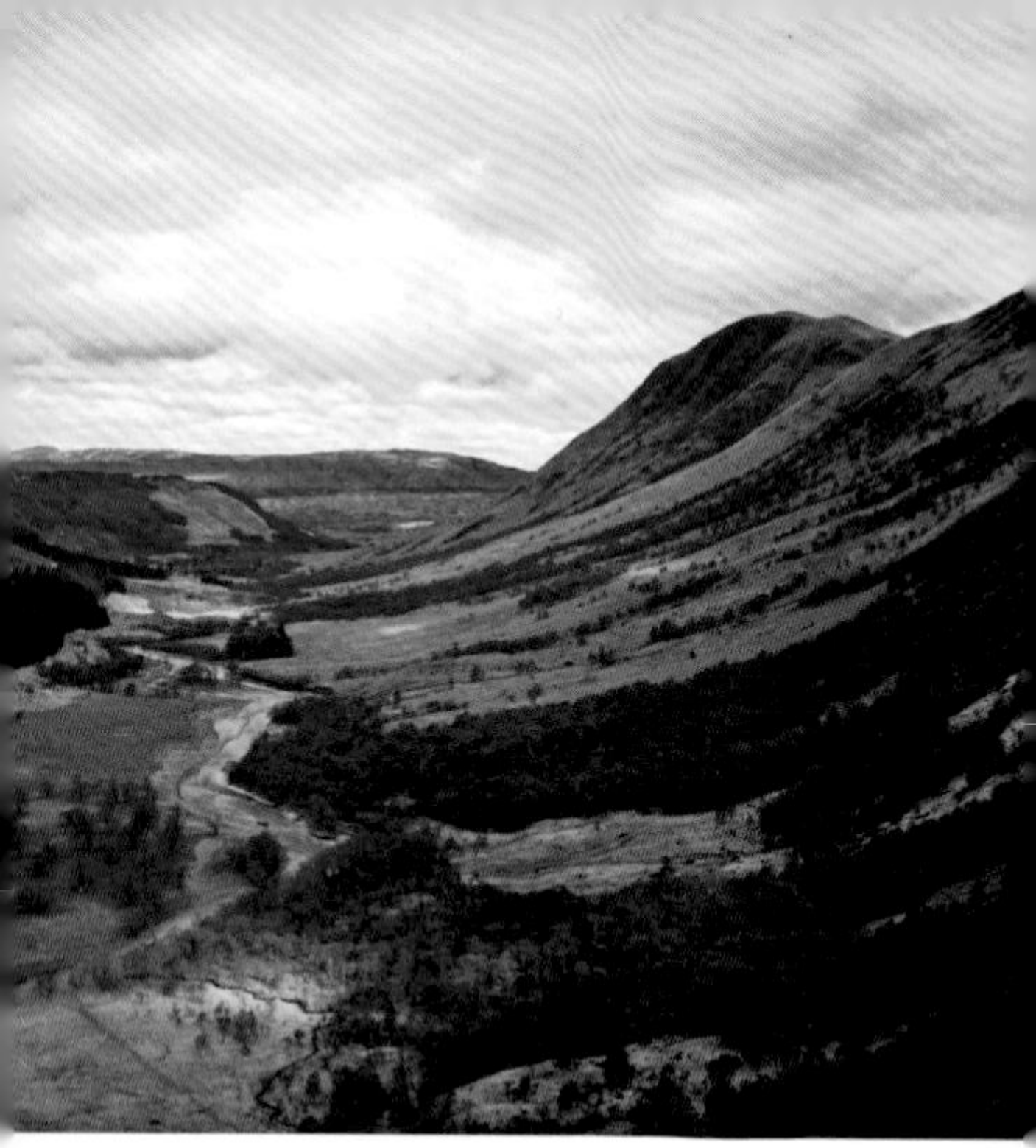

THESE PAGES: A view of the Quidditch Pitch from the Owlery, created by Andrew Williamson for *Harry Potter and the Goblet of Fire*.

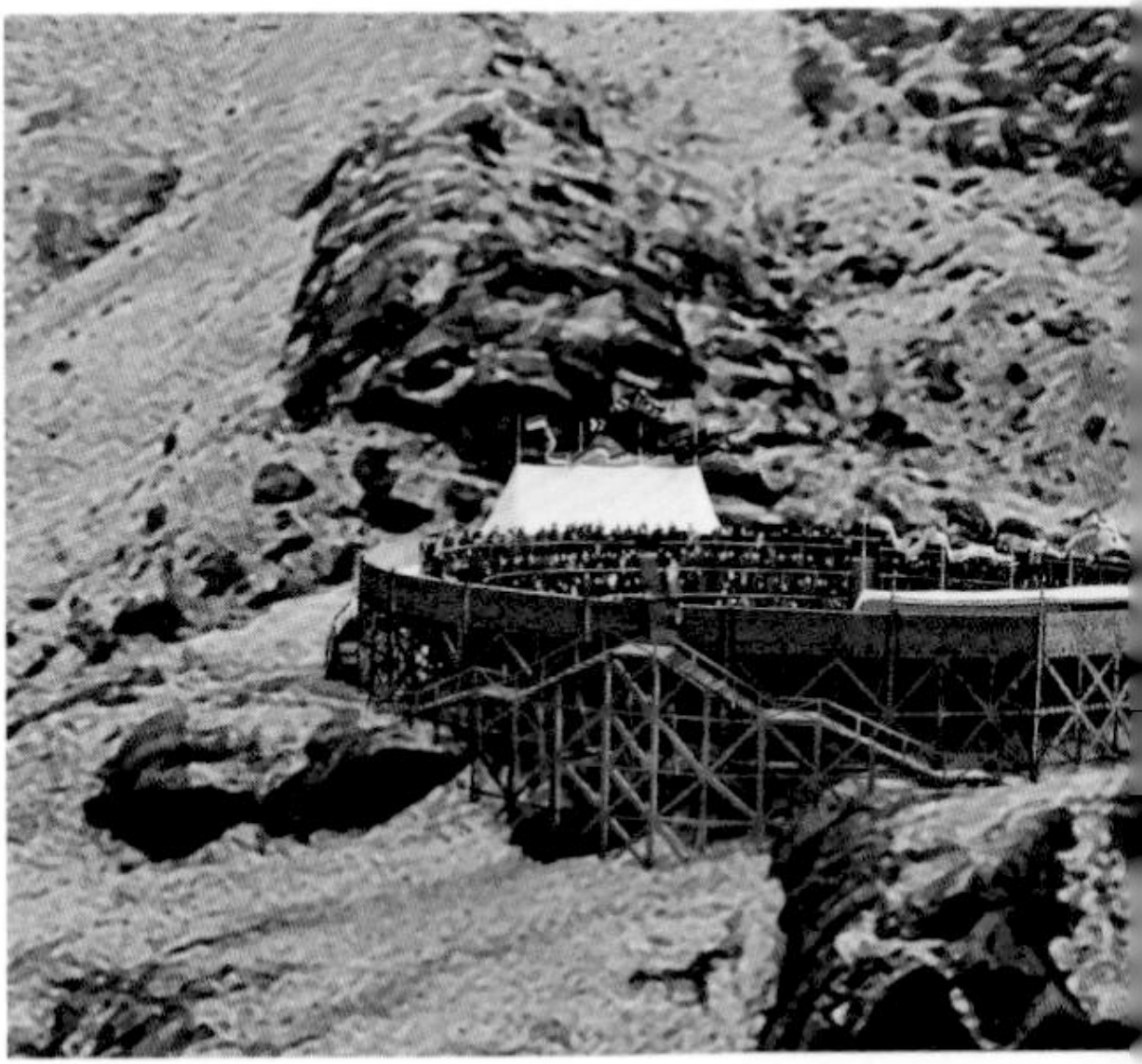

The Triwizard Tournament comes to Hogwarts in *Harry Potter and the Goblet of Fire*, bringing with it two rival schools, Durmstrang Institute and Beauxbatons Academy of Magic.

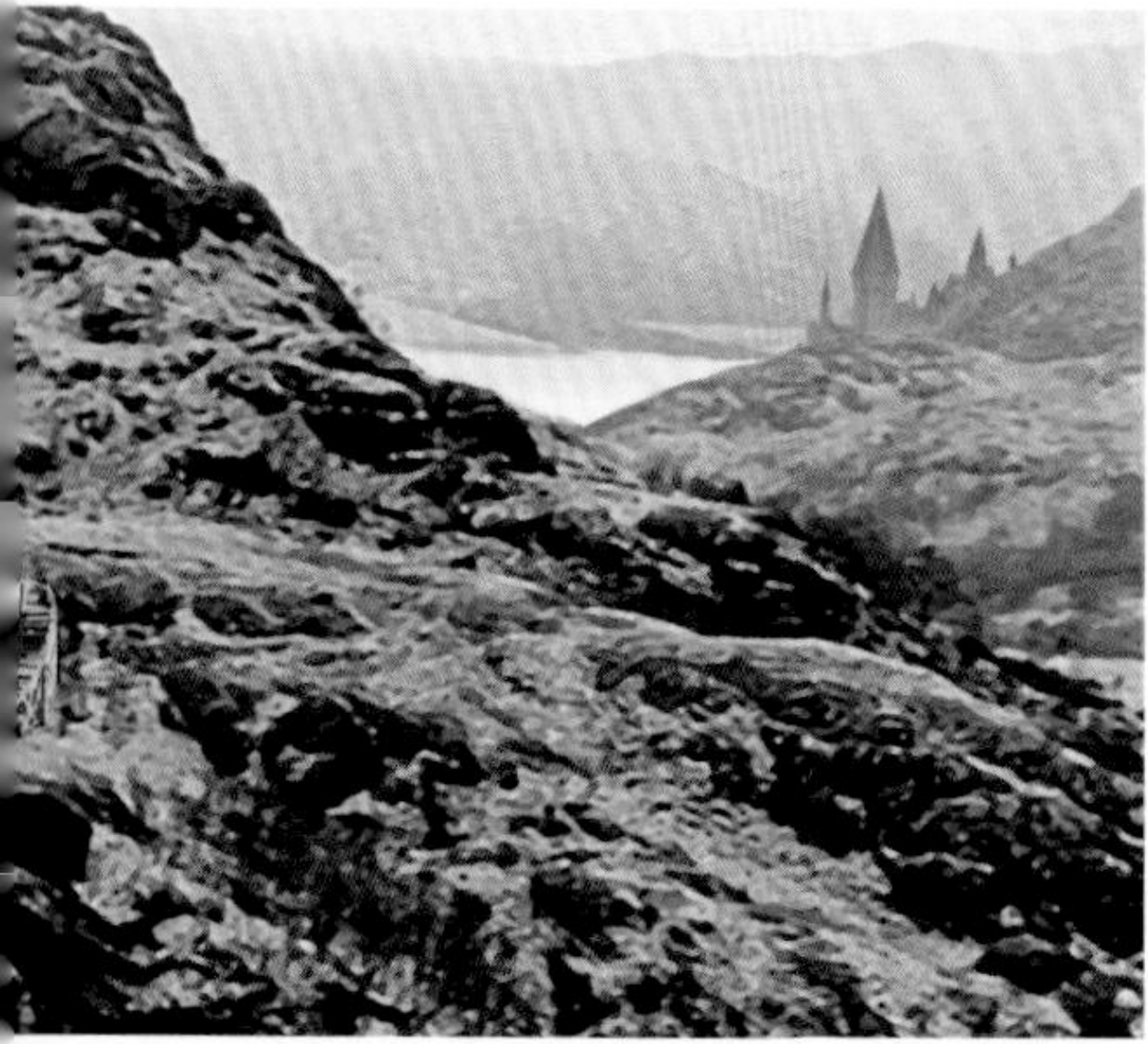

THESE PAGES: Andrew Williamson depicts the arena where the first task took place.

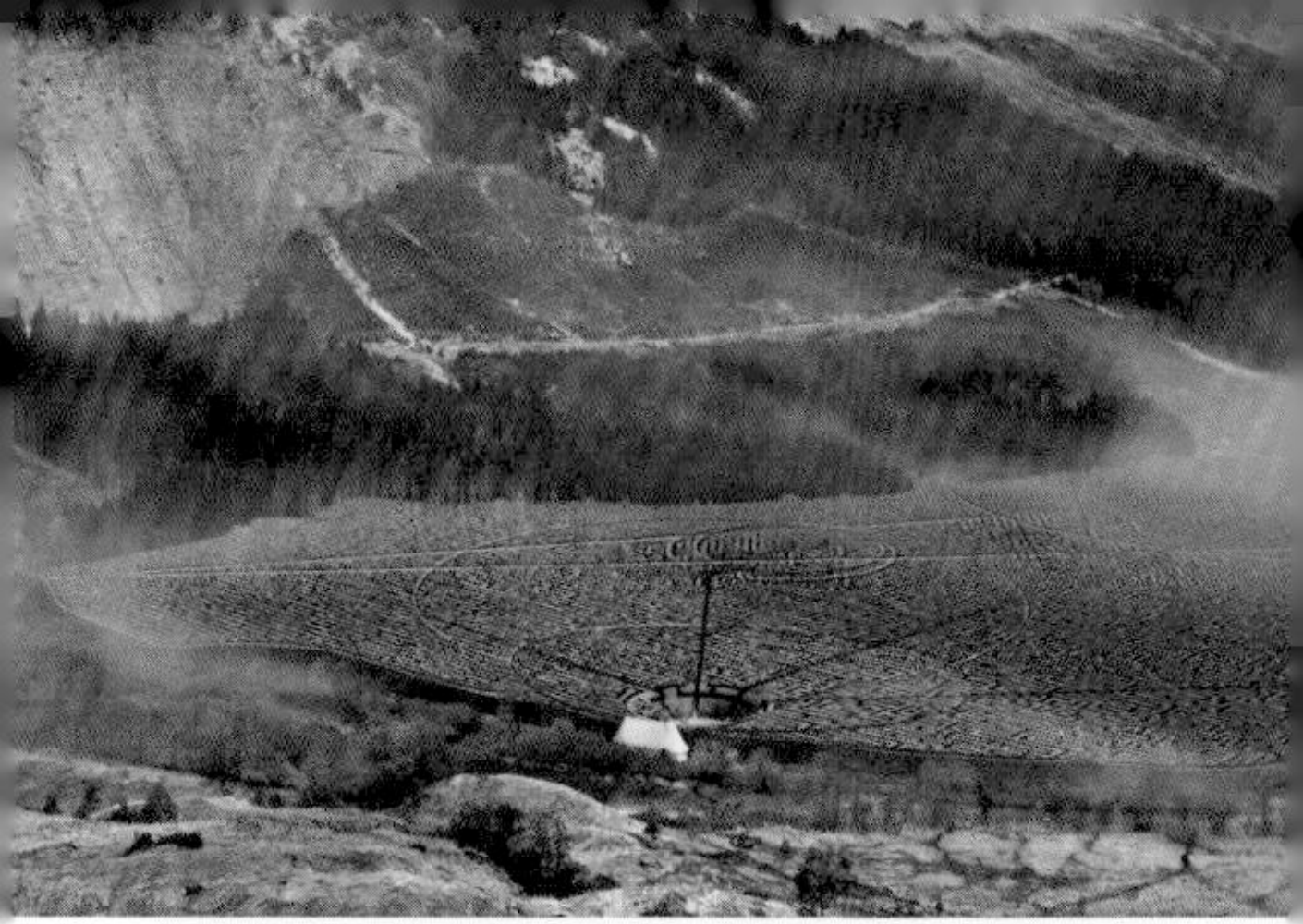

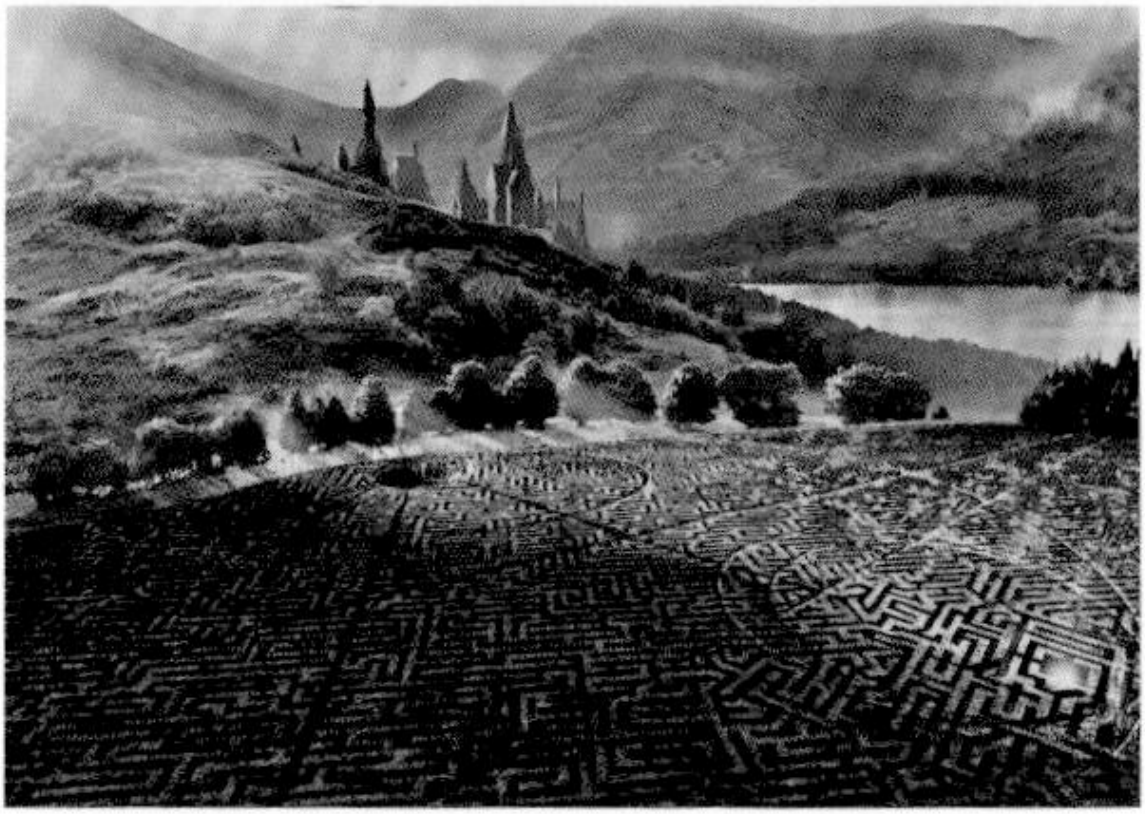

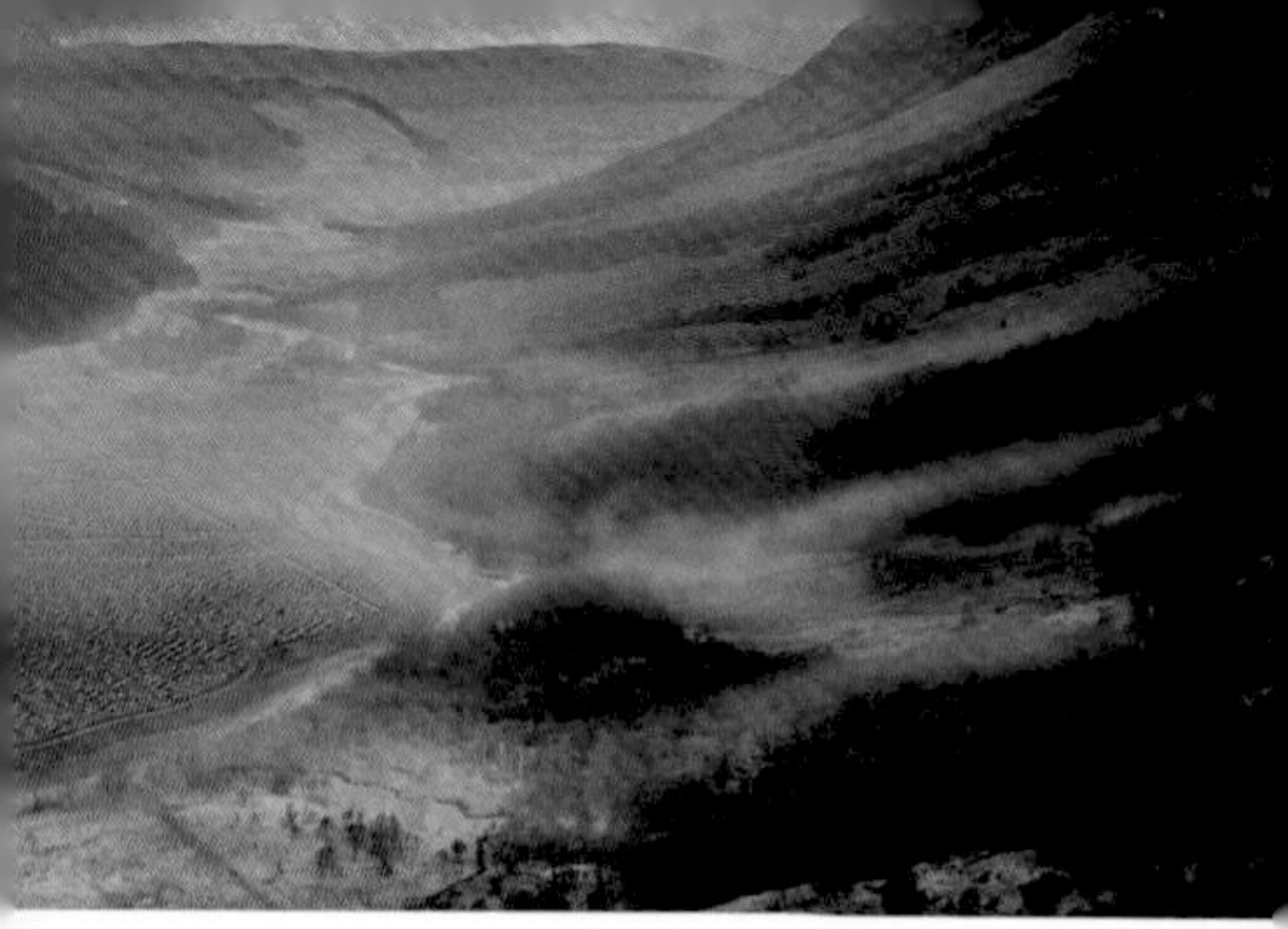

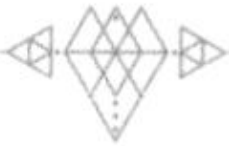

PAGES 210–213: Art by Andrew Williamson showing the exterior and interior of the maze created for the third task of the Triwizard Tournament.

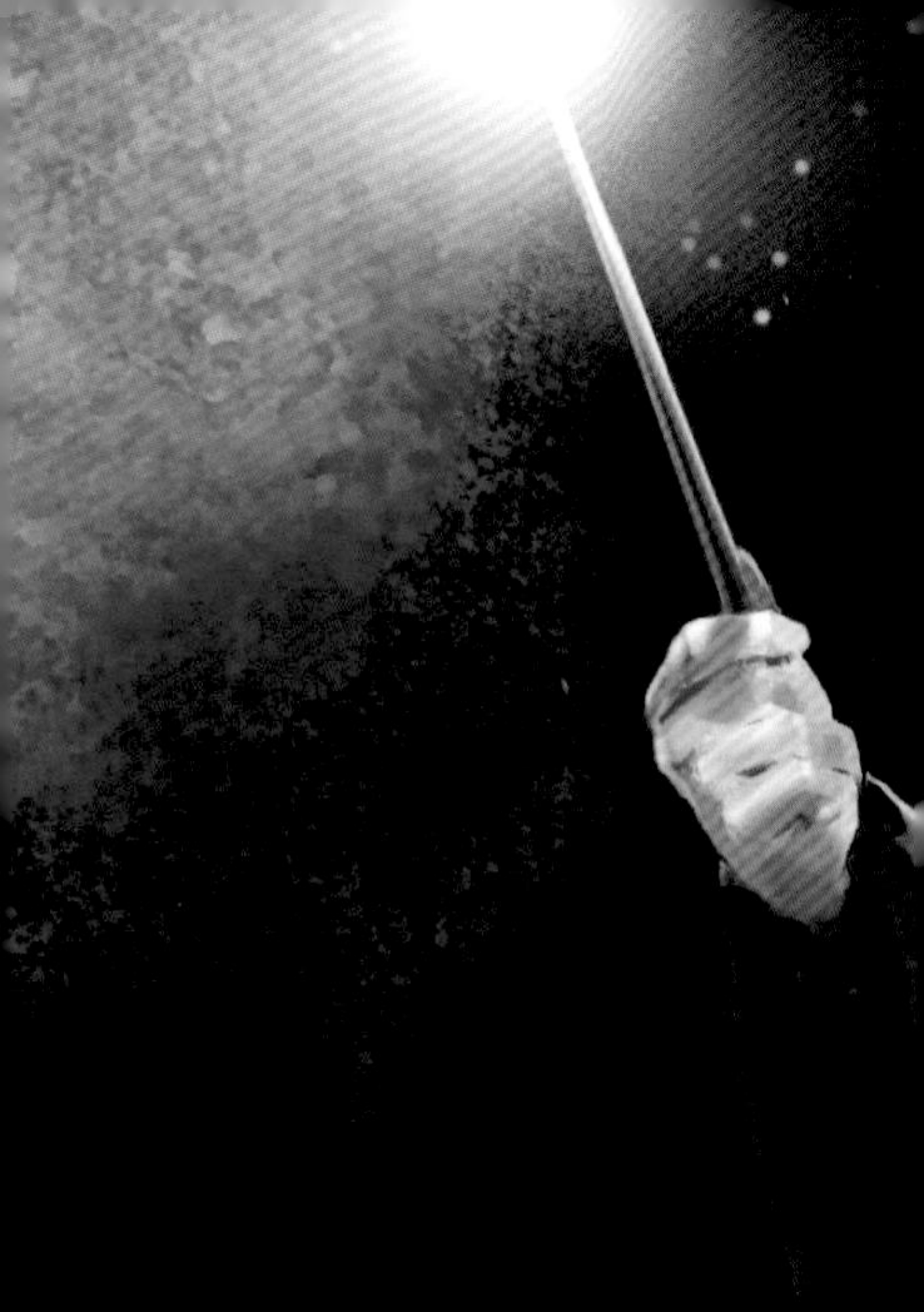

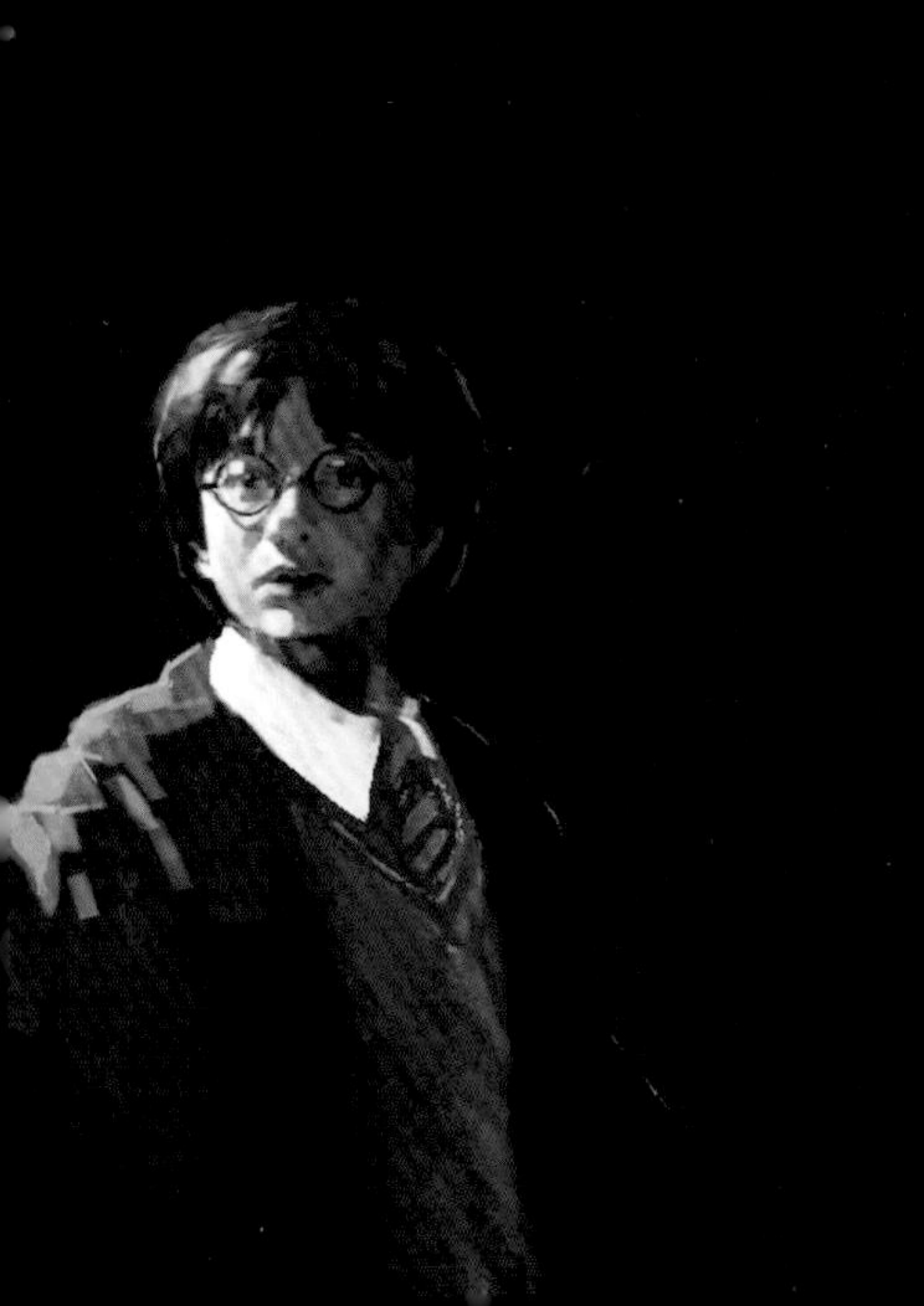

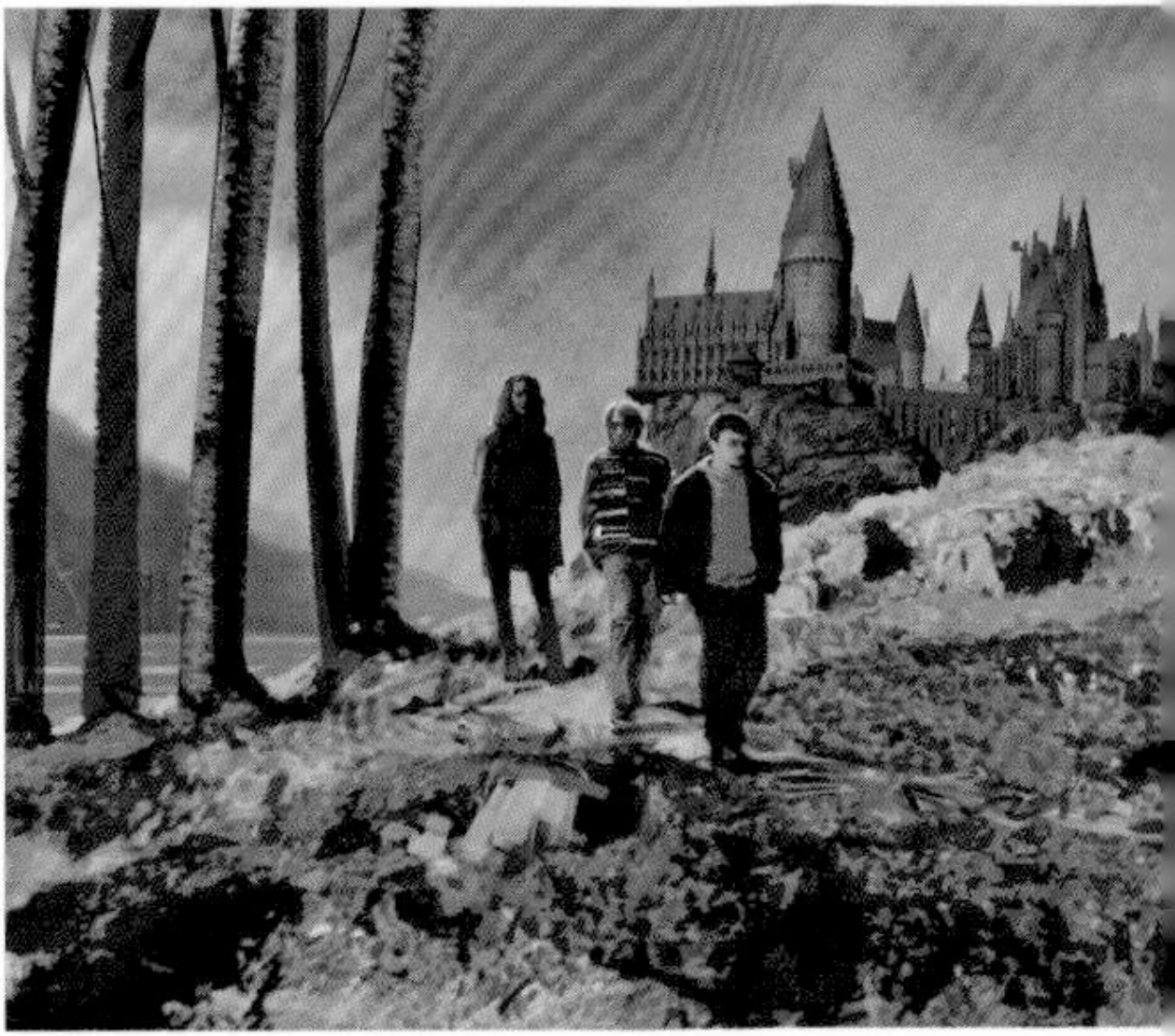

DUMBLEDORE'S TOMB

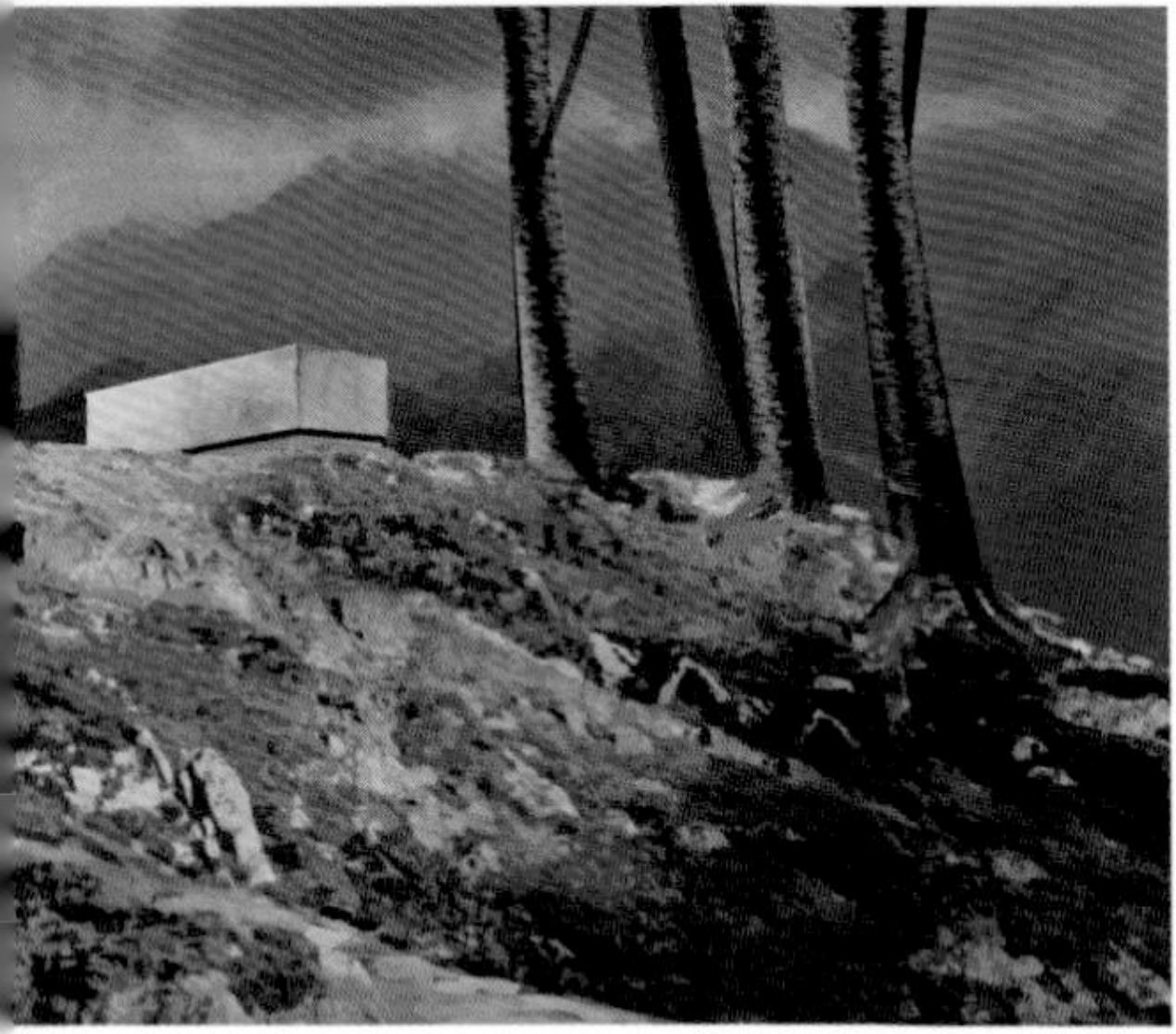

THESE PAGES: Andrew Williamson depicts Harry, Ron, and Hermione next to Professor Dumbledore's tomb on an island in a scene for *Harry Potter and the Half-Blood Prince*. This scene did not make it into the final film.

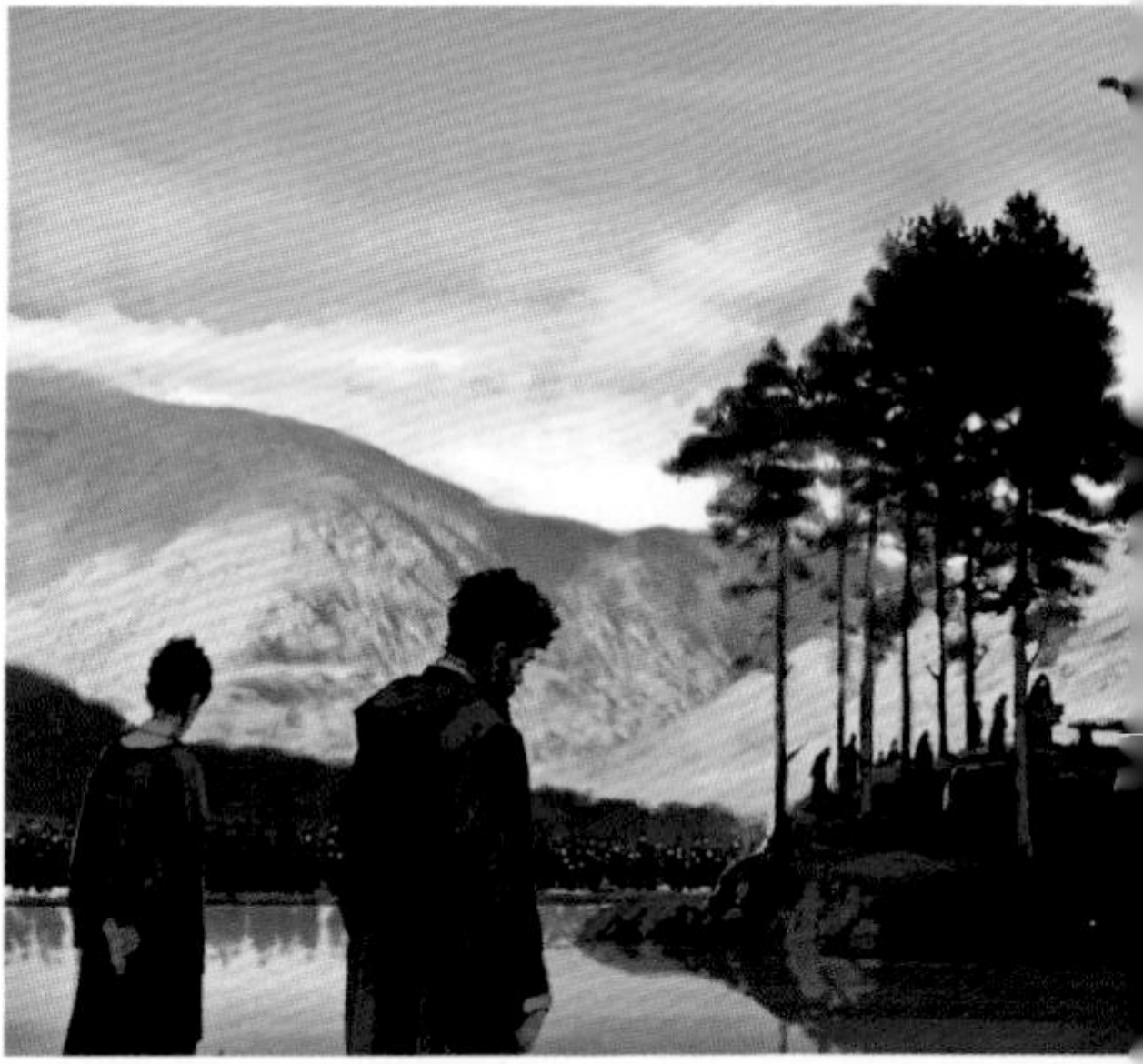

THESE PAGES: Adam Brockbank shows different views of Albus Dumbledore's burial near the Black Lake for *Harry Potter and the Half-Blood Prince*. This scene was not filmed for the movie.

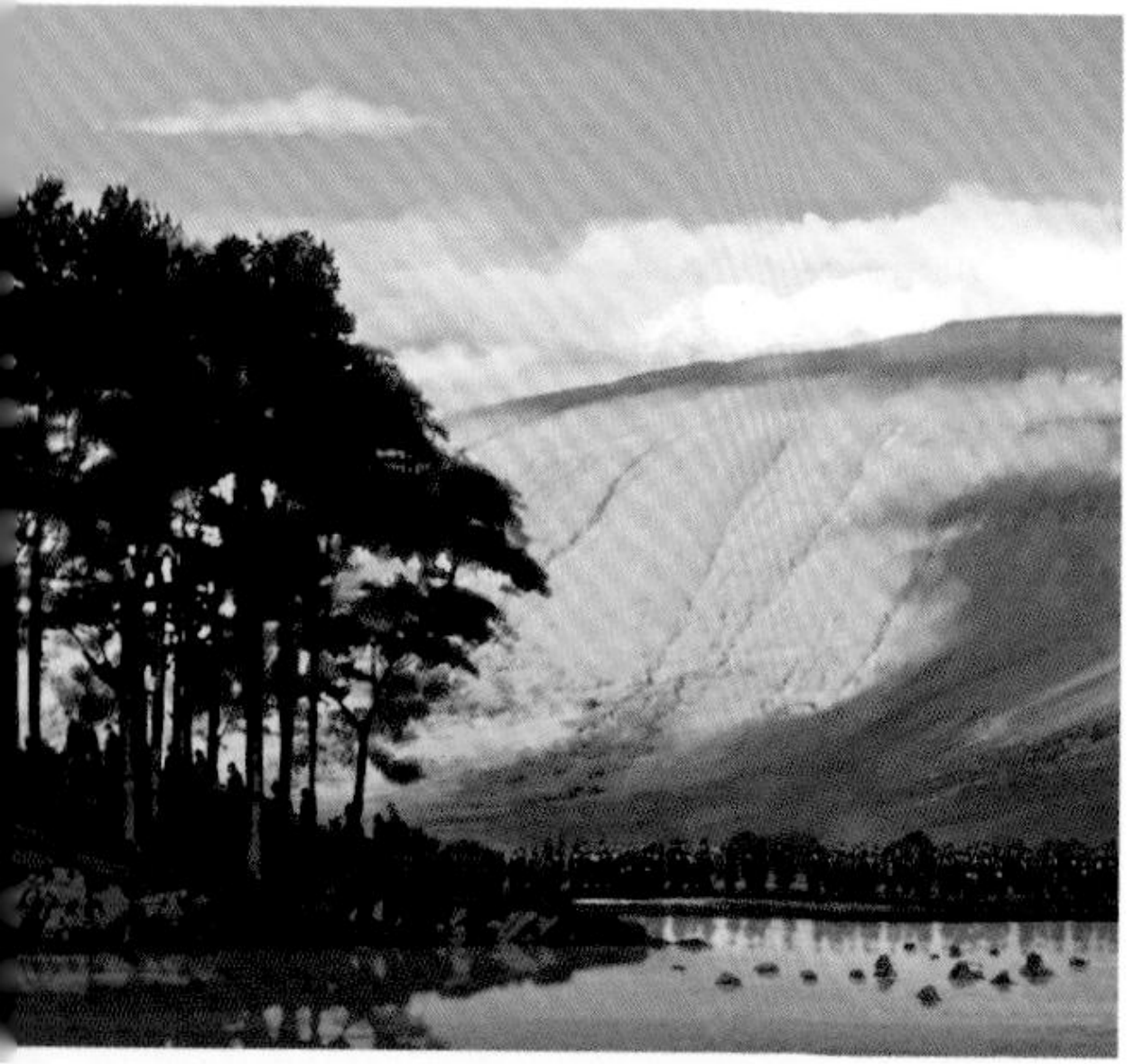

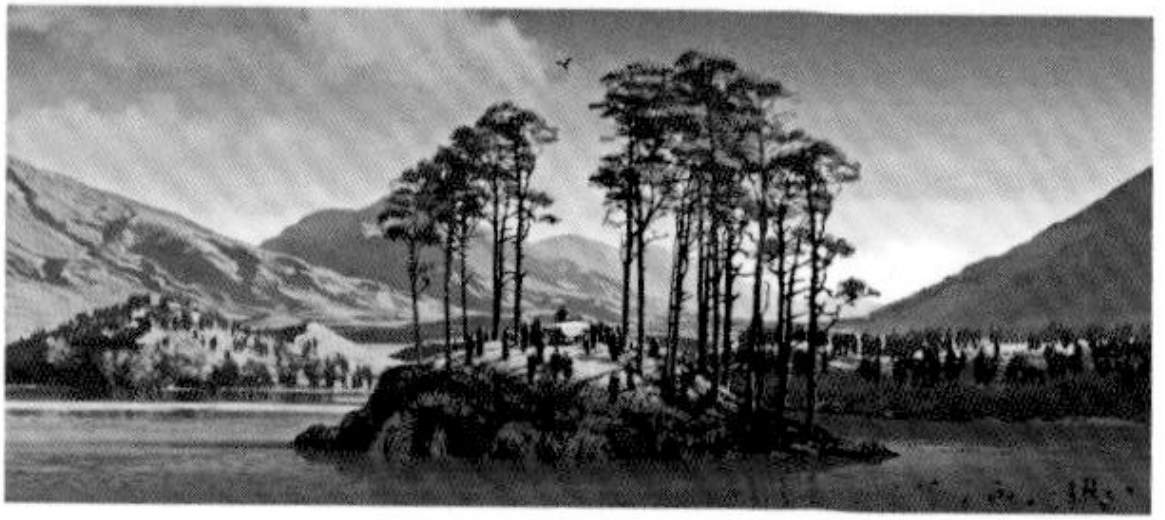

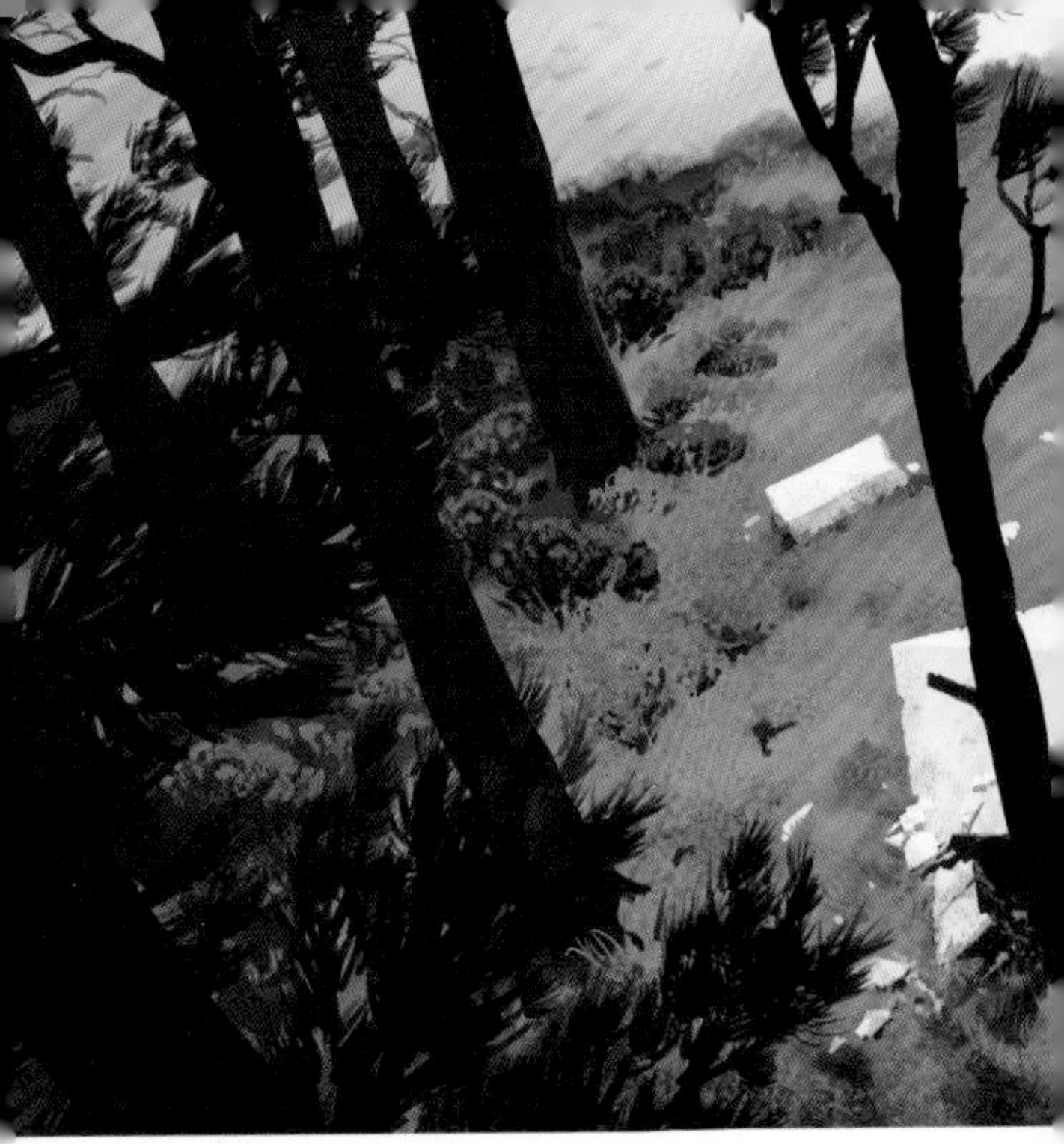

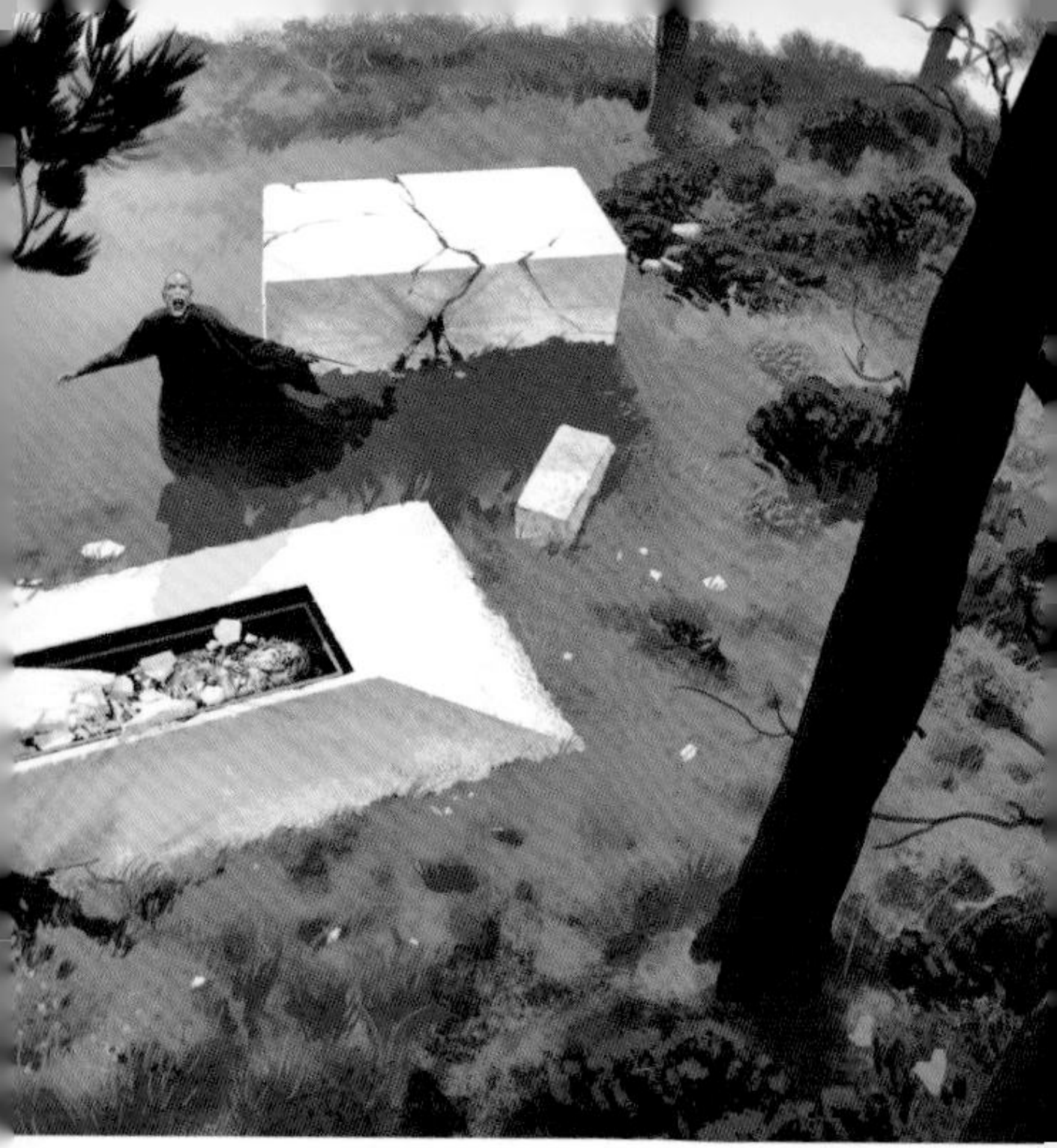

THESE PAGES: Voldemort breaks into Dumbledore's tomb to retrieve the Elder Wand. Art by Adam Brockbank for *Harry Potter and the Deathly Hallows – Part 1*.

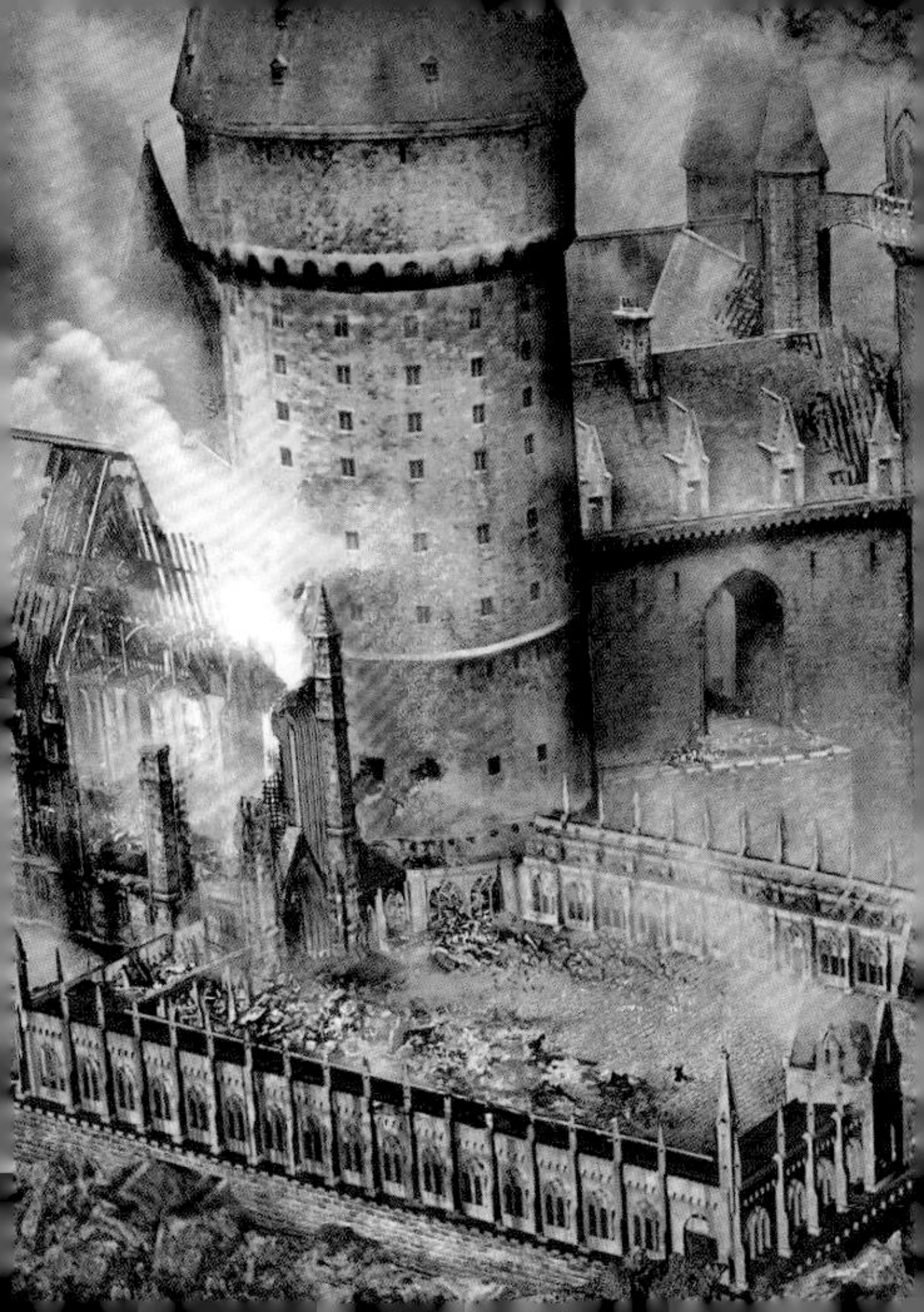

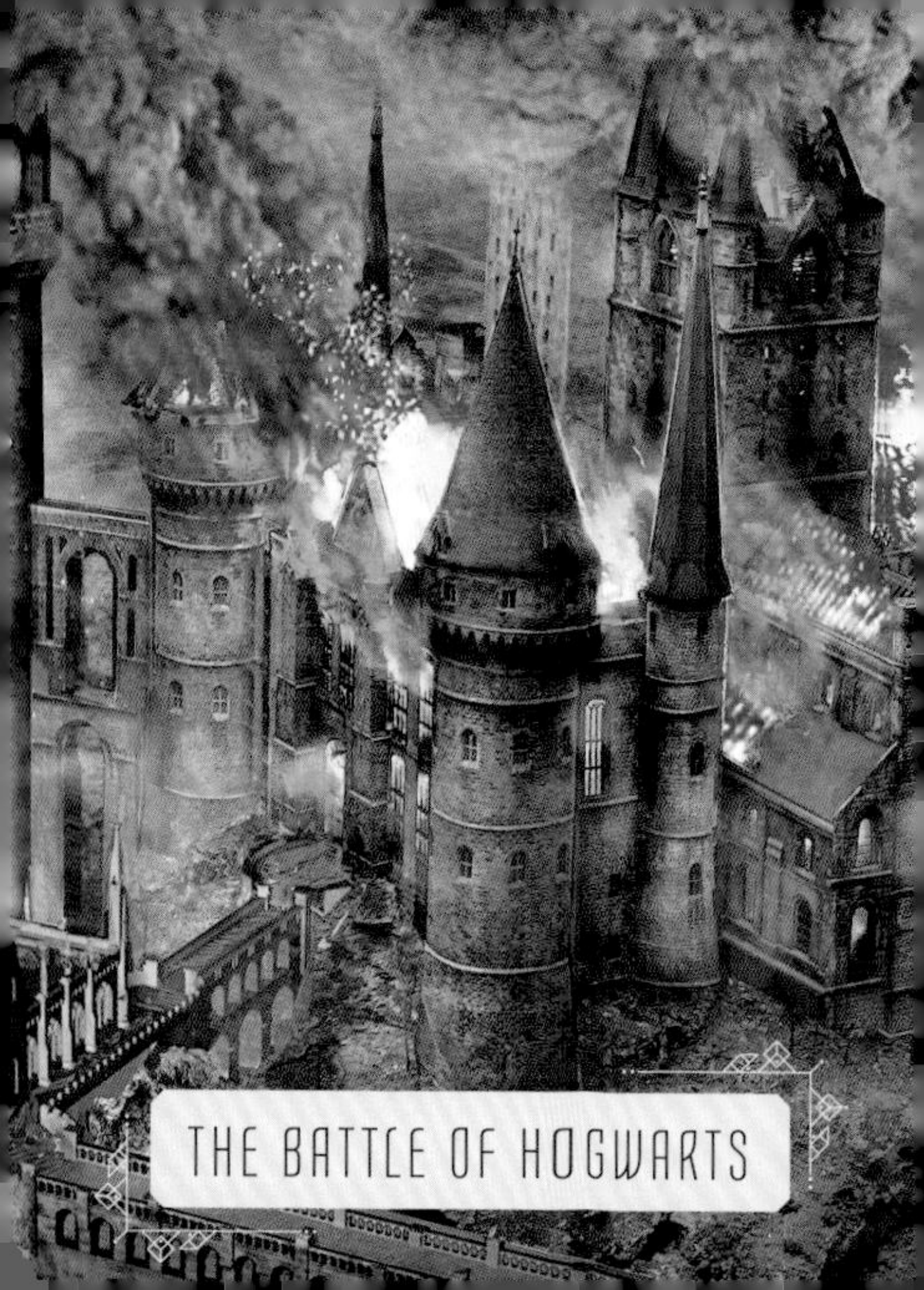

THE BATTLE OF HOGWARTS

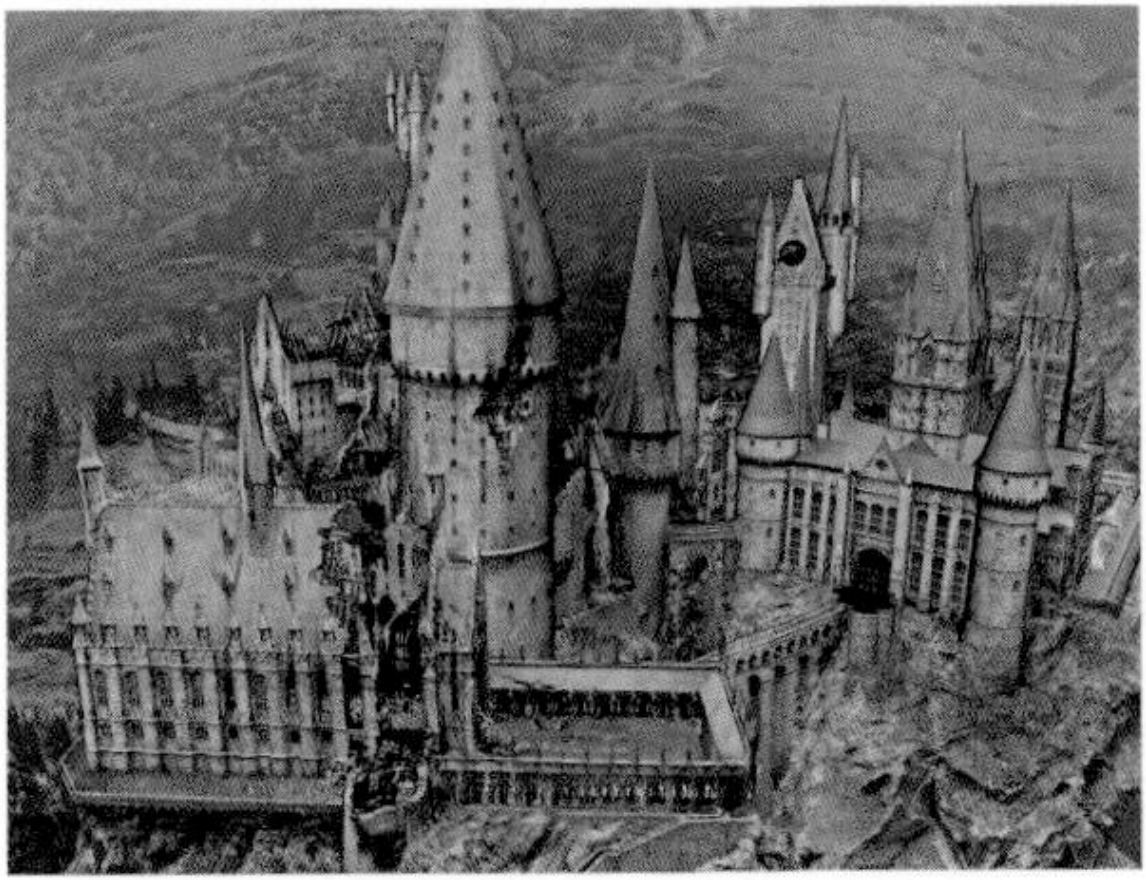

PAGES 220–223: Andrew Williamson depicts Hogwarts castle under attack during the Battle of Hogwarts in *Harry Potter and the Deathly Hallows – Part 2*.

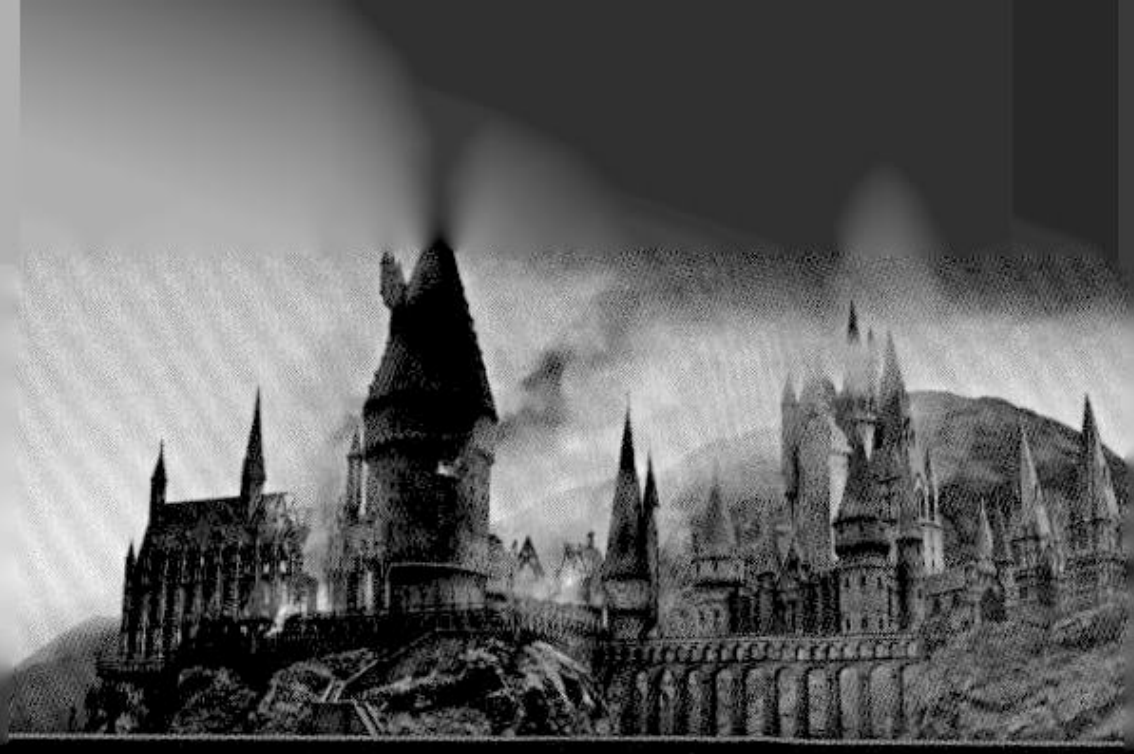

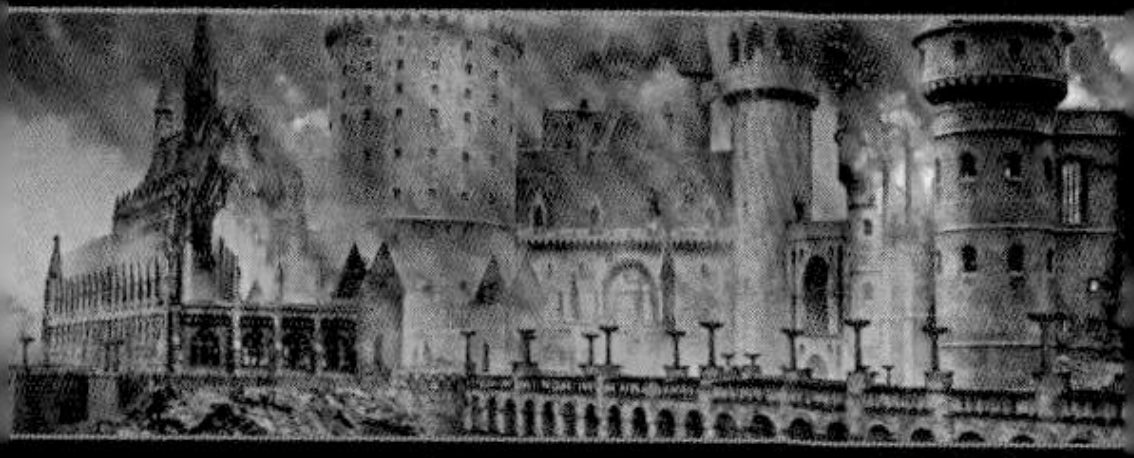

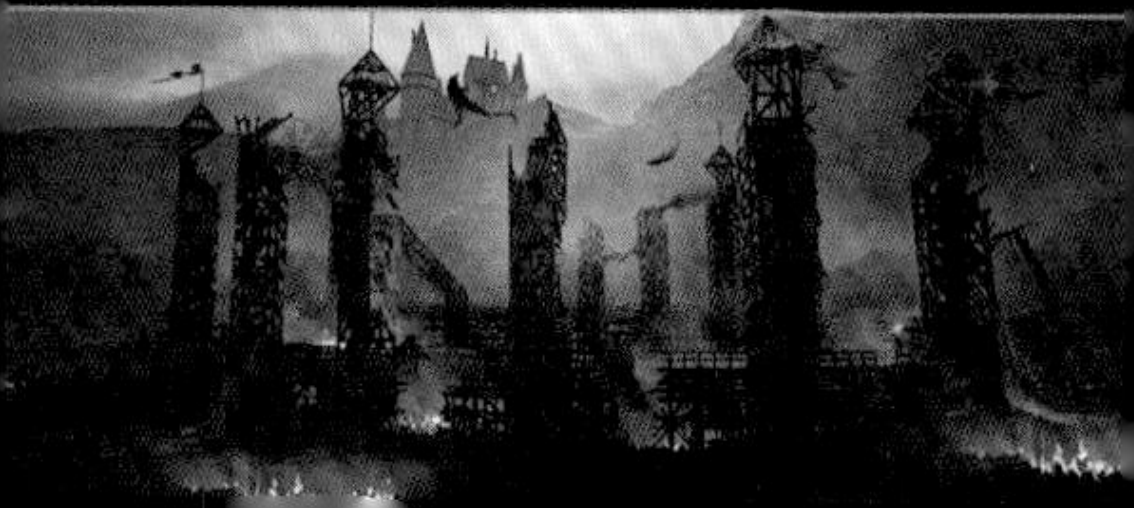

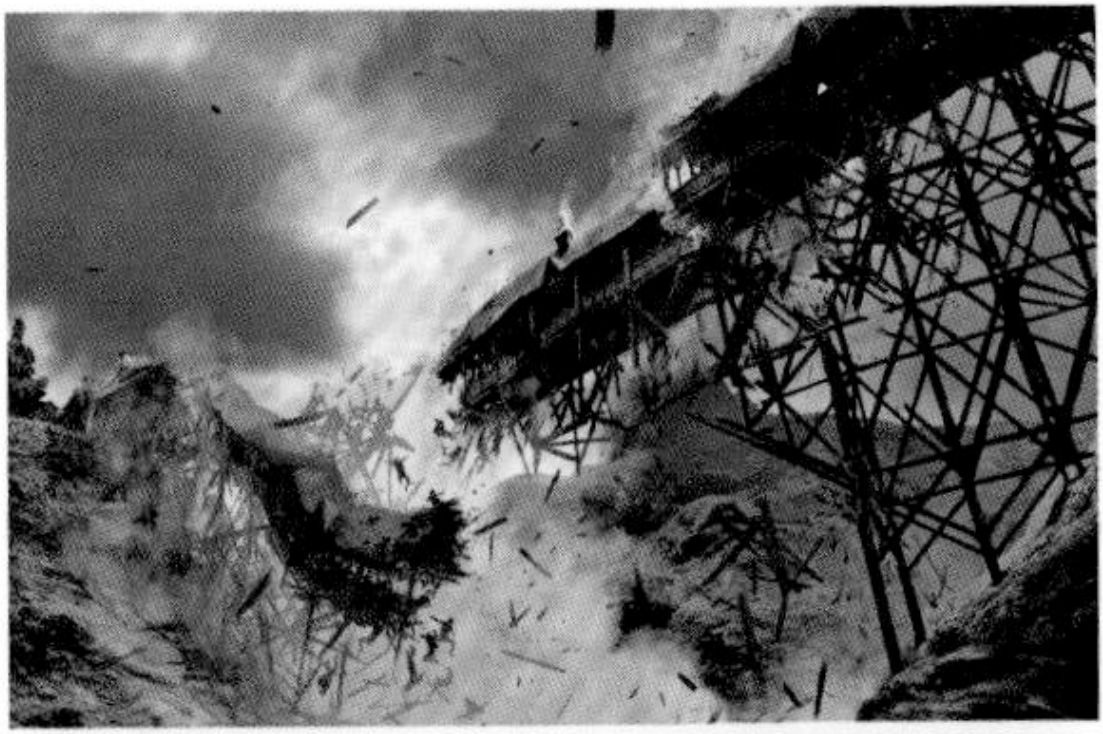

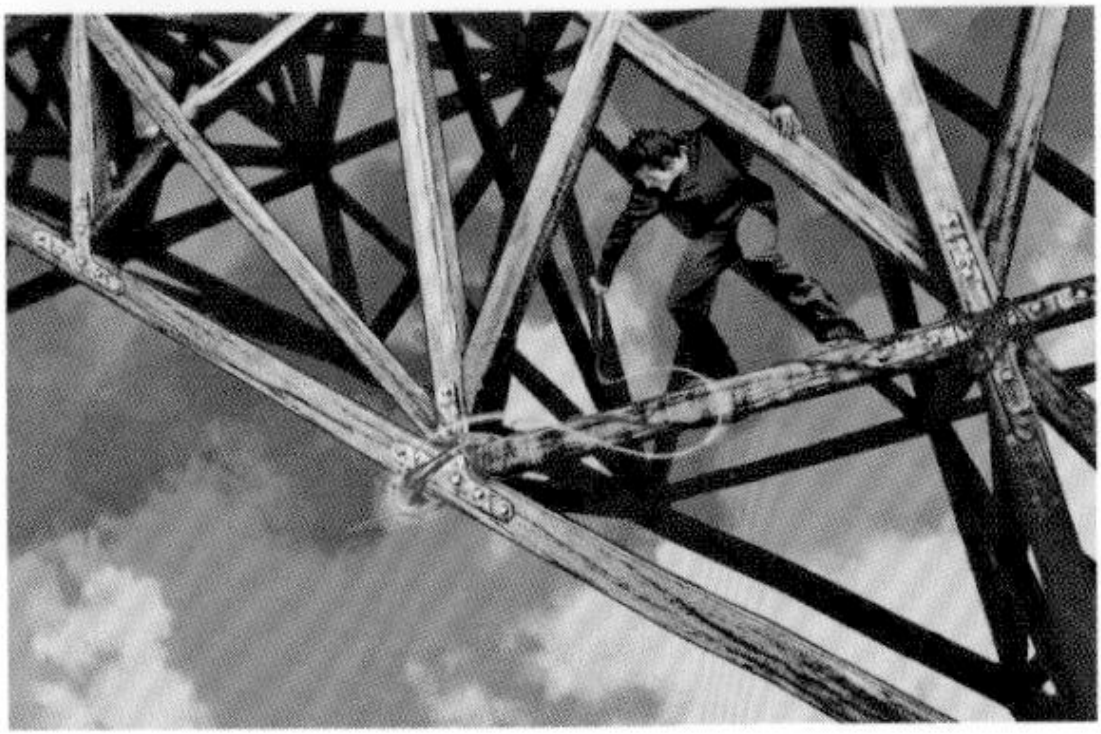

ABOVE: Adam Brockbank depicts the destruction of Hogwarts' covered bridge.

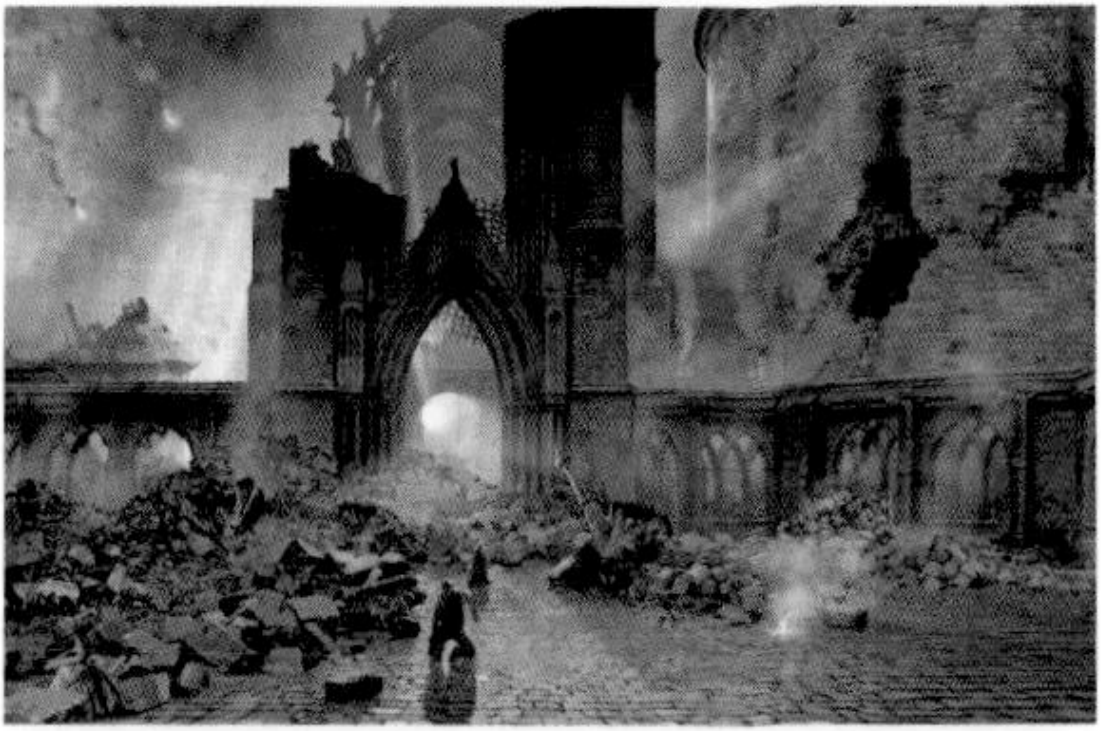

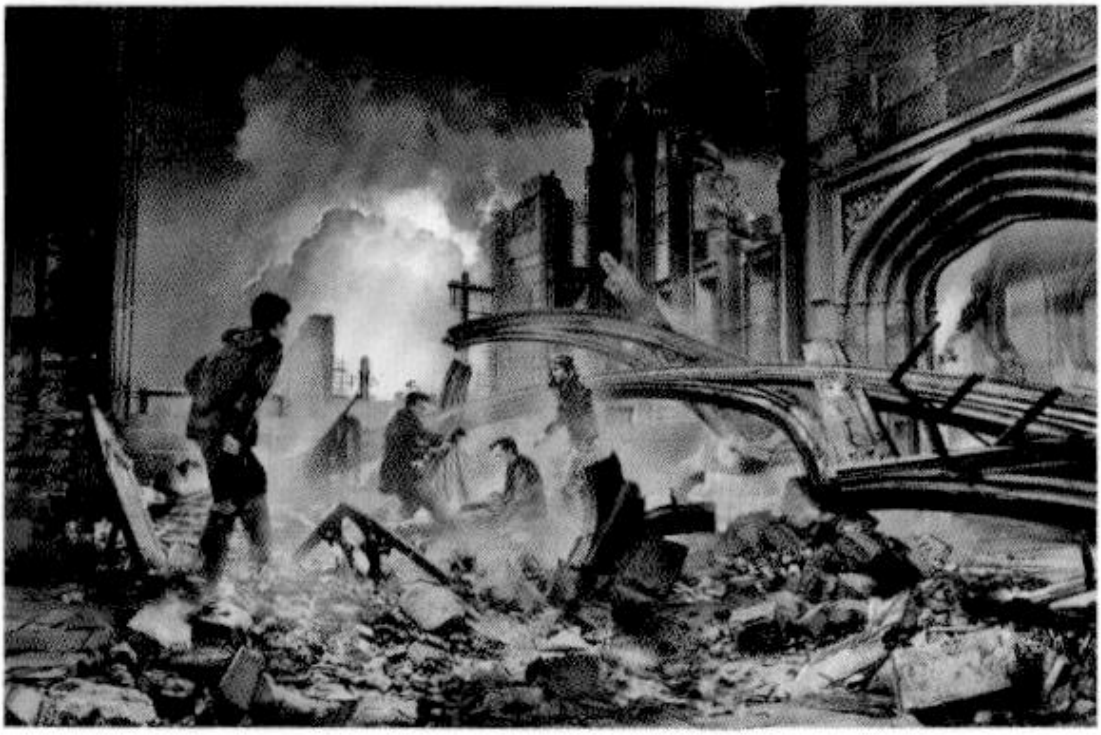

ABOVE: Andrew Williamson pictures various scenes in Hogwarts' decimated courtyard.

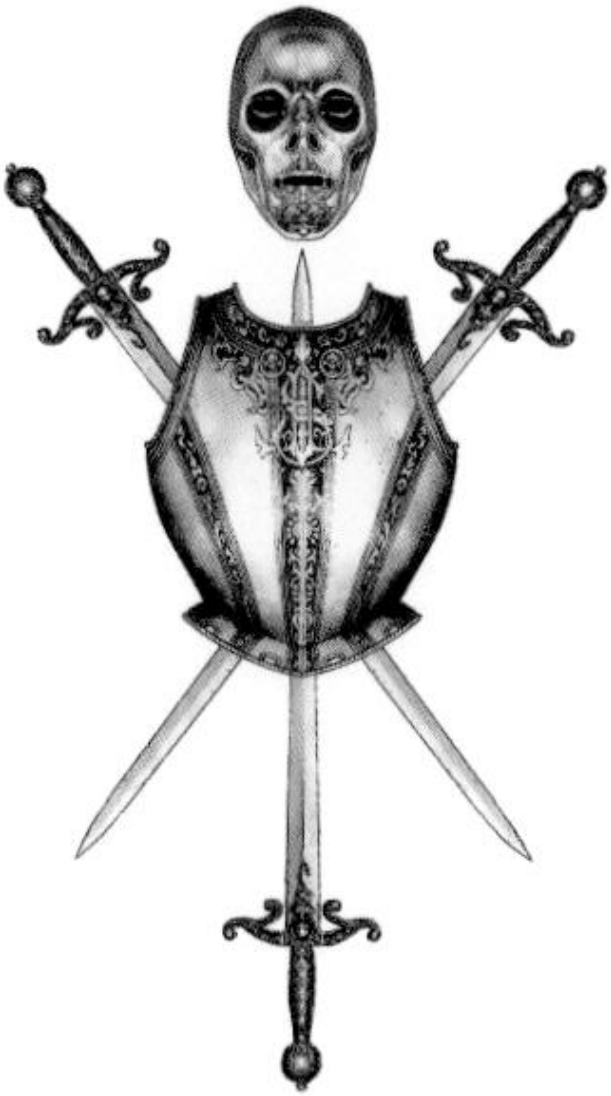

ABOVE: Death Eater armor by Adam Brockbank for *Harry Potter and the Deathly Hallows – Part 1.*

OPPOSITE: The fighting knights of Hogwarts castle by Adam Brockbank. The knights are brought to life when Professor McGonagall casts the spell *Piertotum Locomotor* in *Harry Potter and the Deathly Hallows – Part 2.*

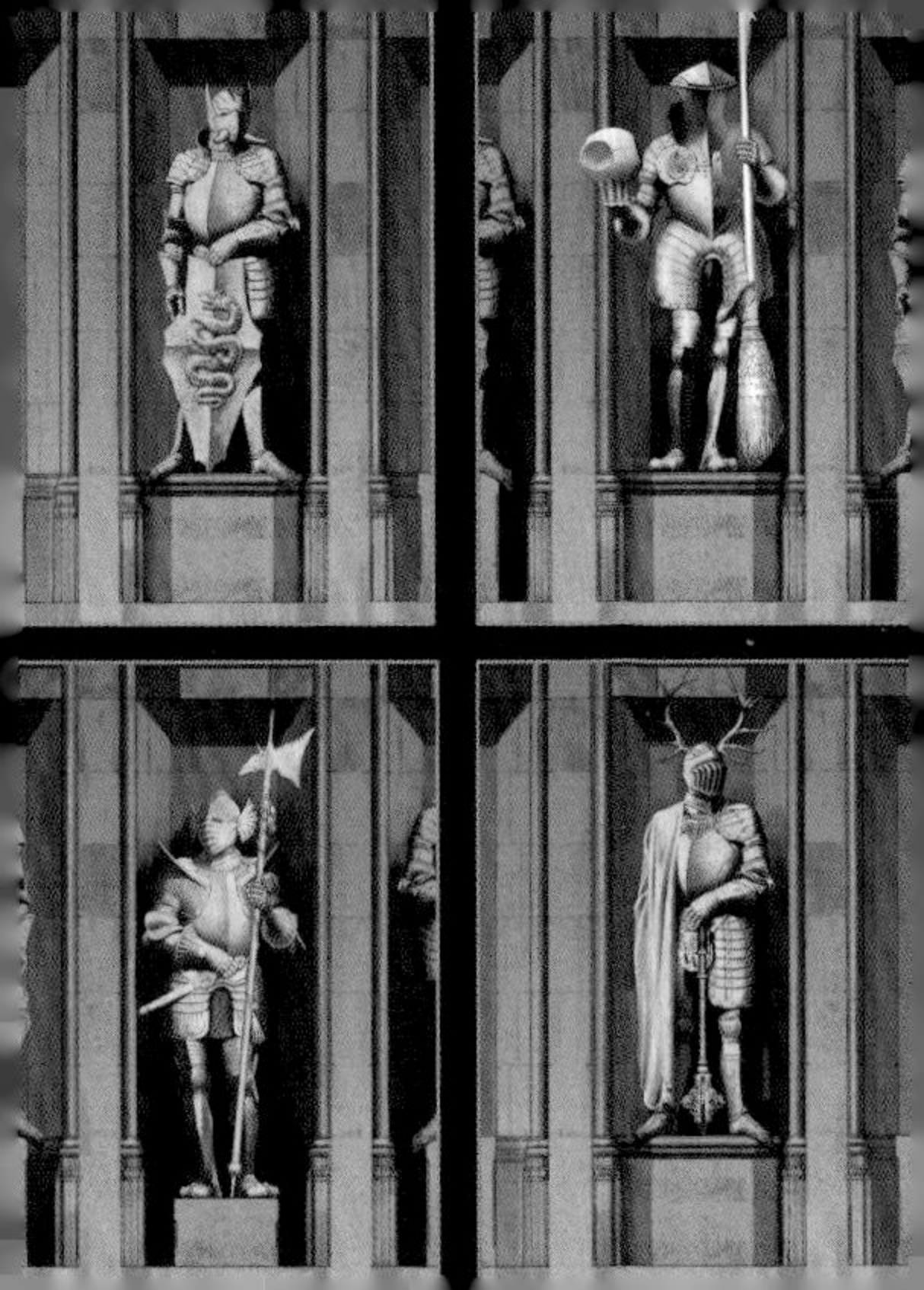

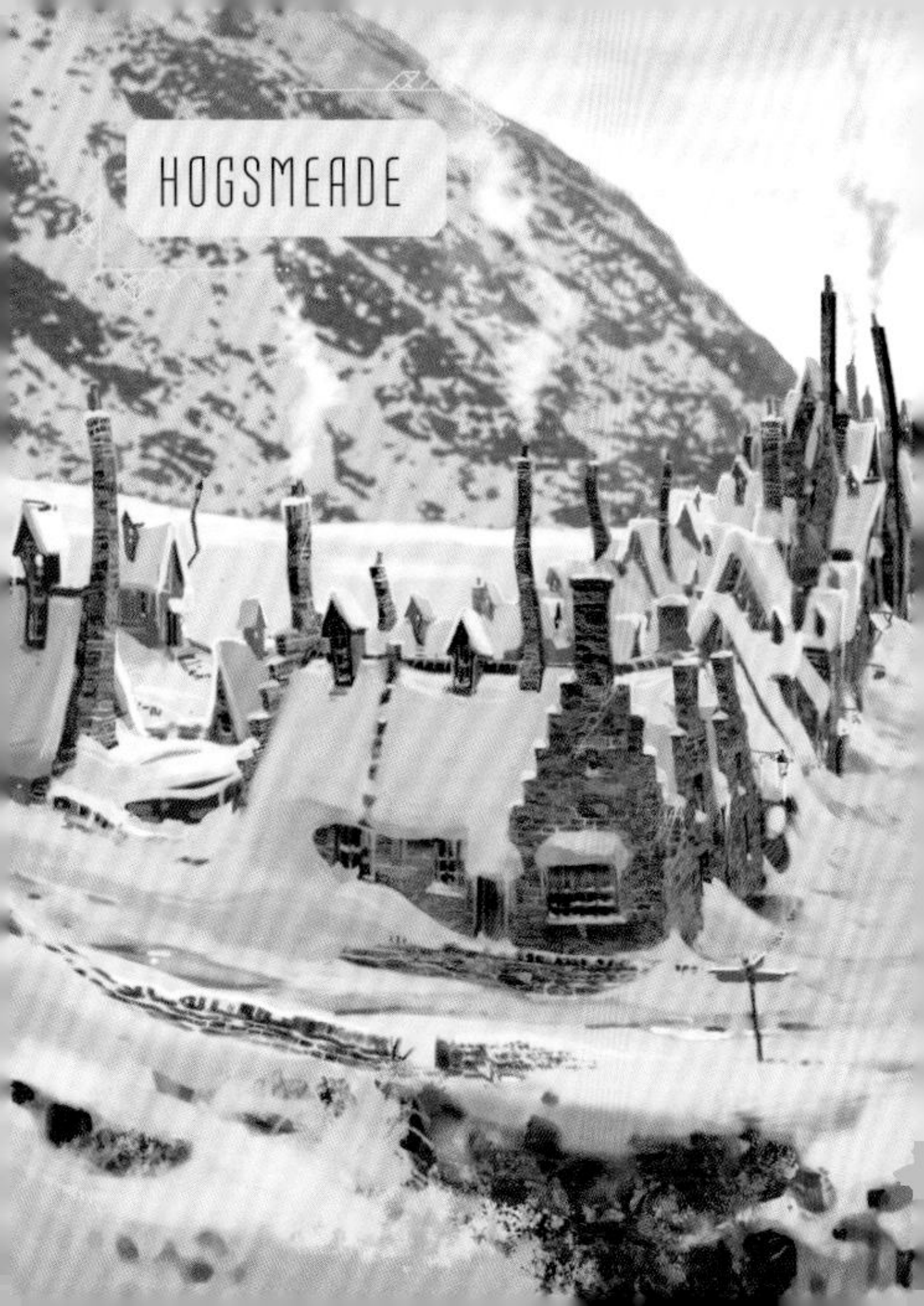
HOGSMEADE

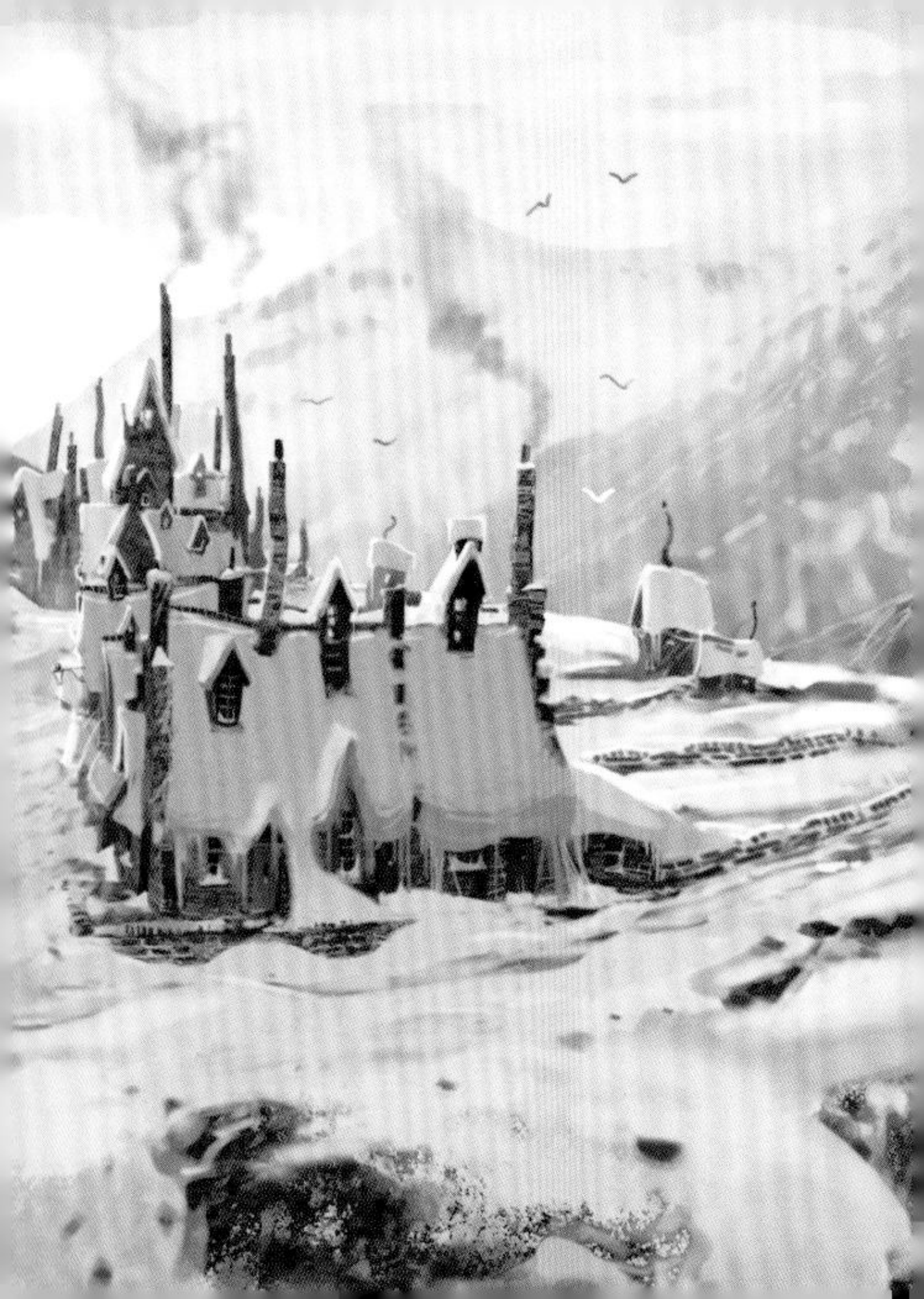

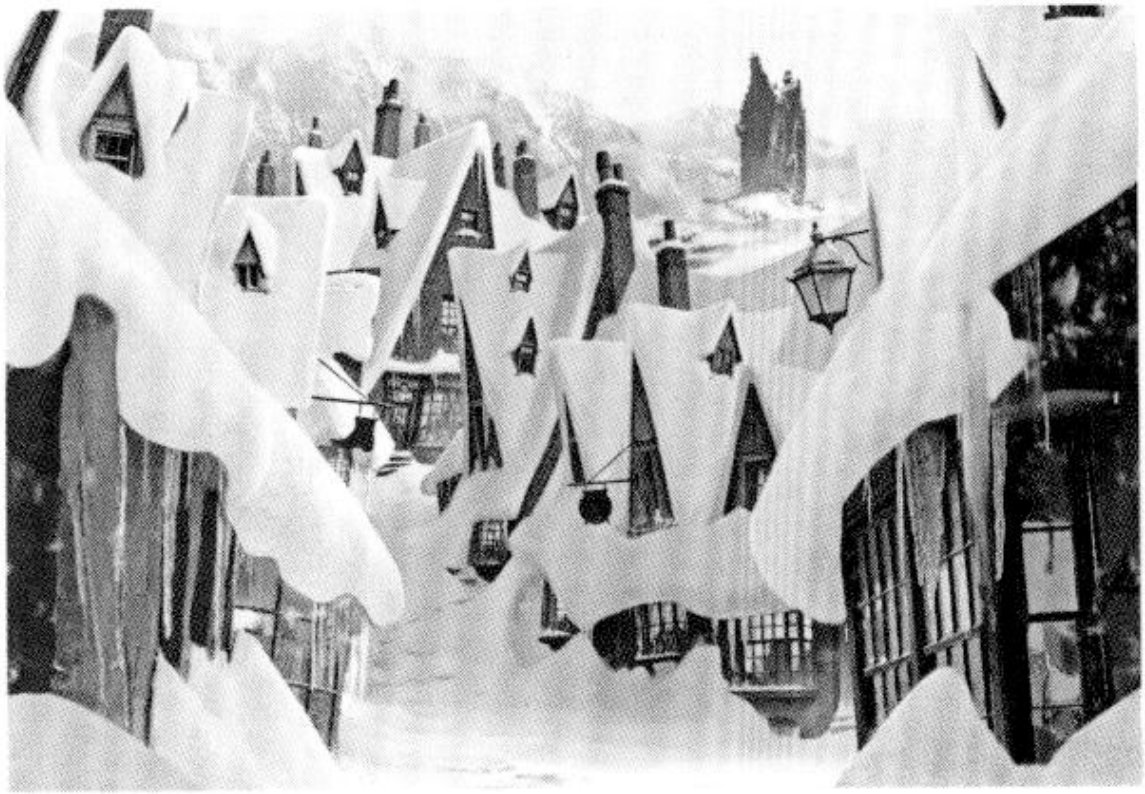

PAGES 228–235: Andrew Williamson paints and sketches various views of the wizarding village of Hogsmeade, which is perpetually above the snowline.

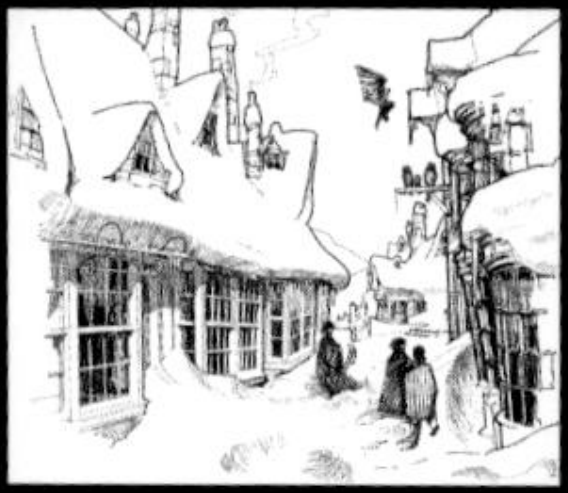

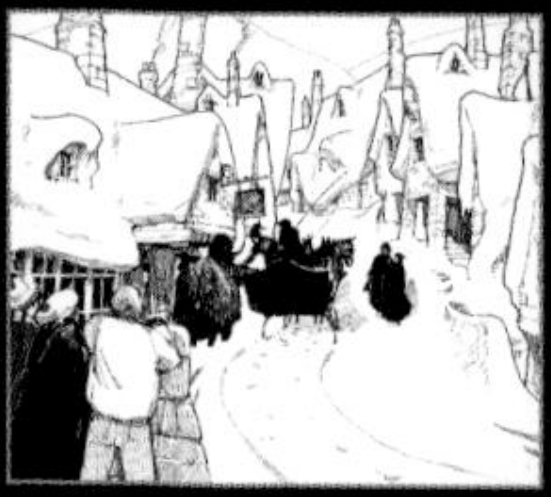

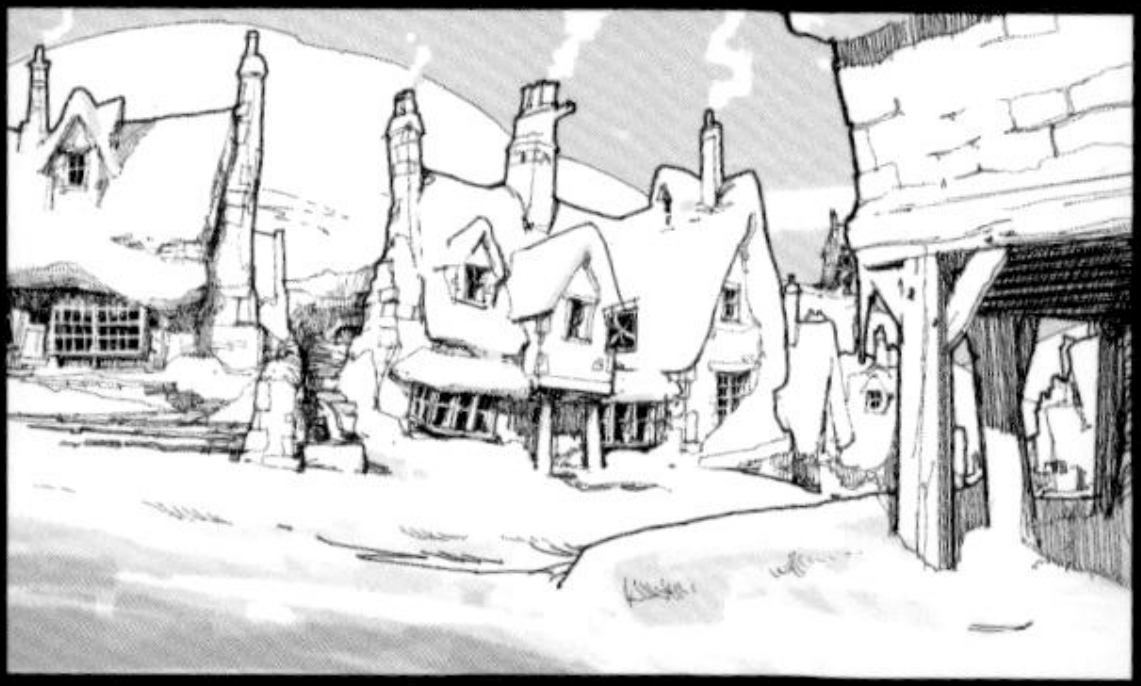

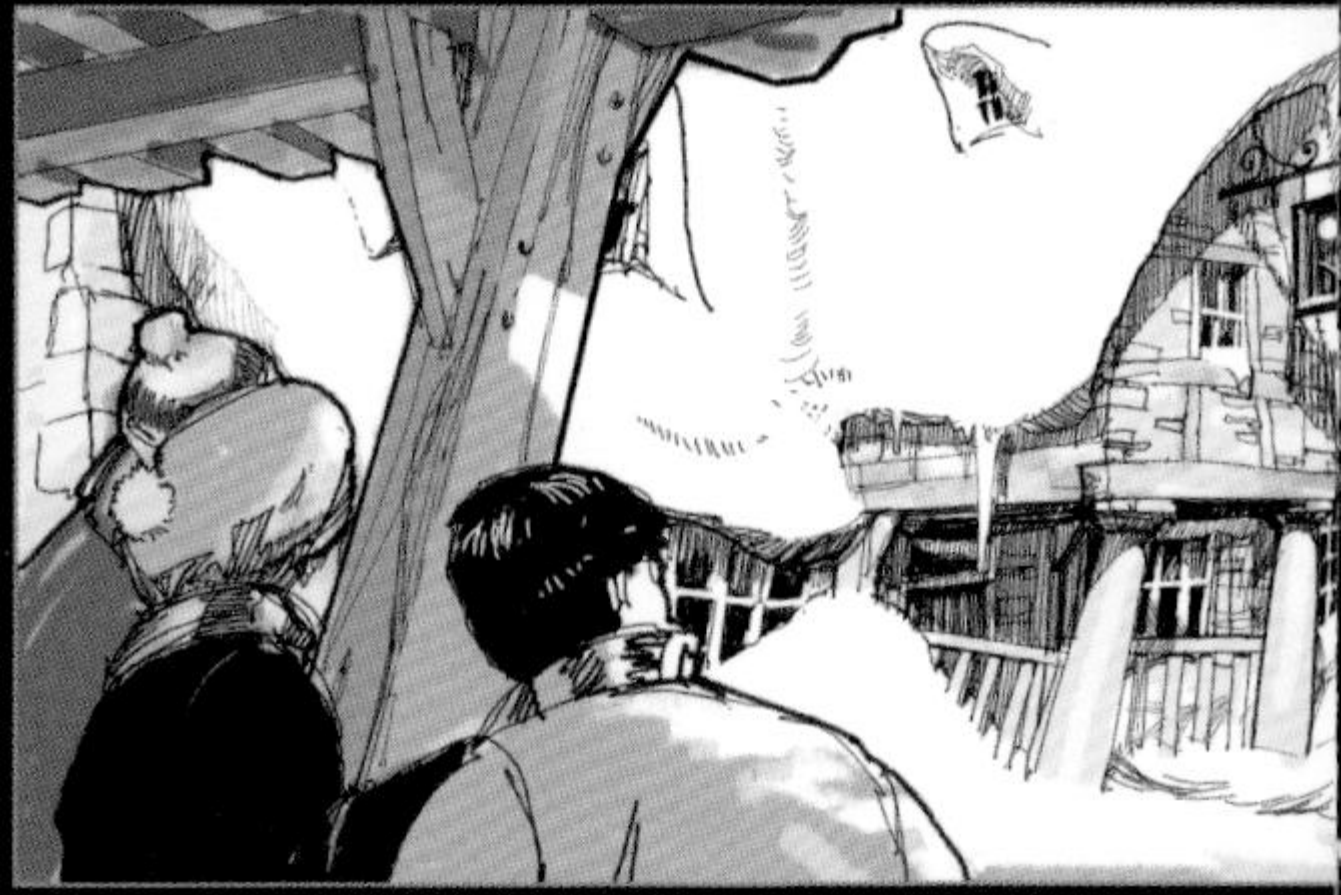

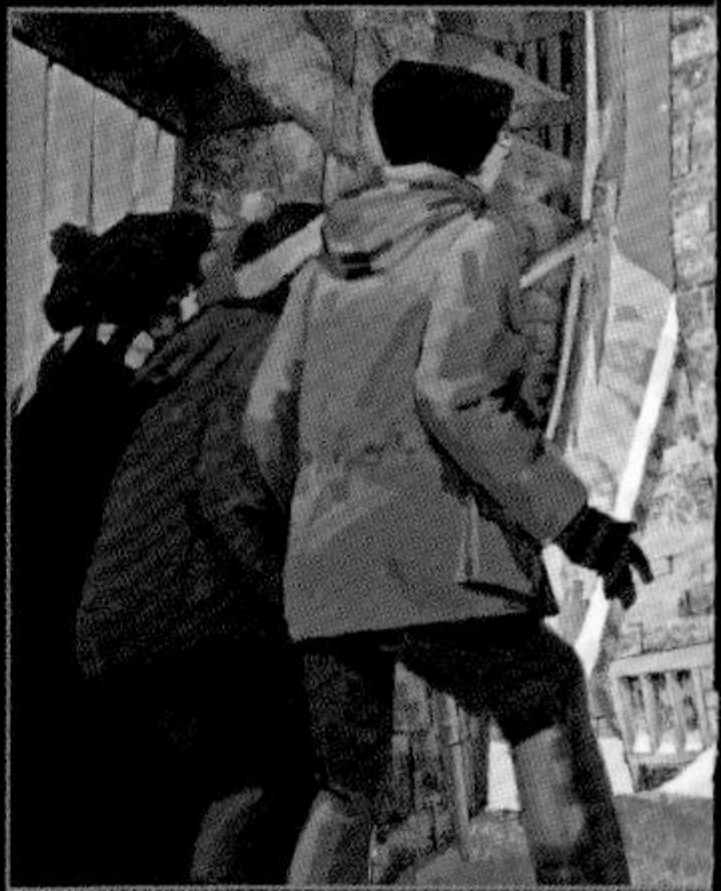

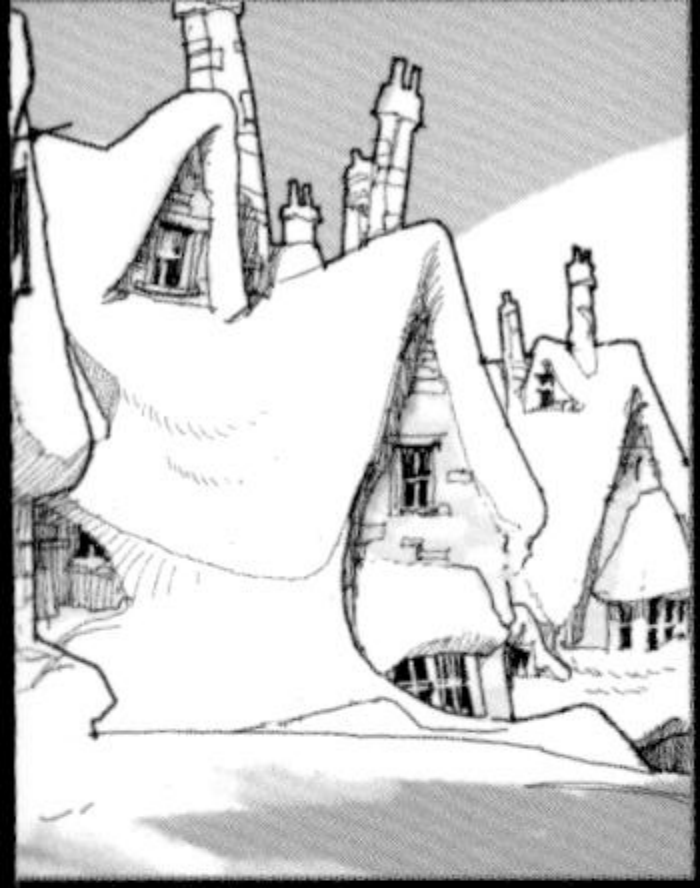

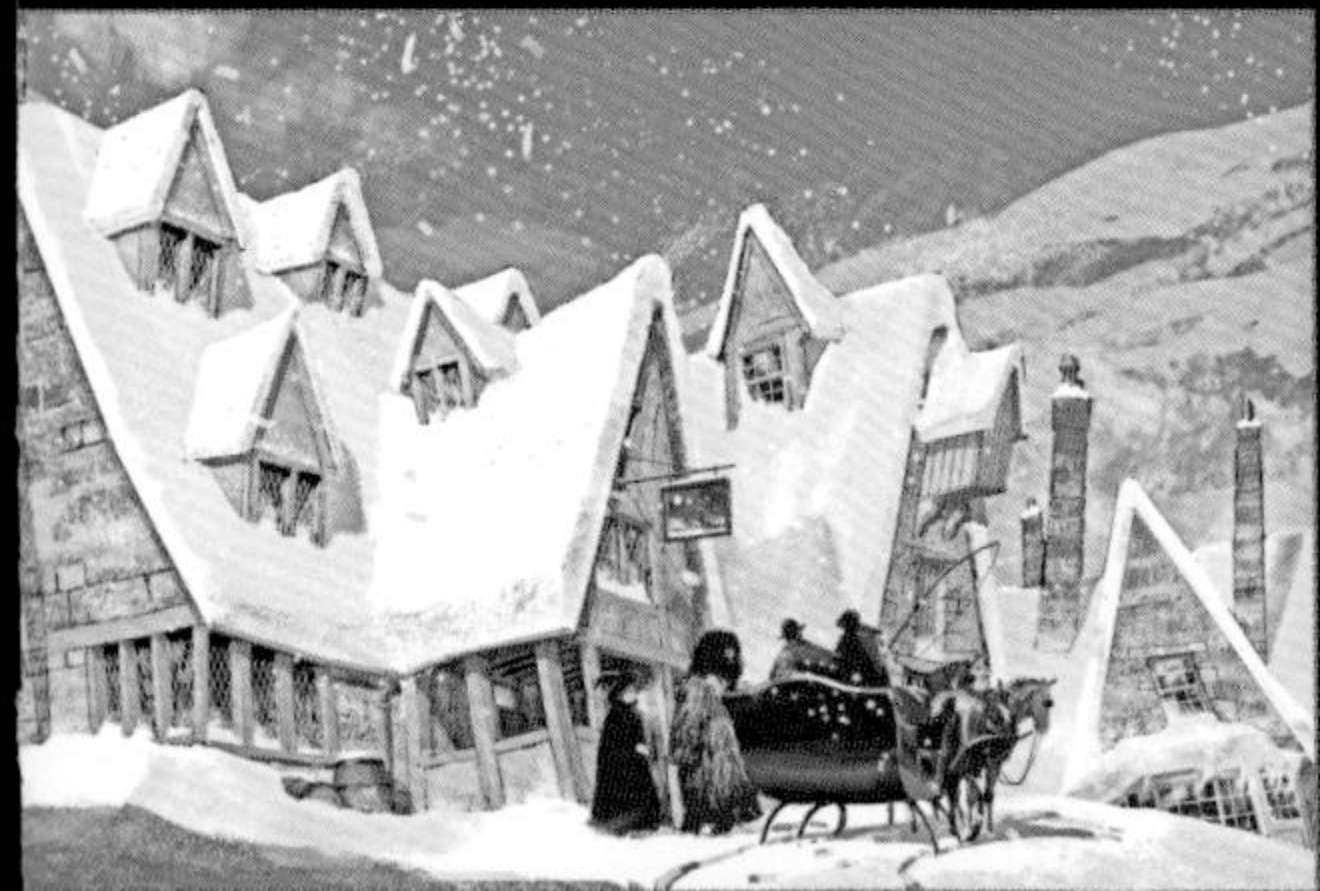

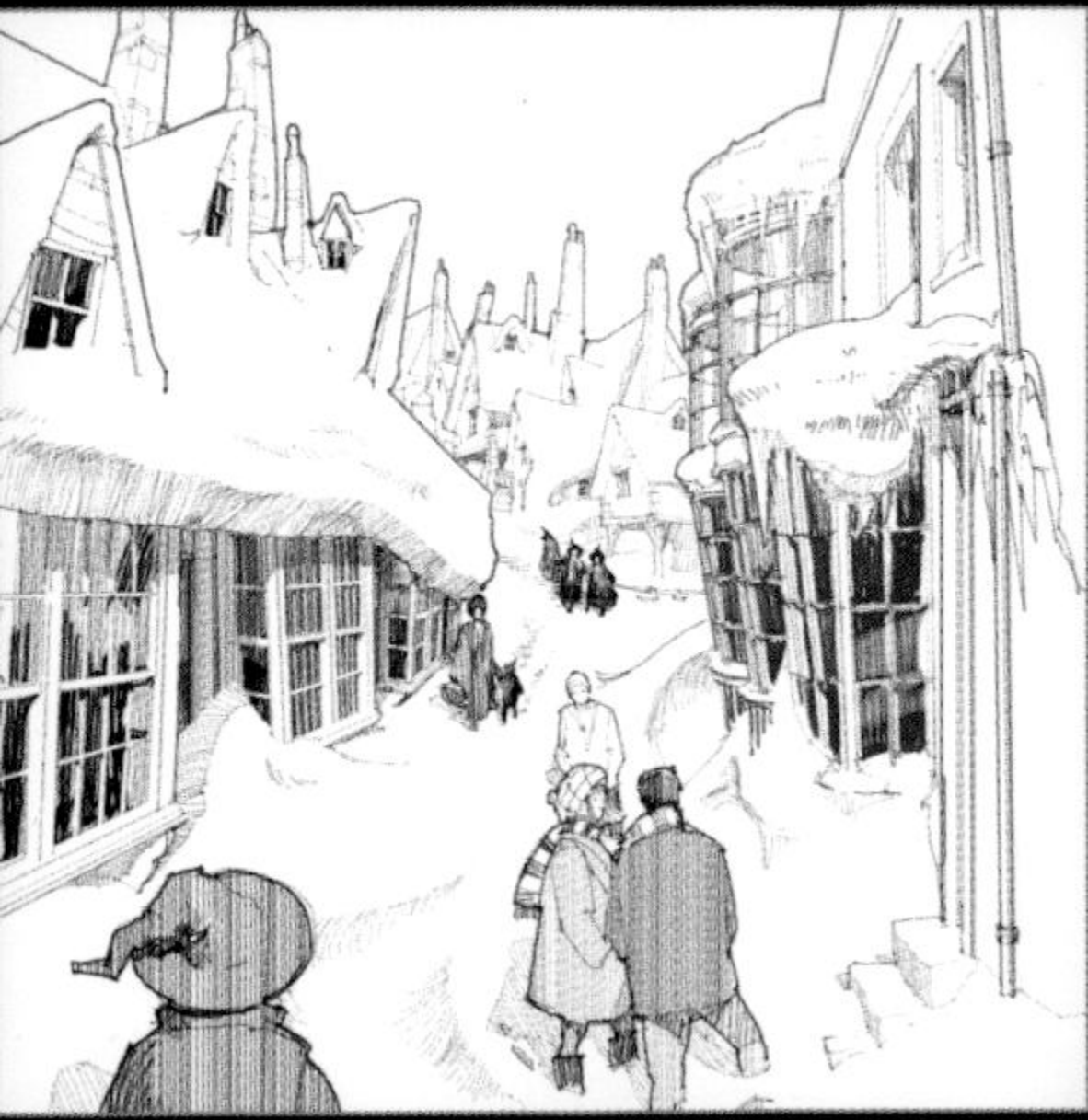

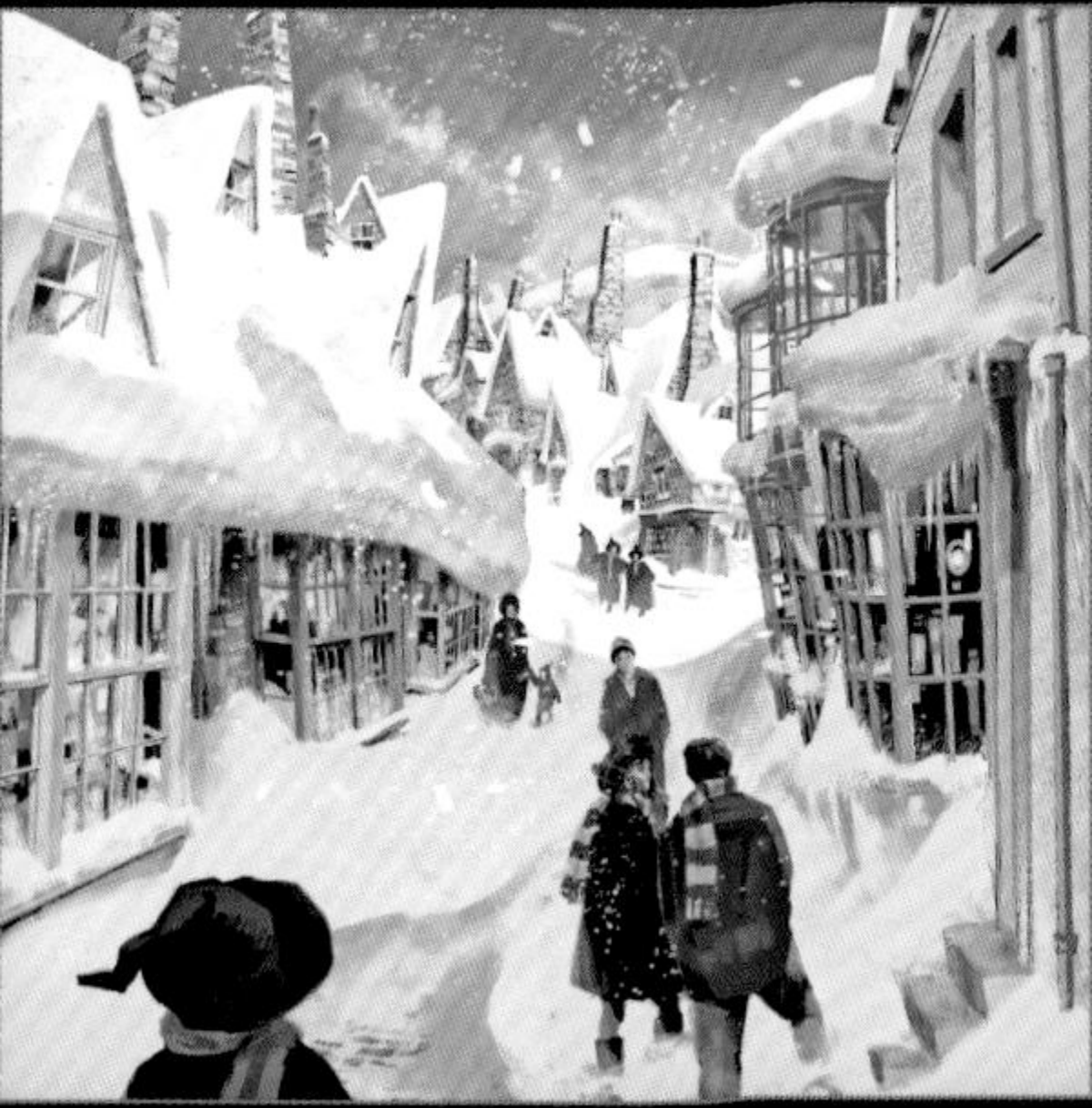

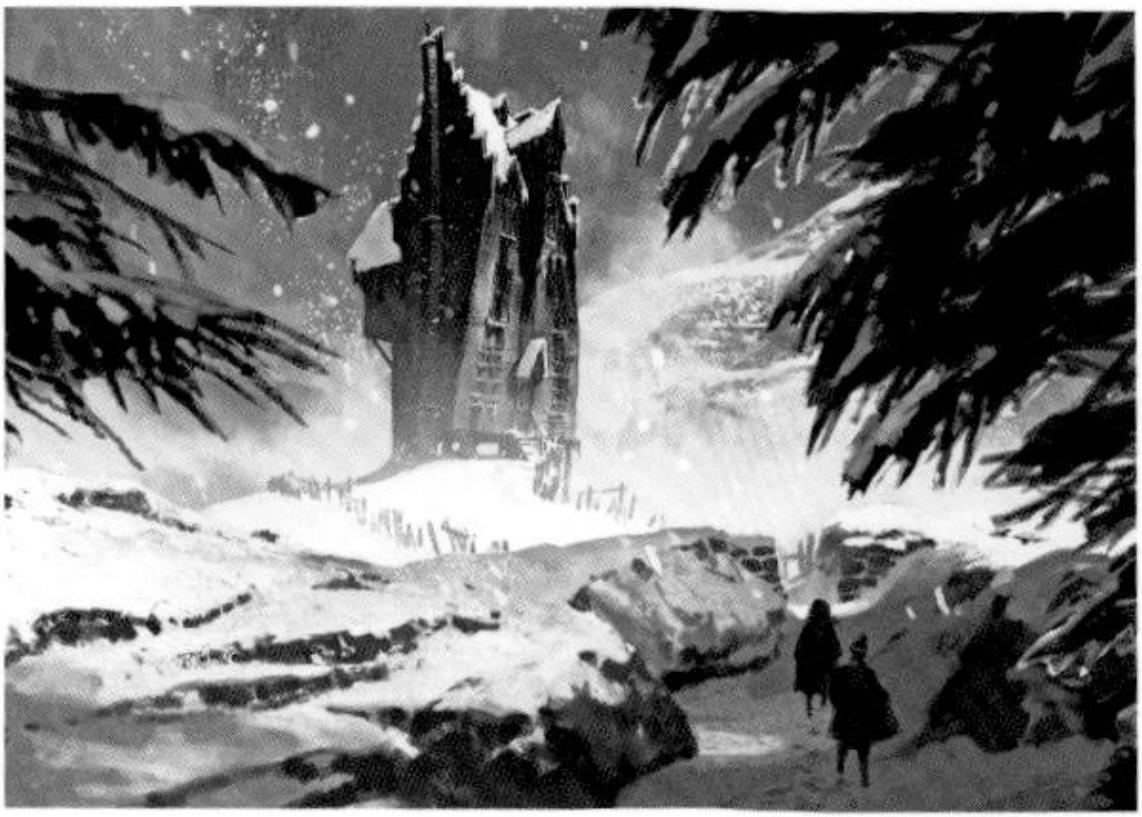

ABOVE: Ron and Hermione walk toward the Shrieking Shack, the most haunted building in England, by Adam Brockbank for *Harry Potter and the Prisoner of Azkaban*.

OPPOSITE: Dermot Power presents a different, though still snowy, view of Hogsmeade.

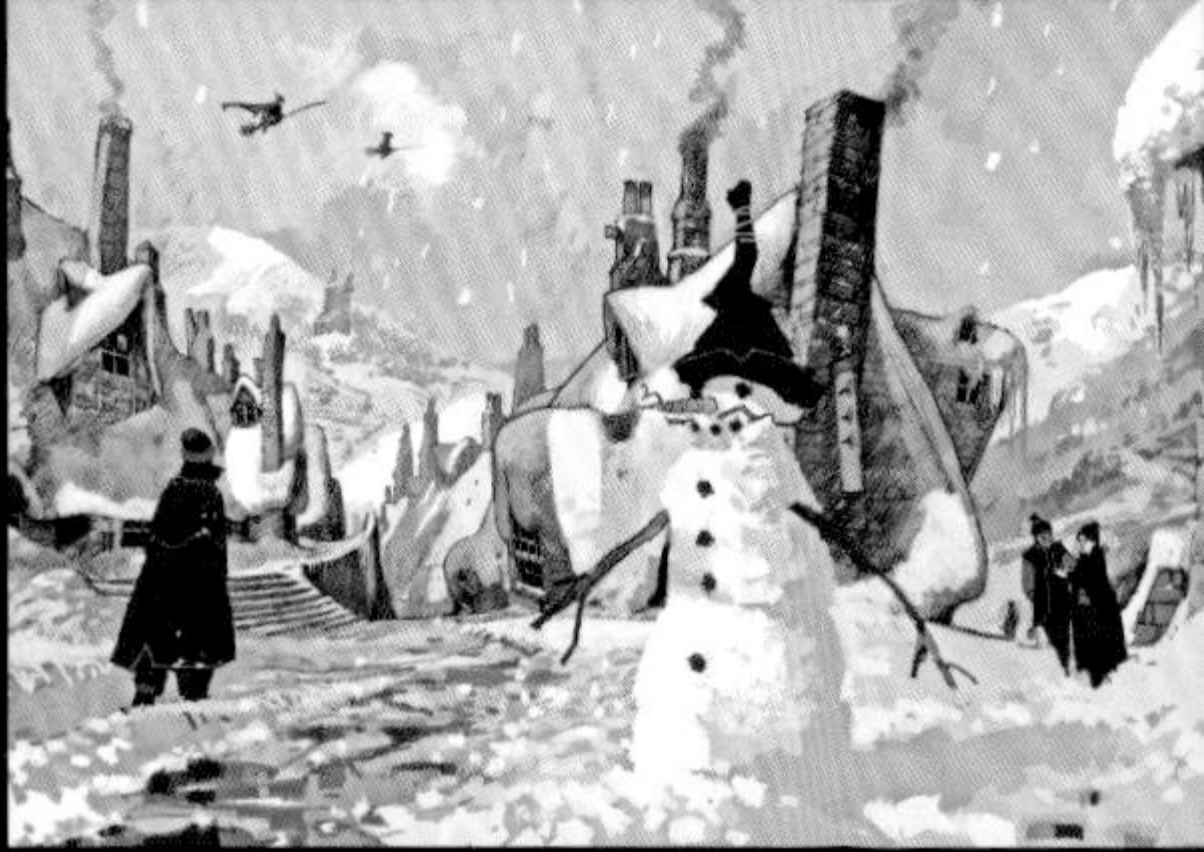

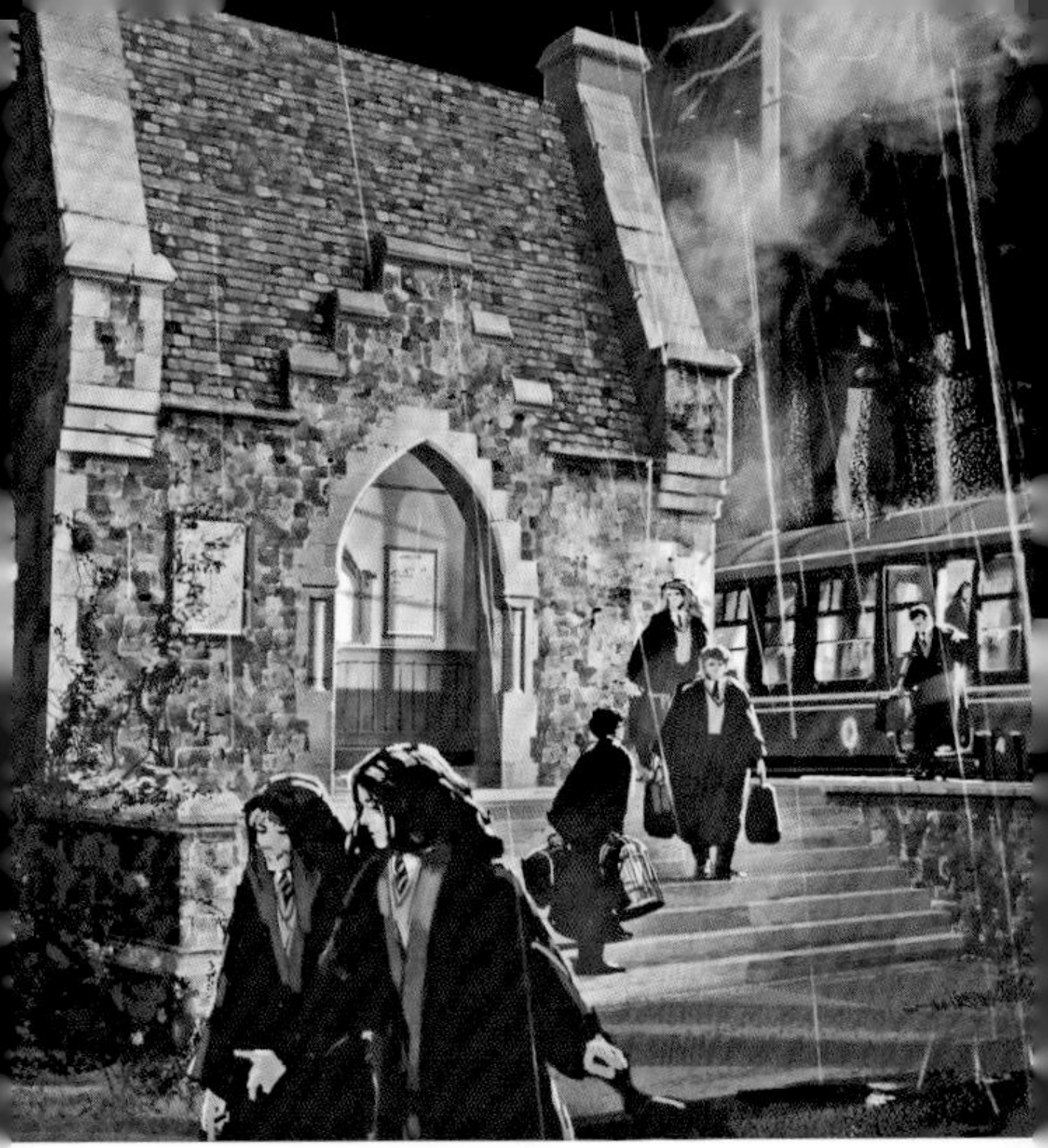

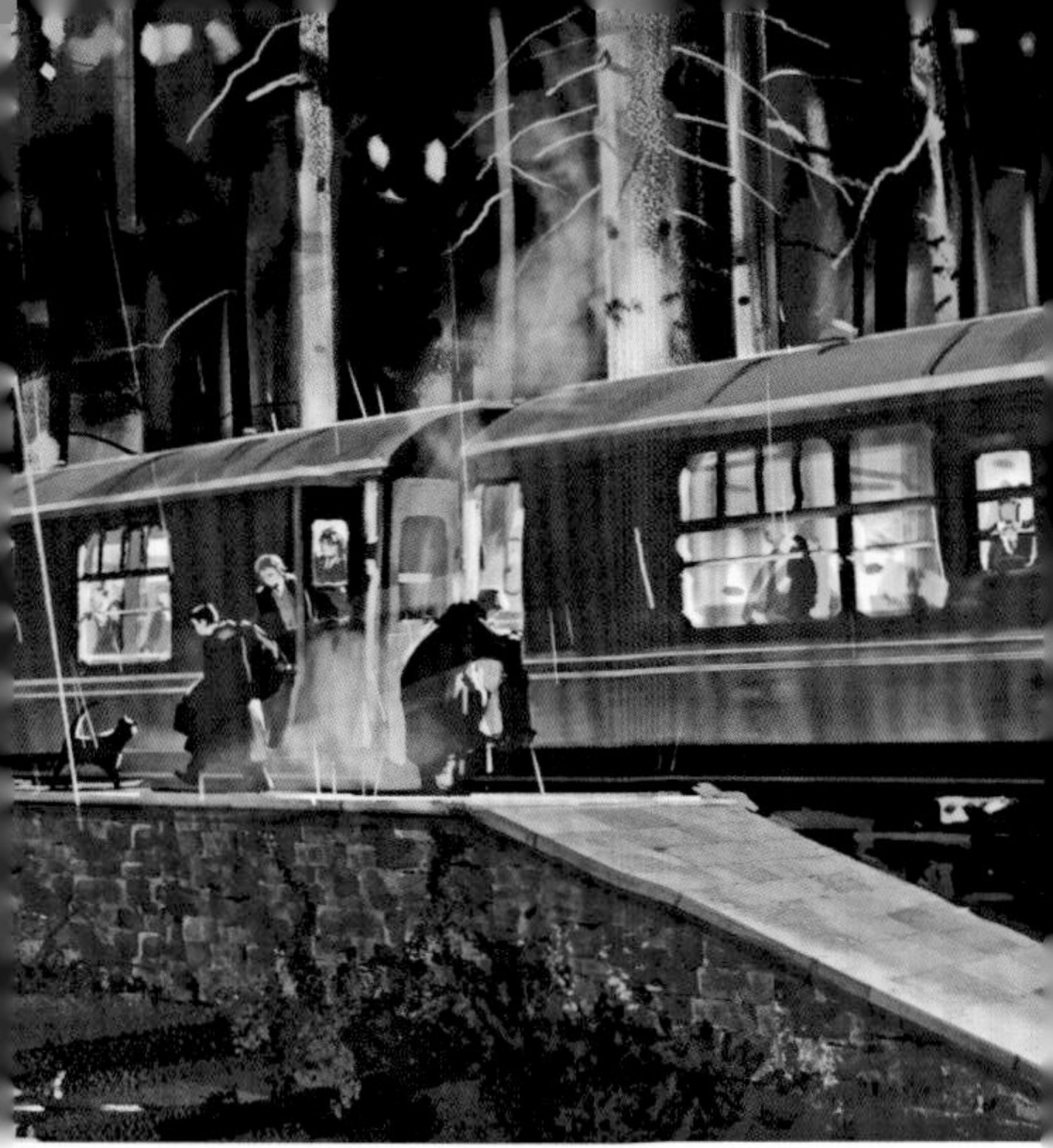

THESE PAGES: Students disembark at Hogsmeade station, by Andrew Williamson for *Harry Potter and the Order of the Phoenix*.

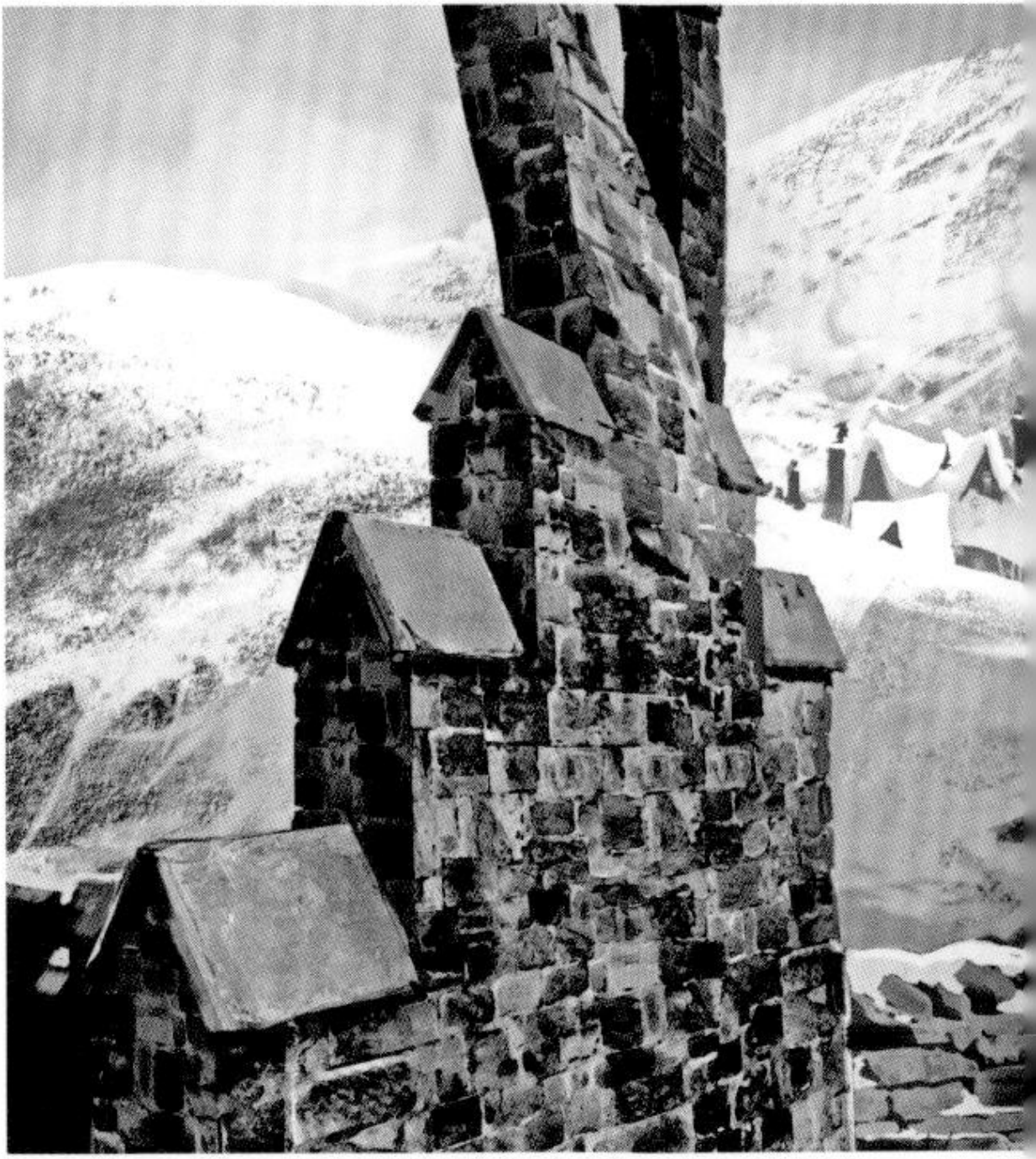

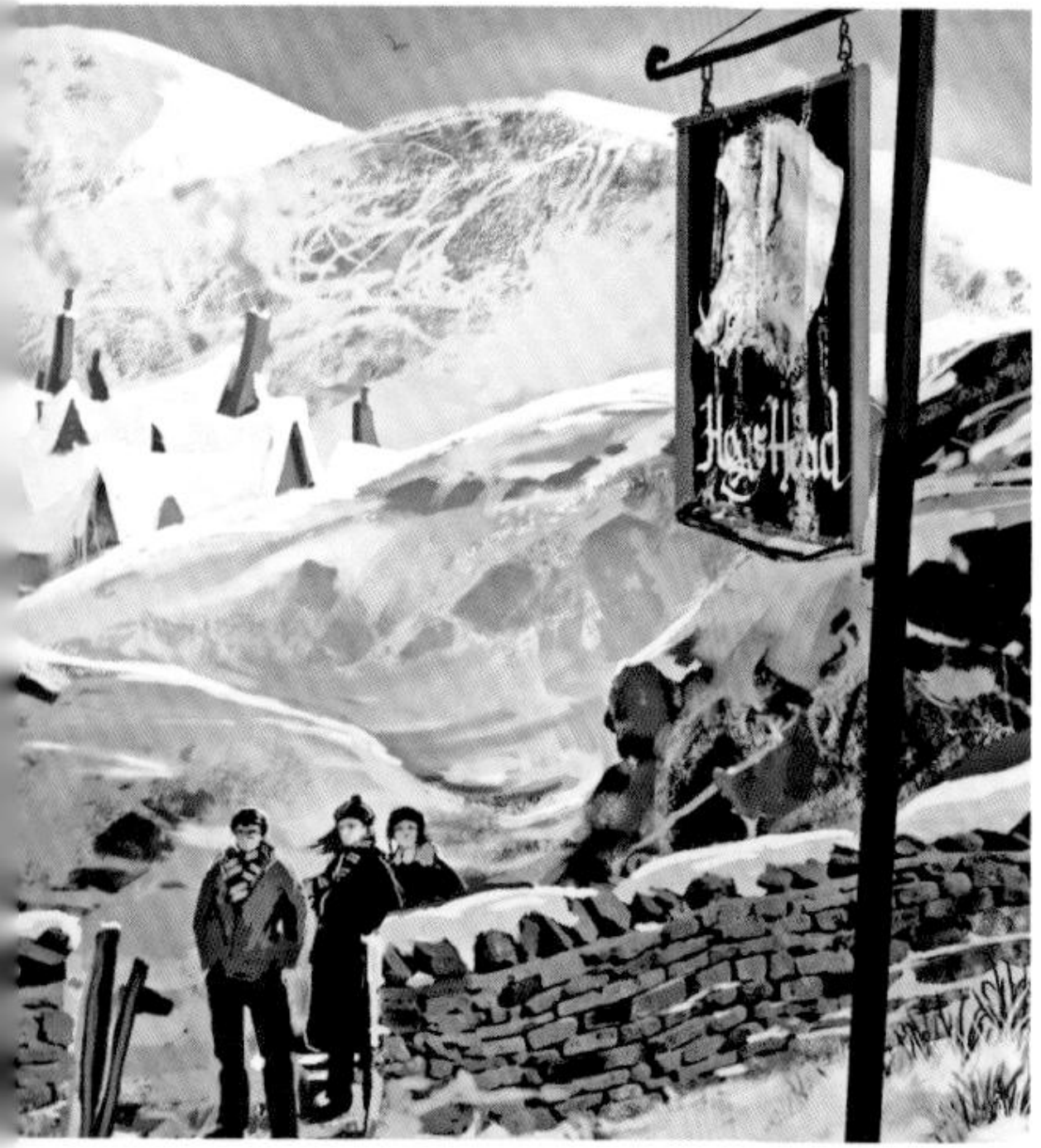

THESE PAGES: Harry, Ron, and Hermione about to enter the Hog's Head, where they will form Dumbledore's Army. Concept art for *Harry Potter and the Order of the Phoenix*.

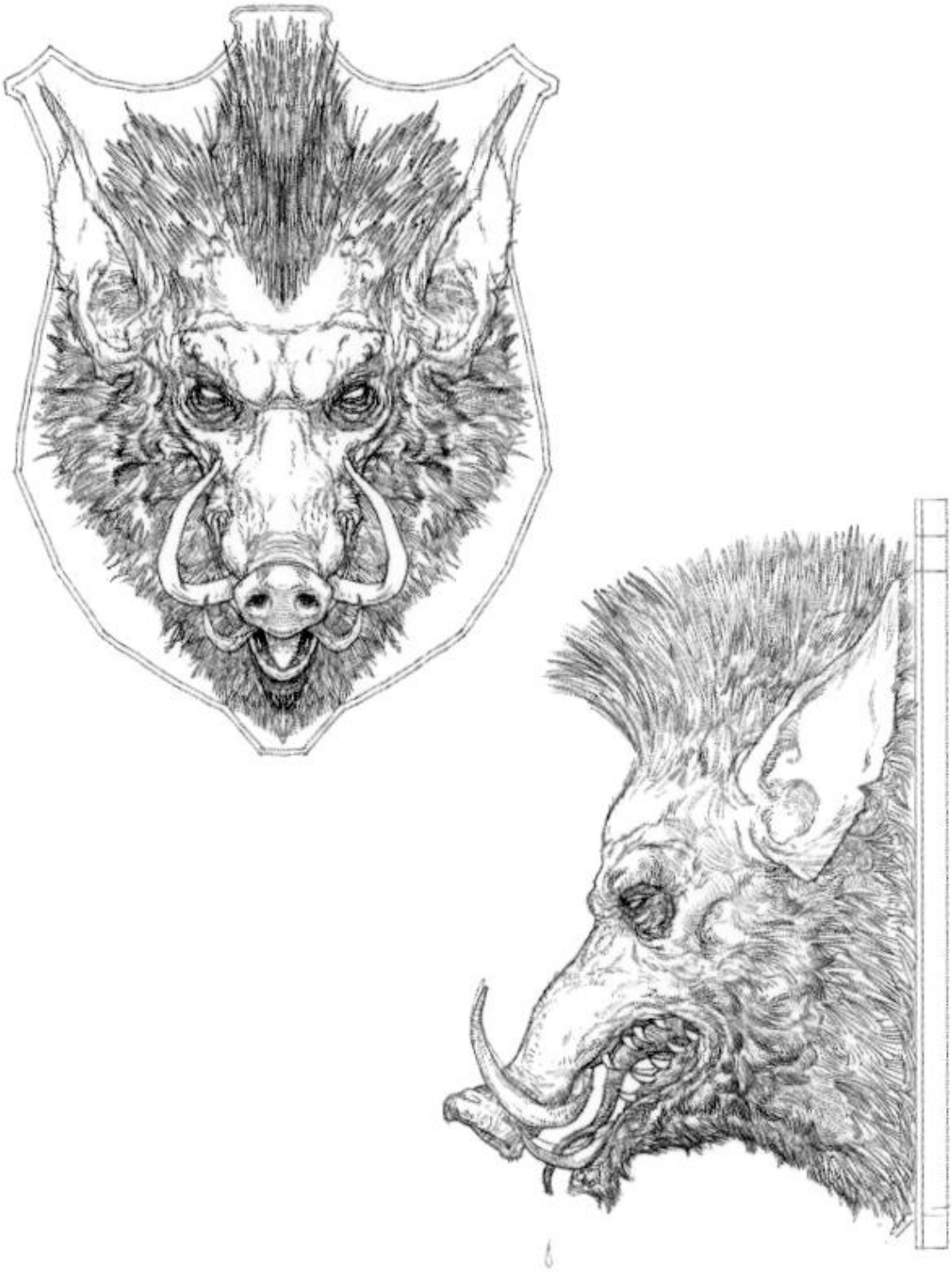

THESE PAGES: The Hog's Head's namesake. Art by Rob Bliss.

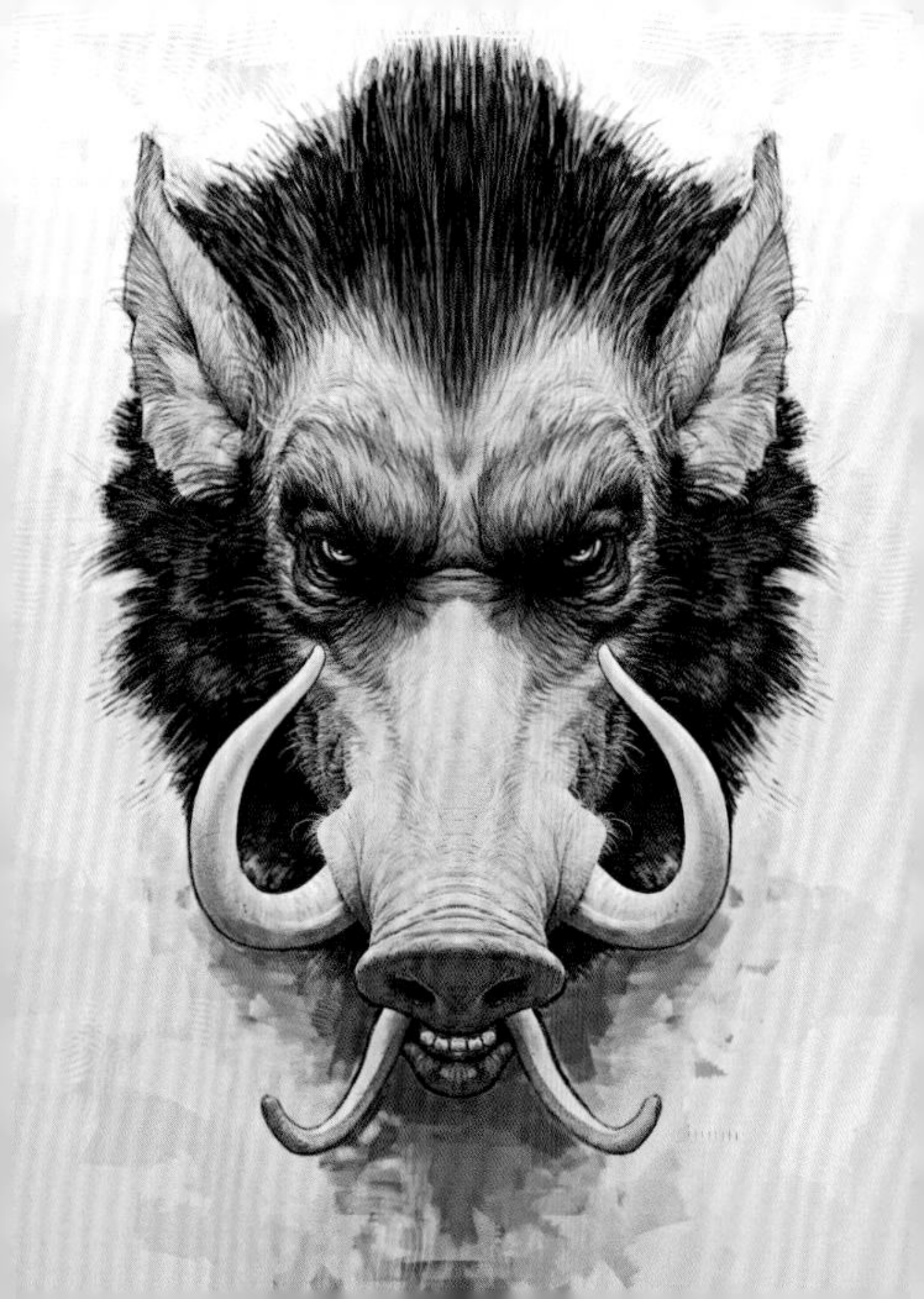

QUIDDITCH WORLD CUP

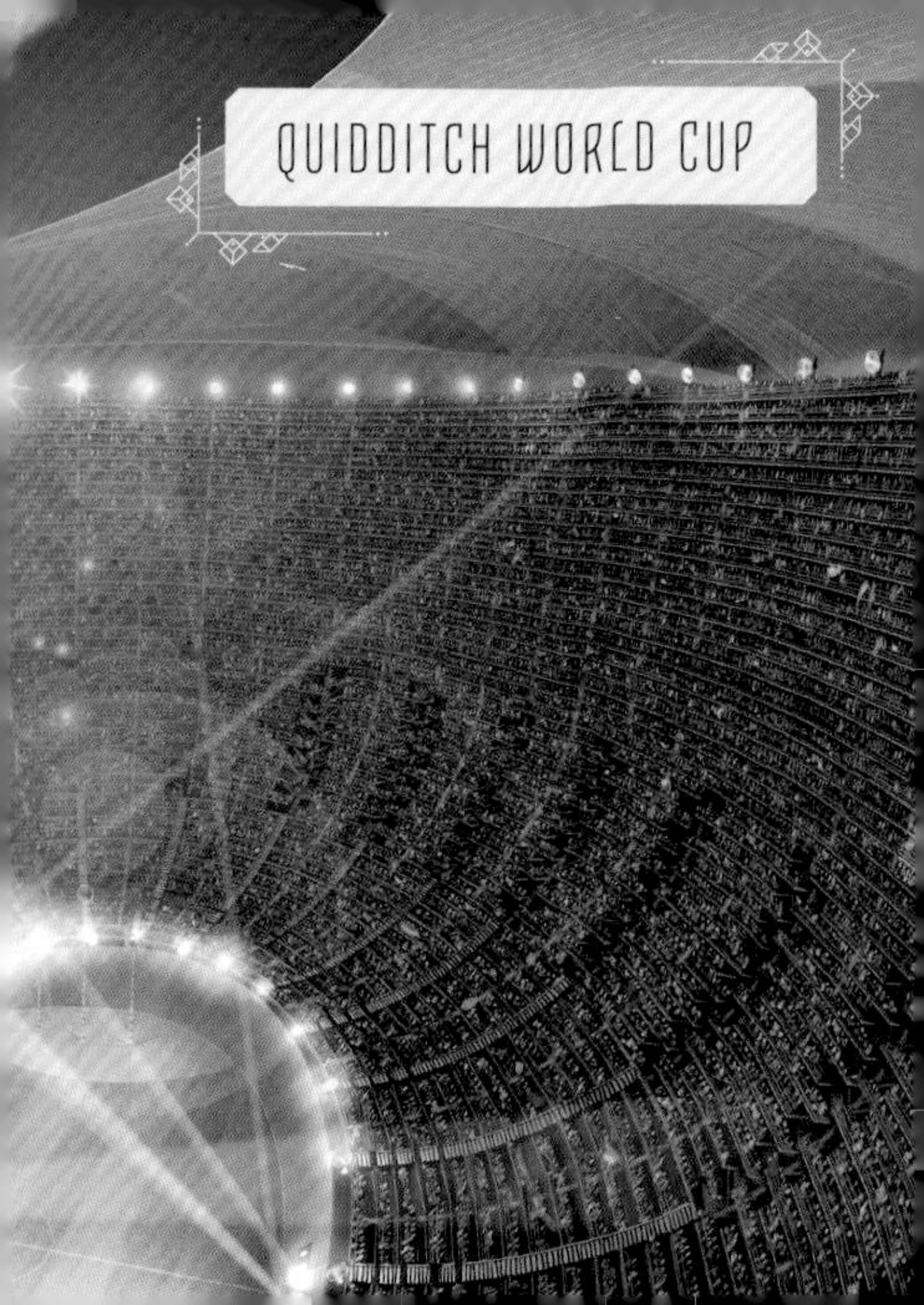

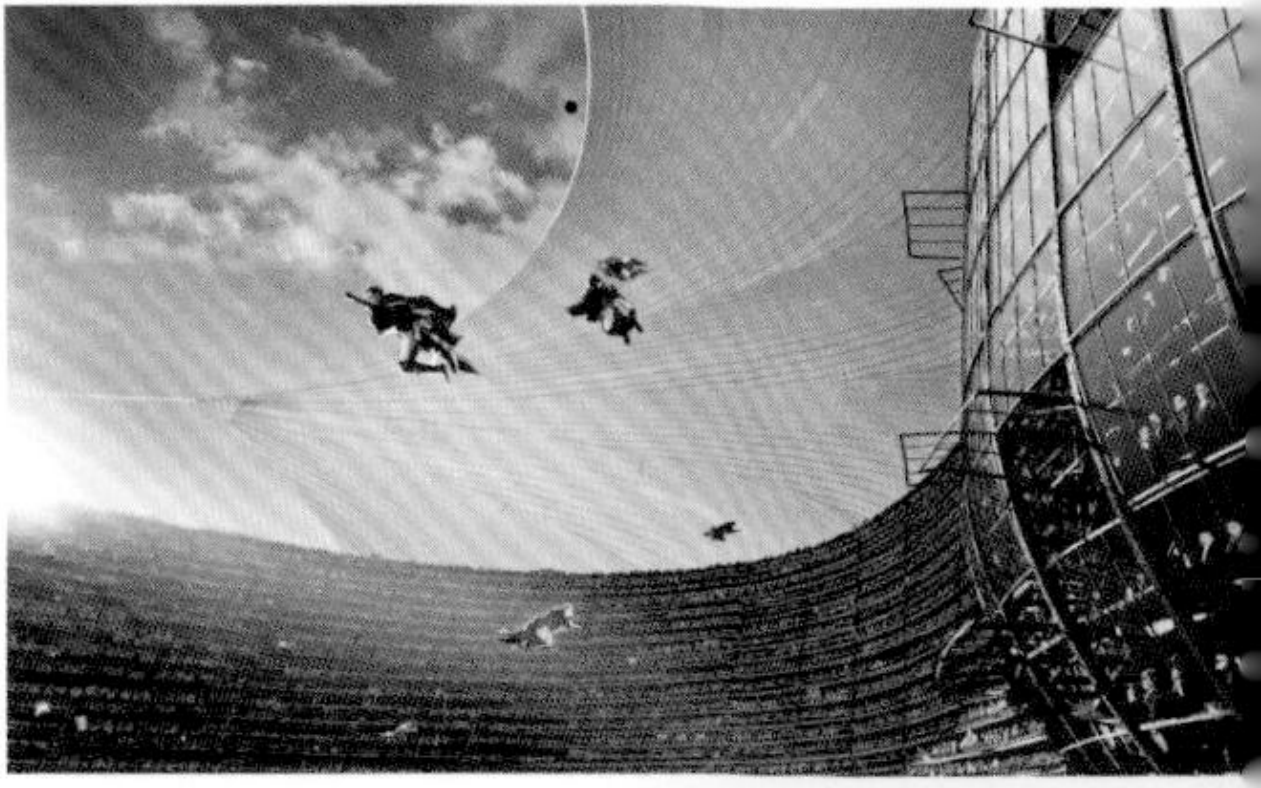

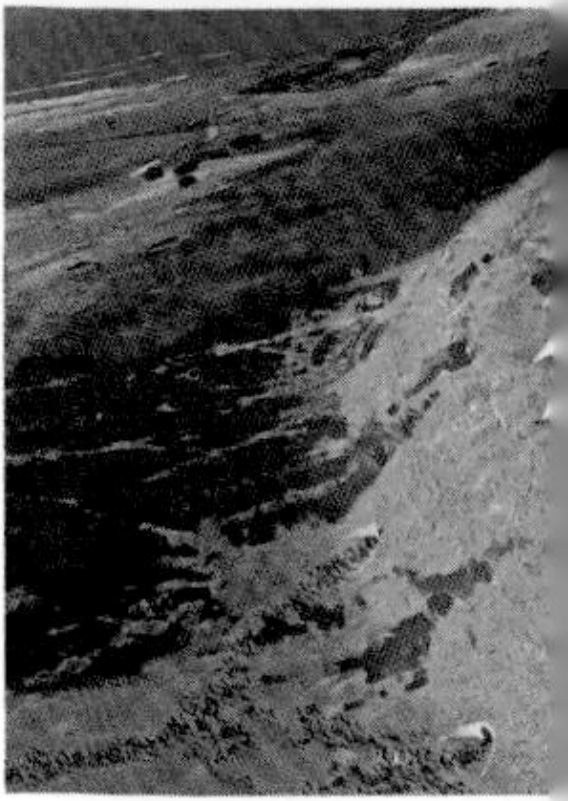

PAGES 244–247: Andrew Williamson illustrates the best views above the stadium hosting the 422nd Quidditch World Cup, as seen in *Harry Potter and the Goblet of Fire*.

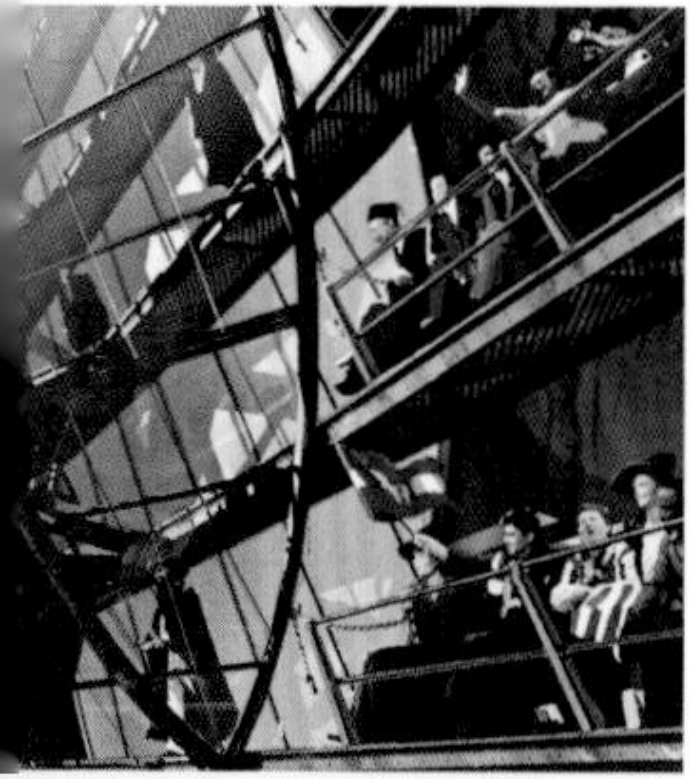

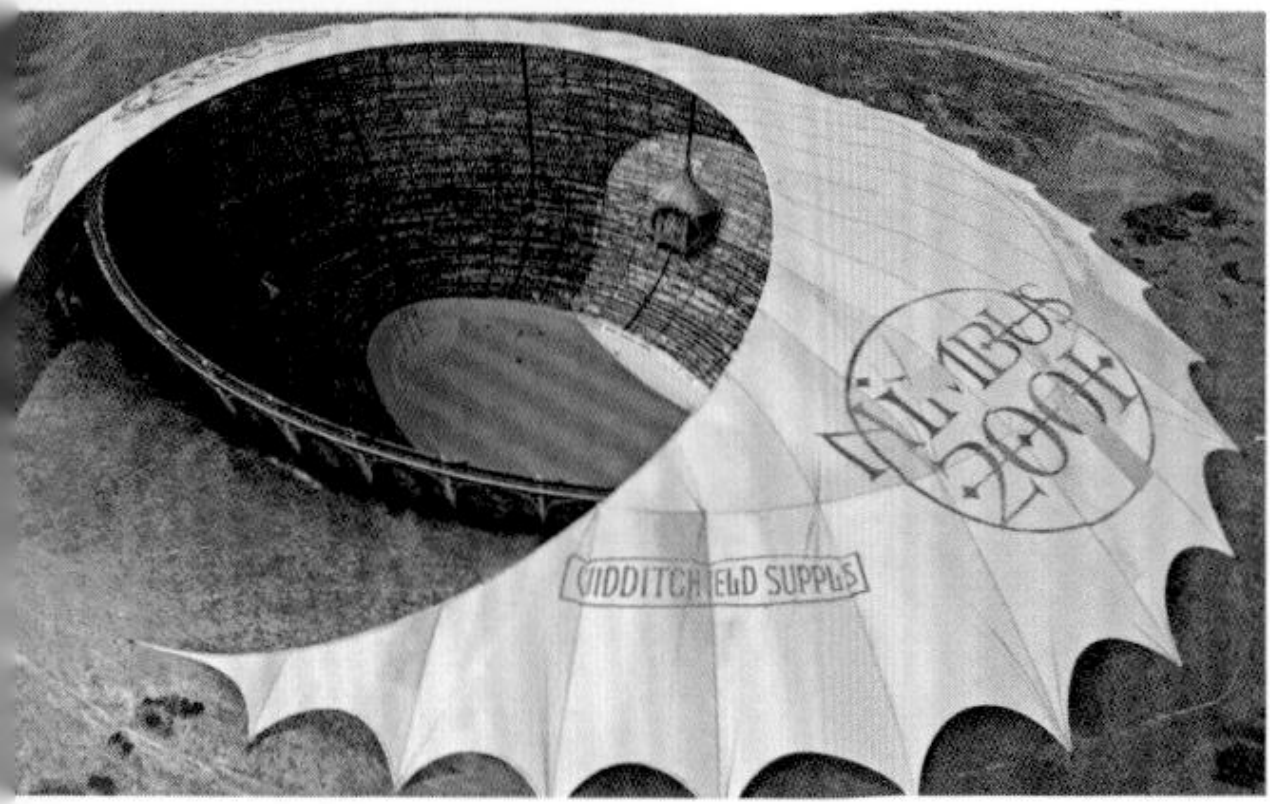
NIMBUS
2001
QUIDDITCH FIELD SUPPLIES

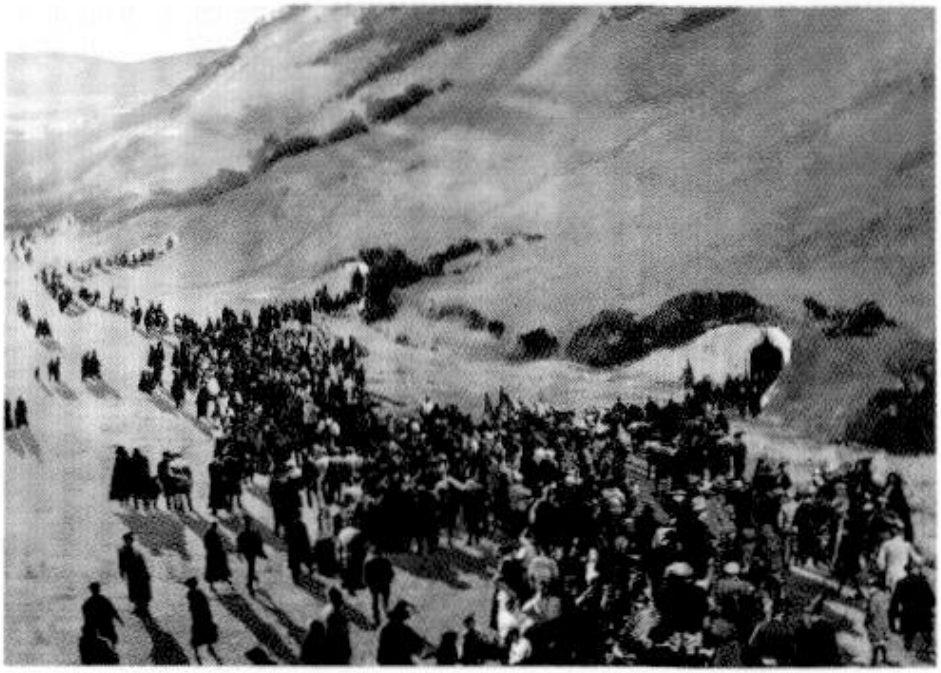

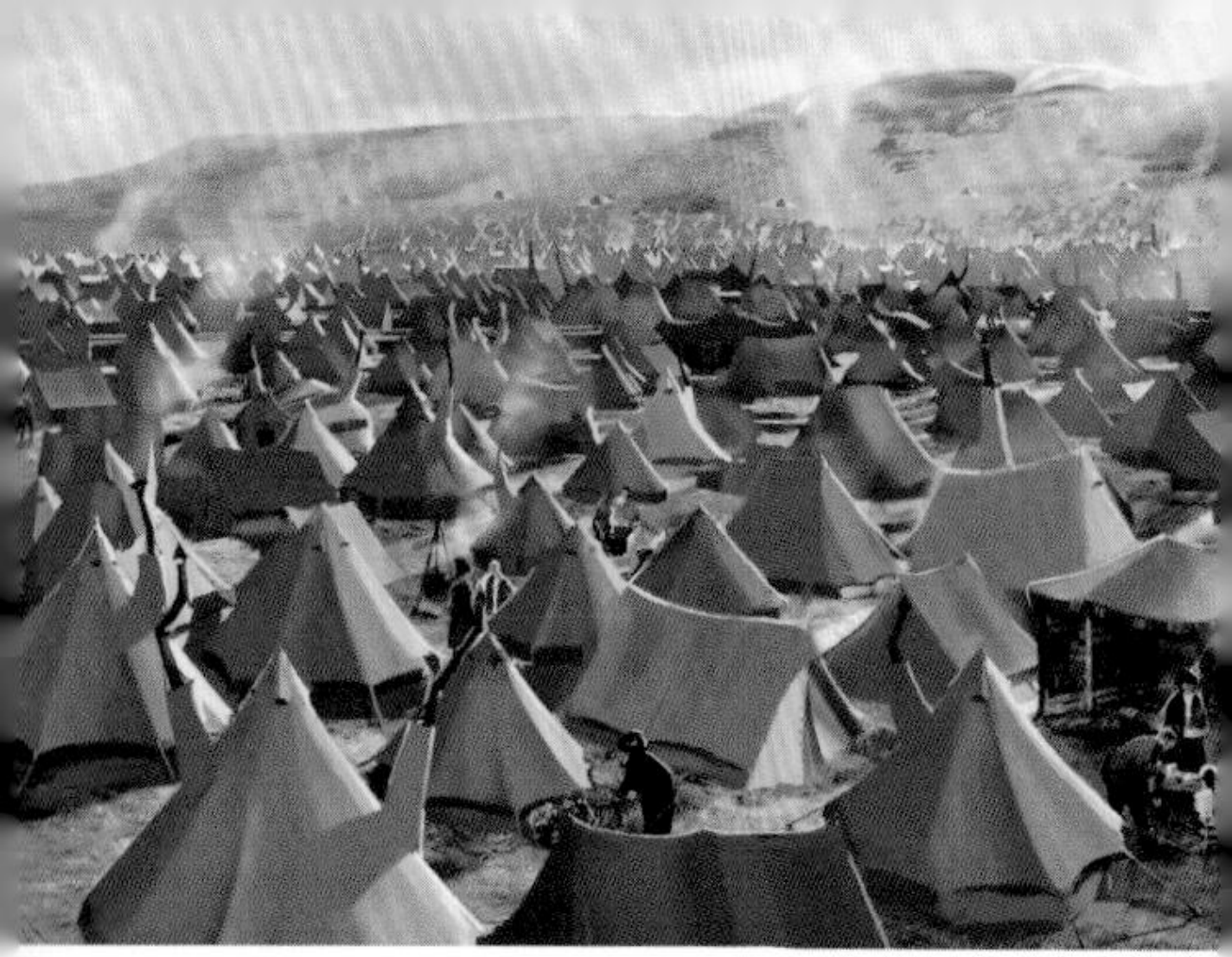

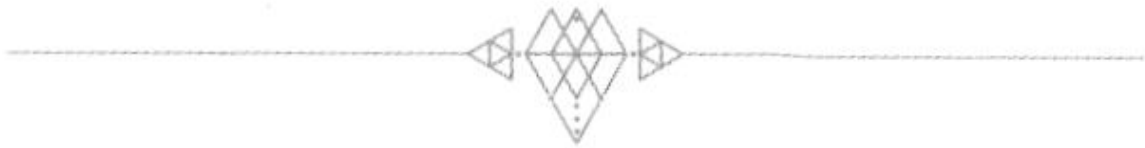

THESE PAGES: The campground beside the Quidditch World Cup arena. Artwork by Andrew Williamson for *Goblet of Fire*.

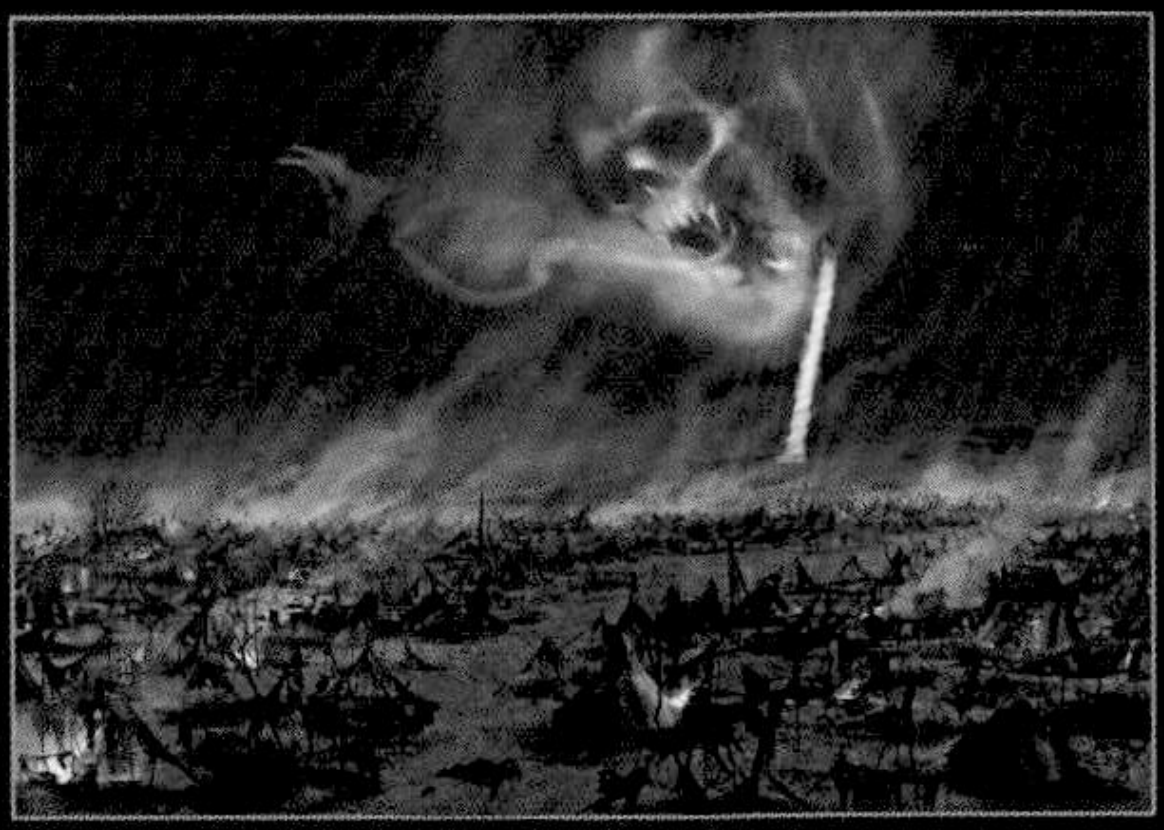

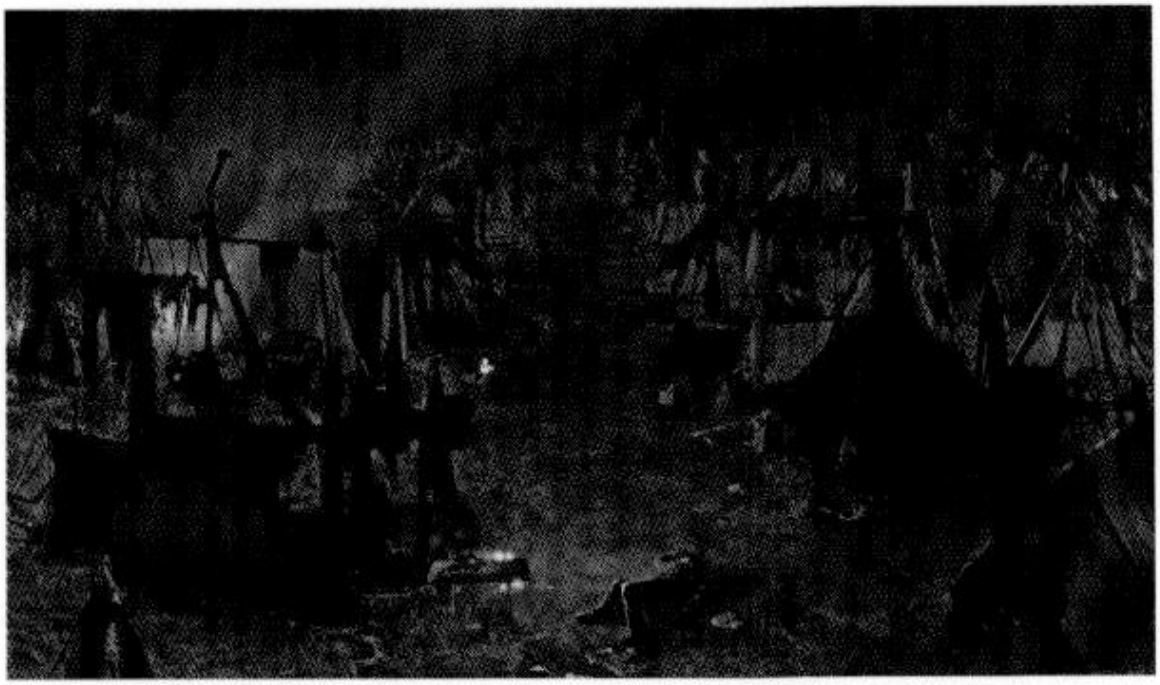

THESE PAGES: Voldemort's Death Eaters invade the camp at night, burning the tents and casting the *Morsmordre* Spell, conjuring the Dark Mark in the sky. Art by Andrew Williamson.

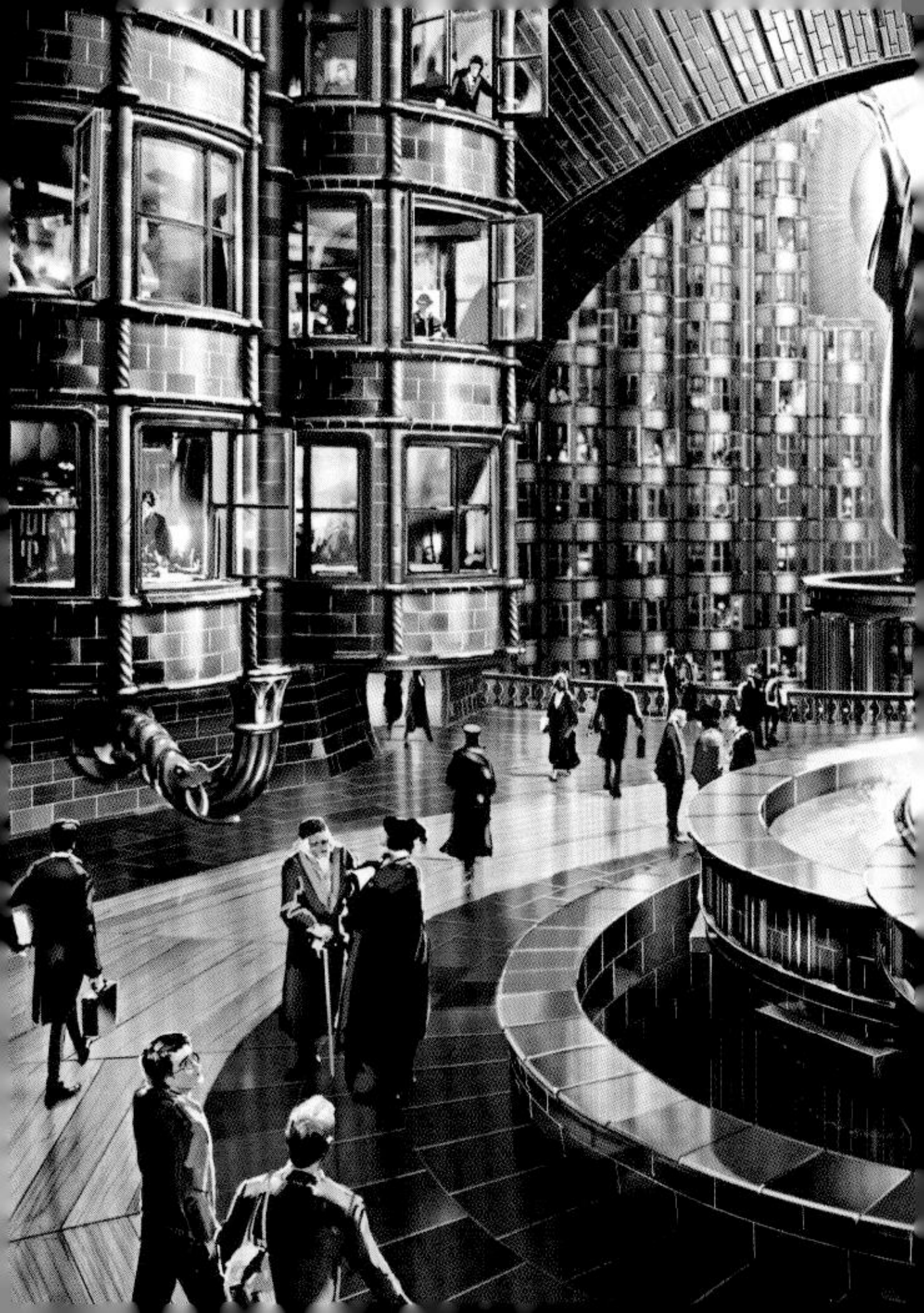

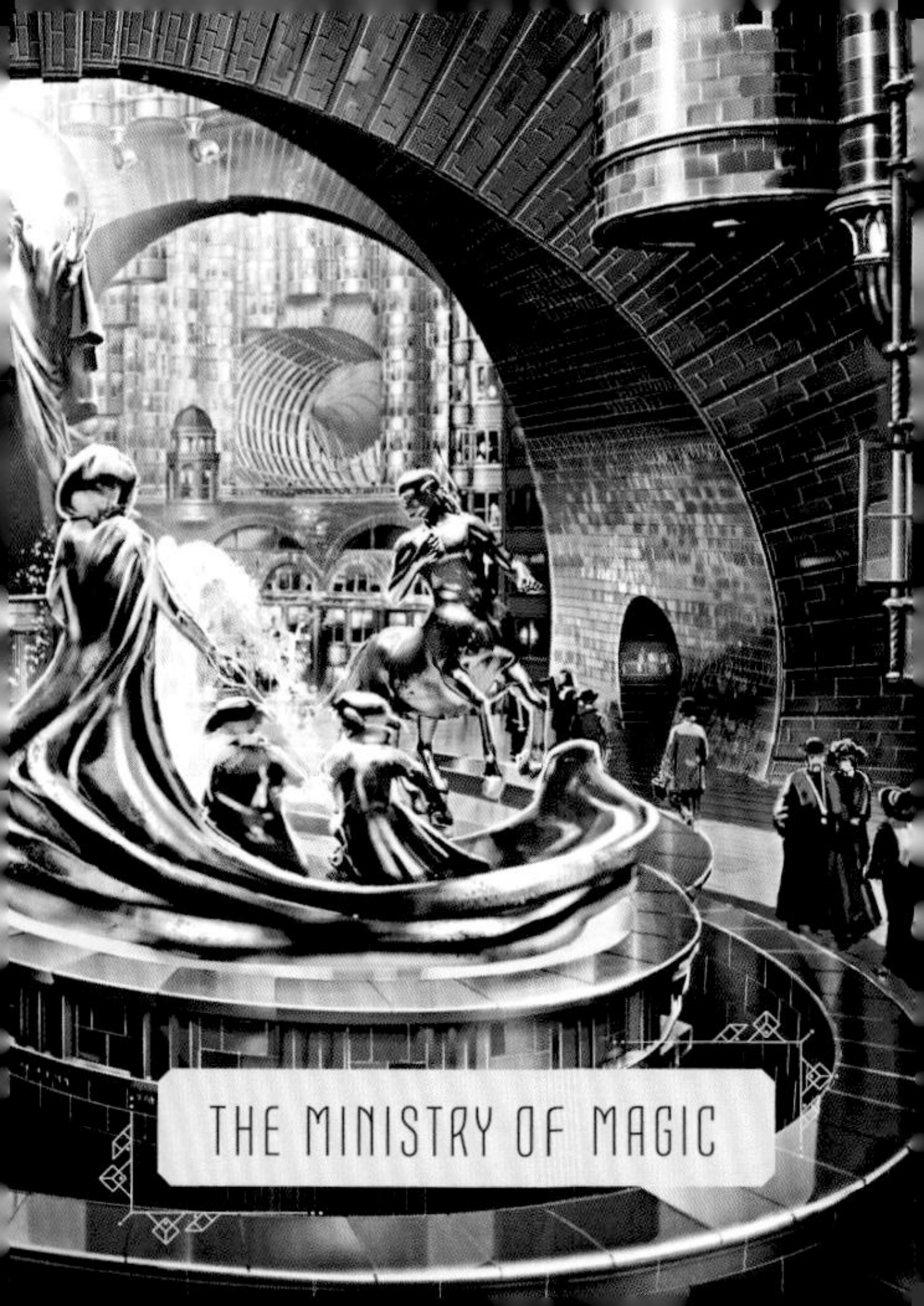
THE MINISTRY OF MAGIC

THE ATRIUM

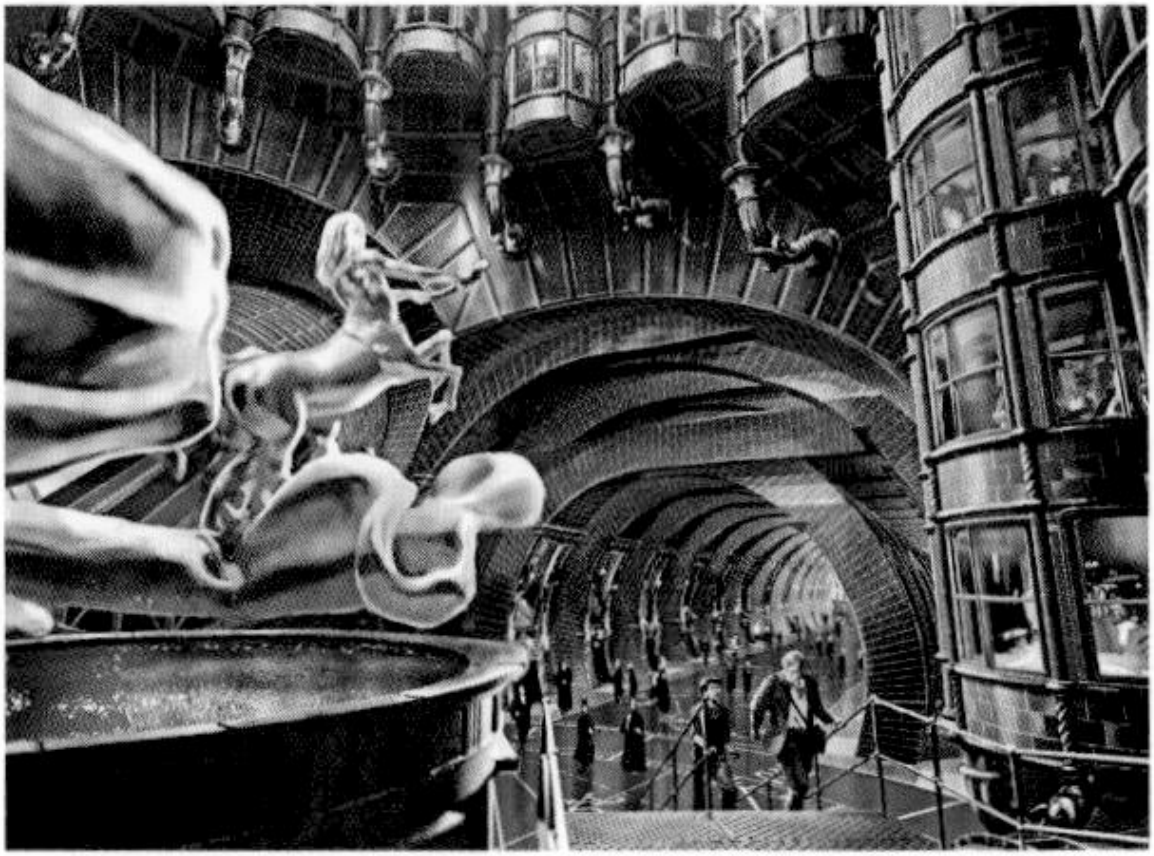

PAGES 252–254: The Atrium of the Ministry of Magic, featuring the Fountain of Magical Brethren, painted by Andrew Williamson as first seen in *Harry Potter and the Order of the Phoenix*.

OPPOSITE: A closer view of the wizard, who floats above his pedestal here, by Adam Brockbank.

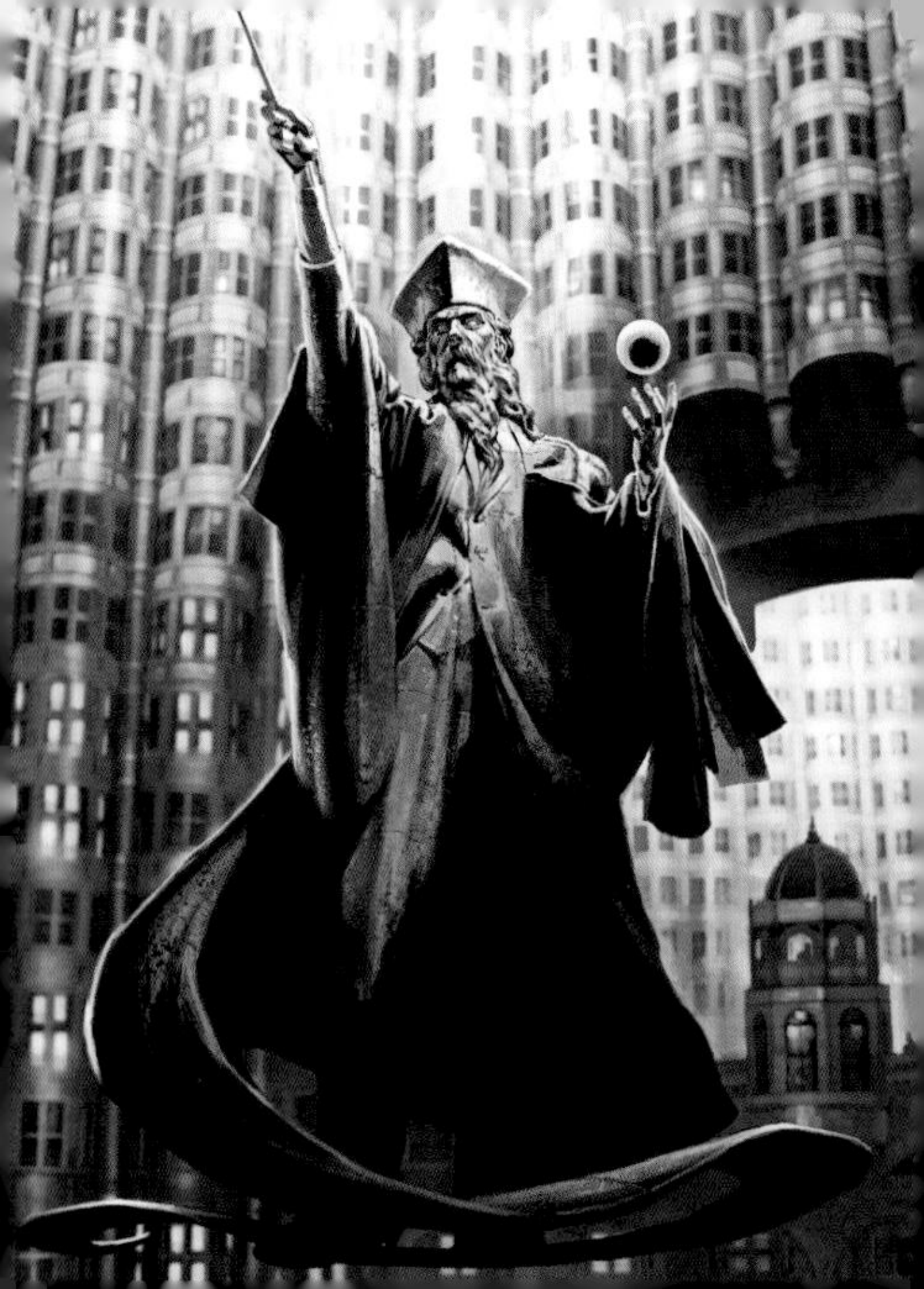

COURTROOMS

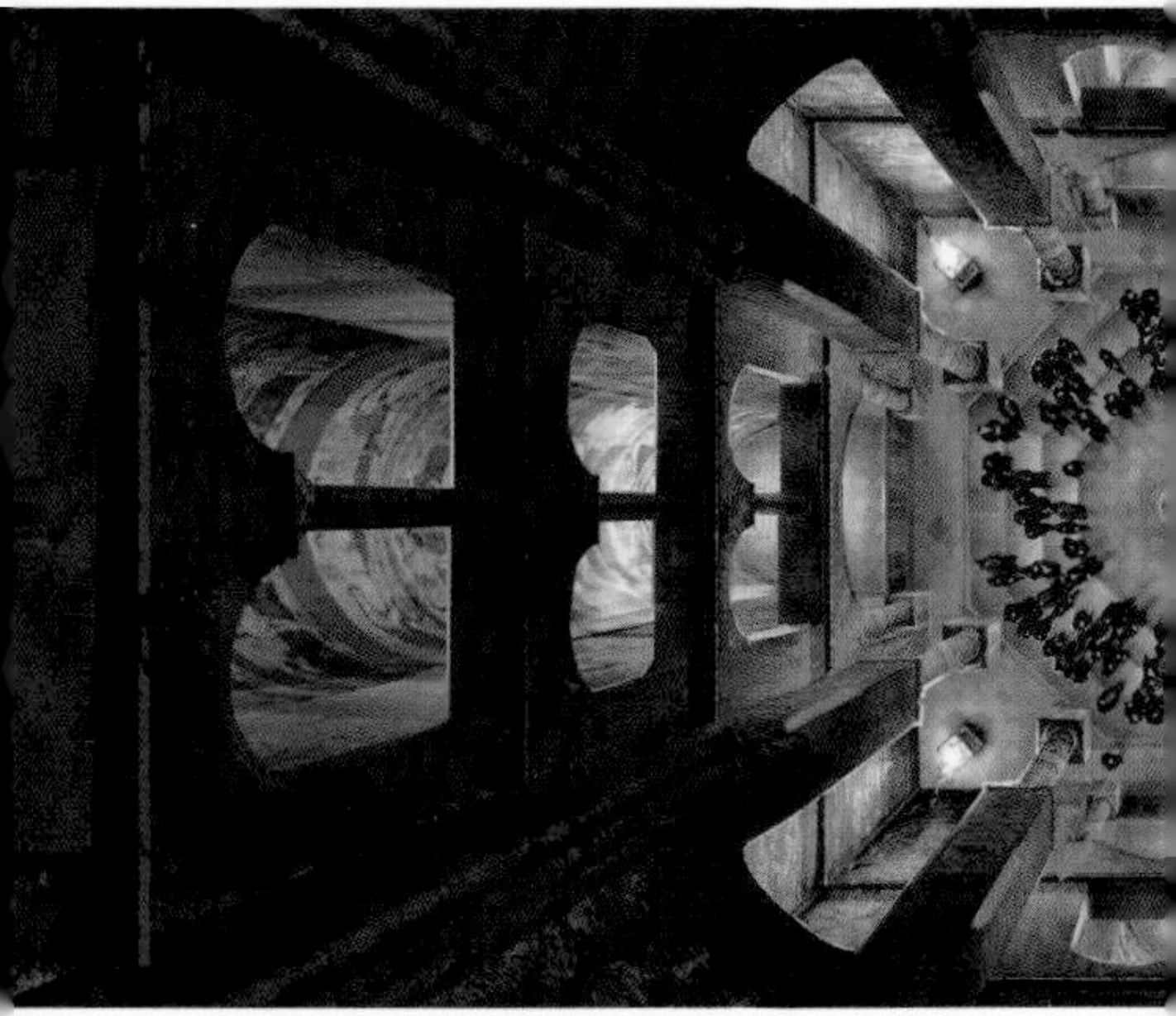

THESE PAGES: The Ministry of Magic courtroom, as first seen by Harry in the Pensieve.

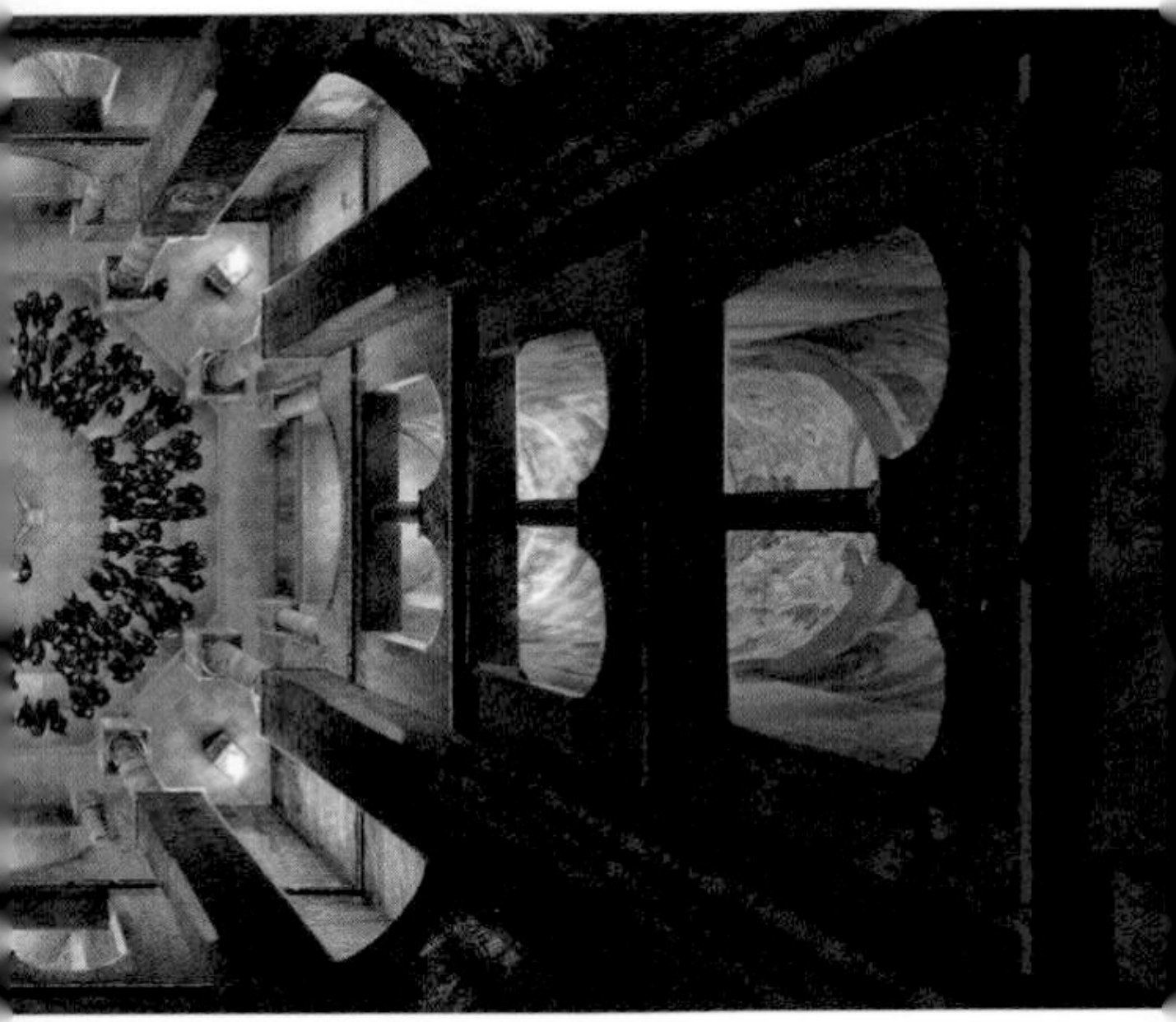

illustrated by Andrew Williamson for *Harry Potter and the Goblet of Fire*.

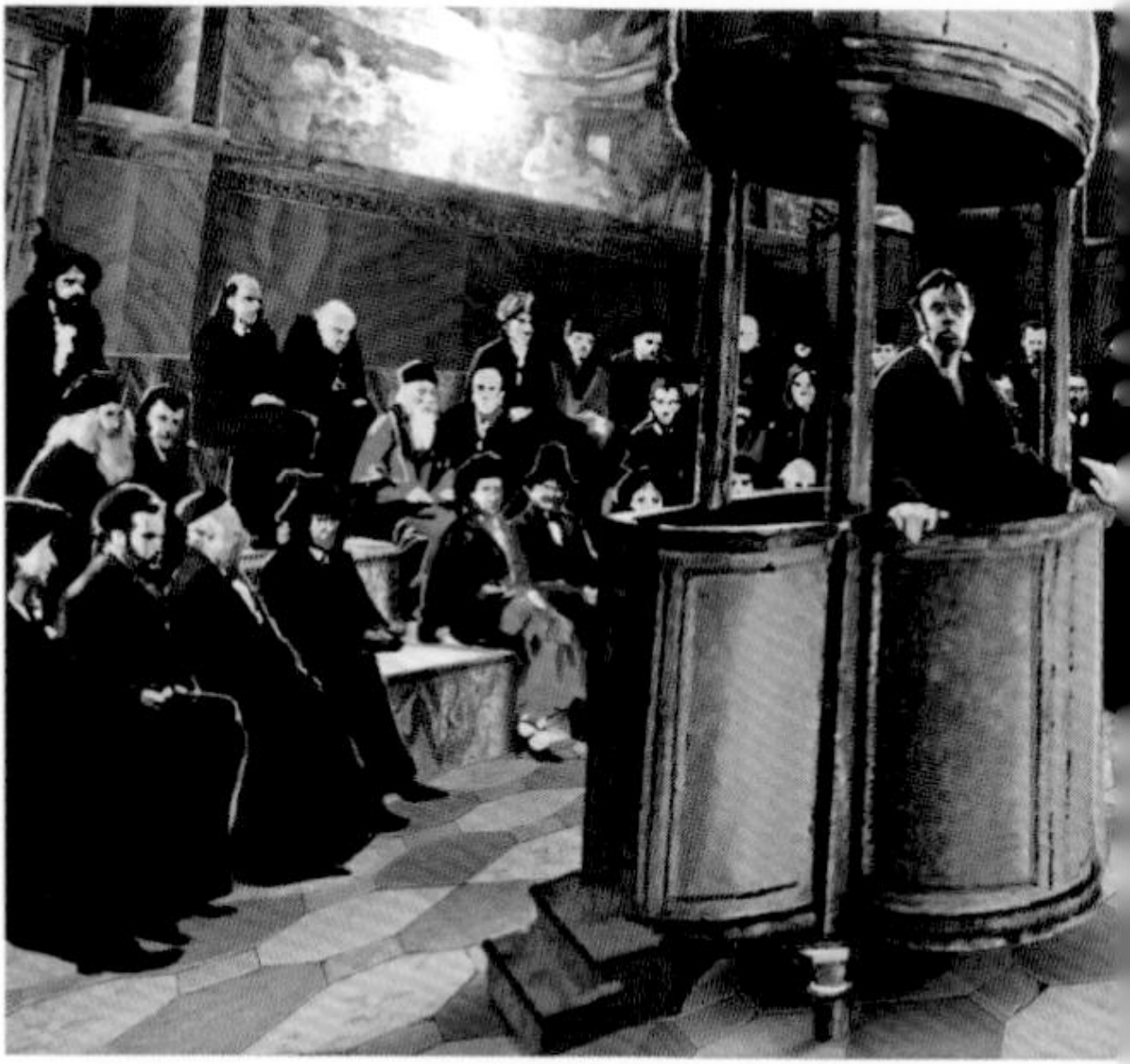

ABOVE: Harry gets a closer view of the trial of the Death Eaters in *Harry Potter and the Goblet of Fire*.

RIGHT: Harry finds himself on trial in *Harry Potter and the Order of the Phoenix*, by Andrew Williamson.

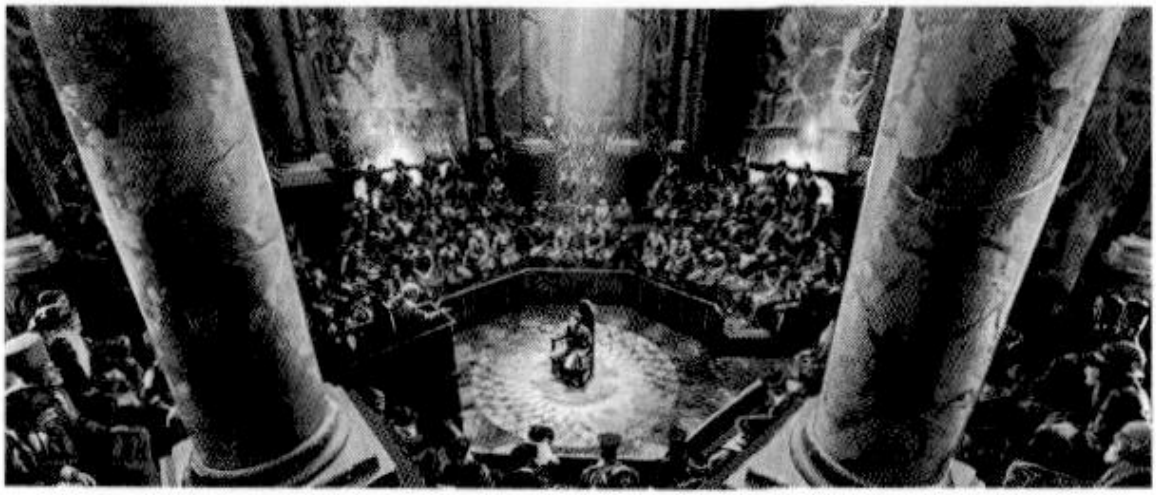

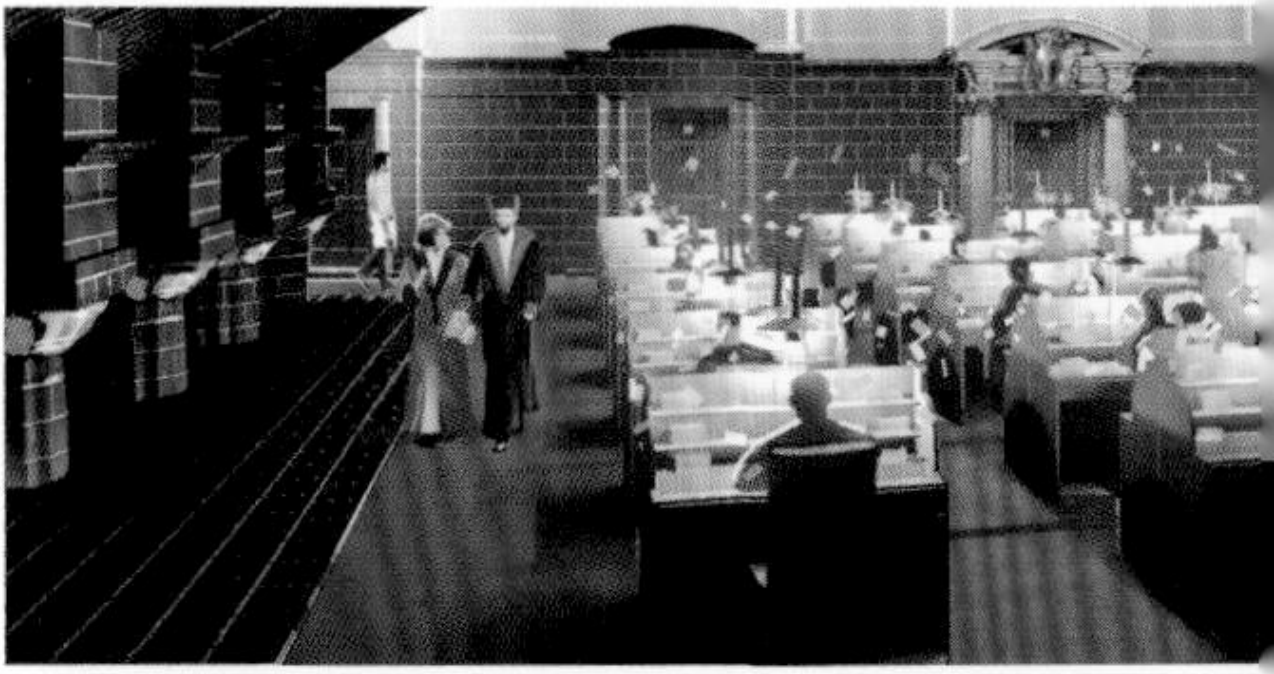

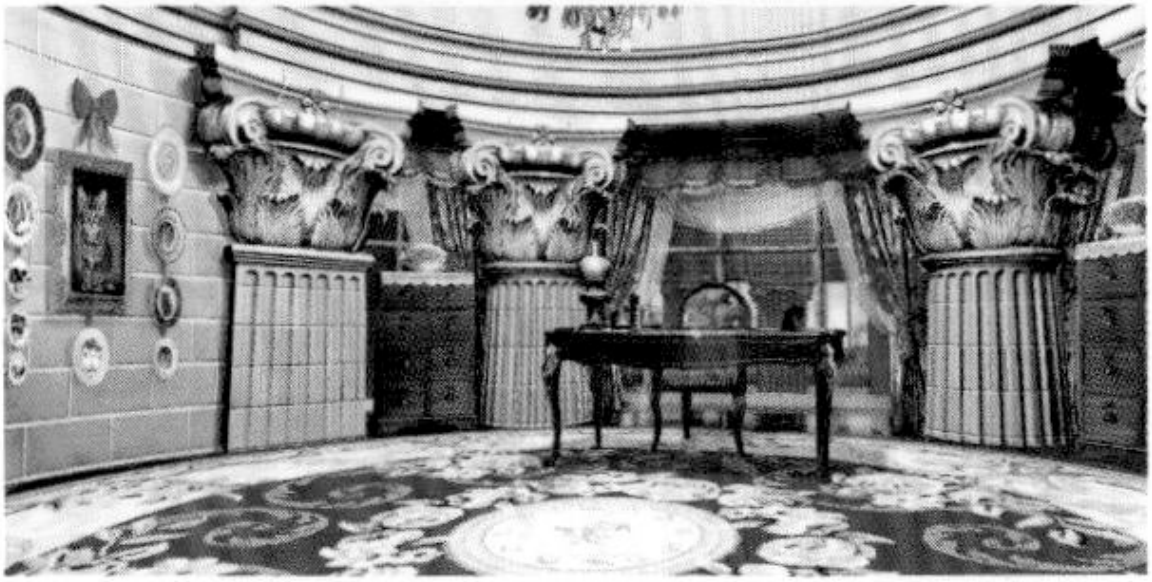

MUGGLE-BORN REGISTRATION COMMISSION

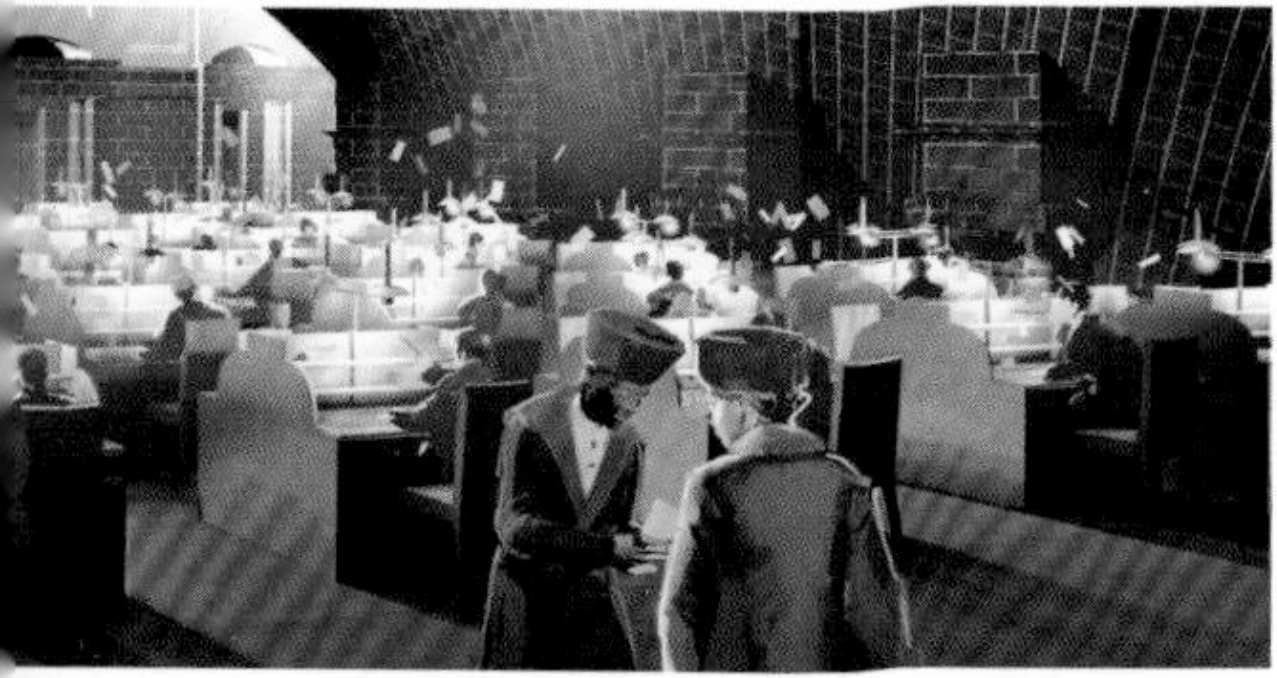

ABOVE: Office of the Muggle-Born Registration Commission, as supervised by Dolores Umbridge. Concept art by Andrew Williamson for *Harry Potter and the Deathly Hallows – Part 1.*

LEFT: Umbridge's office at the Ministry with her familiar kitten plates on pink walls, in Andrew Williamson's depiction for *Harry Potter and the Deathly Hallows – Part 1.*

DEPARTMENT OF MYSTERIES

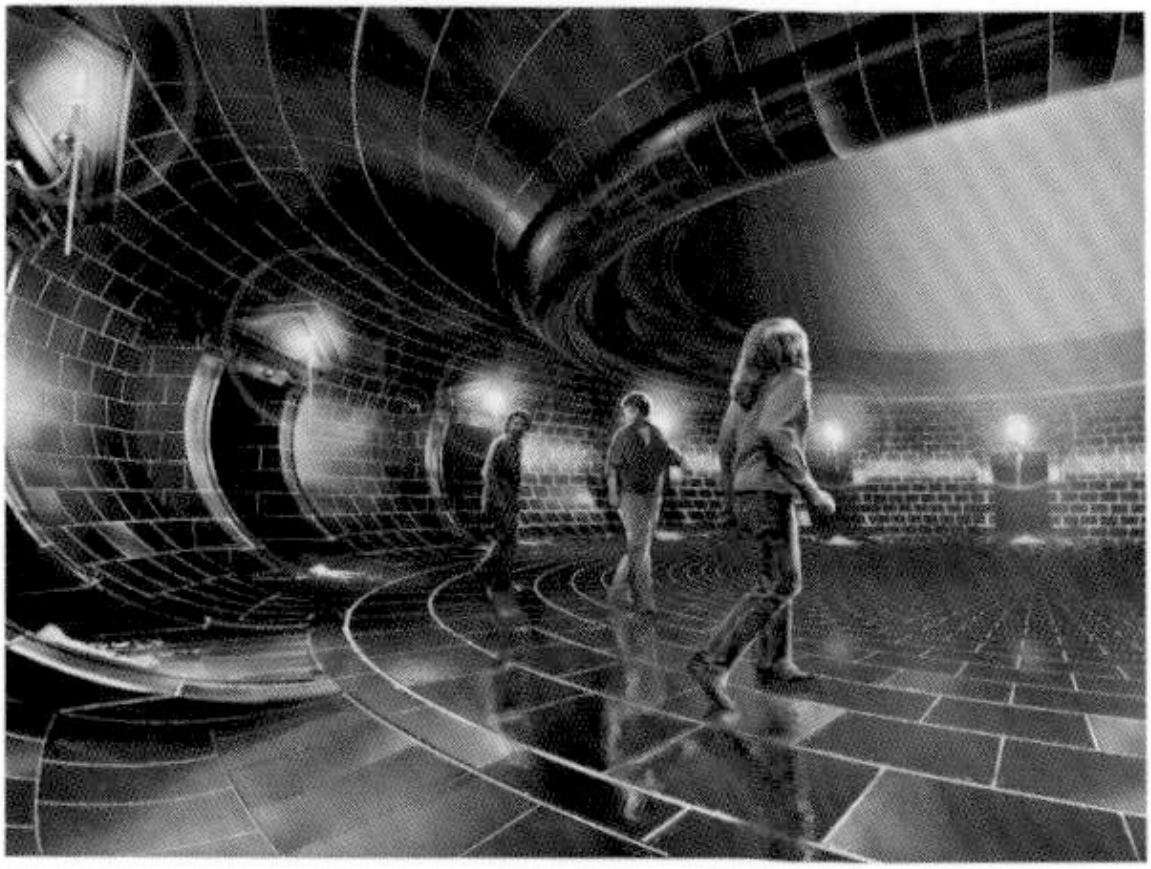

THESE PAGES: The entrance to the Department of Mysteries, by Andrew Williamson for *Harry Potter and the Order of the Phoenix*.

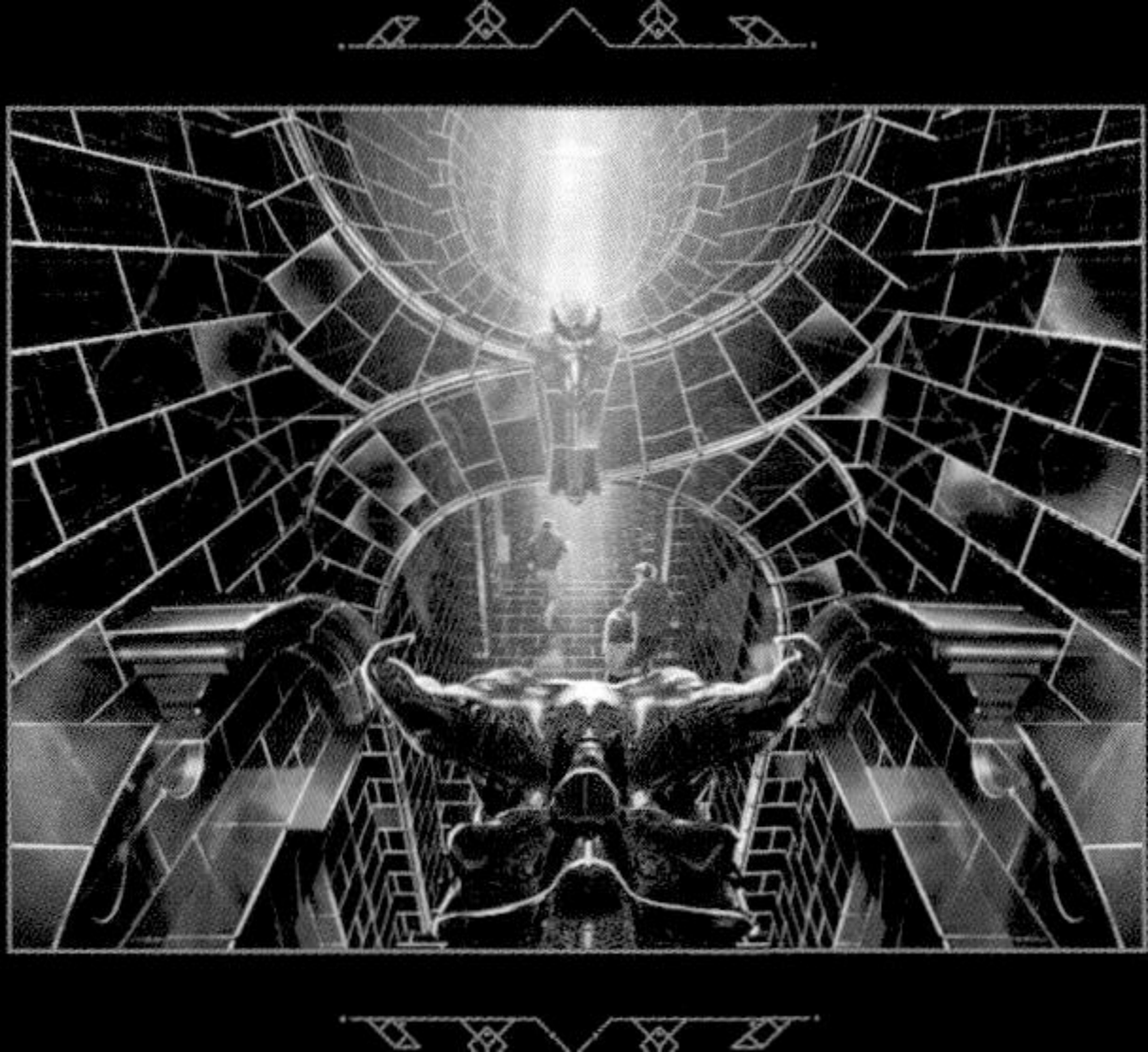

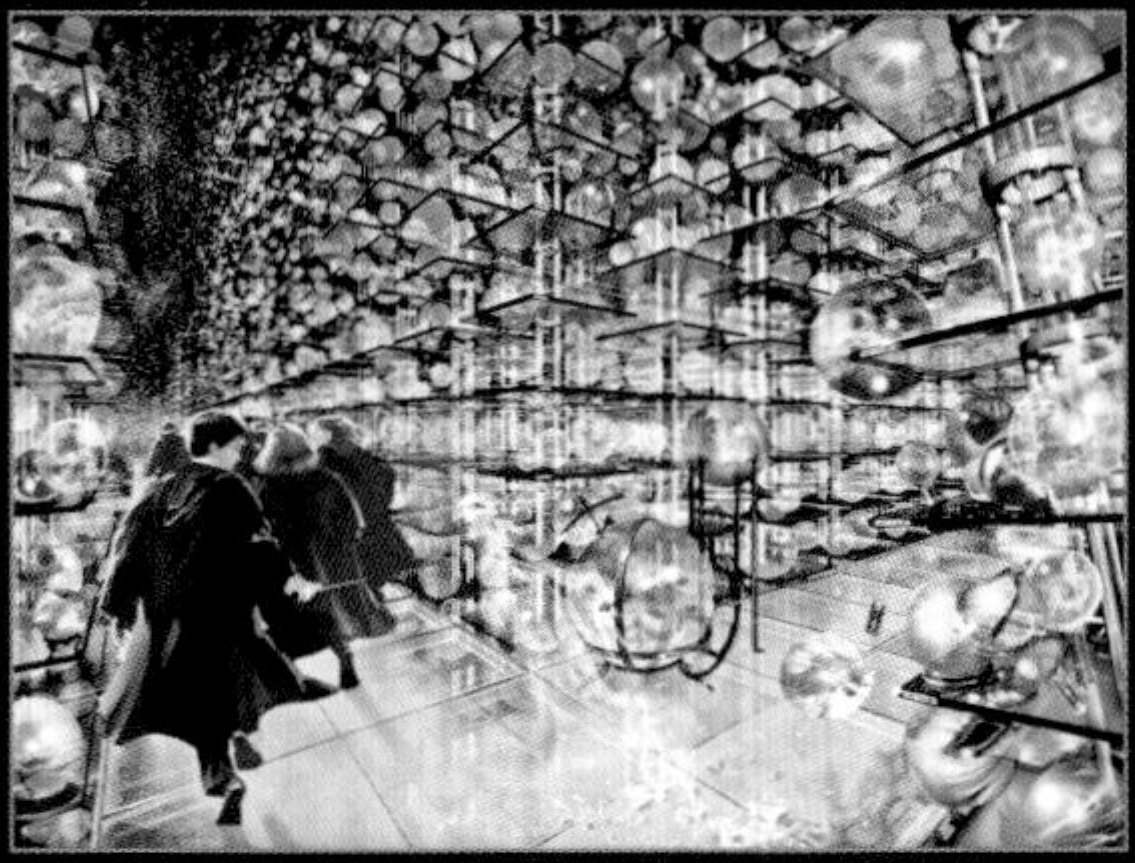

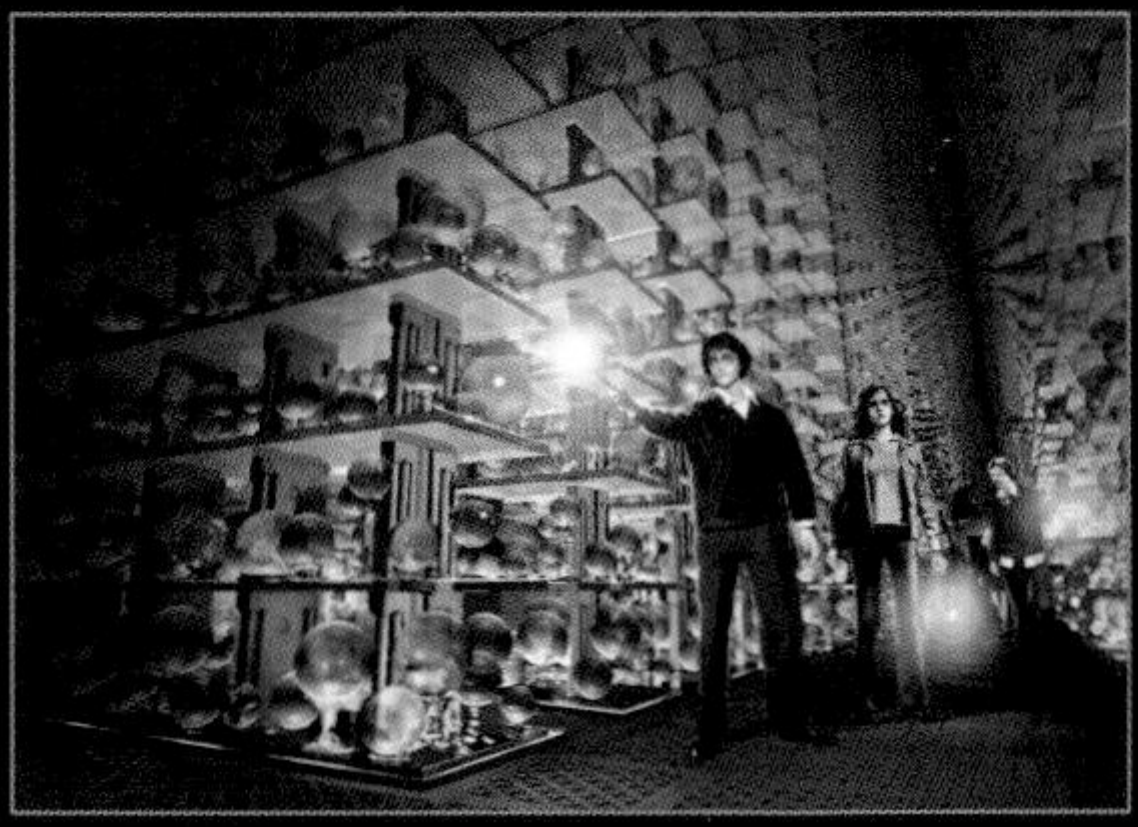

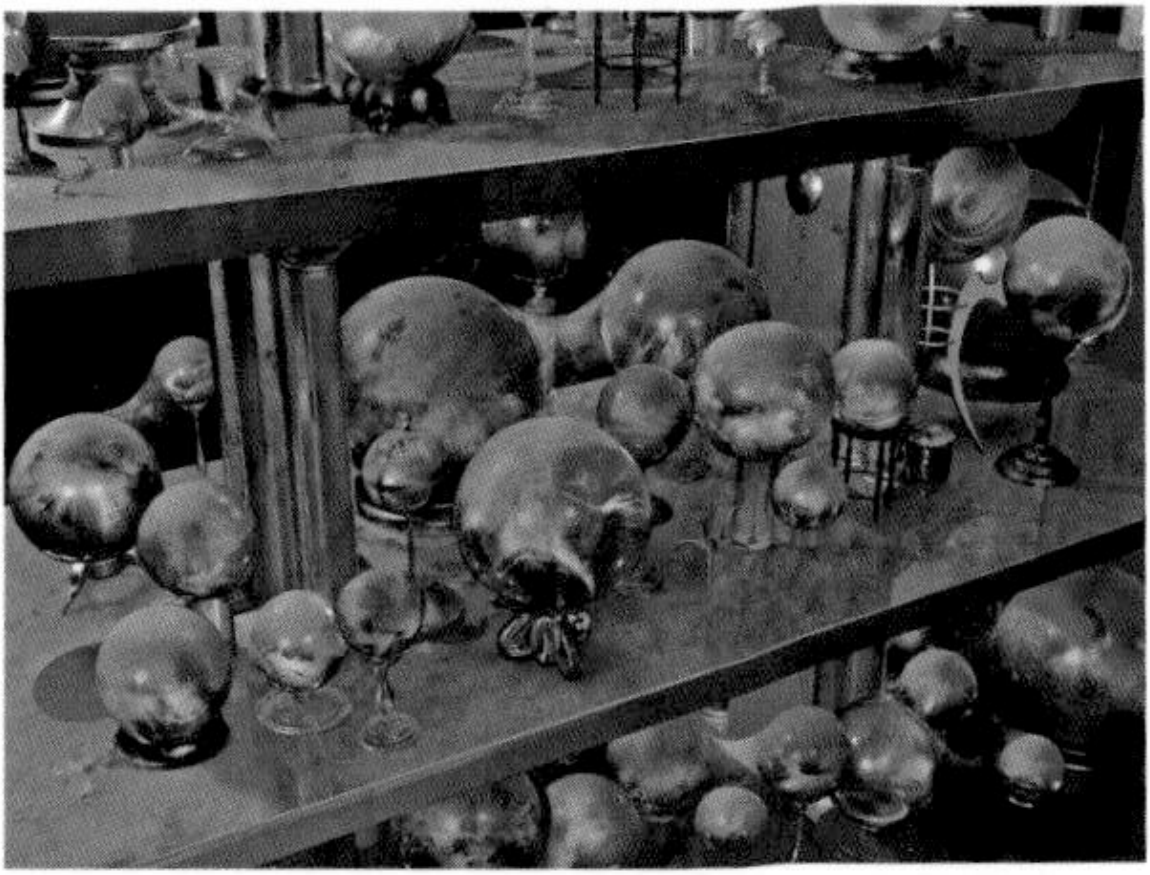

PAGES 264–267: In *Harry Potter and the Order of the Phoenix*, Harry and his friends explore the Hall of Prophecy at the Department of Mysteries in the Ministry of Magic. Andrew Williamson shows the many shelves of orbs in his concept art.

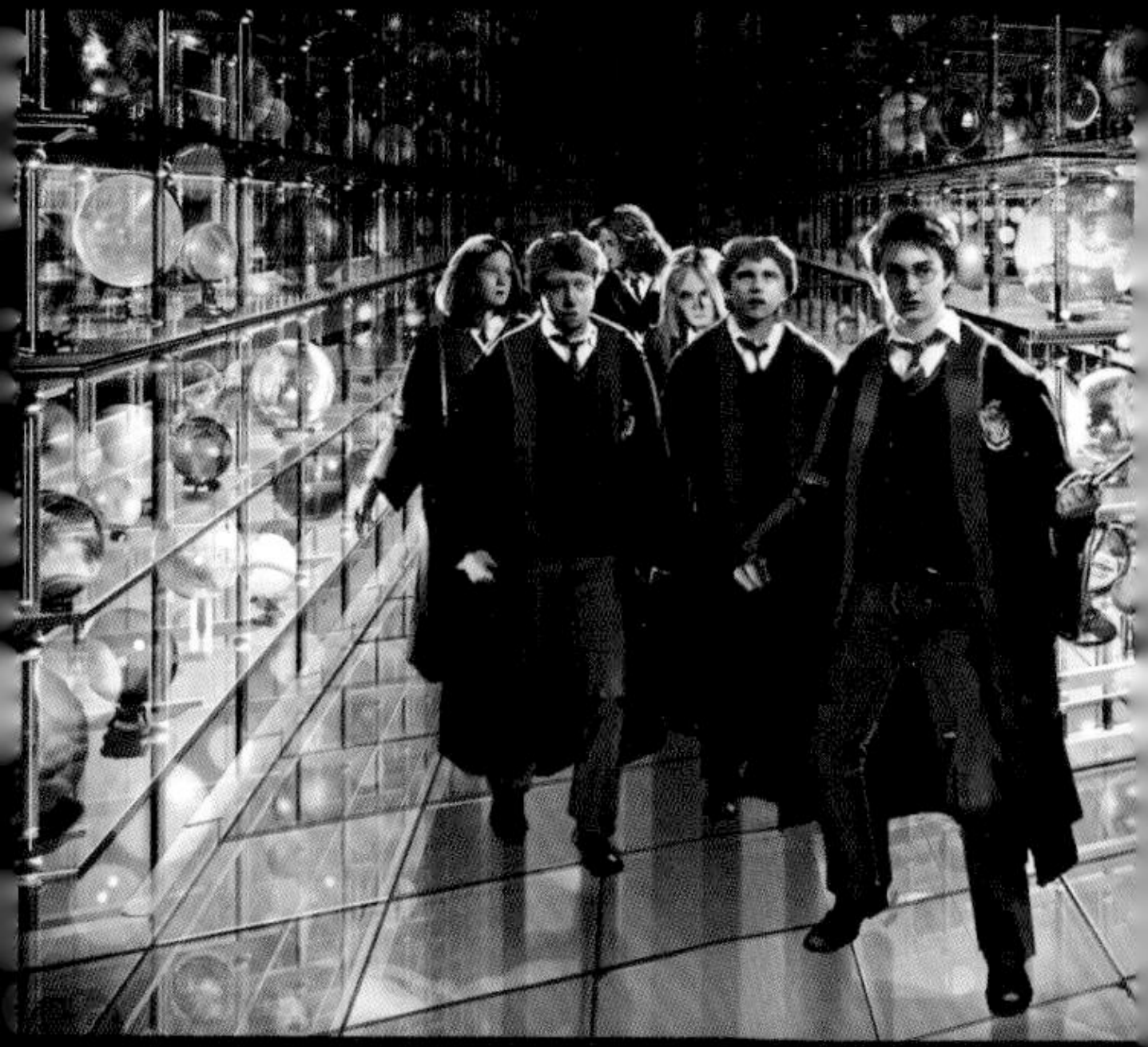

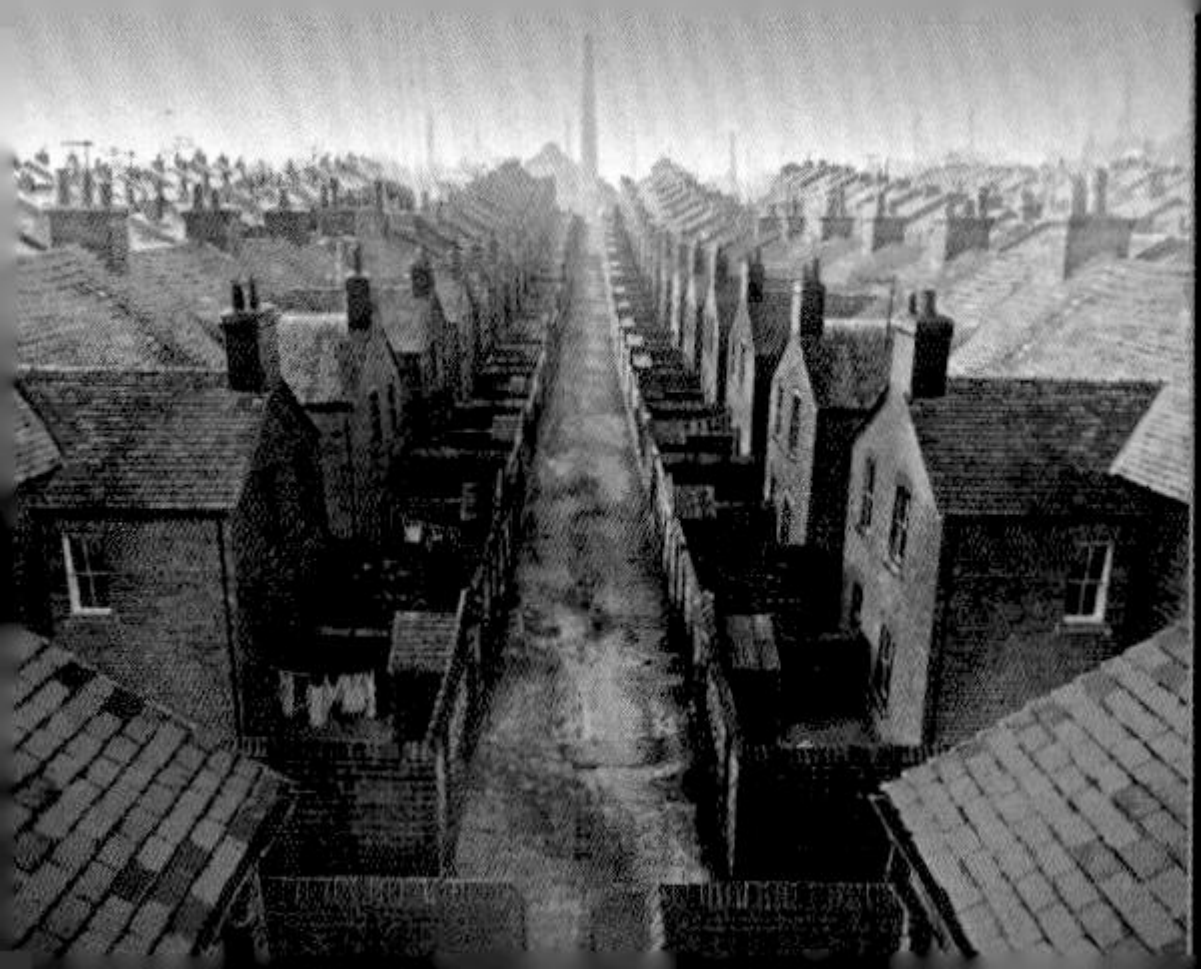